INTERPERSONAL RELATIONS FOR HEALTH PROFESSIONALS

A Social Skills Approach

Thomas W. Muldary, Ph.D.

Department of Psychology
Eastern Michigan University
Ypsilanti, Michigan

MACMILLAN PUBLISHING CO., INC.
New York

Collier Macmillan Canada, Inc.
TORONTO

Collier Macmillan Publishers
LONDON

Macmillan Publishing Co., Inc.
866 Third Avenue, New York, New York 10022

Collier Macmillan Canada, Inc.

Collier Macmillan Publishers • London

Library of Congress Cataloging in Publication Data

Muldary, Thomas W.
  Interpersonal relations for health professionals.

  Includes index.
  1. Medical personnel—Psychology. 2. Interpersonal
relations. 3. Medical personnel and patient. I. Title.
[DNLM: 1. Health occupations. 2. Interpersonal relations.
W 62 M954i]
R727.M825   1983   610.69'6'019   82-20809
ISBN 0-02-384640-2

Printing: 1 2 3 4 5 6 7 8   Year: 3 4 5 6 7 8 9 0 1

With my love and respect
To Pat,
and
my Mother and Father

And, to us all,
May we meet our responsibility
To learn to get along with each other,
To learn to care for one another, and
To show it

PREFACE

Any time that we intervene in the lives of people we love or people whom we are paid to serve, our effects may be constructive or destructive. It depends in part upon the level of interpersonal skills that we offer.

R. R. Carkhuff and B. G. Berenson,
Beyond Counseling and Psychotherapy

Health care professionals with extensive technical training often receive little formal education in psychology and interpersonal relations. Yet, to do their jobs well, they need to be able to relate effectively with other people. The interpersonal nature of their positions requires that health professionals possess reliable conceptual frameworks and practical skills for interacting with health care recipients, colleagues, support staff, and administrators. Human relationships are the media through which technical skills are practiced. A central theme of this text is that all individuals working in health care organizations are integrated into a system of complex human relationships, wherein they function most effectively when they are proficient in the use of interpersonal skills. Certainly, some very important facts of professional life can be observed within the contexts of those relationships. Knowledge of those facts is essential to efficient performance.

Health care practice has been witnessing a transition from primarily curative orientations to a broader orientation which includes prevention and the promotion of well-being. Part of this transition has involved the emergence of different views of health care consumers. No longer the passive receivers of services, they are seen as having a more active role in the total health care process. This expanded view is an expected outgrowth of overall sociocultural change— changes in the values, attitudes, and beliefs which underlie the function of our institutions. And, as change continues to challenge the very foundation of our institutions, individuals resist forces over which they have no control by diverting their energies toward those things which they can control. A strong consumer orientation has been growing, partly because individuals are resisting exploitation by institutional, organizational, and corporate forces which threaten to control them. They are demanding effective health care services, demanding accountability, and demanding that health professionals be more than technicians. The day of the practitioner-as-technician is gone forever. The health professional must now be, above all else, an expert in interpersonal relations. Today, giving service is not enough. Often, the outcome is not enough. The emphasis today includes a sharp focus on the process of service delivery— the way in which care is provided within the contexts of human relationships.

There appears to be a noticeable absence of research and, consequently, good evidence showing that health professionals trained today are demonstrably better skilled in interpersonal relations than those trained 20 years ago. If this is true, then it is probably also true that either we have not emphasized the importance of interpersonal competence in health care practice or we have not gone beyond advocacy to teach prerequisite skills. A good share of the responsibility must be accepted by training programs. Usually, training programs select faculty with demonstrated expertise in academic, research, theoretical, and/or technical areas, as well they should. They appear to have been successful with these selection criteria. Rarely, however, is interpersonal competence considered a quality or credential for these professional role models. As competent as they are in their specializations, they may nevertheless emphasize their areas of expertise to the exclusion of relationship skills necessary for effective health care practice. The outcome is often one in which students learn to be good technical practitioners but not necessarily skilled in relating to people.

In health care practice it may be that we have become more preoccupied with specific medical techniques to the neglect of what may very well account for a notable share of the positive outcomes produced by health care services: the interpersonal relationship itself. Medical research should continue to help improve the quality and precision of techniques. In the meantime, health care professionals have no choice but to deal with clients who bring their total selves to the health care context. It is this aspect of health care services that can benefit from the research and principles of psychology and interpersonal relations.

Many texts in psychology and interpersonal relations are confusing to students who seek information holding some relevance to their own work lives. Often the texts outline highly abstract concepts and theories to persons with technical orientations who are not used to dealing with the gray areas of human functioning. The "black and white" order which they expect from psychology is not found among scattered data, facts, and findings of a seemingly disconnected science of behavior. As a result, students sometimes become disillusioned and avoid further attempts at gaining insight into human behavior. When some of these texts are included in health care training programs, it may also happen that students learn of the various disturbances, disorders, illnesses, and disease processes which well prepare them for *being patients*. All too often, in any case, students are left to wonder how they will be able to relate to real persons, not disease entities or diagnostic labels. Of course, an opposite outcome is equally disturbing. Some students may come to develop a deluded sense of confidence in their newly acquired psychological knowledge. They pick up a few concepts, facts, or skills that are used indiscriminately and with unrestricted application. As the saying goes, "When your only tool is a hammer, it turns out that every problem is a nail."

The challenge, then, appears to be one involving the presentation of material in a representative, relevant, and contemporary fashion. The challenge is met to the extent that students become able to critically evaluate, synthesize, and use information in improving a range of interpersonal skills, while at the same time recognizing the limits of knowledge and application. The student who is able to accomplish this can be a tremendous asset to health care services.

The aim of this text is to (1) acquaint the reader with the processes by which people perceive one another, come into contact, and maintain relationships; (2) demonstrate the connections between cognitive learning and actual practice by bringing information into contact with personally meaningful experience; (3) stimulate assessment and improvement of specific interpersonal skills relative to perception, evaluation, and communication; and (4) present an interesting, accurate, and readable account of the processes of interpersonal behavior in health care organizations.

To attain these general goals the text is organized around three basic processes of interpersonal behavior: perception, evaluation, and communication. Examination of these three areas is preceded by general overviews at the beginning of each major section. The respective chapters are sequenced to facilitate an orderly integration of knowledge. Each section concludes with a brief chapter designed to permit application of learning through assessment of current skills and practice of skills in individual and group exercises. Group discussions and interactions are encouraged.

Part One of the text addresses the fact that each individual brings to his/her position a frame of reference for perceiving events within the health care organization. This frame of reference and his/her characteristic perceptual habits play a major role in influencing responses to others. The purpose of the first part is to examine the factors influencing the perception of persons and the development of individual frames of reference. Effective use of interpersonal skills begins with accurate perception, and knowledge of perceptual influences can contribute to more accurate perceptions.

To have a basis for responding to other people, individuals must encode, process, and evaluate their perceptions. Part Two of the text examines those cognitive and emotional processes which mediate between the health professional's perceptions of people and subsequent response to them.

The focus of Part Three is on interpersonal communication, although the separation of communication from perception and evaluation is arbitrary and offered only for the sake of organization. Interaction with others in health care organizations is partly a function of the ability to use various social communication skills which they simply do not possess. The aim of this section is therefore to provide the opportunity for health professionals to learn and/or improve interpersonal communication skills for maintaining satisfactory work relationships. Work relationships are not restricted to those with health care recipients. In this text equal attention is given to peer relationships, which are just as important to nourish. Indeed, the interpersonal skills discussed in this text are not limited to the health care context, for they belong to life.

In some areas issues are discussed and behaviors are described in cosmetically prettier and conceptually neater ways than experts in those fields would recognize as existing. However, conceptual and methodological nuances are largely ignored on the premise that the student's concern is to acquire an understanding and a feel for the basics of interpersonal relations, and not the latest academic issues which may or may not influence previous thinking. The material in this text is addressed as directly as possible within the limits of our current state of knowledge. The usefulness of the material is to some degree self-evident. To a larger degree its usefulness is a function of the extent to which it bears upon the practical experience of the reader. To that end the reader bears a responsibility for testing applicability and demonstrating relevance, for it is what one *does* with learning that truly matters.

Finally, it should be noted that the humanistic and social-learning orientations reflected in this text make no assumptions about where the focus of interpersonal relations should be limited. It seems to me that it would be a drastic mistake to assume that health professionals should enhance their interpersonal competence solely for the benefit of health care recipients. Such a view has been ingrained for far too long under the valued ethic of "dedication." Health professionals must recognize that they are *their own* mechanisms of health care practice. They must care for their own needs and those of their colleagues as they would care for the needs of health care recipients. With the usual exception of provider-client relationships, most human relationships are symmetrical and characterized by reciprocal give-and-take. It is within the contexts of peer and social relationships that health professionals may find support and strength. Service motives may be important, but so also are the persons holding those motives. In this text there is a strong emphasis on empathy, or understanding others from their points of view. Empathy should not be restricted to health care recipients, but to other health care providers as well. When it is, peer relationships tend to become more complementary and each person's needs have greater chances of being met.

Health care providers and recipients include both males and females. Therefore, masculine and feminine terms are assigned and used interchangeably throughout the text. This format also avoids the constantly cumbersome "he/she" reference, which makes reading difficult.

Sir Isaac Newton once wrote, "If I have seen further, it is by standing upon the shoulders of Giants." Although I doubt that I have seen much further than most people, it is surely upon the shoulders of others that I have stood while translating a vision into the pages that follow. The references cited throughout the text identify many of those persons. However, this text may have remained a mere vision, were it not for the inspiration of author Carmen Germaine Warner, who plied me with wine and irresistible charm and encouragement. For her confidence, urging, and initial direction, I am deeply grateful. Of course, a principal force behind this text came from the insight, expertise, and support of my wife, Pat. Through a project lasting almost three years, she proof read, critiqued, suggested ideas, sacrificed time from her own research, and helped me through periods of writer's block and despair. Finally, I wish to acknowledge the following people, whose contributions came in various forms: Don Eack, Dan Mullis, Charles Muldary, Win Muldary, Adele Spezeski, Joseph Spezeski, Mary Alice Warfield, William Schafer, Judy Schafer, and Sam.

T.W.M.

CONTENTS

PART ONE

The Health Professional and Interpersonal Perception: Perceiving and Understanding Others

In spite of differences among allied health professionals in terms of specialized practices, most share a particular sensitivity toward other human beings. They share a humanitarian commitment to helping others overcome ignorance, achieve health and wellness, and alleviate suffering. Grounded in an altruistic caring for others, this commitment is a principal determinant of their choice to enter a "people-oriented" helping profession in the first place. Yet, entry into a profession of serving other people without sufficient preparation for managing the complexities of interpersonal relationships often leaves many health professionals with a vague sense that something is missing from their repertoire of technical skills. Most of the time, however, their technical training has been adequate. It is in the realm of interpersonal relationships—between health care providers and recipients as well as between providers themselves—that problems often arise, for which solutions are not readily available from the health professional's repertoire of skills. As the famous psychiatrist, Harry Stack Sullivan, once commented (Sullivan, H. S. *Schizophrenia as a Human Process.* New York, Norton, 1962, p. 248):

> People are decidedly the hardest things we have to deal with. Not only does this task require a great amount of skill learning, but also the full value of achievement at this task does not begin clearly to appear to the individual until he is in the second decade of life.

As Sullivan observed, a considerable amount of "skill learning" is necessary. And, just as caring can never be a substitute for technical competence, neither can it replace interpersonal competence. The humanitarian commitment mandates that the health professional become competent in both skill areas.

1

The chapters to follow in Part One are organized around the central thesis that the essential beginning point for interpersonal skills development is necessarily the processes of *perception*. Part One provides a sequence of chapters which stress that each individual brings to her position a unique *frame of reference* for perceiving and responding to events within the health care organization. This frame of reference plays a major role in determining how the individual relates to others. Thus, Part One examines a variety of factors influencing person perception and the development of an individual frame of reference.

The title of Chapter One—Perception as the Foundation of Interpersonal Relations—reflects the basic premise that interpersonal relationships and communication begin with perception. Basic perceptual principles of *selection, organization*, and *stability* are discussed as general influences on perception, which operate regardless of whether we are perceiving an object or another human being. An understanding of these principles should provide some insight into the ways in which we select sensory information, organize often widely disparate information, and used that information to create a sense of order and predictability in our worlds.

Since our world is made up largely of other people, there are special implications for those continuous circumstances where our perceptions of others influence our actions toward them—and where our actions represent data used by others to form their own impressions and respond to us. Chapter Two therefore examines numerous factors affecting *interpersonal perception* in the health care environment. Those factors are grouped in terms of physical and social *context, characteristics of perceived persons*, and the *perceptual tendencies of perceivers*. Accounting for these factors as potential sources of perceptual bias or error should help us to adjust our perceptions for possible inaccuracies, and thereby give us a more reliable data base for responding to other individuals.

In Chapter Three, *self-perception* is discussed. It is argued that we must be able to understand our own experience and behavior if we are to make sense of the way we see others. Self-perception is explored in relation to the notion of *self-concept*, and the effects of the self-concept on *self-presentation* and the need for maintaining *consistency* in our perceptual/experiential world. The *Johari Self-Awareness Model* is presented as a framework for thinking about the ways in which we relate to others. The perception of one's professional *role* is also considered to be an important influence on how a total identity is formed—and how the professional role can be perceived as representing one's whole self, when in fact it is but a part.

The focus of Chapter Four is on understanding other's frames of reference through accurate *empathy*. As a perceptual task, achieving empathy is an integral part of human interactions. Yet, it depends on the ability of the individual to understand his own experience and draw from that experience to gain the perspective of another. An analysis of empathy is highly appropriate for this text in general, for empathic understanding is one of the most necessary of all conditions for satisfactory communication and relationships. Further, even though health professionals are typically viewed as being naturally empathic, the repeated day-to-day contact with people in various states of distress often leads to a decrease in their level of empathic understanding, for it seems somehow much less stressful to detach themselves from suffering than it is to "climb into the skin" of a patient.

Chapter Five provides the opportunity to integrate the material from preceding chapters and to do some personal experimenting in order to demonstrate the connection between cognitive learning and actual practice. Rationale and procedures for assessing social skills are outlined, followed by several individual and interpersonal exercises for enhancing perceptual skills.

CHAPTER
ONE

Perception as the Foundation of Interpersonal Relations

The appearance of things to the mind is the standard of every action to man

Epictetus, circa 60 A.D.

The study of human perception has always been a unique, intriguing, and highly complex field of inquiry. In general, the task has been to explain how individuals extract information from their environment and how they come to experience the world. For centuries this problem belonged to the domain of philosophy called metaphysics, which subsumed numerous theories concerning the nature of reality. With the advent of science, however, the problem of explaining perceptual experience became the province of empirical investigation through the use of objective methods of description and explanation. Yet, even with the methodology of science, the study of perception has continued to be a challenge to those who seek to understand how the same world can be perceived and experienced differently by different persons.

In most other areas of scientific research the phenomena under investigation are objective events: events which are observable by everyone, measurable, and which exist independently of observers. For example, earthquakes are objective events which are noticed by everyone within a specific range of their epicenters, the magnitudes of earthquakes are measurable on a Richter scale, and earthquakes occur with a force and duration independent of observers. In the field of perception, however, the facts to be explained are of a subjective nature: how things appear to individuals. For example, human beings have been puzzled for centuries by the larger appearance of the moon on the horizon, as opposed to its apparent size when elevated higher in the sky. Actually, the distance to the moon is somewhat greater at the horizon, with the retinal image being a fraction smaller (Rock, 1975). Nevertheless, the moon appears to be larger on the horizon. Consequently, any investigation of this phenomenon must necessarily attempt to explain how and why individuals perceive the moon to be larger when, in fact, it is not larger on the horizon. Given the nature of the facts to be explained, it is easy to appreciate the complicated tasks inherent in research exploring the experience, or "private events," of human beings, especially when it is recognized that there is often considerable interpersonal variation among the experiences of individuals exposed to the same objective event.

The Real World Versus the Perceived World

The distinction between an objective world of physical events and a subjective world of experience has been an issue of intense philosophical debate for thousands of years. The issue concerns the question of what is real. One philosophical position contends that only a world of physical objects and events exists in reality. This materialistic argument suggests that subjective awareness is a product of brain functioning, with the brain itself being physical matter. A contrary position holds that reality inheres in our experience of the world. Thus, the idealist maintains that all we can be certain of is that we experience the world in a subjective way, with the world itself being a product of our experience. A third general position acknowledges both material and subjective reality, but the nature of the relationships between the two is an issue upon which proponents of this dualistic position are divided.

To further complicate the objective-subjective reality debate, an epistemological issue mandates consideration of the manner in which individuals can have knowledge of the physical world. Essentially, the questions are "How do we come to have knowledge of the world?" and "How can we be certain that our knowledge is correct?" Special problems arise and confront the idealist, who argues that the world is basically a "creation" of the individual (e.g., if the world is a "creation" of the individual and, therefore, the true reality, then how do we explain phenomena such as the "moon illusion"?). Problems confront the materialist who contends that the world of experience is "given" to us, in correct form, by the physical world (e.g., if the world of experience is "given" in direct and correct form, then how do we explain individual differences?).

In relation to these issues, science has made it abundantly clear that the physical world and the world of experience are not the same. More specifically, the physical world is quite different from the world as we perceive it. The world as we perceive it is a "construction" (Rock, 1975)—a representation in functional, or symbolic, form of physical energy transformations occurring in the nervous system. What we know of the world comes primarily through the senses and is represented in consciousness in a qualitatively different form from that which exists outside of the body. The exact manner in which physical information is extracted from the environment by the senses, the processes determining the creation of symbolic representations of the physical world, and the factors affecting the degree of correspondence between perceptions and physical objects are principal issues confronting theorists and researchers today.

It seems clear that the reason why different people perceive the same world differently is that, psychologically, the world is "not the same" for different people (Hamner and Organ, 1978). As Rogers (1951) suggested many years ago, each person lives in the midst of his/her own phenomenal (experiential) world and responds to that world on the basis of how it is perceived and experienced. According to such a view, "reality" is highly subjective and determined by the individual's perceptions of what is real. Of course, this position does not suggest that perceptions held by individuals are always isomorphic with what is actually out there. When ten persons look at *Ravine in the Peyroulets* by Van Gogh, each person tends to perceive different aspects of the painting and respond to it in terms of the meaning it holds for him. Some persons may see the representation of a looming obstacle in Van Gogh's life, others may perceive an interesting creation of a mountain scene, and still others may see nothing but colorful strokes and daubs of paint on a canvas. What may be objectively real about *Ravine in the Peyroulets* is secondary to each person's subjective perceptions. In fact, some may argue that there can be no objective reality whatsoever in relation to the creation of an artist.

Most people have a feeling of realness about their sensory experiences. Indeed, it is almost as if our perceptions are directly and correctly *given* to us by the stimulus objects or events to which we are exposed. If we perceive a kitten as soft, fluffy, and cute, we tend to assume that it *is* soft, fluffy, and cute. Furthermore, we tend to assume that other persons also perceive the kitten in the same way. If objects in the world did directly and correctly determine our perceptions, every person observing the kitten would experience it in exactly the same way. If mediating cognitive processes intervened between sensory input and perceptual experience, their effects would produce different perceptions of the same kitten among persons with different learning histories. This, of course, seems to be a tenable proposition, since not everyone appreciates animals or sees kittens as soft, fluffy, and cute. Nor do all human beings experience classical music, baseball games, pickles, hospitals, new fashions, or anything else in the same exact way. Thus, although some evidence suggests that certain perceptions can be "given" by stimulus objects, perception is largely an active process of selecting, organizing, and constructing sensory data into stable and meaningful experience.

A significant challenge has been to explain how and why persons select, organize, and create experiences. There are no simple answers, for such complicated phenomena involve the complex interactions of numerous variables intrinsic to objects themselves, the context in which perceptual experience occurs, and, most significantly, perceptual tendencies of perceivers. Untangling these interactions and identifying separate determining factors is no easy chore. Nevertheless, by identifying some of the major factors inherent in objects, context, and perceiver, it is possible to move toward a fuller appreciation of what perception is all about. In addition, an understanding of the role of perception in interpersonal relations requires a consideration of some basic facts relative to object perception, as the fundamental principles governing the perception of objects tend to have direct applicability to the more complex processes involved in interpersonal perception.

Sensation, Perception, Learning, and Cognition

In the realm of human experience it is difficult to establish sharp divisions between interrelated processes which influence behavior. Such is the case regarding the interdependent processes of sensation, perception, learning, and thinking. *Sensation* was once differentiated from perception on the assumption that it was a process limited to the physiological elements from which perceptions developed (Forgus and Melamed, 1976). However, contemporary views hold that sensation is the *initial phase* of the total perceptual process. In sensation, environmental or internal stimuli impinge upon the sense organs, which then translate physical information into messages that the nervous system can use (Forgus and Melamed, 1976). Researchers interested in sensation focus chiefly on the psychophysical correlates of sensory experience, and tend to restrict their focus to the immediate experience of simple or primary aspects of stimuli, such as color, size, shape, or intensity (Rock, 1975).

Perception involves a higher level of processing stimulus input. It involves *the extraction and organization of physical information, as well as the representation of that information in some symbolic form.* As such, perception consists of interdependent sets of relationships with sensation, learning, and thinking. While raw sensory experience (sensation) provides the input for perception to occur, the degree of sophistication of the perceptual process is heavily dependent upon other *cognitive processes* (those processes which are involved in the acquisition and utilization of knowledge), such as learning and thinking. *Learning* has been variously defined throughout the literature as a process through which information is acquired and integrated into the individual's store of knowledge. Since perception is a process of information extraction, the learning process is set in motion through perception, and the results of learning have obvious influences on subsequent information extraction by providing bases for interpreting incoming information. Therefore, as the individual experiences the world, more information becomes available for facilitating the perceptual process. That is, the individual becomes more efficient at extracting information from the environment. Clearly, there is a reciprocal relationship between perception and learning, such that perception facilitates the acquisition of information, and new information broadens perceptual abilities by expanding the capability to extract information and structure it into meaningful experience.

Thinking is inferred to occur when individuals are forced to manipulate existing information in the store of knowledge. When individuals must solve problems, for example, those problems are resolved to the extent that they have both the necessary information in storage and the conceptual tools available for extracting potentially useful information from the environment. The better the individual's conceptual abilities, the better the individual tends to be at extracting information and solving problems. Thus, thinking is influenced by what has been learned, as well as by what can be extracted through perception. There is also a reciprocal relationship between thinking and perception, since thoughts can modify subsequent perceptions of the world. For example, there is little doubt that in thought disorders, such as those found among paranoid disturbances, delusions of persecution influence the person's perceptions of the behavior of those who are suspected of conspiracy. Of course, paranoids are not the only people whose suspicions effectively alter their perceptions of others.

The relationships among sensation, perception, learning, and thinking can be further clarified through reference to your own personal experience. Simply recall the first time that you met your current supervisor. During that initial encounter, visual, auditory, and perhaps olfactory and tactile stimulation were received by the sense organs. That information was translated into nerve impulses to the brain, and further decoded into the perception of an individual. However, on subsequent occasions you perceived the supervisor somewhat differently, based on what you learned about the person and what you thought about him/her. If you have any doubts that your perceptions were influenced by learning and thinking, simply compare your current impressions with your initial impressions.

Perceptual Selection

Human beings live in a world of continuous external and internal stimulation, where physical stimuli unceasingly bombard the senses. In any given situation, countless stimuli impinge upon the sense organs, and yet we do not perceive all of those impinging stimuli. It seems that individuals, although capable of receiving millions of bits of sensory data per second (Haney, 1979), can respond to only a certain number of stimuli at any given moment. In most situations, those stimuli that are relevant for the moment are perceived. They are *selected* and kept in focus, while irrelevant stimuli are ignored. If this perceptual selection process were not activated, all incoming sensory data would be translated and recorded, and the world would be experienced as a chaotic jumble of sensory impressions (Hastorf, Schneider, and Polefka, 1970). For example, while listening to your supervisor discuss a critical personnel problem during a staff meeting, you would also be aware of every other sight and sound within range of vision and hearing, the pressure of the clothes on your body, and all internal bodily sensations.

There is virtually complete agreement among theorists and researchers that individuals play an active part in selecting and processing information from the environment. The question remains as to how and why they selectively perceive a limited number of stimuli from the range available in a given situation. Why, for example, do witnesses to a crime often give such widely divergent accounts of the events to which they were all exposed? An answer to a question of this sort would contribute to our understanding of the manner in which persons go about creating a coherent perceptual experience out of the vastly disparate stimuli which impinge upon the sensory apparatus. Part of the puzzle can be pieced together from the general classes of variables influencing which of the innumerable competing stimuli are selected for attention.

Characteristics of Stimulus Objects and Events

Certain general features of stimulus objects and events have a direct influence on the perceptual selection process. These characteristics include factors related to size, intensity, contrast, and movement. The central notion is that any feature or trait of an object or event, relative to its size, intensity, contrast, or motion, which makes the object or event stand out from others will increase the likelihood of its being perceived. In other words, the most salient stimuli in the environment have a greater probability of being perceived.

The *size* of a stimulus may have an influence on selection if, relative to other stimuli in the environment, the quality of largeness makes the stimulus stand out. For example, while standing on the south rim of the Grand Canyon, one would be immediately captured by the magnificent size of this wondrous work of nature. While strolling along San Diego Bay, it would be difficult to ignore the presence of aircraft carriers such as the USS Constellation, Midway, or Kitty Hawk. Advertisers who seek to draw the attention of potential customers often utilize large, bold lettering in their newspaper advertisements. And, in a hotel lobby it is difficult not to notice the size of a professional basketball player who is standing at the reservation desk.

In addition to the variable of size, the more *intense* the stimulus, the greater the probability that it will be perceived. Most persons have had the unpleasant experience of encountering someone who exuded a pungent odor due to ineffective or unused antiperspirant deodorant, but even such noxious olfactory stimulation may go unnoticed when a skunk is in the area. The noise blaring from an inconsiderate neighbor's stereo system late at night is often difficult to ignore, and so also is the bellicose laughter of the loudest person in the hospital cafeteria at lunchtime. Television executives have long been aware of the effect of sound intensity, and have capitalized on that effect by increasing the loudness of commercials over the regular programs. Movie producers also utilize intensity effects in order to bring viewers to heighten their focus on specific scenes (this was highly effective in the movie *Jaws*, for example).

Contrast is a characteristic which increases the discriminability of specific stimuli from their backgrounds. That is, stimuli which stand out against the background with great prominence, or which differ from what was expected, tend to gain the attention of individuals. A full appreciation of contrast effects must be deferred to subsequent discussions of perceptual *set* and perceptual organization, since the contrasting function of stimuli often depend upon the particular expectations held by the perceiver, as well as the specific relationships between stimuli and their background that are established through perceptual organization. However, some common fundamental examples of stimulus contrast would include fluorescent or luminescent signs which stand out against plain backgrounds, brightly colored clothing which makes individuals stand out in a crowd, and even oases in the middle of deserts. In a hospital emergency department, where there is a constant flurry of activity, emergency personnel typically become accustomed to those conditions. But, if the emergency traffic suddenly stopped, the contrast would surely be noticed. Perhaps you have had an experience with a colleague whose mood or behavior suddenly became different from that which you had come to expect; the contrast probably caught your attention. In industry, for example, many supervisors have been taken for granted as "easygoing" and nondemanding, until severe pressure comes down from upper management, and the supervisor's behavior changes. Finally, at the sophisticated level of literature, "Dr. Jekyll" would have been indistinguishable from "Mr. Hyde," were it not for the genius of Robert Louis Stevenson in providing such a marvelous fictional account of personality and behavioral contrast.

According to the *"movement"* principle, objects which move in the field of vision tend to be noticed more than stationary objects. Imagine sitting on the grass in a public park. In attending to your surroundings, you will most likely notice those objects which move in your field of vision. That is, you will readily perceive movement from people strolling, children playing, pigeons strutting along the grounds, or perhaps dogs chasing one another across the lawn. In the area of advertising, this principle has been employed by business persons who display lighting arrangements on signs to create a stroboscopic effect of apparent movement which attracts the attention of passersby. Even attorneys are often aware of the attention-getting effects of movement, as they frequently manage to capture the undivided attention of jurors by walking back and forth across the courtroom floor while presenting opening or closing arguments.

Stimulus characteristics clearly affect the process of perceptual selection. But, object characteristics are not the sole determinants of the selection process, nor are properties of objects necessarily inherent in the objects themselves, since individuals often attribute properties to objects. Given the active nature of the perceptual process, it is inevitable that certain internal variables, or factors intrinsic to perceivers, become involved and interact with object characteristics to determine the outcome of selection. Prior learning experiences, current motivations, and personality traits and states all tend to influence the selection process by contributing to the formation of what is known as "perceptual set."

Perceptual Set

Perceptual set is a readiness, preparedness, or predisposition to perceive events in a particular way. As indicated above, perceptual sets are influenced by learning experience (which evokes specific expectations to perceive objects or events in particular situations), motivations (which are the products of physical or psychological deprivation and subsequent need states), and personality traits (enduring patterns of behavior peculiar to the individual) and states (temporary psychological conditions). These internal sets can exert powerful influences on perception in general, since they serve to predispose individuals to perceive what they *"expect"* or *"want"* to perceive. To suggest that people may see what they "expect" to see is to imply that prior learning and perceptual experience affect current perceptual functioning; and to say that people see what they "want" to see is to suggest that motivation and unique personality factors influence perception (Reitz, 1977). Accordingly, perceptual sets are determined by factors quite peculiar to individuals themselves, and largely independent from stimulus characteristics.

A classic study by Leeper (1935) demonstrated that, when given a set to process stimulus input, individuals will create a structured perception consistent with the set. Leeper used an ambiguous figure similar to that shown in Figure 1.1 which, upon observation, may be perceived as an old woman or a young woman. One modification of the original figure, which emphasized the young woman, was shown to one group of subjects. Another modification of the original, highlighting the old woman, was shown to a second group of subjects. When shown the original ambiguous picture, all subjects who had previously been shown the adaptation highlighting the old woman saw only the old woman in their first exposure to the ambiguous original. Ninety-five percent of the subjects exposed to the version emphasizing the young woman saw only the young woman in their first look at the ambiguous original. Since two distinct women could be perceived in the ambiguous original, the perception of one or the other depended upon whether the subjects were set to perceive a young woman or an old woman.

The findings obtained by Leeper clearly demonstrated the operation of perceptual sets which were based on prior experience with similar stimuli. In addition, these findings suggested that individuals are indeed actively involved

Figure 1.1 Ambiguous picture of a young woman and an old woman. (*Source: Edwin G. Boring, "A New Ambiguous Figure,"* American Journal of Psychology, *July 1930, p. 444. Also see Robert Leeper, "A Study of a Neglected Portion of the Field of Learning—The Development of Sensory Organization."* Journal of Genetic Psychology, *March 1935, p. 62. Originally drawn by cartoonist W. E. Hill and published in* Puck, *November 6, 1915.)*

in selecting stimuli and processing those stimuli into an organized, structured, functional representation of stimulus impingements. Other implications from these findings are worth noting at this point. Hastorf et al. (1970, 1979) pointed out that subjects in the Leeper experiment did not perceive confusing patterns of light and dark. Rather, they saw either a young woman or an old woman. The subjects apparently extracted features of the ambiguous picture and forced those stimulus features into a meaningful *"category"*: "young woman" or "old woman." The categories they used were derived from learning experience, which is heavily dependent upon language and cultural background (Hastorf, Schneider, and Polefka, 1970). That is, through learning experience, subjects had acquired a system of linguistic coding which provided a basis for categorizing perceived stimuli (i.e., "young," "old," "woman"). The role of language in this categorization process is addressed later. It is sufficient at this point simply to note the role of language and learning in the processes associated with perceptual selection and organization.

Prior learning predisposes individuals to form an expectation that a particular object or event will be perceived in a particular situation. Because the person has learned that in specific situations certain stimuli are virtually always present, or that when one event occurs another event necessarily follows, logical deductions from assumed facts prepare the person to perceive those objects or events, whether or not they are actually forthcoming. For example, a person who has learned of the brilliance of Jean Pierre Rampal may be set to hear a flawless performance of Sonata in E Minor for Flute and Continuo and may indeed "hear" a flawless performance, despite the fact that Rampal missed certain notes. If your prior experience has taught you that "psychologists" and "peculiarity" go together, you may be predisposed to notice something peculiar about the psychologist you have recently met. And, as psychologists know from their own experience, when you expect to find "pathology" in someone, you can always find some. The reality, of course, is that psychologists are no more "peculiar" than any other group of professionals or nonprofessionals.

Perceptual sets do, in fact, frequently influence people to perceive things that are not actually present. But, there are numerous occasions when expectancies are violated, and anticipated objects or events do not materialize. This is a complex psychological experience which is perhaps beyond the scope of the present focus. However, at a simple level, magicians have always been aware of the effects they can produce by violating audience expectancies. That is, magicians capitalize on common learning experiences and perceptual sets in order to misdirect individuals and reveal mysterious and intriguing events which contradict the expectations held by individuals in the audience. Many of the sophisticated tricks which baffle the minds of adults often fail to fool children, whose narrower range of life experiences precludes the evocation of the same expectancies held by adults. Consequently, where adults are set to perceive the logical outcome of a sophisticated stage trick, children often have no such set because they lack the experience necessary for making logical deduction and inferences and are led away from the "magic." Of course, magical misdirection is perhaps a dramatic example of the manner in which perceptual sets can be violated. Yet, the fact remains that people are often misdirected away from making an accurate perception of events simply because their expectations get in the way.

In addition to the effects of learning experience on expectancy formation, the role of learning extends to the attribution of characteristics to perceived objects. Through learning, and with the aid of language, numerous stimuli come to be perceived as having some particular *"value"* or *"meaning."* That is, "value" and "meaning" are not inherent in the stimuli themselves, but are assigned to stimuli when individuals have come to associate them with some relevant value or meaning. For instance, a typewriter has no intrinsic value other than that which has been assigned by people who know what purpose it serves. An Aborigine tribesman may see nothing more than a curious metalic object which contrasts with familiar objects from his world, while the author sees the instrument of his/her trade which may hold special meaning and value. All other things being equal, including the context in which the typewriter is perceived, the Aborigine may selectively perceive the object on the basis of its salience as a strange object, while the author's perceptions are influenced by past experience. By implication, there is yet another variable suggested in this example, and that is *familiarity.* Through frequent exposures to stimulus objects, we often come to perceive them on the basis of their familiarity; and, in relation to the notion of stimulus contrast, we may often fail to notice familiar objects in familiar environments, while quickly noticing familiar objects in unfamiliar environments or unfamiliar objects in familiar contexts.

The role of motivation in the evocation of perceptual sets is also of considerable significance. If you believe that a starving person is especially sensitive to the sight and smell of food, you are correctly basing your belief on an underlying acceptance of motivational bases for perceptual set and selection. You are accepting the possibility that certain motivational factors elicit perceptual sets which, in turn, predispose individuals to attend to highly pertinent stimuli in the environment. The starving person is extremely sensitive to the sight and smell of food because a need state exists which was caused through deprivation. In similar ways, sexually deprived persons may be especially attentive to sexual stimuli in the environment, persons deprived of social contact may be highly responsive to the attention given them by others, and recovering alcoholics may be acutely sensitive to stimuli associated with drinking. Personal "wants," "wishes," "desires," "ambitions," or "aspirations" may also evoke perceptual sets, although these motives do not result from a state of deprivation. Rather, they are acquired through experience; they are learned, or "acquired" motives. In organizations, many individuals "aspire" to top management positions, perhaps due to strong achievement motives. As a result, they may be able to perceive cues for advancement opportunities where less achievement-oriented persons do not. Persons "wishing" for power may be attuned to situational cues signalling the occasion for exercising control over others. Or, the person who simply "wants" to believe that one colleague is more competent than another may be inclined to perceive their respective work performances with a bias toward the favored colleague.

As indicated earlier, people are indeed often motivated to see what they "want" to see. This tendency can be maladaptive at times, because it may prevent individuals from acknowledging important facts about an event. For instance, the reputations of many people were severely damaged, their integrities maliciously impugned, and their lives shattered during the McCarthy Era, when "witch-hunting" fed upon the obsession of seeking out and "exposing" communists throughout the country. The motivational fuel for this obsession was fear, which predisposed many individuals to see "communists" even where there were none. Of course, vestiges of this type of fear and obsession still remain and characterize many persons in our society who equate various social stimuli with communism (e.g., Russians, liberals, peace organizations, social movements, civil rights legislation, college professors). It might also be argued that perhaps few other groups are more predisposed to see and hear what they want to see and hear than some "yellow journalists," who have a distorted sense of what makes news in this country.

The effects of needs and motives on perception are indeed potent, but the effects do not appear to be simple and direct. Various researchers studying perceptual phenomena have noted that motivational influences vary from person to person, with the nature of those influences being relatively stable across situations (e.g., Klein, 1954). That is to say, it appears that individuals possess relatively stable tendencies that determine the form of the influence that motivation exerts on behavior, including perception (Shapiro, 1965). Such stable tendencies have been conceptualized in terms of personality traits, which implicate the pervasive role of personality functioning in the formation of perceptual sets.

The lay person often regards *"personality"* as something related to social charm, attractiveness, or popularity. However, the meaning of personality in psychology extends far beyond the "social image" conception held by the lay person (Hjelle and Ziegler, 1976). Among psychologists, the concept refers to something much more stable, consistent, and essential about persons. There are as many definitions of personality as there are theorists, but most definitions describe personality as some sort of hypothetical internal structure which organizes and integrates behavior; and, as Hjelle and Ziegler (1976) point out, it is this structure which is seen to be that which makes individuals unique. As used here, the concept is meant to refer to the totality of individual characteristics which define the differentness, separateness, and uniqueness of a whole entity: a human being. There are certainly many component aspects to "whole" persons, but some rather definitive aspects of individuals may often be pointed up by reference to unique traits or states. Personality *traits* are relatively enduring patterns of behavior which characterize individuals and set them apart from others. Personality *states*, on the other hand, refer to less permanent, usually transient conditions experienced by individuals. Both of these personality variables exert direct influences on the evocation of perceptual sets.

In relation to personality traits, there are definite patterns of behavior, or certain ways of "being-in-the-world," which cumulatively define specific personality compositions. The orientation individuals have toward the world thus predisposes them to perceive the world in line with the personality factors which make up that orientation. For example, certain people, described in clinical terms as "obsessive-compulsive" personalities, have a peculiar rigidity in their perceptual functioning. They tend to focus intensely and sharply on detail, often to the exclusion of elements at the periphery of their perceptual field and attention. This narrowed perceptual focus often causes them to miss other important aspects of their worlds; they tend to focus so intensely on specific stimuli that they cannot avoid missing other relevant stimulus information. It is as if they cannot see "the forest from the trees." At the other extreme, there are persons who perceive the world in broad, general, vague, and impressionistic ways which lack clarity and specificity. These persons, described clinically as "hysterical" personalities, lack the ability to focus sharply on stimuli, and are instead "struck" by objects and events in the world. Their worlds are composed largely of vague impressions of what is out there. Where obsessive-compulsive persons fail to see the forest from the trees, these persons fail to see "the trees from the forest." Still a different personality type perceives the world as a threatening place in which to live. "Paranoid" individuals tend to live in a more or less continuous state of suspicion and mistrust. The consequent mode of perception is extremely acute and narrowly focused for the purpose of searching the world for confirmation of the validity of existing suspicions. Attention is directed to any aspect or feature of incoming information which lends credence to their delusions. That "delusions," or false beliefs, can indeed influence perception is captured in the amusing story of the "dead man":

> A middle-aged woman arrived with her husband for an appointment with a prominent psychologist. After introducing themselves, the woman proceeded to tell the psychologist that she was at her wits-end with her husband, who insisted that he was dead. The psychologist checked her report with the husband, and he determined that the man did indeed believe himself to be dead. He then instructed the man to stand in front of a mirror ten times each day and repeat to himself out loud that "Dead men don't bleed. Dead men don't bleed." One week later, the couple returned to the psychologist, who immediately asked the husband if he carried out the instructions. The man said, "Ya, Doc, I stood in front of the mirror ten times a day for a week and said to myself 'Dead men don't bleed,' just like you told me to do." The psychologist then took the man's hand and, with a slight prick of a pin, drew blood from the man's index finger. "Well, what do you say about that?", the psychologist asked. The man quickly replied, "Well I'll be darned, Doc, dead men *do* bleed!"

While the above sets of personality traits tend to describe some rather extreme personality dispositions, they are by no means all-inclusive of the diverse perceptual modes which exist. And, of course, most persons are not of these particular types. But, the descriptions provided do illustrate some ways in which personality trait variables influence perceptual functioning. Less extreme illustrations can be gleaned from individuals in work settings, for example. In the hospital environment, the director of nursing who has come to believe that everyone on the staff dislikes her will tend to perceive statements directed to her from various staff members in line with that premise. The radiology technician who believes that everyone eagerly welcomes his presence under all circumstances will have difficulty perceiving the cues given by others who are perturbed by his intrusion into an ongoing conversation. Indeed, the manner in which many persons function in the world suggests that their personalities lack an integrated sense of social intelligence which would enable them to perceive correctly and respond to interpersonal situations.

In contrast to the effects of relatively enduring personality traits, more inconsistent and transient *states* can evoke perceptual sets. Temporary preoccupations and moods are examples of such conditions. For instance, the medical student who is preoccupied with upcoming comprehensive examinations is interested in learning and retaining specific information. Thus, when studying, that student may skim over, give passing attention to, or disregard completely any information which is tangentially or totally unrelated to the knowledge required for performance on the examinations. The respiratory therapist who is focused on a pressing emergency on the fifth floor may fail to notice that others spoke to him as he hurried down the corridor. And, it has often been observed that pedestrians walking down the sidewalks of major cities seem to be so wrapped up in their own worlds that they do not notice other persons or events around them. Clearly, the frequently heard statement, "I didn't notice," often reflects underlying preoccupations which precluded the conscious perception of objects or events in the environment.

Transient emotional states or moods are also effective determinants of perceptual sets. The mother who is frantic with worry over the seriousness of her son's injuries following an automobile accident may hang on every word coming from the mouth of the attending physician who consults her in the emergency waiting room. Later, when she is informed of her son's death, the mother's shock may render her totally oblivious to virtually all other events around her. In a less tragic sense, perhaps you can identify with the person who has a profound fear of flying which predisposes him/her to be highly sensitive to any noise in the airplane which seems abnormal. Finally, if you have ever experienced an earthquake, you can identify with the person who develops a subsequent reactivity to house noises.

Summary

A passive-recording view of perception appears to be untenable in light of the fact that individuals necessarily select stimuli from the countless impingements reaching the sense organs at any given moment. The selection process is influenced by numerous factors related to general stimulus characteristics and internal, organismic conditions of individuals. Stimulus characteristics such as size, intensity, contrast, and motion contribute greatly to the probability of selection from among the available stimuli in the environment. In general, any feature of a stimulus which contributes to its salience will also tend to influence perceptual selection. Internal factors include the primacy of perceptual set, which subsumes the effects of learning experience, contemporaneous motivations, and personality characteristics.

It is important to note that the manner in which these variables contribute to perceptual selection is rarely direct and distinct. In the foregoing discussion, factors were separated and treated independently for the sake of convenience of presentation and for the advancement of a basic understanding of perceptual selection. However, the influence of these factors is virtually always a function of multiple interactions between stimulus characteristics, psychological conditions, physiological functioning of sensory apparatus, and perceptual context. This, of course, is to say that there is multiple causation for perceptual selection.

Finally, selection is only one aspect of the whole process of perception. Perceptual selection cannot independently describe or explain the complexity of human perceptual phenomena; it is but one among many behavioral *"parts"* which make up the *"whole"* of perception. And, as the Gestaltists have suggested, the whole is greater than the sum of its parts. To carry this point even further, perception itself must be recognized as but one aspect of the vast behavioral repertoire of whole persons; also, perceptual processes other than selection must be noted in the service of gaining perspective on the human capacity for constructing meaningful experience from sensory input.

Perceptual Organization

The image of an object, which is reflected on the retina of the eye, is actually an ambiguous prefiguration of what that object represents in the environment. Generally speaking, the retinal image can be thought of as a mosaic of varying sizes, shapes, brightnesses, and colors. Before it can lead to a specific perception, the retinal image must be structured or *"organized"* in some way (Rock, 1975). Contours are attributed to objects, the resulting shapes are seen as geometric patterns against a background, and various stimulus patterns are grouped together for differentiation and discrimination among heterogenous forms. To a large degree, this process is governed by certain principles of perceptual organization, which offer useful descriptions of how objects in the environment come to be structured into experience.

These principles of perceptual organization were posited by Wertheimer (1923) and elaborated further in the writings of other Gestalt psychologists (e.g., Koffka, 1935; Kohler, 1947). *"Gestalt"* is a central concept in theories of perceptual organization. It is a Germanic term which has no direct translation in English, although the terms "configuration," "form," and "shape" are close translations which are frequently used (Lundin, 1979). The most common translation of Gestalt is *"whole,"* and it is this rough version of the term which most approximates the essence of the Gestaltist position: that the whole affects the way in which the parts are perceived. That is, in their early experiments on perception, the Gestaltists noted that subjects tended to perceive whole objects as opposed to successive related elements or components. When perceiving objects, individuals tended to see more than summations of component parts. The parts were dependent upon and given meaning by the "whole object," in that the whole was somehow different from the sum of its parts. For example, when looking at a photograph, we see whole objects and not dots and spots of light; when listening to music, we hear relationships between notes and not disparate, isolated sound frequencies. We create whole perceptions which are different from the parts in isolation.

This contention—that the whole is more than the sum of its parts—came to be a basic tenet of Gestalt psychology, which focused on the study of the "whole" immediate experience of individuals. In the area of perception, this "whole" attitude guided the formulation of principles by which the perceptual field is organized. It must be noted that these ways of organizing perceptions were hypothesized to be innate, as indicated by Wertheimer's reference to the principles of "primitive organization." However, this assumption has been the subject of considerable polemic between nativist positions and those empiricist positions stressing the primacy of learning. Few theorists today would dispute the fact that learning experience plays a significant role in perception, but the question remains as to the "extent" to which the supposedly inborn organization tendencies are modified by learning. Polemics aside, the Gestalt principles of perceptual organization nevertheless offer practical descriptions of a highly complex perceptual process.

Principles of Organization

One of the most fundamental principles of perceptual organization is called *figure-ground*. In figure-ground perception, objects are perceived to exist against backgrounds because perceptions organize themselves in such a way as to permit figures to stand out. As you read these words, for example, you are receiving light wave stimulation in the form of black and white patches, yet you perceive black letters, words, and paragraphs against a background of white paper. Even the illiterate person would tend to see small black symbols surrounded by a white background. This is so because smaller objects tend to be perceived as figures here; also, surrounded objects tend to be perceived as figures, and black is often preferred as figure in many situations (Rock, 1975). It must be noted, however, that figure-ground perception is not limited to the visual modality. For example, when listening to Barbra Streisand sing "People Who Need People," the musical accompaniment remains in the background until she completes a verse, and the melody comes to be figure against the background of silence. This type of perceptual event implies that figure-ground "shifts" often occur, where stimuli organized as figure shift to ground when attention is focused on other stimuli. Furthermore, this implicates the role of selection in figure-ground organization, in that stimuli selected for attention are organized into figure-ground relationships with other stimuli in the environment. Due to the probable malfunctioning of the sensory apparatus, some individuals cannot accomplish figure-ground shifts, however. Such is the case with some learning-disabled children who experience auditory figure-ground distortions which somehow cause background noise to compete with auditory stimuli which should be in the forefront of attention. There is some apparent difficulty in filtering out background stimulation. This type of difficulty is sometimes encountered by anyone who strains to hear another person talk over the roar of machines, the noise of a party, or some other form of interference. In the visual modality, establishing figure-ground relationships among stimuli is extremely hard when objects are camouflaged by their surroundings.

In most instances, however, figure-ground organization is effectively managed by the perceptual system; sometimes, figure-ground organization is even "painfully" effective for the person who suffers excruciating pain from gout, for example (if you will pardon the pun). The pain is at the forefront of focus until an analgesic or anestheic effects a shift of that experience to the background of focus, at which time the individual becomes more attuned to other internal or external events. The unsympathetic jokester has an awareness of figure-ground phenomena, as indicated by the suggestions to the gout sufferer that the pain would hardly be noticed if a severe blow were delivered to the other foot!

A perceptual organization process to which numerous allusions have been made involves the grouping or categorization of stimuli into meaningful patterns. From the Gestalt perspective, stimuli are hypothesized to be grouped into ordered relationships with one another, such that we come to perceive "whole" objects or events which are greater than the sum of their respective parts. One principle which governs this process is that of *"proximity."* According to this principle, objects or events which are closer together in space and time tend to be grouped into a single entity. For example, letters comprising the words on this page are grouped together by virtue of their spacing arrangements. But at a more elementary level, even ambiguous stimuli tend to be grouped in a similar fashion. For example, the symbols below are perceived in groups of two's and three's instead of some random grouping.

XXX XX XXX XXX XX XX XX XXX XXX XX XX

According to the principle of *"similarity,"* stimuli that are alike in some way tend to be grouped together in perception. Rock (1975) indicated that it is not actually clear what "kinds" of similarity affect this type of grouping, but size and color do seem to be two effective dimensions. For example, when looking at a chess board, we tend to see black squares and white squares and black chess pieces and white chess pieces. Pawns are easily distinguishable from other pieces, not only on the basis of their shape, but also on the basis of their size. (For those who are familiar with the game, grouping can also be accomplished on the basis of the "functions" of the pieces, their "values," and their "meanings." Thus, the role of learning becomes involved in higher level perceptual organization, and we shall have more to say about this later.)

Another principle of primitive organization, *"closure,"* states that individuals tend to organize stimulus features into completed wholes even when the figure is not actually complete. That is, the perceptual process fills gaps from incomplete sensory data. It may be quite tempting to extend this principle to the manner in which individuals form complete impressions of others on the basis of partial information, but as we shall see later, such an application would perhaps be too simplistic. At a basic level, the principle of closure can be demonstrated in the tendency to perceive a completed circle and a whole square in the figures below, despite the fact that neither figure is a completed whole.

A converse phenomenon may sometimes occur when individuals are unable to fill gaps from information about a truly completed whole object or event. In such cases, the parts may be so numerous, ambiguous, or complex that individuals have difficulty constructing a whole representation. All of the facts might be in front of the person, and yet he/she experiences difficulty in constructing those facts into a whole perception. You should have no trouble drawing from your own personal experience of objects or events those which were so complicated that you had difficulty organizing those stimuli into something which made sense to you.

Forgus and Melamed (1976) pointed out that, while the Gestalt principles of perceptual organization describe how stimuli are grouped, they do not tell us how elements come together to form a particular meaning or identity which we can recognize. None of the various principles discussed here can adequately describe what it is about another person's face, for example, than enables a person to identify that face as being the face of a particular individual, distinguishable from the face of someone else. It seems that this type of recognition and perceptual organization involves higher mental processes which govern more sophisticated "information processing." While an analysis of theories of information processing is beyond the scope of the present discussion, it is nevertheless appropriate at this point to note the impact of language on perceptual organization and information processing.*

The Role of Language in Perceptual Organization

Perceptual organization is possible to a large extent because individuals have language capabilities. Language functions as a coding mechanism for grouping perceptions into meaningful categories. The linguists Edward Sapir and Benjamin Lee Whorf went so far as to insist that virtually all of our experience is influenced by language (see Whorf, 1956). According to these theorists, the way we perceive and think about the world is heavily determined by the language we use to interpret our experiences (Berkowitz, 1975). This notion has been modified into a qualified version which is generally accepted in contemporary psychology (see Cole and Scribner, 1974; Slobin, 1971). The current view asserts that language makes it "easier" to experience events for which we have an adequate vocabulary (Goldstein, 1980). Thus, language does not dictate specific choices of interpretation of perceptions; it simply makes it more convenient to categorize stimuli. Incoming sensory data have implicative relationships to other data processed from past experience. As a coding mechanism, language facilitates the organization of those relationships into "meaningful" experience. Were it not for this function of language, events would be isolated from one another in perception, and a confusing world of unfamiliar events and objects would be represented in awareness.

It has virtually always been assumed that one of the characteristics of human beings that sets them apart from animal species is their unique capability to use language as a conceptual tool. It is less commonly recognized by the lay

---

*For a representative account of information processing in relation to perception, the reader is referred to Neisser, U. *Cognitive Psychology.* New York, Appleton-Century-Crofts, 1967.

person that language also functions as a "perceptual" tool. Just as the expansion of one's vocabulary facilitates improved conceptual functioning, so also does it enhance perceptual functioning. Language enables the person to make finer discriminations among stimuli in the perceptual organization process. As Hastorf, Schneider, and Polefka (1970) noted, one of the most salient aspects of the individual's participation in organizing and structuring the experiential world is the categorization of stimuli through the use of a linguistic coding system.

According to Hastorf et al. (1970), the categories used by individuals derive from past experience, which is inseparable from language and cultural background. While individuals may use numerous common categories for organizing perceptions within a particular culture, there are also differences among individuals within the culture, such that different individuals may use different categories in organizing perceptions. For example, some individuals may organize their perceptions of a computer around the structural characteristics of the object, while others may organize their perceptions of the computer around its functional characteristics. Countless other categories may be employed in the perception of objects and events. Whatever the nature of those categories and however those categories are used, they are dependent on language learned in the particular culture.

Summary

Perceptual organization is concerned with the manner in which individuals structure their perceptions once stimuli have been selected for attention. The Gestalt principles of organization provide some useful indications of underlying mechanisms in the organization process. Figure-ground, proximity, similarity, and closure are four such principles which have been emphasized as factors contributing to the simple organization of stimuli. Language learned within a specific cultural context also comes to influence perceptual organization by providing a linguistic coding system for categorizing stimuli. While language provides some common categories for grouping stimuli within a culture, the diversity of learning histories of individuals within the culture contributes to the acquisition and utilization of various categories which are unique to individuals. Thus, different individuals may employ different learned categories to organize perceptions of a common stimulus.

Perceptual Stability

If you were to walk around your work area and shift your attention from object to object, you would not be perplexed or bewildered by a constant shift and change in the features of those objects. Obviously, the properties of stimuli remain the same even if we turn our heads or move to the other side of the room. A file cabinet in the corner is five feet high and does not change size, nor does it change shape or color, whether you stand in from of it or 20 feet away. There are enduring aspects of the file cabinet, and there are enduring aspects to our experience as well. Stated simply, our perceptions tend to be characterized by *stability*, and they often remain stable despite the fact that sensory information changes. The ways in which individuals maintain stability in their perceptions have been studied in relation to what is known as "constancy" phenomena. *Constancy* refers to the tendency for objects of perception to remain the same despite variations in the conditions of sensory input.

To clarify the notion of constancy, let us extend the example from above. As you walk toward the file cabinet on the other side of the room, the retinal image of the file cabinet, or *proximal stimulus* (the stimulus impinging upon the sensory receptor), becomes larger. Yet, you do not perceive the file cabinet to change size. Furthermore, you do not perceive the file cabinet to change shape or color, in spite of the fact that the visual angle and incident illumination both change and result in proximal stimulus versions of changing shape and brightness. The size, shape, and brightness of the proximal stimulus all change as you walk toward the file cabinet, and you nonetheless perceive it to be unchanging and invariant. Given the discrepancy between proximal stimuli and perceptual experience, it would seem that individuals necessarily process sensory information in such a way as to produce stability and invariance in the world of objects. Just as we cannot perceive and respond to all stimulus impingements, neither can we perceive and respond to all of the changes in the dimensions of stimulation. That is, while changes occur in the spatial orientation, distance, and incident illumination of objects, we do not process changes in these dimensions.

Whether changes occur in the dimensions of size, shape, or color, the phenomena are basically the same, and are described in terms of the unitary principle of constancy. *Color* constancies have been investigated in relation to both chromatic (brightness) and achromatic (hue) properties of objects which are perceived as invariant in spite of changes in brightness or hue. For example, the color of the surgeon's surgical garments are perceived to be the same whether the surgeon is standing at the operating table or in a darkened room. Illumination in both areas is different, the proximal stimulus versions are different in the respective areas, and the color is perceived to be the same. In *size* constancy, the perceived size of the object remains the same, even though increased or decreased distances from the object result in smaller or larger proximal versions. Thus, the clinical social worker who is 5-feet 6-inches tall is perceived as being 5-foot-6, whether that person is standing next to you or at the end of the corridor. The sizes of the proximal versions are different at the two distances, but the person is perceived as being the same height. *Shape* constancy involves the tendency to perceive the shape of an object as being the same, despite changes in spatial orientation which effect changes in proximal stimulus versions. This book appears to be rectangular no matter from what angle you perceive it. But, as you change angles, or perhaps turn the book in your hand to examine its cover, the proximal stimulus version changes shape from rectangular to trapezoidal and back to rectangular.

Color constancy is apparently determined at the level of stimulus characteristics, while size and shape constancy are dependent on previous learning and higher cognitive functions (Forgus and Melamed, 1976). Once objects become familiar (like the social worker or the textbook), individuals tend to maintain their perceptions of those objects. For example, we know from experience that books are rectangular in shape, and we have all learned that certain objects in our world do not change size, shape, color, or various other characteristics when we change our perspective. In most cases this type of learning serves us well, as it ensures that certain aspects of our world are invariant and stable.

According to Schneider et al. (1979), individuals seem to seek invariance in the physical world even though stimulus information constantly shifts and changes. This perceived invariance is heavily influenced by learning experience and higher cognitive processes which enable us to process stimulus input with existing formulae for immediately creating stable perceptions. It seems that the world must be sufficiently consistent and predictable, or there would be too much variance and uncertainty for adaptation (Forgus and Melamed, 1976). Hastorf, Schneider, and Polefka (1970) compared the stability-seeking tendency of individuals with the process by which scientists go about seeking invariance and order in the universe. Specifically, scientists attempt to determine what aspects of the universe are changing and invariant, so that they can make predictions about the occurrence of events. In a comparable fashion, the lay person attempts to establish aspects of the world that are invariant, so as to create some order, predictability, and stability in the world of experience. In attempting to maintain a stable world of experience, however, the lay person occasionally goes beyond the facts to make inferences about enduring features of the world when, in reality, those features are no longer the same as they once were. Within the area of person perception, for example, you have probably had the experience of perceiving a friend to be the "same 'ol person" despite the fact that he/she has changed; and, how disturbing it sometimes is to realize that this "same 'ol person" is not as predictable as he/she once was.

Summary

Human beings seem to be incapable of perceiving objects in all of their real-life complexity (Goldstein, 1980). We tend to select stimuli from the vast array of heterogenous forms in the environment, organize sensory input into structured perceptions, and utilize higher cognitive functions to impose stability on the world of objects. In short, we "create" our own perceptual experience. The reality is, however, that our creations obviously lack perfect correspondence with the material world. Because perceptions are subjective, a "true view" of the world is an illusion. Yet, we often fail to appreciate this fact, and continue to assume that our view is the one true perspective. We need to realize that *this "one true perspective" has been "selected," "organized," and "stabilized" through our own active efforts at creating meaningful experience.*

The Perception of Persons: Interpersonal Perception

The fundamental processes which characterize object perception also apply to the perception of persons. Principles of selection, organization, and stability are basic to interpersonal perception. However, when human beings are the foci of perception, there are unique aspects to the experience which cannot be sufficiently explained by reference to such elementary processes. In fact, theorists and researchers have traditionally differentiated object perception from person perception on the assumption that the latter is both qualitatively and quantitatively distinct (Taguiri and Petrullo, 1958). There are some rather obvious reasons for noting the distinctiveness of person perception. For one thing, human beings are living entities of unbelievable complexity, who are perceived to behave in predictable or curious ways and to have feelings, emotions, attitudes, values, motivations, and unique personality traits. The perception of persons involves much more than the simple selection and organization of physical characteristics which typifies object perception. In addition, when perceiving the behavior of another person, we tend to assume that there are "reasons" for that behavior. We form hypotheses about those reasons by inferring some internal emotional or cognitive cause, or we may infer that the cause for the behavior lies in the environment.

Whatever forms our inferences take, they are determined not only by the behavior of the other person but also by our own personalities. That is, we tend to perceive others from our own frame of reference, which is the product of myriad factors, not the least of which include our perceptions of self, our assumptions about people in general, our social roles, and our relationships with others. Furthermore, we tend to perceive others as being similar to ourselves. We infer that other persons have attributes which we possess. Other persons, like ourselves, are thinking and feeling persons; they have thoughts and emotions with which we can often identify. And, when other persons express certain emotions across numerous situations, we often tend to perceive them as having that emotional state as an enduring characteristic (Hastorf, Schneider, and Polefka, 1970). For example, the paramedic who responds to medical emergencies without becoming overwhelmed by anxiety and stress tends to be perceived as calm, poised, and in control. Another person who faints at the sight of blood is perceived to be excitable, fragile, or overly sensitive.

You will recall from the previous discussion of perceptual stability that individuals tend to perceive invariance despite changes in the conditions of sensory input. This phenomenon can be extended to the perception of human behavior, which is dynamic, continuous, sequential, and ever-changing. For instance, when you observe the behavior of others on a medical floor of a hospital, you actually perceive a constant flow of activity—a continuous flow of movement in their actions and words. All around you there is ongoing activity, and yet you do not perceive a continuous "flow" of behavior. Instead, you perceive "units" of behavior. You may see a man and woman stepping out from the elevator, an intern walking down the hallway, a volunteer worker pushing a cart, and a patient supporting herself as she walks along with one hand grasping the corridor railing. Each of these perceptions represents specific behavioral segments which are extracted from the ongoing flow of changing behavior on the floor. There is a continuous procession of behavior, and you nevertheless perceive "segments." One of the ways in which we extract ongoing behavior and perceive stable segments is by selecting and organizing acts and their effects. That is, we observe behavior and its consequences, and group them together into manageable perceptual units (Hastorf, Schneider, and Polefka,

1970). However, behavior also has causes, or antecedents, and the inferences of causation for behavior also enter into the process of interpersonal perception.

If you were to watch the snow fall lightly and gracefully to the ground in the wintertime, you would certainly make no inference about the "intentions" or "motivations" of the snowflakes. It would be absurd to make any such inferences about tabular white crystals of water; they result from atmospheric conditions, to which the concepts of intention and motivation do not apply. But, human behavior is a totally different event. If you were to observe a department head shouting at a subordinate, you would probably make some inference about the intentions of the department head. This is because we tend to assume that people are capable of causing their own behavior. They do things in order to bring about certain effects. Thus, our perceptions of others' behavior is typically organized in terms of "cause-behavior-effect" segments. We perceive the actions of others and proceed to infer causes for that behavior in terms of intentions, motivations, or some other antecedent condition. In the above example, you may infer that the department head is angry with the subordinate and is trying to express that anger in order to effect some change in the subordinate's behavior. Or, you may infer that the department head's behavior is due to a nasty disposition, hangover, or some obscure need to intimidate staff members. Any number of inferences could be made, all of which function as tentative explanations for ambiguous behavioral events. It seems that we need to make sense out of the behavior of others, and we attempt to do so by assigning causes to the actions we perceive. This process of assigning causes to behavior is called *attribution*, and it is a variable of principal significance in the perception of persons. Because of the centrality of attribution processes in the perception of persons, considerable attention is devoted to them throughout subsequent chapters. At this point it is sufficient to note the pervasive attribution tendency which, in part, serves to distinguish person perception from object perception.

The role of inference in person perception must not be minimized, for it is perhaps the most significant and perplexing aspect of the entire range of perceptual phenomena. When we observe another individual, the most readily apparent and observable characteristics of that person are physical features, sexual identity, and overt behavior. These characteristics form a type of raw data base for making inferences about the perceived person. From perceived physical features and sexual identity we often draw conclusions about that individual's personality. From perceived behavior we often make inferences about what is going on inside the person. We can never be totally certain of what is happening within another person, but we can be relatively sure that in most cases our senses do not deceive us when providing behavioral information. However, we often do deceive ourselves by drawing unfounded inferences which extend way beyond the behavioral data. For example, on the basis of the outward behavior displayed by the department head in the previous instance, we infer that he/she must therefore be angry. We infer a particular emotion based on the available behavioral cues. The reality is, however, that the department head may not have been angry at all. It is possible that he/she may have been portraying the behavior of someone else for the benefit of the subordinate. Whatever the case may be, the perceptual "facts" derive from the physical features and behavior of others; *inferences are deductions from the apparent facts, and may or may not be accurate.* In contemporary research on interpersonal perception, the chief concern is with the processes by which we come to make such inferences. Subsequent chapters focus on these processes in an attempt to describe how we come to perceive other individuals, evaluate them, and interact with them socially and occupationally.

Summary and Implications

Human perception is a vastly complex and highly subjective psychological process. It involves the interdependent functioning of various physical and psychological mechanisms which facilitate the extraction of information from the environment through the senses. At a higher level, perception involves the organization of that information into meaningful experience. This is accomplished through basic processes of selection, organization, and stability, all of which are influenced to varying degrees by learning, cognition, and motivational/emotional factors. Because of the range of variables contributing to the perceptual process, it is not difficult to appreciate the fact that different individuals perceive the world differently. *Psychologically, the world is not the same for different individuals.* When it comes to the perception of other persons, the complexity of perceptual processes seems almost staggering. This is because interpersonal perception involves the operation of higher cognitive processes which induce perceivers to go beyond the perceptual data and make deductions and inferences from those data about nonobservable events. That is, interpersonal perception involves the processes of attributing personality characteristics, behavioral causes, and internal states to other individuals, subsequent to the extraction of information about their physical features and behavior.

It is essential to satisfactory interpersonal relations that individuals appreciate and understand the critical role which perception plays in the formation and maintenance of relationships with others. Interpersonal relations *begin with perception.* The ways in which your perceptions are selected and organized will influence the ways in which you behave toward other individuals, and your behavior will influence the ways in which others perceive and respond to you. In addition, many interpersonal problems have developed between individuals because of differing perceptions of some common event. In reality, however, there is no "common event" or stimulus which is perceived by two or more persons in any given situation. The event is different for each person. And yet, we often assume that our perceptions are the correct perceptions. When another individual suggests that our perceptions may be wrong, we often become hostile and defensive. We seem to be able to tolerate little disagreement when it comes to matters of assumed fact. That is, we assume that our perceptions are objective, when in fact they only reflect reality *as it appears to us.* If we can develop an understanding that others are "equally inaccurate" in their perception of stimuli in the environment, we will not feel threatened by the views of others. In short, it is important for us to avoid treating matters of subjectivity as matters of "objectivity." As Haney (1979, p. 66) stated, "If I can realize that your 'reality' is not the same as mine, then your statement about your 'reality' is no threat to mine."

References

Berkowitz, L. *A Survey of Social Psychology*. Hinsdale, Illinois, The Dryden Press, 1975.

Cole, M., and Scribner, S. *Culture and Thought*. New York, Wiley, 1974.

Forgus, R. H., and Melamed, L. E. *Perception: A Cognitive-Stage Approach*, 2d ed. New York, McGraw-Hill, 1976.

Goldstein, J. H. *Social Psychology*. New York, Harcourt Brace Jovanovich, 1980.

Hamner, W. C., and Organ, D. W. *Organizational Behavior: An Applied Psychological Approach*. Dallas, Texas, Business Publications, 1978.

Haney, W. V. *Communication and Interpersonal Relations: Text and Cases*, 4th ed. Homewood, Illinois, Richard D. Irwin, 1979.

Hastorf, A. H., Schneider, D. J., and Polefka, J. *Person Perception*. Reading, Massachusetts, Addison-Wesly, 1970.

Hjelle, L. A., and Ziegler, D. J. *Personality Theories: Basic Assumptions, Research, and Applications*. New York, McGraw-Hill, 1976.

Klein, G. S. Need Regulation, in *Nebraska Symposium on Motivation*, ed. M. R. Jones. Lincoln, Nebraska, University of Nebraska Press, 1954.

Koffka, K. *Principles of Gestalt Psychology*. New York, Harcourt Brace Jovanovich, 1935.

Kohler, W. *Gestalt Psychology: An Introduction to the New Concepts in Modern Psychology*. New York, Liveright, 1947.

Leeper, R. The Role of Motivation in Language: A Study of the Phenomenon of Differential Motivation Control of the Utilization of Habits, *Journal of Genetic Psychology,* **46**:3–40 (1935).

Lundin, R. W. *Theories and Systems of Psychology*, 2d ed. Lexington, Massachusetts, D. C. Heath, 1979.

Reitz, H. J. *Behavior in Organizations*. Homewood, Illinois, Irwin, 1977.

Rock, I. *An Introduction to Perception*. New York, Macmillan, 1975.

Rogers, C. *Client-Centered Therapy: Its Current Practice, Implications, and Theory*. Boston, Houghton Mifflin, 1951.

Schneider, D. J.; Hastorf, A. H.; and Ellsworth, P. C. *Person Perception* (2nd ed). Reading, Mass., Addison-Wesley, 1979.

Shapiro, D. *Neurotic Styles*. New York, Basic Books, 1965.

Slobin, D. I. *Psycholinguistics*. Glencoe, Illinois, Scott-Foresman, 1971.

Taguiri, R., and Petrullo, L. *Person Perception and Interpersonal Behavior*. Stanford, California, Stanford University Press, 1958.

Wertheimer, M. Unterschungen zur Lehre von der Gestalt, II, *Psychologische Forschung,* **4**:301–50 (1923).

Whorf, B. L. *Language, Thought, and Reality*. Cambridge, Massachusetts, MIT Press, 1956.

CHAPTER TWO

The Perception of Persons in Health Care Organizations

*What a piece of work is man! how noble in reason! how
infinite in faculty! in form and moving how express and
admirable! in action how like an angel! in apprehension
how like a god!*

William Shakespeare, *Hamlet*

The perception of persons is characterized by rather distinct and intricate in-formation-processing activities which operate at a higher cognitive level than the basic processes involved in object perception. Numerous factors unique to person perception interact with and modify the outcomes of basic selection, organization, and stabilization processes. The present chapter examines those factors and points up their significance to interpersonal relations within health care organizations.

As stated earlier, there is a great probability that many problems in inter-personal relations are grounded in conflicting perceptions held by different in-dividuals. Within health care settings this probability is great enough to sup-port the contention that perception must necessarily be a principal concern of health professionals. Almost everything the health professional does involves face-to-face interactions with others, and unless he can relate effectively, his performance will suffer. At the core of interpersonal relations is perception. Accurate and realistic perceptions of other individuals are crucial to the health professional's ability to function effectively. A prerequisite to competent per-formance is the ability to perceive events and situations correctly. It is no less imperative that the health professional be able to perceive other persons with a level of accuracy that precludes the possibility of responding in dysfunctional or harmful ways. Indeed, distorted perceptions of patients or clients, col-leagues, supervisors, staff, or others within health care settings can lead to consequences which are potentially damaging to those professional relation-ships. Conversely, the ability to see clearly, listen attentively, and utilize all senses to be alert to the appearance, behavior, and changes of others can enhance one's skills at making decisions, solving problems, interacting with others, and, in general, responding in the most situationally-appropriate manner. Therefore, it is a major premise of this chapter that *effective interpersonal functioning in health care organizations requires a recognition of factors influencing perception so that distortions may be prevented or corrected and accurate perceptions developed.*

Interpersonal perception does not occur in a vacuum. *People* are *perceived* to exist and behave in *situations.* This fact suggests the operation of three general sets of variables which influence the person perception process: the characteristics and behavior of persons being perceived, the perceptual activities of perceivers, and the context in which one person perceives others. Perceptual *context* refers to the physical, social, and psychological conditions surrounding the perceptual event. Since person perception occurs within definite spatial, temporal, personal, and interpersonal boundaries, those boundaries define the perceptual context. The first section of this chapter considers the effects of perceptual context on interpersonal perception and addresses the particular role of health care context in influencing perceptions. The second section examines the characteristics and behavior of perceived persons. Just as object features influence object perception, so also do "person features" influence person perception. Effective health professionals must be able to perceive a wide range of "person features" distinguishing those with whom they work. Because it is common for health professionals to become selectively attentive to a limited range of features when perceiving others (e.g., patients being perceived solely in terms of their particular illnesses), the second section presents a variety of person features which must be processed for accurate perceptions to result. The latter portion of this chapter focuses on the perceptual tendencies of perceivers themselves. As we know, two persons looking at the same patient within the same context can perceive that individual differently. Since the stimulus person is the same for both perceivers, and since the perceptual context is also the same for both, it is largely due to their respective idiosyncratic ways of perceiving that their perceptions may differ. Numerous factors affect these individual processes, and many of them are described in this chapter. Hopefully, one by product of the following discussion is the development of insights into those factors relevant to your perceptual experience within health care organizations. However, insights are only as good as the actions that follow from them. The "bottom line" must be in your subsequent actions to prevent perceptual distortions and enhance perceptual accuracy.

Perceptual Context

The influence of context on person perception seems so obvious that it has often been taken for granted. Whatever the nature and extent of its influence, the perceptual context is at least always evident. When perceiving others, individuals must constantly process contextual information and keep in touch with reality. Failure to do so may often lead to perceptual distortions and maladaptive behavior toward the self and others.

Context is conceptualized as the *conditions which surround individuals and qualify the meaning of their behavior.* It is a broad concept which refers not only to the physical stimulus conditions impinging upon individuals, but also to the social and psychological conditions which help to give meaning to perceptions. Often, the terms "situation" or "environment" are used interchangeably with context. However, context is used more expansively to incorporate factors related to time, location, physical conditions, presence and behavior of others, prevailing social and psychological conditions, antecedent events, and even future events if they hold some relationship to current events. Furthermore, *perceivers themselves* are part of the context.

Barker (1968) introduced the concept of behavior setting to refer to regularly occurring patterns of behavior that are compatible with the physical characteristics of the place in which they occur. That is, there are certain spatial and temporal boundaries which tend to indicate wherein specific behaviors may occur. For example, the hospital is a behavior setting for the practice of medicine, community mental health centers are behavior settings for the practice of counseling and psychotherapy, and universities are behavior settings for teaching, learning, and a wide range of behaviors not usually occurring elsewhere. The physical features, or spatial and temporal boundaries, of these contexts tend to lead individuals to expect to perceive certain actions of others within those physical parameters.

More recently, Schneider, Hastorf, and Ellsworth (1979) suggested that contexts have both physical and social features which serve to facilitate or inhibit certain forms of behavior, and which provide bases for determining what is appropriate behavior. The physical and social features of contexts typically "set the occasion" for persons to behave in certain ways and, at the same time, "set the limits" within which they may act. For example, the operating room sets the occasion for the surgical team to perform surgery, while at the same time setting the limits for those actions irrelevant to their objective. Thus, the actions of the surgical team are aimed at treating the patient's illness by operative procedures, and not by spiritual incantations, exorcisms, or "laying on of the hands." Should the latter practices be observed within the context of the operating room, they would be judged as inappropriate by most persons. That judgements of appropriateness could be made in such circumstances suggests that perceivers utilize contextual information as criteria for assessing how others are acting. More attention is devoted to this process later. The important point here is that, to make sense of others and their behavior, individuals must perceive and process contextual data which clarify, qualify, and give meaning to their perceptions. The principal sources of contextual data are physical and social features of perceptual contexts.

The Physical Context

The physical context can affect person perception in numerous ways. At the most basic level, the characteristics of the physical environment can determine whether another individual is perceived at all. Many pedestrians and motorcyclists have been injured or killed by automobiles because drivers "did not see" them. In some cases, however, these victims were within the visual field of the drivers, but they could not be distinguished from their surroundings. Thus, it is occasionally difficult to perceive others because of an inability to establish figure-ground relationships which permit persons to be distinguished from the environment. Hearing a question from a colleague during lunch may be impossible if everyone at the table is talking at the same time. Spotting a particular nursing student amidst others in a lecture hall may be more difficult than spotting the same student in a group of nonuniformed people in the parking lot.

One's physical *location* within any context tends to establish a "perspective" from which to observe events and persons. A patient standing at the end of the corridor may appear to be stable and comfortable when viewed from the central nursing station. From a closer perspective, one may notice that the patient is pallored, perspiring, trembling, and grimacing with pain. Similarly, nurse practitioners learn that they cannot perceive objective symptoms of discomfort expressed by patients over the intercom; only by going to the patient's room can the nurse gain a clear perspective of the patient's condition. To develop accurate perceptions of other individuals, it is therefore prerequisite that one get a clear physical perspective.

Physical contexts exist in *time* as well as in space. While changes in location (space) usually create different perspectives, so also do changes in time often cause altered perspectives. For example, the orderly's perception of orders given to him by a department supervisor at the end of his shift may be different from his perception of those same orders given at the beginning of his shift. A visitor walking toward the nursing station after visiting hours will be perceived differently than he would during visiting hours. And, time alters the perspectives of most people who receive a phone call during the middle of the night; the same telephone ring in the afternoon would not usually be perceived with the same irritation and apprehension. It must also be noted that spatial and temporal features of contexts "interact" to influence perspectives. For instance, the nurse's perception of a compliment for a job well-done, given to her by a physician in the parking lot after work, may be different from her perception of the compliment when given by the physician in the emergency room immediately following successful treatment of a poisoning victim. Thus, in perceiving other persons, contextual characteristics of time and space offer perceptual data which are processed as background information for interpreting the actions of others.

The involvement of physical context in person perception is even more pervasive when time and space features provide cues about others that lead to "snap judgements." According to Schneider, Hastorf, and Ellsworth (1979), physical features of contexts give information that influence snap judgements about the individuals in those contexts. It would seem logical to assume, for example, that people filling out applications in the personnel office are seeking employment, that persons parking their cars in the staff lot are hospital personnel, and that people sitting in the emergency waiting room are friends or relatives of emergency patients. Socialization experiences have taught individuals to make associations between persons and contexts, such that persons perceived in those contexts are assumed to have certain "associated" characteristics. Although many assumptions may be incorrect, contextual information is nevertheless processed to make quick inferences about perceived persons. In relation to health care contexts, it is common for many individuals to apply learned stereotypes and apply generally negative qualities to persons perceived as patients in alcoholism treatment centers, mental hospitals, and drug rehabilitation units. Even hospital personnel who lack an understanding of various patient disorders may tend to make snap judgements about patients, such that patients in an alcoholism unit, for example, are perceived negatively, while orthopedic patients are perceived more positively. In the former case it is common for perceivers to attribute "personal responsibility" to the alcoholic patient, while in the latter case the orthopedic patient is seldom seen as being personally responsible for his condition.

Most people seem to have an intuitive awareness of the tendency to associate persons with context. That intuition is suggested by the behavior of virtually everyone to be seen occasionally in certain places and not in others. It is common for people to enjoy being seen in contexts which influence others to perceive them positively and to feel uncomfortable in contexts which may predispose others to view them negatively. While most individuals do seem to have an intuitive awareness of the effects of context on perception, the evolution of intuition into insight is necessary for enhancing perceptual abilities; and, the translation of insight into "action" is the essential process through which perceptual skills are enhanced. There is abundant evidence that the more clearly an individual perceives the context in which another person is encountered, the more clearly that person will be perceived. Variations in the physical features of contexts will affect the extent to which this is achieved. For the health professional, the implications of such findings are distinct: to be skilled in the perception of persons within health care contexts it is necessary to be skilled in perceiving physical variations within those contexts. It is usually not sufficient simply to be aware of changing physical contexts. It is necessary to utilize awareness by converting it into action. This means that the health professional must be skilled at using perceived changes in physical contexts to adjust perceptions of persons as those contexts vary.

The Social Context

The presence of individuals within physical environments is typically cited as the definitive feature of "social contexts." More specifically, however, social contexts are defined in terms of the *relationships* and *interactive processes* between two or more individuals. A context is "social" when a variation in the behavior of one or more individuals in a physical setting is accompanied by variation in the behavior or experience of one or more other individuals in the same setting. Consider the following dialogue between a client and his psychotherapist:

> CLIENT: Well, I don't know if I can change. I don't know if I even want to. But, at the same time, I know that I have to if things are to get any better for me. I want to be different in some ways, so that certain people like me more. But, I don't care about being different for everyone, just certain people.

THERAPIST: You feel uncertain about changing. You're not sure if you can change, and you're not sure if you even want to. Yet, you feel like you have to become different for those you care about.

In this brief dialogue, two individuals are involved in an interaction with one another. Their interactions in relation to one another define the context as "social," since variations in the behavior of one effect variations in the experience and behavior of the other. In an interactive, reciprocal manner, the statements and nonverbal behavior of each person influence the other's perceptions and subsequent response. As they continue to interact, perceptions will become modified, and behavior may change accordingly. If, early in their dialogue, the therapist acted uninterested in the client's concerns, the behavior of the client could eventually reflect his perceptions of the therapist's insensitivity and lack of respect (e.g., the client may express anger, resentment, frustration, and emotional pain). Regardless of the course of their interactions, the social context changes as their relationship evolves, dissolves, or otherwise changes.

Whereas physical contexts change and thereby affect perceptions of persons, relationships and interactions which define social contexts are more variable and changing. One result is that the same person in the same physical context may be perceived differently as the social context changes. The following case provides an illustration of the role of social context in the perception of a department supervisor:

Ann, a staff nurse in the pediatrics department, was talking with a group of other nurses at the central nursing station during shift change. The department supervisor, Mrs. C., approached the group and interrupted its conversation in order to reprimand Ann for failing to change the I V of a child down the hall. While Mrs. C. reprimanded Ann in an unemotional, matter-of-fact way, Ann became visibly upset and could not focus on the constructive criticism which Mrs. C. provided. In her embarrassment, Ann looked around the group to see how her peers were reacting. As she scanned the group, Mrs. C. commented that Ann would do well to pay attention to what she was saying and not be concerned with the others because, Mrs. C. stated, "It doesn't concern them."

In this case, as with many like it, the supervisor who constructively criticizes a subordinate in the presence of others may be perceived as cold and insensitive by observers, and the subordinate may not process the message clearly because of the presence of her peers. Ann may have heard much of what Mrs. C. said, but it may not have "registered" with her; she may have been worried about what her peers were thinking, she may have been too angry to evaluate critically Mrs. C.'s comments, or she may have been trying to formulate a response to Mrs. C. Given the social context, Mrs. C.'s criticisms were almost guaranteed to have an adverse effect on how she was perceived by Ann and her peers. In addition, Mrs. C.'s contention that her business with Ann "doesn't concern them" is probably a false assumption. That is, while the content of her business with Ann may not concern observers, the "transaction" of that business does, because they are part of the social context through which it is transacted. As indicated earlier, a variation in the behavior of one or more persons in the same physical context will effect a variation in the experience and behavior of others in the same physical context—in this case, the staff's perceptions of Mrs. C. The same criticism communicated by Mrs. C. to Ann in a different social context (in private) could be expected to have different effects: there is a higher probability that Ann would receive the message clearly, Ann would not have been humiliated, her perceptions of Mrs. C. would probably be more positive, and others would not have been exposed to behavior which would negatively influence their perceptions of Mrs. C.

There are other ways in which the presence of other individuals can affect perception. Imagine being in a totally darkened room with three other persons. Your task is to view a tiny point source of light and estimate how far it moves. After a short exposure to the light, you converse with your partners to compare your estimates. Will your estimate be influenced by theirs? From the findings of Sherif (1935) in a study investigating this question, the answer appears to be yes. In the original study, the "autokinetic effect" was used by Sherif to determine the effect of group influence on individual behavior. The autokinetic effect refers to the tendency of a stationary point of light in a completely darkened room to appear to move. While the light does not actually move, it appears to move up or down, right or left, because perceivers lack visible reference points in the darkened room. Without reference points, there are no sources of information available for estimating the distance of light movement. The situation is thus highly ambiguous. Sherif hypothesized that the effect of social influence is maximized under such conditions, where sensory information is ambiguous. In testing this hypothesis, Sherif had subjects view the point of light individually and then state their estimates of movement. When viewing the light individually, subjects created their own frames of reference for judging light movement and expressed their estimates on the basis of their respective frames of reference. After three sessions alone in the room, subjects were put into groups of two or three. In stating their estimates, the subjects were initially at odds because they had each previously established a different frame of reference. However, as they continued to express their judgements, their estimates began to converge on a common norm concerning light movement. This convergence appeared to reflect a true perceptual change among subjects, rather than verbal conformity to the judgements of others. There has been an accumulation of supportive findings from subsequent studies which clearly indicate that, in ambiguous conditions which provide individuals with no stable frame of reference for making perceptual judgements, other individuals can exert considerable informational social influence which modifies the perceiver's perception of stimuli.

In relation to the findings just reviewed, it must be recognized that the health professional's work group exerts an influence on perception, judgement, and performance. Health professionals tend to incorporate many of the values, attitudes, and perspectives of their peers. Consequently, they may often come to perceive and respond to situations on the basis of how those situations are defined by a group. While health professionals also define situations as individuals, the tendency for perceptions to be influenced by others is common in ambiguous situations where individuals cannot depend upon their own sensory information. When individuals cannot rely on the evidence of their own senses, they rely on the social context to clarify their perceptions. Usually, this is an adaptive way of responding to ambiguity. For example, if a radiologic technician cannot readily discriminate certain discrete and rarefied areas on a radiogram, he may seek assistance from a colleague to make those discriminations. However, a reliance on others for clarification of perceptions does not always yield accurate information, nor is it always appropriate to depend on others in such circumstances. The new staff member who has had infrequent contacts with her supervisor may develop a distorted perception of the supervisor if she relies too heavily on the impressions of other staff. Conversely, the supervisor who has not taken the time to observe closely the performance of a subordinate may be unable to appraise accurately his performance if she relies on reports from others.

Because social context implies the presence of individuals, it might be expected that people occasionally are perceived in relation to the "company they keep." Indeed, this ancient aphorism has received some empirical support in the findings of Gurwitz and Dodge (1977) which indicated that perceivers are willing to infer characteristics about others simply by knowing the typical behavior of their friends. In health care organizations it is common for people to form small social groups, or cliques. Thus, an observer may perceive one individual from a particular clique solely on the basis of knowledge about the behavioral history of others comprising the group. However, even though this tendency may be common, it is seldom sufficient to base perceptions of others on "the company they keep."

Schneider, Hastorf, and Ellsworth (1979) noted that the same behavior in different social contexts may lead perceivers to use different "labels" for the behavior of others. For example, singing to oneself might be called gleeful, annoying, strange, or entertaining, depending on whether the social context was on the street, in a library, on a bus, or in front of an audience. Such behavior could also be termed appropriate or inappropriate, depending upon the social context. It is usually considered appropriate for athletes to pat one another on the rump during a game, for example. However, it would be judged inappropriate if a psychiatric social worker went around the state hospital patting everyone on the rump.

When perceivers judge another person's behavior to be appropriate, no attempt is made to go beyond that assessment and explain "why" the behavior was appropriate. Most persons tend to assume that others usually act in appropriate ways; and, when they do, the assumption is verified, and no residual curiosity forces perceivers to seek explanations. On the other hand, when the behavior of others is judged to be inappropriate in the social context, perceivers are induced to seek an explanation for that behavior. To develop a satisfactory explanation, perceivers tend to make inferences about the actor. In the case of the psychiatric social worker, observers might therefore infer that he lacks social intelligence, that he misjudges situations, that he defies social norms, or that he intends to affect people in some peculiar way. Whatever inferences are made, perceivers must know something about the social contexts in which the behavior occurs before they can arrive at a satisfactory explanation. Earlier in this section it was pointed out that the physical and social features of contexts "set the occasion" and "set the limits" for behavior. Unless perceivers are able to perceive those contextual cues which set the boundaries for behavior, they will be unable to make reliable discriminations between appropriate and inappropriate behavior. In health care organizations, the individual who is unable to make necessary discriminations by utilizing contextual information will himself tend to respond inappropriately across a range of situations. Such has been the case for some foreign-born and educated psychiatrists, deficient in their knowledge of cultural norms in the United States, who have made psychiatric diagnoses on individuals whose behavior was within the limits of social conventionality and normality. To make accurate and responsible psychiatric diagnoses, it is imperative that the practitioner know something about the context and the forces within the context that might influence the individual's behavior. Clinical diagnosis, as well as other forms of assessment, are exercises in person perception. The consequences of misperception and, hence, misdiagnosis on nonpathological behavior can be devastating for the individual. It is, therefore, mandatory that health professionals develop the perceptual acumen to make accurate discriminations and respond to others in the most helpful and adaptive ways.

Characteristics of Perceived Persons

In point of fact, human beings present themselves to others as perceptual stimuli. Like inanimate stimuli, human beings have some readily perceptible physical characteristics. Individuals come in distinct sizes, shapes, and colors. They speak in different languages, dialects, volumes, pitches, rates, fluencies, and qualities, or perhaps they do not speak at all. They emit different odors and scents, they have varying skin textures, appendages, and physical limitations. Of course, physical characteristics such as these make up only part of the total stimulus pattern of human beings. People also have characteristics that are not readily perceptible. Not being outwardly observable, thoughts, attitudes, values, and feelings must be "inferred" from the behavior of individuals. What people *say* and what people *do* are the data bases from which perceivers infer these and other nonobservable characteristics. Health professionals come into contact with people who are often perceived mainly in terms of their physical characteristics; but, those individuals are also encountered at various times of fear, apprehension, pain, stress, mental preoccupation, relief, optimism, and happiness. How these cues are perceived and integrated with physical characteristics will affect the extent to which health professionals form perceptions of "whole persons." Patients, for example, are more than "illnesses." Yet, there is often a tendency among health professionals to perceive patients in terms of their respective illnesses (e.g., "the amputee," "the epileptic," "the diabetic"). People are much more than severed limbs, seizures, and sugar imbalances. As targets of perception, human beings present characteristics offering a wealth of information extending far beyond mere physical data. Many of these considerations are discussed in this section in relation to *physical features* and *artifacts* (accessories to appearance), *nonverbal behavior*, and *verbal behavior*.

Physical Features and Artifacts

The perception of physical features is an area that has lagged behind other areas of psychological research (Wrightsman, 1972), despite the fact that physical appearance is a key factor in determining one's "attraction" to another.

This section reviews some of the limited findings concerning inferences that are commonly made from perceptions of various physical features. Physical features do indeed influence perceptions, and it would benefit the health professional to be aware of the types of inferences that are often drawn from perceptions of particular physical characteristics.

The essayist, Walt Whitman, once wrote the following about Abraham Lincoln (*Specimen Days*, 1867):

> None of the artists or pictures has caught the deep, though subtle and indirect expression of this man's face. There is something else there. One of the great portrait painters of two or three centuries ago is needed.

The human face can indeed be perplexing, posing challenges not only to essayists and portrait painters, but also to anyone casting a glance upon the facial features of another. In many respects, the face is the central channel through which individuals manifest themselves to others. It is typically the most compelling feature to which perceivers attend, because of the kind and amount of information it can convey in a short period of time. Truly, "there is something in a face," as the poet, William Somerville, suggested (*The Lucky Hit*, 1727):

> An air, and a peculiar grace,
> Which boldest painters cannot trace.

For centuries, enduring physical qualities of the face (its *physiognomy*) have been regarded as keys to personality and character (Weitz, 1979). "Face reading" is as old as palm reading, phrenology, and the reading of tea leaves. Many enduring facial features have been associated with specific personality types, despite the fact that inferences from facial features are complicated, compounded by stereotypes and false assumptions, and potentially damaging to human beings. Research has failed to find any relation between facial type and character (Harrison, 1974), yet the misconception still persists (Harrison, 1974, p. 117):

> . . . you might have a man with a low forehead who was demonstrably a very intelligent individual. But show his picture to a group of judges and they would tend to agree that, yes, this person was not very bright.

A variety of facial characteristics tend to lead to inferences about persons. For example, persons with high foreheads are often thought to be intelligent, persons with thin lips may be seen as serious and conscientious, persons with full and rosy faces are often perceived as warm, jolly, and friendly. The implicit assumption that many individuals make is that certain traits can be detected in specific locations of the face. Certainly, beauty and ugliness are culture-bound value judgements which are almost exclusively made on the basis of perceived facial features. Numerous studies have shown that one's assessment of facial attractiveness tends to have a direct influence of subsequent interactions with individuals. In this connection, it is possible that "blonds do have more fun" because they tend to be perceived as more attractive and social, while brunettes are seen as more dependable and intelligent (Lawson 1971). The listing of facial features and presumed associated traits could comprise an encyclopedic account of unsubstantiated assumptions. It should suffice at this point to reiterate the highly tenuous and contestible nature of inferences drawn from perceptions of facial features. It should, however, be helpful to note some of the facial cues which can be used to generate some reasonable hypotheses about perceived persons.

Harrison (1974) noted that the face and head provide appearance cues which are enduring, semifixed, or momentary. *Enduring* cues are static features which reveal information concerning the individual's sex, age, race, and possibly ethnic background, status, or occupation. Cues that are often used to infer these characteristics include hair color and density, wrinkles, muscle tone, fat deposits, eye color, skin pigmentation, scars, and the shape and configuration of features. *Semifixed* cues are not permanent characteristics of an individual, but are likely to remain fixed during an interaction. These cues include length of head and facial hair, hair style, cleanliness, facial cuts and abrasions, and blemishes. *Momentary* cues are changing facial expressions that indicate emotions. They represent a class of nonverbal behaviors to be discussed later: head movements, eye movements, mouth and lip movements.

Overall *body appearance* can provide information about an individual's age, sex, race, and other demographic characteristics. The belief in a correspondence between body appearance and personality goes back to the ancient Hindus, the physicians of Greece and Rome, and extends to modern civilization. Perhaps the best known of the various body typologies relating physique to personality is the system devised by Sheldon (1940, 1954). Sheldon posited that individuals could be classified according to three dimensions of physique, with each dimension being associated with specific "temperamental" characteristics. The *endomorphic* body build was described as round, heavy, fleshy, and soft. The major temperamental characteristics associated with endomorphy were sociability, sympathy, relaxation, laziness, and agreeableness. *Ectomorphic* physiques were described as thin, tall, and fragile. Individuals with ectomorphic body builds were said to be tense, ambitious, pessimistic, nervous, and suspicious. The *mesomorphic* type was seen as having self-reliant, mature, energetic, and assertive temperamental characteristics that accompanied a muscular and athletic body build. Such a simplified typology has been regarded as minimally useful in accounting for the complexities of human development and behavior.

Nevertheless, physique and general body appearance *do* influence the kinds of inferences perceivers make. Numerous studies have found that individuals *are* willing to infer personality characteristics from others' body appearance (e.g., Beck, Ward-Hull, and McLear, 1976; Dibiase and Hjelle, 1968; Sleet, 1969; Wells and Siegal, 1961). For example, Kleinke and Staneski (1980) recently found that women with large bust sizes were perceived by male and female subjects to be relatively unintelligent, immodest, immoral, and incompetent; women with small bust sizes were seen as being the opposite. These perceptions reflect the influence of stereotypes which are no more reliable in predicting personality characteristics than body types are in predicting temperament. Yet, body appearance seems to hold some implicit predictive value for naive observers. There are various possible explanations for why individuals associate personality with body appearance. One possibility is that the culture holds different expectations for different kinds of physique, and a perceived congruence between physique and behavior may be a function of individuals' attempts to conform to social expectations. An endomorph is expected to be agreeable and affable; it may therefore be easier for that person to act agreeable and affable than to be disagreeable and deviant. Acting amiably not only increases the liklihood of receiving social reinforcement, but it also satisfies a "self-fulfilling prophecy." That is, if others perceive the individual as amiable, they may behave in ways that make him amiable. When he behaves as expected, he is socially rewarded, and others come to perceive him as "fitting the type."

It is no news to anyone that the color of a person's *skin* leads to inferences about personality characteristics. Many studies on prejudice and stereotyping have made it clear that in this society people with dark skin are assigned more negative characteristics than those with light colored skin (Schneider, Hastorf, and Ellsworth, 1979). It is also relatively common knowledge that persons with *physical handicaps* are perceived differently than nonhandicapped persons. Handicapped persons are often perceived to be less happy and more self-conscious, less selfish, and more gentle than nonhandicapped individuals. In most cases, handicapped persons are readily perceived in social contexts due to stimulus features such as contrast and movement. That is, as social stimuli, handicapped persons tend to contrast with other stimulus persons who are ablebodied and more mobile. Persons with different handicaps also tend to be perceived differently, as indicated by the findings of Richardson et al. (1961). Their findings revealed a preference among observers for different types of handicapped individuals. Ablebodied persons were rated most preferred and then, in decreasing order of preference, persons with a leg brace, persons in a wheelchair, persons with a hand missing, and persons with a facial disfigurement. These data suggest that individuals differentially perceive physical deformities, and that persons with particular types of handicaps are perceived more favorably than others.

There are various other physical appearance cues which influence perceptions, not the least of which include *age* and *sex*. Adolescents are often perceived as immature, troubled, naive, and insecure; young adults are typically seen to be more mature, confident, secure, and responsible, despite the fact that it seems to be increasingly difficult to determine where adolescence ends and young adulthood begins. At any rate, both age groups are perceived differently than persons in the oldest age groups, who are also frequently misperceived due to age-group stereotypes. Women have historically been perceived differently than men, with men being assigned more positive qualities. With changing sex roles in our society, it may be expected that perceptions based on sexual stereotypes will change. Indeed, perceptions of women are presently changing, with women being seen by both sexes as more assertive, ambitious, and competent than at other times in history. This trend highlights a significant point: perceptions are influenced by culture and time. They are culture-bound and may change as time and events ring in new values and standards of interpersonal judgement.

Personal *artifacts* often reflect changing values and standards. Artifacts are accessories to appearance, such as clothing, which communicate a wide range of information about individuals. Clothing styles can give information about the sex, age, occupation, status and, in some cases, inner feelings, values, and attitudes of different persons. Choices of clothing often reflect concerns about physical appearance, conformity to fashion, social approval, and self-expression. The mere fact that we have fashion may suggest this. One only needs to note how quickly some individuals made the fashion change from the "disco" outfits of the late 1970s to the Western attire of the early 1980s to make some reasonable inferences about those persons' concerns with appearance, fashion, approval, and self-expression. Clothing conveys important information about how to approach individuals, how to interact, and what to talk about. But, clothing can also serve as a basis for misperceptions. During my first winter in Southern California, after moving from Michigan, I found the weather to be delightfully warm by contrast—so warm, in fact, that I frequently basked in the sun, clad only in cutoff blue jeans. It seemed appropriate to me, but apparently not to many longtime residents who strolled by, bundled up in their sweaters and jackets, shaking their heads in amazement that anyone could be so foolish. I, too, shook my head in disbelief that anyone could be so sensitive and fragile as to insulate oneself with heavy clothing on such warm and sunny days. In these instances, clothing was a basis for a wide range of negative inferences and so also were our respective assumptions that the other was obviously misperceiving the physical environment.

While enduring physical characteristics are difficult to change, individuals can often embellish, disguise, or hide them with the aid of various artifacts. For example, many women use artifacts to highlight different facial features, disguise bulging waistlines, or hide graying hair. Many men use artifacts such as toupees to hide baldness, high-heeled shoes to appear taller, or sunglasses to mask crow's-feet. Some individuals resort to more radical measures of changing enduring features through plastic surgery, face-lifting, or hair implants. While some individuals may choose to alter permanently their physical features in these ways, it is much more common for people to use personal artifacts in modifying their appearance. The kinds of artifacts that people use, as well as the ways in which those artifacts are used, can provide informative data about individuals that can be obtained without having to ask questions. In this regard, health professionals may be able to gather important information concerning patients' feelings and self-perceptions by noting their use of artifacts such as clothing, cosmetics, deodorants, and even prosthetic devices.

In summary, it is important that health professionals utilize "tangible" physical appearance cues when perceiving others in health care contexts. As the foregoing review has suggested, there is often a tendency to rely upon stereotypes and false assumptions when perceiving individuals displaying specific facial and body characteristics. A caveat must be advanced because misperceptions often result from underlying assumptions that individuals with particular physical characteristics "necessarily" have associated personality traits.

Nonverbal Behavior

There are differences of opinion among psychologists as to what actually constitutes "nonverbal behavior." Various definitions may be found throughout the literature on nonverbal phenomena. Furthermore, the distinction between verbal and nonverbal behavior may represent more of an arbitrary division than a true state of affairs. The verbal and nonverbal aspects of a human interaction cannot actually be separated if one wishes to gain a full appreciation of the nature of that interaction. However, for the purpose of highlighting those broad categories of nonverbal cues which communicate information to perceivers, the following discussion is limited to a survey of *nonsemantic responses of perceived persons*: facial expression, body movements and gestures, proxemics, and paralanguage.*

Just as facial "features" have been assumed to reveal personality traits, so also have facial *expressions* been assumed to reveal personality traits. Research interest in facial expression goes back to the pioneer work of Charles Darwin, who wrote a book entitled *The Expression of Emotions in Man and Animals* (1872). Darwin argued that his theory of evolution was supported by similarities that could be observed between facial expressions of emotions in humans and in different animal species. While his argument for a biological basis of emotional expression has been an issue of continued debate, it is a matter of agreement among many researchers that emotions and facial expression are related on a neurophysiological level. Tomkins (1962, 1963), for example, maintained that when an emotion is aroused in a person, neural messages are transmitted to the face and cause constriction and relaxation of specific facial muscles. A question that plagued researchers for years was whether or not others could accurately perceive these resultant facial configurations and identify specific emotions. There now seems to be ample evidence that observers can indeed accurately identify facial expressions of emotion (Harper, Wiens, and Matarazzo, 1978). Some people, however, appear to be more skillful than others in recognizing facial displays of emotion. Even skilled observers may have difficulty in perceiving certain emotions, for various reasons. For instance, Harrison (1974) suggested that the occurrence of *partials, blends,* and *micros* may complicate the recognition of facial displays of emotion. *Partials* are expressions in which only one portion of the face is active (e.g., the expression of surprise through only a raised eyebrow or a slight opening of the mouth). *Blends* are expressions of different emotions in different parts of the face (e.g., enjoyment showing in the eyes, while indifference is showing at the mouth). *Micros* are facial expressions that are displayed at almost imperceptible speeds; thus, they are "micro-momentary" expressions. Misperception of emotions can also result from "false displays," where individuals "put on" an emotion designed to affect the perceiver in some way. For example, a medical patient may try to elicit the sympathy of a visitor by "putting on a sad face." A great deal of information is communicated through head and facial movements, but perhaps the movement of another person's eyes can provide more clues than any other facial structure.

One's *gaze* is a major nonverbal signal to others. It has been defined as looking at another person in or between the eyes, or in the upper half of the face (Cook, 1977). Research on gaze patterns of individuals has revealed some

*For comprehensive analyses of nonverbal phenomena, the reader is referred to the texts of Argyle (1975), Harper, Wiens, and Matarazzo (1978), Harrison (1974), Knapp (1972), or Weitz (1979).

interesting and significant findings. For example, Argyle and Ingham (1972) found that in social interaction people look at each other about 60% of the time, on the average, they look more while listening than while talking, and *mutual gaze* (making eye contact) tends to take up only one-third of the time of their interaction, with each eye contact being fairly short. Argyle and Ingham also found that women tend to look more, especially when interacting with other women. Kendon and Cook (1969) found that each individual has his own characteristic gaze pattern that remains relatively consistent from one encounter to another. However, these researchers also found that gaze patterns are influenced by numerous factors: who the person is with, what he thinks of that person, and what sort of meeting it is. In this regard, one's dislike for another person can be indicated by gaze (Cook, 1977), as well as can one's liking for another (e.g., Rubin, 1973). Numerous studies have found that eye gaze is an important element in the establishment of dominance relationships within various animal species. But, despite the fact that "stare downs" often seem to lead to many barroom brawls among humans, the inability of research to demonstrate the existence of similar dominance patterns among human beings precludes any tempting generalization of the findings from animal studies. Staring another person in the eye can be used intentionally by individuals to communicate anger, hostility, or dominance; but, the gaze itself does not seem to function as a type of "innate releasing stimulus" calling forth an instinctively aggressive response from another person.

In most cases, when people notice that others are looking at them, they will draw the simplest and most immediate conclusion: that the person is interested in them (Cook, 1977). As Cook (1977) pointed out, when an individual is looked at by someone with whom he is not interacting, he expects that something will happen (perhaps an interaction will start). Because many individuals feel vaguely pressured to initiate an interaction after catching someone's eye, they may become adept at avoiding eye contact (have you ever tried to catch the attention of a waitress in a busy restaurant?). Of course, Darwin (1872) noted that people who feel ashamed or embarrassed tend to avoid eye contact and look down. This observation was supported in the findings of Exline et al. (1970). Exline and his associates also found that people who look more are seen as being more truthful, and people who look less are aften seen as being less truthful. People who avoid eye contact, however, are most frequently perceived as being nervous and unsure of themselves (even though there is no empirical evidence that nervous people do look less). People may also avoid eye contact because they have learned that looking at strangers may precipitate an unpleasant event. It should be noted here that the amount of time an individual looks at another is additionally influenced by topics of conversation. Persons who are embarrassed by a particular topic tend to look less than persons who are comfortable with the conversation topic (Exline, Gray, and Shuette, 1965).

It is particularly informative to note *when* people look at others during social interaction. According to the findings of numerous studies (e.g., Bakan, 1971; Levine and Sutton-Smith, 1973; Kendon, 1967), an individual tends to look away when starting to speak, when answering a question, when hesitating, and when trying to avoid the distracting effects of the person to whom he is speaking. When individuals finish their statements to others, they tend to look toward the person to whom they are speaking. When looking away, individuals are relatively consistent in glancing to one side or the other. The average person makes about 75% of his head and eye movements to the right side or to the left side (Harrison, 1974). "Right-lookers" seem to have left-hemisphere cerebral dominance. The left hemisphere of the brain is dominant on verbal and rational matters and digital information processing. "Left-lookers" apparently have right hemisphere cerebral dominance. The right hemisphere is dominant for spatial concepts as well as metaphoric and analogic thought processes. Left-lookers are said to be inclined toward the classics and humanities, while right-lookers are supposedly found mainly in science and mathematics (Cook, 1977). If this is true, it would be predicted that you and most of your colleagues are right-lookers. You might do some casual investigating to assess the extent to which prediction holds by posing questions to your colleagues and observing whether they look mainly to the right or to the left.

Body movement and *gesture* (or "kinesics") are central phenomena in nonverbal behavior and communication research (Weitz, 1979). The study of body movement and gestures have led to the marketing of provocative bestsellers which promise readers that they can "read people like a book" (e.g., Nierenberg and Calero's *How to Read People Like a Book*, 1971) by tuning into such cues as "body language" (e.g., Fast's *Body Language*, 1970). In spite of the secret keys to which readers become privy, the promise of uncovering the dark motivations and deep feelings of others cannot be fulfilled because of the inaccessibility to those covert processes through a simple glossary of body movements to which many spurious meanings have been attached. Weitz's comments are noteworthy here (1979, p. 4):

> At the heart of such books . . . is the rather disturbing vision of a world populated by detectives each busily reading the body signs of the other, while disregarding the intentional words spoken, and all the while trying to disguise one's own verbal and nonverbal displays so that equally skilled readers cannot discover one's true ploys by the same means one is trying to use on the others.

Within the context of interpersonal relationships, the diagnostic "body language" approach of ferreting out clues to hidden meanings can be more damaging to those relationships than helpful. Obviously, body movements *can* indicate certain things about individuals. But, it is often difficult to specify precisely what message is being communicated at a nonverbal level because such behavior is frequently ambiguous and can have multiple meanings. A person being interviewed by the personnel director for a staff position may move about in her chair for various reasons. Her movements may indicate that she is nervous, uncomfortable, physically ill, or even anxious to terminate the interview because she has changed her mind about wanting the job after the personnel director indicated a lower salary than that for which she had hoped.

There are different ways of approaching the study of body movement. Duncan (1969) distinguished two: the *structural approach* and the *external variable approach*. Most of the research conducted has followed the latter approach (Harper, Weins, and Matarazzo, 1978). The external variable approach is best represented in the work of Ekman (e.g., Ekman and Friesen, 1969; Ekman, Friesen, and Ellsworth, 1972). This approach attempts to attach the meaning of body movements to certain psychological variables. Implicit in this approach is the assumption that individuals have characteristic "expressive styles" which cross all categories of movement and which reveal certain underlying states. The approach does not represent an effort to catalogue a grammar of "body language." Rather, it is a framework for conceptualizing the meaning of nonverbal behavior in terms of its usage, origin, coding, and classification. Ekman and Friesen (1969), following this approach, outlined five descriptive categories of body movement. Those categories are presented here as a useful scheme for basing inferences of the possible meanings of perceived nonverbal behavior.

The first category of body movements identified by Ekman and Friesen consists of *emblems*. Emblems are culturally stylized movements which are readily translatable into verbal messages. They are intentionally used by individuals to communicate a message without words, and perceivers usually assume that the person deliberately sent the message. Examples of emblems with direct verbal counterparts include waving ("Hello" or "Good-bye"), thumbs up ("Good job," "Well done," "A-Okay"), a student's raised hand ("I want your attention" or "I want to ask a question"), or even the raised middle finger as an obscene gesture.

Illustrators are movements used to illuminate what is being verbalized. They are often intentional efforts to accentuate, clarify, or underscore verbal statements. However, individuals may sometimes use illustrators without awareness of the extent to which they are "talking with their hands." Some illustrators include pointing to objects or to one's self, extending hands apart to show how wide a patient is, holding the stomach or touching the head to indicate the source of pain, or moving the hand laterally from left to right to illustrate the peaks and valleys of an oscilloscope.

Regulators are movements which adjust and control the interaction between two individuals. They indicate to one another how the interaction is going. Examples include head nods, postural shifts, distancing, or gestures to stop or start talking.

Affect displays are involuntary or intentional behaviors which indicate particular emotions. The facial expression of emotion was briefly discussed earlier. Here, it must be noted that such expressions are usually informative in an "interactive" sense. They give more personal information than any of the foregoing classes of cues and often possess unique meanings in individuals. That is, while most humans produce similar facial expressions when experiencing a particular emotion, social learning experiences modify those expressions by teaching individuals from different cultures and subcultures the "display rules" (Ekman, 1972) for expressing emotions. The interaction effect is to alter the type of feedback responses from another individual. For example, a display rule can call for the "intensification" of an emotion, as seen in exaggerated expressions of grief in some Asian and Mediterranean cultures; an "understatement" of emotion, as seen among the British; a "neutralization" of emotion, which has been required of American males through messages such as "Men don't cry"; or "masking" an emotion with a different one, as some persons do when masking their disappointment over being passed up for promotion by smiling and heartily congratulating those selected over them (Harper, Wiens, and Matarazzo, 1978). Thus, the perception and interpretation of affect displays are subject to error and must be viewed relative to the individual's background and current situational context.

Adaptors are learned movements which originated in the necessity of responding to personal needs, but they eventually become habits performed out of awareness. They are responses that were originally used to "adapt the self" to internal or external demands (e.g., scratching the head, licking the lips or teeth, sniffling, rubbing the nose). These and other movements can become habitual and serve no self-adaptive purpose (e.g., stroking one's mustache, picking or rubbing one's face when there is no skin irritation, fingernail biting or tearing). Such behaviors are aften perceived as "nervous habits," although the reduction of anxiety through these responses represents only one possible interpretation. For example, a person may stretch or sigh when relaxed and satisfied, and may have a habit of communicating relaxation in that way.

Emblems, illustrators, regulators, affect displays, and adaptors can have important information value for perceivers. They may tell a great deal about an individual: how he feels about himself, you, the situation, or the interaction; his habits, background, sincerity, and perhaps even his relationships with others. These categories of nonverbal cues are rich sources of information which should not be ignored when processing information about perceived persons. It must also be recognized, however, that nonverbal behavior does not always originate from the same sources and operate in the same ways from one situation to the next. Nonverbal cues can be ambiguous and can have multiple meanings which must be considered against the broader social context in which they occur, as well as the verbal behavior that may accompany the nonverbal. The old joke that "she couldn't talk at all if you made her hold her body still" may capture the ways in which some people communicate. But, it must be remembered that "she wouldn't *bother* to 'talk' in that way if it weren't for the social context"; nonverbal behavior must be viewed against, and relative to, all existing conditions in order to mean something.

There is one other aspect of nonverbal behavior that deserves attention, and it is reflected in the reaction of a psychiatric intern in the following case:

> Dr. K. was a psychiatric intern who had been working closely with a recently admitted patient. The patient had been admitted to the psychiatric ward for observation and diagnosis subsequent to his arrest for disturbing the peace by shouting obscenities at customers in a department store. Dr. K. presented her observations of the patient to her supervisor and stated her clinical impressions. The supervisor, who had also observed the patient, stated that he did not agree with Dr. K.'s opinion that the patient was in need of further observation and possibly intensive treatment. The supervisor believed that the patient had simply "acted out" his anger and frustration over being fired from the same department store that day. "We both talked to him yesterday, Dr. K.," noted the supervisor, "and you heard what he said. He said that he was just angry at the time, and that he was no longer angry about being fired." In support of her opinion that the patient's anger had not dissipated sufficiently to preclude further antisocial behavior, Dr. K. replied, "It wasn't *what* he said about his anger, it was the *way* he said it that concerns me."

There are two noteworthy aspects of this particular case. The first is that the patient was arrested and admitted for observation, not so much as a result of "what" he said, but because of the "way" in which he made his statements. It was not the obscenities *per se* that brought him to the attention of the police; it was the "delivery" of those obscenities (i.e., shouting) in a public context. Secondly, while Dr. K. had heard the patient's statements about his anger, she was less concerned with "what" the patient said then she was with "how" the patient discussed it. In both of these aspects of the case, the significant features of the patient's behavior were the *paralinguistic cues* to which perceivers responded.

Paralanguage refers to the nonsemantic elements of speech that lead perceivers to make inferences about the speaker. It is a "language of language" that includes cues which give additional meaning to spoken words. Paralanguage subsumes cues such as voice quality, pitch, tone, range, tempo, intensity, resonance, and control. An individual's *range* of voice is indicated by fluctuations in pitch from high to low. Some persons demonstrate a wide range of voice by being able to vary pitch, while others speak in a monotone without varying pitch. Voice *resonance* is determined largely by the individual's vocal endowment, with great variation from person to person on a range from booming voices to frail and delicate voices. *Tempo* refers to the speed of verbalizations, which usually fluctuate as a function of emotional states such as excitement or boredom. *Control* is of three different types (Harrison, 1974): lip control over transitions in speech that are smooth versus sharp; articulation control which regulates forced versus relaxed streams of sound; and rhythm control for producing smooth, broken, or shaky cadence. Range, resonance, tempo, and control are enduring voice "qualities" that help distinguish one person from the next (Harrison, 1974).

Intensity and pitch are voice *qualifiers* which vary as a function of the situation, topic under discussion, or emotional state of the individual. Thus, in different circumstances voice production may be loud or soft (intensity), high or low (pitch). These and the other paralanguage cues help to regulate interpersonal communication, offer indications of the states of individuals (Harrison, 1974), and offer bases for identification of individuals.

There are some important implications concerning the perception of paralinguistic cues in health care organizations. Patients are individuals under stress. They are often apprehensive and fearful of their illnesses. They may therefore be highly sensitive and hyperalert to paralinguistic cues signalling feared news about their conditions. Just as the person who fears rejection is hyperalert to any cue of rejection, so also is the person who fears the worst from test results hyperalert to any indication that his fears are confirmed. Health professionals must recognize that their *manner of speech* is data for perception by others. In relation to patient care, if manner of speech is perceived by patients as calm, controlled, and yet sincerely concerned, patients may not become unnecessarily worried and upset over a condition which is less serious than they may think; a calm, controlled, and sincere manner of speech may be perceived by seriously ill patients to mean that the health professional is concerned. Conversely, a calm, controlled, and unaffected manner of speech may be perceived by any patient as meaning that the health professional doesn't care.

It could logically be argued that *all* behavior is communication. Indeed, some writers have based extensive theories on the premise that "one cannot *not* communicate" (e.g., Watzlawick, Beavin, and Jackson, 1967) or that any mobile feature of the body is a medium for expression (e.g., Freud, 1905). Whether communication is intended or not, whether language is used or not, and whether or not the verbal message is congruent with the nonverbal, people express their personalities continuously. All modes of expression have information value. Here we have been concerned with the nonverbal mode, a rich source of information which can highlight the spoken word, qualify it, contradict it, provide context, or even replace it. And, as Harrison noted (1974, p. ix):

> It provides all the challenge of a good intellectual puzzle. Yet it also promises practical applications in your daily life. It has implications for you as a communicator—and as a human being.

Some of the material presented in the foregoing discussion should serve as useful "clues" for constructing the challenging puzzles represented by other human beings. It should also bear upon your daily professional encounters as health care providers. Finally, it should relate directly to you, who are not only the perceiver, but also the "perceived."

Verbal Behavior

Verbal behavior represents an extremely complex system of coding sounds in terms of language elements, the rules for using and organizing those elements, and the rules for relating those elements to infinite internal and environmental referents. In the English language, the 26 letters can be combined into countless words, phrases, and sentences; and sentences can be combined following still other rules of syntax. With the aid of a few simple rules we can order and reorder letters and words to create an immense vocabulary of usable symbols (Harrison, 1974).

Our concern here is not with the generation and utilization of words per se, but with those characteristics of verbal behavior not associated with language itself. The principal aim of this section is to examine vocal cues, their functions, and the information from vocal cues which extends beyond the actual words spoken. When listening to someone speak, we hear a verbal message of words *and* a vocal message of emotions. Sometimes the vocal message supersedes or even contradicts the verbal message. This fact has led some researchers to conclude that, when given the choice between the spoken word and its vocal expression, perceivers will tend to rely on the vocal expression as the primary data base for inferring the actual meaning of the speaker's words. The most important information gained from vocal cues seems to be in relation to the emotions of the speaker. Various emotions can be identified on the basis of how the speaker uses vocal cues such as pitch, range, resonance, control, and tempo of speech. Perhaps you have been confronted by someone who responded to your vocal expression by angrily stating, "Don't use that tone of voice with me!" And, from the ways in which that person manipulated vocal cues, you could in turn infer her emotional state.

While vocal cues carry important indications of the emotional state of the speaker, they are often used to make other kinds of inferences. Personality traits are often inferred from vocal cues. For example, many people who attend seminars conducted by individuals who project their voices loudly, vary the pitch and tempo of speech in an expressive manner, and control the articulation of specific points of emphasis conclude that the person is "dynamic." Many organizations arrange to have such "dynamic" individuals present motivational-type seminars to their sales personnel; and, it could be argued that part of the popular Dale Carnegie course is aimed at teaching people how to maximize the effects of vocal cues in order to ultimately influence others' perceptions of their personality. Even though people often make inferences about personality based on vocal cues, such inferences are based more on vocal stereotypes than on true relationships between vocal cues and personality (Tubbs and Moss, 1980).

As indicated, perceivers attend to vocal cues of pitch, range, resonance, control, and tempo of speech. *Pitch* refers to the frequency level of the voice. It may be high or low, depending of the size and shape of the vocal bands within the larynx. However, speakers tend to vary pitch according to their learned expressive habits, such that some individuals vary pitch in a naturally expressive voice which is spontaneous and relatively pleasing, while others speak in a monotone with unvaried pitch or in dramatic and exaggerated pitch changes. Apparently, pitch level influences the perceiver's attitude toward the speaker as well as the content of the message (Tubbs and Moss, 1980). And, while monotones are generally disliked by most individuals, exaggerated pitch changes are even more disliked (Eakins, 1969). Speakers with naturally spontaneous voices tend to be perceived more favorably. They use a moderate *range* of pitch, as opposed to a wide range or a narrow band.

Resonance is determined by one's vocal apparatus and often corresponds to one's physical size. It is a voice quality which is typically judged by perceivers in terms of its "pleasantness." Thus, pleasantness is often equated with resonance, although the equation is not necessarily correct. In addition, resonance is often equated with the physical size of the speaker, such that a 6-foot, 200-pound man, for example, is expected to have a more resonant and booming voice than a frail man of much smaller proportions. When this expectancy is violated, the speakers do not fit vocal stereotypes, and perceptions must be adjusted.

Another important vocal cue is *control*. There are various types of vocal control identified by Harrison (1974). "Lip control" involves manipulations which produce smooth, as opposed, to sharp, transitions in speech. "Articulation control" regulates forced versus relaxed streams of sound. "Rhythm control" produces a smooth flowing rhythm instead of halting, broken, or jerky rhythm. This aspect of vocal production is clearly affected by one's emotional state, in that the flow of speech may be interrupted by emotional preoccupations. Thus, various pauses, half-stated words, quick transitions, or even long, drawn out speech may reflect particular emotions.

Control is also closely related to the *tempo* of speech—the speed of vocal production. Fast tempo and frequent pauses are often associated with emotions such as fear or anger, while slow tempo is often associated with sadness or depressed states (Barnlund, 1968). A slow tempo with frequent pauses and utterances such as "uh," "er," "um" can indicate uncertainty, and perhaps suggest that the speaker is stalling while he searches for a response. These kinds of vocal cues are often disturbing to perceivers, who frequently become impatient, bored, and anxious to finish sentences for the speaker. The comedy team of Bob and Ray captured the frustration of individuals forced to listen to speakers with slow speeds of vocal production in their skit about *Slow Talkers of America*.

It should also be noted here that some persons are able to control their vocal production in spite of their emotions, but the strain of controlling emotions can often leak out through other nonverbal cues such as facial expression and body movements. For example, many patients do not want to show their emotions when told by their physicians that they must undergo surgery, so their voices may not be a source of information about how they are reacting. Nevertheless, their shock and apprehension is usually reflected in their faces and body movements.

The scheme for classification of body movements (Ekman and Friesen, 1969), presented earlier, is a useful framework for understanding vocal cues. You will recall from the preceding section that *emblems* are culturally stylized movements that are readily translated into verbal messages. The verbal complement of the emblem is, of course, a "word." But, as Harrison (1974) pointed out, there are "nonword" vocal sounds that simulate emblems. For example, sounds such as those identified above ("uh," "um," "er") may communicate uncertainty, the sound "hm-mm!" may indicate surprise, the sound "huh" may substitute for "what?" or "tsk'tsk" may indicate disapproval.

Vocal *illustrators* are essentially inflections used to stress one word or one meaning over another. For example, if one's pitch goes down at the end of a sentence, the sentence is perceived as a statement, but if pitch goes up, it is taken as a question. Subtle shifts with the use of verbal illustrators can be demonstrated by noting the emphases in the following by Sir Alan Patrick Herbert: (*I Can't Think What He Sees In Her*):

> I'm not a jealous woman, but I *can't*
>   see what he sees in her,
> I can't see *what* he sees in her, I can't
>   see what he *sees* in her!

Perhaps most people have perceived the question differently, depending on which words were emphasized by speakers in the following common query:

> *What* are you doing here?
> What are *you* doing here?
> What are you *doing* here?
> What are you doing *here*?

Each of these interrogatives may communicate a different message, depending on the vocal illustrators used by the speaker.

Vocal *regulators* adjust and control the interaction between two or more persons on a verbal level. For instances, if one's pitch goes up at the end of a sentence, the other individual will tend to feel obliged to respond in some way. If one's pitch goes down and is followed by a pause, the other person will usually take it as an indication that he may begin speaking. Some vocal emblems may be used as regulators, as in the case of an individual trying to communicate that he will continue speaking as soon as he finishes searching for the right words or idea. In such cases, individuals often use "ummmm" or "uhhh" as a clear "wait" signal.

Verbal *adaptors* function much like nonverbal adaptors. For example, clearing the throat is often used to respond to a personal need, but it may also be used to catch someone's attention, communicate disapproval, or to prepare for speaking. It was pointed out earlier that perceivers will often choose the vocal expression rather than the words spoken as the main data base for inferring the meaning of the speaker's words. Mehrabian (1971) described the results of studies which suggested that, when communicating feelings, the actual words spoken account for a very small percent of the impact on others. Vocal cues seem to influence more than one-third of the impact, and facial expressions influence more than one-half of the impact on others. Such findings would imply that perceivers tend to optimize the value of vocal cues and facial expressions when attending to the spoken words of persons expressing their feelings. While not as influential as facial expression, the *verbal affect display* provides cues to which perceivers have a great proclivity to attend. This might suggest that if you don't have them all in sync, others may not perceive your behavior the way that you may have intended.

The Role of the Perceiver

Stimulus properties of contexts and perceived persons are basic data sources for person perception, but these stimuli are external to perceivers and tell us very little about *how individuals extract and interpret them*. Certainly, the information that one gets about an individual can be construed in various ways. If John walks down the state hospital corridor at a fast pace toward a group of ward attendants and then greets them with a smile as he quickly passes by, John has provided numerous appearance and behavioral cues for perception by the attendants. Yet, we still don't know *how* the attendants will go about interpreting those cues. The same person in the same context may be perceived differently by different individuals, or even differently by the same individual at different times.

A major issue of person perception research has concerned the tendencies that *perceivers* bring to interpersonal encounters and how those tendencies influence perceptions of others. Any or all of the factors discussed so far may operate to distort perceptions. It is more likely, however, that perceptual distortions frequently result from the particular ways in which perceivers extract and interpret external stimuli. *The ways in which individuals process information are the most significant influences on perceptual accuracy and subsequent "impressions" of others.*

Two lines of research are based upon this premise. One thrust has focused on identifying factors affecting the accuracy of perceptions. The second line of research has been concerned with how information is used to judge individuals and form impressions. This approach has emphasized that the information we acquire about individuals can modify our ideas of what persons are like and thereby alter the kinds of evaluations and judgements we make about them.

Special attention is given to these processes of *impression formation* in Part Two. In the present section, our concern is primarily with the former line of research and its guiding question: "What perceiver tendencies affect the clear perception of others?" Studies have revealed several tendencies that are so pervasive as to characterize the perceptual inclinations of virtually *all* individuals. Because these tendencies are relatively consistent and invariant across different situations, they are described here as *uniform perceptual tendencies*. These include perceptual set or readiness, implicit personality theories, stereotyping, the halo effect, projection, and attribution. Other tendencies are less uniform and more idiosyncratic, characterizing the particular "perceptual style" of different persons or reflecting their current emotional states. These tendencies are discussed separately as *idiosyncratic tendencies*.

Uniform Perceptual Tendencies

Through social learning experience, people come to assume that certain aspects of the world remain more or less constant. Most persons assume that the world tomorrow morning will be pretty much the same as the world is today. Most persons also assume that friends and relatives will appear no different tomorrow or next week from how they appear today. Stated simply, most persons learn that various aspects of the world are *predictable*. It seems to be prerequisite to adaptive interaction with the world that individuals learn about its invariant properties. If individuals did not learn of the relatively constant aspects of life and living, then the world would be perceived as a chaotic, ever-changing, unpredictable place which stifles every action and produces unexpected outcomes.

In addition to learning of predictability in the world, human beings develop a concomitant *need* for it. A need for order and predictability in the world is assumed by some theorists (e.g., Maslow, 1970) to reflect a basic human motivation to ensure a degree of "safety" in one's environment. Whatever the underlying motivation, it is through the striving for order and predictability that individuals come to develop *expectancies*. Expectancies are states of anticipation in which the individual makes an implicit prediction about the probability of occurrence of an event. Expectancies are based on past experience in situations which are somehow similar to the one in which the individual may currently find himself. The extent to which the individual perceives a relationship between the former situation and the present situation tends to determine the relative strength of the expectancy. Thus, expectancies may generalize from specific situations to various other situations perceived as similar and, as a result, come to determine how the person behaves in those situations (Rotter, 1966). It would stand to reason that, as a person gains more experience in a specific situation, the more narrow an expectancy becomes and the higher the prediction that results for the individual. In the absence of experience in certain situations, individuals often rely on the more "generalized expectancies" (Rotter, 1966) for some degree of predictability. It is important to grasp this notion of expectancy, because we develop expectancies of almost everyone's behavior, and those expectancies represent extremely potent influences on how we perceive them. Let us turn to some illustrations to emphasize the effects of expectancies and, at the same time, note some of the factors which may alter expectancies.

> Mary was a student nurse in a large metropolitan hospital located in a neighborhood with a high indigent population. Because security was often lax in the hospital, some derelict individuals would occasionally sneak in from the cold winter nights and find a concealed place to sleep. While Mary was making her rounds alone one evening, she passed Mr. D.'s room. She shined her flashlight into the room and noticed that Mr. D. seemed to be resting comfortably. However, she was startled at the sight of two legs protruding from under Mr. D.'s bed. Afraid to investigate alone, Mary rushed to the central nursing station, called her supervisor, and then phoned security for assistance. Her supervisor and two security guards arrived shortly and were taken directly to Mr. D.'s room. After quietly entering the room, the guards shined their flashlights under the bed, then exited the room with smiles on their faces. The two "legs" that Mary had reported seeing turned out to be prosthetic limbs that Mr. D. had placed under his bed for the night. It seems that Mary was not aware that Mr. D., a new patient, was a double amputee.

In this case (which, incidentally, is true) various factors influenced Mary's perceptions. The physical location of the hospital, the hospital's poor security system, and the knowledge that derelicts often sneaked in for the night all influenced Mary's readiness to perceive a person under Mr. D.'s bed. In a sense, she expected to perceive a human being under the bed and was thus predisposed to see one. However, her perceptions were also influenced by the physical darkness of the room and her perspective from the hallway. And, of course, had she been familiar with Mr. D.'s condition, she may not have been inclined to perceive a derelict under the bed.

As indicated above, we develop expectancies about almost everyone with whom we come in contact, even strangers. When walking down a hospital corridor, you don't expect an approaching stranger to grab you. However, late at night, in a hospital such as Mary's, you may have a different expectancy. You may also have a different expectancy when walking down the street in the neighborhood of that hospital. What you have learned about the neighborhood and the behaviors likely to occur in that neighborhood will tend to alter your expectancies and your subsequent perceptions of persons in that neighborhood. Contextual factors often influence expectancies in very direct ways. For example, when in a bar, one would expect to perceive behavior that would not be perceived at the opera, in church, or in numerous other places. One would not expect to hear loud conversation, joke telling, haughty laughter, or arguments about football games in places such as these. In these types of contexts, we expect more inhibited and reserved behavior. As contexts change, expectancies change. In many organizations, this phenomenon has stressful consequences on personnel, who are informed that budget constraints may necessitate staff reductions. If they are asked to come into the supervisor's office, they may expect to receive bad news, whereas prior to the announcement of cutbacks they may have had a totally different expectancy.

The notion of expectancy implies, also, that people may tend to see and hear what they want or expect to see and hear. This *perceptual set* phenomenon was discussed in Chapter One, but is no less applicable to the present concern.

In fact, *expectancies are perceptual sets*. If, for example, an individual has had a bad experience with a hospital social worker, he may come to expect that all subsequent experiences with hospital social workers will be negative and, therefore, be *set* to have a bad experience regardless of how the social worker behaves. If you have learned from the repeated stories of friends that a certain professor is very enthusiastic, then you may expect to perceive enthusiasm when you take a course from her; because of your set, you may indeed perceive enthusiasm even if it is not objectively manifested. In general, *if you hold certain expectations about an individual, your perception of that individual will be affected to varying degrees by those expectations*. One result is that your expectations may effectively "distort" your perceptions.

In order to facilitate predictability in relation to other persons, individuals develop expectations and inferences about "what goes together with what" in the personalities of others. Intuitive assumptions and concepts about the nature of personality collectively represent what is referred to as the perceiver's *implicit personality theory*. Although the overwhelming majority of perceivers are naive observers of human beings and not "real" personality theorists, they nevertheless have their own ideas about human nature. These ideas, implicit personality theories, provide a framework for perceiving and making sense of other individuals.

The naive assumptions that certain personality characteristics are associated with each other reflect the need to simplify, integrate, and predict the complexities of human behavior that we encounter in everyday life (Wrightsman, 1977). In the absence of complete information about an individual, a perspective is gained by inferring that the person has characteristics that go along with those of which you are aware. For example, if you know that Dr. Smith is quiet and reserved, you might use your implicit personality theory to complete the picture of Dr. Smith by inferring other characteristics. Thus, you may infer that Dr. Smith is also introspective, sensitive, intelligent, and whatever other characteristics your "theory" holds as going together with "quiet and reserved." The inferences that you make from your theory may not be valid, but they serve a purpose, even though you have gone beyond the information available; they help you to *order and predict your world to your satisfaction*. This is an important aspect of implicit personality theories. Individuals tend to keep their theories and rely on them as long as they function as they are supposed to. When other persons behave in ways that violate expectancies, or when certain personality traits are not perceived to go with some others in a particular individual, perceivers can tolerate a few "exceptions to the rule." But, when expectancies are violated too often, perceivers are forced to modify their implicit personality theories to account for the discrepancies. In some ways, this process parallels "formal" academic theorizing. That is, new research findings often cannot be explained by existing theories and, consequently, modifications of those theories become necessary. When theories cannot be modified to account for new data, they have "run their course" for all intents and purposes. New theories must then be developed to replace them. Unlike "real" theorists, however, the implicit personality theorist is more resistent to changing his assumptions because it threatens to disrupt the order and predictability which those assumptions have provided for so long. Changing his assumptions means unpredictability, which threatens to undermine his sense of reality. The person who is unable to incorporate new and incongruous information into a modification of his implicit assumptions may become much like Toffler's (1970, p. 361) "Super-Simplifier," who " . . . seeks a single neat equation that will explain all the complex novelties threatening to engulf him."

Fortunately, most persons do not become like the "Super-Simplifier" and, instead, modify their theories to varying degrees as needed. The fact that persons have implicit personality theories that influence perceptions suggests that there may be individual differences in these theories. This is probably to be expected, since people tend to have some differences in their respective notions about human nature. It follows, then, that in order to understand how an individual perceives another person, it is necessary to determine the underlying assumptions that guide his perceptions. Research has not been particularly informative about what personality factors correlate with different implicit personality theories. However, it is clear that the assumptions individuals hold about human nature reflect their past experiences with other individuals. Consequently, their assumptions often give an indication of the nature of those experiences and the probable effects which those experiences will have on subsequent perceptions.

Each individual is socialized within a particular environment which provides language and concepts for relating to the world. Perceptions of the world are often filtered through the language and concepts that one has learned. When different individuals have different learning histories and, hence, different concepts available to them, they may view a common event differently. For example, if you have learned, through your training, the concept of "nasal cannula," you will tend to see an instrument for giving oxygen or compressed air to a person in need of assistance in breathing. An individual without your training may not have the same concept and, therefore, see nothing more than a strange plastic band across the person's face. Having learned the concept, you are able to look at the object, assign a name to it (nasal cannula), and place it in a proper category (respiratory care). You may then ignore other aspects of what is before you because you have perceived the essence of the object. This same process often occurs in relation to human beings. For example, if you have learned the concept of "homosexuality," you may perceive individuals of the same sex who share a common sex-object preference. A person who has not learned the concept of homosexuality may see nothing more than same sexed persons together. It is likely, however, that the perception of homosexual persons extends beyond the simple categorization on the basis of sex-object preference because the concept carries social implications which most individuals have learned. For many individuals the conceptual category is replete with traits and behaviors that are supposed to "go with" homosexuality. Thus, when perceiving an individual who manifests behaviors or traits that "go with" homosexuality, that individual may be thrown into a perceptual category from which other traits are assigned. In a word, the individual is "stereotyped," and *important aspects of the individual are ignored.*

It is worth noting that implicit personality theories are often constructed from or tied together by stereotypes that individuals have about others. *Stereotypes refer to sets of characteristics that are assumed to belong to a group of people.* The most socially significant and devastating kind of stereotyping, of course, is *prejudice.* While the concept of stereotyping has negative social connotations, it does seem to serve a purpose as a "perceptual process." Stereotypes are actually inevitable by-products of the need to predict and order the world of experience. They allow individuals to treat new information rather quickly, without having to attend to its full details and implications. Processing large amounts of information can be simplified by organizing that information in terms of general "categories." The category information can then be used as a data base for responding. In relation to person perception, this would suggest that individuals may tend to perceive certain persons in terms of the categories that they "fit into," and not in terms of their distinctive personal characteristics. This would also suggest that information about particular individuals within those categories may not be perceived and processed sufficiently to permit the formation of an accurate impression of the individuals. Furthermore, information about particular persons "within" those categories can become lost through the grouping. Thus, in order to recall information about a specific individual, the perceiver may refer to "category information" and not "person information." The result is that the perceiver may recall only that Judy was black, Jewish, feminist, Southern, or blond, and therefore basically the same as all other blacks, Jews, feminists, Southerners, or blonds.

Stereotypes are not restricted to groups of individuals. In our culture, we have many stereotypes concerning forms of behavior. We have stereotypes about nonverbal behavior, for example, that are widely shared and which form a basis for rules of social interaction. Through socialization we are told, "Don't stare," "Don't point," "Don't pick your nose," "Sit like a lady," and "Act like a man." We hold stereotypic beliefs about persons who violate these norms and stare, point, pick their noses, sit in "unlady-like" postures, or fail to act like a man. Our culture also provides stereotypes about verbal behavior, the use of poor grammar, CB language, sophisticated words, and even "silence." There are stereotypes concerning artifacts such as white socks, fur coats, cowboy hats, football jerseys, white uniforms, Mercedes-Benz automobiles, and bleached hair.

This tendency to rely on stereotypes reflects a tendency to overgeneralize from available information. The use of stereotypes reinforces a point made earlier that *individuals go beyond the available data to make inferences about others.* Despite the fact that the use of stereotypes can often be counterproductive to good interpersonal relations, individuals would be at a loss without stereotypes. They serve a purpose of enabling the individual to predict (with varying degrees of accuracy) the behavior of others. As Schneider, Hastorf, and Ellsworth (1979, p. 175) observed, "The fact that we sometimes make mistakes and frequently overgeneralize is the penalty we pay for the glory" (of being able to generalize in the first place). However, on the other side of the coin, it may be helpful to consider Jourard's assertion (1974, p. 67):

> . . . the ability to see what is there, to transcend labels and classes and apprehend the thing before one's view, is a means of enriching one's knowledge of the world and of deepening one's contact with reality.

Another common phenomenon, which often derives from one's implicit personality theory, is an evaluative bias know as the *halo effect.* The halo effect describes the tendency to draw a favorable or unfavorable inference about an individual's total personality on the basis of a "single" characteristic. The halo effect can occur when the health professional isolates a single trait in a patient and then allows a total evaluation to be based on how he judges the patient on this one trait. For example, the patient may be friendly at first contact, and this friendliness may lead the health professional to conclude that the patient is also warm, generous, sociable, understanding, genuine, and various other things.

That certain traits can affect overall perceptions of others is amply demonstrated in the findings from Asch's classic study (1946). In this study Asch presented subjects with a list of traits which supposedly characterized a particular person. He then asked the subjects to write a paragraph describing that person. Next, he presented another list of characteristics and asked the subjects to write a description of this person. Asch found that the descriptions were quite different. Subjects tended to perceive the second person quite differently from the first person. The interesting aspect of this study is that Asch substituted *only one trait* on the second list. On the first list, subjects were presented with the following traits: intelligent, skillful, industrious, *warm*, determined, practical, cautious. On the second list, subjects were presented with the same traits, except that *cold* had been substituted for "warm." It seems that subjects perceived the second person differently *on the basis of a single trait*. The substitution of a single trait on the second list was sufficient to produce a qualitatively different perception of the hypothetical person.

Subjects in the Asch study apparently organized the perceived person characteristics into a meaningful system. Asch suggested that, when one judges another person, one will attempt to fit isolated experiences of that person into a more comprehensive context. A few experiences are used to form a total perception. Furthermore, since "warm" elicited a different overall perception than "cold" did in the same context, Asch concluded that a change in one trait was enough to produce a change in the other six. It seems that a person cannot perceive one quality and another quality in the same person without their affecting each other. The interaction of both qualities tends to produce a new quality. For example, the person who is "warm and intelligent" is somehow different from the person whose is "cold and intelligent"; both are intelligent, but the quality of their intelligence is different.

There are other implications of the halo effect. Think about a colleague that you like very much. Now think of a colleague that you dislike. Chances are pretty good that at times these two persons may behave exactly the same. They might even make the same recommendation about how to handle a disruptive patient, for example. But, chances are also good that when the favored colleague makes the recommendation, you will respond more positively than you will to the same recommendation made by the disliked colleague. Once we have established a person favorably or unfavorably, we tend to base further perceptions on these initial evaluations. Consider how your subsequent perceptions of an individual might be affected if, on your first contact with that person, she ignored you and walked away. The halo effect would predict that you would form an overall negative impression of that person from this one encounter and that subsequent perceptions would be strongly affected by the negative view that you have established. On a more positive note, suppose that you meet someone for the first time and that person treats you with respect. If you then make the assumption that this person is always respectful of others, your perception of the person has been influenced by an aspect of the halo effect known as *temporal extension*. Temporal extension is a halo effect phenomenon in which the perceiver extends a perceived trait in time. An inference is made that, because the individual has manifested a specific trait in one situation, he must *always* be that way. For example, many people have met other persons and assumed that those people would be great fun to be around on a continual basis: "He's so much fun; he must be great to live with." Finally, a related halo effect phenomenon called *functional inference* involves the perceiver's tendency to infer that, because an individual has one particular trait or characteristic that makes her skillful on a task, she must therefore be skillful on other tasks. For example, if a person is seen as being a good organizer, the perceiver may conclude that she is also a good thinker, a good problem solver, or a good leader. Or, if a psychologist is seen as being skilled at working with alcoholics, a perceiver may infer that he must also be skilled at working with other populations of substance abusers.

A notion introduced from the classic psychoanalytic perspective is that individuals may attempt to defend against the recognition of an undesirable trait in themselves by assigning that trait to someone else. This is known as *projection*, and not only is it an ego-defense mechanism for maintaining a stable self-concept, but it is also a uniform perceptual tendency. This tendency often clashes with reality because the perceiver may see some trait in another person that the person *does not have*. For example, the inhalation therapist who sees his co-workers as lazy may be projecting his own desire to avoid work. The LPN who sees all patients as being helpless may be projecting her own wish to be taken care of. And, the person who accuses his friend of being "cheap" because the friend will not lower his asking price for a lawnmower should probably think about "who is really being cheap." The tendency to project traits, thoughts, feelings, or motivations onto others is not uncommon, even among professionals who need to guard against it. For example, I once had a colleague who perceived most of his female psychotherapy patients as "hysterical" and most of his male patients as "submissive." His perceptions may very well have been projections of his own dependency conflicts, since such conflicts are assumed to underlie both "hysterical" and "submissive" behavior.

It is often easier for perceivers to project unacceptable traits onto members of a different social group. This may occur, for example, when some individuals accuse members of an ethnic or racial minority of being lazy, unproductive, oversexed, or unscrupulous in business dealings. By projecting traits onto members of an "out-group," the perceiver can distance herself from those traits more comfortably than by assigning them to members of her own social group. Once the traits have been "put into" the out-group person, the individual convinces herself that the person truly has those traits. The effect is a clear distortion of reality.

There is a form of projection which involves the assignment of traits to others for the purpose of justifying one's own behavior toward them. Schneider, Hastorf, and Ellsworth (1979) refer to this as *complementary projection*. While many examples can be given of complementary projection in relation to prejudice, the following case illustrates how certain individuals may use this ploy in group psychotherapy and various treatment programs:

> Kevin was a Seaman Apprentice in the Navy who had been referred for treatment at an alcoholism rehabilitation center. Upon admission, he was assigned to a therapy group which met each morning. During his first few sessions in group therapy, Kevin said very little and interacted minimally with other group members. However, his silence concealed the perceptual work that he was doing. Kevin was sizing up each group member, forming impressions based largely on the particular sensitivities that he perceived each person to have. Soon, he began interacting in group therapy in a disruptive fashion. He began "pinging" on other group members, deliberately provoking their anger by treading on sensitive personal issues which they had yet to work through. Within a very short period of time, Kevin had successfully alienated himself from the rest of the group by turning everyone against him. Perhaps without his clear awareness, Kevin had "set up" the entire group to reject him. It seems that Kevin saw himself as being inherently unlikable, other people as basically disapproving of him, and the world as a threatening place. Kevin was afraid to take risks in relationships because opening up to others also meant the possibility of ultimate rejection. To be accepted would mean that his view of self and others was incorrect and that he would therefore have to change his ways of relating to people. Because change was more threatening than being disliked, Kevin could maintain his view of the world by setting things up to ensure rejection. Thus, he could effectively project disapproving motives into others, reinforce his beliefs of being unlikable, and justify his behavior.

Kevin's behavior was much like the traveling salesman who could not find a jack in his car trunk after getting a flat tire. He saw a farmhouse down the road and decided to ask the residents if they would let him borrow a jack. As he walked toward the house, the salesman began to grumble that the residents probably wouldn't answer their doorbell when he rang. Walking across their lawn to the porch, he grew angrier because he "knew" that they wouldn't help him out. "Nobody helps anyone anymore," he scoffed. Then, upon ringing the doorbell, a middle-aged woman greeted him with a cordial smile and asked if she could be of some help, for she could see from her window that he appeared to be having car trouble. "No!" roared the salesman, "I just came to tell you that you can keep your damned jack!" Thus, the salesman had convinced himself that he wouldn't receive help from anyone, and pretty much ensured it by responding as he did. Somewhat like Kevin, the salesman projected motives, set up rejection, and created a "self-fulfilling prophecy" (see Chapter 10 discussion on this).

If someone were to observe the salesman, the question would probably arise as to why he acted to rudely. There are times when perceivers want to know the reasons behind another person's actions. To explain perceived behavior, perceivers often *assign causes*. This process of assigning causes is known as *attribution*, and it is a process which has received great attention among researchers interested in person perception.

One might wonder what perceivers can gain from making causal attributions. One thing is an understanding of behavior by simplifying perceptions into manageable proportions (Shaver, 1975). Thus, observers are probably not interested if the salesman acted at noontime or late afternoon, in the rain or in the sunshine, summer or winter, on a workday or weekend, 5 miles or 50 miles from his office. Observers are more interested in the fact that he shouted and acted in a hostile manner. Causal attributions may disregard important information, but they nevertheless permit observers to attend to those aspects of behavior that are most important to their attempts at understanding it. A second function of attribution is to increase the perceiver's ability to predict what an individual is likely to do in the future (Shaver, 1975). In order to respond to others, it is often necessary to have some idea about how they might respond to us. By inferring causes to behavior, we can make a prediction that similar actions may be forthcoming from the person under similar circumstances in the future. We then derive an expectancy in relation to the other's probable behavior and utilize this expectancy as a type of data base for interaction.

Perceivers often make *reactive* attributions in an attempt to explain behavior seen as involuntary, unconscious responses to some internal or external stimulus (Schneider, Hastorf, and Ellsworth, 1979). In the case of the salesman, a reactive attribution might be that the man responded out of an emotional state of frustration or anger, or that he had previously experienced rejection of his requests for help, or even that his perception of reality was disordered. Any number of attributions could be made. It is often difficult to make reactive attributions that are accurate, because internal states are not always obvious and not all of the necessary contextual circumstances are known. In short, perceivers often have to do a lot a guesswork. Without the necessary information to explain a person's behavior clearly, observers might ask themselves, "What kind of person would behave in this way?" An answer would require a *dispositional* attribution of certain personality characteristics to the actor.

From an attribution framework (Heider, 1958; Jones and Davis, 1965; Kelley, 1967), it is assumed that perceivers make an inference about whether the behavior is caused by *personality dispositions* of the actor or by *situational factors*. The key to differential attribution to one of these alternatives is in the knowledge that the perceiver has about forces in the situation that may relate to the behavior. In the salesman case, an observer would most likely infer that the causes of his actions related to some personality disposition, because little information is available about possible situational influences. But, consider a more likely example involving an RN and a patient. If a perceiver observed an RN helping a patient out of bed, he may conclude that this behavior is helpful and humane, and that it is due to the nurse's virtuous, humanitarian, and noble "intentions." However, a different attribution could occur if the observer is aware of the helping norm within the hospital environment. Thus, if this aspect of the "context" is taken into account, the attribution might be that the RN is merely "doing her job." This type of attribution to situational factors would also be influenced by "social desirability." According to Jones and Davis (1965), the social desirability of a person's behavior tends to decrease the strength of attribution such that, when a person behaves in an expected, socially desirable way, we really obtain little information about the person's personality. You might speculate about what characteristics would be inferred for the RN if she had behaved in a socially undesirable way and tripped the patient intentionally! Jones and Davis also noted that "hedonic relevance" affects attributions. Thus, if the *perceiver* were helped by the RN (instead of the patient being helped), the perceiver would tend to infer positive characteristics to her, since her actions were directed toward him and not someone else. Whatever the nature of the particular attribution to the RN's behavior, the issue of "intentionality" must somehow be resolved by the observer. Unlike the reactive attribution that is made in cases involving behavior such as the salesman's outburst, the nurse's behavior is more deliberate, purposeful, and intentional. A *purposive* attribution must be made which accounts for the actor's purposes and intentions. The attribution of intention is a matter which has been debated for centuries by philosophers and in more recent years within our legal system when judges and jurors attempt to establish "intent" behind a defendant's actions. The attempt to establish intent is nothing new to human beings, nor has it ever become a simple process. It is not a simple process in relation to person perception, yet perceivers tend to make purposive attributions in order to make sense out of perceived behavior.

Most psychologists would accept the formula that $B = f (FP, E)$; behavior (B) is a function (f) of personality (P) *and* the environment (E). *Behavior is always a function of both*. And, herein lies the principal significance of attribution in relation to perceptual accuracy: when perceivers emphasize P as the cause of behavior, while ignoring E in the equation, they are committing a major perceptual error. A high degree of perceptual distortion can be expected from causal attributions which place too much emphasis on personality dispositions. If one were to examine carefully the environment in which behavior occurs, it might be possible, in a large number of cases, to recognize stimulus factors which exerted direct influences on the individual. It is interesting to note that perceivers are quite adept at identifying environmental/situational influences *on their own behavior*, but are less able or willing to consider relevant situational influences on the behavior of others. That is, there is a pervasive tendency for perceivers to attribute personality dispositions as causes for the behavior of others and situational factors as the causes for their own. For example, Jane may see her interest in psychology as being due to the nature of the subject matter, while others may believe that her interest derives from a need to learn how to deal with her own problems. This phenomenon will be discussed in greater detail in the next chapter. For our present purposes, it is both necessary and sufficient to emphasize that differential attributions such as these clearly overrate one set of factors in relation to the other.

Idiosyncratic Perceptual Tendencies

Idiosyncratic perceptual tendencies are accounted for in terms of individual differences in general. It should not be surprising that perceivers may differ in terms of to what they pay attention, how they organize their perceptions, and what kinds of inferences they make from what they perceive, nor should it be surprising that such differences are based on different learning experiences. Differential learning experiences may account for differences in certain perceptual tendencies that have been noted between men and women. According to Reitz (1977), women tend to be more intuitive, rely more on visual cues, and use more stereotypes than men. Women also seem to seek out more information about others than men do. Although research has indicated these types of differences, there are no data to support a conclusion that one sex is more "accurate" than the other in person perception. Because of sex role learning, however, men and women are probably differentially "set" to perceive messages aimed at their own sex. One only needs to watch a few television commercials to see that advertisers have some grasp of what is "salient" information for men and what is salient for women.

In Chapter One, the concept of "perceptual set" was introduced as a predisposition to perceive certain aspects of the environment. Perceptual sets are influenced by learning as well as by current psychological and physical states. The factors discussed in Chapter One in relation to perceptual set come into play in accounting for many individual differences in person perception. Other factors that were not discussed include training and occupation, purpose, social roles, relationships, and self-perception.

Training and *occupation* can predispose individuals to attend to stimuli that others may ignore. For example, the psychologist is trained to attend to certain symptoms of psychopathology which aid in diagnosis and treatment of mental disorders. Individuals without such training would probably have difficulty in perceiving some indications of disorder because they would not be predisposed to notice them. The same applies to physicians who are attentive to patients' conditions and notice symptoms of cancer that the individual "just didn't pay any attention to." One's *purpose* is observing others also influences what is observed. Because it is crucial to monitor the heart patient, for example, one may purposely attend more carefully to that individual than to the person with a compound fracture of the tibia. *Social roles* can predispose individuals to perceive others from the framework of their group membership or responsibilities. For example, Rich (1974) found that blacks perceive certain specific traits in whites and that whites perceive certain traits in blacks. This type of finding may confirm an assumption that many individuals have made already: that one is predisposed to view members of another social group somewhat differently from members of one's own social group. From a professional standpoint, one's role within an organization can affect perception. Indeed, the hospital administrator often perceives budget and personnel problems differently than on-line personnel. Supervisors often perceive a staff member's performance differently than other staff members do. And, occasionally some physicians' perceptions of patients become distorted when they take their role as "healer" to its extremes. *Relationships* can influence perceptions in a wide variety of ways. The more we get to know someone, the more we come to expect certain behavior from him. More will be offered about this relationship influence later, but here it is important to note that the relationship between two people can create a "defensive bias" that predisposes them to *see or not see* certain aspects of the other person's behavior. For example, I once worked in a state prison where an inmate told me that, although he had been arrested several times in his life, his sister always maintained his innocence and refused to acknowledge that her brother had any personal responsibility for his actions in each case. He admitted that he was personally responsible for his actions in each case, but his sister would not accept that possibility. This prison example is a tragic complement to the tendency which many parents have when they argue that "my child simply wouldn't do such a thing."

The number of factors which can influence individual differences in person perception tendencies is almost countless. As we compare one person with the next, individual differences may increase not proportionally but exponentially. One variable on which no two persons are comparable is that of *self-perception*. This variable is so important to person perception that a special chapter is devoted to a discussion of its significance.

Summary and a Model of Person Perception

This chapter has provided a framework for identifying perceptual determinants in terms of three interdependent categories of factors. Contextual factors, perceived-person characteristics, and perceiver tendencies *interactively* determine the outcome of person perception. The separation of these factors represents an arbitrary division aimed at highlighting predominant effects of various aspects of human experience and interaction. It is important, however, to stress the totally *interdependent* nature of these perceptual influences.

As stated at the beginning of this chapter, "People are perceived to exist and behave in situations." This fact can be represented in an equation derived in part from the formula $B = f(P, E)$ cited earlier. The equation is as follows:

$$P_n = f(P_{BP}, A_{BP}, C)$$

where P_n is person perception, P_{BP} is the behavior (*B*) and personality (*P*) of the perceiver, A_{BP} is the behavior (*B*) and personality (*P*) of the actor, and *C* is the context. Thus, *person perception is a function of the behavior and personality of the perceiver, the behavior and personality of the actor, and the context*. All three sets of factors are intrinsic components to the equation, and they cannot be separated out in "reality" as they have been here for convenience.

In closing, the process of person perception requires *skill*. In Chapter Five you are given some exercises and cases designed to assist you in improving your perceptual skills. Within your profession, your skills at perceiving others can be among the most important skills you will ever need. The use of skills rests upon a knowledge base. This chapter is intended to help you expand the knowledge base for improving perceptual skills. Being effective at interpersonal perception requires that you have an awareness of some of the things that can affect the process. A "perceptive" person is one who is able to process a range of perceptual information by integrating it with existing knowledge, correcting for possible errors, and adjusting for accuracy. This is no easy process, but a step toward improved perceptual skills is taken when you begin to expand your *knowledge base*.

Finally, the step toward skill enhancement is taken when individuals come to realize fully that a living person is *more* than the sum of "behavioral" and "personality" *parts*. You are more than your perceptions, more than your skills, more than your personality traits, and so also are the individuals who are the targets of your perceptions. This is perhaps no more important to realize than in the health care setting, where individuals are fit into roles as "patients," observed in terms of their "symptoms," and often perceived as diagnostic entities whose essences lie only in their "illnesses." Patients are more than "cases," just as you are more than a health professional. An effective health professional is a whole person who has the ability and the willingness to perceive others in their totality. In short, the effective health professional is a person whose efforts at perceiving people in their totality reflect an attitude that is consistent with the current philosophy of holistic health.

References

Argyle, M. *Bodily Communication*. New York, International Universities Press, 1975.

Argyle, M., and Ingham, R. Gaze, Mutual Gaze, and Proximity, *Semiotica,* **6**:32–49 (1972).

Asch, S. Forming Impressions of Personality, *Journal of Abnormal and Social Psychology,* **41**:258–901 (1946).

Bakan, P. The Eyes Have It, *Psychology Today,* **4**:64–67 (1971).

Barker, R. G. *Ecological Psychology: Concepts and Methods for Studying the Environment of Human Behavior.* Stanford, California, Stanford University Press, 1968.

Barnlund, D. C. *Interpersonal Communication: Survey and Studies.* Boston, Houghton Mifflin, 1968.

Beck, S. B., Ward-Hull, C. I., and McLear, P. M. Variables Related to Women's Somatic Preferences of the Male and Female Body, *Journal of Personality and Social Psychology,* **34**:1200–10 (1976).

Cook, M. Gaze and Mutual Gaze in Social Encounters, *American Scientist,* **65**:328–33 (1977).

Darwin, C. *The Expression of Emotions in Man and Animals.* New York, D. Appleton, 1896 (First published in 1872).

Dibiase, W., and Hjelle, L. Body-Image Stereotypes and Body-Type Preferences Among Male College Students, *Perceptual and Motor Skills,* **27**:1143–46 (1968).

Duncan, S. Nonverbal Communications, *Psychological Bulletin,* **72**:118–137 (1969).

Eakins, B. The Relationship of Intonation to Attitude Change, Retention, and Attitude Toward Source. Paper presented at the Annual Convention of the Speech Association of America, New York, December 1969.

Ekman, P. Universal and Cultural Differences in Facial Expression of Emotions, in *Nebraska Symposium on Motivation.* Lincoln, Nebraska, University of Nebraska Press, 1972.

Ekman, P., and Friesen, W. V. The Repertoire of Nonverbal Behavior: Categories, Origins, Usage, and Coding. *Semiotica,* **1**:49–98 (1969).

Ekman, P., Friesen, W. V., and Ellsworth, P. *Emotion in the Human Face.* New York, Pergamon Press, 1972.

Exline, R. V., Gray, D., and Shuette, D. Visual behavior in a Dyad as Affected by Interview Content and Sex of Respondent, *Journal of Personality and Social Psychology,* **1**:201–9 (1965).

Exline, R. V., Thibaut, J., Hickey, C. B., and Gumpert, P. Visual Interaction in Relation to Machiavellianism and an Unethical Act, in *Studies on Machiavellianism,* ed. R. Christie and F. L. Geis. New York, Academic Press, 1970.

Fast, J. *Body Language*. New York, M. Evans, 1970.

Freud, S. Fragment of an Analysis of a Case of Hysteria. *Collected Papers*, Vol. 3. New York, Basic Books, 1905.

Gurwitz, S. B., and Dodge, K. A. Effects of Confirmations and Disconfirmations on Stereotype-Based Attributions, *Journal of Personality and Social Psychology*, **35**:495–500 (1977).

Harper, R. G., Wiens, A. N., and Matarazzo, J. D. *Nonverbal Communication: The State of the Art*. New York, Wiley-Interscience, 1978.

Harrison, R. P. *Beyond Words: An Introduction to Nonverbal Communication*. Englewood Cliffs, New Jersey, Prentice-Hall, 1974.

Heider, F. *The Psychology of Interpersonal Relations*. New York, Wiley, 1958.

Jones, E. E., and Davis, K. E. From Acts to Dispositions: The Attribution Process in Person Perception, *Advances in Experimental Social Psychology*, Vol. 2, ed. L. Berkowitz. New York, Academic Press, 1965.

Jourard, S. *The Healthy Personality: An Approach from the Viewpoint of Humanistic Psychology*. New York, Macmillan, 1974.

Kelley, H. H. Attribution Theory in Social Psychology, in *Nebraska Symposium on Motivation*. Lincoln, Nebraska, University of Nebraska Press, 1967.

Kendon, A. Some Functions of Gaze Direction in Social Interaction, *Acta Psych.*, **26**:1–47 (1967).

Kendon, A., and Cook, M. The Consistency of Gaze Patterns in Social Interaction, *British Journal of Psychology*, **69**:481–94 (1969).

Kleinke, C. L., and Staneski, R. A. First Impressions of Female Bust Size, *Journal of Social Psychology*, **110**:123–34 (1980).

Knapp, M. L. *Nonverbal Communication in Human Interaction*. New York, Holt, Rinehart, and Winston, 1972.

Lawson, E. Haircolor, Personality, and the Observer, *Psychological Reports*, **28**:311–22 (1971).

Levine, M. H., and Sutton-Smith, B. Effects of Age, Sex, and Task on Visual Behavior During Dyadic Interaction, *Developmental Psychology*, **9**:400–5 (1973).

Maslow, A. *Motivation and Personality*. New York, Harper and Row, 1970.

Mehrabian, A. Nonverbal Betrayal of Feeling, *Journal of Experimental Research in Personality*, **5**:64–73 (1971).

Nierenberg, G. I., and Calero, H. H. *How to Read a Person Like a Book*. Hawthorne, 1971.

Reitz, H. J. *Behavior in Organizations*. Homewood, Illinios, Irwin, 1977.

Rich, A. *Interracial Communication*. New York, Harper and Row, 1974.

Richardson, S. A., Hastorf, A. H., Goodmen, N., and Dornbusch, S. M. Cultural Uniformity in Reaction to Physical Disabilities, *American Sociological Review*, **26**:24–47 (1961).

Rotter, J. B. Generalized Expectancies for Internal Versus External Control of Reinforcements, *Psychological Monographs*, **80**:1 (1966), Whole No. 609.

Rubin, Z. *Liking and Loving: An Invitation to Social Psychology*. New York, Holt, Rinehart, and Winston, 1973.

Schneider, D. J., Hastorf, A. H., and Ellsworth, P. C. *Person Perception*, 2d ed. Reading, Massachusetts, Addison-Wesley, 1979.

Shaver, K. G. *An Introduction to Attribution Processes*. Cambridge, Massachusetts, Winthrop, 1975.

Sheldon, W. H. *The Varieties of Human Physique: An Introduction to Constitutional Psychology.* New York, Harper and Row, 1940.

Sheldon, W. H. *Atlas of Men.* New York, Harper and Row, 1954.

Sherif, M. A Study of Some Factors in Perception, *Archives of Psychology,* **27** (187): 1-60 (1935).

Sleet, D. A. Physique and Social Image, *Perceptual and Motor Skills,* **28**:295-99 (1969).

Toffler, A. *Future Shock.* New York, Bantam Books, 1970.

Tomkins, S. S. *Affect, Imagery, and Consciousness. The Positive Effects,* Vol. 1. New York, Springer, 1962.

Tomkins, S. S. *Affect, Imagery, and Consciousness. The Negative Effects,* Vol. 2. New York, Springer, 1963.

Tubbs, S. L., and Moss, S. *Human Communication,* 3d ed. New York, Random House, 1980.

Watzlawick, P., Beavin, J. H., and Jackson, D. *Pragmatics of Human Communication.* New York, Norton, 1967.

Weitz, S. *Nonverbal Communication: Reading With Commentary,* 2d ed. New York, Oxford University Press, 1979.

Wells, W. D. and Siegal, B. Stereotyped Somatypes, *Psychological Reports,* **8**:77-78 (1961).

Wrightsman, L. *Social Psychology in the Seventies.* Monterey, California, Brooks/Cole, 1972.

Wrightsman, L. *Social Psychology.* Monterey, California, Brooks/Cole, 1977.

CHAPTER
THREE

Self-Perception and the Health Professional

"I can't explain myself, *I'm afraid, sir," said Alice,*
"because I'm not myself, you see."
"I don't see," said the Caterpillar.

Lewis Carroll, *Alice's Adventures in Wonderland*

What could be simpler than perceiving one's own self? It was easy enough for Alice to see that she was not "herself," and because it was obvious to her, she assumed that it was apparent to the Caterpillar as well. Yet, Alice had the advantage over the Caterpillar since she had access to information about herself that the Caterpillar did not have. Her perceptions were different because she had a different *frame of reference*. This fictional encounter captures certain significant aspects of person perception that go far beyond the simple realm of fantasy into the complex phenomenological world of human experience.

The statement, "I'm not myself," is one which most persons have heard and probably used at one time or another. Health professionals, for example, often hear this type of statement from patients who claim, "I don't know what's wrong with me these days. I just don't seem to be myself." Of course, this is a common statement from people who are under stress and confused by the effects of their illnesses, but such statements also reflect the probability that the individual has perceived her own behavior and dissociated it from herself because the behavior is inconsistent with her *concept of self*. When a person acts "out of character," she experiences a threat to her sense of identity. Because of these threats, the individual will often go to extremes to maintain a stable view which does not violate that identity. By claiming that "I am not myself" the individual can separate her behavior from her self and deny that there is a connection. Outside observers, however, usually see her as the actor of her own behavior.

This type of experience points up the significant issues of self-perception which constitute the focus of the present chapter. These issues pertain to the notion of *self*, the *self-concept*, the effects of self-concept on self-perception, the need for *cognitive consistency* (i.e., the need for order and predictability in relation to the self), and the distinction between self- and other-perception. In the first part of this chapter, a theory of personality (Rogers, 1951) is outlined as a viable conceptual framework for approaching these issues. Self-perception is then described against the frameworks of both Rogers's theory and attribution theory as a process distinct from other-perception. The issues are then elaborated in relation to *perceptual biasing* processes and *cognitive dissonance* phenomena. The implications of the focal issues for increasing self-awareness and accurate self-perception are discussed within the context of a model called the Johari Window, and the effects of role perception on interpersonal relations in health care organizations are considered from the perspective of this model. The final section of this chapter addresses the importance of integrating accurate role perception as a health professional into a basic view of oneself as a total human being with a subsumed professional identity that forms only "part" of the whole self.

It must be recognized that nowhere in the science of psychology do we come closer to the basic unresolved issues of philosophical controversy than we do in the area of self-perception. It is not the purpose of this chapter to debate those issues. Rather, it is the purpose of this chapter to point up the significance of self-perception as the very core of interpersonal relations.

A Model of Self-Perception: Rogers's "Self Theory"

Contemporary psychology has taken up a renewed interest in the role of "self" in social interaction—an interest that was formerly seen in the works of William James (1890), Charles Cooley (1902), and George Mead (1934), but which faded when the concept of self fell into disrepute with the then-emerging behavioral school of thought with its focus on overt behavior. Mentalistic, immeasurable concepts, such as the self, were unpopular for many years in psychology when the science went through its phase of growth in radical behaviorism. However, it was this very emphasis on overt, observable, stimuli and responses that eventually led to a reappearance of theories about the self. Partially in reaction to behavioral concepts which described human beings as organisms responding to environmental stimuli, an attempt to "humanize" psychology was undertaken by various theorists. Perhaps the most notable among the "humanistic" writers was Carl Rogers, a psychologist who introduced a theory of self which gained and sustained respect and applicability. A process which lies at the very core of Rogers's theory is that of perception. More specifically, the process of self-perception is treated as a basis for personal growth, the development of a self-concept, and social interaction. Rogers's theory of personality was outlined in a series of propositions in *Client-Centered Therapy* (1951). Those propositions are indicated here (Table 3.1) to outline the framework of his theory. Our discussion of the theory will focus only on those aspects which seem essential to developing an understanding of self-perception per se.

Table 3.1   Basic Propositions of Rogers's Theory of Personality

I. Each individual lives in the midst of his own continually changing world of experience.

II. The individual reacts to the world as it is perceived; the perceived world is "reality."

III. The individual reacts as an organized whole to the experiential world.

IV. The individual has one basic tendency—to actualize, maintain, and enhance the self.

V. Behavior is a goal-directed attempt to satisfy needs as experienced, in the world as perceived.

VI. Emotion accompanies and facilitates goal-directed behavior; the kind of emotion is related to the seeking aspects of behavior, and intensity of the emotion is related to perceived significance of behavior for maintenance and enhancement of self.

VII. The best perspective for understanding behavior is from the internal frame of reference of the individual.

VIII. A part of the perceptual field becomes differentiated as the self.

IX. A structure of self is formed through interactions with the environment; this structure is an organized pattern of perceptions of characteristics of "I" or "me," with values attached to these concepts.

X. Values attached to self and experience are in some instances values experienced directly by the self, and in some instances values of others which have been distorted and taken as one's own.

XI. Life experiences are either (a) perceived and organized into relationship with the self, (b) ignored because they are not perceived as related to the self, (c) denied or distorted because the experience is inconsistent with the self-concept.

XII. Individuals mostly behave in ways which are consistent with the concept of self.

XIII. When behavior occurs in response to organic causes and when such behavior is inconsistent with the concept of self, it is not "owned" by the individual.

XIV. Maladjustment exists when the individual denies awareness of significant experiences, and does not organize those experiences into the self-structure; when this situation exists, there is a state of psychological tension.

XV. Adjustment exists when experiences are assimilated on a symbolic level into a consistent relationship with the concept of self.

XVI. Experiences inconsistent with self-concept may be threatening; the more threat perceived, the more rigid the self-structure.

XVII. When self-structure is not threatened, experiences inconsistent with the self may be assimilated.

XVIII. When the individual comes to accept himself, he is necessarily more accepting of others.

XIX. As the individual continues to accept his experiences, he finds that he is replacing his dysfunctional value system with an organismic valuing process.

Source: Rogers, C. Client-Centered Therapy. Boston, Houghton Mifflin, 1951.

As Proposition One suggests, each individual lives in the midst of his own experiential world. Most of what the individual experiences is not consciously perceived, but nevertheless organized at some level of consciousness as "ground" of the perceptual field. Those experiences may become "figure" if and when a need arises for the individual to retrieve them from unconscious experiences. Thus, while the individual's actual awareness of his total perceptual field is limited at any given moment, it is the individual and *only the individual* who has direct access to his experiences. Each individual lives in a private world of experience which can ultimately be known only to the individual himself.

Each individual responds to the world on the basis of how it is perceived. What is perceived constitutes reality, such that reality is, for the individual, his perceptions. The individual, then, interacts with the world as he sees it. If others are perceived to be hostile, then for the individual, they *are* hostile. Some theorists would dispute this proposition on the grounds that, just as the "map is not the territory," neither is perception reality. However, Rogers is concerned with "reality-as-perceived," and does not choose to debate the issue of what "really" constitutes reality; for Rogers, "the map *is* the territory."

According to Rogers's fourth proposition, all persons have an innate tendency toward developing their capacities in the service of continued growth. This is an assumption that human behavior is goal directed and purposeful. It is not a new notion, nor is it unique in psychological theorizing, but it is a notion that appeals to the sense of optimism which most persons seek to have about human nature—the idea that we are not bound by destiny to remain in any state but can actualize those capacities which we have and gain fulfillment in life.

As part of this actualizing tendency, individuals begin to differentiate experiences that are part of their own being and experiences that belong to others. Those experiences which are differentiated as belonging to oneself come to form the "self." They are "symbolized" through language and words, and are elaborated into a *concept of self*. The self-concept is an organized configuration of perceptions of what is characteristic of "I" or "me" (the self); the self-concept also includes perceptions of our relationships to others and to the world, as well as the *values* attached to these perceptions (Rogers, 1959).

As the consciousness of self develops, the individual acquires a need for "positive self regard"—that is, the individual develops the need to regard herself in a positive way. At the same time, the individual develops a need for positive regard *from others*. This need to be prized, accepted, liked, and loved by others is so strong that it becomes the most powerful need of the individual. The ever-present challenge of the developing individual is to look into the faces of others and interpret signs to determine if they hold her in positive regard. Whenever another person, especially a significant-other, such as a parent, communicates positive regard, the individual's overall self-concept is strengthened. However, when a significant-other communicates negative regard, the individual's total self-concept is weakened and undermined. Thus, the feedback that the individual receives from others is so compelling that it becomes the dominant motivational force for behavior. This, for some individuals, means that their behavior comes to be guided by the need to receive acceptance and approval from others. From a social learning perspective, it might be said that the experience of "approval" and "acceptance" becomes a potent reinforcer to the individual—so potent that his behavior comes under the control of it.

As the individual develops, he begins to regard himself in much the same way as he experiences regard from others. The individual *learns* to regard himself in the same way that significant others do, even though the experience of his own behavior may be different. For example, the individual may not "himself" be particularly elated about receiving a good grade on an examination but, because others approve, *he* "approves." Or, even though the individual may have enjoyed the sensation of masturbation, his experience of it is negative because it is viewed negatively by significant others. When this sort of experience results, the individual has acquired *conditions of worth*. The person regards himself positively only when he meets the conditions set by others for approval. For some individuals, this means that they can only feel good about themselves when they act in accordance with the expectations of significant others. For example, they can only feel good about themselves when they achieve, when they are nice, when they are agreeable, or when they "do the right things." These persons become controlled by the values of others. They have exchanged their own values and substituted their actualizing tendency for the approval of others.

Because of the need for positive self-regard and for positive regard from others, the individual begins to perceive his experiences selectively, in relation to the conditions of worth that he has learned. Experiences and behaviors that are consistent with conditions of worth are allowed into awareness and represented accurately in consciousness. For example, individuals who learned that they were prized when they behaved in nice ways toward others are often able to recall those instances where they exercised kindness. Or, if an individual learned that he could receive special attention by achieving something, he may be able to recall his grades, touchdowns, home runs, and contest awards very easily. It may be more difficult to recall experiences that conflicted with conditions of worth because such experiences are usually *distorted* to fit the conditions of worth, or they may even be kept out of awareness altogether.

As some experiences are distorted or kept out of awareness, there develops an incongruity between what is experienced and what is symbolized as part of the person's self-concept. That is, the individual truly experiences something, yet keeps it out of awareness because it is inconsistent with his self-concept. If, for example, you believe yourself to be a fair and just person, and *yet you do not always feel fair and just* and instead feel prejudiced and angry, your prejudice and anger may not be allowed into awareness because it is incongruent with your perception of your self. More specifically, it is incongruent with your *ideal self*. According to Rogers, the incongruence between self and experience is the basic conflict in human beings. Individuals often therefore become only a part of who they really are. Their lives represent their *concepts of self* and *not* their *real self*. Individuals become like the proverbial "house divided against itself."

For the purpose of keeping the positive regard of others, the individual no longer remains true to who he really is. The individual falsifies himself and denies to awareness those aspects of self that are incongruent with what he holds to be his ideal self. Various mechanisms are used in an effort to prevent experiences from coming to awareness. Rationalizations, projections, and even denial of experiences are used to maintain the conditions of worth that have been internalized. Should the individual become aware of experiences that are not worthy of positive regard, his concept of self would be threatened. To preserve his self-regard, the individual resorts to overutilization of these types of defenses.

The problem with using defenses is that they keep accurate information out of awareness. They cause inaccurate perceptions by distorting experience and selectively incorporating information into the self-concept. The result is that the gap widens between the *real self* and the *ideal self*. For example, suppose that a particular person, after donating blood at a "bloodmobile," begins to see herself as a great humanitarian. This single experience of herself has provided the basis for an inflated self-concept. The same person may completely ignore the fact that she has for the last 20 years refused to donate blood under any circumstances. Thus, through selective perception she has experienced herself as humanitarian, and through denial she has distorted information that would threaten that view. When the incongruity between the real self and the ideal self becomes large, defenses may not function effectively, and the individual comes face-to-face with previously disowned experiences which are now accurately represented in awareness.

There are many implications from this theory of self. For example, perceivers view others *from their own frame of reference* and impose their own values on perceived behavior. We evaluate others from "our own perspective," which is far removed from the *individual's view* of his own behavior. Furthermore, we view our own selves from the same frame of reference, a vantage point that no one else has. The obviousness of this fact makes it no less important to our understanding of human behavior. In fact, it poses a special challenge to researchers to find out what "processes" underlie differences in frames of reference. It is consistent with Rogers's theory to predict that the actor's perceptions of his own behavior are different from others' perceptions of his behavior. If this is so, and we can safely assume that it is, then the research should be able to account for differential processes specific to actors and perceivers. That is, the research should provide evidence in support of Rogers's theory.

Self-Perception and the Perception of Others

Jones and Nisbett (1972) reviewed some earlier studies on person perception and concluded that there are distinctive differences between self- and other-perception. Upon examining the studies, Jones and Nisbett noted a peculiar tendency for experimental subjects to offer qualitatively different explanations for their own performance versus the performance of others on research tasks. Subjects in the studies tended to favor *personality dispositions* as causes for the performance of others, while favoring *situational influences* as determinants of their own performance. An example may be useful in highlighting these findings. If you are required to perform a task which supposedly measures your level of professional competence and you fail completely, you are more likely to challenge the validity of the test than your level of competence. You know your competencies, and you are not going to let the results of a test tell you that you are not competent. On the other hand, if you are asked to assess the level of competency of a stranger who has failed the test, then, unless you have also taken the same test, you will most likely see that person as relatively incompetent. In other words, you make a personality attribution to the other individual and a situational attribution to yourself. Jones and Nisbett posited that the bases for these different perceptions and attributions were in the "available information" and the "information processing activities" of different persons.

Within their own frames of reference, actors and perceivers usually have different information available to them about the actor's behavior in the present situation. Actors usually have *more* and *better* information about their behavior than do perceivers. The actor has knowledge of his feelings, thoughts, and motives, as well as personal history. The actor may perceive his current behavior in relation to these pieces of information, while the perceiver must usually base his perceptions mainly on the current behavior of the actor. For example, a patient who is not aware that night-duty nurses check on everyone with the aid of a flashlight may think that the nurse who enters his room during the night is sneaking in for some ignominious reason. Or, the new personnel director might think that his secretary is inept because she files records in a peculiar way, while she sees herself as being efficient in using a long-established filing system.

Jones and Nisbett also noted that actor-perceiver differences are due to differential processing of the information that is available. That is, while certain bits of information may be available to both the perceiver and the actor, they may respond to that information differently. The perceiver usually attends to the *behavior of the actor* and not to causal factors in the situation. According to Heider (1958, p. 54), the actor's behavior tends to "engulf the total field," such that situational influences are organized into the background of attention, while the actor's behavior becomes figure; the actor's behavior comes to the forefront of attention and is perceived more readily than situational forces. Conversely, for the actor, the focus is on those situational factors that the perceiver ignores (Shaver, 1975). In short, the actor does not focus on *herself*, but focuses on the situation and the forces in the situation to which she must respond. This would seem logical, since most persons do not go around observing themselves all the time. It is very difficult for "the eye to observe itself," and when it does, then there is an indication of some pathology. In a similar vein, the person who continually observes himself is usually described as "narcissistic" or perhaps even "schizophrenic." In most situations, our "selves" retreat to the background of attention, and the context comes to the foreground. Most of the time, we attend to what is happening around us and not to what is happening within us. Of course, from what we know of figure-ground organization, the relationship between figure and ground can shift. For example, it is common for individuals to begin focusing more on themselves when they are about to speak before a large group. Many persons become aware that their hearts are pounding, that they are nervous, and that they are about to become the focus of attention for everyone present. Just as everyone else is focusing on the actor, so also does the actor turn his focus toward the self. Perhaps you have had this type of figure-ground shift of awareness when you presented a case before a group of colleagues at a staff meeting. The important point here is that individuals attend to those features of a situation that they find "salient" (those features of the situation that are distinctive and which stand out). For the observer, the actor's behavior is most salient. For the actor, it is the situation or the context that is most salient.

The findings reviewed here suggest that self-perception and other-perception are different and relate to one's particular frame of reference. The actor's frame of reference is different from the observer's frame of reference. They have different information available to them and they process that information somewhat differently, largely as a function of what they consider to be salient in the situation. It might also be expected that the processing of perceptual information is influenced by the self-concept, and that perhaps the actor and perceiver are differentially motivated to select and deny relevant behavioral data. This would be predicted from Rogers's theory, but what does the research show?

Perceptual Biasing and Cognitive Consistency

In Rogers's theory, the self-concept plays a critical role in the perception of one's own behavior. As it evolves, the self-concept tends to guide the admission of new experiences into consciousness by selectively accepting congruent information about the self and selectively distorting incompatible information. This aspect of Rogers's theory is simple in its formulation and far-reaching in its scope. Nevertheless, predictions generated from this component of the theory should be able to yield empirical support after they have been stated narrowly and specifically. For example, if the self-concept does operate to modify incoming perceptual information, then research should be able to demonstrate that individuals *bias* perceptions of self and others. Furthermore, the research should also be able to demonstrate that individuals attempt to maintain *cognitive consistency* through processes of selective attention and defensiveness. Two separate but related lines of research, from attribution theory and cognitive dissonance theory, have obtained findings which are consistent with the type of predictions that may be generated from Rogers's sweeping personality theory. A brief discussion of the findings from the attribution framework, on *perceptual biasing*, is followed here by a more detailed consideration of *cognitive consistency* research and the compatibility of those findings with Rogers's self theory.

Perceptual Biasing

Schneider, Hastorf, and Ellsworth (1979) reviewed several studies which suggested that "ego-enhancement" and "ego-defensiveness" needs are involved in person perception. In tasks where the individual's self-concept is heavily involved, for example, it might be expected that experiences of success are attributed to self, while experiences of failure are attributed to task difficulty. This prediction has been supported in the findings of studies which showed that when a task was "ego-involving" (i.e., a task in which the individual identifies himself with the situation), subjects tended to attribute success to ability and failure to task difficulty (e.g., Miller, 1976). There may be various reasons for these kinds of causal attributions, but motivational differences would certainly seem to be involved. Subjects were most likely "motivated" to attribute performance to the cause (ability or task difficulty) which was most consistent with the self-concept. That is, to reinforce the self-concept, subjects could attribute their performance to ability; to minimize damage to the self-concept, subjects could attribute performance to task difficulty. Most individuals are more likely to attribute personal causation to good performance and find some external causal agent for poor performance. It is difficult for most persons to observe their performance as being poor and then explain that performance by referring to a lack of ability. Such an admission often serves to devalue the self-concept. Thus, if a clinical psychological report was poorly written, the intern is most likely to attribute his performance to a lack of information, stress, unclear instructions, poor supervision, or any number of other factors which place the locus of causation "outside" of him. In all probability, the intern will not attribute his performance to a lack of clinical ability.

To maintain a stable self-concept, individuals are often eager to take credit for success and deny responsibility for failure. When I worked in a state prison, for example, I rarely heard the so-called "I'm innocent" rap from inmates. Most of the time, the men would admit to the crimes for which they had been convicted. However, they did not often see the locus of causality as being within themselves. Rather, they claimed that "circumstances" led to their crimes. It might be argued that their self-concepts had already undergone terrible abuse by virtue of their arrests, trials, and incarcerations. To keep their self-concepts as intact and generally positive as they could, they often resorted to projecting responsibility outward for their behavior—somewhat of a last-ditch effort at maintaining the self-acceptance and integrity of which they were being stripped within the prison environment. No matter what the context is, however, it seems that people usually want to take more credit for their successes than for their failures. Teachers tend to take more credit for students' successes than for students' failures (Beckman, 1970), winners of competitions tend to see their own wins as due to ability and their losses as due to external factors (Streufert and Streufert, 1969), and some health professionals may frequently take credit for "curing" patients while denying responsibility for "conditions beyond their control." This tendency to take credit for success and project blame for failure has been called "ego-biasing" by Schneider, Hastorf, and Ellsworth (1979).

There are various factors which relate directly to this motivationally based bias to protect the self-concept. For example, one's history of past performance tends to influence the extent to which an individual biases self-perceptions. If an individual has a history of failures on some particular task, then self-confidence suffers, and the person eventually begins attributing failure to lack of ability. However, if a person feels that he has some control over events, such that trying harder may improve performance, then he may increase his effort to succeed and not perceive himself to have a lack of ability. Conversely, if the person believes that he has no control over events in his life and that no amount of effort will do him any good, then he may attribute a lack of ability to himself and stop trying. The person who has a long history of success may find it hard to attribute failure to a lack of ability (and perhaps this is justified on the basis of that history), so his attributions would most likely be toward external factors. We could expect that this is the case with the clinical psychology intern who failed to write an acceptable case report for his supervisor. In most instances, persons who get to that point in their professional lives have achieved numerous successes along the way and are more inclined to see their performance as reflecting ability, except when they do poorly.

It should be noted here that ego-biasing does not occur only in relation to self-perception, but in relation to other-perception as well. For example, because of some vague threat to the self-concept, certain individuals have a personal investment in seeing Blacks and other minorities as responsible for discriminations against them. And, it is interesting to note that when women succeed, their successes are seen as being due to external or chance factors, but when they fail, they are seen as causing their own failures (Schneider, Hastorf, and Ellsworth, 1979). The findings of Bramel (1962) indicated that ego-biasing occurs also in cases where one has been accused of having unfavorable traits. That is, when an individual is accused of having traits that she does not have, that individual will tend to project those attributed traits back onto others. In this connection, it might be pointed out that people are less likely to throw back "desirable" traits that have been attributed to them. Just as individuals are prone to taking credit for successes, so also are they inclined to take credit for having desirable personality traits. When Russ is told by a peer that he is kind and understanding, he is more likely to accept that praise than he is to accept an attribution of callousness from the same person. Finally, imagine how frightening and disconcerting it would be for a patient to perceive incompetence in his physician. Most persons have a need to see their caretakers as skilled and knowledgeable. This need may predispose them to overlook contradictory information and selectively attend to only those aspects of the physician's performance that conform to their existing views. It seems that most patients assume that their doctors are the best, and the admission that one's physician is not skilled has numerous implications for the patient. Specifically, the admission is incompatible with having chosen the doctor in the first place; it may be taken as a reflection of the individual's poor judgement if he were to note his physician's lack of skill; and, it may shake his view of the world as a relatively safe and predictable place.

Cognitive Consistency

Rogers's notion that the self-concept operates to enhance the self through selective perception and defensive distortion of information is compatible with the notion that individuals strive to maintain *cognitive consistency*. There are various theories of cognitive consistency which seek to explain how and why individuals try to keep their cognitions (thoughts, beliefs, and attitudes) stable and consistent. The most prominent of these theories was introduced by Festinger (1957), and it has stimulated a wealth of research.

According to Festinger, individuals have a need for "consistent" information about themselves and their world. They need to see themselves in certain ways over time and across situations. Inconsistent information causes them to experience a disturbing state of "dissonance" (psychological tension or discomfort). To eliminate the psychological tension, they must reduce the inconsistency between existing information and contradictory information. This can be achieved in many ways, such as rejecting the new information, adding additional qualifying information, or changing existing information. In relation to cognitions, it means adding new cognitions (for example, attitudes) or changing the old ones. This does not have to be a rational or logical process, as long as the individual can successfully relieve the dissonance. In fact, it is often the case that individuals are illogical and irrational when reducing dissonance and trying to eliminate inconsistencies. For example, the theory would predict that, if you are a smoker and you are exposed to the Surgeon General's findings that "cigarette smoking is dangerous to your health," you will experience cognitive dissonance. You would hold two incompatible cognitions: (1) cigarette smoking is dangerous to health and (2) I smoke. The logical response to this cognitive inconsistency is to quit smoking. That would restore consistency. But, such a course of action is obviously not the only one that can be taken to regain consistency. There must be others, for why else would people continue to smoke in light of the facts? If you are among the millions of people who persist in cigarette smoking, you have at least one other thing in common. You have successfully reduced cognitive dissonance by rejecting the Surgeon General's report or by qualifying the data in some way. Except perhaps when you are in a group of nonsmokers, you experience little discomfort about your smoking, and you therefore have little motivation to quit. You and countless others may have used some form of the following types of rationalizations to justify your behavior: "I don't smoke that much," "The evidence is not conclusive," "Lots of smokers never get cancer or any other kind of disease," "My father smoked for 50 years and nothing ever happened to him," "Maybe I'll die sooner, but at least I'm going to enjoy myself," "I stay healthy by exercising." In each of these statements, there is an effort to minimize the danger of smoking. The speaker can thus avoid seeing himself in a negative way.

Of course, many of these statements fail to reflect true rationality, and that is what the theory would predict: *to reduce dissonance, the individual does not have to be rational or logical* (see Figure 3.1). The irrationality in justifying cigarette smoking is reflected in the person's attempt to convince himself that he is neither self-destructive or foolish by taking actions that inevitably endanger his life! This type of dissonance reduction is evident among alcoholics as well. To justify drinking and prevent realization of a problem, the alcoholic develops a system of denial that is extremely hard to penetrate. The entire system of denial represents a massive effort at dissonance reduction. Rationalizations run the gamut of possibilities: "I don't drink any more than lots of people," "I can stop any time I want," "I've never gotten into trouble after drinking," "It's not interfering with my job or my family life at all." In an attempt to convince themselves that they have no problems with drinking, many alcoholics will stop drinking for a period of time "just to prove to themselves and others that they can," but once they have supposedly "proved" this, they

Oh, Mr. Shoddy is very strong indeed! He can bend *facts*, stretch *truths*, twist *stories*, and distort *reality*!

Figure 3.1 Dissonance reduction is often irrational.

resume drinking, further convinced that they have no problem. Unlike the cigarette smoker, the alcoholic has more at stake in reducing dissonance. His entire self-concept is threatened by the possibility that he may be an "alcoholic"—a label with such profound connotations as to imply that he is out of control and in social disgrace. This brings us to the most important implication of cognitive dissonance theory: the implication that cognitive dissonance represents a form of threat to the self-concept.

Many writers have emphasized the possibility that much of the tension an individual experiences in dissonance reactions is produced by a threat that he detects to his self-concept. When individuals are exposed to information that is incompatible with their self-concepts, a state of dissonance is produced. In an attempt to maintain a stable view of self, information is rejected or distorted in some way. This implies that people are often like ostriches who stick their heads in the sand to avoid seeing unpleasant things. It may be difficult to see what survival value there is for the ostrich in this behavior, but for the human being it serves the purpose of protecting the concept of self. We have all had the experience of not wanting to hear unflattering things said about us, and we have probably tried to avoid many situations where that possibility existed. We can avoid reading newspaper editorials that conflict with our views of the world, we can avoid discussions of various topics, and we can avoid placing ourselves in positions where we are subjected to the scrutiny of others. Of course, we can do the opposite also. We can read those articles that reinforce our views, we can discuss topics that reflect our wealth of knowledge, and we can select situations that offer the probability of receiving praise for our behavior. In general, we can arrange many aspects of our lives to provide maximum reinforcement of the self-concept while minimizing potential threat.

In Festinger's original formulation of a cognitive dissonance theory, there were actually two additional ways in which dissonance could be produced. One way was hypothesized to be through the choice of one behavioral alternative over the other—in other words, through decision making. Let's take your choice of training programs as an example. Let us first assume that you were faced with different choices, such that you could select School A or School B, both being equally attractive to you. School A has a good reputation, a reasonable tuition rate, and it is closer to your home. School B also has a good reputation, a slightly higher tuition rate, but it is known for its "personalized approach" to training. After struggling with the decision in which training program to enroll, you select School B. Even though you go ahead and enroll at School B, the issue is not yet completely resolved. The knowledge that you selected School B is incompatible with the advantages of attending School A. You have rejected a school with desirable qualities, so cognitive dissonance results. Now what do you do? Essentially, you lessen the dissonance by altering your view of the two schools, so that your chosen school becomes more attractive and the rejected school becomes less attractive. For example, you may seek out additional information about your chosen school in an attempt to convince yourself that it is the better of the two, and you may be selectively attentive to bad reports about the rejected school. Certainly, you don't want to hear about how great the other school is, because that kind of information is inconsistent with having chosen the school in which you enrolled. So, you may justify your enrollment by emphasizing that, even though it may cost a little more money and is farther away from home, School B has a better training program because it takes a "personalized approach." This kind of dissonance experience is quite common after people make decisions, because the selected alternative is seldom "entirely" positive. There is often some trace of doubt about the wisdom of the choice. If you labor over a decision about going to a party, for example, and you decide to stay home, then you probably are not going to want to hear from your friends the next day that you missed a great time. Or, if you finally decide to buy a small car instead of a large car, you are not going to want to learn about all of the disadvantages of owning a small car.

According to Festinger, dissonance can also be produced through an action in which the individual would not normally engage. When a person behaves in a way that would normally be avoided, the behavior conflicts with the self-concept and causes dissonance. For example, if you see yourself as being an honest person, and yet you cheat on an examination, lie on your income tax return, or tell someone that her dress is pretty when you really don't like it, you will experience dissonance because you have acted in a contradictory way. But, you may not have too much dissonance in cases like these because the "situation" provides ready-made justification for your actions. That is, when you cheat on an exam, you do so because if you don't, you'll pay severe consequences; when you falsify your income tax return, you do so because you're already being squeezed to the bone financially; and when you compliment a friend for her dress, you do so because you don't want to hurt her feelings. But, even if you do the opposite in each of these situations, you'll still be able to justify your behavior by referring back to your self. When you don't cheat, you can convince yourself that you are indeed an honest person; when you fill out your tax return completely and honestly, you're being a good citizen; and when you tell a friend that her dress is unattractive, you can claim that you just want to be honest with her. All of these latter alternatives reinforce your sense of honesty about yourself. The former alternatives can be justified by the situation so that you lose no self-respect.

When the situation does not provide adequate justification, however, the individual must justify his actions from "within." For example, suppose that I asked you to write a paper in which you expressed views that actually ran counter to your real views; suppose also that I asked a friend of yours to do the same, but I also offered your friend $50 for writing the paper. To you, I offered nothing, save for my sincere appreciation. Cognitive dissonance theory would predict that you would experience *more* dissonance than your friend. Your friend has clear justification for advocating a position contrary to her beliefs—she has $50! You, on the other hand, have no money for your cooperation and, therefore, no ready-made justification for your advocacy statement. You have written a statement that contradicts your supposed views, so you must justify those actions somehow. To resolve the inconsistency, you can *convince yourself* that your previous beliefs were incorrect and that you *really do believe* in what you have written. In all probability, this is exactly how you would justify your behavior. This is not only predicted from cognitive dissonance theory, it is supported through the findings of numerous studies (e.g., see Aronson, 1976). In fact, a study which tested this very prediction (Brehm and Cohen, 1962) showed that persons who wrote a counterattitudinal essay without monetary compensation changed their attitudes on the topic as a function of *internal* justification. They could not justify their statements by referring to a monetary reward because they received none, nor could they justify their compliance with the experimenter's request on the grounds that he was an attractive person. Subjects could only justify their actions by convincing themselves that their essays reflected their true beliefs. Individuals who received the largest sum of money for their essays showed the least change of attitude toward the topic, those who received token payment showed slight changes of attitude, and persons who received no payment showed the greatest overall change of attitude toward the espoused position. This further suggests that attitude change may increase as external justification decreases. The effects of cognitive dissonance on consistency-seeking can easily be inferred from these findings. At the very least, results such as these suggest that cognitive consistency is important to individuals, and a direct implication is that persons may begin to alter their self-concepts when they can find no situational justification for acting in ways that they would normally avoid. But, why should this be so? Why do people strive for cognitive consistency? And, more importantly, what are the ultimate effects of consistency-seeking for the person?

As indicated in the preceding chapter, people have a need for order and predictability in their worlds. Unless they can see those qualities in the world, they experience difficulty in working out adaptive responses to events. Nowhere is the need for order and predictability more important than in relation to the self. We seem to demand a view of ourselves that is consistent from day to day. We need to know that we are still basically the same persons, no matter how much we change or the world changes around us. Without a relatively stable view of ourselves, each day would bring us face-to-face with a stranger—unknown and unpredictable. Since variations threaten to disrupt a stable experience of the self and the world, meaningful perceptions can be maintained by seeking consistency of experience. Thus, individuals strive for consistency for the purposes of *maintaining* an orderly and predictable sense of self and *preventing* variations from disrupting their lives.

Because incongruent perceptions of self often conflict with conditions of worth that have been internalized, the individual strives to maintain positive regard by preventing accurate awareness of those incongruencies. Instead of accommodating new information about the self by adjusting the concept, the individual "assimilates" information by distorting it to fit the existing self-system. The need for positive self-regard assures that the individual will act in ways that are compatible with the self-concept. He tries to avoid behaving in ways that are inconsistent with the self-concept because it would frustrate his need for positive self-regard. As Rogers argued, the need for positive self-regard and the positive regard of others becomes so strong as to dominate the individual's life. Maintenance strivings to *protect* the self come to take precedence over actualization strivings to *enhance* the self.

The process of protecting the self and maintaining positive self-regard is a defensive process which functions much like the physical self-regulatory process of the body to maintain a steady, balanced state of *homeostasis*. The systems of the body function in ways which preserve levels of physiological balance necessary for survival. When any of these mechanisms fails to maintain or restore homeostatic balance, illness or death supervenes. In a corresponding way, psychological defenses and strivings operate to maintain or restore homeostasis, so that damage to the self does not disable the person. Part of human living necessarily involves this sort of tension reduction and homeostatic maintenance on both levels of functioning. But, it is also necessary for human beings to grow and develop, both physically and psychologically. On the physical level, it is necessary for human beings to develop in accordance with their genetic possibilities, and this is *not* guided by any homeostatic mechanisms, because growth is the complement of stability. Growth and development imply movement, direction, and the process of *heterostasis*. The psychological counterpart of this physical process is *self-actualization*, a process of movement in the direction of improving relatedness to the world, enriching the range and quality of experience, fulfilling potentialities, and "becoming" what one can become. This is the process which becomes blocked when individuals strive for cognitive consistency in order to meet conditions of worth and maintain positive self-regard. To seek consistency at the expense of growth is to block the fulfillment of possibilities, to derail from the proper course of development, and to substitute stability for stimulation, challenge, and a world of novel experience. Thus, while cognitive consistency serves the purpose of maintaining a homeostatic sense of self, the ultimate effect when this becomes an overriding motive for behavior is that the need to grow and develop is tragically deprived.

Individuals may move in the direction of self-actualization through *exposure* to the world of experience, not through insulation from it. It would seem that individuals could come to see themselves more accurately by exposing themselves to feedback from others and by combining that feedback with information available only to the self. This is a viable proposition from a model of self- and other-perception known as the Johari Window.

The Johari Window

Figure 3.2 represents a person as she relates to others. It is called the *Johari Window* (Luft, 1969), and it is named after two psychologists, Joe Luft and Harry Ingham (Joe-Harry Window). According to the model, each person who relates to another has certain information available to *self only*, to self *and* the other, to the other but *not* to self, and to *neither* self nor the other. Information which is available to self and others is represented in the upper left quadrant as *open*. Information known only to self is represented in the lower left quadrant in the *hidden* area. Information available to others but not to the self is represented in the *blind* area at the upper right corner of the grid. The last quadrant in the bottom right corner is the *unknown* area, where neither the self nor others have information about the individual.

To understand how the concept applies to perception and interpersonal relations, note the names *Marie* and *Carl* which correspond to each quadrant. Figure 3.2 represents Marie *as she relates to* Carl. All of the information contained within the total window is "valid" information, and it is "relevant" to Marie's relationship with Carl. The window panes only distinguish the two persons in terms of "who has knowledge of what information."

The *open* area comprises all aspects of Marie that are known to both herself and Carl. It includes their awareness that Marie is Carl's immediate supervisor in the emergency department, that Marie has two children, that she has always been considerate of Carl, that she gives him responsibility and holds him accountable for his performance, that they both like mystery novels, and so forth. This area delineates "public" knowledge for Marie and Carl. It is mutually perceived information and forms a common ground for their interactions. If a problem should arise in this area, both persons would recognize that something is wrong, and they would have a mutually congruent basis for working out their difficulties.

The *hidden* area denotes those things which Marie prefers to keep private and not disclose to Carl. It may include information about her salary, her sexual preferences, her feelings toward her husband, her debts, and so on. In short, this is the area which includes information that Marie knows about herself but which Carl does not.

The *blind* area consists of all the things that Carl and others perceive about Marie, but which Marie fails to see about herself. Perhaps Carl has no-

	Known to Self (Marie)	Not Known to Self (Marie)
Known to Others (Carl)	OPEN	BLIND
Not Known to Others (Carl)	HIDDEN	UNKNOWN

Figure 3.2 The Johari Window.

ticed that Marie has a habit of tapping her fingers when she is nervous, that she leaves conversations when topics shift to politics, that she is the most respected person on the staff, or even that Marie looks pale, drawn, and tired toward the end of her shift. Carl could reduce Marie's blind area if he is willing to share information and if Marie is willing to accept it.

The *unknown* area is that part of Marie which is not known to her or to Carl and others. It symbolizes that part of Marie's self which has not been revealed to her because no one knows about it. It may contain such unknowns as untapped capabilities, latent conflicts, or even insidious disease processes. Marie is powerless to change this aspect of herself until she or others explore the unknown area and reveal some of its content. This is perhaps the most ambiguous and questionable area within the window. It is hypothesized to exist, but it is only revealed on a *post facto* basis; in retrospect, the person may look back and note that there was a time when she did not know certain aspects of herself.

The four sectors of the Johari Window are *interdependent*, such that a change in the size of one quadrant effects a change in others. The actual size and shape of the four areas are determined by two principal factors related to interpersonal behavior: *self-disclosure* and *feedback processing*. Self-disclosure is on the "giving side" of an interpersonal encounter and involves the revelation of thoughts, feeling, values, or attitudes to self and others in an open and honest manner. One can "give" information to self and others which may change the configuration of the four quadrants. The *open* area becomes larger, with the effect of reducing the sizes of the other areas. Feedback processing is on the "receiving side" of the transaction, but it involves far more than the mere passive receptivity to information. It is an active process of encoding, evaluating, integrating, and utilizing information from self and others. To process feedback requires that the individual not only pay attention to information, but also organize and respond to the information without "passing it off" as unimportant, irrelevant, or necessarily inaccurate.

The nature of the relationship between two people at any given time will affect the extent to which those persons disclose themselves and process feedback. This means that the nature of the relationship will affect the relative sizes of each sector in their respective windows. Luft (1969) assumed that it is desirable to expand the open area of the window through self-disclosure and receipt of feedback. To borrow Jourard's (1971) concept, this means that individuals should become more *transparent* in relation to self and others. Luft assumed that this would contribute to improved self-acceptance and enhanced self-esteem. Before it is concluded that this is always desirable, the proposition needs to be put in perspective.

The central quality around which a relationship is built is *trust.* Here, trust is used to mean the *expectation that self-disclosure will be treated with respect and that feedback from the other can be relied on.* When mutual trust exists between two people, each person feels free to be genuinely himself, without fear of rejection because of what is expressed. Under conditions of mutual trust, it is possible to alter the shape and size of each sector in the Johari Window. Open areas can be expanded, hidden and blind areas can be reduced, and unknown areas can be explored and revealed (see Figure 3.3).

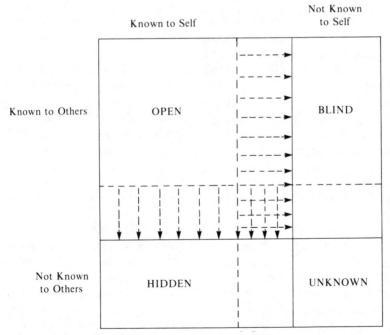

Figure 3.3   An enhanced Johari Window with a broader open area and narrower blind, hidden, and unknown areas.

Without trust, self-disclosure is limited, selective, guarded, and inauthentic. Feedback is either resisted altogether by the target person or distorted at the source. Each person tries to influence the other's perceptions by presenting an image that limits vulnerability to threatening feedback. Numerous factors can influence the growth or erosion of trust in a relationship. Of special significance here are those factors which affect trust in health care organizations, where individuals have relationships that exist on more than one level. That is, health professionals relate to one another within the contexts of personal friendships, on the one hand, and role relationships, on the other. Personal relationships tend to overlap with professional relationships, and the same overlapping relationships may characterize interactions with patients. Under these conditions, the *role* that an individual occupies can have a direct bearing upon trust and the configuration of cells within her window. Consider the aforementioned relationship between Marie and Carl, for example. These persons have a personal friendship of sorts, but they also have a professional relationship which is defined by their respective roles within the health care organization. Both persons occupy positions of responsibility within the organization, and those positions carry *expectations* about the ways in which Marie and Carl are to relate to one another. Marie, being Carl's supervisor, is expected to act the role of supervisor and display a whole range of behaviors which reinforce that role in relation to Carl, who is expected to act within the boundaries of his role as subordinate. It could be, then, that opening up and giving feedback to Marie constitutes a *role violation* for Carl. Giving certain forms of feedback to supervisors is usually considered to be inappropriate within most organizations. The message is usually communicated within organizations that personnel must do their jobs, "know their place," and not "step out of line." To violate this norm may jeopardize the individual's job. If Marie, for example, has communicated that there is a limit to which Carl may offer feedback, he may avoid open expression because he has learned the limits to which he can be open with Marie. They have allowed their roles to set the limits of openness in relation to each other.

Within health care organizations, it is possible for personnel to function in their roles for years and never get to know the persons who are acting the other roles. An individual can work under his supervisor for 10 years and never really get to know her. He knows her as "supervisor," "head nurse," "department head," and she knows him as "subordinate," "staff nurse," or "one of my people." It is difficult for individuals to be open with one another when their relationships are defined by the organization for the purpose of maintaining the *status quo*. Moreover, it is difficult for individuals to be open when they are in conflict between the need for personal relationships and the demand for role enactment. Thus, it seems to be consistent with the individual's need to survive in the organization that he learn to conceal his real self and project an image that conforms to normative expectations. Under such conditions, where it is perceived to be unsafe to express oneself openly, the individual may become obsessed with defending himself in his role. The effects on individuals *and on the organization* may be far-reaching. Because interpersonal trust is not promoted through open interaction, individuals are placed under conditions of *stress* above and beyond that which they experience by virtue of their professional responsibilities in working with patients. This additive stress can be expected to have a cumulative effect over time and thus interfere with effective performance. Furthermore, when individuals spend inordinate amounts of time in peer relationships protecting images, warding off threatening feedback, seething over criticism, passing the buck, scapegoating, and "playing it close to the vest," *it is difficult to see how the organization can benefit.* More confusing is the issue of how service consumers can benefit! There is a curious paradox in all of this that should be noted. In the eyes of health service consumers, health professionals are persons who are "trustworthy." Their professional roles define them as persons who can be trusted by the public to accept self-disclosures and provide reliable feedback. Yet, the same perception of trust does not always characterize their peer relationships within health care organizations!

This state of affairs does not characterize all peer relationships within health care organizations, and *it need not characterize any.* Health professionals *can* balance personal relationships with role expectations. The two are not mutually exclusive, where the maintenance of one precludes the existence of the other, but the fulcrum upon which they are balanced is *trust,* which is the natural outgrowth of genuine and open interaction. The very things that are avoided when there is an absence of trust (i.e., self-disclosure and receptivity to feedback) *can be used to build it.* Trust does not develop from avoiding others and taking refuge within the protective confines of role norms; it develops through the willingness of individuals to *risk* disclosure of self *as one human being to another.* The building of mutual trust requires that individuals risk the whole relationship for the sake of letting it grow. It requires that they *lay the relationship on the line* and share hidden aspects of themselves that may be misunderstood, criticized, or rejected. As Rogers (1972) pointed out, there is an effect of this vulnerable communication which most people cannot believe until they have tried it. Specifically, the expression of hidden feelings from within oneself almost always elicits similar sharings from others. As a result, the interacting persons have data in a mutually shared open area which provide bases for tending to the importance of the relationship. By responding to the opportunity for appropriate self-expression, both persons accept the invitation to move the relationship to a more personal level. Through the sharing of previously hidden aspects of self, individuals come to perceive themselves and the other more clearly; their real selves and ideal selves gradually shift toward greater congruency. A common ground is established for understanding one another as *both* persons *and* professionals.

Role Perception and the Self-Concept

If you were to ask someone in the health professions to answer the question, "Who are you?" the answer would most likely be, "I am a nurse, an occupational therapist, a laboratory technician, a physician, a psychologist," and so on. The person would probably state the role with which he identifies, but the name of a role does not tell us *who* the person is! It tells us something about *what* the person is. Being a nurse, an occupational therapist, or a psychologist does not by itself make the person unique. It is clearly *part* of the total person, but is does not separate her from the rest of humanity. Nevertheless, this aspect of the self is important to the individual's overall self-concept—so important for some individuals that they spend a great portion of their lives trying to find out who they are, and once they have discovered and settled on their *roles*, they spend the rest of their lives trying to act out the part (Jourard, 1959). You have spent considerable time and effort, and you will probably spend much more, in pursuit of a professional role in the health care field. Your perceptions of self will be strongly influenced by that role. Hopefully, as you grow in the profession, you will not lose sight of the fact that it is *just a role*, and it does not define you in your totality. To point up the full significance of this fact, it is necessary to delineate various concepts of *norms* and *roles* and then differentiate the components of roles, so as to highlight their functions and the wide range of effects which they exert on behavior and the self-concept. The following discussion is intended to emphasize the importance of these factors as *social context influences* on behavior.

Concepts of Norms and Roles

The functioning of any social system, including health care organizations, depends on the existence of standardized *norms* for regulating uniformity and diversity of behavior within the system. Norms are uniform rules of conduct that are accepted by the system as specifications for the behavior of individuals. They denote the acceptable behavior patterns that individuals may pursue within society, a subculture, an institution, an organization, or a group. They regulate the performance of individuals within health care organizations by prescribing those actions that are necessary to insure the survival of the system and move it toward particular objectives. As conservative devices for maintaining the *status quo*, norms indicate the *range* of behaviors that are acceptable within the organization. This range of acceptable behaviors may be explicitly defined in terms of *formal norms* (e.g., uniform dress codes, standards of practice, ethical norms) or implicitly communicated through *informal norms* that are tacit, unstated, and yet fully understood and accepted by individuals within the system (e.g., the implicit norm that you do your job and not overextend yourself by performing extra duties).

When formal and informal norms become "institutionalized" within the health care organization, they come to regulate the interrelated functions of personnel. Patterns of norms are established for each position occupied by individuals within the system, such that a common set of expectations is shared by personnel regarding the behavior of individuals occupying each position. In short, patterns of norms are used to define *roles—the behaviors expected of persons occupying specific positions in the organization*. The roles of health professionals can be conceptualized in various ways. It is therefore useful to examine different conceptions so that the implications from each approach can be identified as they pertain to the health professional's functioning in a role within the health care organization (Bower, 1979).

Normative Concepts of Role

A normative concept of role is based on the values and expectations of society. Social norms suggest the behavior that is to be displayed by an individual in a particular position. This means that health professionals' roles are seen as determined by the norms which society attaches to their positions. For example, society expect health professionals to be dignified, nurturant, and controlled in their behavior. These and other characteristics are supposed to be manifested by health professionals because they are the "expected" characteristics representing a norm. The health professional who is not dignified, nurturant, or controlled stands out noticeably because he does not project the image that others expect.

> Doctor D. was a successful internist in private practice in a small midwestern city. After several years of medical practice in the same city, Dr. D. began to develop new social interests for pursuit during his leisure hours. His main interest became dancing. He pursued this interest with great vigor by frequenting local dance halls and bars that featured "disco" music—his newest passion. Within a short period of time, Dr. D. developed a reputation as "Disco Danny." The local citizens were appalled by his behavior, since it was considered "undignified" for an eminent physician to be seen in such places, dancing to the beat of disco music several nights each week. Gradually, many of his patients became disgusted with his social behavior and terminated their relationships with him. These patients and most of the townspeople could not accept his behavior because it violated a traditional normative expectation concerning the role of physicians.

Normative roles prescribe that "doctors are supposed to look and act like doctors." Professionals like Dr. D. are often cast into their professional roles like molten iron into a vat—after it has had time to set, it takes permanent form which is highly resistant to change unless it is melted down into its essence and recast into a different form. As long as roles are defined according to normative standards, individuals will find it hard to change roles and "break out of the mold." From the perspective of normative roles, role change depends on redefinition of the role *by others* (Bower, 1979). When society resists redefining the role, the consequences for the individual may range from personal frustration to social censure, as in the case of Dr. D.

Many people like Dr. D. reach a point in their lives when they feel the need to redefine themselves and their roles. Their long-standing patterns of living become incompatible with their changing self-concepts. When they try to act on their changing self- and role perceptions, they often meet resistance because *others* have not changed *their* normative expectations and perceptions of the role. Under circumstances like these, it is truly difficult to change one's role when others are not prepared to accept that change. It should be noted that, in the case of Dr. D., he did not attempt to change his perceived role as "medical practitioner," and his social behavior had nothing to do with his performance as a physician. But, the role of physician ascribed by social norms extended beyond medical practice and into his personal life. Thus, it should be clear that normative roles defined by society are broad and include areas of functioning that are removed from the specific performance requirements of a position.

Situational Concepts of Role

Situational concepts of role refer to actions which are socially appropriate to the demands of a situation. Conceiving of roles in these terms means that behavior is enacted in accordance with the expectations deriving from context and circumstance. For example, in crisis situations, it may be appropriate for an RN to help an individual in the emergency department by implementing crisis intervention skills. It would not be appropriate for the same RN to provide long-term psychotherapy on an outpatient basis. The latter situation requires different role behaviors by professionals trained to provide that service. It would be a rare situation where an RN would attempt long-term psychotherapy. But, it is not uncommon for some health professionals to violate situational role expectations by attempting to render services that they are not trained to perform. It would seem that most situational role violations occur when individuals fail to recognize and accept their limitations. In health care settings, it is of paramount importance that staff recognize the limits of their training and skills. Situational norms dictate that professional skills are prescribed and performed in light of their fit with the situation (Bower, 1979). Health professionals cannot be all things to all people. They must be able to account for situational demands and respond appropriately. To do this, they must first have an accurate perspective toward their roles and their abilities.

Functional Concepts of Role

A functional concept of role takes a perspective on what individuals actually *do* when given a particular function within the organization (Bower, 1979). From this perspective, roles refer to the *enacted behaviors of persons in particular positions*. Roles are not conceptualized in terms of expectations; they are viewed in terms of actual performance. In a limited sense, for example, this means that the nurse's role is "nursing," the therapist's role is "therapy," the social worker's role is "social work." But, these are very general descriptive categories of functions, and they really tell us little about the actual behavior manifested in nursing, therapy, and social work. Thus, a functional definition of roles would attempt to narrow the role to specifics. For example, the psychotherapist's role may include such functions as interviewing, psychological testing and evaluation, clinical diagnosis, treatment planning, record keeping, implementation of a therapeutic technique or strategy, outcome measurement, and follow-up. The actual behaviors performed in this role are too numerous to list, but a functional definition of the psychotherapist's role would account for most of those activities.

When roles are defined in functional terms, there is often considerable overlap of the behaviors enacted by persons in different positions. For example, the social worker and the nurse may also perform some activities that define the role of the psychotherapist. Both of these positions require occupants to interview, evaluate, plan, and keep records on patients. The social worker may also perform the identical functions of the psychotherapist by implementing a treatment approach. When roles are defined in this way, there are not conflicts among persons in different positions as long as they recognize that their positions require the performance of similar functions. Problems arise when they become overly protective of their roles and object to the performance of similar activities by persons in different positions. From a functional perspective, then, individuals within organizations are not actually differentiated on the basis of their respective roles, since their role behaviors may be the same; individuals are differentiated on the basis of their *positions*—the particular "slot" within the organizational structure that is occupied by an individual.

Interaction Concepts of Role

Roles do not exist in isolation. Since they subsist as parts of a broader structural system, roles take meaning only "in relation to" other individuals. From an interactional perspective, roles are seen as constellations of behavior patterns that emerge from the interactions between individuals (Bower, 1979). They acquire meaning and relevance from their connections to significant others in the system. For example, the role of physician has meaning only in connection with the reciprocal interactions between the person in that position and persons in complementary positions who *behave* as patients, staff, or other physicians. The role of "leader" is another example of one which takes on meaning only when others behave in a reciprocal manner as "followers," and so it goes with all other roles, such as mother (to children), husband (to wife), supervisor (to subordinates), client (to service provider), in which the roles are defined by interactions. Thus, in the health care organization, the individual may learn his functions, the expectations that accompany his position, and the special demands of specific situations, but unless others in the organization respond to his behavior in ways which affirm his position, the role is not established.

From an interactive view, neither the individual herself nor the organization per se determines roles. It is the *reciprocal behavior between persons* in different positions that determines roles. This perspective is not incompatible with the foregoing concepts of role, since it does accommodate the notions that normative expectations, situational demands, and enacted functions represent essential *components* of roles. None of these "components" represents the "whole," and none is meaningful until it is attached to referents in behavioral interaction. To complete the development of this concept, try to recall an occasion when you were placed in a newly formed group of people without a designated leader. In situations like these, it is common for certain individuals in the group to make a bid for the leadership role. Perhaps in your experience you attempted to assert yourself and offer some direction for the group. Perhaps a few other persons also tried to make some suggestions as to how the group should function. As "candidates" for the leadership role, you probably engaged in overt or subtle competition, with people gradually withdrawing and backing out of the mainstream of interaction until one or two people emerged in the leadership role. This is an inevitable dynamic in unstructured groups which highlights the point of the interactional concept. Specifically, the leader does not assume that role until others accept and support his bid for leadership. For the individual to take the role of leader, others must respond to his behavior in complementary ways. *Leaders cannot lead if there are none who will follow.*

Synthesis of Role Concepts

The concept of role is a global concept that attempt to account for all of the relevant patterns of behavior displayed by an individual occupying a position within an organization. It is a concept which is broad enough to be described in numerous ways. Several specifically defined concepts have been used to describe fully what is meant by "role." The different concepts of role reviewed here have certain elements in common which can be pulled together in an integrative fashion. First, each approach ties the concept of role to the *behavior* of an individual in a *position*. Second, both the behavior and the position are viewed against a broader *social context*. Third, the social context gives meaning to the role primarily through the *expectations and behavior of others*. Finally, the process which constitutes the essence of roles is *human interaction*—the *reciprocal* relationships between individuals that mutually influence interacting parties.

Implications for Health Professionals

From the foregoing discussion, it should be clear that the functioning of any organization depends on the existence of norms and standards of reciprocal behavior among members of the system. One of the most efficient ways of assuring the maintenance and survival of the organization is in the execution of these norms through roles enacted by individuals in specific positions. Roles therefore have an intrinsic value for the organization. While roles are not necessarily the most efficient ways of promoting the welfare of *individuals*, they do tend to hold some value in relation to self-perception and the self-concept.

Each of the preceding approaches to the concept of role carries implications for self-perception that are relevant to the positions of health professionals. Specifically, these approaches suggest that the health professional can:

Use her position in the organization as a medium for self-observation of performance by attending to behavior with clients and colleagues

Give herself feedback by approving or disapproving or suggesting to herself some ways of changing performance, if necessary

Evaluate her performance against normative expectations and situational demands

Assess her special capabilities and strengths, identify limitations, and account for the extent to which she acts out of those strengths and limitations or dwells too much on either

Seek and process constructive performance feedback from others in positions related to the role

Observe her performance and compare it against the performance of others who carry out the same function

> Attend to her feelings about her role so as to assess the extent to which it may be restricting or promoting personal and professional development

In general, the role provides a vehicle for learning about the self. As such, a role is an integral component of total self-perception, for it provides useful information about the self—information that can be integrated into the self-concept. Of course, the frequent problem is that individuals assign too much weight to this kind of information about the self. All too often, individuals define their total selves in relation to their professional roles. As a result, they commit themselves to a course of living directed by a prescription for carrying that role into other areas of their lives. They perceive themselves to be "onstage" most of the time, so they continue to "play the role" when it is not appropriate. Healthy individuals enact their roles and derive satisfaction from their jobs, while at the same time growing through the ability to be true to their real selves (Jourard, 1959). They do not define themselves in terms of their roles. They also realize that their professional roles are among the many other roles that they play in society.

As individuals move from one context to another, they move from one role to another. A necessity of everyday life is the ability to change behaviors to meet the requirements of changing circumstances and changing expectations. For example, the psychologist may occupy the roles of father, husband, church parishioner, club member, civic group leader, neighbor, golf partner, and others which demand that he continuously shift out of one role and into another. Each one of these roles causes him to perceive himself in slightly to markedly different ways from his perceptions of self as a psychologist. For him to function optimally across all of these situations, he must *integrate his roles into an organized pattern of diversity.* In all probability, his success *in any one of these roles* will depend on his ability to integrate all of his roles into an organized gestalt (whole pattern). He would probably be a relatively unsuccessful father, husband, and golf partner, for example, if he continued to act as a psychologist in these other roles.

Through this continuous shifting out of one role and into another, the person's concept of himself may shift in very subtle ways. Under such circumstances, it would seem natural for him to be somewhat inconsistent and "chameleon-like." Since some persons are unable to tolerate this inherent inconsistency, it occasionally happens that they consolidate their identity within one predominant role because it offers the most congruent information about the self. We see this type of phenomenon across all occupations, from the sailor who literally "tattoos his identity" to his arm, to the physician who bristles when someone calls him by his first name. And, in one of America's greatest political tragedies, the country witnessed the downfall of a president who desperately resorted to unconstitutional acts in order to maintain the position which formed the essence of his identity. This tragic example serves to highlight the additional fact that roles may be perceived incorrectly. There is not always a direct correspondence between perceived and enacted roles. A person, like the former president, may be perceived more or less objectively by others who observe his behavior (enacted role), but in dramatically different ways by the individual himself (perceived role) and those close to him. This, of course, would suggest that more accurate role perception may derive from the constructive feedback of others on how one is enacting a specific role. There is clearly a lesson to be learned about role perception from the behavior of our past president.

In summary, it should be noted that changing and varied perceptions of self in different roles continuously present the individual with new elements for integration into the self-concept. These elements will increase as the number of roles increase. More specifically, these elements will increase as the number of roles "acknowledged" increases. To develop a broader, more accurate self-concept, it is necessary to utilize the wealth of information available about the self in *multiple roles*. You are aspiring to be successful in a position as a health professional. You will be successful partly as a function of how accurately you perceive your role in relation to your whole self. The "healthy" professional is one who subsumes her professional identity within an integrated concept of self as the player of many roles united by an essential core—the discovery of which represents a lifelong task.

Summary and Conclusion

Human beings have a need for order and predictability in the world. Nowhere is this need greater than in relation to one's own self. Through life experience, each individual comes to differentiate characteristics that belong to the "me" or the "I," and to symbolize those characteristics of self, each person develops a self-concept. The self-concept is a cognitive abstraction about the nature of one's self "as perceived." This concept of self becomes the interpretive framework for processing experiences of the self in relation to the world. Experiences that are consistent with the self-concept are incorporated and allowed into awareness, while inconsistent experiences are distorted or denied into awareness.

The self-concept comes to function as a mechanism for maintaining consistency in the experience of self. In the service of maintaining consistency, the self-concept may ultimately become distorted; it comes to represent more of an "ideal" concept of self. When the gap between the real self and the ideal self widens, the individual experiences an increased need for consistency. To enhance the preferred concept of self, the person thus increasingly biases and distorts perceptions of self in social interaction. To narrow this gap, it is necessary for the individual to be receptive to accurate feedback from self and others. It is also necessary for the individual to disclose himself to others and to himself. Within health care organizations, personal relationships may conflict with role relationships in such a way as to inhibit the individual from open self-disclosure and receptivity to feedback. This obstacle can be removed through the very actions that are avoided. Individuals can risk their relationships in a responsible fashion through appropriate self-disclosure and move toward improved relationships fostered by an emergent mutual understanding. Understanding of self and others as both persons and professionals depends partly on the ability of interactants to understand their respective professional roles. When professional roles are put into proper perspective as "parts" of integrated "whole" persons, individuals become freer to move toward an elaboration of their self-concepts and more accepting of the natural inconsistencies that characterize their beings. The challenge for most individuals is to learn to accept themselves "as they are," to move toward unconditional positive self-regard, to become fully aware of what they think, feel, and want.

There is a profound implication from this chapter for effective health care services. A prerequisite for effective health care service is the ability of the health professional to *know* and *care* about clients. *Knowing* and *caring* are inseparable in health services, yet their interdependence is often not realized. But, in health care you can never know how truly sick a client is unless he discloses himself to you (Jourard, 1971). As Jourard maintained, you cannot help that person in any meaningful way unless you have allowed him to express himself. You can monitor and check objective signs and symptoms, but if you want to understand anything about that person—explain his illness, predict its course, prescribe treatment, control the outcome—you must get as much information as possible. This aspect of health care is probably implicitly understood by most health care practitioners. However, it seems to be less understood that knowing and caring for the self and others (including clients) rests upon the same basic processes of self-disclosure; *you cannot care for someone you do not know. To care for others, you must come to know them. Similarly, to care for the self, you must come to know the self. And, unless you know and care for your own self, you cannot come to fully know and care for another person. You cannot understand his frame of reference because you do not understand your own.* As Mayeroff stated (1971, pp. 41–42):

> To care for another person, I must be able to understand him and his world as if I were inside it. I must be able to see, as it were, with his eyes what his world is like to him and how he sees himself. Instead of merely looking at him in a detached way from outside, as if he were a specimen, I must be able to be *with* him in his world, "going" into his world in order to sense from "inside" what life is like for him, what he is striving to be, and what he requires to grow.

References

Aronson, E. *The Social Animal*, 2d ed. San Francisco, W. H. Freeman, 1976.

Beckman, L. Effects of Students' Performance on Teachers' and Observers' Attributions of Causality, *Journal of Educational Psychology*, 61:76–82 (1970).

Bower, F. L. Nursing Process Roles and Functions of the Nurse, in *Fundamentals of Nursing: Concepts, Roles and Functions*, ed. F. L. Bower and E. O. Bevis, pp. 178–81. St. Louis, C. V. Mosby, 1979.

Bramel, D. A. A Dissonance Theory Approach to Defensive Protection, *Journal of Abnormal and Social Psychology*, 69:121–29 (1962).

Brehm, J. W., and Cohen, A. R. *Explorations in Cognitive Dissonance*. New York, Wiley, 1962.

Cooley, C. H. *Human Nature and the Social Order.* New York, Scribner, 1902.

Festinger, L. *A Theory of Cognitive Dissonance.* Evanston, Illinois, Row, Peterson, 1957.

Heider, F. *The Psychology of Interpersonal Relations.* New York, Wiley, 1958.

James, W. *Principles of Psychology.* New York, Holt, Rinehart, and Winston, 1890.

Jones, E. E., and Nisbett, R. E. The Actor and Observer: Divergent Perceptions of the Causes of Behavior, in *Attribution: Perceiving the Causes of Behavior,* ed. E. E. Jones et al. Morristown, New Jersey, General Learning Press, 1972.

Jourard, S. *The Transparent Self.* New York, Van Nostrand, 1971.

Jourard, S. Healthy Personality and Self-Disclosure, *Mental Hygiene,* **32,** 499–507 (1959).

Luft, J. *Of Human Interaction.* Palo Alto, California, National Press, 1969.

Mayeroff, M. *On Caring.* New York, Perennial Library, 1971.

Mead, G. H. *Mind, Self, and Society: From the Standpoint of a Social Behaviorist.* Chicago, Illinois, University of Chicago Press, 1934.

Miller, D. T. Ego-Involvement and Attributions for Success and Failure, *Journal of Personality and Social Psychology,* **34:**901–6 (1976).

Rogers, C. *Client-Centered Therapy.* Boston, Houghton Mifflin, 1951.

Rogers, C. A Theory of Therapy, Personality and Interpersonal Relationships, as Developed in the Client-Centered Framework, in *Psychology: A Study of a Science. Formulations of the Person and the Social Context,* Vol. 3, ed. S. Koch. New York, McGraw-Hill, 1959.

Rogers, C. *Becoming Partners.* New York, Dell, 1972.

Schneider, D. J.; Hastorf, A. H.; and Ellsworth, P. C. *Person Perception,* 2d ed. Reading, Massachusetts, Addison-Wesley, 1979.

Shaver, K. G. *An Introduction to Attribution Processes.* Cambridge, Massachusetts, Winthrop, 1975.

Streufert, S., and Streufert, S. C. Effects of Conceptual Structure, Failure, and Success on Attribution of Causality and Interpersonal Attitudes, *Journal of Personality and Social Psychology,* **11:**138–47 (1969).

CHAPTER
FOUR

Alternative Perceptions: Toward Empathic Understanding

If . . . you can learn a simple trick . . . you'll get along a lot better with all kinds of folks. You never really understand a person until you consider things from his point of view—until you climb into his skin and walk around in it.

Atticus Finch to his children in
Harper Lee's *To Kill a Mockingbird*

There is something of an irony about human relationships in that we spend so much time interacting with others and yet so little time in really *trying to understand one another*. Of course, we do develop some notions about most people we encounter because our perceptions of them need to be meaningful to us. From our own frames of reference, we observe their behavior and process that information in order to make sense out of our perceptions. The meanings we attach to our perceptions lead us to assume that we "know about" those with whom we interact. There are limits to this type of "knowledge about" or "understanding of" other persons, however. For one thing, when two people interact in close proximity, they both send and receive verbal and nonverbal messages that *may mean different things to each person*. Rarely do we achieve perfect correspondence between the exact meanings intended by the sender and the subsequent meanings attached by the receiver of a message. This must be expected, since each person operates from his or her own personal frame of reference, but this very fact often represents the major obstacle to *real interpersonal understanding*. Specifically, we ordinarily rely on our own perspectives and fail to achieve deeper understanding of others by trying to perceive things as they might see them. It is entirely within our capabilities to increase our understanding of others by broadening our frames of reference to include their perceptions—that is, we can "put ourselves in the other person's shoes" or, as Atticus Finch advised in the excerpt above, "climb into his skin and walk around in it." We can re-create an individual's experience in our own frames of reference and move toward *empathic understanding*.

Empathic understanding—the unique capacity of human beings to feel and understand what another person is experiencing—is a learned skill which has its roots in the processes of human interaction and development. In the first chapter it was noted that we perceive the behavior of others to be meaningful most of the time. It is perceived as meaningful partly because we tend to assume that they are *similar* to ourselves. Behind all interpersonal transactions is the tendency for individuals to relate to one another at the most basic level of *species similarity.* Everyone can at least recognize a member of the human race. Even higher animal species behave in ways which clearly suggest that they "know" when they encounter members of their own species. This was even a theme of Hans Christian Anderson's "The Ugly Duckling." Among humans it is automatic that we identify others as being basically like ourselves. Furthermore, because we have complex personalities and intellects, we are likely to see a great deal of similarity between ourselves and others in terms of *experiences* and *behavior.* For example, I can appreciate the fact that Dan feels lousy because he had no sleep the night before, that Sue feels proud of graduating from college, and that Elaine enjoyed visiting with her old friends at Christmastime. I, too, have had similar experiences, and I know what they feel like. So, on the basis of our similarities as living persons, we have a foundation for basic mutual understanding. This is not the only basis for our understanding, however.

If you observe an infant, you will notice that she cannot resist the expressed emotions of others around her. In a real sense, she has no means for preventing the "spread of others' emotions to herself." When her mother smiles and tickles her, she squeals with delight, and when her parents shout and yell at one another, she cries. This spread of affect (emotions) has been called *emotional contagion.* Empathy is a later form of emotional contagion (Holt, 1971). For emotional contagion to mature into a capacity for empathy, the developing individual must first grow out of the contagion state and learn to be "appropriately indifferent" to emotional expressions of others. That is, she must learn to control her own emotions as others express theirs. This occurs through normal development as the self becomes differentiated from the total perceptual field. In Chapter Three, it was pointed out that each person develops a concept of self, with definite boundaries which separate the self from the rest of the world. The experience of self includes perceptions of personal feelings and thoughts—those that are perceived to be *our own.* We learn that our own feelings are distinct from the feelings of others. Emotional experiencing thus comes to involve a differentiation among our own feeling states as well as those which belong to other persons. Emotional contagion, then, may be viewed as a stage which precedes the controlled awareness of the feelings of others that we call "empathy" (Holt, 1971).

In this chapter, the concept of empathy is presented as a necessary condition for establishing and maintaining satisfactory human relationships. Whether those relationships are professional or nonprofessional, a basic necessity of good interpersonal relationships is the ability of interacting persons to achieve and communicate adequate levels of empathic understanding. Therefore, the primary focus of the present chapter is on the achievement of empathy through accurate perception and the expression of empathy through effective communication. Later chapters of this text are devoted to specific communications skills, whereas communication is treated here in terms of its complementary relationship to perception as integral processes which together define the essence of empathic understanding. The importance of empathy in the provision of health care services rings clear when it is recognized that empathy is at the very foundation of true altruism—the helping of other human beings with no expectations of receiving self-serving benefits. Thus, the present chapter ends with a consideration of the implications of empathic understanding for effective health care services.

Empathic Understanding

The word *understanding* has come to mean a "knowledge of or about" something. It is a concept which is typically viewed as a cognitive or intellectual grasp of the nature, significance, explanation, or general relations of particulars, but this is *not* the type of understanding with which we are concerned when we speak of "empathic" understanding. The term *empathy* is an English derivation of the German word *einfulung*, which means "feeling into." As a psychological phenomenon, this "feeling into" has been conceptualized in various ways by different writers. For example, Rogers (1961, p. 284) defined empathy as an understanding of the other's world as seen from the inside—a sensing of the other person's private world "as if" it were your own, "but without losing the 'as if' quality." Clark (1980, p. 187) also emphasized the "as if" quality when he defined empathy as "that unique capacity of the human being to feel the experiences, needs, aspirations, frustrations, sorrows, joys, anxieties, hurt, or hunger of others *as if* [italics added] they were his or her own." Pearce and Newton (1963 p. 52) defined empathy as "experiencing in ourselves *some reflection* [italics added] of the emotional tone that is being experienced by the other person." Each of these definitions contains elements which imply that the experiences of others are not taken on "as one's own." Empathy is therefore seen as an understanding *with* others, not "as" others or "about" others. As conceptualized here, empathy involves the *re-creation of the experience of another person within your own frame of reference*. It requires the broadening of our frames of reference to where we share some part of another person's experience. This is the process through which real interpersonal understanding emerges and, as Keen pointed out (1975, p. 33):

> In order to reveal the many meanings of an event, we must come to see clearly the experiences of the participants, whose intentions and perceptions *are* the event's meanings. Then we understand.

Empathic understanding should not be confused with the simple acknowledgement of another's point of view. It is not difficult for anyone to see that points of view are like names—everybody has one. However, it does seem to present a problem for many people to go beyond a recognition of the obvious toward an understanding of what those points of view actually represent. Empathy involves an understanding of how another person *feels* and *thinks* and *perceives* things, including himself and the world around him (Patterson,

1974). This kind of understanding is rare in our society because we neither give it nor receive it very often. We rarely persist in a mode of perception that allows us to attend to the "real facts" of an interaction—the feelings, ideas, and perceptions of another person, as well as the sources which give rise to those experiences. This is not to suggest that people are incapable of achieving empathic understanding, for the *potential* is certainly there for most individuals. Nevertheless, in our society, empathic understanding is like an untapped natural resource which remains concealed within our midst. Once it is "discovered," however, the means for releasing its potential can be developed in the form of behavioral *skills* which transform empathic understanding into an *actuality of interpersonal relations*.

At present, the means for developing empathic skills are described primarily within the literature on counseling and psychotherapy. Within this context, virtually all theorists and practitioners regard empathy as a prerequisite condition for establishing and maintaining the relationship between client and therapist. Without empathy being communicated by the therapist at consistently high levels, the relationship does not evolve satisfactorily, and the client is less likely to move toward positive change. The client-therapist relationship is really the medium through which change occurs, but this relationship actually represents an "ideal," characterized by high levels of empathic understanding on the part of the therapist. And, it is indeed interesting to note that, not only is such a relationship considered an "ideal" relationship, but also as a condition so basic to good human relations, empathy itself is described as an ideal condition which is found mainly within the supposedly ideal context of a psychotherapeutic relationship! In fact, Patterson (1974) remarked that society has reached a low point when the provision of a good human relationship is found primarily within this context. In reality, psychotherapy is probably *not* an ideal model for interpersonal relationships. Psychotherapy is typically a one-way process in which the person taking the "role of therapist" helps the person in the "role of client." The therapist may move toward the client in understanding, communicating, caring, and support, but there is no reciprocity by the client toward the therapist. Everyday relationships are characterized by more *mutuality* of communication, more "give-and-take" between individuals, and less clear-cut roles. Nevertheless, the *skills* of the therapist are skills that people need to be effective with one another in all kinds of interpersonal relationships (Egan, 1975). The skills of achieving and communicating empathy should not belong solely to a trained psychotherapist, but to life and interpersonal relations in general!

Achieving and Communicating Empathy

As indicated, most people have the capacity for achieving empathic understanding. The irony here is that the capacity is so latent in most cases that we have to educate and train people in the skills necessary to actualize it. Empathy is based on the effective use of *perceptual* and *communication* skills. The first essential ingredient for empathy is the perceptual skill of perceiving accurately the experience and behavior of another person. This is accomplished to the extent that one is able to re-create the experience of another within one's own frame of reference. Most persons may very well accomplish this. The second ingredient, the catalyst which moves "insight into action" and makes empathy part of the interpersonal relationship, is *communication*. The insights gained from accurate perceptions of another are meaningless unless they can be revealed to the other through communication. In fact, we have no way of knowing if a person really has achieved empathic understanding in the perceptual sense if it has not been communicated in the behavioral sense. Conversely, an individual can try to communicate to another person that she "understands" his experience, but, if her understanding is not based on *accurate perception*, she has not only failed to achieve empathy—she has also failed to communicate it! Empathy is very much a function of *both* ingredients. Without *accurate perception* and *effective communication*, there is simply no empathy.

Achieving Empathy

Patterson (1974) described empathy as involving three aspects or stages. First, the individual must be *receptive* to another's communications. Second, the individual must *understand* the communication by putting himself in the other's place. Third, the individual must *communicate* that understanding to the other person. The first two aspects are contingent primarily upon accurate perception, although receptivity can be communicated to the other person very easily. The third aspect is clearly a matter of verbal and nonverbal communication. As indicated in a later section of this chapter, empathy can be blocked anywhere along the way—from the communication of the sender, to the perceptions of the receiver, to the receiver's communications back to the sender. Here the focus is on perception and its relationship to the first two aspects of empathy.

The first aspect involves "receptivity" to the communications of the other person. Being receptive to another individual is not a difficult task to learn, but in deep interpersonal transactions, there is a certain "intensity of presence" (Egan, 1975) that is sometimes difficult to sustain. When you are receptive to someone's communications, you have first of all accepted her as a person who merits attention. Then you focus "attentively" on what she is communicating. This means that you must attend to her physically and psychologically. Physical attending means that you adopt a *posture of involvement* (Egan, 1975) with a person by facing her squarely, maintaining appropriate eye contact, and leaning toward her with uncrossed arms and without leaning back with your legs crossed and your hand supporting your head. It also means that you put down whatever you have in your hands at the moment, like a pen or pencil, cigarette, or some other object. All of these behaviors tell her a great deal about your receptivity to what she has to say. How often have you encountered someone who read a newspaper or watched television while you were trying to talk her? How many times have you encountered someone who would not stop working at a task when you tried to relate something important to him? How many times have you sensed that a person was just not listening to you? And, better yet, how many times have you done the same? You probably have done so many times in each instance. The lack of physical attending in interpersonal relations is very common, and its effect is to cause a disruption in the relationship, temporarily or permanently. Physical attending is at the base of receptivity and increases the likelihood that you will be able to attend *psychologically*. Psychological attending goes beyond the "being with" quality of physical attending to *active listening* and "behavioral-data processing." Active listening as a communication skill is discussed in Chapter 13. It is sufficient to note here that, as a perceptual skill, active listening involves selection, organization, and complex cognitive processing of verbal and nonverbal cues provided by a communicating individual. This means that you hear not only the words spoken by the other person, but also the ways in which those words are modified by nonverbal and paralinguistic cues (Egan, 1975). You perceive the experience and behavior of the individual as well as the feelings that permeate them, and you move toward understanding by laying the cornerstone of empathy through total active listening.

The greatest obstacle to the achievement of empathy occurs in the reception stage. When you judge, evaluate, approve, or disapprove of the statements of the other person, you have failed to be receptive. Instead of being open to the other person, you are biasing your perceptions and resultant communications, and you are not receptive to the meanings which those experiences have *to that person*. Suppose that your response to a friend who stated that he did not like Joe was something like this: "Joe's not a bad guy. You just don't know him. I like him." Your response indicates that you have ignored and discounted the experience of your friend; you have made no attempt to understand his feelings about Joe and, instead, have evaluated what he has said to you from your own frame of reference. "Joe is not a bad guy" is a statement which negates your friend's experience. "You just don't know him" is an evaluative statement about the legitimacy of your friend's comment. "I like him" is a communication of *your* appraisal of Joe. Because you were not open or receptive to your friend's experience of Joe, you do not understand how he feels about Joe *from his perspective*. You may understand the words spoken by your friend, but you have not picked up the real meaning of those words.

The second aspect of empathy is the ability to understand the communications of another person. Anyone speaking the same language as a communicator can understand the words spoken. That is, anyone can understand the *content* of a message, but it is only when the individual puts himself in the place of the communicator that he can derive the same *meaning* which those words have to that person. When this is accomplished, the individual has gained an understanding of the *essence* of what is being communicated. The essence of a communication is found in the *experience* of the communicator—in feelings, thoughts, and perceptions which suffuse the verbal content of the message. Furthermore, when one understands the essence of another's experience, he understands the sources which gave rise to that experience. For example, he not only hears Jane *say* that she doesn't like Joe, he perceives Jane's expressed *feelings* which underlie her statement, and he knows that Jane dislikes Joe *because* Joe always ignores her when she tries to talk to him. Obviously, no one can feel toward Joe in exactly the same way that Jane does. No one can actually "be" another person, for we are always outside of the person's subjective frame of reference. We cannot experience anything exactly as someone else does. So, how can we possibly gain another person's frame of reference and see things as she does? How can we possibly achieve empathic understanding if it means re-creating another person's experience in our own frames of reference? Often, demographic characteristics make it especially hard to understand another's experience. No male can fully understand what it is like to be a woman, nor can an adolescent fully understand what it is like to be a grandparent. Even the nurse cannot fully understand the experience of the dying patient, just as the psychologist cannot fully understand the psychotic experience of one of her patients. The fact is, however, that we do not have to be exactly like another person, nor do we need to have the same exact experiences to gain empathic understanding. I do not need to bang my head against the wall to understand what my friend's headache is like for him, and I certainly don't have to make myself sick to understand what physical illness is like! Most of the experiences communicated by an individual have some relation to our own perceptual experiences, our own feelings, and our own thoughts. We can achieve empathic understanding on the basis of our *similarities* as human beings! *We can relate their experiences to some of our own!* All of us share the experience of being human—of feeling, thinking, and interacting with the world—something which, in spite of our differences, we cannot escape sharing.

Once when I was working with alcoholic persons, I was challenged by a patient who insisted that I couldn't possibly understand his problems since I was not an alcoholic (even some "experts" in the field would believe this to be true). Even though his accusation was a defensive ploy to justify his resistance to treatment, this person needed to know that I, too, had experienced a range of feelings, thoughts, and actions similar to his. For example, in my life I, too, have felt compelled to do some things that were not in my best interest, and I have been perplexed by self-defeating behavior that I didn't know how to stop. I have also felt anger, guilt, shame, despair, loneliness, and resentful of others whose lives appeared to be more rewarding; I have on occasion felt unappreciated, unloved, exploited, and misunderstood; there have been times when I have felt inadequate and lacked confidence in myself, just as there have been times when I have felt threatened by others, when I thought I had to defend my actions, rationalize my behavior, and deny responsibility for the consequences of those actions. True, there were important differences between us, but our overriding similarities were undeniably and inescapably grounded in these and many other common life experiences. *Using my own experience*, I could understand this person very well! I could achieve empathy because I could recreate his experience in my own frame of reference by relating those experiences to some of my own.

By drawing from my experience of living—of feeling, thinking, and acting—I can relate to another's experience without having to "be that person" and without having to go through the same exact circumstances. As a side note, it frequently happens that a person will claim that you cannot possibly understand what it is like to have experienced something as she did. This argument should not prevent us from surmounting the obstacle that has been put in front of us. Some people will make this contention because they do not want to go any deeper in the transaction, and they use the argument to terminate discussion of a sensitive issue. However, others actually believe that no one can understand. In either case, it is usually sufficient to acknowledge that you *may not* fully understand, and then encourage the person to help you gain some understanding by describing *what it is like for her* to have had such an experience. This kind of response has the effect of "putting the ball back in her end of the court," placing some responsibility on her to help you achieve the understanding which you have indicated to be important. You will communicate that you think her experience is *worth the effort* of understanding. By communicating that we *want to understand*, or that we are *trying to understand*, the other person will often show remarkable persistence in helping us to attain it.

Perceiving Feelings in Oneself. Empathy can be achieved when we re-create another's experience in our own frame of reference by relating his experience to some of our own. Understanding a person in this way depends on numerous factors, including the perception of feelings in self and others. Feelings are consciously experienced states of physical arousal. Before we can relate to the feelings of someone else, we must be able to perceive accurately the cues to their feelings. We never really "see" someone's feelings—we see outward expressions of current internal states, and from those cues we make inferences about what he is experiencing at the moment. We perceive overt behavior and then make *attributions*. Our degree of accuracy often depends upon how clearly we have been able to discriminate our own feelings under similar circumstances.

The commonsense view of feelings is that they occur in response to the perception of some stimulus and that they then cause behavioral expressions that are recognized as *emotions*. For example, when a person encounters a threatening stimulus, she experiences anxiety or fear, and then trembles. Perception of the stimulus is assumed to "cause" the feeling of "fear" which, in turn, "causes" trembling. This commonsense view of a causal chain of events has never been the most popular view among psychologists, to which numerous theories of emotions over the last 100 years can attest. In the nineteenth century, William James, the "father of psychology," posited that the important factor in our felt emotions is the feedback we receive from bodily changes in particular situations. In an eloquent proposition that seemed to put the cart before the horse, James claimed that we do *not* tremble because we are afraid—*we are afraid because we tremble* (1890, Vol. 2, p. 449):

> . . . the bodily changes follow directly the perception of the exciting fact, and that our feeling of the same changes as they occur *is* the emotion.

Strange as it might seem, this proposition has some plausibility when you apply it to some of your own life experiences. For example, recall a time when you were driving your car and suddenly had to slam on your brakes to avoid an accident. Before you even had time to recognize a state of fear, the emergency had passed—*then* you probably noticed your feelings. Health professionals often experience this sort of thing in emergency situations where they react quickly, calmly, automatically, and then after the crisis has passed, they often notice that their hearts are pounding, their breathing is rapid, and they feel a weakness or trembling in their legs; it is then that they recognize the feeling of anxiety or fear!

Cannon (1927) objected to James's theory on the grounds that internal bodily changes often occur too slowly to be a source of emotions and that those changes do not seem to differ much from one emotional state to another, even though we tend to be fairly clear about what feeling we are experiencing at the moment. According to Cannon, bodily changes and the subjective experience of emotion *occur at the same time* and are products of the activation of certain portions of the brain. Thus, you are trembling *and* you are afraid at the same time because the brain has activated those responses simultaneously. Research evidence has shown that the time distinction between Cannon's theory and James's theory is not very useful or meaningful. On some occasions, such as threatening or dangerous situations, feelings may be preceded by bodily activity (giving credence to James's theory), while on other occasions one's awareness of a feeling precedes bodily activity (lending support to Cannon's theory). A major contribution of these theories is that both have pointed to the importance of bodily changes or physiological arousal as an intrinsic component of emotional experience. But, neither has answered some important questions. For example, *do people always interpret these bodily cues accurately? Do they always know exactly what they are feeling?* To gain a full appreciation of empathy, it would be helpful to have some answers to these questions.

Most people take it for granted that they can recognize their own feelings and that they can discriminate among different feelings. They believe that they know whether they are angry, afraid, or just excited, for example, but a large body of empirical evidence suggests that people may be deluding themselves. It seems that people are not always accurate in recognizing bodily changes that characterize feelings, nor are they necessarily good at discriminating one feeling from another. Physiological responses of the body are usually the same for most of our emotions. For example, when we experience anger, our hearts beat faster, our blood pressures become elevated, our breathing changes. *These are the same bodily responses which occur when we experience fear or excitement* and a range of other emotions! The research has failed to show that there are distinct patterns of bodily responses that characterize different emotions. No single pattern appears to be unique to any emotion! How then can people discriminate their feelings? It seems that feelings have other important sources which come from behavior, past experience, and current situations.

Bem (1965) argued that when internal cues about our feelings are weak or ambiguous, we must *infer* our feelings from observations of our own behavior and situational influences. Bem's contention is that we must function like "outside observers" and make inferences as if we had no access to our own internal experience. In effect, this means that we observe our behavior in a particular situation and use behavioral and contextual information to infer that we must therefore be feeling a particular emotion. It does not mean that a person knows he is happy by observing his laughter and concluding that "I must be happy because I'm laughing." In circumstances such as these, internal cues are not ambiguous, nor are they vague, so we do not rely heavily on behavioral cues. It is only when we are unable to make much out of the cues from within that we use the cues from "without." It might be hard to accept this idea, since we usually believe that internal cues are unmistakable and that we can always rely on those cues. "I know what I'm feeling" is the typical assumption. Given that the evidence contradicts this assumption to some extent, it appears that there are occasions when we do rely on our own behavior as a source of information about what we are feeling. Bem's hypothesis is somewhat radical in its form, but there is a simplicity in the assertion that does have some value in understanding possible influences on the perception of feelings. But, Bem is not the only theorist who maintains that internal cues may be insufficient sources of information about feelings.

Schachter (1964) introduced a "cognitive-physiological theory" of emotional self-labeling, based on findings which showed that *different feelings can be induced in individuals given the same physiological arousal*. In a classic experiment on which the theory is based, Schachter and Singer (1962) injected subjects with epinephrine (adrenalin). Increases of adrenalin in the bloodstream produces feelings of arousal. All subjects receiving the injection experienced this experience of arousal. Each subject had been told that the injection was a vitamin supplement, but one group was told that the symptoms it would experience were "side effects" of the drug. When symptoms then appeared (usually in five minutes), these subjects would have an explanation for their feelings. A second group was given no explanation about the symptoms that would follow. A third group was told that the side effects would be numbness, itching, and a slight headache; thus, subjects in this group were misdirected with a false explanation. A fourth group was given a placebo injection of saline solution and no information about the subsequent symptoms. Subjects were then joined by a confederate of the experimenter, and this person had been trained and instructed to act angry or euphoric. For subjects who had not been given an explanation for their symptoms, the behavior of the confederate could thus provide a "label" for their feelings. The confederate displayed either anger or euphoria in the presence of subjects individually while they sat in a waiting room "presumably" prior to an experiment. When he showed anger, the confederate complained about the experiment and about a questionnaire that they had to fill out, and then tore up the questionnaire and stormed out of the room. When he acted euphoric, he behaved playfully and joyously by playing with objects in the room. The findings revealed that, when the confederate was angry, subjects who had not been informed about their symptoms reported more subjective feelings of anger than did subjects who had been informed. When the confederate showed euphoric behavior, uninformed subjects reported more euphoria than did the informed group. Schachter concluded that internal physiology *interacts* with the situation to determine the felt emotion. People tend to determine their feelings by appraising the emotion-producing situation. When feeling aroused, they will label their feelings as happiness, sadness, anger, or fear, depending on the circumstances.

In light of the foregoing theories and research findings, it is difficult to say whether physiological responses precede, accompany, or follow emotions, As Hilgard, Atkinson, and Atkinson (1979) pointed out, an emotion is not a "momentary" event, but takes place over a period of time. Even though the feeling may be activated by the perception of stimuli in the environment, the body is also activated immediately in such a way as to provide physical feedback about the experience. The resultant experience of a particular feeling involves the combination of physical information and information about the stimulus. Other findings have made it clear that people perceive their own feelings by including an observation of their own behavior, an appraisal of the situation, and then integrating that information with internal cues to make a quick, high-level cognitive deduction. Schachter's theory advanced the idea that feedback to the brain from internal bodily activity gives rise to an undifferentiated emotional state, and that the resultant feeling is determined partly by the "label" that the person assigns to this aroused state. This also points to the role of learning and language in emotional experience. People will describe their feelings in the language terms that they have learned within their culture. They will use the language of their culture to label or name their feelings, and the exact label that they use will be determined by the various internal and external cues available to them. It therefore appears that the perception of personal feelings is a very complex process, influenced by numerous factors.

Given the apparent facts of emotional experiencing, it would clearly seem that the ability to perceive one's own emotions is a skill that is learned. Many people have difficulty recognizing their feelings, discriminating among various feelings, and describing their experience of those feelings because they have not learned the skill adequately. They are not used to *attending* to their feelings, so it is often hard for them to really know what they *are* feeling in different situations. They are not as effective as they could be in extracting available internal and external cues. And, it is indeed difficult to *describe* an experience that you cannot clearly perceive in the first place. Perhaps this is yet another reason why some people insist that you cannot possibly understand what they are feeling—they don't understand it either!

One of the keys to achieving empathy is found in the ability to perceive one's own feelings accurately. When you have the skill for perceiving and processing available experimental information, you can identify your own feelings and learn to be "in touch" with your own self. Being "in touch" with your own self is more than a popular cliché. It means that you are skilled in perceiving your own feelings. You cannot be "in touch" with another human being's experience if you are not "in touch" with your own. You have no reliable basis for re-creating his experience in your own frame of reference. In short, you cannot achieve empathy. Learning how to attend to yourself, to others, and to the situations in which you interact with others is essential if you are going to enhance the kind of understanding that is the foundation of empathy! As the old saying goes, "It all begins at home," *with your own experience.*

Perceiving Feelings in Others. It has been established that people do not always perceive their own feelings accurately. But, can people perceive *others'* emotions accurately? This question was entertained by Charles Darwin in 1872, who proposed that there are certain universal emotional expressions that are innate and recognizable by everyone. Darwin argued that most of the ways in which we express emotions are inherited patterns of behavior that originally held some survival value to the human species. As an example, he assumed that the expression of disgust represented an attempt by the human being to dispose of something which he had consumed. It is an expression which can be manifested toward another person also:

> Extreme disgust is expressed by movements around the mouth identical with those
> preparatory to the act of vomiting. The mouth is open widely, and the upper lip

strongly retracted . . . the partial closure of the eyelids, or the turning away of the eyes or of the whole body, are likewise highly expressive of disdain. These actions seem to declare that the despised person is not worth looking at, or is disagreeable to behold. . . .

Many of Darwin's insights went largely ignored for many years until recently, when researchers began to take a more respectful attitude toward some of his notions. For example, the research by Izard (1971) and Ekman, Sorenson, and Friesen (1969) established unequivocally that there are certain basic universal emotional expressions displayed by human beings that can be judged with a high degree of accuracy. Of course, these findings were restricted to *facial* expressions of emotion, and do not imply that all we have to do is look in another person's face to quickly determine what they are feeling. Not all emotions can be detected so readily. Some people may not be experiencing a strong emotion when we encounter them, and others may be trying to conceal an emotion by not letting it show on their faces. Izard and Ekman obtained findings which indicated that there are certain *basic emotions* which can be detected from *facial expressions*. People all over the world seem to be able to recognize facial expressions of happiness, disgust, anger, interest, and even fear, sorrow, shame, and surprise (Schneider, Hastorf, and Ellsworth, 1979). This fact implies that there is a definite connection between emotional *experience* and emotional *expression*, for if the two were not related, people could not identify or agree upon perceived expressions (Schneider, Hastorf, and Ellsworth, 1979). This fact implies the additional possibility that Darwin's original contention of an innate connection between emotion and expression may indeed be quite tenable.

As indicated in Chapter Two, there are rules of "affect display" in every culture, such that emotions are typically expressed in accordance with the contingencies of the situation in which a person finds himself. For example, you may be invited to a friend's house for dinner, and when the main course of liver and onions is put on the table, it would be unacceptable and inappropriate for you to show disgust at the sight of a meal which you deplore. Or, in many of our interpersonal encounters, we are expected at least to show interest in the other person and be polite and cordial. Even though we may be quite bored by the other person, we are expected to maintain expressions of respect and politeness. Thus, when we disguise our true feelings because of affect display rules for specific contexts, others will have a hard time reading our true feelings. Unfortunately, sometimes we think that our expressive disguises are working well for us when, in reality, our masks are slipping as our true feelings leak out in subtle ways that are perceived by others. Then we begin to appear somewhat differently to others. In general, however, when people are experiencing genuine feelings and are making no attempt to hide those feelings, others can usually perceive them accurately. There are ways of expressing basic emotions which are not culture-bound, and people are normally quite good at perceiving those expressions. It is when we come to more subtle emotional expressions, where differences begin to be less clear, that we often have difficulty in discriminating the feelings of another person. As Schneider, Hastorf, and Ellsworth noted, this type of conclusion would have to be true (1979, p. 214):

If people could never accurately perceive emotions, then people could never accurately communicate whatever emotions they happen to be feeling. Not only would that make for considerable interpersonal mischief, but actors would not be able to create any emotions on the stage.

All of this is not to imply that we are invariably accurate in our perceptions of feelings expressed by others, but we can develop an extremely high degree of accuracy by improving our perceptual skills.

Understanding another person's feelings when emotional expressions are subtle is quite challenging. There is simply an absence of some much needed information in cases like these. However, there is an effective way of generating some useful information that can enhance our perceptual accuracy: *When you are not clear about what emotion is being expressed by a person, take into account the circumstances, and then check out your own feelings! If you are being empathic, chances are that your feelings may approximate hers!*

Communicating Empathy

Accurate perceptual discriminations of the experience of self and others are necessary conditions for empathic understanding. Perceptual accuracy is a basic ingredient for empathy. However, like any "ingredient," perceptual accuracy represents only "part of a whole." The second essential ingredient of empathy is effective communication, and there is an interesting relationship between interpersonal perception and communication: persons who make accurate perceptual discriminations are not always able to communicate effectively, but those who can communicate effectively are usually able to discriminate accurately (Carkhuff, 1969). This is not to say that if you communicate effectively you will naturally perceive others accurately. However, just as communication can be enhanced when two persons perceive each other accurately, perception can be enhanced when they are able to communicate effectively.

Carkhuff (1969) developed a five-point scale for assessing communication of empathic understanding in interpersonal processes. This scale has been widely used as a means for demonstrating various levels of empathic communications. As Carkhuff and Berenson (1977, p. 9) noted, the individual's ability to communicate at high levels of empathic understanding involves his ability to "merge with the experience" of the other and "reflect upon his experience while suspending his own judgements, tolerating his own anxiety and communicating this understanding." Accordingly, it is the "manner" of the individual that communicates understanding (Carkhuff and Berenson, 1977).

Level One. This is the lowest level of empathic communication. The person's responses to the other either *do not attend to* or *detract significantly from* the verbal and behavioral expressions of that person, in that they communicate significantly less of the other person's feelings than he has communicated himself. The first person communicates no awareness of even the most obvious surface feelings expressed by the second person. The first person's frame of reference totally excludes the frame of reference of the second person. He operates entirely out of his own frame of reference and is responding to his own feelings, while being undiscerning of the other's expressions. The first person does not communicate that he is listening, hearing, understanding, or sensitive to the feelings and thoughts expressed by the second person. Here are some examples of individuals communicating low levels of empathy:

PATIENT: Sometimes I feel so depressed because I'm not making faster progress in my recovery from the operation.

NURSE: You had a serious operation and it takes time to recover. Most people who undergo that kind of surgery feel the same way.

PATIENT: Well, sometimes I just feel like giving up.

NURSE: You shouldn't feel that way. Everything will turn out fine. You just have to be patient.

The nurse's first response was in relation to the surgery and not to the person's feelings. She communicated little sensitivity to the patient's expressed feelings about his recovery and implied that he was no different from others in his reactions. The fact that others may also have felt the same way is probably no consolation to him, and such a communication from the nurse ignores and discounts his feelings as a separate and different person. Her second response was highly judgemental and evaluative. It was a moralizing response which scolded the patient for having a legitimate feeling. The nurse clearly operated from her own frame of reference, predicted that everything would turn out fine, and preached to him about what he "had" to do. In both of her responses, she failed to communicate anything but a low level of empathic understanding.

STUDENT NURSE: I'm really scared. I'm about to finish my training and I feel like I don't really know enough to begin working in a hospital and take on all of that responsibility.

INSTRUCTOR: I remember when I finished school. I felt the same way. But, I found out later that it's a normal feeling. Lot's of us get nervous before we take our first job.

First of all, the instructor responded to the "content" of the communication and failed to attend to the student nurse's feelings at the moment. But, he also responded to her communication by relating it to his own experience and then staying in his own frame of reference. Empathy is achieved by relating the other's experience to some of your own, but it requires that you use those experiences to re-create the other's experience in your own frame of reference—not to recall and reflect upon your own experiences! The instructor also discounted the student nurse's "personal" experience by minimizing its importance; he passed her feelings off as being "normal." Normal or not, the feelings are hers, and this is what must be recognized. Finally, the instructor managed to throw her into the masses of others who get nervous before they take their first job. The important thing is *not* whether "other people" have felt this way. Again, the important thing is that *she feels this way*.

Level Two. At level two, the first person responds to the expressed feelings of the second person, but he does so in such a way that he *subtracts noticeably* from the feelings communicated by the other person. The first person may show some awareness of surface feelings expressed by the other, but his communications take away from the level of feeling and distort the level of meaning. In brief, the first person responds to something other than what the second person is expressing.

> TECHNICIAN: I don't know how I'm going to handle all of this extra work. They give me all of this responsibility and expect miracles. But, I asked for it when I told them I didn't have enough to do, and that I *wanted* more responsibility. So, I guess I should be happy because they gave me what I asked for.
>
> ORDERLY: I can see how you'd be really mad with them dumping all that extra work on you. You shouldn't have to take on so much. Boy, if they ever did that to me, I'd tell them where to go.

The orderly responded to what he perceived as anger being expressed by the technician. Then he added his own feelings of resentment over being expected to do extra work. In effect, the orderly subtracted noticeably from the ambivalence communicated by the technician, and he distorted the actual meaning of what was being expressed by the technician.

Level Three. This is the level which Carkhuff (1969) called "interchangeable responses." At level three, the verbal and behavioral expressions of the first person in response to the expressed feelings of the second person are essentially *interchangeable* with those of the second person, in that they express essentially the same feelings and meaning. The responses of the first person neither subtract from nor add to the expressions of the second person. He is able to communicate accurate understanding of the other's surface feelings, but he does not communicate understanding of deeper feelings. Egan (1975) referred to this level of empathic understanding as *primary empathy.* According to Egan, this is the stage where the first person communicates "basic initial" understanding of what the other is feeling as well as the experiences underlying those feelings. At this level of "interchangeable responses," or "primary empathy," the individual merely tries to communicate that he understand what the other has *explicitly* expressed about himself. She communicates this in her own words and in her own style and manner. She does not try to "read between the lines" and make inferences about what is being expressed *implicitly.* Level three is regarded by Carkhuff and Egan to be a minimally facilitative or effective level of functioning.

> SUBORDINATE: I'm behind in my work. My desk is covered with papers, memos, and reports that I haven't even read yet. I have to finish the draft of the new project by tomorrow noon. And now I find out that I have to write a bid proposal by Friday!
>
> SUPERVISOR: You're really feeling overwhelmed because you can't catch up on your work and you have these deadlines to meet.

Even though there is a clear and present work-related problem that has to be resolved in the above case, the first order of business should be attention to the stress experienced by the subordinate. A step in this direction was taken by the supervisor, who communicated primary empathy at level three. The supervisor communicated an understanding of the content of the subordinate's message as well as the feelings being expressed. Her communication neither added to nor subtracted from the subordinate's experience. It captured the essence of the message and indicated that she understood at a basic level what he was feeling and why he was feeling that way.

> PETER: How's your job going these days, Hank?
> HANK: It's okay. I make a living, and I can pay the bills. I've got security and that makes Barb happy. But, it's the same old thing day after day, and I get tired of doing some little job that anyone can do.
> PETER: So, you're both satisfied and dissatisfied because, on the one hand, your job does have its financial advantages, but, on the other hand, you really don't get a lot of satisfaction for *yourself*.

Most of the time, people communicate more than one feeling in a message. In the interchange above, Peter communicated his understanding of Hank's conflicting feelings about his job, and his response implied that he also discerned the reasons for Hank's feelings.

Level Four. According to Carkhuff, responses above level three are "additive" in nature. That is, the first person's communications add noticeably to the expressions of the second person in such a way as to express feelings a level deeper than the second person was able to express. Responses at this level, as well as responses at level five, are *facilitative*, in the sense that they enable the second person to experience and/or express feelings that she was unable to express previously. Responses such as these represent what Egan (1975) has called *advanced accurate empathy*, in contrast to Carkhuff's *additive empathy*.

> ELLEN: God, that man makes me so upset! I don't know who he thinks he is. He's such a phoney, and I can't stand being around him anymore. And, I get mad at myself. I don't want to be bothered with him anymore, but I haven't done anything about it. I'd like to tell him to take this job and shove it. But I just can't bring myself to do it.
> KAYE: Boy, he makes you furious! But it's not just him, because you're mad at yourself for not acting on how you feel.

Ellen's feelings were blurred and kept her from recognizing their meanings and implications. Kaye responded by going beyond Ellen's words and even beyond her expressed feelings to the real meanings of her statements as well as to the implications which those statements held. It was almost as if Kaye understood Ellen better than Ellen understood herself. Of course, in reality this is probably not true, nor is it desirable for Ellen to get the feeling that it even *might* be true. Should Ellen come to believe such a thing, she could very well close herself off to further disclosures to Kaye, or she may come to assume that she needn't express herself because Kaye "understands anyway." Therefore, this type of high level empathic communication should probably not be used with great consistency, for it could represent a threat to the other individual. As relationships develop to a point where there is a mutual sharing and understanding, this sort of additive empathic response could be used effectively with greater frequency. But in the initial phases of developing relationships, extremely high levels of empathy may inhibit open communication, since the first person appears to come on like "gang busters," showing a level of understanding beyond that which would normally be expected at that stage of the relationship. These types of responses should be used discriminatingly.

Level Five.   At level five, the first person's responses *add significantly* to the feelings and meanings of the expressions of the second person in such a way as accurately to express feeling levels beyond what the person herself was able to express or, in the event of apparent searching on the part of the second person, to be fully with her in her deepest moments. The first person responds accurately to all of the other's deep as well as surface feelings. He is "tuned-in" to the other's wavelength and, in a sense, merges with the other's frame of reference to become "with" her. Thus, "together" they could proceed to search for those areas of experience which are hard for the second person to reach. In contrast to primary empathy, or interchangeable responses at level three, this highest level of advanced accurate empathy goes beyond relevant *surface* feelings and meanings to get at feelings and meanings which are somehow not available to the immediate grasp of the second person. Often, the first person will see the other's world more clearly than she, because he has maintained a sense of his own self and, thus, is not trapped within the experience of the other. Consider the following example:

> LARRY: I get a lot of attention at work for relating my experiences. Almost every-one perks up and pays attention when I talk about all the great things I've done in my life. But when I do this at home, I flop. When I try to relate these things to my wife, she scoffs at me and tells me to "knock it off." I really have to watch what I say at home.
>
> ROY: What you see as an interesting story just doesn't go over at home, and it irritates you.
>
> PAT: You get irritated when your wife reacts to you so differently. You want to talk about yourself, but she doesn't want to listen, and that can hurt when you want someone to know something special about you.

Roy tried to understand Larry from Larry's frame of reference, and he dealt with Larry's feelings and the experience underlying those feelings. However, Pat probed a bit further because she picked up something that Larry did not express overtly—that he has a need to impress people and that they will not accept him as he is. Larry can gain a different perspective on himself through the understanding communicated by Pat. She has provided some information which Larry can take a look at—information which he has probably denied to awareness. Thus, advanced accurate empathy, or level five empathy, goes beyond the expressed to the implications of the expressed. The communication of this level of empathy is a way of sharing your understanding of those implications with the other person.

Concluding Note.   An individual's effectiveness in relating to another human being is related to his depth of understanding of self and the other. Equally important is her ability to communicate an ever-growing awareness of the other, at least at the level of interchangeable responses (level three). In Part Three of this text, more attention is given to the particular communication skills that are involved at this and higher levels of empathy. A word of caution must be offered at this point. It has been emphasized repeatedly in this chapter that empathy involves the "re-creation of another person's experience in your own frame of reference." This means that you *never really lose your own perspective.* Some element of merging with the other's frame of reference is required to achieve empathic understanding. Some individuals have the misconception that empathy is akin to *sympathy*—feeling sorry for the other person—and therefore never really get out of their own frame of reference. Some people assume that empathy is *identification*—the selfsame experiencing of the other's feelings "as one's own"—and therefore often come close to losing their frames of reference. When empathy is equated with "feeling sorry for" another person, communications are thus *sym-pathetic*, and when the other's feelings are taken "as one's own," communications are *em-pathetic*. There is truly a "pathetic" quality to the expressions of some individuals who misunderstand the meaning of empathy. I strongly prefer the term "empathic" as an adjective, which connotes the *"as-if"* quality of the experience of empathy, while reserving the term "empathetic"—with the emphasis on the adjunctive modifier "pathetic"—to denote the *pathetic* or pitiful quality of those communications indicating overidentification. Overidentification can often be a problem for health professionals, and its consequences can be more disastrous than being sym-pathetic.

For example, I once cofacilitated group therapy sessions with a paraprofessional counselor. It frequently happened that, as group members expressed deep feelings, he would express the identical feelings. He *identified* with their feelings so much that, when a group member cried, so also did he! He tried so intently to achieve the other's frame of reference that he became absorbed in it. As a result, he lost his perspective, his sense of self, his objectivity, and, ultimately, his effectiveness as a counselor. But, this type of experience is not limited to paraprofessional counselors. It occurs among professionals as well—across the allied health professions—and extends into the lay population. It is a form of *emotional contagion* which represents an immature and developmentally premature response to others, as indicated at the beginning of this chapter. Passive, uncontrolled sensitivity and involuntary overidentification do not constitute functional empathy.

Paradoxical as it may seem, empathy requires a clear *separation* of self and others. There must be a proper distance which allows you to slip back into your own frame of reference and your own sense of self. Overidentification precludes this by causing a subordination of one's own sense of self to the peremptory influence of another's identity. The individual simply loses himself in his empathic imaginings. Thus, a continuous anchoring to your own experience of self must be one factor which enables you to achieve empathy, while at the same time keeping you from losing yourself in your empathic response. In summary, empathy is not identification any more than it is sympathy—it is not a feeling "as," nor is it a feeling "for" another person. Empathy is a feeling *with*, and the "as-if" quality must not be lost.

Summary and Implications for Health Professionals

Empathic understanding is a basic, core condition for good interpersonal relationships. As a prerequisite condition for effective personal and professional interactions, empathy involves an experiencing within ourselves of the meaning and implications of the experience of another person. The attainment of empathy has been variously described as a "merging" with the experience of another, a "sensing" of another's private world, a "feeling" of the experiences of others, and a general experiencing "with" others "as-if" we perceived the world from their frames of reference. In the present chapter, empathy was defined as the *re-creation of the experience of another person within your own frame of reference*. This definition implies that the achievement of empathic understanding requires a "broadening" of one's own frame of reference to "include" some aspect of another's experience. Since we can never "be" another person and, hence, experience the world totally within his frame of reference, we are forever within our own experimental "spheres." Therefore, we achieve empathy only when we are able to bring the experience of others within our own spheres. By permitting access of another's experience to our own perceptual spheres, we can move toward an understanding of such experience *as if* it were our own. This process is not only an active one, it is "interactive" as well. Empathy is a skill which is learned through the interplay of perception and communication. By consistently trying to respond appropriately to what another person is striving to communicate, we learn to be more and more alert to cues indicating covert or unexpressed thoughts and feelings. Thus, through human "interactions," we develop the *perceptual* skills and the *communication* skills that constitute the inseparable core ingredients of empathic understanding.

The first essential ingredient for empathy is *accurate perception* of the experience and behavior of another person. It is influenced by factors relating to *receptivity* to communications and, therefore, "attention" to others, the *suspension of evaluative tendencies*, the perception of both *content* and *essence* of communications, the perception of *feelings in oneself*, the perception of *feelings in others*, and the cognitive processing of *relevant contextual information*. The second basic ingredient of empathy is *communication*. As an "interactive" process, empathy must be converted from perceptions to action toward another person. It is communicated in one's own "manner" at various levels of effectiveness. At the lowest level, there is a *detraction* from the expressed feelings of others, while at minimally facilitative levels of empathic communication, the first person's communications are essentially *interchangeable* with those of the second person. At higher levels of empathy, communications are *additive*, in that they add significantly to the feelings and meanings of the expressions of the second person. A caveat was advanced so as to clearly differentiate empathy from sympathy and overidentification. Basic implications of overidentification were considered. Additional implications related to the achievement and communication of empathy within health care organizations will be pointed up.

Implications for Health Professionals

Across the allied health professions there is a central motive among practitioners which represents a common denominator amidst the diversity of their functions. It is the commitment to *helping others* achieve health and wellness. This altruistic motive—a caring and concern for others—is usually a major influence behind one's decision to enter a health profession in the first place. Indeed, anyone who wants to be a "helper" of some sort needs an adequate measure of caring, concern, and good will. The very act of helping presupposes this, as some degree of altruism is assumed to underlie even the routine performance of health service activities. Thus, helping behavior clearly suggests a "caring" for people.

As emphasized at the conclusion of the last chapter, the intrinsic relationship between "caring" and "knowing" is rarely appreciated for its implications to health services. To really care for another person we must know him, not as an embodiment of medical symptoms, but by understanding him and his world from his frame of reference. Clearly, *the type of real caring that underlies effective health services must be rooted deeply in empathy.* At the most elementary level, the connection between caring and empathy is so conspicuous that it would seem redundant to dwell on the obvious—that caring involves an ability to relate to the experience of another person. We need to look no further than the basic nursing function in hospitals, for example, to witness the most fundamental instances of helping behavior influenced by the sensing of patients' experiences. It is the *behavior* of nurses in such cases that gives testimony to the actual existence of basic levels of caring and empathy. Behavior is always the principal clue to inner experiences, including caring and empathy. Without "actions" in relation to self and others, caring, concern, good will, and empathy are no more than highly speculative "possessions" of an individual's private world. Given this fact, we can look again to the basic nursing function and note the unfortunate reality that, all too often, nurses remain at the most basic levels of caring and empathy, across patients and over time. Then, we can look across the health professions in general and note that there is something about the "manner" of experienced practitioners which suggests they are perhaps more "concerned" with taking care of "business" than taking care of "persons." This is not an indictment against health professionals, for they are typically committed to "giving" of themselves for the expressed purpose of helping others, and they usually accomplish this admirably. However, many experienced health professionals have seemingly internalized the credo, "You can't get too involved with patients or you won't be able to handle your job," to the point where this conviction has blocked them from moving beyond the most elementary levels of expressed caring and empathy.

Obviously, it is important that health professionals do not burst into tears during an operation, become paralyzed with fear during a Code-Blue, or take clients' problems home with them at night. There are necessary role-behaviors that must be enacted to perform efficiently. The point is that many health professionals assume a "professional manner" in order to carry out role-expectations. The "professional manner" is usually manifested in detached, unaffected, rigid, and stereotypic behavior within the context of the health care setting. I've known certain psychotherapists, for example, who have dressed and acted the part so intently that you couldn't tell the copy from the original role-model. These are persons who have learned through observation of other professionals to put on a professional manner as soon as they put on their professional "uniforms." They step into a role as easily as they step into a room— and sometimes they do both at the same time! In relation to others, they remain detached and seemingly unaffected by others' communications; they strive to maintain objectivity, poise, control, and a "clear head" when interacting with others; and, their expressions to others are usually stereotypic, "canned," ungenuine, often stilted, and lacking spontaneity. What does this "professional manner" have to do with caring and empathy?

For one thing, the "professional manner" is a major obstacle to empathy. By staying in this mode the health professional makes it almost impossible to understand the experience of others from their frames of reference. Empathy cannot be achieved or communicated beyond the lowest levels; even the level of "interchangeable responses" at level three is virtually out of reach when the individual is locked into a manner which insulates him from the experience of others. If empathy cannot be achieved or communicated at minimally acceptable levels, then it is difficult to comprehend how caring—which is rooted in the experience of empathy—can be anything more than a capricious fantasy in the depths of private imaginations.

The professional manner serves a purpose for health professionals. It is a logical outgrowth of the internalized belief that "You can't get too involved." It is an effective defense against "overinvolvement" with consumers of health care services. Health professionals are in continuous contact with persons experiencing various kinds of illness and distress. All around them they see human suffering. Clients show signs of physical suffering, and they also express feelings of discomfort, worry, despair, fear, apprehension, depression, and countless other emotions. With the constant exposure to the distress of others, health professionals learn to use a "protective armor" in the form of a "professional manner." The professional manner helps to reduce the anxiety caused by close contact with the experience of suffering persons. It is a means of coping with the stress of repeated encounters with pain and suffering. However, in addition to this function as a "defensive" tactic, the professional manner is also used as a means for disarming the feelings that clients threaten to express. Unconsciously fearing that clients will express deep feelings, which cause considerable discomfort for the health professional who is unable to cope with those expressions, the professional manner is used to stifle and block those expressions. For example, the so-called "bedside manner" of nurses is often noticed by even the most detached observer. Smiling, humming, and bubbling with enthusiasm, some of these nurses display a bedside manner replete with meaningless questions such as, "How are *we* doing today?," and condescending directives like, "You have to take your pill; it's good for you, and it'll make you feel better." Parenthetically, for those patients in need, perhaps the best emetic that we can offer is the bedside manner of certain staff members! Others display a bedside manner which indicates an aloof, impersonal, and unaffected posture of involvement with patients—no smiling, no humming, no apparent feelings, just "business." In either case, bedside manners are used in such a way as to reduce effectively the probability that patients will express themselves. And, in both cases, the bedside manner is level one empathy—the lowest level of empathic communication. Whatever form the professional manner takes, it is usually an indication of level one empathy; it detracts noticeably from the expressions of clients, and, too frequently, it doesn't even reach level one because it effectively prevents expressions from the outset!

There are three major points that need to be made in regard to the professional manner. First, while there is some justification for the contention that "You can't get too involved" with clients, the reality is that being "too involved" is *overidentification*—it is the taking of another's experience *as one's own*, and it is helpful to no one. To care for others does not mean that you must take on their pain, and it can be argued that to try to do so communicates a lack of respect for the ability of that person to handle his own suffering. To care for others means that you can *empathize* and feel *with* them, not sympathize and feel "for" them or overidentify and feel "as" they do. Empathy can therefore be achieved and communicated in spite of the suffering and amidst the suffering that health professionals perceive all around them. But, of course, it requires something which represents the second major point concerning the professional manner. Specifically, the achievement of empathy is based partly on one's ability to know one's own feelings and the professional manner cuts the health professional off from her own feelings. By developing a detached, unaffected manner, the health professional alienates herself from her own experience. If she is cut off from her own experience, she will either fail to recognize pertinent communications from clients or she will be threatened and unable to respond appropriately. Clearly, the professional manner reduces personal insight and, hence, empathy. Third, the professional manner is learned as a coping device, and it is learned primarily through observation of other health professionals. It has its origins in training programs where health professionals are taught how they should and should not act in their professional roles, *and how they should and should not feel.* Explicit and implicit messages are communicated that "You can't let it bother you," "You have to stay calm," and "You'll get used to it." *These messages come from the top down*—from instructors to students, from supervisors to staff. Cultivating (not stifling) the capacity for empathy should be a goal of training programs, but it is difficult to understand how students can develop empathic skills when their instructors, for example, fail to communicate it in the classroom. If instructors behave toward students in a detached, unaffected manner, then students will come to accept their behavior as the normative model to emulate. They will learn to act in some fancied "professional" style of controlled feeling and superficial dignity. Conversely, when empathy is communicated throughout the training program, when it is part of the relationships between staff and students, then empathy becomes the norm, and the professional manner can at least include this aspect of genuine human functioning.

The importance and significance of empathic understanding across the health professions cannot be overemphasized. When medical patients, for example, express their emotions, they are trying to communicate how they are reacting to their illnesses. This kind of communication holds essential information that is directly pertinent to the purpose of health care services. The health professional is actually "obliged" to tune-in to clients and obtain measures of psychological functioning, just as they are obliged to sample pulses, temperatures, and blood pressures. To really understand clients, we must become acquainted with their thoughts, feelings, perceptions, and the implications of these for their problems or illnesses. We accomplish this through the skills of accurate perception and communication—the bases of empathy. As Jourard

(1971, p. 192) argued, the person's communications constitute the "equivalent of the numbers on a thermometer," and we must know how to perceive and interpret these data. Most health professionals can do this with little trouble. It requires but five simple steps, which collectively represent a forward movement in the process of really coming to "know" the persons about whom we are supposed to "care."

The first step requires that the protective facade of the "professional manner" be suspended long enough to enter into genuine interaction with clients. Gradually, as the health professional grows accustomed to open interactions, the professional manner will become less necessary as a defensive armor.

The second step is almost effortless, as it simply requires taking at least a few moments of available time to interact with clients and allow them to express themselves.

The third step requires receptivity, attention to client communications, and "active listening." The third step rests upon the first two, such that the health professional must be "free to listen."

The fourth step involves the re-creation of the client's experience within one's own frame of reference by "climbing into his skin and walking around in it."

The final step toward real understanding brings the process full circle and feeds into a cycle of reciprocal interpersonal transaction. It requires the conversion of perceptions into communications back to clients—the second basic ingredient of empathy.

Without the effort of progressing through these steps toward real understanding, we are left with an incomplete picture of the client's illness, at the very least. *We do not know how his feelings affect or are affected by his illness?* It is not beyond the realm of possibility that, as a result, diagnosis and treatment may be deficient—and then, all of the supposed "caring" in the world may not undo the outcome!

References

Bem, D. J. An Experimental Analysis of Self-Persuasions, *Journal of Experimental Social Psychology*, **1**:199–218 (1965).

Cannon, W. B. The James-Lange Theory of Emotions: A Critical Examination of an Alternative Theory, *American Journal of Psychology*, **39**:106–24 (1927).

Carkhuff, R. R. *Helping and Human Relations. Selection and Training*, vol. 1., New York, Holt, Rinehart, and Winston, 1969.

Carkhuff, R. R., and Berenson, B. G. *Beyond Counseling and Therapy*, 2d ed. New York, Holt, Rinehart, and Winston, 1969.

Clark, K. Empathy: A Neglected Topic in Psychological Research, *American Psychologist*, **35**(2):187–90 (1980).

Darwin, C. *The Expression of Emotion in Man and Animals*. New York, Philosophical Library, 1872.

Egan, G. *The Skilled Helper: A Model for Systematic Helping and Interpersonal Relating*. Monterey, California, Brooks/Cole, 1975.

Ekman, P.; Sorenson, E. R.; and Friesen, W. V. Pan-Cultural Elements in Facial Displays of Emotions, *Science*, **164**(3875):86–88 (1969).

Hilgard, E. R., Atkinson, R. L.; and Atkinson, R. C. *Introduction to Psychology*, 7th ed. New York, Harcourt, Brace, Jovanovich, 1979.

Holt, R. R. *Assessing Personality*. New York, Harcourt, Brace, Jovanovich, 1971.

Izard, C. E. *The Face of Emotion*. New York, Appleton-Century-Crofts, 1971.

James, W. *The Principles of Psychology*. New York, Holt, Rinehart, and Winston, 1890.

Jourard, S. *The Transparent Self*. New York, Van Nostrand, 1971.

Keen, S. *A Primer in Phenomenological Psychology*. New York, Holt, Rinehart, and Winston, 1975.

Patterson, C. H. *Relationship Counseling and Psychotherapy*. New York, Harper and Row, 1974.

Pearce, L., and Newton, S. *The Conditions of Human Growth*. New York, Citadel, 1963.

Rogers, C. *On Becoming a Person*. Boston: Houghton-Mifflin, 1961.

Schachter, S. The Interaction of Cognitive and Physiological Components of Emotional State, in *Advances in Experimental Social Psychology*, vol. 1, ed, L. Berkowitz, pp. 49–80. New York, Academic Press, 1964.

Schachter, S., and Singer, J. E. Cognitive, Social, and Physiological Determinants of Emotional State, *Psychological Review*, **69**:379–99 (1962).

Schneider, D. J.; Hastorf, A. H.; and Ellsworth, P. C. *Person Perception*, 2d ed. Reading, Massachusetts, Addison-Wesley, 1979.

Schneider, D. J.; Hastorf, A. H.; and Polefka, P. C. *Person Perception*. Reading, Massachusetts, Addison-Wesley, 1979.

CHAPTER FIVE

Skills Assessment and Applications for Part One

I hear and I forget,
I see and I remember,
I do and I understand.

Confucius

In this chapter, some issues are examined relative to the assessment of social skills and the application of learning. The objectives are to (1) present the rationale for assessing your social skills, (2) describe *what* to assess, (3) suggest some methods of self-assessment, and (4) provide some individual and interpersonal exercises for skills improvement. The particular skills of concern in this chapter are those related to accurate perception—skills which can be enhanced, coincidentally, through skills assessment itself.

Assessment of Social Skills

Assessment, or taking account of existing skills, is central to new learning. Enhancing interpersonal effectiveness is often contingent upon identifying samples of how individuals function in interpersonal situations. In this section, important considerations concerning skills assessment are outlined, followed by suggestions on how and when to obtain samples of your own interpersonal behavior.

Goals of Assessment

The primary goal of assessment is to gain an understanding of your current interpersonal skills. From a *broad* perspective, it is necessary to get an idea of *how you tend to respond across a range of situations.* That is, it is necessary first to identify how you "typically" act across certain kinds of interactions. For example, let's suppose that you typically have problems asserting yourself with people; that's a pretty general statement, a broad enough perspective. With this broad perspective on your assertiveness, you can then describe the usual kinds of problems you have in those situations where assertion would be more appropriate. This means that you describe a general pattern of behavior that seems to occur in many different interpersonal situations. Suppose that your pattern is one in which you generally have difficulty meeting people, saying no to unreasonable requests, expressing your personal opinions in a group, or confronting someone who violates your rights. Suppose, further, that in all of these situations you feel nervous, self-conscious, unsure of yourself, and you make others feel uncomfortable even though you don't intend to. Now that you have obtained a broad perspective on a mode of behavior exhibited in a variety of situations, you can begin to narrow it down. The broad view of your social behavior, which you have labeled "nonassertion" or "passivity," has only put you in the ball park, so to speak. The next step in assessment is to break that general pattern of nonassertion down into its component parts. The rationale is that it is much easier to make changes in your level of general assertiveness if you have identified the *specific* behaviors which define it.

After gaining a broad understanding of your social skills in various situations, the next step is to sharpen your understanding by *assessing specific behavioral and cognitive components* of the general pattern identified. In the example above, it was observed that you usually have difficulty meeting people. If we look at this pattern more closely, we may discover that in those situations you tend to avoid eye contact, you tend to lower your head slightly, you orient you body away from others, you clasp your hands in front of the waist, and you don't show signs of interest on your face. If you give it some thought, you'd probably also note that you have a persistent desire to say something, but you're afraid that what you say will be all wrong. You're somewhat self-conscious to begin with, but you're afraid of being embarrassed and more self-conscious if you say something that draws attention. At this point, you have broken down your broad view of nonassertion into specific behavioral and cognitive components.

Hopefully, you are beginning to see the value of specificity in skills assessment. All too often, individuals make general impressionistic statements about themselves and their behavior: "I'm a shy person," "I get along well with people," "I've got a bad temper," "I'm sure of myself." Such statements lack the precision necessary for accurate self-assessment and, where needed, change. But, even the identification of specific responses and cognitions requires further precision. Continuing with our example, we might ask if you are *always* uncomfortable when you meet people, regardless of circumstances. Maybe you are, but maybe not. To answer this question, it is necessary to account for specific *characteristics of situations* in which you experience your difficulties. Skills assessment therefore requires that you describe as fully and representatively as possible the distinguishing features of the social contexts in which you are nonassertive. Let's suppose that we examine your response patterns, and we find out that you are *not* passive in *all* social situations (this is most assuredly what we would discover). For the purpose of illustration, we will assume that you find it most difficult to meet department heads, administrators, and people from utilization review committees—people who you perceive as having some power to reward or punish you for professional performance. If you were to meet these people on the street, you might not feel as anxious. It turns out in your case that your passivity is manifest in the health care environment. But, more precisely, it is manifest when these persons—male or female—happen to enter your work area. We could probably become even more specific here, but I assume that you have gotten the point about skills assessment: *it demands specificity of behaviors and cognitions in particular situations.*

To summarize to this point, when assessing your own interpersonal skills:

1. *Identify a pattern of behavior which you tend to follow across a range of situations.* At this point it may be helpful to tag a label on your behavior (e.g., "I'm shy," "I'm outspoken," etc.).
2. *Break your general impression down into its component parts.* Identify exactly *what you do* when you are shy or outspoken, for example, also identify what you think and how you feel when the pattern is followed.
3. *Specify characteristics of the situations in which you typically behave in those ways.*

Targets of Assessment

Social skills are comprised of numerous discrete verbal statements, vocal speech responses, and nonverbal behaviors used by individuals to communicate with others. Social skills also relate in very important ways to covert processes, such as thoughts, feelings, attitudes, values, and social intelligence. Furthermore, social skills and cognitive responses interact with situational factors to determine their effects for all persons concerned. Each of these interrelated areas needs to be accounted for in social skills assessment.

Assessing Observable Behaviors. When assessing your social skills, you must be aware of verbal, vocal, and nonverbal responses defining the skills in question. For example, if you are interested in assessing your empathic skills, you will need to specify examples of the *verbal contents* of your empathic statements in particular situations. You will also need to assess *vocal characteristics* of empathic communications (e.g., is your tone of voice matched with the tone of voice of the other person? do you speak at an appropriate speed?). Furthermore, you will need to account for your *nonverbal behavior* (e.g., do you maintain eye contact? do you lean forward? do you face the other person squarely?).

Assessing Cognitions. In assessing cognitive components of social skills, it is important to note your *attitudes and beliefs* about particular kinds of behaviors. You may find that certain beliefs about expressing anger, for example, are limiting your interpersonal effectiveness. If you believe that anger should never be expressed under any circumstances, then the response alternatives available to you are necessarily limited. In order to find better ways of dealing with anger, it may be necessary to change your beliefs about its expression. It is also important to assess your *perceptions of others*. There are numerous exercises in the latter part of this chapter which should help you in determining how well you can read other people's behavior, as well as your own. These aspects of social skills can often be assessed more effectively by comparing your attitudes, beliefs, and perceptions with those of others or with whatever objective comparisons are available.

Assessing Situations.   Social skills cannot be evaluated apart from the situational context. Some skills show deficits in highly specific kinds of situations (e.g., inability to communicate empathy to alcoholic patients), whereas other skills may be deficient across many situations (e.g., difficulty receiving compliments from co-workers, patients, friends, and instructors). Therefore, it is important in skills assessment to distinguish those skills deficits which are situation-specific from those which are more generalized. The task is one of *classifying situations* which lead to the inefficient performance of a particular skill.

The Process of Skills Assessment

Two principal forms of assessment are suggested here: self-observation and observation by others. *Self-observation* methods include self-report inventories, such as pencil and paper questionnaires and various self-monitoring techniques. Many of the individual exercises offered here are designed to facilitate self-observation, so that you can begin identifying those social skills which may be in need of improvement. While there are no formal structured inventories provided in this section, several series of questions are presented to stimulate personal observations. Some self-monitoring techniques are also described as means for "checking yourself out" as you engage in certain interpersonal behaviors. In addition to self-observation methods, this chapter provides numerous exercises involving interpersonal contact. Interpersonal exercises are extremely useful, since they offer you the opportunity to learn from others, to obtain valuable feedback on your own behavior—feedback which is used in assessing your levels of particular skills. It should also be noted that the exercises to follow are not only means for assisting skills assessment, they are exercises for *practicing and enhancing your skills* at the same time.

As a way of summarizing the material to this point, take a moment to identify a pattern of behavior you would like to change for the better. Then respond to the questions in the inventory in Figure 5.1.

Describing Your Behavior

As a preliminary exercise in describing your interpersonal skills concretely, read each of the statements in Figure 5.2 and place a check next to those which describe behavior in terms of specific components. Those which are non-descriptive should be "operationalized"—described in terms of observable actions. After completing this exercise, proceed to the next one and expand those statements as well.

1. What label have you assigned to this pattern of behavior (e.g., "short temper," "shyness")?	
2. What do you typically do when you follow this pattern of behavior?	
3. What are the response components of this pattern of behavior?	
4. Give examples of specific verbal statements, vocal cues, and nonverbal responses which characterize this pattern.	
5. What beliefs or attitudes do you have about behaving in this way?	
6. What do other people do before and after you respond in this way?	
7. Identify and describe situations in which you find yourself behaving this way.	

Figure 5.1   An inventory format for assessing social skills. In your assessment, move from the general to the specific. Be as specific as possible with all answers. Note that item 6 asks for identification of others' behavior before and after you act in this way. Item 6 is designed to help you identify antecedents and consequences of your behavior. Are there any common antecedents (things which usually happen before you act) or consequences (things which usually happen after you act)?

I Am . . .

Take the words "I am . . ." and complete the sentence in at least ten different ways. After looking at your list, determine which of your sentences identify *what* you are, and which identify *who* you are; see Chapter Three for help in making the distinctions, if necessary. Each statement that describes *what* you are should be supplemented with another statement describing *who*.

1. I am _____.
2. I am _____.
3. I am _____.
4. I am _____.
5. I am _____.
6. I am _____.
7. I am _____.
8. I am _____.
9. I am _____.
10. I am _____.

Statement	Acceptable as is	Concrete Description
1. The patient turned over on his stomach.	X	
2. The patient was tired.*		The patient yawned, nodded his head, and had difficulty keeping eyes open.
3. Joanne is a very good nurse.		
4. I cried when I was awarded the honor last night.		
5. That physician is really wrapped up in his work.		
6. He drinks 1 quart of rum per day.		
7.		
8.		
9.		

Figure 5.2 "Operationalizing" (expanding) descriptions of behavior. Provide your own examples for the last three spaces. *Note*: This is an inference from nonverbal cues. When describing behavior, try to identify the overt responses made.

Expand each statement indicating *who* you are. For example, if you said, "I am a sensitive person," describe *what you do* that makes you sensitive and what specific feelings accompany your "sensitivity."

Some Questions About Your Interpersonal Style

The following questions ask you to reflect on some aspects of your interpersonal behavior about which you may not be used to thinking. After reflecting on these questions, there should be a lot you could say about yourself, but of course, it's all up to you. Your responses to these questions should help you in the process of skills assessment. They should stimulate your thinking sufficiently to enhance your awareness of yourself and your relation to other people. Some of the questions pertain directly to self-perception, some concern other-perception, and some deal exclusively with your feelings. Although there may seem to be a lot of questions, in reality there is no limit to the questions we may put to ourselves.

No doubt some of your answers will be that "it depends." By responding in this way, you automatically suggest the operation of various classes of influences that must be accounted for in skills assessment. The very fact that your perceptions, for example, "depend" on different factors attests to the complexity of your interpersonal experiences. Whatever your answers happen to be, they should highlight the complexity of interpersonal perception and communication. I believe that one way to make your perceptual experiences mean something, come alive, and be brought to awareness is to take some time to consider carefully each of these questions:

1. Am I good at understanding people? What kind of feedback to I get that lets me know that?
2. Am I a good listener?
3. Do people feel understood after disclosing something to me?
4. Do I value it when others open up to me?
5. Do I value my disclosures to others? Do I disclose very often?
6. How do I encourage others to be open with me?
7. What do I do when I see that someone is not really being honest with me?
8. Do I ever reject others who want to be close to me? How?
9. When do I try to hide things from others? From myself?
10. In what ways am I good to myself?
11. In what ways am I unkind to myself?
12. In what ways do I neglect myself?
13. What are some of my interpersonal strengths?
14. What are some of my interpersonal weaknesses? Limitations? Pet peeves?
15. Do I spend too much time thinking about myself?
16. Do others perceive me as a sensitive person? A caring person?
17. How do I know that others perceive me as sensitive and caring (or not)?
18. When am I a mystery to others?
19. Do I ever act as if I don't see another person? When?
20. Do other people ever act as if they don't see me? When?
21. How do I perceive people in authority?
22. What are my stereotypes about the "mentally ill"?
23. What do I usually notice first about people?
24. Am I my real self when I'm with casual acquaintances?
25. When am I not my real self with people?
26. Am I willing to talk about myself with others? When am I not willing?
27. What do I like to hear about myself? What do I not like to hear?
28. How do I show that I care for someone?
29. Do others usually know that I care when I try to show it?
30. Do others care for me? Who does and how do they show it?
31. How much do I care about myself?
32. What feelings are easy for me to express? What feelings are hard?
33. Is it usually easy or hard for others to know what I'm feeling? Why?
34. Do I ever use my emotions to manipulate others?
35. What makes me feel good about other people?
36. When I make a mistake, do I try to make myself "right"?

37. How did I feel when someone accused me of being something I wasn't?
38. What risks am I not willing to take in most of my relationships?
39. What are some of the norms I see in my current occupational role?
40. How important is my current role? My aspired future role?
41. What do I want my professional role to say about me as a person?
42. How do I feel when I'm criticized unjustly?
43. How do I react when I'm criticized unjustly?
44. What feelings are difficult for others to express to me?
45. Why are those feelings hard for them to express to me?
46. What feelings are hard for me to express to close friends? Acquaintances?
47. Why am I entering this profession?
48. What are my perceptions of the kinds of people who work in my profession?
49. Why do I want to help people?
50. Which questions were hardest to answer? Easiest? Why?

Identifying Contexts for Feelings

Take some time to fill in the following incomplete sentences. These sentences are designed to steer your thinking toward particular circumstances in which you commonly experience certain kinds of feelings. Where those feelings are negative, you may want to consider some ways for effecting change.

1. I like myself when _____.
2. I like myself most when _____.
3. I like myself least when _____.
4. I feel really great when _____.
5. I feel proud when _____.
6. I feel angry when _____.
7. I am confused about myself when _____.
8. I "beat myself up" when _____.
9. When I am successful, I feel _____.
10. When I fail a task, I feel _____.
11. When I hurt someone, I feel _____.
12. When I am criticized, I feel _____.
13. When I am complimented, I feel _____.
14. When I help someone, I feel _____.
15. When there is nothing I can do for someone, I feel _____.
16. When a patient is crying, I feel _____.
17. When a patient goes home healthy, I feel _____.
18. When a patient dies, I feel _____.
19. When a colleague experiences a crisis, I feel _____.
20. When there is something I could have done, but didn't do, I feel _____.
21. When I'm having a good day at work, I feel _____.

22. When things go wrong at home and at work, I feel _____.
23. When I help someone with a problem, I feel _____.
24. When I am not treated as an equal, I feel _____.
25. When I am with my family, I feel _____.

Perceiving Nonverbal Cues

The behavorial descriptions below are intended to help you assess your skills relative to perceiving nonverbal behavior. The context in which behavior occurs always provides some information for interpreting the meanings of nonverbal cues, and so also do other nonverbal responses and verbal and vocal cues. This kind of information is absent in this task, so you may conclude that many of the behaviors listed can be interpreted in two or more ways. In those cases, you should identify at least two possible meanings.

1. A supervisor shakes her head from side to side.
2. A patient tenses up when you place your hand on his shoulder.
3. A young man rolls his eyes upward as you tell him about drug effects.
4. A woman looks at the floor as she tells you about her abortion.
5. As you talk to an administrator, he folds his arms and leans backward.
6. As you talk to an instructor, he faces you squarely and leans forward.
7. A patient lying in bed rolls his head to one side and looks out the window as you walk in the room.
8. A colleague slouches in her chair with knees crossed as you converse.
9. A physician taps his fingers and then picks lint from his coat while you describe a case.
10. A patient furrows her brow and scratches her head as you describe a medical procedure to her.

Perceiving Nonverbal and Verbal Cues

Read each verbal statement and its accompanying nonverbal message. In the space provided, indicate your perceptions of the overall meaning of the communications.

1. LONNIE: I've felt misunderstood, also, but I haven't seen anyone here really make an effort to get to know me.

   Nonverbal message: Lonnie's eyes are moist, he is blinking rapidly, and frequently breaking eye contact.

2. YOLANDA: It's the same for me, too, but I haven't reached out to anyone. I haven't let anyone close to me.

   Nonverbal message: Yolanda is speaking with a pressured voice, her jaws are clenched, and she is staring at the floor.

3. ELLIE: I don't know why you should be so concerned about being accepted in this group. All we have to do is work together. We don't have to be "buddies."

Nonverbal message: Ellie is talking with her arms and legs crossed. She is leaning back in her chair. A corner of her mouth is turned upward as she speaks, making a dimple in her cheek.

4. BARRY: Sure, we do have to work together, but we can work better if we respect and care for each other.

Nonverbal message: Barry's upper body is leaned forward as he sits squarely in his chair. His arms are outstretched, and the palms of his hands are turned upward.

Some of Your Assumptions About People

The items below are designed to help you clarify some of the assumptions you make about people and human nature. There are no right or wrong answers here. It is intended as a stimulus for personal reflection. These assumptions may have an effect on your perceptions of those with whom you interact.

1. People are responsible for everything they do.   True   False
   People are not responsible for their behavior.   True   False
2. Human behavior is guided mainly by reason.   True   False
   Human behavior is guided mainly by emotion.   True   False
3. People are born to be whatever they are.   True   False
   People learn to be whatever they are.   True   False
4. People are careful of their actions if they are held accountable for what they do.   True   False
   People tend to disregard the effects of their actions if not much is expected of them.   True   False
5. It's better to be honest with people and tell them the facts, no matter how painful it might be for them.   True   False
   It's better to withhold unfavorable information from people, because most people don't want to hear it.   True   False
6. You lose respect if you admit you're wrong.   True   False
   It's better to face up to your mistakes.   True   False
7. Certain kinds of people go into the health professions.   True   False
   There are no common personality types among health professionals.   True   False
8. The vast majority of people are only out for themselves.   True   False

The vast majority of people are not out for themselves only.	True	False
9. People are basically good.	True	False
People are basically not good.	True	False
10. People are what they are; they'll never change.	True	False
People tend to change more than they remain the same.	True	False

At this point, perhaps you have been stimulated enough to outline your own theory of personality. Take a moment to gather your ideas and then write them down on a sheet of paper. Your theory should contain statements about why people do the things they do.

Exercises

The following exercises are designed to assist you in learning more about your perceptual skills and, at the same time, to facilitate the enhancement of those skills. Exercises which are intended for *individual* use are identified by a single asterisk (*), and those which require *interpersonal* involvement are identified by two asterisks (**).

Exercise 1*

To demonstrate how the principle of selection limits your capacity for responding to all stimuli in your immediate environment, close your eyes for one minute, orient your body toward the center of the room, then open your eyes.

What objects did you immediately perceive? What features of those objects did you respond to? Size? Intensity? Contrast? Movement?

Exercise 2**

Ask a friend to rearrange a few objects in the room while your eyes are closed. When she/he instructs you to open your eyes, try to identify the alterations. Perhaps there are certain rearrangements you were more sensitive to. How do you think your perceptual set influenced your perceptions? What is the role of "familiarity" here?

Exercise 3*

Do something different, like trying a new food, attending a sports event to which you've never been, a hospital department in which you've never been, or a part of town you've never seen. To make the most of this experience, try something you think you wouldn't enjoy—one which you would otherwise avoid. After your experience, answer these questions: What was the experience like for you? Was it different from what you expected? What did you expect? How were your expectancies confirmed? Violated? How did you approach the experience? Were you open to it? Nervous? Apprehensive? Skeptical? How did these feelings influence your perceptions?

Exercise 4*

Read a book on magic and then attend a magic show. How can you explain some of the effects produced by the magician? Can you explain them at all? What do you think were some of the expectancies the magician was trying to violate?

Exercise 5**

Prepare a list of behaviors that you think others expect from you in your normal interactions. Then answer these questions: What would happen if I acted differently? How would I feel if I acted differently? Having answered these questions, you've established your own expectations, so now you can check them out. Behave in a (responsibly) different manner and note how you feel and what happens.

Exercise 6**

Carry on a conversation with another person for five minutes. Discuss an issue around which you have some strong opinions. After you interaction, provide feedback to one another on the following:

1. When expressing your own opinions or responding to the other's, what words did you use? "I think," "I feel," "I know," "I see," "I hear"?
2. Did you personalize your statements by using personal pronouns (e.g., I, me, mine, myself), or did you distance yourself from your own opinions by using "you," "people," "it," "they," "we"?
3. When expressing your views, what nonverbal messages did you send?
4. How was your eye contact during the conversation?

Exercise 7*

Write a list of 10 "characteristics" that you think the public expects to see in health professionals. Ask yourself: "Do I have these characteristics?", "How do I know?", "Is it necessary that I confirm these expectations?", "Which ones should I confirm?" How do you expect people to react when you, as a health professional, fail to meet their expectancies on some dimension?

You may want to share your list with another person and see if your assumptions are accurate.

Exercise 8*

You may have certain expectancies about the ways in which certain patients will act when you encounter them. For example, you may expect children to be afraid, to cry and need nurturing and support in addition to medical attention. How would you expect the following patients to behave, given the extremely limited amount of information provided? Do your expectancies say anything about stereotypes you may hold? Are there implicit assumptions about people in general? How is your implicit personality involved in your expectancies?

1. An 80-year-old woman with arteriosclerosis.
2. A 35-year-old female attorney with a peptic ulcer.
3. A 16-year-old high school cheerleader with appendicitis.
4. A 40-year-old businessman with essential hypertension.
5. A 45-year-old woman with migraine headaches.
6. A 68-year-old Catholic nun with a broken pelvis.
7. A 37-year-old Mexican-American laborer, father of eight children, hospitalized for diabetes.
8. A 43-year-old chronic alcoholic man admitted for malnutrition.
9. A 51-year-old male physician admitted for detoxification from alcohol.
10. A 26-year-old male prison inmate admitted for emergency surgery.
11. A 19-year-old street gang member with multiple lacerations from a knife fight with another male.
12. A 23-year-old male member of a religious sect admitted for treatment of hepatitis.
13. A 30-year-old female police officer with a gunshot wound.
14. A 9-year-old orphaned boy injured when struck by an automobile.
15. A 40-year-old woman weighing 350 pounds.
16. A 17-year-old girl admitted for anorexia nervosa.
17. An 18-year-old boy admitted for a PCP reaction.

Exercise 9*: The Blind Men and The Elephant

There was once a city in which all of the inhabitants were blind. One day a king arrived nearby and camped in the desert with his army. He had an elephant, which he used in attacking cities and to increase the awe of the people.

The inhabitants of the city became anxious to learn about the elephant, and some of the sightless from the community ran like fools to find it. Since they knew not even the form or shape of the elephant, they groped blindly, gathering information by touching some part of it. Each thought that he knew something, because he could feel a part.

When they returned to their fellow-citizens, eager bands of people clustered around them, anxious to learn the truth from those who themselves were astray. They asked about the form, the shape of the elephant, and they listened to all they were told.

The man whose hand had reached an ear said: "It is a large, rough thing, wide and broad like a rug."

One who had felt the trunk said: "I have the real facts about it. It is like a straight and hollow pipe, awful and destructive."

One who had felt its feet and legs said: "It is mighty and firm, like a pillar."

While this tale (Version adapted from Idries Shah, *Tales of the Dervishes*, New York, Dutton, 1970) can be found in many cultural traditions to convey various messages, there are certain implications for perceptual *selection* and *organization*. Clearly, in relation to selection, the blind men had experienced only certain selected aspects of the total stimulus (the elephant). Less apparent may be the factors which influenced the "organization" of their perceptions. What do you think were the roles of the following in the organization of their perceptions?

1. Proximity
2. Closure
3. Language
4. Learning

Now that you are aware of the contributions of the principles of perceptual organization, discussed in Chapter One, and the role of selection in this tale, what generalizations can you make to the effective practice of your profession in the health care field? What are the implications of this tale for health professionals? Upon answering these questions, think of a similar set of circumstances as they could occur in health care settings, and write your own "tale."

Exercise 10**: A Social Incident

Design an illustrative experiment for the purpose of demonstrating the effects of selection and organization on the perception of a "social incident." This could be conducted as a class project, for example. Simply enlist the aid of a person whom your classmates do not know. Instruct you confederate to enter the classroom and create a minor disturbance in full view of everyone. The incident should be harmless but serious enough to convince your classmates, that they may have to report to the dean exactly what they witnessed if they are later called on to do so. You can tell them that it would help if all took a moment to write down what they did see, thereby saving them the trouble of later having to submit a report at a more inconvenient time. After collecting their "statements," you can compare them for accuracy.

1. How accurate were their descriptions?
2. What did some perceive that others did not perceive?
3. What words were used to describe their perceptions?
4. What were the differences and similarities in terms of descriptions of appearance cues, the actions of the "perpetrator," and the effects of his behavior?

Share your findings with the group and use them to point up the influence of these basic principles of selection and organization.

Exercise 11*: My Ways of Organizing Perceptions

There are certain general principles of perceptual organization that apply to perception in general. However, each person tends to have his or her own ways of organizing the world of experience. These idiosyncratic organization processes are influenced by learning experiences and are largely unconscious and automatic. To stimulate your awareness of some of the ways in which you organize your perceptions, listen to some music, look at a painting, and try to determine whether you focused on details to the exclusion of the whole, or vice versa. Is this typical of the way you perceive the world around you?

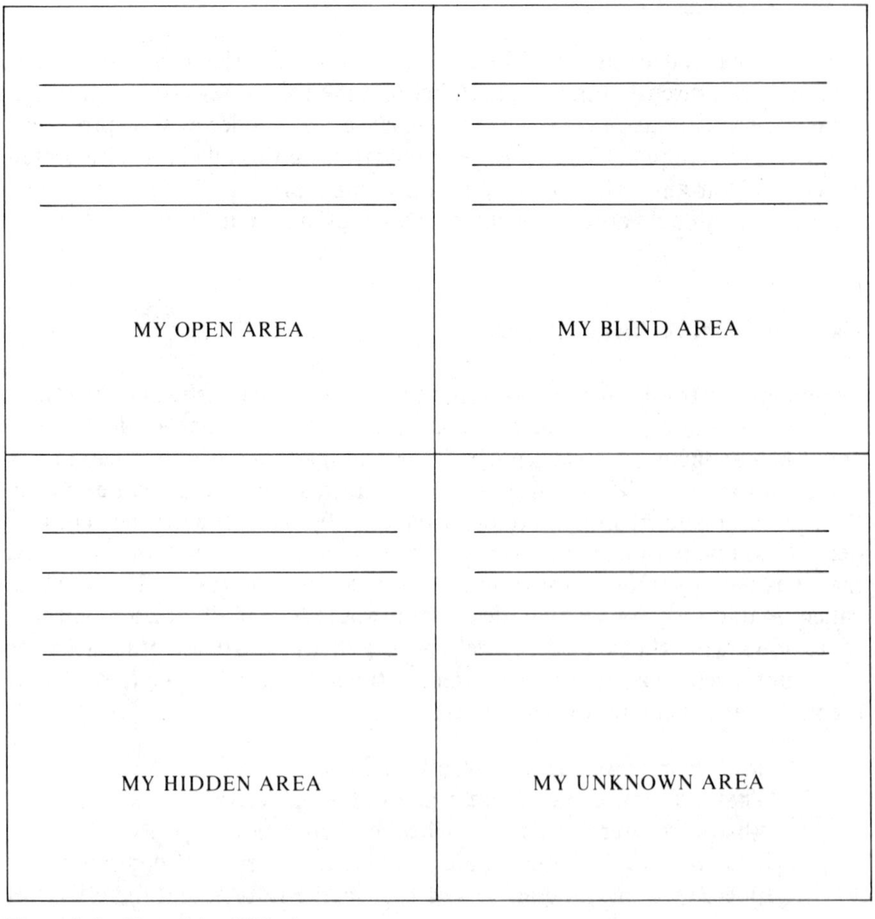

_____ _____ _____ _____ MY OPEN AREA	_____ _____ _____ _____ MY BLIND AREA
_____ _____ _____ _____ MY HIDDEN AREA	_____ _____ _____ _____ MY UNKNOWN AREA

Figure 5.3   Your Johari Window.

Exercise 12*

Refer back to Chapter Three and the discussion of the Johari Window. After familiarizing yourself with the Johari Window, fill in your own as best you can. The two areas you can describe by yourself are the "open" and "hidden" areas. To fill in the "blind" area of your window, you will need to solicit feedback from someone who is willing to help you learn of characteristics of which you are not aware. You may want to ask a close friend to help you fill in the "blind' area. Through you interactions, you may begin to discover some things that exist in your "unknown" area.

Not that the interpersonal part of this exercise depends upon your willingness and the appropriateness of discussing your "hidden" area, and the other's willingness and ability to discuss your "blind" as well as open areas. The exercise should probably not be practiced just for fun, therefore. Use the window in Figure 5.3 as a guide.

After processing feedback from your friend, what does your window look like? Have the panes been altered in relation to that person? Is your "open" area now larger? Hidden area smaller? Blind area smaller?

PART TWO

The Health Professional and Social Appraisal: Between Perception and Communication

The chapters in Part One looked at major influences on our perceptions of self and others. Those influences and our resultant perceptions impact on our actions toward others in a variety of situations under numerous different conditions. Having examined a host of factors, it may be hard to conceive of any way in which interpersonal relations could be approached meaningfully when perceptual processes are not established at the core of our relationships with other people.

Another significant and frequently neglected aspect of interpersonal relations in health care concerns the role of cognitive processes that intervene between perception and communication: what we *think* of other people. Certainly, a person's *appraisal* or evaluation of an individual or situation plays a key determinate role in how that perceiver responds. In Part Two, we are concerned with a variety of factors affecting the interpretations we attach to our perceptions through cognitive processes. Clearly, the images of others that we form in our minds, the degree of liking that we have toward others, as well as our existing values, beliefs, and attitudes are among the most fundamental influences mediating perception and communication.

Chapters Six through Ten explore cognitive events taking place "under the skin," as it were. Chapter Six focuses exclusively on *impression formation* and the role of *attribution* processes in creating impressions of others. Chapter Seven surveys determinants of *self-presentation* and the role of *impression management* in interpersonal relations. Whereas Chapter Six explores the images of others that we form, Chapter Seven examines the *images of ourselves* that we try to project in our relationships. Then, in Chapter Eight, *Values, be-*

137

liefs, and *attitudes* are identified as criteria for judgements we make about ourselves and others. Their influences on processes of impression formation and impression management are discussed. Chapter Nine addresses the bases for our *attraction* to other people. Several models of interpersonal attraction or liking are presented, followed by an analysis of major determinants of attraction and liking. Chapter Ten examines the effects of *accidents, harmdoing,* and *self-fulfilling prophecies* on our impressions of others. In particular, Chapter Ten is concerned with our efforts to maintain consistent views of others in the face of evidence which challenges the validity of those views. Chapter Eleven concludes Part One with an opportunity to apply cognitive learning to practical matters. The primary focus of the exercises in Chapter Eleven is on impression formation and self-presentation.

CHAPTER
SIX

Forming Impressions of Others

*The power to guess the unseen from the seen, to trace
the implications of things, to judge the whole piece by
the pattern . . . this cluster of gifts may almost be said to
constitute experience. . . . . If experience consists of impressions, it may be said that impressions are experience.*

Henry James, *The Art of Fiction*

It is almost time for your first class to begin. You are awaiting the arrival of
your instructor, wondering what she will be like. A classmate told you that she
has an excellent reputation as a teacher, and she has written three books on
health assessment; beyond that, you know nothing about her. Soon, the instructor walks into the classroom, and you are surprised to see that she walks
with a severe limp. She places a huge pile of papers on her desk, turns and
writes her name on the chalkboard, and, without looking at anyone or saying
anything, proceeds to distribute the papers to the class. You have observed her
long enough to draw some tentative conclusions about her. What are your impressions?

Before the instructor even entered the classroom, you probably concluded
that she must be intelligent, because she has written three books. She must be
quite knowledgeable about the field, so it should be a good class. Also, being a
woman in a male-dominated profession must mean that she's hardworking,
achievement-oriented, ambitious, determined, assertive, and dedicated to the
profession. When she entered the classroom, you noticed that she was younger
and more attractive than you had expected, and she looked sophisticated in her
expensive clothes. You were struck by her appearance, because most of your
former teachers were older and looked and dressed like "ordinary teachers";
they all look as if they have the wisdom of their years behind them, as well as
their long lost appreciation for style and fashion of dress. The question then
crossed your mind, "What can I learn from her? She doesn't seem to be much
older then I am!" But, then you also noticed her limp. Why does she have this
difficulty walking—some type of congenital myopathy, muscular dystrophy,

poliomyelitis? Perhaps she was disabled in an automobile accident, or maybe she has a simple sprain from a fall while skiing. Maybe you decide that, because of her disability, she feels insecure and overcompensates for a poor self-concept by absorbing herself in academic and professional pursuits. If this is the case, she probably doesn't have a satisfactory social life; she probably avoids social activities by overloading herself with work. She may not know how to relate to people, and she's probably lonely. You might decide that this is true when you consider the fact that she hasn't spoken a word or made eye contact with anyone; she is shy and nervous, probably self-conscious, and aware that everyone is watching her. Yes, she must be shy, because your experience with intelligent people has taught you that they are usually shy, and authors are usually so preoccupied with ideas that they don't relate well with others. She does seem nervous to you, but, on the other hand, maybe she's just worried about making a good impression on the class; people who want to make a good impression often do act nervous. Maybe that's it. After all, she is attractive and very nicely dressed in expensive clothes. She must have "intended" to make the most of her appearance. So, on second thought, maybe she is outgoing and has a rich social life. She would have to be able to relate well to people in order to be a successful teacher. Then again, maybe she's not nervous at all. It could be that she is simply cold, aloof, and impersonal; professors are often like that.

Throughout this entire process, you are considering possibilities and drawing tentative conclusions on the basis of a very limited amount of information. You have gone beyond the information available to make inferences about the instructor. You have drawn from your own experience to make those inferences. You have seen the instructor and observed a sample of her behavior, and you have identified certain traits and matched them up with those which you have learned to be related. Certain aspects of her appearance and behavior seem to stand out, while other aspects have not been attended to. Stimulus information is selected, integrated with information from past experience, and organized into a meaningful whole pattern or impression. As you know, we all possess certain basic assumptions about human nature, and these assumptions collectively represent our implicit personality theories. In forming an impression of your new instructor, your implicit personality theory has played an important part. Your implicit personality theory also reflects specific stereotypes which you hold, and these have influenced your impression. In addition, your implicit personality theory contains assumptions about why people do the things they do. Those assumptions encourage you to make attributions about the causes of a person's behavior. In relation to your instructor, you relied on certain causal assumptions to make inferences about her silence and lack of eye contact. Numerous factors have influenced your overall impression of the instructor.

In this chapter, the processes of impression formation are explored. The value of learning about these processes lies in the fact that they are essential in getting to know another person. As you become acquainted with other people and develop relationships with them, you perceive and organize stimulus information into meaningful "wholes." The impressions which you form during your daily encounters with newly admitted patients, clients seeking services for the first time, new staff in the organization, or even new instructors will have critical influences on how you respond. Impressions serve as bases for deciding how to respond to and interact with others; as relationships develop, impressions are altered and refined, and your behavior changes accordingly. By examining the various influences on impression formation, you should become more skilled at adjusting perceptions for potential distortions and biases and, in general, become more careful in making inferences about those with whom you interact. Furthermore, by learning of the ways in which you form impressions *of others*, you should become more aware of *how others probably form impressions of you*! You spend considerable time perceiving others, but you spend equal time as an actor who is being perceived by others. The same factors which influence you as a perceiver also apply to others as perceivers.

Elements of Impression Formation

When we encounter an individual for the first time, we immediately begin forming an impression of him. Since it is highly unlikely that we would obtain enough information to form a final conclusion, our initial impressions are usually tentative. Some individuals are quick to form rigid and final impressions during first encounters, but most persons make tentative judgements about those they meet and automatically refine their impressions as more is learned about others. Of course, some individuals even claim that they make no judgements whatsoever during first encounters and, instead, "try to get to know" the person before they form an impression. In point of fact, our need to make sense out of our perceptions makes it a perceptual necessity to form impressions. That is, one way in which we try to make our perceptions of people meaningful is to form, alter, or radically change "impressions" of them. If we made no judgements—formed no impressions—then our perceptions would be meaningless, and we would be devoid of an informational basis for guiding interactions with new acquaintances.

For years, researchers in person perception have focused on the processes of impression formation in an attempt to determine (1) how individuals integrate diverse bits of information into a total impression and (2) how this information, once organized, is manipulated by individuals to make judgements of others. The former issue is essentially one of "organization," while the latter issue addresses the problem of "utilization" of information. These two areas of research have turned up some revealing evidence about the actual processes of impression formation. In the following section, relevant findings are discussed, but the prefatory note should be added that the research has not covered everything that happens as people get to know one another. It has tended to focus primarily on the issues identified above.

Organizing Information into Impressions

Asch (1946) was the first researcher to take a serious interest in what happens when we form impressions of others. His original explanation of impression formation might be described as a "holistic" approach, since he assumed that an impression is an *organized whole conception of another person's total personality*. *Traits* are perceived in others and immediately organized into a gestalt, with each perceived trait affecting another. Stated differently, all available bits of information affect each other and somehow organize into a total configuration or pattern. The resultant pattern, or impression, is more than the sum of its component traits; the final impression is not easily predictable from each of the traits taken separately. This is to say that the meaning of each bit of information is dependent upon the meaning of the whole pattern—the whole impression. From this holistic perspective, then, the overall impression of an individual gives meaning to each of the perceived traits of that person. This would imply that you may perceive the same trait or characteristic in two different individuals, but the meaning of that trait will differ for each person. For example, you may know that Dr. Smith and Dr. Jones are witty, but you may also be aware that, while they both seem witty, they have different personalities. Dr. Smith is sincere, thoughtful, and modest, whereas Dr. Jones is rather critical, aloof, and boisterous. According to Asch, these other characteristics would interact with each doctor's "wit" in such a way as to cause you to interpret differentially the meaning of their respective wittiness. Thus, it would be predicted that the wit of Dr. Smith may be interpreted as playful and good-natured, while the wit of Dr. Jones may be seen as sarcastic and ostentatious. The relative meanings of their respective wit are determined by the other information you have about the doctors.

In Asch's proposition there is the suggestion of an "interactive" effect of information. It is assumed that you cannot perceive two or more characteristics in an individual without those characteristics interacting in such a way as to create a different characteristic. By analogy, just as red and green lights can be combined to produce yellow, so also can two personality characteristics be combined by the perceiver to produce a different characteristic (e.g., a person who is "witty" and "critical" may be seen as "sarcastic," "derisive," "offensive," or "insensitive"). Asch also noted that our impressions of others are heavily influenced by characteristics that are important to us. In the case of the two doctors above, for example, you *may not care* if either doctor is "witty," but you may care if they are thoughtful. You may not attend to characteristics that are unimportant to you, but you will be inclined to focus on those characteristics that are important to you. Your overall impressions of the two doctors will be influenced by your perceptions of important traits, which Asch called *central traits*. Central traits are those perceived traits of another person that carry greater weight than others and thus modify the whole impression. By assigning greater weight or importance to certain traits, we therefore establish a core around which our perceptions are organized into total impressions. We perceive central traits in others and proceed to organize other personality information around those traits. In a sense, these central traits represent information about individuals that "stick out in your mind," while other information, being less important, is more difficult to articulate when relating your impressions of them. If I were to ask you to recall the first job you had and then to give me your impression of your first supervisor or boss, the first things you remember about that person would be those that "stick out in your mind"—the person's central traits, as perceived by you.

One of the noteworthy aspects of Asch's formulations is his assumption that impressions are "organized" through the interaction of perceived traits; the meaning of one trait will be influenced by the meaning attached to other information about the person. To investigate this assumption, Asch read a description of an unknown person to a group of subjects. To a second group, he read the same description, but the adjectives describing the unknown person were presented in reverse order. In the former case, the descriptive adjectives were "favorable" at the beginning of the list and became increasingly "unfavorable" or negative toward the end of the list. In the latter case, the descriptive adjectives were just the opposite—unfavorable at the beginning and more favorable toward the end. Asch predicted that subjects in the two groups would form different impressions, and that is precisely what he found. Subjects in the first group developed more "favorable" overall impressions of the unknown person, and subjects in the second group developed relatively "unfavorable" impressions. In explaining these findings, Asch maintained that the early information at the beginning of the lists created a set for the interpretation of information toward the end of the lists. He argued that the "order" in which information is received can have an impact on the total impression. One such "order effect," called the *primacy effect*, occurs when information received early in a series has a greater impact on impressions than later information. The primacy effect was demonstrated in Asch's study. An opposite order effect, the *recency effect*, occurs when information received later in the series has a greater influence on the resulting impression. Subsequent studies have pointed up the fact that the relative effects of primacy versus recency variables are dependent on other factors, to be discussed later. A point of significance here is that the meaning of a certain trait appears to be influenced by the *context* of the other information that we have about an individual. So, again it must be emphasized that our assessments of any particular characteristic of another person are directly influenced by the overall impressions that we hold. The whole impression appears to be greater and more significant than any single aspect of the impression.

Asch's seminal work provided some preliminary indications of the influence of specific factors on impression formation. His findings revealed that our impressions of others are well organized and that bits of information about others do not remain as independent data, but interact in an orderly fashion to produce an integrated whole impression of each person we perceive. However, Asch's findings do not explain impression formation in its entirety. For instance, his notions and his findings fall short of explaining how we actually do "combine" and "utilize" information to make an evaluation of another individual. Suppose I told you that your new supervisor is soft-spoken, tolerant, honest, trustful, and highly respected. She has many years of successful supervisory experience, she is a competent practitioner, and she treats staff with respect. She is middle-aged, attractive, a mother of three, and has lived in the same city for the last 20 years. Now, if I asked you to tell me how well you think you will like her, you will first have to combine all of this information in a way that permits you to make a single judgement. Asch's notions are unable to explain how you actually go about manipulating this information and what your resultant impression will be. To move toward an understanding of these processes, it is necessary to examine the findings from a separate line of research.

Combining Information to Make Judgements

In the example above, it was assumed that I asked you to tell me how you think you will like your new supervisor. In organizing your thoughts, you may attend to certain central traits from my description and then integrate other bits of information around those central traits. You will probably develop an organized impression, but I still don't know how well you think you'll like the supervisor. For purposes of illustration, let us assume that I told you that your new supervisor is demanding, critical, intolerant, authoritarian, and impersonal. Consider the former description that I gave you and then think about how your impressions would differ. How would you arrive at two different impressions? Two models have been proposed as possible explanations: the *averaging* model and the *additive* model. Both of these models have been described as "linear combination models" (Schneider, Hastorf, and Ellsworth, 1979), which are based on the assumption that responses to trait information can be made along a single evaluative dimension by adding or averaging the relevant information from the perceived traits; that is, we assign a particular value to each perceived trait, and our evaluation of an individual is then determined by adding or averaging the values of those traits. These two linear combination models are essentially mathematical formulations that have been applied to impression formation in an attempt to explain the processes by which we combine information in order to evaluate others' characteristics. Therefore, they are not concerned with the total impressions that you form, but with the bases for evaluating others' characteristics and arriving at the total impressions.

Anderson (1965, 1974) hypothesized that we combine information by adding the values of each perceived trait and then use the mean (average) of these values to form our impression of a person. This is not a conscious process; rather, it is hypothesized to be automatic and routine. The averaging model is nothing more than a "conceptual representation" of how we think the process works. The averaging model therefore postulates that it is "as if" we assigned a numerical scale value on a scale of one to ten to each trait and then divided the sum by the total number of traits. To illustrate the process, let us use the first description of your new supervisor. Let us assume, further, that you are able to assign a particular value to each of the descriptive traits. The process would occur in this manner:

$$
\begin{array}{ll}
\text{Soft-spoken} = 5 & \\
\text{Tolerant} \quad = 6 & \\
\text{Honest} \quad = 9 & \dfrac{5+6+9+9+6}{5} = 7 \\
\text{Trustful} \quad = 9 & \\
\text{Respected} = 6 &
\end{array}
$$

Given that the value of 10 is the highest on the scale from "least valued" to "most valued" traits, we can now say that your impression of the new supervisor is rather favorable. Your liking for this person could be reduced if we introduced other traits which are less favorable; being less favorable traits, their effect would be to bring down the average. Your impression will therefore remain favorable as long as the averaging process results in values at or above 5.

In contrast, the *additive* model suggests that judgements are based not on the average of the traits' values, but on the *sum* of the traits' values (Anderson, 1962). According to this model, the favorability of an impression is determined simply by adding the trait values summarily. To illustrate the operation of this process, let us use the second description of your new supervisor:

Demanding   = 2
Critical   = 1
Intolerant   = 2 $2 + 1 + 2 + 3 + 2 = 10$
Authoritarian = 3
Impersonal   = 2

The resultant value of the additive process does not imply that the supervisor is highly regarded. In this instance, the value of 10 would be considered rather low in light of the fact that the maximum possible value of the sum is 50 (i.e., on the scale of 1 to 10, each trait's highest value is 10, and if all traits were weighted with the value of 10, the sum would be 50). Table 6.1 shows the application of both the additive and averaging models to each of the descriptions. As Table 6.1 indicates, no matter which process is engaged, the second set of descriptive adjectives results in a less favorable impression of the supervisor. The appropriate question at this point would be "Which one is correct?" The answer is that there is some evidence in support of each, but recent evidence (e.g., Anderson, Lindner, and Lopes, 1973) has been strongly supportive of the averaging process (Wrightsman, 1977). As Wrightsman (1977) noted, it seems that at least "part" of our response to others involves some kind of averaging of available information in order to form a total impression of them. This may seem logical, but the logic of the additive model is perhaps even easier to follow—that the more positive information we have about a person, the more positive our overall impression becomes. Clearly, the process is not just a matter of averaging, because certain information necessarily carries more weight than other information. This fact is worth exploring further.

Weighting of Information

The actual value, or *weight*, that we give to each perceived trait is contingent upon the relative importance of those traits to us. The import of perceived

Table 6.1 Application of Additive and Averaging Models in Weighting Information About Persons

Characteristic	Value	Characteristic	Value
Soft-spoken	5	Demanding	2
Tolerant	6	Critical	1
Honest	9	Intolerant	2
Trustful	9	Authoritarian	3
Respected	6	Impersonal	2
Sum	35	Sum	10
Average	7	Average	2

traits is often contingent upon the particular circumstances in which an impression is being formed. For example, if you were given the opportunity to take over as a supervisor and revitalize an inefficient department, you would no doubt weigh certain information about each of your staff. Some information would be more important to have than other information. You probably wouldn't care if Judy is a good tennis player or whether she has caps on her teeth. Your impression of her would be influenced primarily by those traits and behaviors you see as being directly related to her performance. Therefore, you might give considerable weight to perceived traits of "dependability," "conscientiousness," and various other traits related to her performance and your new responsibilities. On the other hand, if you were interested in finding a good tennis partner with a bright smile, your overall impression of Judy would be somewhat different because of the weight now attached to her tennis skills and pearly teeth. That context and circumstance influence the relative weights of perceived traits can hardly be disputed, even at the level of common sense. One only needs to consider the different impressions that are likely to result when health professionals have an opportunity to see patients walking on the streets at a lively pace, as opposed to lying flat on their backs in hospital beds, with somber expressions and intravenous tubes sticking in their arms. The context of the health care environment often influences a "set" to weigh differentially diverse bits of information about others. Several factors have been identified which appear to exert direct influences on the values we attach to perceived traits and behavior.

Order Effects

It was pointed out earlier that the order in which information is received affects subsequent impressions. The *primacy effect* occurs when information first in a sequence exerts the dominant influence on our overall impressions. A *recency effect* occurs when later information (the most recent in the sequence) exerts the dominant influence on impressions. The primacy effect occurs to the extent that perceivers attach more "weight" to information received first, while the recency effect involves the assignment of more weight to later information. The primacy effect is reflected in the old saying that "first impressions are lasting impressions." While there may be some truth to this old belief, it is certainly open to qualification, since various factors tend to affect the relative impact of information primacy.

One such factor is called *attention decrement*, which involves a decrease in attention to incoming information over time. In most situations, we tend to be more attentive at the beginning of an interaction and gradually become less attentive as time passes and more and more information comes in. As a result, information which has received less attention is automatically deemed less important and, hence, receives less weight in the impression formation process. There have been two basic hypotheses for attention decrements. One hypothesis is that individuals simply get tired or forget to pay attention to later information. This type of explanation is, of course, contradicted in those instances where we are able to recall recent information but cannot recall information received at the beginning of an interchange. A second hypothesis is that individuals may assume that later information is presented later because it is less credible or less important and, therefore, deserves less attention. This hypothesis is limited also, in that we occasionally focus on information which we suspect is being "camouflaged" by prefatory statements. In other words, we sometimes filter out preliminary information and attend to later information which carries the essence of for what we were looking. This often happens as we listen to politicians' rhetoric.

While attention decrements may very well contribute to the relative impact of primacy over recency effects, there must be some factors which determine opposite outcomes. To appreciate what those factors might be, it should be acknowledged that both primacy and recency exert their influence through the interplay of *learning* and *retention*. That is, before impressions can be dominated by primacy or recency effects, information must first be acquired (learned) and retained. Research in the psychology of learning has made it clear that the recall of information learned early in a sequence is often "inhibited" by the learning of material later in the sequence. Given that later information interferes with the recall of early information, we would be inclined to conclude that recency effects dominate impressions. Before we reach such a conclusion, it should also be noted that the research has established that the learning of information later in a sequence is not as complete or thorough as the learning of information early in a sequence, simply because the mere existence of the first information inhibits the learning process. A primacy effect therefore occurs. From these findings, it may seem as though we have reached an impasse and cannot say whether primacy or recency are dominant in impression formation. We have not reached a "dead end." We have simply arrived at the point where the qualifications must be introduced. It seems that there is an assortment of miscellaneous factors which contribute to the relative impact of primacy in some instances and recency in others. Certainly, the relevance of information within the total communications context is an important determinant. Relevant and important information tends to exert a dominant influence on our impressions, and does so whether such information comes early or late in an interaction. Other factors include interesting information, as well as familiar, unexpected, or controversial information. Thus, the "kind of information" we perceive may, in fact, underlie or even supersede the effects of primacy and recency.

Negativity Effects

The weight attached to a bit of information reflects the importance of that information within the context of the evaluation process. One type of information which tends to receive heavy weighting in impression formation is *negative* information. Research has shown that when we have both positive and negative information about a person, the negative information will have more weight in determining our impressions of that person (Anderson, 1965; Hodges, 1974). As unmerciful, unfair, or unkind as it may seem, individuals tend to be relatively sensitive to negative information about others. Even in our magnanimous attempts to "look for the good in others," we have an apparent difficulty in overlooking negative information. One possible explanation for this tendency is that we are "selectively attentive" to such information. Negative information suggests to us that an individual may not be the kind of person with whom we would like to become involved. The negative traits which we perceive represent potential liabilities in relationships with persons manifesting those traits. Because we have learned to be sensitive to information signalling a possible threat to our well-being, we are therefore "set" to avoid interactions wherein we may have to pay a cost. From this perspective, it would seem to be an adaptive response on our parts to attend to significant negative information. Of course, the problem is that an orientation like this can often become maladaptive and predispose individuals toward a "fault-finding" mode of perception and impression formation.

There is a second possible explanation for negativity effects that is particularly interesting. Suppose I told you that next semester, your Pharmacology instructor would be Ms. White. She is ethical, intelligent, modest, friendly, she has taught the same course for the last 5 years, and she is basically well-liked by the faculty. However, she is not well-liked by students. With this information, you could form a tentative impression of Ms. White, and you would most likely attach heavy weight to the last bit of information—that she is not well-liked by students. This last bit of information tells you more about how Ms. White *differs* from other instructors than does any of the preceding information. Most instructors are ethical, intelligent, modest, and friendly. Most of them have experience teaching a particular course, and most of them are basically accepted by other faculty. So, there is nothing in this information which helps to distinguish Ms. White from any other instructor. But, because most instructors are usually liked by students, at least at a basic level of general acceptance, her reputation for being disliked sets her apart from other faculty. Until you learned that she was disliked, you had little information about Ms. White as a unique individual. Having learned of her reputation, you could then make inferences about her personality, and information as useful as this could receive greater weight in the impression formation process. Let us assume that, instead of being disliked by students, Ms. White is very popular. Given this information, you would obviously develop a more favorable impression of Ms. White. Her relative popularity carries the most weight in forming your impression. Now, wouldn't the implication be that positive information also carries heavy weight in impression formation? Indeed, it does, but the "kicker" is that *positive first impressions are less resistant to change* than are negative impressions; *perceivers have a pervasive tendency to weigh negative information more heavily than positive information* (Hamilton, 1980). Thus, a second possible explanation for negativity effects is that there is a *differential informativeness* between negative and positive information about people (Hamilton, 1980). Since we generally *expect* others to behave in socially acceptable ways, and because *we usually do* see others acting in socially acceptable ways, *deviations* from a norm of acceptability tend to be especially informative and thus, are given more weight in impression formation.

Salience Effects

Salient information is that which stands out, that which is prominent, or that which is noticeable about an individual. In impression formation, those traits and behaviors which are most salient to the perceiver tend to be weighted heavily. What is salient to one person may not be salient to another person, or even to the same person in a different context. Information salience is a function of any number of stimulus person, perceptual context, or perceiver variables (see Chapter Two). In relation to impression formation, information salience is often a function of what the perceiver considers to be *relevant* under the circumstances of the judgements being made.

Imagine that you are an experienced psychologist who has been asked to serve as an examiner on a licensing board. For purposes of illustration, let us assume that a nonpsychologist has been assigned to work with you in conducting oral examinations of candidates for licensure. Somewhere in the political bureaucracy, it was decided that the public interest would be served by balancing your evaluations with those of a naive examiner who would have no professional biases. After conducting your first oral examination of a candidate, Dr. Green, your lay associate describes his impressions. He says that Dr. Green seemed honest, sincere, good-natured, sociable, warm, and that he seemed to know about what he was talking. Your associate recommends that Dr. Green be granted a license. Although you happen to agree with your associate on the final decision, the reasons for your conclusion are probably different from those of the nonpsychologist. Your associate has apparently attended to "social" characteristics, with only a vague sense of Dr. Green's professional competency. You, on the other hand, focused on Dr. Green's knowledge of therapeutic techniques, his clinical judgement, awareness of strengths and limitations, problem-solving skills, adherence to ethical codes, knowledge of laws and standards of practice. You did not pay special attention to Dr. Green's social characteristics, because you considered them peripheral to the centrality of "professional/intellectual" characteristics. In short, you have formed an impression of Dr. Green by weighting information heavily on a dimension which is most salient to you as a psychologist and most relevant to the judgement you must make. The lay examiner formed an impression weighted heavily on a social desirability dimension—an evaluative dimension which is most relevant to him, given his inability to weigh information along the relevant dimension of professional competence. Even though you were both favorably impressed with Dr. Green, your individual impressions were influenced by the weighting of differentially salient information.

This example illustrates a phenomenon which often occurs in everyday interactions: two persons can be in agreement about a third person, despite the fact that their impressions are constructed from different bits of information, differentially weighted on a salience dimension. People can come to the same end point from different directions. The opposite outcome may occur as well. In the course of normal events, it often happens that we develop impressions of people which are in contrast to the impressions held by others. It seems to be a universal fact of life that not everyone feels the same way about a given person. Differences of opinion about individuals result from the interplay of numerous factors, one of which involves the weighting of salient information.

Isolating one set of factors as the sole determinants of information salience is not possible. Information salience is determined by the interaction of stimulus features which make the perceived person "stand out," relevant physical and social circumstances, perceptual tendencies and information processing activities of the perceiver. Of these influences, perceiver variables probably exert the strongest impact. *Stimulus information is salient if one has learned to attend to it and weigh it heavily.* The very acts of attending to, selecting, and weighing information implicate the underlying effects of learned values and attitudes as well as perceptual set. Finally, the differential assignment of weights or values to information about others suggests a direct relationship to the perceiver's *implicit personality theory.* As you may recall from Chapter Two, implicit personality theories are intuitive assumptions about human nature. They are cognitive frameworks for organizing and integrating information about others, and they help us to ascertain "what goes with what" in the personalities of human beings. Let us turn to a consideration of the special role of implicit personality theories in impression formation.

The Role of Implicit Personality Theories

Impression formation is extraordinarily complex, owing as much to the intricacies of perception as to the complexities of learning and thinking. It is a complicated perceptual-inferential process, determined at the outset by the same factors which apply to person perception in general, and in the interim by such additional factors as primacy and recency effects, averaging and adding, weighting of information. That an individual's impression of another person is influenced by these factors suggests *ipso facto* the existence of some sort of cognitive framework for processing information. Perceivers employ some type of system, structure, or framework filled with meaningful categories for organizing and interpreting perceptions. It is within this framework that stimulus information is processed and impressions formed. A "behavioral" fact which permits such an hypothesis is that *perceivers make inferences based on limited information.* For instance, when a hypothetical person is described as rigid, malicious, and prejudiced, a large number of people would assume that the person is also mean, narrow-minded, obnoxious, and aggressive. The mere fact that these latter traits are assumed to belong with the former traits is an indication that people have cognitive frameworks for processing information and generating inferences about the hypothetical person. These cognitive frameworks represent *implicit personality theories,* and they allow individuals to go beyond the particular information given to form a general overall impression.

One of the key features of the implicit personality theory is that it contains a set of *trait relationships.* It consists of separate assumptions about "what traits are related to other traits." People seem to have clear notions about "what goes with this and what goes with that" in the personalities of other individuals. That is, most people believe that when a person has one specific trait, he must therefore have other related traits. Consequently, we are often able to take a single trait and develop an overall impression of someone by *grouping* the trait with other associated traits. However, the simple awareness that certain traits go together is really not sufficient for making inferences about how a person with those traits is likely to "behave."

There is another feature of implicit personality theories which makes it possible for us to make inferences about behavior. *Trait-behavior relationships* are learned, and they allow us to predict a person's behavior from the traits we perceive. To clarify the importance of trait-behavior relationships, let us assume that you are to have a blind date, and the only thing you know about your date is that he/she is "shy." Replete with trait relationships, your implicit personality theory allows you to develop a composite picture of this person. You may associate shyness with introversion, self-consciousness, low self-confidence, feelings of inadequacy, and social sensitivity, but in and of themselves, these traits tell you nothing about how your date is likely to act. Your main concern under such circumstances is probably whether or not you're going to have a good time with this person. Your impression becomes meaningful only when you relate these traits to the behaviors with which they are associated. Thus, you may have learned that shy people make little eye contact, often have a downward gaze, initiate few conversations, aviod active involvement in group events, often display little interest in social activities, and remain quiet and inhibited in their interactions with others in novel situations. In short, you may have learned that these types of actions go along with shyness. A pertinent question would be "How did your implicit personality theory come to contain these relationships?" The answer is that you learned of these relationships through your interactions with people; you observed their behavior and learned that certain descriptive adjectives can be used as labels for different forms of behavior. You observed the behavior and then learned that trait name for it. On subsequent occasions, you could simply infer behavior from the trait name you have learned. When someone tells you that your date is "shy," you can immediately infer the person's probable behavior, because you have interacted in the past with shy people and you think you know how they act. You have also learned other trait names which represent behaviors that are similar to those displayed by shy persons. Those trait names are grouped together in the same category with their associated behaviors. When forming impressions of others, we can therefore go beyond the information given by drawing information from the categories of trait relationships and trait-behavior relationships.

As indicated in Chapter Two, implicit personality theories are constructed from and tied together by learned *stereotypes*. Stereotypes are, in turn, constructed from trait relationships and trait-behavior relationships. Stated differently, stereotypes are what hold these types of relationships together. They are simplistic categories of relationships which are used for organizing information and forming impressions. By learning some general relationships between traits and behavior, as well as general relationships among traits per se, we come to develop an implicit personality theory tied together by stereotypes. Although stereotypes have a negative connotation and are usually taken to represent beliefs about groups of people with shared demographic characteristics, they are certainly not limited to sociocultural variables. The following passage from Shakespeare's *Julius Caesar* illustrates a different kind of stereotype:

> Let me have men about me that are fat;
> Sleek-headed men, and such as sleep o' nights.
> Yond Cassius has a lean and hungry look;
> He thinks too much: such men are dangerous.

The assumption that "fat" and "sleek-headed" men are loyal and reliable, while persons with a "lean and hungry look" are dangerous is a kind of stereotypic impression which probably involves the same processes of grouping traits and behaviors as those leading to the assumptions that blacks are lazy, the Irish are heavy drinkers, and college professors are absentminded. Stereotypes can also apply to individuals. For example, if you have a friend whom you have always known to enjoy drinking beer in the tavern with his peers, you may find it hard to believe when your friend tells you that he is tired of drinking in bars. If you have a hard time taking him seriously, it is probably because you have overgeneralized from his past behavior: "What do you mean you don't want to go to the tavern anymore? That's not like you at all!" Stereotyping specific individuals probably results from our basic need for stability of experience. No doubt, you have been the "subject of this need" in others when you encountered people who knew you "way back when." Not being aware of changes in your personality, these persons relied upon overgeneralizations from past information in order to relate to you in the most meaningful way they had.

The implicit personality theory clearly encourages one to go beyond information given to form an overall impression. It has been described here as a cognitive framework, constructed from a wide range of stereotypes, with stereotypes representing broad categories which subsume trait relationships and trait-behavior relationships. These underlying relationships are learned through our interpersonal experiences as well as through vicarious, or nonsocial, experiences. We can therefore expect important individual differences in the implicit personality theories held by persons within any given context. In relation to individual differences, it should be noted that, because of differences among perceivers' implicit personality theories, the kinds of inferences perceivers make about others may tell us a great deal more about the perceivers themselves than about stimulus persons (Schneider, Hastorf, and Ellsworth, 1979). There is a definite link between an individual's personality and his own implicit personality theory. The "theory" is an extension of one's personality and life experience. Dominant thoughts, feelings, and themes in one's own life may be reflected in the nature of the impressions formed of other people. Therefore, in addition to stimulus information (about perceived persons), the perceiver's own personality and cognitive framework directly affect the formation of impressions. Although it is not possible to determine the relative importance of these determinants, Hamilton noted that certain circumstances favor the influence of perceiver variables over stimulus information (1980, p. 187):

> . . . when the information available about the stimulus person is extensive and compelling, we may expect that implicit personality theories will be less influential than when only impoverished information is available. The particular judgement being made may also be an important variable; implicit personality theories may be particularly important when we make abstract inferences about a person's personality attributes, but have less influence on our interpretation of behavioral cues.

In spite of the varying conditions under which implicit personality theories exert dominant effects on impression formation, the inescapable fact still remains that the contribution of the perceiver to the entire process is quite substantial. With meager or extensive information, trait or behavioral data, the perceiver is actively engaged in categorizing diverse bits of input into an integrated total impression. Impressions of stimulus persons are not smatterings of incidental perceptual cues; they represent the perceiver's conceptions of other human beings.

In the course of your daily interactions, you are active in constructing your own personal conceptions of those with whom you come into contact. From the first moment you lay eyes on a client or peer to the last moment of encounter, you are the creator and reconciler of meaningful impressions of those persons. The raw material for your impressions are perceptual data, your "tools" are perceptual and cognitive skills. As you construct and adjust your impressions, all of the factors identified here will come to exert some effect on the final product.

There is yet another major influence on your impressions that must be recognized: the *attribution of causality*. The assignment of causes to perceived behavior was discussed in Part One as a basic process involved in person perception as a whole. Recently, psychologists have become interested in the role of attribution in impression formation per se. One reason for this interest comes from the wealth of research data showing that we organize our conceptions of others at least partially around our assumptions of causation. Our implicit personality theories also contain *learned relationships between behavior and its causes*. Therefore, it is helpful to examine the ways in which our notions about the causation of behavior influence impression formation.

Attribution Processes in Impression Formation

Perceivers function very much like informal theorists. They have intuitive notions about the ways in which traits are related, how traits are connected to behavior, and what goes together in the personalities of others. Being informal theorists, we also have our ideas about "why people do the things they do." These ideas are contained within our implicit personality theories, and they help us to explain the causes of behavior. Perceivers as informal theorists are in some respects like philosophers and scientists—discontent with organizing information into simple "descriptions" of experience and satisfied when able to "explain" what has been described. It seems that we satisfy our need for meaningful experience only when we achieve understanding through some form of explanation. When it comes to other people, meaningful impressions often result only when we explain their actions in some way. Of course, as informal theorists, we are much less systematic than the philosopher and the scientist when we embark on this task. In most of our everyday encounters, our causal explanations of others' behavior are derived intuitively, automatically, and usually without much conscious thought.

When forming impressions of others, it is often necessary to make some inferences about the reasons for their actions. There are various kinds of inferences, or attributions, which are germane to impression formation. These include attributions of dispositional and situational causes of behavior, attributions of intention and reaction, and attributions of responsibility, ability, effort, and the causes of success and failure. In this section, we will examine some of the factors which influence one's choice of these types of attributions.

Dispositional and Situational Attributions

Attribution research has its roots in the original writings of Fritz Heider (1944, 1958). Heider advanced the notion that individuals perceive behavior as being

caused by either the perceived person (actor) or the enviornment or some combination of both. In a naive attempt to determine the causes of another's behavior, the perceiver assesses the relative strengths of forces within the person
and forces within the environment. Causal forces intrinsic to actors are called
dispositional causes and include personality characteristics such as traits, ability, effort, intentions, and individual motives. *Situational* causes are environmental factors which facilitate or block the performance of some action. Situational causes include available resources, assistance with a task, task difficulty,
luck, and countless other external forces. You will recall from the discussion in
Chapter Three ("Self-Perception and the Perception of Others") that perceivers lean toward dispositional attributions as explanations for the behavior of
others, whereas actors tend to attribute their behavior to situational causes.
Actors usually have more and better information about their own behavior,
and they sometimes have an attributional bias related to their self-concepts.
They may use their accumulated information in combination with ego-enhanc-
ing biases to attribute causes to their actions. When the consequences of the actor's behavior are positive or successful, the actor prefers a dispositional attribution to self, and when the consequences are unsuccessful, the actor supports
a situational attribution. Perceivers tend to do just the opposite; they attribute
the actor's successes to situational factors and failures to personality dispositions. This is, of course, a general tendency. The fact that perceivers can infer
causes from different possible sources suggests that there are factors which affect the choice of dispositional versus situational attributions. A principal concern of attribution research has been the identification of conditions influencing the kind of attributions perceivers make.

Attributions of Ability and Effort

According to attribution theory, when we perceive a person's behavior, we attribute the cause to the actor if we believe that the results of her actions were
produced through *ability* and *effort*. We attribute the cause to situational factors when we believe that ability and effort are not involved. For example, I realize that my wife is intelligent and hardworking. As a clinical psychologist,
she is competent and committed to the highest standards of practice. If she
were to be promoted from her staff psychologist position to a senior staff position, I would attribute the promotion to her special competencies; I would
make a dispositional attribution as to the cause of the promotion, because I see
the promotion as a direct consequence of her ability and work effort. However,
if I did not see her as being very intelligent or hardworking, I would not see her
promotion as resulting from anything special that she did. I would attribute
her promotion to situational factors; perhaps she was promoted "just because
she is a woman," or maybe it was due to "hospital politics," or maybe no one
else wanted the job. But, promotions are usually considered to be positive
changes; they are achievements and represent some level of success. An outside
observer, unaware of her intelligence and work effort, may take it for granted
that she earned the promotion on merit. On the other hand, he may be inclined
to attribute her promotion to situational factors. As indicated in Chapter
Three, when women achieve, their successes are often attributed to situational

factors, and to dispositional factors when they fail. For the outside observer to attribute her promotion to dispositional factors, he would have to know something about her ability and work effort. Otherwise, he would fall back on a situational attribution.

It should also be noted that my wife's attributions are likely to be different from those of casual observers. Actors attribute more responsibility to themselves for their successes than for their failures, whereas perceivers attribute more responsibility to the actor for failures than for successes. The conflicting attributions are due, in part, to the amount and kind of information available to actors. Actors usually have *more and better* information about their behavior than perceivers do. While I may be an outside observer of sorts, my attributions are probably going to parallel those of my wife. Why should this be so, given the differences in attributional tendencies between actors and perceivers? First, I favor a dispositional attribution because I, too, have more and better information than others by virtue of my relationship with her. I know of her ability and work effort. Second, the fact that I happen to like her and love her would further increase my attributional bias. I have a favorable impression of her already, and, because of that positive concept, I would probably have a motivationally-based attributional bias to protect the impression I hold. Finally, I have had the opportunity to observe my wife's long history of performance. Therefore, I would be inclined to infer dispositional causes and attribute *another success* to her ability and effort.

Perception of "Can"

Dispositional attributions based on the perception of ability and effort are related to the *perception of "can"*. Can is a dispositional factor which involves the relationship between the actor's ability and environmental forces. Ability is attributed to the actor when she successfully performs a task under difficult conditions; the actor is perceived as being *capable of producing specific consequences*. That is, she *can* produce specific outcomes as a result of some particular ability. When I offer a dispositional attribution to explain the causes of my wife's hypothetical promotion, the perception of can is an important consideration. As indicated, I am aware of her intelligence and hard work, but I am also aware of her working conditions—I know that the job is demanding. I would lean toward a dispositional cause for her promotion because environmental forces were strong enough to make effective performance dependent on ability. She merited promotion because she was able to perform successfully in a difficult job. If her job were so easy that anyone could handle it, then ability would not be an issue, and I would probably attribute her promotion to situational factors; I would attribute success to the nature of the job. If her job were so difficult that no one could handle it, then I still couldn't make an inference about her ability, and I would attribute her promotion to situational influences. But, the possibility remains that maybe she got the promotion on the basis of plain old "hard work" and sheer perseverance.

Perception of "Trying"

Ability is obviously not the sole determinant of behavior. We are all able to produce countless effects on our environments, but whether we do or not is another issue. Often, this other issue relates to effort. When both ability and effort are perceived to underlie an individual's behavior, perceivers tend to make dispositional attributions. When either one or both are absent, perceivers favor situational causes for behavior. Ability is often inferred subsequent to the perception of can—when the actor is seen as being capable of producing certain behaviors. Effort is inferred subsequent to the *perception of "trying."* *Trying* is a dispositional property that is related to the actor's motivation to perform an action. Being a function of *intention* and *exertion*, trying refers to "what" the actor wants to do and "how hard" she tries to do it. When the actor is perceived to have "intended" to act in a certain way by "exerting" her ability to perform that action, then the actor is perceived to have "tried." The attribution of dispositional causes then become more probable. For example, after an appendectomy a patient is asked to get out of bed and walk for a few moments. When he slowly swings his legs over the side of the bed, places his feet on the floor, and gradually pushes himself upward with all the strength he can muster, we would infer that he intended to act in that way and exerted his ability to do so. Because we perceive that he tried to produce those actions and that he was able to perform them, we would naturally attribute his behavior to personal causes. This is a simplistic example, but the principle extends to any form of behavior. To illustrate, let us return to the example of my wife's promotion.

I would infer dispositional causes for my wife's job performance if I knew that she "intended" to perform well and that she "exerted" her ability to do so. I would infer effort because I have perceived her to have tried to act as she did. If I knew of her ability, but that she did not "intend" to perform as well as he did, I would not infer effort and, therefore, I would probably not attribute her success to dispositional causes. Similarly, if I knew that she wanted to perform well, but never really got around to exerting herself, then I would not infer that she was trying very hard. I would not perceive much effort, and, consequently, I would look to situational factors as predominant causes for her promotion. When the perceiver is unable to infer intention, exertion, or both, the cause for the actor's behavior is not likely to be attributed to effort. Even though the perceiver may know of the actor's ability to bring about certain consequences, the general attribution will refer to situational causes if ability cannot be complemented with perceived effort.

Attributions to Multiple Causes

To this point, attribution theory may seem remarkably simple. Indeed, Heider termed his attribution framework a form of "naive" psychology. The perceiver attributes an actor's behavior to dispositional factors upon the inference of both ability and effort. When either one or both are absent, a situational cause for behavior is inferred. Ability is inferred when the perceiver determines that the actor "can" produce a behavior under certain conditions. Effort is inferred subsequent to the perception of "trying," which is a function of intention and exertion. If either one or both are absent, behavior is not likely to be attributed to dispositional causes.

Given these conditions, it may seem that attributing the causes of behavior is a simple matter of choosing between two possible sources. Heider's approach goes no further than to say that we make a dispositional attribution, a situational attribution, or, in some cases, an attribution to both. Even though the perceiver may make a dispositional attribution, for example, we are still left with the question, what *specific* dispositional characteristics are inferred by the perceiver to have caused the behavior? If a person makes a donation to a charitable foundation, is it the result of her "generosity," her "sympathy," a sense of "guilt," or is it a self-serving attempt to get a tax deduction? How the perceiver goes about making *specific inferences* is a matter which has been taken up by other attribution theorists (e.g., Jones, 1979; Jones and Davis, 1965; Kelley, 1967, 1972). These theorists have developed elaborate frameworks for explaining the complicated ways in which perceivers use available information to make causal inferences. In general, these theories and the research generated by them have demonstrated that perceivers do not engage in a thorough consideration of all possible explanations for an action. They often fail to consider some information which is relevant to the attribution being made. Perceivers seem to search for *sufficient* explanations, feeling no obligation to go beyond the most obvious explanation and account for alternative possibilities. In many cases, the perceiver will simply attribute the cause of an actor's behavior to that aspect of the stimulus information which is most *salient* to him. Perhaps there are various reasons why a person would make a charitable donation. But, most often, the cause is attributed to "generosity," and perceivers—*especially the recipients of the donation*—do not consider other possible donor motives. In cases like these, perceivers seem to assume that generosity is self-evident and clearly sufficient to explain the donor's actions. However, even in a case like this, there may be other causes—*multiple causes in a chain of events leading up to and surrounding the behavior in question.*

Of all the possible explanations which may account for a perceived action, the perceiver will usually opt for those that are *sufficient*. According to Kelley (1972), the perceiver often finds it difficult to attribute a single cause to an actor's behavior. In most cases, there are "multiple sufficient causes" for behavior. The perceiver then uses a *discounting principle* (Kelley, 1972) to infer sufficient causes: he will discount a given possible cause as the sole source of a given effect if there are other possible sufficient causes present. This is almost a person-perception counterpart to the medical diagnostic process of ruling out a given possible cause for symptoms of illness when there are various other sufficient causes for those symptoms. However, unlike the medical examiner, the casual perceiver is rarely as systematic and deliberate, and often goes no further than the most salient information.

Most forms of human behavior occur in a causal sequence or *chain*. For you to get to these words on this page, you had to proceed through a chain of behaviors, which could probably be pushed back *ad infinitum*. Obviously, we are not concerned here with tying behavior to The Initial Cause, but let us take an example to point up the significance of causal chains in behavioral attributions. If a friend tells you that he will pick you up for work in the morning and fails to do so, you might be angry, but before you accuse him of thoughtless irresponsibility, you need to determine why you were stranded in the first place.

Deciding upon an ultimate cause may be a complicated process if you look at events in sequence. For example, your friend may have failed to pick you up because his car broke down—simple enough, but maybe you won't stop with a situational attribution. Maybe his car broke down because he didn't make repairs that were needed and overdue. Perhaps you'll stop here and attribute the cause to his negligence. Or, perhaps you know that he didn't make repairs on the car because he couldn't afford them, and he couldn't afford them because he was spending his money on leisure, and he was spending his money on leisure because . . . well, the causal chain could go on and on. The important point is that it is often difficult to stop at any given point in a chain and assign a cause for behavior with complete confidence. If an individual entertains the probability of a causal sequence for behavior and searches the chain for a reasonable and sufficient cause, his "stopping point" will have implications, not only for dispositional or situational attributions, but also for evaluations of the actor based on the assignment of *responsibility*.

Attributions of Responsibility

Heider originally assumed that the distinction between dispositional and situational causes is important for perceivers, because, without such a distinction, *responsibility* for behavior could not be assigned. He assumed that before a person can assign responsibility to the actor, a dispositional attribution must be made. The motivation to assign responsibility for behavior probably stems from our basic need for an orderly, organized, stable, and meaningful world of experience. But, the fact is that Heider was incorrect in his basic contention. Research evidence is conclusive that people are often held responsible for actions that they neither intended nor tried to cause. Sometimes, people are even held responsible for actions or events that they *could not possibly cause*: weather forecasters are sometimes blamed for bad weather, the President is sometimes blamed for every inflationary trend, and health professionals are sometimes held responsible for not "curing" certain patients.

One of the problems with attribution of responsibility relates to the various meanings of the term. When a person claims that someone is "responsible" for an action, she could mean that the individual: (1) caused something to happen, (2) intended for something to happen, (3) failed to prevent the occurrence of an event, (4) has a legal liability for an effect, or (5) is morally responsible for something. It is not always clear what a person means by "responsibility." Shaver (1975) concluded that the term as used by attribution theorists refers primarily to an *"evaluation of moral accountability."* He added that perceivers may still use the term in various other ways.

There are three sets of factors which can influence the attribution of responsibility—three sets of factors that we have pointed out throughout this text: characteristics of the perceived person (actor), characteristics of the context, and characteristics of the perceiver.

The Actor and the Context

People are usually held responsible for the effects they try to produce. As Shaver (1975) noted, this is probably the strongest statement that could be made about the relationship between behavior and responsibility. However, we do not often hesitate to attribute responsibility for many "unintentional" acts, nor do we always attribute complete responsibility for intentional ones. For example, nurses working in an emergency department treat many victims of automobile accidents. How many of those nurses do you think honestly believe that those car accidents were nobody's fault? Probably, none of them—automobile "accidents" are by definition *unintentional*, yet someone invariably is held to be responsible. Emergency department personnel occasionally treat children injured while trying to imitate a stunt they saw on television. Are the children held responsible for their injuries? The answer is yes and no. It is yes in the sense that they would not have been injured if they had not attempted the stunt. On the other hand, they would not have attempted the stunt if they had not seen it on television. In cases like these, complete responsibility is not attributed to the children for their intentional acts. But, there is something else in this latter example that should be noted: for the injuries to occur, *both* the television model *and* the attempted stunt were *necessary*. The television model was not sufficient to cause an injury, nor was playing per se sufficient to cause the injury. Even so, one of these two necessary causes is likely to receive more causal responsibility; which one? An answer was suggested by Feinberg's (1965) assertion that the "more ordinary" event will be assigned less responsibility. If it is common for a child to try every stunt witnessed on television, then less responsibility will be attributed to television models, because it is "ordinary" for the child to observe and imitate. If it is uncommon for the child to try a television stunt, more responsibility will be attributed to the television model, because it is not "ordinary" for the child to attempt such a thing.

Intention is a difficult basis for assigning responsibility, because the actor's motivation and ability and various situational factors all bear upon the attribution decision (Shaver, 1975). Consider the behavioral outcomes of success and failure, for example. When most people set out to do something, they don't set out to fail, yet they sometimes do fail at a task, and some people fail more often than others. How do we attribute the responsibility for failure? The research has been informative here (e.g., Jones and deCharms, 1957; Lanzetta and Hannah, 1969), in that persons who fail for lack of trying are held more responsible than are those who fail because they lack the requisite ability. We are more lenient with persons of low ability because it is not under their control, whereas we are less tolerant of those with adequate ability who are not motivated to put forth an acceptable amount of effort. For example, when a patient's improvement is hampered by her unwillingness to help herself when she can, she will be held responsible for her continued ill health, and the staff's frustration may have an effect on the quality of treatment it provides. The more an action appears to be under the control of the actor, and the more he controls the consequences of his actions, the more responsibility will be assigned to him.

Perceiver Influences on Responsibility Attributions

Shaver (1975) identified three sets of factors contributing to differences among perceiver attributions: personality differences, perceivers' views of the perceptual task, and perceivers' motivations. According to Shaver, personality differences may account for different attributions to the same behavior when individuals generalize from their own life experiences. An implicit assumption of similarity may lead perceivers to conclude that others do things for many of the same reasons they do. If I am standing in a long line, waiting for a ticket window to open up so that I can purchase tickets for a football play off game, I may well conclude that everyone else in the line is there because, like me, they want to get tickets for themselves. History has shown, however, that some of these folks are probably purchasing tickets so that they can "scalp" them at higher prices. Or, if you are enrolled in a class because you wish to learn something about preventive medicine, you may conclude that everyone else is there for the same reasons. It often happens, though, that people enroll in certain classes simply to pick up necessary credits for meeting licensing requirements, and they may not care whether they learn anything at all.

The perceiver's view of a perceptual task may also influence his attributions of responsibility. For example, the task of the clinical social worker is often to provide supportive counseling without passing judgement on the legitimacy of feelings expressed by clients. The social worker is predisposed or *set* to be impartial. Whereas trial judges are also predisposed to be impartial, their professional task is different, and they *must* make responsibility attributions. Thus, depending upon the circumstances, different persons may be predisposed to attend to aspects of behavior that others might ignore.

The third set of factors influencing perceiver attributions of responsibility pertains to the motivations of the perceiver. A person who is losing money in a poker game may blame the dealer for his losses. A person may also blame the victim of an act of violence in order to protect himself from the upsetting possibility that *he too could be a victim*. And, as probably happens more frequently than we would like to admit, health professionals may very well blame numerous patients for their diseases on the assumption that "they got what they deserved" because they didn't take care of themselves. To attribute sole responsibility for lung cancer to the patient who smoked cigarettes does help to insulate the perceiver somewhat from the realization that he, too, could die from the exact same disease. This type of attribution reflects a strategy for self-protection that has been called the *belief in a just world* (Lerner, 1966). It is upsetting for people to accept the possibility that misfortune could befall someone purely by chance, so perceivers often opt for explanations of negative events which place the responsibility on the victim, whose misfortune is deserved for one reason or another. Responsibility attributions based on the belief in a just world have special relevance for interpersonal attraction and liking. A broader discussion of this phenomenon is provided in Chapter 10. It is sufficient here to note that attributions of responsibility can be influenced not only by the perceiver's past experience, beliefs about similarity, perceptual sets, needs, wants, and various other motivations, but also *by the perceiver's fears and hopes*.

Summary and Implications for Health Professionals

The moment we encounter another human being, we begin forming an *impression* of that person. From our need to make sense of our perceptions, we immediately try to fit together bits of information into an overall pattern that is meaningful. The resultant pattern, or impression, is an *organized whole conception of another person's total personality*. This organized whole gives meaning to each of the component parts, such that the overall impression we have of someone gives meaning to each of the perceived traits of that person. Some traits seem to be perceived more readily than others, and these are called *central traits*. Central traits are the core around which the total impression is organized.

One factor which has a significant effect on our impressions of others pertains to the *order* in which information is received. A *primacy effect* occurs when information received early in a series has greater import than later information. A *recency effect* occurs when information received later in the series has a dominant effect on the resulting impression. Two models have been proposed to explain how we go about combining information in order to arrive at a single judgement about a perceived person. An *averaging model* assumes that we assign values to each perceived trait and then add those values and use the average to form an impression. The *additive model* suggests that judgements are based on the sum of the traits' values. While both models appear to be useful in explaining how we combine information, the averaging model has received the most empirical support. The actual value or *weight* that we give to each perceived trait is dependent upon the relative importance of those traits to us, and the importance of each trait is often contingent upon the circumstances in which an impression is being formed. Factors which influence the weights given to perceived traits include *order effects, negativity effects, salience effects*.

Implicit personality theories are used by perceivers to draw inferences which go beyond the information given to form overall impressions of others. Two key features of implicit personality theories are *trait relationships* and *trait-behavior relationships*. Perceivers have learned that certain traits go together in the personalities of others, as do certain traits and certain behaviors. These relationships are held together by *stereotypes*, and groups of stereotypes are tied together in order to establish the implicit personality theory. Implicit personality theories also contain assumptions about why people do the things they do. Perceivers are able to assign causes to perceived behavior because they have also learned relationships between behavior and causes. Perceptions that events are caused are grounded in our own experiences as causal agents of change in the environment. We have learned through experience that we can have an impact on our surroundings by acting in specific ways. When forming impressions of others, it is often necessary to make inferences about the causes of their actions. This helps us to make sense out of their behavior.

Whether we make *situational* or *dispositional attributions* of causes depends on our perceptions of the actor's *ability* and *effort* to act as he did. The perception of ability rests upon the *perception of can*, and the perception of effort is dependent upon the *perception of trying*. The perception of trying is, in turn, determined by the perception of *intention* and *exertion* on the part of the actor. When multiple causes are apparent to us, we opt for those which are *sufficient* to explain the actor's behavior. Often, this amounts to attributions to the most *salient* causal information. In cases where there are multiple sufficient causes for the actor's behavior, we use a *discounting principle* in which we discount a given possible cause as the sole source of a given effect if there are other possible sufficient causes present. The attribution of *responsibility* is often made when the perceiver wishes to hold someone morally accountable for an action. Responsibility attributions depend first and foremost upon the assignment of dispositional causes, and then on other factors related to the actor and context, as well as on perceivers' personalities, view of the perceptual task, and perceivers' motivations.

Our examination of impression formation is by no means exhaustive. But, the processes outlined here appear to apply to impression formation in general and, therefore, have implications for health professionals in applied settings.

Implications for Health Professionals

Your profession is a "person-centered," "people-oriented" profession requiring continuous interaction with others. The nature of your work demands that you become skilled in impression formation, since the impressions you develop are carried with you as you enter into each of those interactions. In most cases, all of the processes involved in impression formation serve an "adaptive" function, helping you to determine the most appropriate ways of interacting with others. In a sense, your professional responsibilities include a mandate that you optimize the adaptive function of impressions: you must prevent or reduce biases, distortions, and errors that can lead to ineffective or even contraindicated responses to clients. *The reality is that in professional practice you cannot afford to be as casual as you might otherwise be in social relationships.*

In this chapter, you have learned a great deal about those factors which have an influence on the ways in which we form impressions of others. Now that you are aware of some of these factors, you can begin to improve your skills in forming impressions of people. If you know that impressions are organized around the perception of *central traits*, take time to consider what traits tend to have a strong impact on your impressions of those you know. Reflect on the various impressions you have formed of clients and challenge your assumptions, your inferences, and your overall evaluations. Make a habit of challenging yourself in this way from time to time. If you know that inferences are subject to error, since they are deductions and presumptions from limited information, try to validate inferences you have made. You can do this by checking your assumptions against other information and corroborating your "findings" before settling on a definite conclusion about someone. If you know that your impressions are strongly influenced by *primacy effects*, you may want to guard against possible bias by attending more to later information. If you are aware that people have a tendency to assign more weight to *negative information*, you can compensate for this tendency in yourself by trying to identify particular strengths and personality assets in others. If you know that *implicit personality theories* influence impressions, you may want to look at your own assumptions about human nature in general. Perhaps you will discover that many of your impressions are colored by assumptions which you have never before questioned. If you realize that *stereotypes* influence the tendency to group people into simple categories, you can correct for overgeneralizations and oversimplified impressions by identifying stereotypes which you have incorporated. If you are aware of differences in causal attributions between perceivers and actors, you may try to be more careful in attributing causes to others' behavior, especially since they have *more and better information* about their actions then you do. And, if you know that a person's behavior tends to cover a major part of the entire "perceptual field," obscuring possible situational influences and preventing you from clearly recognizing environmental causes for the behavior, you may work on being cautious when deciding upon *dispositional* and *situational attributions.* If you recognize the various factors which influence causal attributions, you may develop more accurate impressions as you try to account for the "why" of another person's behavior. By focusing on attribution processes in general, you should learn about the ways in which perceivers might come to understand their own behavior, as well as the behavior of others. Finally, if you recognize that sometimes you are the perceiver and *sometimes you are the perceived*, you can use your own experience as a perceiver to develop some insights into how others might perceive you.

In health care settings, we encounter staff whose behavior is influenced partly by their professional roles and clients or patients whose behavior is influenced by *their* roles as well as their problems or illnesses. We must therefore be aware of the ways in which *contexts* influence our impressions, for we would no doubt view both staff and clients differently if we all attended the same Christmas party at the local reception hall. You must account for the special effects of physical illness in the case of the medical patient, for example. Illness may force a patient to be much more *dependent* than she would be otherwise. She is a person under stress, and part of her behavior is in response to that stress. She may be somewhat demanding, attention-seeking, and express feelings of helplessness. Before you conclude that this person *is a dependent person* (a particular *type* of individual), you must consider the conditions surrounding her behavior. She may not be responding *out of* dependency at all; instead, she is probably responding *to* her current *life circumstances.* Medical patients do not necessarily behave in accordance with underlying personality *traits.* It is most probable that their behaviors reflect their feelings about their conditions: physical conditions, conditions of isolation from friends and family, and/or even the physical conditions of the hospital. As you interact with clients, be sensitive to each person as an individual. *Be attuned to their illnesses, but also be attuned to their feelings about their illnesses. Be not focused solely on illness, but also on wellness; learn to recognize strengths and indications of wellness that can be used for their benefit.*

In many ways, a major influence on the health professional's impressions of patients comes from repeated encounters with particular health problems. You may encounter a specific health problem many times in your career, *but the persons presenting those problems have not*! Their only shared characteristic may be that they have manifested similar symptoms. So, it may require a concentrated effort to avoid the tendency to group individuals in terms of their illnesses—to avoid stereotyping. In certain health professions, this tendency is especially hard to avoid when it has been formalized and systematized into an institutionally sanctioned ritual. For example, in the mental health field, where systematic attempts are made to formulate reliable clinical impressions, personality evaluations occasionally represent little more than methodized stereotyping. That is, when information is gathered through testing and interviews and integrated for the purpose of making a "psychiatric diagnosis," individuals are subsequently reduced to diagnostic entities, tagged with a label, and grouped with others having the same label. Fortunately, there has been an increasing trend away from this type of process, but some institutions have found it hard to abandon archaic traditions. The consequences for those tagged with psychiatric diagnoses have been far-ranging. When clinical "impressions" are summarized in terms of labels such as "schizophrenic," there are immediate connotations which spread out to all who learn of the judgement. The "schizophrenic" is essentially stripped of his individuality, stereotyped, and treated like all other members of the "schizophrenic" group. Staff begin seeing the person as "the schizophrenic" and relate to him accordingly; family and friends begin relating to the label and no longer to the person whose complexity defies any label; the person begins accepting himself as others are defining him. These are a few of the consequences which can accrue for "victims" of what might very well be termed "institutionalized impression formation processes." Granted, the consequences can be devastating on a scale such as this. However, you may give some thought to the potential consequences of impressions which you form as you get to know clients. Hopefully, your conclusions bear no resemblance and, instead, attest to your skills in interpersonal relations.

References

Anderson, N. H. Application of an Additive-Model to Impression Formation, *Science*, **138**:817–18 (1962).

Anderson, N. H. Averaging Versus Adding as a Stimulus Combination Rule in Impression Formation, *Journal of Experimental Psychology*, **70**:394–400 (1965).

Anderson, N. H. Cognitive Algebra: Integration Theory Applied to Social Attribution, in *Advances in Experimental Social Psychology*, vol. 7, ed. L. Berkowitz, pp. 1–101. New York, Academic Press, 1974.

Anderson, N. H.; Lindner, R.; and Lopes, L. L. Integration Theory Applied to Judgements of Group Attractiveness, *Journal of Personality and Social Psychology*, **26**:400–8 (1973).

Asch, S. Forming Impressions of Personality, *Journal of Abnormal and Social Psychology*, **41**:258–290 (1946).

Feinberg, J. Action and Responsibility, in *Philosophy in America*, ed. M. Black, London, Allen and Unwin, 1965.

Hamilton, D. L. Person Perception, in *A Survey of Social Psychology*, 2d ed., ed. L. Berkowitz, pp. 179–213. New York, Holt, Rinehart, and Winston, 1980.

Heider, F. Social Perception and Phenomenal Causality, *Psychological Review*, **51**:358–74 (1944).

Heider, F. *The Psychology of Interpersonal Relations*. New York, Wiley, 1958.

Hodges, B. H. Effect of Valence of Relative Weighting in Impression Formation, *Journal of Personality and Social Psychology*, **30**:378–81 (1974).

Jones, E. E. The Rocky Road from Acts to Dispositions, *American Psychologist*, **34**:107–17 (1979).

Jones, E. E., and Davis, K. E. A Theory of Correspondent Inferences: From Acts to Dispositions, in *Advances in Experimental Social Psychology*, vol. 2, ed. L. Berkowitz, New York, Academic Press, 1965.

Jones, E. E., and deCharms, R. Changes in Social Perception as a Function of the Personal Relevance of Behavior, *Sociometry*, **20**:75–85 (1957).

Kelley, H. H. Attribution Theory in Social Psychology, in *Nebraska Symposium on Motivation*, ed. D. E. Levine, Lincoln, Nebraska, University of Nebraska Press, 1967.

Kelley, H. H. Attribution in Social Interaction, in *Attribution: Perceiving the Causes of Behavior*, ed. E. E. Jones et al., Morristown, New Jersey, General Learning Press, 1972.

Lanzetta, J. T., and Hannah, T. E. Reinforcing Behavior of "Naive" Trainers, *Journal of Personality and Social Psychology*, **11**:245–52 (1969).

Lerner, M. J. The Unjust Consequences of the Need to Believe in a Just World. Paper presented at the meeting of the American Psychological Association, New York, September 1966.

Schneider, D. J.; Hastorf, A. H.; and Ellsworth, P. C. *Person Perception*, 2d ed. Reading, Massachusetts, Addison-Wesley, 1979.

Shaver, K. G. *An Introduction to Attribution Processes*. Cambridge, Massachusetts, Winthrop, 1975.

Wrightsman, L. *Social Psychology*, 2d ed. Monterey, California, Brooks/Cole, 1977.

CHAPTER
SEVEN

Shaping Impressions
Through Self-Presentation

*I have entered on a performance which is without prece-
dent, and will have no imitator. I propose to show my
fellow-mortals a man in all the integrity of nature; and
this man shall be myself.*

Jean Jacques Rousseau, *Confessions*

So far, impression formation has been described as a process determined
largely by perceptual and cognitive operations of perceivers. A *unidirectional*
approach was taken in the preceding chapter in order to describe the perceiver's
experience. Most of the research has taken this approach. However, it was also
stressed that the perceiver is an actor as well; she forms impressions of others at
the same time they form impressions of her. In addition, it has been emphasized repeatedly that our perceptions of others influence our reactions to them,
and our reactions affect the ways in which others perceive and respond to us.
These realities clearly suggest that person perception and impression formation are *interactive processes* mediated by reciprocal communication. A unidirectional approach therefore gives us only part of the real picture.

In your interactions with others, you usually know that you are being perceived and evaluated in some way. This realization often influences you to try
to present a certain image of yourself. The person with whom you are interacting may know you are trying to project a specific image, and he may use various discounting tactics to tone down the image you're presenting. In a spiral-
ing interaction, you, in turn, may use some of your own tactics to offset his. In
effect, your behavior is influenced not only by your impression of his personality, but also by your *impressions of how he sees you*. His behavior is affected in
similar ways. To make the interaction even more complicated, you also form an
impression of *what he thinks you think of him* (see Figure 7.1). During this spi-
raling interaction, both of you are attempting to present yourselves to one another in strategic ways. You are both conspiring and maneuvering to control
and shape each other's impressions. Thus, in interpersonal transactions, it is

Figure 7.1 Reciprocal views.

not only the perceiver who creates impressions of an actor. The actor is something of a coproducer, in that he shares in the creation of the perceiver's impressions: he promotes an image of himself that he hopes will be received as intended.

Without question, our own efforts to create images of ourselves in the minds of others are potent influences on the impressions they ultimately form. In this chapter, we will examine the ways in which individuals present themselves to others and attempt to influence the impressions others develop. The manner in which individuals display themselves to others is called *self-presentation*. The process of controlling one's appearance and behavior in order to influence others' impressions of oneself is known as *impression management*. There are various reasons for bringing these processes into focus here. First, because each individual brings herself to any encounter with another, impression formation phenomena cannot be fully appreciated without a recognition of the ways in which they present themselves and shape others' perceptions. Second, as a health professional, you are expected to present a certain image of yourself to those with whom you work. Broadly speaking, your image must include evidence of "professionalism," "caring," and "competence." It should therefore be helpful for you to understand some of the factors affecting your style of self-presentation as well as some of the consequences. Such an understanding may assist you in influencing responsibly the kinds of impressions you want others to form. Third, self-presentation and impression management involve specific sets of skills which are necessary for effective and satisfactory interpersonal relations in general. Your professional life is only part of your total life situation, and, as such, it is directly affected by other social events and relationships. You play an active role in determining the quality of those events and relationships, which is often a direct function of how you present yourself to others. Self-presentation and impression management skills can be used in a repertoire of interpersonal skills to enhance the quality of those nonprofessional experiences. A frequent result is a positive "carry-over effect," wherein professional relationships become more rewarding as one's personal life becomes more balanced and satisfying. Finally, there are important social implications which make impression management a highly relevant topic for health professionals as well as the public in general.

Specifically, human beings have been at least intuitively aware of some of the causes and effects of impression management for thousands of years. However, it seems that in this century the desire to make a good impression has erupted and intensified into a profound, and yet generally accepted motive for behavior. Prior to the self-improvement motif, which has gained increasing popularity since emerging forcefully in the 1960s, Dale Carnegie's best-selling advice book, *How to Win Friends and Influence People* (1936) and then Norman Vincent Peale's *The Power of Positive Thinking* (1952) contributed greatly to the illusion that simple formulae do exist for self-promotion and how to project a "winning-image." During the so-called me-decade of the seventies, as people seemed to retreat from the heights of social awareness to the depths of self-consciousness, we witnessed a tremendous surge of demand for self-enhancement books. A great number of these books reflected the pervasive concern with self-presentation and impression management. For example,

Dyer (1977) offered advice on *Pulling Your Own Strings*, Weinberg (1978) revealed the basics of *Self-Creation*, Molloy (1975) gave instructions to men on how to *Dress for Success* and then added *The Woman's Dress for Success Book* (1977) so that both sexes could improve their appearances; the man reputed to be "the world's greatest salesman" had his own tips on *How to Sell Yourself* (Girard, 1979), and Ringer (1974) introduced his secrets to self-promotion in the chillingly manipulative title *Winning Through Intimidation*. We will have to look someday in retrospect at the 1980s to see how this trend proceeded. At this time, however, it appears to be continuing, as people are still seeking the answers that were promised, but which turned out to be less simple than expected. The preoccupation with self-improvement, personal advancement, and public images still appears to be strong. For example, Juian Fast has parlayed *Body Language* (1970) into *Body Politics: How to Get Power with Class* (1980), cosmetics executive Adrienne Arpel has published her beauty hints in *How to Look Ten Years Younger* (1980), and Landau and Bailey (1980) have outlined the ways in which "working women win top jobs" in *The Landau Strategy*. Indeed, there are hundreds of books which become immensely popular each year, and each book has its own "strategies" for improving one's lot in life by creating the right public images and making the right impressions. Glamour and menswear magazines display the newest fashions, countless new diets are introduced for looking healthy and slim; toothpastes, deodorants, breath mints, acne "cover-ups," and hair conditioners are advertised much like food staples for those who wish to have "sex appeal," the "dry look," or who simply wish to "smell like a man"; automobiles, furniture, and even wallpaper are often selected according to the public image individuals want to project. The fact that the proliferation of products and strategies for self-promotion is continuing unabated says a great deal about the culture in which we live. It also attests to the fact that either there are no simple strategies for making good impressions, or impression management is far too complicated to be explained by popularized self-improvement books. Both of these appear to be not only logical observations, but empirical facts.

In this chapter, self-presentation and impression management are examined as normal behavioral phenomena. The nature of impression management is discussed, with special attention given to the need for social approval. Factors affecting self-presentation are then examined in relation to the effects of other persons as well as social context. Since not all self-presentation is impression management, the final section addresses self-disclosure as a mode of interaction which can improve the quality of interpersonal relationships.

The Nature of Impression Management

Many social observers have commented that Americans seem to have an obsession with "keeping up appearances" and maintaining favorable "public images." Indeed, a frequent observation is that we place more value on appearances and outward images than on reality and personal authenticity. With all that has been written in recent years concerning discrepancies between public appearance and private experience, it would seem that a preoccupation with social acceptability is endemic to twentieth-century America. The fact is that human beings have attempted to create images of themselves in the minds of others for as long as civilization itself, and they have done so for numerous reasons, not the least of which is the need for social approval or acceptance. A whole range of phenomena associated with what we now call "impression management" has been discussed and written about for centuries by poets, philosophers, novelists, politicians, and even religious leaders. The interpersonal behaviors subsumed under the term impression management have long been favorite themes of literature. However, samples from the works of famous writers reveal that, historically, impression management has been discussed in rather unflattering ways. From the early works of the Greek fabulist Aesop, for example, numerous admonitions are given that "appearances are deceptive" (*The Wolf in Sheep's Clothing*):

> The Lamb that belonged to the Sheep, whose skin the Wolf was wearing, began to follow the Wolf in the Sheep's clothing.

Appearances can, indeed, be deceptive, and a great many literary masterpieces seize upon this fact in the development of their themes. Shakespeare's works are rife with this theme, but in *Measure for Measure*, he expressed the view that people project images that best serve their own personal interests:

> It oft falls out,
> To have what we would have, we speak
> not what we mean.

The French writer, Francois Duc de La Rochefoucauld, expressed similar views throughout *Maximes* (1665), with the biting conviction that self-interest is the basis for human social behavior in general:

> To succeed in the world, we do everything we can to appear successful.

Charles Dickens, the English novelist, contended that individuals are naive if they believe that others will not try to deceive them when there is something to be gained by the actor. He held the opinion that self-serving motives are often concealed behind a pretense of sincerity (*Little Dorrit*):

> I have known a vast quantity of nonsense talked about bad men not looking you in the face. Don't trust that conventional idea. Dishonesty will stare honesty out of countenance, any day of the week, if there is anything to be got by it.

However, the French novelist, Marcel Proust, recognized that, although self-interest may influence our attempts to deceive others through impression management, we are not necessarily malicious, calculating, or even conscious of our behavior (*Remembrance of Things Past*):

> Untruthfulness and dishonesty were with me, as with most people, called into being in so immediate, so contingent a fashion, and in self-defense, by some particular interest, that my mind, fixed on some lofty ideal, allowed my character, in the darkness below, to set about those urgent, sordid tasks, and did not look down to observe them.

Niccolo Machiavelli is one person whose name has become synonymous with interpersonal manipulation and calculated deceit. This sixteenth-century political philosopher outlined a blueprint for political exploitation in his literary masterpiece, *The Prince*. The term *Machiavellianism* is a well-known label for an approach to human behavior guided by the belief that personal gain justifies any means for obtaining it: the ends justify the means—including deception (*The Prince*):

> The prince must be a lion, but he must also know how to play the fox.

Self-interest and personal gain are not the only motives cited by early writers. For example, the Dutch philosopher, Spinoza, recognized the necessity of consistent self-presentation and impression management when one is dependent on the approval of others (*Ethics*):

> He whose honor depends on the opinion of the mob must day by day strive with the greatest anxiety, act and scheme in order to retain his reputation.

And, Jean Paul Sartre, the French philosopher, revealed a basis for impression management which is relatively independent of self-interest and the need for approval (*The Words*):

> I was escaping from Nature and at last becoming myself, that Other whom I was aspiring to be in the eyes of others.

Finally, some writers have simply acknowledged the necessity of impression management in general, without discussing the relative goodness or badness of such behavior. Ralph Waldo Emerson, for example, stated that (*Conduct of Life. Behavior*):

> Your manners are always under examination, and by committees little suspected— a police in citizen's clothes—but are awarding or denying you very high prizes when you least think of it.

Perhaps Mark Twain put it more simply than anyone before him (*Following the Equator*):

> Everybody is a moon, and has a dark side which he never shows to anybody.

From this sampling of literature, it would appear that impression management is a deceptive practice. Certainly, many of the world's most prominent wordsmiths have reinforced this impression. They have made human beings seem like actors on a stage: changing our lines and our faces to fit the roles we play, never quite able to resist our cues for the correct performance at the right moment for the right person. In spite of the grains of truth that may lie in many disapproving literary portrayals of human behavior, most of us would be hard pressed to welcome such views as representing all persons in their totalities. Surely, some persons are consistently deceptive and calculating, and all of us manipulate our images to suit our own purposes on occasion. But, as the famous German poet and novelist, Goethe (*Elective Affinities*, 1802), said, "One is never satisfied with a portrait of a person that one knows." Thus, it is difficult for us to be content with an unflattering portrait of ourselves as cunning masters of misrepresentation; most of us know ourselves to be different.

Impression management continues to be a favorite theme of novels, plays, and movies. It has also become a topic of considerable interest to psychologists, who are in general agreement that impression management is necessary for effective social interaction. Impression management skills enable us to be flexible and adaptive, to adjust quickly and efficiently to the diversity of roles required of us in modern society (Snyder, 1977). Impression management skills represent a repertoire of self-presentation options, from which we may select a mode or style of interaction most appropriate for the circumstances in which we find ourselves. It is frequently necessary that we project an image of ourselves that is not misinterpreted by others, and to accomplish this, we must be adept at impression management. Imagine yourself on trial for a crime you did not commit, or imagine being accused by your supervisor of doing something you did not do. In both cases, it would be imperative that you effectively present a true and honest image of yourself. Without the necessary skills, your innocence could easily be misperceived. In everyday interactions, we often find it necessary to put our "best foot forward," show our "best profile," and make the best impression we can. When meeting new people, we often try to be on our "best behavior"; when interviewing for a job, we try to appear alert, sharp, knowledgeable, personable, and we often tailor our images to meet the expectations of the interviewer. When working with patients and clients, we try to appear confident, competent, and self-assured, even when we're not. As health professionals, we recognize our obligations to our clients, and because of this, we must often subordinate our own feelings and present ourselves in ways which assure and promote their welfare.

The literary excerpts cited above are examples of countless similar personal or philosophical points of view concerning the relative goodness or badness of impression management phenomena. However, in and of itself, impression management is neither good nor bad. It is human behavior, the practice of which is the same, regardless of the reasons for its use. People may employ the same strategies to convey an honest image or a deceptive image; they may do so for altruistic reasons, for social approval and acceptance, for material gain, professional advancement, personal growth, or to avoid something unpleasant. Whether we approve or disapprove of one's motives for impression management does not alter the fact that its occurrence is most assuredly an integral part of daily human interactions.

The Necessity of Impression Management

Sociologists and psychologists alike have maintained that impression management is necessary for effective interpersonal functioning. From the sociological tradition of what is know as *symbolic interactionism*, C. H. Cooley (1922) argued that individuals develop a notion of self on the basis of the appraisal of others. We use those appraisals much as we would use a mirror to see what we are like. This concept of the *looking-glass self* was elaborated by G. H. Mead (1934), who suggested that individuals develop an awareness of self by taking the perspective of others—by trying to see themselves as others see them. From back-and-forth interactions with others, individuals develop an awareness of self which not only enables them to know how they are coming across, but which also allows them to adjust and direct their behavior to have desired effects on others. For example, by taking the role of the other, a pharmaceutical salesman can select the right suit and tie and the right selling technique and style of presentation to please family practitioners in a rural community, and then change each of these to win the favor of cosmetic surgeons in metropolitan areas. Similarly, by considering the perspectives of each medical patient, The RN can alter her style of communication so as to facilitate meaningful interactions with geriatric patients or children.

The sociologist, Erving Goffman, made impression management the foundation of his theory of the *Presentation of Self in Everyday Life* (1959). Goffman described our interactions as performances in which we are like actors in theatrical productions, presenting ourselves in roles that are consistent with one another and which keep the play moving. Accordingly, we must determine how others are interpreting our lines, and we must find correct interpretations of their lines. We are constantly checking our behavior against contextual cues and adjusting it as needed. Changing situations require that we shift roles, change our lines, and present ourselves in ways which fit the circumstances. For example, an individual can shift from a role as generous friend to fierce competitor when the cards are laid on the table in a poker game; or the disinterested student may wax poetic about the enchantment of psychology when confronted by his professor about his excessive absences from class.

According to Goffman, individuals try to control the impressions they present to others when they interact. They also have numerous motives for doing so. One particularly strong motive is the desire for *social approval*: people frequently project images of themselves of which they hope others will approve. When a person is successful in securing approval of his image, he is said to be "in face," and when his image fails to be approved, he is "out of face." Goffman contended that one of the implicit rules of social interaction is for each participant to work to keep each other participant "in face." To this end, each person uses various face-saving devices to manage his own impression for the benefit of the other. For example, it is common for patients to experience a blow to their sense of dignity when their illnesses cause them to lose control of eliminative functions. They cannot present themselves to others as they would like and, therefore, feel considerable embarrassment. To help them save face, medical staff typically try to appear unaffected. Health professionals have a repertoire of impression management tactics that permit patients to save face, they are aware that patients fear the reactions of others, they have a desire to help the patients keep face, and they are willing to use those tactics to serve such purposes. Goffman would maintain that this is also done to prevent any interference with the conduct of the interpersonal relationship. Often, people will help others apologize for blunders they commit just to help them save face and keep the relationship going smoothly. Perhaps you have done this in a restaurant after a waitress spilled water in your lap. And, there have probably been many instances in your life when you relied on the phrases "don't worry about it," "that's all right," or "forget it, no harm done," in attempts to help others save face by trying to convince them that you are not thinking what they think you are thinking!

The viewpoints of Goffman, Mead, and Cooley all share the common assumption that people are always forming impressions of one another and using those impressions as guides for interactions. This being the case, it would certainly seem to be to our advantage to try to understand how others perceive us and to present images that are acceptable to us and which foster the enhancement of our relationships. It would also seem that impression management is a *natural consequence of the fact that others do form impressions of us and act on the basis of those impressions.*

Sociological perspectives may have pointed up the necessity of impression management in everyday social relationships, but they do not offer insights at the level of individuals. That is, a psychological perspective must be taken if we are to identify specific factors which determine the particular image a person will present in given situations. An examination of psychological theory and research can provide some tentative answers to important questions about impression management processes.

Securing the Approval of Others

Poets, novelists, sociologists, and psychologists have all recognized that there is at least one clear benefit received by individuals as a consequence of controlling the way they come across to others: *social approval.* By acting one way instead of another, by choosing one mode of self-presentation over the next, individuals frequently try to maximize their chances of receiving the approval and acceptance of others. But, what is this need for approval? Where does it come from? And, why do people seek it out?

Approval as Positive Reinforcement

If there is any one finding which is consistently supported in psychological research, it is that our behavior is often under the control of its consequences. That is, whenever we do something, our actions are followed by some set of consequences. In most cases, these consequences do not occur unless we behave in specific ways. For instance, you don't obtain a job if you don't get out and look for one (although some people seem to believe that consequences occur randomly and that employers will beat a path to their doors just for the privilege of having them in their employ). Thus, the consequences of our behavior—which usually occur in the form of rewards and punishments—are *contingent* upon specific actions on our parts. A contingency here refers to an "if-then" relationship between our behavior and its consequences, such that "if" we behave in a particular way, "then" specific consequences will follow. To get a Coke (rewarding consequence) out of a machine, you must put the exact change required into the slot (specific response). Most of the time, when you make all the correct responses, you will receive your Coke—"most of the time." As we all know, machines sometimes steal our money without paying off. Yet, this knowledge doesn't prevent us from continuing to make similar responses and putting more money into other machines. That is because we develop expectations based on *probabilities*: we learn that certain consequences do not *always* follow certain behaviors, but they have a high probability of occurring.

In effect, our behavior "operates" on the environment to produce some sort of change in the environment. *If* our behavior causes the environment to change, *then* the environmental change can be said to be *contingent* upon our behavior (i.e., the change occurs *only* when the behavior is emitted). For instance, getting certain specific answers from people is contingent upon asking the right questions, and effecting positive changes in a person's physical health is contingent upon many things, not the least of which include accurate diagnosis and application of the proper medical treatments. Now, in the same way, *getting the approval of other people is contingent upon making the right responses*. People manage their impressions in accordance with the contingencies of a situation. The greater one's awareness of those contingencies, the greater the probability that he will act appropriately and, thus, receive the approval he is seeking.

The mere fact that people seek approval suggests that approval functions as a positive consequence for behavior. This positive consequence, or reward, is commonly referred to by psychologists as *positive reinforcement*. Positive reinforcement is any response consequence which increases the probability of future occurrence of similar behavior. In very simple terms, it is anything pleasant or satisfying. Food, water, and sex are innately rewarding and satisfying for most persons, especially following periods of deprivation. When a person is deprived of these reinforcers for extended periods, they can become extremely powerful behavior control devices. Approval also functions as a powerful reinforcer for most people, and if a person is deprived of approval for a period of time, it, too, can become even more potent. Logic might lead you to assume that, if a person receives sufficient approval from others, she would experience little need for more approval. However, if often happens that reinforcers begin to lose their potency, and what was originally sufficient for the individual no longer functions to produce an acceptable level of satisfaction. Thus, some people become almost "addicted" to the approval of others, needing more and more to produce a level of gratification once produced by lesser amounts. If this insatiable appetite for social approval seems to you to be similar to the experience of the alcoholic or substance abuser who comes to need more and more of a chemical reinforcer, you are right. The reinforcers are different, but the processes are similar in the sense that the potency of the reinforcers must be increased or they will not function as reinforcers. A similar thing happens to all of us when inflation changes the real value of our salaries, and what might have been sufficient at one time is no longer sufficient—and often not sufficient compensation to justify the work we do. Consequently, our salaries may gradually become less and less effective in influencing our work behavior.

Disapproval as Punishment

Not only do individuals seek to gain the approval of others, they also wish to *avoid* censure and disapproval. Communications of disapproval are punishing to most persons; they hurt, cause varying degrees of emotional pain, and undermine self-esteem. Therefore, behavior also often comes under the control of potential punishing consequences, and people act in various ways simply to avoid those consequences. The principle is simple: if a cat sits on a hot stove and gets burned, he will avoid sitting on that stove again. But, there is often another consequence, which Mark Twain described so well (from *Pudd'nhead Wilson*):

> We should be careful to get out of an experience only the wisdom that is in it—and stop there; lest we be like the cat that sits down on a hot stove-lid. She will never sit down on a hot stove-lid again—and that is well; but *also she will never sit down on a cold one anymore* [italics added].

As applied to social approval and disapproval, individuals may become overly sensitive to possible rejection and disapproval and avoid interactions where they expect to be censured. We certainly need to be sensitive to such possibilities, but sometimes we can get carried away with our fear of punishment. For example, in health care settings, it is not uncommon for nurses to have had an unpleasant interchange with a physician. As a result, they may refrain from approaching the physician in the future because they fear unpleasant consequences. But, by avoiding the physician successfully over a period of time the avoidance tendency grows stronger, and the possibility of reconciliation decreases. In effect, we prevent the occurrence of something unpleasant by avoiding it. If we are successful in avoiding it, we are *negatively reinforced*. Negative reinforcement refers to any satisfying responses consequence which occurs when aversive consequences are prevented or removed. The effect of negatively reinforcing consequences is the same as the effect of positive reinforcement; they both increase the likelihood that the person will act in similar ways under similar conditions in the future.

The distinction between "punishment" and "negative reinforcement" is important. Punishment refers to the *presentation of something unpleasant* or the *removal of something pleasant* to us. Traffic tickets, insults, and physical assaults are punishing because they involve the presentation of unpleasant consequences. The revocation of one's driver's license or the "silent treatment" from our friends are punishing because they involve the removal of pleasant consequences. The effects of punishment are generally to *decrease* the likelihood of behaving in *unacceptable ways*. Thus, people often show their disapproval in order to influence others to stop acting in certain ways. Now, negative reinforcement involves the *prevention* or *removal* of something *unpleasant*. For example, people pay their bills in order to avoid the aversive consequences of nonpayment (they do not pay their bills because it is a fun thing to do); women and men use contraceptive devices to avoid undesired consequences, not because those devices are inherently satisfying; and, many persons avoid parties and other social gatherings because they do not feel comfortable in those situations—they can prevent great discomfort simply by not attending the events. Similarly, an individual is negatively reinforced for her behavior when she leaves an unpleasant situation, because she has removed herself from an aversive experience. Unlike punishment, the effects of negative reinforcement are to *increase* the likelihood of behaving in *acceptable* ways. In this connection, we may often receive the communication from others that we can maintain their approval so long as we avoid doing certain things and perhaps even "keeping out mouths shut." In short, we may recognize approval is contingent upon keeping quiet, and disapproval is contingent upon saying the wrong things. As a result, we may manage our impressions by responding to the contingencies of the situation.

From our discussion to this point, it should be clear that approval functions as a behavioral consequence with strong positively reinforcing effects. When individuals manage their impressions to gain the approval of others, they are, in effect, seeking to obtain the positive reinforcements that others hold. When others reinforce our self-presentations with approval, our self-esteem is enhanced, and we become more inclined to seek out those reinforcements in the future by presenting ourselves in ways which increase that probability. At the same time, we wish to avoid social censure and disapproval because those consequences are punishing to us; they often cause a lowering of our self-esteem. So, we also manage our impressions in ways which help us to avoid the unpleasant consequences of social deprecation and disfavor.

Development of the Need for Approval

People learn at an early age to seek the approval of others. By direct implication, they also learn at an early age to manage their impressions. In our culture, children are at first influenced almost entirely by their parents, upon whom they are dependent for their very survival. Parents, then, are the principal dispensers of reinforcements to the child. At first, these reinforcers come in the form of life-sustaining nourishment. But, soon the child learns that parents are also the sources of affection, and they can give or withhold affection as they please. As the child's cognitive abilities mature, she comes to learn that her parents' affection is often contingent upon her behavior—when she is good, her parents approve, but when she is bad, her parents withhold their approval and affection. When the child learns the relationships between her behavior and her parents' affection, she learns that securing her parents' approval is a key that unlocks many doors; "please" and "thank-you" go a long way toward opening those doors to new rewards. The child also begins to develop an intuitive sense of how to present herself to her parents. As other adults become more prominent in her life space, she learns that they, too, are holders of approval and affection, and some of her behavior comes under the control of the reinforcements they promise to dispense.

As time passes, the peer group becomes a significant source of social influence, although it does not entirely supplant the influence of parents and other adults. The transition from parental influence to predominant influences of peers is a gradual process occurring over a period of many years. Over the course of normal development, what was once a form of infantile dependency (on the parents) changes into an approval-seeking motive, manifested through various forms of attention and approval-seeking behavior, including impression management. As interaction and affiliation with others becomes more valued, the possibility of social acceptance becomes increasingly important as a reinforcer, and the threat of rejection becomes increasingly feared. The individual learns to be increasingly sensitive to the approval of others, and she gradually incorporates standards for approval as her own. These standards are then used as forms of internal control—she can approve or disapprove of her own behavior. It is at this point that problems are especially likely to develop for the individual if those standards are accepted and internalized without question. In Rogers's (1951) words, the person may unquestioningly incorporate the *conditions of worth* of others (see Chapter 3) and gauge her own self-worth on the basis of those conditions. The major problem is that the individual may be so concerned with the approval of others that she is no longer true to who she really is. Impression management becomes more than an adaptive interpersonal strategy—*it becomes a way of life*. The challenge to most persons is to balance personal genuineness with impression management as needed. This can be accomplished partly through appropriate self-disclosure, a topic to be reexamined shortly.

Impression Management and Social Desirability: Do Some People Need More Approval than Others?

By internalizing social standards for acceptable behavior, the individual acquires a useful means for controlling his own behavior. There is usually an experience of personal satisfaction for most persons when they adhere to those standards, because they have incorporated measures by which they can appraise their actions and reinforce themselves accordingly. However, for some persons the reinforcement—self-approval or approval from others—becomes an end in itself: instead of experiencing personal satisfaction as a *by-product* of acceptable performance of some behavior, *approval becomes the goal, the whole purpose of an endeavor*. For those persons, what was once a form of nurturance-seeking dependency in infancy evolves into an *adult version of dependency* in the form of unrelenting generalized approval-seeking. Rather than managing impressions to secure approval where appropriate, there is a pervasive effort to gain universal acceptance "across the board." The means for obtaining this unobtainable goal include continual, persistent, unremitting impression management based on the deeply ingrained sense that one must "measure up" and "never let down." Of course, the approval motive does not ascend to a position of ultimate priority in the lives of most persons. But, for some individuals, the need for approval is so formidable as to permeate their very existence.

Crowne and Marlowe (1964) developed an instrument for the purpose of identifying the tendency of people to present themselves in socially desirable ways on personality tests. This instrument, the Marlowe-Crowne Social Desirability Scale, is a test in which high scores reflect strong needs for social approval. Individuals high in the need for social approval tend to endorse such items as "I am always courteous to people who are disagreeable," "I have never intensely disliked anyone," and other statements reflecting characteristics commonly assumed to be socially desirable. It is assumed that individuals who endorse such statements do so because they wish to present themselves in the best way they can. Underlying this mode of self-presentation is a craving for approval. Crowne and Marlowe (1964) provided evidence through their research that individuals high in the need for approval do tend to make socially desirable responses across a wide range of situations. Furthermore, such persons tend to be more socially conforming than persons with low approval needs, and they display less overt hostility toward those who have insulted or exploited them. Crowne and Marlowe also noted that these individuals are often described by their peers as loners who don't try to make friends, socialize, or act friendly when they do encounter others. It is possible that such persons either misperceive and misinterpret their own behavior or are simply more aware of themselves around persons who have the type of approval they need.

Dimensions of Self-Presentation

How would you present yourself to a person who is arrogant, boisterous, and opinionated? Would you act the same if you encountered a mild-mannered, timid, and self-conscious person? You would most likely present yourself in different ways to each of these persons. You might act rather guarded with the arrogant person and more open with the shy person, and you might be more honest, consistent, and humble as well. The fact that you can adapt your mode of self-presentation in accordance with the personalities of other individuals suggest that their behavior plays an important part of how you manage your impressions. It also suggests that there are various dimensions along which you can vary your own behavior. And, the nature of the interaction context will further influence your choices of self-presentation strategies along dimensions such as positiveness and negativeness, openness and defensiveness, genuineness and pretense, consistency and inconsistency.

The Influence of Other People

Gergen and Wishnov (1965) simulated a situation which permitted investigation of questions similar to those above. One group of subjects was paired with persons who acted egotistical and boastful. After a simulated task, these subjects were asked to describe their own personalities. Their descriptions were compared with self-descriptions provided one month earlier, before they were paired with others. Gergen and Wishnov found that the subjects described themselves more positively than they had in their earlier descriptions. However, a second group of subjects who had been paired with humble and modest persons tended to discount their own positive qualities, while emphasizing their deficiencies. It appeared that subjects in both conditions presented self-images similar to those displayed by their partners. It may have been that the ambiguity of the experimental situation made it difficult for subjects to decide how to act. Being unsure of how they should present themselves, subjects relied on their partners for cues for self-presentation. As a result, they presented themselves positively or negatively, depending on what their partners implied was appropriate.

Awareness of others' attitudes also influences the way we present ourselves. For example, imagine that you are an authority on the subject of socialized medicine and you have been asked to present your views to a group of health professionals who are in favor of socialized medicine and then to a group which is opposed to it. Being the objective professional that you are, you understand both sides and take a moderate stance. Is it possible that you will present your views differently to each audience? It is not only "possible," it is "probable" that you will tailor your presentation according to the attitudes of the respective groups. A study by Newtson and Czerlinsky (1974) revealed that, even when students were told to present their own views accurately, they still presented themselves as being more similar to each audience than they actually were when expressing views on the Vietnam War issue before a group of "hawks" and a group of "doves." Snyder (1977) suggested that perhaps the students were trying to win the approval of their audiences by *exaggerating their similarities*. This is a plausible hypothesis, especially when one considers the great vulnerability to extreme disapproval which individuals experience when standing before a potentially hostile audience. It would therefore seem that individuals might exaggerate their similarities to others, not only to gain their approval, but also to *avoid* public censure. In this same connection, it is worthwhile to note the findings of Hovland, Harvey, and Sherif (1957) that, if a communication differs greatly from one's own position, it is thus outside of one's "latitude of acceptance," and one will not be very much influenced by it. This would suggest that if an individual even has an intuitive sense that he will make no impact on another person by expressing his personal views, he may avoid such communications altogether. The realization that we may be speaking upon "deaf ears" often causes us to change our mode of self-presentation and, indeed, occasionally causes us to withdraw from the interaction entirely.

Whereas there are situations in which we choose a self-presentation style that maximizes similarity with others, there are also situations in which we elect to maximize our *differences*. Cooper and Jones (1969) found that subjects changed their stated attitudes whenever an "obnoxious" interaction partner communicated views similar to the subjects' original attitudes. It seems that there are occasions where we will go to great lengths to put interpersonal distance between ourselves and others by emphasizing the differences between us. When we do not perceive similarity to be particularly desirable or advantageous, we will use impression management to establish social distance (Snyder, 1977). Perhaps you have had an experience in your life when a person you did not really like told you, "You and I are just alike," "We're cut out of the same mold," or "You're no different from me." You probably tried very hard to get out of that trap, and you probably emphasized your differences!

The Influence of Social Context

The social context also influences the image a person presents to others. You will recall from Chapter Two that "social context" implies the presence of other people, and when a group of people is present in an interpersonal situation, it exerts varying degrees of influence on the ways in which each individual acts. Common sense would tell us that we present ourselves differently to our friends than to a group of strangers or new acquaintances. Any number of variables can account for the types of influence different people exert on our style of self-presentation—familiarity, intimacy, status, similarity, attractiveness, power, reputation, to name but a few. However, common sense often falls short of telling us about the nature of social influence and the *manner* in which others come to have an effect on our self-presentations.

Informational Social Influence

Several years ago, Deutsch and Gerard (1955) offered a useful distinction between *normative social influence* and *informational social influence*. The former was described as a form of social influence exerted by a group on an individual when the person wishes to be in agreement with others and not violate their expectations of her. In response to this type of influence, individuals manage their behavior in order to receive approval from the group. They present themselves in accordance with expectations. The latter form of social influence, however, occurs when there is some informational value to the individual. That is, the behavior of the individual is influenced by the group to the extent that the group offers useful information about what is most appropriate under the circumstances. Essentially, the individual uses the group's influence as a source of guidance. It is alleged, for example, that in Turkey it is considered proper for guests to belch after a meal prepared by their hosts. But, let us suppose that you didn't know this. Let us also suppose that you had been invited to dinner at the home of a Turk whom you had met through your American friends who were living in Turkey and whom you had been visiting while touring the Mediterranean. If, after the meal, your friends began belching, you might be somewhat astonished, but, chances are, you would belch too. You would probably pick up additional cues and catch on that "etiquette" dictates that belching is expected. If you did not belch, your host might easily form the impression that you are unappreciative or even rude. Thus, you use the information others provide to project the right image.

Informational social influence has a direct bearing on impression management when individuals are not sure of what to do or how to act. It follows, then, that anything which increases the ambiguity of a situation would increase the informational influence of a group. As situations become more and more unclear to individuals, they become more and more inclined to look to others for guidance. Informational social influence also increases as the size of the group increases and as the amount of agreement among persons in the group increases. Furthermore, if an individual perceives members of a group to be competent, then the informational influence of the majority increases. With these factors in mind, let us now suppose that you are in a staff meeting where the topic of discussion centers on the results of a psychological evaluation of a patient, Mr. Jones. Let us also assume that you know a little about psychological testing, but not as much as you should know, given your clinical position. The senior psychologist holds up Mr. Jones's personality profile for everyone to see. The test data seem to be plotted out nicely on a profile scale which you don't understand. When the senior psychologist asks for the group's impressions of the test profile, other staff psychologists and colleagues begin stating their opinions about what the data reveal. You know that they know what they're talking about when they give their opinions and that they're not just making impressive talk. After noting that everyone seems to be in agreement on their interpretations of the profile, the senior psychologist recognizes that you have not had an opportunity to express your opinions. The probability is extremely high that you will state opinions that are consistent with those expressed by the rest of the group. It is not necessarily because you are seeking their approval or avoiding their disapproval that you agree—it is because the situation is ambiguous (you are unfamiliar with the test) and because there is a consensus among a group of competent professionals who know about what they are talking. Not being sure of how to present your opinions, you simply follow their lead.

Normative Social Influence

It would probably be incorrect to assume that your behavior in the preceding case is solely a function of informational social influence. When the senior psychologist asked for your impressions, he turned the spotlight on you and set the stage for you to express yourself *publicly*. Under such circumstances, normative social influence plays a role in how you present yourself. For instance, you may communicate agreement with the rest of the group in order to avoid the embarrassment of being deviant. You may feel that, by disagreeing with the group, you would call unnecessary attention to yourself and expose yourself to criticism. It seems that normative social influence is enhanced to the extent that publicity is given to a person's behavior. When our identities are made public, we experience more pressure to present ourselves according to expectations. In addition, normative social influence is increased to the extent that a person feels insecure about her status in a group. So, if you felt less competent than your colleagues, your stated impressions would come under normative influence. To carry the possibilities further, if you are attracted to the group and value your membership a great deal, you would probably have a strong fear of disapproval and rejection, and, therefore, present your views as being compatible with everyone else's. Finally, let us assume that in addition to being unsure of the meaning of Mr. Jones's personality profile, you have no investment in any clinical interpretation at all. Not only are you unable to interpret the profile, you don't care. If you lack a commitment to any clinical impression, normative social influence becomes stronger. There is simply nothing to gain and much to lose by deviating from the group's consensus. Conversely, if you were able to develop a firm clinical conviction based on reliable interpretation skills, you may very well stand your ground and risk deviating from the opinions of others.

In summary, when the situation is ambiguous, other people become an important source of information on how to behave. When the individual seeks to be in agreement with a group, secure its approval, and avoid rejection, he will tend to present himself in line with social expectations.

Reference-Group Identification

One of the most powerful contextual influences on self-presentation is the particular social group with which the individual identifies. Such groups are called *reference groups*: any group to which the individual refers for guidance concerning attitudes, values, and behavior. Reference groups provide individuals with a frame of reference, a way of looking at the world and other people. They also provide people with whom individuals can identify and to whom they can relate. Interestingly, we need not actually be a member of a particular group in order to identify with it. Conversely, although we may be actual members of a specific group, we may not identify with it. In the latter case, the group is called a *membership group* because, without psychological identification with the group, we belong only in name or body. As persons with only nominal associations with a group, we do not necessarily become genuine psychological participants in the system. A group is truly a reference group for an individual when there is an identification with the group's purpose and values and an adherence to its regulative norms. For example, although an aspiring young athlete may not be on the player's roster of the San Diego Chargers football team, he may nevertheless identify with the team, and his style of self-presentation may reflect his efforts to emulate his heroes. "Weekend bikers" may identify with Hell's Angels and every Saturday trade their corduroys and loafers for denim jackets, swastikas, engineer's boots, and steel-studded gauntlets. In the area of inpatient psychiatric treatment, by the way, it sometimes happens that a patient perceives staff professionals as a reference group, identifies with the treatment staff, and effectively blocks out the recognition of his true status. This also happens occasionally in medical treatment, especially when health professionals become the patients!

Psychological identification with a particular group can have profound effects on the ways in which some people present themselves to others. This was vividly demonstrated in the sensationalized kidnapping case of Patricia Hearst in 1974. In February of that year, a radical group called the Symbionese Liberation Army (SLA) kidnapped the 19-year-old granddaughter of William Randolph Hearst, magnate of a vast newspaper and magazine empire. As ransom, the SLA demanded that the Hearst family give away several million dollars' worth of food. At the time she was to be released, Patty publicly denounced her family, disowned her former life-style, and proclaimed that she had joined the SLA. Two weeks later, Patty and the SLA robbed a bank, with Patty standing in full view of the bank's security cameras to ensure that her identity would be clear. When she was finally captured after 20 months, Patty listed her occupation as "urban guerrilla" and gave her name as Tania. While she was in jail, Tania, the urban guerrilla, gradually began to transform back into Patty, the "newspaper heiress." At her first court appearance, Patty was again the sweet young woman described by the media at the time of her kidnapping.

The case of Patty Hearst led to considerable public speculation concerning what had happened to her. For a period of time, there was also renewed interest among psychologists in processes of conformity, obedience, attitude change, and numerous phenomena related to "brainwashing." But, Patty also underwent significant changes in her manner of self-presentation. Having identified with the purported "cause" of the SLA, she acquired a reference group which exerted a tremendous impact on her behavior in general. She "tried on" a totally different value system and style of behavior, only to discard that value system for her "old self" when she determined after her capture that it didn't quite fit. Apparently, Patty had identified with the SLA and temporarily adopted their radical ideology. At the same time, however, she had not entirely replaced her old beliefs; she had initiated changes in herself through identification with the group, but she had apparently not *internalized* those values with unchanging conviction.

The behavior of Patty Hearst is only an extreme example of the kinds of behavioral changes many people undergo as they adopt and discard different values and move into and out of identification with different reference groups during their lives. It is not at all uncommon for people to adopt styles of dress, mannerisms, and speech patterns characteristic of one group and then exchange these for still newer sets when they are no longer consistent with their self-images. The process of "trying on" and "taking off" different ways of living is a natural part of human growth and development. As people struggle to establish their identities, it is commonplace for them to experiment with assorted value systems and modes of conduct—especially during the college years when identification with traditional values is challenged by novel ideas from diverse sources in the academic environment. However, as Hilgard, Atkinson, and Atkinson (1979) pointed out, the process really never ends for those who remain open to new experiences.

When Appearance Creates Reality

With all of the shifting around that individuals do in their self-presentations, it might seem that they would occasionally become confused as to their true identities. As Nathaniel Hawthorne wrote in *The Scarlet Letter*:

> No man, for any considerable period, can wear one face to himself, and another to the multitude, without finally getting bewildered as to which may be the true.

One particularly notable effect of shifting our public appearances is that we sometimes come to believe our own performances: we may become the persons we appear to be (Snyder, 1977). For example, Jones, Gergen, and Davis (1962) instructed subjects to win the approval of an interviewer by presenting complimentary images of themselves. One-half of the subjects then received favorable responses from interviewers, while the other half did not. Subjects were later asked to indicate how accurately they portrayed themselves to the interviewers. Those subjects who gained the approval of the interviewers contended that their self-presentations were honest, while those who did not win the approval of the interviewers claimed that their self-presentations were less honest. As Gergen (1968) suggested, subjects in the interview conditions apparently had self-concepts which were rather pragmatic: self-presentations which produced the most positive outcomes were taken to be accurate reflections of their real selves. Snyder (1977) observed that impression management can sometimes blur the distinction between public appearance and private reality. A factor which influences the extent to which we believe our own performances is the behavior of other people. If they take our self-presentations at face value, they may relate to us as if we really are what we purport to be. For example, if you try to appear glamorous for people and receive frequent feedback from others about your attractiveness, you may come to see yourself as being quite appealing, even though your grooming was originally stimulated by an unsatisfactory body image. Or, if you act as if you like a new supervisor, chances are good that she will like you and act friendly toward you. Because of her friendliness, you may very well develop a true liking for her, even though you disliked her in the first place.

Psychologist have a name for certain instances where our performances do not reflect our real feelings: *reaction formation*. This psychoanalytic concept refers to the manifestation of behavior which is the *opposite* of what the person actually feels. When reaction formation underlies overt behavior, the behavior often has a forced character, appearing rather strained. Observers are thus frequently alerted to the fact that the actor is expending extra energy to keep up a "front." Thus, a supervisor may become rather suspicious of the subordinate who communicates a fawning subservience and continually defers his own judgements to her "wisdom and expertise," while insisting that "you're the boss, you know what's best." The irony is that the observer may not "buy the performance," but the actor actually believes it is real! In such cases, it is simply too threatening for the individual to acknowledge his true feelings; he feels guilty or ashamed about having those feelings, so he covers them up by acting in a totally contrary fashion. Then, by observing his own behavior, he comes to believe in his own act. It is tempting to offer a medical example, where persons sometimes try to appear as if they are sick and then come to believe that they *really are* sick, even when they have *not* convinced others.

The Ingratiation Process

The pervasive desire to make a good impression has continued to be an overriding reason for the popularity of one of the best-selling books of all time, *How to Win Friends and Influence People*, first published by Dale Carnegie in 1936. This book, which still sells at the rate of more than 250,000 copies each year, has been viewed by many social scientists as a twentieth-century version of Machiavellian strategies for interpersonal manipulation. Manipulation or not, Carnegie's advice comes in the form of deceptively simple formulae for how to win the acceptance of others—and this seems to be precisely for what people have been looking. His recommendations are straightforward: become genuinely interested in other people, smile, remember their names, encourage others to talk about themselves, sincerely try to make them feel important, and talk about things which interest them. Due to the simplicity of this advice, it is easy to make light of Carnegie's approach. Yet, the advice is nonetheless reasonable and practical. The Carnegie approach is based on a sweeping *reward-cost theory* of human behavior: we like people who provide us with rewards at a minimum of cost to us. So, to win friends and influence people, Carnegie suggests that we use our own behavior to provide others with rewards. Unfortunately, underlying this reward-cost notion are misconceptions about what is *universally* rewarding to people. Praise and favors, for example, are seen as uniformly rewarding to people. The fact is that praise and favors do not always function as rewards. Interpersonal situations are usually of sufficient complexity to render a general reward-cost theory inadequate for predicting the behavior of others. Unless our definition of what constitutes a reward in a given situation is clear and specific, we could end up behaving in ways which are actually offensive to others.

Essentially, the Carnegie prescriptions involve *ingratiation* tactics. Jones (1964, p. 11) defined ingratiation as *"a class of strategic behavior illicitly designed to influence particular other persons concerning the attractiveness of one's personal qualities."* Thus, the method of self-presentation proposed by Carnegie is one in which a person consciously uses specific tactics to increase others' liking for him. Jones (1964; Jones and Wortman, 1973) conducted in-depth analyses of the ingratiation process and suggested that there are various sets of ingratiation tactics frequently used by individuals.

Positive Self-Presentation

One of the most obvious ways in which a person can ingratiate himself is to present a favorable image. You will recall that this is what subjects were instructed to do in the Jones, Gergen, and Davis (1962) study cited earlier: they presented themselves to interviewers in very flattering ways. These tactics are often used by individuals when they seek particular reinforcements from others. By presenting oneself as a paragon of virtue, for example, an individual may increase her chances of receiving approval (Schneider, 1976). While virtuosity may be a desirable image to project, it is not the only characteristic we can use to enhance our public images. Circumstances would largely determine which traits we wish to project and which ones to conceal. Circumstances also tell us that it is sometimes wiser to be *modest* instead of self-enhancing. For example, the study by Gergen and Wishnov (1965), which was described earlier, revealed that individuals paired with humble and modest partners tended to downplay their positive qualities while emphasizing their shortcomings. It appears that the behavior of others, as well as the relative clarity of the interpersonal situation, provides cues for guiding our self-presentations. Without the ability to integrate this kind of information, self-enhancing presentations may come across as vain and egotistical. The successful ingratiator is one who is *appropriately* self-enhancing.

A more subtle self-enhancing strategy involves *name-dropping*. When individuals seek to have others form favorable impressions, they may "casually" or blatantly mention the name of a significant other person. This often represents an attempt by the ingratiator to imply some kind of relationship with the significant other. And, some people carry this a step further by implying that the relationship is on a "first-name basis." For example, instead of trying to impress upon a new staff member that you happen to be on speaking terms with the chief of staff, you would be implying a more intimate relationship if you stated, "I was talking with Jane in the hall yesterday, and. . . ." It so happens that occasionally the relationship is not quite as intimate as the ingratiator would have us believe. In this regard, I must confess a personal delight in being present when self-enhancing name droppers encounter their "intimates," whose behavior disavows the true depth of their relationship! Of course, name-dropping is not limited to persons. Ingratiators may seek to enhance their self-presentations by citing the names of places, objects, or experiences: "While crossing the channel to Martha's Vineyard on the Van Snob's yacht, we ate caviar shamelessly and toasted our friendship with champagne in crystal glasses."

Other-Enhancement

As Dale Carnegie suggested, we can win friends and influence people by "doling out praise"—by outright flattery. It would seem to make sense that we could win friends by flattering them and trying to make them feel good about themselves. But, flattery is not necessarily rewarding to people. Praise and compliments are rewarding *if* the recipient perceives them to be *sincere*, with no ulterior motives behind them. Insincere flattery is often detectable, and, when it is, it may have the *opposite effect* of what was intended by the ingratiator. As Jones (1964) put it, flattery will get you "*somewhere*," but maybe not where you want to be.

Recipients of praise may attribute ulterior motives to the praiser. For example, suppose that you have delivered an excellent presentation to the staff on cardiopulmonary resuscitation. Your supervisor praises your thoroughness and says, "Great presentation, Joe." Her reactions will undoubtedly function as rewards, and your liking for her will be strengthened. But, let's say you were not as prepared as you wanted to be, and you know that the presentation was inadequate. Your supervisor comes by and gives the exact same praise in the exact same way. Given the circumstances, it is difficult to say if the praise would function as a reward. You could conclude that the supervisor is trying to offer some support and reassurance after an obviously poor presentation, and that she is simply trying to help you save face. If this is your conclusion, you could end up liking your supervisor even more, because of her apparent thoughtfulness. On the other hand, you may interpret her remarks as sarcastic, patronizing, condescending, nondiscriminating, or even stupid. As a result, your liking for the supervisor may decrease. This latter possibility was reflected in Groucho Marx's famous quip, "I wouldn't want to belong to any club that would accept me as a member." When we perceive that others have made poor judgements of us, our liking for them often decreases.

Carnegie seemed to recognize that the ingratiator must enhance his credibility by appearing *sincere* when giving praise. *Being* sincere and *seeming* sincere are two different things, however. But, this is really not the crucial issue in praise-giving, as the bottom-line consideration is *how the recipient perceives the praise. Perceived sincerity* is apparently more important than real sincerity. Thus, to maximize his credibility, the ingratiator must be *discriminating* in his use of praise. Telling the ugliest woman of the staff that she is beautiful won't necessarily make her like you. Similarly, telling the most beautiful woman on the staff that she is beautiful won't necessarily make *her* like you. In the former instance, your praise would probably be taken by the woman as either an indication of your poor judgement or as biting sarcasm. In the latter case, the beautiful woman has probably heard such compliments many times, so that telling her something she is used to hearing may not impress her very much. In *both* cases, it would be much more effective to compliment the women on something about which they are uncertain (Jones, 1964). Clearly, one thing about which they are probably very certain is their relative beauty. Thus, to be effective, praise must be discriminating and have some degree of realism.

Doing Favors

As an ingratiation tactic, favor-doing is based on the same assumption as praise-giving: that people are reinforced by the favors others render. The same qualification therefore applies: all other things being equal, favors will serve as rewards *if* the recipient perceives them to be freely given, with no "strings attached." Favors generally do function as rewards, and we usually do like people who provide us with such rewards. However, we do not like to be manipulated either, and when we believe that there are hidden reasons for the favors we receive, we may indeed feel manipulated. Consequently, our liking for the favor-doer may decrease.

In general, most persons do not like to receive favors or gifts that cause them to feel indebted to the giver. Furthermore, most people do not like to receive favors that are inappropriate. For example, do you think that your instructor would like you more if you did her some favors or gave her a gift or two? She might, but numerous factors would determine whether your generosity is perceived to be sincere. One principal factor would be your relative standing in the class—if you're a borderline student, your instructor may look askance at your "kindness." And, your chances of gaining her approval could possibly diminish further if your indulgences were given just as she was about to record your final grade! Favors are not universal rewards, in the same sense that food is always rewarding to a starving person regardless of who gives it or when it is provided. When favors and gifts appear to be freely given and appropriate, they are much more likely to function as the ingratiator intends. Without this qualification, Carnegie's advice to win friends by doing them favors would seem risky.

Conformity

There is also a simple assumption upon which this ingratiation tactic is based: the people generally appreciate those who hold similar beliefs, attitudes, values, or interests. There is considerable evidence to be reviewed in Chapter Nine that *perceived similarity* enhances the attractiveness of others. The ingratiator can increase another's liking for him by trying to appear similar—by expressing agreement with the other's opinion, judgements, and behavior. For conformity to work as an ingratiating tactic, however, the individual must be credible and mix disagreements on unimportant issues with agreements on important matters. The proverbial "yes-man" of corporate repute may fail to win the liking of others because of the nondiscriminating use of ingratiating conformity. Often, his tactics are so obvious that they are largely ineffective. Furthermore, because he makes a habit of agreeing with others, his opinions eventually lose their potential as reinforcers: they don't effectively validate our own beliefs and give us the feeling that we are right. Finally, it is likely that people make negative inferences about someone who always agrees with everyone. Because of this, it is easier to discount their opinions in general.

The Goals of Ingratiation

The ingratiator uses various tactics designed to increase his attractiveness to a target person. Jones (1964) cited three primary motives for ingratiating behavior. *Acquisition* or *personal gain* is a motive when the person's goal is to receive favorable treatment from a target person. The "yes-man" may ingratiate himself with the boss in order to secure the boss's approval or a promotion, or a student may be ingratiating with a professor in order to "grease the skids" and increase chances for a higher grade. *Protection from harm* is a goal when the person tries to prevent the target person from exercising some form of coercive power over him. He seeks to avoid either physical or psychological harm. Thus, the yes-man may engage in fawning obedience to his boss in order to avoid being demoted or fired, or the student may do favors for a professor as an attempt to make it hard for the professor to justify giving her a low grade. *Enhancement of self-worth* is a goal when the approval of a significant other increases the ingratiator's feelings of self-esteem. Being the "right-hand man" of the boss may make the yes-man feel important, or the student who successfully engages her professor in frequent conversations may come to believe that the professor finds her to be particularly interesting. Indeed, many people try to "rub shoulders" with "important" people. It often makes them feel as if they're a "cut above the average."

Self-Disclosure

Not all self-presentation is impression management. We can and do present ourselves openly and honestly when we judge the circumstances to be right. And, when we do this, we are actually engaging in *self-disclosure*. Self-disclosure is essentially *free-information* that you give about yourself during an interaction with someone. It involves the honest revelation of something about your own personal life: your feelings, thoughts, actions, values, attitudes, and so on. Moreover, self-disclosure is an index of personal *genuineness*: the nondefensive communication of personal experience. You will recall from the discussion of the Johari Window in Chapter Three that self-disclosure increases the size of the individual's "open area." Although it is often assumed that increasing the size of this area is generally desirable, it was noted that there are circumstances which may contraindicate self-disclosure. Unfortunately, individuals often appear to be so guarded in their interactions as to suggest a pervasive belief in the overall inadvisability of self-disclosure. The need to receive approval and avoid disapproval often seems to outweigh the desire for intimacy. This section examines self-disclosure, its determinants, consequences, and value. Self-disclosure as a facilitative communication skill is examined further in Chapter Sixteen.

The Emotional Issues: Too Much or Too Little?

The issue of self-disclosure is a highly charged emotional one for most people. Most people feel there is a lot at stake concerning what to say about ourselves, how to say it, when and where to say it, and, most of all, *to whom*. There are many diverse and even multiform attitudes among the public regarding these issues. Some people believe that we're too private and keep too much to ourselves because we're afraid of getting close to others. Some carry it further and suggest that the unwillingness to reveal oneself to others is a sign of psychological disturbance, which reflects upon society itself. In this group there are those who are only too willing to undress their personalities before others as an *exhibition of inhibition*, a public show of how "well adjusted" they are. For some of these persons, self-disclosure is nothing more than reaction formation—they fear self-revelation, so they reveal themselves to show they are not afraid. For others, self-disclosure is an adult psychological version of the childhood "doctor" game, where "I'll show you mine, if you show me yours": people are encouraged to bare their souls for the benefit of the *observers*. Finally, on the "pro" side of self-disclosure, there are those who force self-revelations down our throats, telling us about themselves, whether we want to hear it or not. A brief scan of the autobiography section of a local bookstore attests to the fact that we are inundated with revelations by second- and third-rate "personalities" who somehow reasoned that we need to know about their most intimate life experiences.

On the "con" side of the issues, there are those who argue that we have lost proper control of ourselves and that we need to exercise more restraint on our public behavior. Some persons assume that people are too eager to talk about themselves and that their self-disclosures are nuisances. Among those in this group are individuals who argue that they have enough of their own problems and that they don't need or want the burden of someone else's. Finally, there are individuals who believe that others are simply not to be trusted with highly personal information about oneself. In defense of their position, they interpret almost anything pertaining to their nonpublic lives as being "personal." As a result, they often resemble a walking "classified secret" under the lock and key of a supercontrolled and impenetrable exterior. The mere task of living becomes a challenge to "keep the wolves from the door" of privacy.

The opposing views discussed above reflect varied and, in some instances, antithetical values held by people in our society with respect to self-disclosure. Whereas some individuals value transparency very highly, others value personal privacy just as much. The value issues underlying self-disclosure cannot be resolved here by introducing other sets of values to evaluate which ones are right and which ones are wrong. Such determinations simply cannot be made on value issues. From a behavioral standpoint, however, it is possible to steer a course down the middle between *overdisclosure* and *underdisclosure*. As Egan (1977) suggested, one way of looking at self-disclosure is to consider these two extremes. Some persons are *overdisclosers*, in that they talk too much about themselves and/or they talk too personally about themselves when the situation does not call for it (Egan, 1977). For example, suppose your colleague, Helen, was doing an intake report with a patient being admitted to the hospital. If, while doing the intake, Helen began telling the patient all about her problems at home with her husband and her children, she would be *overdisclosing* because she is saying *too much* about herself and she is being *too personal*, given the circumstances. Overdisclosure is a problem of *too much quantity* and *too much quality* in the communication about oneself. Conversely, *underdisclosers* don't offer enough quantity or quality in their self-revelations. Even when the situation might call for it, they avoid talking personally about themselves. For instance, you may know someone who encourages you to talk about yourself and disclose your thoughts and feelings, but who does not reciprocate. I have worked professionally with many married couples where one or both of the partners do not know what the other is thinking or feeling. Sometimes, they don't even know what the other person is doing! Underdisclosure becomes the norm of interaction in a context where it may do the most harm.

Egan (1977) used the term *appropriate self-disclosure* to describe self-revelation which cuts between the two extremes of overdisclosure and underdisclosure. Both the *amount* and the quality or *intimacy level* of the disclosure are proper and fitting *under the circumstances*. Situational factors which affect the appropriateness of self-disclosure also include the amount of *time* spent in revealing oneself and the *person talked to*. It would be appropriate for a patient dying of lymphosarcoma (circumstance) periodically (time) to express her fears of dying (intimacy) in their full extent (amount) to her husband (person). On the other hand, it would be inappropriate for a man to corner a psychologist (person) at a party (circumstance) and pour out his sexual problems (intimacy) at great length (amount). It may not matter whether he describes these problems for one minute or one hour (time), because other factors have already defined his behavior as inappropriate.

Underdisclosure

I am not disclosing much intimate information when I reveal that my favorite college football team is the University of Michigan, that I don't like to wash dishes, and that I long for the beaches of Southern California as I write this text in the clutches of a cold Midwestern winter. Indeed, most of the people who know me know these things about me. But, none of these are central to my personality, nor do they control much of my behavior. So, if this is all the information I have chosen to give to people, I haven't really come close to revealing things that you would call intimate. However, if I expressed my religious or political beliefs, deep feelings for my friends, or the frustrations I sometimes feel with my psychotherapy clients, I would be offering more intimate information. It comes closer to my most important concerns and private experiences. It is the kind of information that reflects my private world. And, all things considered, it is not appropriate for me to disclose my private world here. Besides, *I really don't want to*! But, why don't people want to share themselves more deeply with others? What are the reasons for underdisclosures?

Many of our attitudes toward self-disclosure were learned at home. Egan (1977) noted that the willlingness of individuals to talk about themselves deeply with other members of their families depends partly on whether their parents talked personally to one another. In many families, intimate self-disclosure is simply not the norm. More often, individuals will talk about personal things with friends outside of the home. Thus, to some extent our willingness to self-disclose depends on the kinds of *role-models* to which we were exposed in our families.

Jourard (1971) suggested that one of the reasons for not sharing ourselves more deeply with others is that we sometimes fear that we will *make contact with parts of ourselves that we would rather ignore.* According to Jourard, self-disclosure is not only a means for communicating with others, it is a means for communicating with ourselves. To disclose something to others or to our own selves, we have to dig down, as it were, and retrieve information. We have to pull that information up and out so that others can see it or so that we can see it ourselves. The problem is that sometimes we just don't want to see what we've dug up!

When we reveal aspects of ourselves to others, we usually become somewhat closer to them. Thus, fear of self-disclosure may for some people reflect a *fear of growing close* to another person. Being close to someone means certain interpersonal responsibilities have to be met. Some persons do not want to accept that responsibility because they perceive it to be a restriction of their freedom. They want no "strings attached," they want some sort of "platonic" relationship, they want an "understanding"—they want *"no commitments."* For other people, getting close to someone introduces the obvious possibility of eventual pain. They fear rejection, and one sure way to prevent rejection is to set it up that they don't get close enough to be hurt. Many people vow, after a relationship break-up, that they'll never get hurt again. Most of those same persons change their perspective eventually, but, for a period of time, they may actively avoid intimate relationships.

In relation to rejection, people often avoid self-disclosure because they think that "If other people knew what I am *really* like, they wouldn't accept me." They assume that there is a part of themselves that must remain forever hidden if they are to keep the approval of others. Self-revelation means certain rejection.

Jourard (1971) believed that underdisclosure (as well as overdisclosure) can be psychologically unhealthy. The person who never discloses anything about herself would be trapped in a life of stressful solitude, unable to establish any close and meaningful relationships with others. Even in a type of interpersonal "bubble" in which the underdiscloser lives, self-revelation is still important for psychological adjustment, according to Jourard. An individual cannot be herself unless she knows herself, and it is very difficult to know oneself without disclosing to others and to one's own self. People with emotional problems are often persons who have difficulty sharing their feelings with others, and they often work very hard to avoid self-disclosure. As a result, stress mounts, problems magnify, and the cycle becomes more and more difficult to maintain. It is interesting, in this connection, that many of these same people are helped tremendously when they ultimately seek professional help, *where they pay another person to listen to their self-disclosures*!

Jourard maintained that the psychologically healthy person is one who is able to make herself known deeply and fully to *at least one other person.* People stop growing psychologically when they stop making themselves known to others. And, Jourard pointed out quite nicely that love is a gift of self, and the person who finds self-disclosure difficult is one who therefore has difficulty loving another human being.

Reciprocity of Self-Disclosure

One of the most consistent findings in psychological research is that self-disclosure is reciprocal (Schneider, 1976). We tend to reciprocate or imitate the quantity and quality of self-disclosure defined by others as being appropriate. When one person discloses something about himself, a signal is sent to the receiver that he is willing to trust her with personal information. The receiver then responds with an equally intimate self-disclosure, and a signal is sent back to the original communicator that his self-disclosure was received and accepted. A back-and-forth interaction then serves to escalate levels of intimacy and trust in a manner similar to that represented in Figure 7.2. When a mutually acceptable level of intimacy is reached, the quantity and quality of self-disclosures stabilize. Further increases in self-disclosures might be uncomfortable for the interacting persons, so they remain at an optimal point until they are ready to move toward greater intimacy (Argyle and Dean, 1965). Taylor (1968) provided some evidence that self-disclosure increases with the length of the relationship. It appears, then, that this reciprocal self-disclosure and intimacy-building process is often a direct function of time factors. When more time is perceived to be available for a relationship to develop, individuals may take longer to disclose themselves. And, as most people know, when little time is available, people often cram a great deal of intimacy into a very short period.

Summary and Implications

In social interactions, we form impressions of others at the same time they form impressions of us. The manner in which individuals display themselves to others refers to a set of behaviors known as *self-presentation*. As a natural consequence of the fact that others do form impressions of our self-presentations, we attempt to influence or shape their perceptions. *Impression management* is the general process of controlling one's appearance and behavior in order to influence the impressions others form. One goal of impression management is to secure the *approval* of others and, at the same time, avoid their disapproval. The need for social approval is a particularly strong motivational base of behavior, with roots in infantile dependency. Throughout the course of most people's lives, approval functions as a potent form of *positive reinforcement*, and disapproval serves as a *punishing* consequence of behavior. Some individuals develop an insatiable need for social approval and, as a result, impression management becomes a habitual mode of interaction. Most people, however, are appropriately discriminating in their use of impression management strategies. They effectively adapt their self-presentations in accordance with the behavior of others as well as social context. Nevertheless, it sometimes happens that people come to believe in their own performances; the reactions of others lead

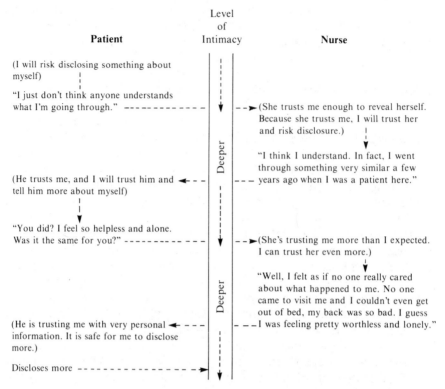

Figure 7.2   Individuals tend to reciprocate the quantity and quality of self-disclosures defined by others as being appropriate. If two people contribute increasingly greater amounts of personal information, the relationship will usually move to more intimate levels. The kind of information shared will often determine whether a conversation stays at a superficial level or moves to a more personal level.

them to assume that they are who they appear to be. In trying to make a good impression, individuals may use various *ingratiation* tactics: consciously used strategies designed to increase one's attractiveness in the eyes of another. Ingratiation tactics identified by Jones (1964) include *positive self-presentations, other-enhancements, favor-doing,* and *conformity* to the beliefs or interests of others. The goals of ingratiation include *acquisition* or personal gain, *protection from harm,* and *enhancement of self-worth.*

Some forms of self-presentation do not involve impression management. *Self-disclosure* is the open revelation of genuine information about oneself— information pertaining to one's personal or private experiences. Differences of opinion exist as to whether self-disclosure is good or bad. Because these are *values issues,* no definitive characterization of self-disclosure as good or bad can be made. From a behavioral standpoint, however, differences can be established between *underdisclosure* and *overdisclosure,* with *appropriate self-disclosure* falling between the two extremes. Appropriateness of self-disclosure is defined in terms of the *quantity, quality* or intimacy, *time, circumstance,* and *person* to whom one reveals oneself. A highly replicable finding in psychological research is that self-disclosure tends to be *reciprocal*: individuals tend to reciprocate the quantity and quality of self-disclosures defined by others as being appropriate. Reciprocal self-disclosure functions effectively as an intimacy- and trust-building mechanism in interpersonal relationships.

As indicated at the beginning of this chapter, impression management is a *necessary* social skill. Because people are always forming impressions of us, it is clearly to our advantage to try to present the most favorable image we can. Unfortunately, for too many persons, the only identities they can construct are those they build out of the materials from Madison Avenue advertisers, movie themes, television programs, magazines, and self-improvement books. They try to emulate and model themselves after practically perfect physical specimens who have been made up, trimmed down, combed out, and given scripts with all the right things to say. With fraudulent standards of acceptability, many individuals constantly assess the extent to which they measure up, checking themselves in the mirror daily, just to see if they've added a pound here, a wrinkle there, or a blemish that bears witness to their imperfections.

Countless books have been written by human potential gurus and self-styled experts on living, proclaiming that people are just not making it until they change themselves to satisfy needs which they never knew they had. So many psychological needs have been manufactured that wearing an aura of self-actualization has become as necessary for appearance as the latest hairstyle. A constant beating of the self-awareness drum has made hyperreflection, introspection, self-analysis, and self-consciousness a way of life for many people. What is actually a pseudo-self-awareness has caused many individuals to lose their genuineness and spontaneity—their ability to freely express themselves without meditating on the possible effects of their behavior on others. Virtually everyone has been bombarded with the same messages about unconscious motivations, hidden potentials, "real" feelings, and body language. As a result, many people have become terrified of inadvertently revealing themselves through their actions, expressions, and even their clothes. Innocent and inconsequential quirks of behavior are no longer insignificant for many persons—they have become hang-ups, symptoms, or social signals. Public appearances and performances thus become more and more necessary to control. The norm for social interaction becomes an unrecognized contradiction: *controlled genuineness and spontaneity.*

At times, individuals cannot avoid noticing the inauthenticity of their own behavior. Consequently, they cannot help doubting similarly ungenuine expressions from *others* who may be equally skilled in the art of impression management. The entire interaction may thus resemble an interchange of lines designed to assure one another that each has been truly moved by the other's performance. To play this game effectively and to ensure continued acceptance in the eyes of the other, each person must first be a critic of his *own* performance and a connoisseur of "fine lines."

References

Argyle, M., and Dean, J. Eye-Contact, Distance, and Affiliation, *Sociometry*, **28**:289–304 (1965).

Arpel, A. *How to Look Ten Years Younger.* New York, Rawson, Wade, 1980.

Carnegie, D. *How to Win Friends and Influence People.* New York, Simon & Schuster, 1936.

Cooley, C. H. *Human Nature and the Social Order*, rev. ed. New York, Scribner, 1922.

Cooper, J., and Jones, E. E. Opinion Divergence as a Strategy to Avoid Being Miscast, *Journal of Personality and Social Psychology*, **13**:23–40 (1969).

Crowne, D. P. and Marlowe, D. *The Approval Motive.* New York, Wiley, 1964.

Deutsch, M., and Gerard, H. A Study of Normative and Informational Social Influences on Individual Judgement, *Journal of Abnormal and Social Psychology*, **51**:629–36 (1955).

Dyer, W. *Pulling Your Own Strings.* New York, Avon, 1977.

Egan, G. *You and Me: The Skills of Communicating and Relating to Others.* Monterey, California, Brooks/Cole, 1977.

Fast, J. *Body Language.* New York, Evans, 1970.

Fast, J. *Body Politics: How to Get Power with Class.* New York, Tower Books, 1980.

Gergen, K. J. Personal Consistency and the Presentation of Self, in *The Self in Social Interaction*, ed. C. Gordon and K. J. Gergen, pp. 299–308, New York, Wiley, 1968.

Gergen, K. J., and Wishnov, B. Others' Self-Evaluations and Interaction Anticipation as Determinants of Self-Presentation, *Journal of Personality and Social Psychology*, **2**:348–358 (1965).

Girard, J. *How to Sell Yourself.* New York, Warner Books, 1979.

Goffman, E. *The Presentation of Self in Everyday Life.* Garden City, New York, Doubleday Anchor, 1959.

Hilgard, E. R.; Atkinson, R. L.; and Atkinson, R. C. *Introduction to Psychology*, 7th ed. New York, Harcourt Brace Jovanovich, 1979.

Hovland, C.; Harvey, O.J.; and Sherif, M. Assimilation and Contrast Effects in Reaction to Communication and Attitude Change, *Journal of Abnormal and Social Psychology*, **55**:244–252 (1957).

Jourard, S. *The Transparent Self.* Princeton, New Jersey, Van Nostrand, 1971.

Jones, E. E. *Ingratiation.* New York, Appleton-Century-Crofts, 1964.

Jones, E. E.; Gergen K. J.; and Davis, K. Some Reactions to Being Approved or Disapproved as a Person; *Psychological Monographs*, **76**:521 (1962).

Jones, E. E. and Wortman, C. *Ingratiation: An Attributional Approach.* Morristown, New Jersey, General Learning Press, 1973.

Landau, S., and Bailey, G. *The Landau Strategy.* Rockville Centre, New York, Playboy Paperbacks, 1980.

Mead, G. H. *Mind, Self and Society*, ed. C. W. Morris. Chicago, University of Chicago Press, 1934.

Molloy, J. T. *Dress for Success.* New York, Warner Books, 1975.

Molloy, J. T. *The Woman's Dress for Success Book.* New York, Warner Books, 1977.

Newtson, D., and Czerlinsky, T. Adjustment of Attitude Communications for Contrasts by Extreme Audiences, *Journal of Personality and Social Psychology*, **30**:829–37 (1974).

Peale, N. V. *The Power of Positive Thinking.* Englewood Cliffs, New Jersey, Prentice-Hall, 1952.

Ringer, R. J. *Winning Through Intimidation.* New York, Fawcett, 1974.

Rogers, C. *Client-Centered Therapy.* Boston, Houghton-Mifflin, 1951.

Schneider, D. J. *Social Psychology.* Reading, Massachusetts, Addison-Wesley, 1976.

Snyder, M. Impression Management, in *Social Psychology*, 2d ed., L. S. Wrightsman, Monterey, California, Brooks/Cole, 1977.

Taylor, D. A. The Development of Interpersonal Relationships: Social Penetration Processes, *Journal of Social Psychology*, **75**:79–90 (1968).

Weinberg, G. *Self-Creation.* New York, Avon, 1978.

CHAPTER EIGHT

Criteria for Interpersonal Judgement and Impression Management: Values, Beliefs, and Attitudes

*I have a dream that my four little children will one day
live in a nation where they will not be judged by the
color of their skin, but by the content of their character.*

Martin Luther King, Jr.,
August 28, 1963

A young girl has been in a coma for a long time following a drug overdose. Now she is dying. The physician wants to prolong life, the nursing staff wants to let her die with dignity, and the girl's parents are torn between the two alternatives. What do you think should be done?

Sandra is a head nurse in a coronary care unit. She has always had problems relating to her staff. When a conflict over duty schedules developed, she implemented a policy that was very unpopular among the staff. They responded by withdrawing even more from interactions with Sandra. The administration felt she was right, but did not support her decision in the face of protests by staff. Whose behavior is the most objectionable?

Janet is a second-year nursing student whose performance in course work has been marginally acceptable. She is currently enrolled in a course wherein her grade is determined primarily through self-evaluation. Because her grades in other courses are quite low this semester, her only hope of maintaining a passing average is to inflate her self-evaluation and present herself to her instructor as being more knowledgeable than she really is. Should she evaluate herself highly and try to shape the impression her instructor forms of her?

Your responses to each of these hypothetical situations rest upon specific sets of evaluative criteria. Your evaluations of situations and people—including yourself and your styles of self-presentation—are ultimately grounded in your own personal *values*, *beliefs*, and *attitudes*. These are the *criteria* against which we judge ourselves and others. They also account for many of the differences between ourselves and others. As the bases for interpersonal judgements which underlie impression formation and impression management, values, beliefs, and attitudes represent *essential* areas for you to explore.

Values pertain to what you consider to be right or wrong, good or bad, just or unjust, desirable or objectionable. From the moment of birth, society and all of its agencies make demands on individuals by communicating different sets of cultural values, and each individual is socialized to internalize these values (Rokeach and Regan, 1981). Values are organized into relationships with one another, and a general priority system evolves where certain values take precedence over others. Priorities can and often do change with circumstances and new learning, but, for the most part, the system is relatively stable and enduring across the life span. As such, values are always with us, guiding our choices, our decisions, and our judgements of ourselves and others. They affect the impressions we form, the impressions we manage, and the behavioral exchanges in our interactions.

Values, as notions about the way things "should be," are different from *beliefs*, which are convictions about the way things "are." Beliefs consist of facts, general knowledge, and assumptions acquired through our interactions with the environment and other people. They, too, are organized into relationships with one another and, while some fundamental beliefs tend to endure over time, with new learning they may change with less resistance than values. Our assumptions about human nature are contained in our implicit personality theories, and, as you know, our personal theories exert powerful effects on the judgements we make and the impressions we form.

Beliefs and values are different from one another and still different from *attitudes*, which incorporate beliefs and values into a broader system consisting of an emotional component and a readiness to action. They are also learned, relatively enduring, and can be changed. However, because of the rather inconsistent relationships among our attitudes, they are often very hard to change (this phenomenon is addressed in Chapter Ten). Because attitudes "predispose" us to react in specific ways toward those with whom we interact, it should not be surprising that they play a key role in impression formation and impression management. One purpose of this chapter, then, is to present some convenient ways of thinking about the nature of values, beliefs, and attitudes, to explore their respective roles in impression formation and impression management, and to develop the view that they are the ultimate criteria for interpersonal judgement and impression management.

In this chapter, each concept—values, beliefs, and attitudes—is briefly examined. The first section provides an overview of values and a scheme for identifying the values associated with your own style of self-presentation. The role of values as criteria for interpersonal judgements is then examined, and information weighting is reconsidered in light of those criteria. Beliefs and attitudes are discussed in the latter sections of the chapter, where attention is also given to the kind of information beliefs and attitudes reveal about people. Upon summarizing the content of the chapter, implications for health professionals are emphasized.

It is important to point out here that the following sections are necessarily limited in scope and do not address the controversial conceptual issues surrounding these notions. Values, beliefs, and attitudes have been defined in myriad ways across and even within social science and medical science disciplines. Frequently, conceptualizations clearly differ. More often, however, formulations have overlapped, thus making it difficult to draw clear lines between interrelated concepts. Theory and research on these concepts is controversial at most and confusing at least, but the general problem is understandable: if theorists cannot agree on the best definition of each concept, how could they be expected to agree on where to set the conceptual boundaries? In spite of this problem, the position taken here favors basic distinctions between values, beliefs, and attitudes. They are conceived differently, and they are presented as such. It is assumed that your interest and need to explore purely conceptual and empirical issues are less compelling than your desire to gain some functional ways of using these concepts in your everyday encounters.

Values

When fully conceptualized, values are seen as *criteria* for evaluations, judgements, and choices. They are the bases for selecting one state of existence or one mode of conduct over another. As Rokeach (1973, p. 5) defined the concept, *value* refers to "an enduring belief that a specific mode of conduct or end-state of existence is personally or socially preferable to an opposite or converse mode of conduct or end-state of existence." Examples of preferred end-states would include values such as peace, freedom, equality and preferred modes of conduct would include valued ways of acting, such as being honest, cooperative, self-controlled. Recognizing that values exist in some relationship to one another within each person, Rokeach (1973, p. 5) defined a *value system* as an "enduring organization of beliefs concerning preferable modes of conduct or end-states of existence along a continuum of relative importance." Each person has a value system in which, for example, certain values like freedom, happiness, and equality have priority over other values considered less important (e.g., excitement, pleasure, wisdom). The relative importance of each value differs from one person to the next, although Rokeach and Regan (1981) argued that the *number* of values that humans possess is limited. Thus, there are a limited number of end-states, or *terminal values*, and modes of conduct, or *instrumental values*, which serve as criteria for judgements and choices. As a result of each individual's social learning experiences, a relatively small number of basic values are arranged in different orders of priority into a system of standards and criteria that guide virtually all aspects of behavior (Rokeach and Regan, 1981). Values underlie our social behavior, occupational choices, our positions on religious and political issues, *and the impressions we form of others as well as the ways in which we present ourselves and evaluate our own personalities.* In fact, some theorists and researchers contend that *all* of our behavior is "value-expressive."

Implicit in the definition above is the relationship between values and *purposive* or *intentional* behavior. Purposive behavior refers to actions performed "on purpose," with the intention of reaching some goal or bringing about a certain result. The assumption is that purposive behavior is based on decisions or choices to act in certain ways. Decisions or choices are, in turn, dependent on underlying values. Thus, your decision to enter the health professions instead of becoming a coal miner is a value-based decision. You have purposely chosen to become a health professional because you perceive a direct relationship between this line of work and what you want for yourself and others. Coal mining is apparently not high on the list of your priorities.

Decisions and choices can obviously be made without awareness. Indeed, if you were asked why you sat in the red chair and not the green one, you would probably think the question was strange, because such choices are not the kind to which people usually give a lot of thought. Similarly, if someone asked you why you answered the telephone when it rang, you'd probably think that person was odd, because somebody was obviously trying to get in touch with you. But, these kinds of actions are so basic, so automatic, that they can cloud the realization that choices are still involved. Yet, how many people really acknowledge that they have a *choice* to answer the phone! Decisions and choices guide virtually every action except reflexes and other responses determined by physiological factors. Once we have made certain choices a number of times, a consistent pattern of responding often becomes habitual and seemingly under the control of situational forces or stimuli. When this happens, we often become farther removed from the values underlying that behavior. For example, people often fall into routines of living after doing certain things for a period of time. Often, they don't even recognize the routine, and, when it is pointed out to them, they have a very hard time trying to figure out how they even got into it! One of the common tragedies for many people is that, even when they realize they are in a routine they don't like, they *fail to realize that they can choose to change*! When lecturing on this issue, a common response from some of my students is that there is nothing they can do about their life circumstances: "I'd love to quit my job, but I can't," "I'd like to get away from my family, but I can't," "I'd like to go to graduate school, but I can't." Such complaints rarely reflect reality. Rather, they reflect priorities which people have set for themselves. Top on their lists of priorities is the desire to avoid *the costs of change*. Change is difficult, demanding, sometimes painful to self and others. In short, the process of change is often unpleasant. Thus, quitting one's job, leaving one's family, and enrolling in graduate school involved costs to individuals which they seek to avoid. You will recall from the preceding chapter that individuals often do things, not to obtain positive reinforcement, but to avoid unpleasant consequences. The bottom-line is that they *choose* to avoid those consequences because they have negative value.

Values can be *positive* or *negative*. Positive values are views about what is *desirable* or how things *should be*. Positive values should not be confused with positive reinforcers, since positive values are broad, general, and relatively abstract *views* about what is desirable, while positive reinforcers are specific and relatively concrete response consequences. For example, some professionals feel that the holistic model is desirable and should be followed by practitioners (positive value). Overall improvement of personal well-being is the positive consequence predicted from this model (positive results are the reinforcers). Conversely, negative values are views about what is *undesirable* or how things should *not* be. Thus, some persons consider moody people to be undesirable, and most health professionals feel that they should not jeopardize the welfare of their clients by breaching confidentiality for any reason. "Moodiness" as a negative value is a *criterion* of undesirability, and "revealing private information" about clients is a mode of conduct that should not occur. The discomfort one feels when interacting with moody people is a negative *consequence* which is avoided, and harming clients by violating confidentiality is also a negative consequence.

Values and Impression Management

Virtually every voluntary action we perform can be traced back to one or more positive or negative values. Determining the precise value or values that influenced the behavior in question is sometimes a problem. It is difficult because some people simply do not have access to their own values and cannot identify the reasons for their behavior; their values are as invisible to themselves as they are to everyone else, and their explanations for their behavior are often as speculative as the attributions observers make. In other cases or at different times, multiple values may have a combined effect on the behavior in question; trying to sort them out and discover the predominant influences may be almost impossible. As an example, think about your reasons for entering a health profession. On what basis did you choose this particular occupation? Was it a deep concern for humanity (involving values of love, respect, compassion, altruism)? Was it a desire for status, recognition, admiration? Did you think the work would be rewarding in terms of stimulation, challenge, self-fulfillment? Was your choice based on a sense of obligation, responsibility, duty? Did you think you could achieve prosperity, financial security, a comfortable life? Did you want to feel autonomous, independent, and in greater control of things? Or, was it because you thought you could gain more self-respect? These are some of the many values that underlie choices to enter the health professions, and your own decision could have been based on any one or several of them. You may even have some values that aren't cited here. Identifying the dominant value influences can be difficult for you, and, if it is, you can bet that it would be even harder for perceivers who are much farther removed from your personal experience.

Other people can only *infer* what your values are by observing your behavior, and some psychologists (e.g., Bem, 1970) would argue that that's all *you* can do, too. Certainly, there are times when we can only discover our own values by noting how we act and how we present ourselves and relate to others. *The only real "facts" about values are your actions.* Let's suppose you claim that helping people is a high priority in your value system. Let us suppose, further, that every time a friend asks for help with something, you tell him that you can't because you're too busy, you're waiting for a phone call, you have to study, or you'll help him tomorrow. In reality, you rarely put yourself out for someone; you help people when it is convenient for you, not when they need it. If this is what you discover, then you should learn the difference between a value and a "good idea." That is, many people claim to have certain values, like helping people, yet they fail to act on those reputed values. We would therefore have to wonder if they really hold the values they claim. You might contend that courage is a value for you, but it is no more than a good idea if you never stand up for your beliefs or "go out on a limb" for someone. You might say that compassion and forgiveness are important to you, but they are little more than passing notions if you carry grudges and always manage to get revenge. Or, maybe you occasionally try to verbalize a belief in racial equality and yet engage in overt or subtle discrimination, which can even take the form of patronizing individuals from minority groups. *Values are truly important to you if you act in accordance with them.* You may *assume* that you're projecting a specific image of yourself as a person who values kindness, social justice, or any number of other things, but you may be conveying an entirely different image if you're not "walking like you're talking." Helping is a value for you if you help others when they need it, just as honesty is a value if you are honest, or cleanliness is a value if you are clean. Your deeds will attest to your values, and they may do so whether you want them to or not. Your values will speak for themselves *through your behavior!* This clearly applies for those who feel that actions involving generosity, giving, and sharing are good things—as long as they are on the receiving end! Even in their roles as passive recipients, they communicate exactly where their real values are. Unfortunately, we are often quick to identify with certain values when we are on the receiving side of actions based on those values. It seems that, if it is really better to give than to receive, there are times when we are more than willing to let the other person bask in the greater glory.

Identifying Values in Your Self-Presentation Styles

There is a way to conceptualize values in relations to your style of self-presentation. First, let us clarify what is meant by your self-presentation *style*. Your self-presentation style is part of your overall interpersonal style, your usual manner of interacting with people. If I were to ask one of your friends what you are like when you are with people, that person would give me a description of your interpersonal style and how you usually present yourself to others. For example, if your friend told me that you are usually very open with people and that you frequently relate some of your deep feelings about things, I could infer that intimacy is important to you. I could also infer that intimate communication is part of your interpersonal style and that you present yourself as a relatively open and genuine person. By making the further inference that intimacy and genuineness are values for you, I could predict that you talk openly and honestly about your feelings in a wide range of interpersonal situations. Now, these two values—intimacy and genuineness—are actually instrumental values. They are valued modes of conduct, as opposed to end-states of existence. It is with this distinction firmly in mind that we can turn to a conceptualization of values in self-presentation.

Our social learning experiences teach us about the world around us. We acquire information about our environments and about the people in them, and we organize our experiences in ways that will help us interact effectively. We develop expectations about the consequences of our actions as well as the consequences of others' behavior, and these expectations of the contingencies between behavior and specific outcomes lead us to act in ways that bring about expected results. The results we hope to achieve are reinforcements; the results we hope to avoid are punishments. As indicated earlier in this section, reinforcements and punishments are *not the same* as positive and negative values, *but they are clearly related.* Reinforcements and punishments are specific response consequences that are associated with general positive and negative values. That is, a response consequence is reinforcing if it is positively valued, punishing if it is negatively valued. Values are the criteria by which response consequences are judged to be reinforcing or punishing. Once response consequences are judged to be reinforcing or punishing, we may set out to achieve reinforcing outcomes and avoid punishing ones. In a sense, we seek to attain certain goals or end-states (terminal values) by bringing about specific behavioral consequences. We bring about those consequences and, hence, attain our goals through actions that serve as *means to our ends*. Behavior that is a means to an end is *instrumental* behavior. Instrumental behaviors are modes of conduct that can be positively or negatively valued. Thus, instrumental behaviors are associated with instrumental values.

Our self-presentation styles actually consist of repertories of instrumental behaviors designed to bring about desired consequences and avoid undesired ones. When we graciously compliment someone on her appearance, we do in order to create some particular effect for us and for her. In most cases, the specific effect we seek to create can be traced to a more general value, in this case perhaps "friendship" or "happiness" or "intimacy." The behaviors we select to attain our reinforcing consequences and satisfy our terminal values are chosen if they are positively valued (i.e., if they have been associated with the achievement of our goals). Behaviors are not selected if they are negatively valued—if they will not help us achieve our desired goals. Thus, if you sought to develop a deeper friendship with someone, you would not tell her that her appearance is disgusting—unless you have found that with this person "honesty" is the best instrumental act in which you can engage. In short, your self-presentation style consists of interpersonal behaviors that you have evaluated positively or negatively, depending on whether or not they lead to response consequences associated with your terminal values. Even though your style of self-presentation is designed to bring about reinforcing consequences, the ultimate function of your behavior is to accommodate your values. To accommodate the terminal values that are important to you, you must take into account the impressions you make on others.

To identify your own values, then, you can easily begin by considering your self-presentation style. What behaviors describe you in relation to other people? With patients, do you usually put on your "bedside manner" and act cheerful? What are the values associated with this kind of behavior? What effects are you trying to produce, and what are the terminal values associated with those effects? With authority figures, are you usually willing to accept everything they say and do, whatever they tell you to do? If this is part of your interpersonal style, is your behavior related to the priorities you place on obedience, respect and duty? What terminal values are served through these positively valued instrumental behaviors: recognition, interpersonal harmony? In relationships in general, do you try to do and say all the right things and gain the acceptance and approval of others? What are the terminal values associated with these behavioral consequences? That is, if approval as a specific consequence of your behavior is important to you, what are the values underlying approval: self-esteem, a sense of security, inner harmony?

Again, something is a value for you if, and only if, it becomes part of your behavior. By looking at what you *do* and by reflecting on the goals you try to achieve, you can move closer toward clarifying your own values. The process can be difficult and at times painful. Sometimes we're rather shocked to learn from our friends that we haven't come across as we thought we did: "What do you mean I'm not sensitive?"; "How can you say I'm narrow-minded?"; "I can't believe you don't think I'm affectionate." By examining our interpersonal style and revealing our values to ourselves, we are occasionally forced to modify our self-presentation styles. Often, we discover that what we thought were our values are really not our own, but someone else's. Therefore, it is frequently a major effort for most persons to present themselves in ways that are *consistent with their own values* and not *dependent* on the perceived values of others. As indicated in Chapter Three, individuals often experience an incongruence between their real and ideal selves when they accept the conditions of worth (values) of others and behave in ways that accommodate others' values and not their own. The falsification of oneself for the sake of keeping the positive regard of others is essentially a *distortion or denial of one's own values.*

The Role of Values in Impression Formation

The *averaging* and *additive* models described in Chapter Six are useful hypotheses about the ways in which individuals combine information when making judgements of others. According to these models, individuals assign specific *weights* to stimulus information and then average or add the weights to arrive at an overall evaluation of someone. The weights attached to information are contingent upon the relative importance (to the individual) of each perceived trait and behavior. Importance is largely a function of the individual's system of *value priorities* as well as situational factors. Therefore, to promote a deeper understanding of impression formation and the role of values in the process, we will reexamine information weighting and approach this central element of impression formation from a slightly different perspective.

A Value-Related Hypothesis of Information Weighting

The relative weights attached to stimulus information are ultimately contingent upon the individual's value system, where certain traits and actions are higher in the organization of positive and negative values than others. At times, circumstances may effect a rearrangement of value priorities, such that a less valued behavior comes to be more valued, or vice versa, as information about the interaction context changes. For example, when meeting someone for the first time, it may be more desirable to be modest, quiet, and unassuming; as time passes, it may become more desirable to be extroverted. Or, in one context, it may be desirable to be tolerant and obedient, while in a different context, assertiveness may be highly valued. Nurturant behavior is an example of something that is positively valued in health care settings, but if a health professional tries to be just as nurturant of others at a party, they might see her as patronizing, condescending, or egocentric. In a similar way, when mental health counselors shift from a context wherein open, honest, spontaneous, and genuine communication of feelings is usually highly valued, they must alter their interpersonal styles. In the so-called real world outside of the mental health context, it is not common, nor is it particularly desirable, for people to express themselves so freely. A more constrained and controlled style of interaction is usually required in the broader society.

One factor contributing to differential weighting of information is *negativity*. You will recall that this involves the tendency to attach greater importance to negative information about people. Two hypotheses were offered to account for negativity effects, and those explanations are reconsidered below. The basic premise for reviewing these hypotheses is the assumption that information is judged to be negative *if it is consistent with the individual's negative values or incompatible with positive values.*

One hypothesis for negativity effects was that we are sensitive to information that implies a potential threat to ourselves and our relationships. Negative information indicates potential liabilities or problems in relationships. From the perspective of personal values, problems in relationships cover a multitude of negative values which probably rest upon a basic belief in the *undesirability of interpersonal conflict and tension*. Interpersonal conflict and tension are undesirable because they threaten our sense of inner harmony, can make us feel unhappy and generally miserable, and, in essence, *disrupt the order and balance we value in life*. In extreme conditions, interpersonal conflict and tension can completely upset the balance in our lives by threatening our very *survival*. From a values-perspective, then, *survival* appears to be the chief value that underlies the heavy weight we attach to negative information about people.

In most interpersonal relationships, our lives are not directly threatened. We usually have conflict and tension without consciously feeling a threat to our survival, but we can still be upset by the conflict. Some theorists (e.g., Rokeach and Regan, 1981) maintain that whenever a person encounters problems in relationships, value-conflicts exist. In simple terms, value-conflicts exist when one person's positive values are another person's negative values, or when one person places high priority on a value that is low in the other's system of priorities. For example, clear and concisely written communications may be highly valued by a supervisor but not by staff, and tension could develop if the gap between their respective priorities remains wide. Actually, it is not *conflict* per se that people tend to dislike; conflict as an interpersonal phenomenon can be very beneficial to relationships, and even sought after. At moderate levels, it can stimulate personal growth and the quality of relationships by provoking the search for new solutions to problems, new ways of interacting. It is conflict at high levels that leads to overstimulation, overarousal, and pervasive discomfort that people do not like. High levels of conflict are generally unpleasant and avoided. Now, for a person to anticipate problems in a relationship, she must evaluate the traits and actions of the other person. Traits and actions are negative and problems or value-conflicts are predicted if those traits and actions are judged undesirable. Social learning experiences have taught us that certain negative qualities of people go with certain kinds of relationship problems. If you like people with a good sense of humor, you would probably expect to have a dull and unsatisfying time with someone who is very sober and solemn. You take the person's interpersonal style as a predictor. In summary, the hypothesis that negativity effects are due to the expectation of threat or conflicts in relationships is a hypothesis based on the implicit premise that threat and conflict are negative values.

A second hypothesis for negativity effects was that negative traits and actions are more informative about people than positive traits and actions. Because we usually expect people to look and act in socially acceptable ways, and because they usually do, deviations may be especially informative. Regardless of one's culture, deviations from anything are not tolerated very well. Surely, we do value change, variety, and some degrees of unpredictability in life, but *order*, *sameness*, *regularity*, and *predictability* are often more potent values. People are supposed to do what they say they're going to do, treat one another the same from day to day, express consistent thoughts and feelings, and be generally predictable. Those who are inconsistent are unpredictable, and people who are unpredictable are judged harshly and punished (Gergen and Jones, 1963). What this suggests is that we have other values that are also related to the heavy weight we give to negative information. These values include *order*, *prediction*, and *control*, and they follow from one another: an orderly world enables us to predict the occurrence of events, and if we can predict events, then we may also be able to control them. We place a premium on an orderly world of experience because such a world allows us to feel *secure* and *safe*—two values that are still more basic in our systems of priorities.

Although it was not offered in Chapter Six, an alternative hypothesis for negativity effects might be that negative information about others is weighed heavily because it *raises the perceiver's self-esteem*. In a social comparison process (e.g., Festinger, 1954), individuals can affect their own levels of self-esteem by judging themselves against others. While this is a complicated process studied extensively in social psychology, it is sufficient to note here that individuals may attach greater weight to negative information when that information can be used to support their beliefs that they are "better" by comparison. We have very strong needs to feel good about ourselves, and self-esteem is one of our most fundamental values. When we receive negative information about others, it can sometimes make us feel pretty saintly if we've never done the same things, or at least less guilty if we have!

Finally, it was noted earlier in the text that we attach heavy weight to information that is *salient*: information that stands out. Salience is often a function of *relevance* (i.e., information is salient if it is relevant to the judgement being made). Relevance, in turn, depends on circumstances. It also depends on the individual's values. Ultimately, salient information has some value to the individual, given the priorities assigned to it.

Beliefs

Beliefs are assumptions or convictions about the way things are. They pertain to what you know or assume to be true. As such, beliefs can be and often are convictions about values. Most Americans believe in the value of democracy and free enterprise, and the majority of those same persons are split in their beliefs in the relative value of a two-party system of government, split again in their beliefs about the respective values of Republican and Democratic parties, and further divided in their beliefs about the respective values of Republican and Democratic parties, and further divided in their beliefs about liberalism versus conservatism. Several years ago, Fishbein and Raven (1962) differentiated "beliefs in" from "beliefs about." *Beliefs in* involve the acceptance of the existence of some object, issue or person. For example, one may believe in capitalism, civil rights, God, Machiavellianism, and many other things. *Beliefs about* are convictions regarding the relationships between objects, issues, or persons. Many clients believe that health professionals are compassionate, that physicians are omnipotent, and that psychologists can read people's minds. Most of the beliefs that pertain to interpersonal relations are of this type, where relationships are assumed to exist between people and their behavior, motives, needs, feelings, and countless other variables, including values. The exact relationship between beliefs and values is highly complex and not fully understood. A common view is that many of our beliefs rest upon values. For example, you may believe that people are basically good, that tighter gun-control laws are needed, or that nursing is a noble profession. If you hold such views, you have accepted that certain relationships exist between some object and a value (i.e., "people" and "goodness," "guns" and "control," "nursing" and "honor"). You have taken these relationships as self-evident facts. Beliefs such as these are sometimes referred to as *value-judgements*.

Beliefs do not always involve values. You may simply believe that the moon is made of green cheese or that full moons bring out the craziness in people. Some people even believe they are God. But, most of us would regard such beliefs as false, because our own beliefs happen to be different. One of the interesting aspects of beliefs is the underlying primitive belief in the validity of our own beliefs. *We believe that what we believe is true.* We take it for granted that our beliefs are correct, because we have an *ultimate belief in the reliability of our own senses.* Thus, when a person claims that he is the Messiah, we assume that he is delusional because our senses tell us that he is not the Messiah any more than he is green cheese. At this point, we simply have a difference in beliefs about reality, and the differences are not as important as what each individual believes. Regardless of which belief is true and which is false, each individual believes he is right. And, this is the real significance of beliefs: what is taken as true *by the individual*. When divergent beliefs exist about some issue, value-judgements often become involved. As soon as we evaluate a person and his behavior and conclude that there must be something wrong with him, we have made a value-judgement. Thus, when the self-styled Messiah informs us of his identity, we immediately make a value-judgement that he is psychotic, paranoid, insane, and accept that our pejorative labels accurately describe him. And, just as the real significance of the belief lies in what the "Messiah" assumes to be true, so also does the real significance of our own beliefs about him lie in what we accept as being true. In other words, he may not be psychotic at all, but the important thing is that *we believe that he is*.

To say that you have a belief about something does not necessarily mean that you also care very deeply about it (Berkowitz, 1980). Millions of Americans believe that gun-control laws should be changed. Yet, those same persons do not feel compelled to do anything with their beliefs! They don't seem to feel strongly enough about gun control to pressure their congressional representatives to pass new legislation. History has recorded a great hue and cry from the public after the assassinations of President John F. Kennedy, Martin Luther King, Jr., and Robert Kennedy. Similar reactions occurred following the shootings of Governor George Wallace and President Ronald Reagan. But, the surge of negative public opinion about guns never seemed to get beyond the point of venting personal convictions that "there ought to be a law" or "somebody ought to do something." Apparently, people must become emotionally "charged" about an issue before they feel motivated to respond. Beliefs per se do not provide the charge. As Berkowitz (1980) noted, beliefs produce relatively little effect, if any. For individuals to be moved to action, what they *think* about something is less important than what they *feel* about it.

Attitudes

Beliefs are basically expressions of what people *think* about an issue, object, or person. Attitudes, on the other hand, include more of what people *feel* about something. *An attitude is a relatively stable affective predisposition to respond in a particular way toward a person, object, or issue.* Being "relatively stable" means that attitudes tend to endure over time, remaining basically the same, without significant change. As "affective predispositions," attitudes involve an emotional readiness or preparedness to act in particular ways. Predispositions are hypothetical processes which are assumed to intervene between stimulus events and subsequent behavior. They are not observable. Therefore, attitudes are nonobservable cognitive/emotional processes which function like "inclinations" toward some particular target person, object, or issue. The fact that we have attitudes *toward* things and people means that attitudes *always have an object* to which they are attached. In this sense, attitudes are "target-specific" and simply do not exist independent of some specific object. When viewed in this way, it therefore makes absolutely no sense to assert that someone has a "bad attitude," unless that bad attitude is attached to something (e.g., work, authority, people). Furthermore, when conceptualized this way, the difference between attitudes and values becomes easier to identify. Attitudes are narrow and restricted, specific, and concrete, whereas values are broad, general, and abstract. Examples would include the value of "freedom," which is an abstract concept not directly tied to a specific target, as opposed to one's attitude toward licensing laws—identifiable concrete, specific, and narrowly defined targets. Rokeach (1973) noted, however, that values can serve as criteria for choices and judgements through which an individual develops attitudes. Thus, a person's attitude toward a health profession that requires intensive study and training may be influenced by the degree to which "helping," "health," "health care," or some other criterion is an abstract value for her. If, for example, helping is a strong value for her, then intensive study, hard work, and sacrifice may not weaken her positive attitude toward the profession.

The number of attitudes people have is almost limitless, and every person has an attitude toward virtually everything he or she experiences in life. We have attitudes toward baseball, salt-free diets, exercise, meter maids, supervisors, self-fulfillment, bumper stickers, identification badges, the IRS, FBI, CIA, LSD, IBM, and AMA. Our attitudes concerning these and other issues and persons express our relationships to every aspect of social life. As clusters of thoughts and feelings, our attitudes help us to achieve a relatively organized and meaningful view of the world which, in turn, helps us to function more effectively in that world. To say that these clusters of attitudes are "organized" is not to suggest that all our our attitudes are necessarily *consistent* with one another. In fact, one of the perplexing characteristics of human beings is their remarkably inconsistent attitude structure. For example, you may have strong attitudes toward human rights in general, and those attitudes can be totally inconsistent with your attitudes toward civil rights in particular. Members of such groups as the Ku Klux Klan express so many inconsistent attitudes on these issues as to leave observers in utter confusion over how they can possibly fit their inconsistencies within the same attitudinal and belief system. Some insights into how we all resolve our attitudinal inconsistencies are provided in Chapter Ten.

Components of Attitudes

The general view today is that attitudes consist of three basic components: cognitive, affective, and conative. The *cognitive component* includes beliefs and factual information about the attitude target. Examples would include beliefs that nursing is an occupation for men as well as for women, the knowledge that trauma teams work under high stress conditions, or the awareness that funding for mental health research has been drastically reduced. Stereotypes make up part of the cognitive component and so do implicit personality theories. Therefore, this component of attitudes does not necessarily consist of purely objective information.

The *affective component* is perhaps the central component in the structure of attitudes. It consists of *feelings* connected with beliefs and other cognitions as well as feelings about the attitude target. As you know, feelings can vary in their intensities, such that one person may feel slightly perturbed when the entire work group is reprimanded unjustly by the supervisor, while another person might be absolutely livid. And, each individual has feelings of different intensities concerning different issues. Your attitude toward bowling on the hospital team may be one of relative indifference, but your attitudes toward two inescapable facts of life—death and taxes—are probably much more intense. These are central issues for all of us, and, the more important the issue, the more intense our feelings become and the stronger our attitudes become. What is important is, of course, dependent upon circumstances and one's values. Thus, the affective component, which is sometimes referred to as the "evaluative" component, is heavily rooted in one's values—one's criteria for judgements.

The third component of attitudes is an *action tendency* implied by the term *conative*. The conative aspect is characterized by the inclination to act.

This reflects the readiness or predispositional property of attitudes. It also reflects one's particular "stance" or "policy orientation" on an issue. Your particular stance on issues such as budget cuts and breaches of confidentiality would predispose you toward specific actions in relation to these issues. Your stance on any issue and your orientation toward any person are assumed to effect a state of preparedness where you are actually on the "verge of responding." In a rather dramatic sense, perhaps, the conative function of attitudes is to move you close to the edge. To appreciate this aspect, you might think of certain issues or certain people and determine how close you are to the edge of responding. For example, your attitude toward an acquaintance might be that "if she does that one more time, I'm going to. . . ." If you've ever felt this way about someone, then you were close to the edge of responding.

An example may help to tie together the three components of attitudes. Let us assume that your attitude toward encounter groups is based on the *knowledge* that they involve groups of people interacting with one another. That's all you really know about them, but people have told you some things that have led you to *believe* that encounter groups are highly volatile situations in which participants criticize one another relentlessly—group members just tear one another down. What you know and what you believe about encounter groups represent the cognitive component of your overall attitude. Let us also suppose that when you think about encounter groups, you feel somewhat nervous and apprehensive. In fact, every time a person tells you that the ought to try it, you immediately feel anxious, tense, threatened, and repulsed by the idea. Your *feelings* comprise the affective component of your attitude. Finally, given your thoughts and feelings about encounter groups, you have a *behavioral tendency to avoid participation*, ignore information that the experience can be very rewarding, reject invitations to join a group, and resist persuasive efforts to change your mind. The real force behind your negative attitude is not so much the knowledge and beliefs you have, but your feelings of *fear*.

Even if I tell you here that encounter groups *are not what you think they are* and that you *needn't be afraid of them*, your attitude is not likely to change very easily. This is because attitudes are highly resistant to change when emotional involvement is intense. They are not usually altered by the acquisition of a few new facts or bits of information. It would be much easier to change your beliefs and perhaps even your values where emotions are largely neutral. This latter point may seem somewhat difficult to accept, since most people assume that there are intense feelings that go with many firmly held beliefs and values. Indeed, our convictions are sometimes so powerful and irrepressible, our values so precious and sovereign, that we are willing to sacrifice, endure immense suffering, and even die for them. Is this not irrefutable evidence that we clearly have feelings about our values and beliefs? It would be hard to argue that we don't have feelings *about* our important beliefs and values. However, the fact should not be obscured that such feelings are *components of our attitudes toward our beliefs and values*. Beliefs and values do *not* have emotional components. Beliefs and values are actually the *targets* of our feelings, the *objects* of our attitudes. Our feelings about the things in which we believe and the things we cherish are manifested through attitude expressions. If we are prepared to suffer for the sake of our beliefs and values, it is our *attitude* that predisposes us to personal sacrifice.

What Attitudes and Beliefs Reveal About People

Individuals can disclose information about themselves by expressing verbally or nonverbally their attitudes and beliefs. Moreover, they can use those expressions to control information revealed and project the image they want others to form. People can claim desirable images and disclaim unfavorable ones by publicly expressing thoughts, feelings, and inclinations. Politicians have made an art of this, and, as you know, there can be a wide gap between what they say and what they privately accept. Publicly communicated beliefs and attitudes do not have to parallel private experience. Attitudes are often expressed for the sake of making a good impression; the new hospital administrator who wants to improve the organizational climate may claim that staff's complaints about salary inequities are justified and that she intends to correct the problem. Beliefs can be expressed for impression management purposes: "I've always thought that we should receive more training in interpersonal skills." Attitudes and beliefs make up part of your social identity. When they are expressed, messages are conveyed to others about what kind of person you are and how you function interpersonally. According to Schlenker (1980), attitudes and beliefs can reveal at least five types of information about individuals.

First, attitudes and beliefs can reveal an individual's *positive or negative orientation toward a social context or interaction*. A patient may remark, "This is a wonderful hospital. The staff has been so kind to me, and I've received such good personal care." She communicates what she thinks and how she feels about the situation she is in and the people with whom she is interacting. She conveys a feeling of satisfaction and a positive orientation toward the hospital in general and the staff in particular. She might then be seen as a person who is grateful for quality care, a person who knows that everyone is doing his best for her, and a person who is very much inclined to cooperate with treatment efforts.

Second, attitude and belief expressions can indicate *the role a person wants to take in an interaction*. "I don't think you know what you're talking about" is a clear expression which is designed to help the speaker ascend to a dominant role in the interaction. Conversely, by expressing beliefs that are tentative and weak, a person can indicate uncertainty and thereby assume a submissive role in relation to someone he thinks is more knowledgeable: "I'm not really sure what to put in this report. I just haven't had your experience in writing these kinds of case summaries." And, it is quite common for people to try to hold the center of attention by relating their own thoughts and feelings, while ignoring those expressed by others:

> MAC: Say, John, wasn't that something about that patient they had in emergency last night? He really tore up the place before they restrained him. Why do you think people take PCP, anyway?
> JOHN: Some people don't know they're getting it. They think they're smoking an exotic joint, and "bang!"
> MAC: No, I don't buy that. I think they know just what they're getting into. I think they just don't care. What do you think?

JOHN: Well, I don't know if very many people really suspect—

MAC: How can they not suspect it? Look, you gotta figure that these people will take anything to get high. They don't care what gets 'em high, so long as it works. And, look at the trouble they cause for everyone up here. Right? One big mess, ain't it?

JOHN: It'd be worse for them if we weren't here.

MAC: Worse for them?! Who cares? I couldn't care less if it's worse for them if they have no place to turn for help. They got themselves into their own messes; let them get themselves out. I tell you what I think we ought to do with them, we ought to . . .

Third, attitude and belief expressions can *associate a person with a particular group*. Recall the case of Patty Hearst, for example, who associated herself with the SLA by public attitude and belief statements in addition to illegal acts. She probably created the image of herself as an "urban guerrilla" more through attitudes and beliefs that she expressed than she did by any other means. Most of us don't go to such extremes to associate with particular groups or types of people, but we do consciously identify with certain groups and reveal our identification through the kinds of beliefs and attitudes we express. Occasionally, people will try to get themselves identified with the "kind of person" they want others to think they are (e.g., intellectual, liberal, humanist). For example, Woody Allen captured a phenomenon we have all witnessed at one time or another—a person trying to pass himself off as an "intellectual." In his Academy Award winning movie, *Annie Hall*, a character in line for a movie tried to impress his date by interpreting Marshall McLuhan's works, only to have McLuhan himself appear before the man and pronounce him wrong!

Fourth, individuals can use attitudes and beliefs as *explanations for their behavior*. By citing our thoughts and feelings, we can let others know why we did what we did. The old explanation that "I only did it for your own good" is supposed to let you know that the other person believed he was acting in "your best interest." Sometimes in the medical literature, we read lucid accounts of what it is like to live with a certain illness. The authors explain that they want to share their experiences, so that we will have an idea of what it means to live with those illnesses. In everyday life, we explain our actions constantly by referring to our attitudes or beliefs: "I spent some extra time with Mr. Jones today because I thought he seemed pretty depressed," "You didn't return my call, so I went ahead and ran the tests anyway."

Finally, information about an individual's *personality* can be communicated through belief and attitude expressions. We have examined inferences about personality elsewhere in this text. Suffice it to say here that attitude and belief expressions are additional data sources for making inferences about the personalities of others. For example, what would you infer about Ron's personality from his expressed beliefs and attitudes?

I believe that male nurses are every bit as good as female nurses. They may even be better because of the hardships they have to overcome trying to break through stereotypes. They're sometimes discriminated against in subtle ways, and other men sometimes look at them like they're gay. But, through it all, they manage to make it because they have their goals in mind. I have a lot of respect for male nurses, and that's one reason why I'm thinking about becoming one.

There are probably a number of diverse personality characteristics that you could attribute to Ron. Regardless of what they are, the fact is that you *can* make inferences based upon his expressed beliefs and attitudes, and your inferences about Ron's personality are probably different from your inferences about Ted:

> Why any man would ever want to become a nurse is beyond me. Nursing is for women, and men don't belong in that profession—unless they got some identity problems, if you know what I mean. If a man wants to go into the medical field, let him be a doctor and leave nursing for women. I don't want no male nurse taking care of me, any more than I want a female doctor taking care of me. Hey, that's just that way it is, man!

Summary

Interpersonal evaluation and impression management are ultimately dependent on our criteria for judgments. These criteria are found in our values, beliefs, and attitudes. *Values* were defined here in terms of preferences for specific end-states of existence or broad modes of conduct. Preferred end-states were identified as *terminal values* and preferred modes of conduct as *instrumental values*. The relationship between values and voluntary or *purposive* behavior was described as one involving *choices* to act in one way as opposed to another. It was also noted that values can be *positive* or *negative*. Positive values are views about what is desirable or how things should be. Negative values are views about what is undesirable or how things should not be. The only way in which we can determine what values an individual holds is by observing his behavior and attributing specific values to him. This is because the only real "facts" about values are the *actions* of individuals. Values are truly priorities for individuals *if* they act in accordance with them. A way of conceptualizing values in relation to *self-presentation styles* was presented, where instrumental behaviors (means to ends) are associated with instrumental values and designed to bring about specific behavioral consequences which are associated with terminal values. It was emphasized that, in order to identify and clarify your own values, you must first examine your behavior. The *averaging* and *additive* models of information weighting in impression formation were reexamined from the perspective of values. *Negativity effects* were hypothesized to be grounded in basic values pertaining to survival and the undesirability of interpersonal conflict, as well as in the values we hold for *order, prediction, control,* and *security*. Salience effects were briefly noted as contingent upon individual values.

Beliefs were defined as assumptions or convictions about the way things are. *Beliefs in* involve the acceptance of the existence of some object, issue, or person. *Beliefs about* are convictions regarding the relationships between objects, issues, or persons. Many of our beliefs rest upon values, and when we express evaluation beliefs, we have revealed our *value-judgements*. Underlying our system of beliefs is the primitive belief in the reliability of our own senses. We implicitly trust that what our senses tell us is necessarily true and accurate.

In impression formation this has important implications, in that the attributes which actually *do* characterize an individual are often overshadowed by the ones we *believe* describe him. What we believe about people is often a criterion of more importance than the real "facts."

Attitudes were described as affective predispositions to behave in particular ways toward a person, object, or issue. The definition implies that attitudes involve an emotional readiness or preparedness and that they are *always attached to an object*. Attitudes simply do not exist in a vacuum, independent of a target. Three components of attitudes were identified. The *cognitive component* includes beliefs and other information about an attitude object. The *affective component* is a central evaluative tendency consisting of feeling about an attitude target. The *conative component* is essentially an action tendency which reflects the individual's particular stance on an issue or his behavioral readiness. Individuals can manage the impressions they convey by expressing particular attitudes and beliefs to others. Attitude and belief expressions reveal at least five types of information about people: (1) their positive or negative orientation toward a particular social context or interaction, (2) the role that individuals want to take in an interaction, (3) the group with which they identify with which they want others to associate them, (4) the reasons for their behavior, and (5) characteristics of their personalities.

Implications for Health Professionals

When taken together, values, beliefs, and attitudes comprise our individual philosophies of life and our orientations toward the world. Yet, we rarely consider our philosophies and orientations until some situation emerges and causes us to pause and reflect: "What *do* I want in life?"; "What *are* my beliefs about terminating life-support?"; "How *do* I feel about authority figures?"; "How *does* my stand on abortion fit with my beliefs about professional responsibility?" Hopefully, this chapter serves a heuristic function in leading you toward a reappraisal and clarification of your views about life. Life is what your profession is all about.

Values hold a place at the very center of human life. If values are central to life, then they are undeniably central to health care services. It is therefore incumbent upon you to examine and clarify your values and the ways in which they enter the health care process. If your thinking is truly stimulated, you will consider the potential impact of your values on your performance and on your clients, the effects of clients' values on you, and the conflicts that may arise when your values differ. It is difficult to understand how a health professional could work so intimately with the foremost issues and problems of living on a day-to-day basis without having a firm grasp on her own values and a clear idea about their significance.

Some general value-issues that are essential to confront pertain to the reality of *individual differences*. Health care clients come from the entire spectrum of possible characteristics, varying in terms of demographic differences, mental status, habits, sexual orientations, and almost any other variable one chooses to use to differentiate one person from the next—including value-systems and physical well-being. As a health professional, you have a responsibility to be sensitive to individual differences. Part of your training stresses the importance of observational skills in recognizing signs of illness. Those same observational skills must alert you to signs that you may be in conflict with clients whose values are different from yours. It is imperative that you have the ability to recognize those signs, lest your differences lead you to be less responsive to some persons in providing health care services. By clarifying your own values, you should be able to identify potential obstacles to efficient performance when caring for persons of various backgrounds. Consider, for example, how your values might differ from and, hence, predispose you toward differential treatment of:

Elderly patients
Persons with same sex relationship preferences
Persons from racial and ethnic minorities
Alcoholic and drug-dependent persons
Obese patients or anorexic patients
Persons with fundamentalist religious backgrounds
Physically deformed or disfigured patients
Dependent, hypochondriacal, hysterical, or brain-damaged patients
Patients who express radical political views
Lower class, middle class, upper class patients

Persons who fall into some of the above categories will have values contrary to yours. If you privately object to their values and disapprove of them, can you really respect them as human beings? If you cannot give them your full respect, can you really care for them to the best of your ability? If you cannot care for them to the best of your ability, what are the consequences for them? What are the consequences for you? It is not wrong for your values to differ; value differences must be expected rather frequently. *You can hold antithetical values and still provide quality care, as long as you recognize those differences and do not allow them to interfere with the responsibility you have to those persons who are nonetheless expecting and entitled to the best you have to offer.* There may even be some persons for whom you truly feel unable to care, and, in those cases, you must acknowledge the conflict that exists and still meet your responsibility. This may require that you arrange for someone else on the staff to attend to their needs.

Another value-issue for you to consider is the fact that you may often have to recognize value-conflicts *within patients themselves.* Those conflicts may represent serious impediments to their health and well-being. Just as you are sensitive to signs of illness, so also must you be alert to factors which may prolong or aggravate illness or make treatment difficult. Examples of value-conflicts within patients include the following:

A young male resists treatment for a serious medical condition because he fears that those treatments will endanger his masculinity.
A woman struggles with a decision to give permission for her surgeon to perform a necessary mastectomy.
A middle-aged male with cirrhosis of the liver refuses to accept that he is an alcoholic and will die if he continues drinking.

It would be much too simple to suggest that each of the above examples is reducible to basic conflicts of personal values. Nevertheless, value-conflicts are involved for each person, and it so happens that in each case the conflict is between two positive values: *survival* and *self-esteem*. This is a basic conflict which may exist for many hospitalized persons who want health, well-being, and survival, on the one hand, and who want to feel good about themselves, on the other hand. Sometimes, our methods of treatment strike a serious blow at an individual's self-esteem, especially when those treatments cause significant changes in physical appearance or when individuals must subsequently alter their habits and life-styles. These are the kinds of conflicts of which you must be aware and to which you must be alert. They are also the kinds of conflicts through which you may have to help people work, for their own good. *If you have not examined your own values, then it will be quite difficult for you to provide a climate in which they may explore theirs.* The knowledge of and respect for others' values can be a major determinant of your effectiveness as a health professional. And, it all begins with a knowledge of and respect for your own values!

Beliefs and attitudes are no less important to recognize in yourself. Just as value-differences may underlie differential treatment efforts, so also may belief and attitudinal dissimilarities predispose you toward preferential treatment for some and deferential treatment for others. Reconsider the persons in the categories mentioned earlier, and you may find that you have different attitudes toward each group. Or, you may have certain beliefs that you have simply taken as true, without question. It could be that you have implicitly assumed that alcoholics, for example, are weak-willed, that they can quit drinking if they want to, and that it's a waste of time to help them achieve sobriety when they're just going to leave treatment and get drunk again. If these are your beliefs, you should know that they are also misconceptions which would make it highly unlikely that you could be effective in working with alcoholic patients. Or, let us suppose that you have been assigned to care for a young male patient who was recently admitted to the hospital following a motorcycle accident. Let us also suppose you heard that the young girl who was riding on the back of his motorcycle was killed in the accident. What do you think your attitude toward this young man would be if you also heard that he was driving recklessly while high on a hallucinogenic drug? Many beliefs and attitudes would probably come into play here, as most people seem to have rather clear stands on motorcycles and drugs, reckless driving, and deaths of innocent victims. If, in your own mind, you judged the young man to be "guilty," how would your treatment of him be affected?

The latter example is one in which numerous variables come into the picture and influence your impressions. Most situations involving interpersonal judgment are quite complex, and circumstances can weigh heavily in our judgements. It is therefore sometimes hard to predict how we will react to people, even if we know ourselves fairly well. Nevertheless, there is a general question that you must attempt to answer as you examine your personal beliefs and attitudes about people: *Do you see yourself as being able to work effectively with "all" patients to whom you are assigned?* Your answer to this question will point you toward a recognition of what some of your beliefs and attitudes are!

References

Bem, D. *Beliefs, Attitudes, and Human Affairs.* Belmont, California, Brooks/Cole, 1970.

Berkowitz, L. *A Survey of Social Psychology,* 2d ed. New York, Holt, Rinehart, and Winston, 1980.

Festinger, L. A Theory of Social Comparison Processes, *Human Relations,* 7:117–40 (1954).

Fishbein, M., and Raven B. H. The AB Scales: An Operational Definition of Belief and Attitude, *Human Relations,* **15**:35–44 (1962).

Gergen, K. J., and Jones, E. E. Mental illness, predictability, and affective consequences as stimulus factors in person perception. *Journal of Abnormal and Social Psychology,* **67**:95–104 (1963).

Rokeach, M. *The Nature of Human Values.* New York, Free Press, 1973.

Rokeach, M., and Regan, J. F. The Role of Values in the Counseling Situation, *The Personnel and Guidance Journal,* **58**(9):576–82 (1981).

Schlenker, B. R. *Impression Management: The Self-Concept, Social Identity, and Interpersonal Relations.* Monterey, California, Brooks/Cole, 1980.

CHAPTER NINE

Interpersonal Attraction:
Liking and Disliking Others

*I joked about every prominent man in my lifetime, but I
never met one I didn't like.*

Will Rogers, Epitaph

*Down on me, down on me,
Looks like everybody in this whole round world
Is down on me.*

Janis Joplin, Down on Me

There are few things we experience in life that go without some form of evaluation. After dining at a new restaurant, browsing through department stores,
completing a course of study, or even driving through different cities, we can
usually offer some evaluative comment about our experiences. Most of the
time, we translate our positive and negative evaluations into simple statements
about how much we *liked* or *disliked* something. The same holds for our evaluations of the people about whom we know or with whom we come into contact.
In general, if we find others to be pleasant, we like them more than those
whom we find unpleasant. Psychologists would say that we are more *attracted*
to those we evaluate positively and less attracted to those we evaluate negatively. Somewhere in between are people to whom we are neither attracted nor
by whom repulsed, because we don't know enough about them to like or dislike
them. In this chapter, we are concerned with the factors that move us one way
or the other and influence our liking or disliking of the people we encounter in
our lives.

As a health professional who comes into contact with literrally thousands
of people during your career, you are continuously forming impressions and
evaluating people. From preceding chapters, you should now be aware of some
of the factors influencing these processes. Here, the focus is on a highly significant outcome of evaluation and impression formation—one which carries important implications for your professional relationships. Specifically, the impressions you form often include judgements about whether you like or dislike

persons with whom you interact. Your liking for someone has a direct effect on your manner of self-presentation, which, in turn, influences the other's impressions of and liking for you. In one way or another, your attraction to one another affects virtually every interaction and every phase in the development of your relationship. That feelings of attraction and liking may determine how you behave toward someone is hard to dispute. Simply think about a person you like and a person you dislike. Do you act the same toward each person? Do you present yourself in the same way to each person? Are you not friendlier and more open to the person you like? Are you not inclined to seek out the person you like and avoid the person you dislike? And, are you not more willing to help the person you like, even going out of your way sometimes to do things you wouldn't do for the disliked person? *Can you see how this might apply to your relationships with patients and colleagues?*

In the course of your work, you'll have positive feelings about some people, negative feelings about others, and even mixed feelings toward still others. Nowhere in the professional literature will you find it written that you *must* necessarily like every person with whom you come into contact. The plain fact is that we just don't feel the same way about everyone we know. This is normal and to be expected, even in the performance of your duties. What *is* written in the literature and what is also to be expected is that you do not permit your negative feelings about certain people to interfere with providing the best possible services you have to offer. The material to follow should provide you with a knowledge base for identifying various sources of your feelings toward other people. Although our relative attraction to others may sometimes seem to be mysterious and beyond explanation, the reasons why people like or dislike one another are really not so elusive. In the first part of this chapter, different models of interpersonal attraction are presented in order to help you gain a perspective on the experience of perceivers. The second part actually addresses the question, "What is it about people that makes them likable or unlikable?"

The Meanings of Interpersonal Attraction and Liking

Interpersonal attraction is essentially a positive or negative *attitude* toward someone. In the preceding chapter, attitudes were defined as affective predispositions to behave in particular ways toward persons, objects, or issues. In the context of interpersonal attraction, attitudes are toward *persons only.* As such, they predispose individuals to respond toward others in favorable or unfavorable ways, depending on how others are evaluated. If an individual judges someone positively, then he is inclined to *approach* her and interact with her. If he sees her in a predominantly negative light, then he is predisposed to *avoid* interactions with her. As an attitude, then, interpersonal attraction is defined as *"an individual's tendency or predisposition to evaluate another person or symbol of that person in a positive (or negative) way"* (Walster and Walster, 1976, p. 280).

Liking is the term we use most frequently in everyday language to describe our preference for and attraction to another person. It is a very general semantic index of our overall orientation toward someone. It is also a term with various dimensions of meaning. To illustrate this point, let's imagine that you've gone to the hospital cafeteria for lunch with a colleague because you *like* her company. As you discuss various topics over lunch, you tell your friend about a male patient whom you *like* very much because he is conversant on a wide range of subjects and he entertains you with fascinating stories about people he has met. Then you tell your friend about this man's handsome young son who visits him every day and always stops at the nursing station to talk with you. After describing him to your friend, you confide in her that you really *like* him. No one would question the general meaning of *liking* as you use it in relation to each of the three individuals above. Nevertheless, the same word does *not* indicate that you have the same feelings about each person, nor does it indicate that your feelings come from the same source. About the only thing the term does indicate is that your *overall* evaluation of each person above is positive.

To say that liking and attraction have various dimensions of meaning is to suggest that they are *multidimensional* and not unidimensional in nature. If we were to view liking and attraction as unidimensional concepts, then we would be suggesting that there is *only one kind* of attraction for others and that we *cannot like and dislike the same person*. From a multidimensional perspective, we recognize that our liking for other people is very complex and that we are attracted to different people in different ways. For example, in the hypothetical cases above, you may have been attracted to your colleague because you enjoy her company, attracted to the male patient because of his intelligence and wisdom, and attracted to the young man because of a romantic interest. From a multidimensional perspective, we also recognize that we may like and dislike the same person, love and hate the same person, like but not love or love but not like the same person. In the cases above, you may like your colleague but dislike various things she does or says, you may like your male patient but dislike his manners and personal habits, and while you may be attracted to the young man, you may also be repulsed somewhat by his insistence on hanging around the nursing station to make public "passes" at you. Virtually all of the people with whom we come into contact in our lives engender ambivalent feelings in us. Seldom do we evaluate a person *entirely* positively. And, it would be hard to conceive of a situation in which we are attracted to two people for *identical reasons*.

Thus, to discuss interpersonal attraction and liking is not a simple matter of describing a single evaluative dimension. The unfortunate fact is, however, that the unidimensional view has figured prominently in the line of research on interpersonal attraction. We *have* learned a good deal about attraction and liking through the research, but in guiding the research, the unidimensional view has ensured that we still have a long way to go toward fully understanding the kinds of attraction one person may have for another (Berscheid and Walster, 1978).

Models of Interpersonal Attraction

The bulk of research findings to be discussed support the already overwhelming acceptance that each of the conditions listed above is a determinant of our attraction to others. We like people who share our views more than people who disagree with us; we like people with pleasant qualities more than people with unpleasant qualities; we like competent people more than incompetent people; we like people who like us more than people who dislike us. When taken at face value, perferences like these would suggest that we are simply attracted more to people who reward us than we are to people who do not reward us. While this may be a sweeping generalization, the role of reward or *reinforcement* in interpersonal attraction does appear to be significant. In one form or another, the principle of reinforcement is represented in most theories of interpersonal attraction. Some of those models are discussed here.

The Reinforcement-Affect Model

Byrne and Clore (1970) proposed that our liking for people is based on the extent to which positive or negative feelings are aroused. In essence, their positions are that our liking for a person is based on the positive feelings we associate with that person, while our disliking for someone is based on the negative feelings we associate with him. For example, let's suppose that you have driven a friend to the hospital for emergency treatment of a rather severe laceration. After what seemed to you to be an eternity of waiting, you stepped out into the corridor and stopped an orderly who had helped your friend into the emergency room earlier. You asked him how much longer your friend would be in there, and he quickly snapped back at you with almost unrelenting hostility over the nature of your question. It was as if your innocent question unleashed all of his pent up frustrations and you happened to be the nearest target. If you were asked about your reaction to that experience, you would obviously report that you didn't like getting yelled at and didn't like the person who yelled at you. Your negative feelings would probably not end there, however. It is quite likely that they would generalize to the whole context of your interaction—the corridor, the waiting room, the emergency department, and to anyone who happened to be around when the incident occurred. Conversely, if everything had happened differently—if the orderly was extremely kind and helpful, seeing if he could find out how your friend was doing and offering to get you some coffee—then your feelings would be positive and your liking for the interaction context would be much different. It would be hard to dispute the differential effects of getting yelled at versus getting coffee, congeniality, and the information for which you asked. According to the reinforcement-affect model, the differential effects relate to positive and negative feelings which, in turn, become associated with particular people and surroundings. The essence of this model is summarized in four basic propositions (Baron and Byrne, 1976; Baron, Byrne, and Griffitt, 1974);

1. Most of the stimuli to which we are exposed can be said to be either reinforcing or punishing. We tend to seek out and approach reinforcing stimuli and we try to avoid punishing stimuli. We learn to behave in ways which help us obtain reinforcements and minimize punishments.

Note that the first proposition reflects the basic reinforcement paradigm which was discussed in Chapter Seven. Thus, the entire model is built around the fundamental principle of reinforcement.

2. Reinforcing stimuli arouse positive feelings and punishing stimuli generate negative feelings. It is assumed that positive feelings exist at one end of a continuum which extends to the opposite extreme of negative feelings.
3. The evaluation of any given stimulus as pleasant or unpleasant depends on whether it arouses positive or negative feelings and how strong they are. Consequently, we can order our likes and dislikes along a rough scale.

For example, you may like working in a hospital more than you like working in a public health center, and you may like working in both settings better than in a storefront clinic. In all probability, you would prefer a storefront clinic to a makeshift clinic in a mud hut along the Amazon River.

4. Any neutral stimulus that is associated with a reinforcer will acquire the capacity to arouse positive feelings and will be liked as a consequence. A neutral stimulus that is associated with punishment will acquire the capacity to arouse negative feelings and will be disliked as a consequence. If the neutral stimulus is a person, he or she will be liked if associated with reinforcers and disliked if associated with punishments.

For example, if the orderly in the case above yelled at you in the presence of strangers, those people would become associated with the unpleasantness of the situation and, therefore, those people themselves can rekindle your negative feelings. Consequently, it becomes something of a "guilt by association" process, whereby those people are evaluated negatively *as if* they were the ones who yelled at you. Innocent bystanders who are simply present will be liked if you receive reinforcements and disliked if you receive punishments (Griffit and Guay, 1969).

The final aspect of the reinforcement-affect model pertains to the effects of *combined* reinforcements and punishments. According to the theory, if a person (for example, your supervisor) is associated with *both* rewards and punishment, your feelings toward that person are the outcomes of an *averaging* process which is not at all unlike the averaging process described in Chapter Six. Attraction is the net result of the value we attach to reinforcers versus the value we attach to punishments.

Social-Exchange Theory

Another type of reinforcement theory, proposed by Thibaut and Kelley (1959), as social-exchange theory, holds that individuals remain attracted to one another in a relationship if the rewards from the relationship are greater for each person than the costs. By introducing the concept of *comparison level* (CL), Thibaut and Kelley hypothesized that individuals compare their profits in a relationship with the profits they "expect" from the relationship. That is, individuals stack up their actual gains in a relationship and compare them against all possible gains which they could expect to receive. The comparison level is conceptualized as some average value of all reinforcing outcomes known to an individual by virtue of what he has experienced or seen others experience in relationships. The individual's attraction to another is dependent on a ratio of actual outcomes-to-expected outcomes in the relationship. If actual outcomes exceed the CL, the individual is satisfied with the relationship; as those outcomes exceed the CL by greater and greater degrees, the individual becomes more and more attracted to the relationship and the other person. On the other hand, if the outcomes are below the CL, the individual is dissatisfied with the relationship and less attracted to the other person. For example, if you think about one of your most important relationships from the past, you can apply this model. In that relationship, you probably carried certain expectations about how the other person should treat you, how the relationship should work, and what you should get out of it. From your experience in other relationships and from your observations of others in separate relationships, you probably developed some ideas about what rightly to expect and what not to expect. Let's take "respect" as one variable. Around that notion, you may have developed expectations that the other person should accept you for who you are and not try to make you something or someone else, that he or she should recognize your right to your own opinions, that your feelings should not be criticized, and so on. If you stacked up these expectations against the ways that person actually treated you, you arrived at your own CL. According to social-exchange theory, if the other person consistently showed respect for you as a person, then you would find the relationship to be satisfactory (all other things being equal, of course—repsect is the only variable in this example). If the actual outcomes of your relationship fell short of what you could realistically expect, then your dissatisfaction with the relationship in general probably diminished the attractiveness of the other person in particular (see Figure 9.1).

Whereas the comparison level determines how content an individual is in a relationship and how attracted he or she is to the other, a different concept was used by Thibaut and Kelley to indicate the person's *commitment* to the relationship and the other. This concept, called *comparison level for alternatives* (CL_{alt}), permitted an important distinction between our liking for others and our actual commitment to them (see Figure 9.1). CL_{alt} is seen as the criterion for making the ultimate decision about continuing in a relationship. It is arrived at by comparing the cost/reward ratio of one relationship with the cost/reward ratio of available alternatives. If the outcomes received in a relationship are below the CL_{alt}, the individual may abandon the relationship when he thinks a better one is available. Nevertheless, even if the individual is not attracted to the other, he may continue in the relationship if nothing better has come along. The concept of CL_{alt} permits a distinction between an individual's "attraction" to another person in a relationship and his tendency to "remain" in the relationship. As Thibaut and Kelley suggested, attraction and association (or liking and commitment) are not synonymous. Just because two people are in a relationship does not necessarily mean that one or both like the other!

A Note on Reinforcement

The basic principle of reinforcement is reflected in the widely accepted view that we like people who reward us and dislike people who punish us. The

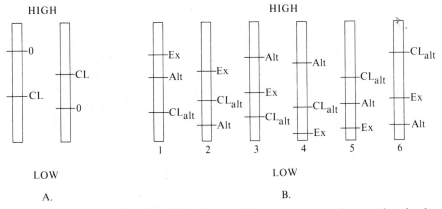

Figure 9.1 (A) According to social-exchange theory, outcomes and comparison level are factors affecting satisfaction with a relationship and attraction to the other. Comparison level (CL) is an average value of all reinforcing outcomes an individual can expect in a relationship. When actual outcomes (O) exceed (CL), as in 1, satisfaction is high and attraction is strong; when O falls short of CL, as in 2, the opposite occurs. (B) Comparison level for alternatives (CL$_{alt}$) is a hypothetical gauge for deciding whether to remain in a relationship. Individuals are hypothesized to compare their existing relationships (Ex) with available alternatives (Alt). Six possible consequences are represented above: (1) although an alternative relationship may be seen as satisfactory, the individual is sufficiently content in her present relationship; for example, if you received several enticing job offers, you would remain in your current position if it was even more rewarding than the alternatives. (2) Even the best alternative would not be satisfactory because it is below CL$_{alt}$ and well below the level of satisfaction being derived in Ex; if your best job offer didn't meet your expectations and was less appealing than your current job, you may remain in your present position. (3) The individual is satisfied with her Ex, but the best alternative is even more attractive; you might change jobs if you received a terrific offer. (4) The individual is dissatisfied with her current relationship and perceives the Alt to be much more rewarding; if you were dissatisfied in your job and received a good offer, you would probably accept it. (5) The individual is not attracted to Ex or Alt, but Alt is lesser of "two evils"; you don't like your job, but you don't want to be unemployed, yet you'd take unemployment because you're so unhappy in your job. (6) Nothing appeals to the individual, and she may feel hopelessly trapped; you may do any number of things, from remaining in an intolerable job to continuing your search for a better one, to changing your whole line of work.

principle is widely applicable to a range of attraction phenomena, but it may be too simple to account for the real complexity of those phenomena. Those whom we like may provide numerous rewards, but they also provide numerous punishments. Deriving an index of attraction by balancing rewards against punishments seems hardly practical in a world where individuals vary in what they regard as reinforcing and punishing and even in what they find to be reinforcing from one time to the next. The simple labeling of something as reinforcing may not be adequate for making predictions about who will be attracted to whom, how, when, and with what effect. As Wrightsman (1977) argued, several theoretical models may be necessary in order to advance our understanding of the reasons why one individual is attracted to another individual. At the present time, however, most theories of interpersonal attraction assign a dominant role to reward, and few minimize its importance or subsume its operation under other theoretical concepts. It seems as if the more fundamental presupposition of *hedonism*—the view that individuals are motivated to seek pleasure and avoid pain—is so widely accepted that the real question about the role of reinforcement in interpersonal attraction is *not whether* it is important, but *how important* it is in determining our liking for others. As we shall see shortly, it has been possible to identify some general reinforcers that are "transsituational" in nature—they function as rewards for *most people most of the time*. These general rewards appear to be very important as determinants of attraction. Before describing those conditions, we will examine another model of attrraction in which the role of reinforcement is equally conspicuous.

Equity Theory

Equity theory was introduced by Adams (1965) and elaborated by Walster, Berscheid, and Walster (1970, 1978). The theory is quite simple, consisting of four basic propositions resting upon a few broad assumptions about human nature. A basic assumption of equity theory is that every human being tries to get as much as he or she can out of life. Since there is a limit to everything available to people, rules evolve for determining who gets what and when. Equity theorists have been interested in how people determine who gets what and how they react when they think they're getting more or less than to what they're entitled (Berscheid and Walster, 1978). The four propositions of equity theory are conveniently summarized by Berscheid and Walster (1978):

1. Individuals try to maximize their rewards and minimize their costs (rewards minus costs equal "outcomes").
2. Groups of people evolve systems for maximizing their collective rewards by "equitably" apportioning available rewards and costs among group members. Groups will induce individual members to adhere to the system, and will usually reward members who treat others equitably and punish those who behave inequitably.
3. Individuals become distressed when they find themselves participating in inequitable relationships. The more inequitable the relationships, the more distress they feel.
4. Upon discovering the inequity in a relationship the individual will attempt to eliminate distress by restoring equity. The greater the inequity, the greater the distress, and the harder she will try to restore equity.

Thus, equity theory suggests that people like to maintain a balance in their relationships between what they give and receive and what the other gives and receives. It is assumed that people like to have their rewards proportional to their investments in a relationship. Consequently, individuals are contented when they believe they are getting just what they deserve out of relationships. From these assumptions, equity theory would predict that the way in which we treat a person in a relationship will have an effect on our feelings toward him. We may be attracted to those we treat fairly and not attracted to those we treat unfairly, especially if we feel we've done everything within reason to compensate for our unfair treatment of individuals (and it still doesn't restore equity in the relationships). There is ample evidence to be discussed later that we often come to dislike those we treat unjustly and like those whom we benefit.

Cognitive Dissonance Theory

All three of the preceding theories would have difficulty accounting for an individual's attraction to someone who has treated him poorly or caused him to expend great effort for the sake of the relationship. Yet, there are times when we seem to like others even though they have treated us badly, times when we may be attracted to someone who is "beyond our reach" so to speak, and times when our expenditure of effort makes another person or group seem even more desirable. For example, data reveal that the more severe an initiation is, the more attractive the group becomes to the person being initiated for membership (e.g., Aronson and Mills, 1959). Reinforcement-based theories seem inadequate in explaining such findings. There is a model, however, which is useful in accounting for instances where it is difficult to identify the rewards inherent in our attraction to others: *cognitive dissonance theory* (see Chapter Three for details) (Festinger, 1957). When applied to instances of attraction such as those described above, cognitive dissonance theory would predict that we will find another person *more attractive* when our efforts to promote a relationship with that person are *great* and *less attractive* when our efforts are *minimal*. The assumption is that, when we expend effort in behalf of another person, we must justify our effort to ourselves. We do so by convincing ourselves that the other is a worthy fellow and by making him more attractive. To acknowledge that the other person is unlikable or somehow unattractive is inconsistent with having expended considerable effort in his behalf. Thus, we convince ourselves that he is likable and attractive. Why would we go to all the bother if we disliked him?

To illustrate this point, let's suppose you have a roommate who asks you to do a big favor and run down to the drugstore and get her some cigarettes. If you refuse to do this favor, you may subsequently justify your refusal by telling yourself that she's always asking you to do things for her, that she never reciprocates, that if she wants something as mundane as cigarettes she can go to the drugstore herself, and so on. All of these are actually negative commentaries about your roommate, and they may make her less attractive to you. After all, you're a decent, helpful person who is willing to do things for people, and you wouldn't turn anyone down unless you had a good reason. Right? I don't know if your reasons would necessarily be good, but they would probably suffice *for you*. On the other hand, if you decided to put on your coat and walk through the snow for three blocks to the drugstore, it would be hard for you to dislike your roommate and at the same time brave the winter cold to do her a favor. Even if you let her know that "I wouldn't do this for just anyone," you'd still have to make her more attractive in your own mind in order to justify your efforts.

Cognitive dissonance theory is a model with considerable utility in the area of interpersonal attraction, and it can account for various phenomena which the other theories discussed here have difficulty explaining. Rather than using this model as a broad theory of attraction, most theorists who recognize the value of dissonance theory see its major contribution in relation to hypotheses concerning the *cognitive component* of attraction. Remember, interpersonal attraction is an attitude, and, as such, it consists of three components, one of which is the cognitive aspect. Dissonance theory appears to be useful in generating hypotheses about the variables affecting our thoughts. For example, if you know that there is no way you can get out of having to care for a certain patient—that it is inevitable for you to come into frequent contact with and spend time with him—you may end up trying to convince yourself that he really isn't so bad. If you're successful in selling yourself on that idea, you could even end up liking him in the long run! Obviously, factors may enter into this process—factors for which we have not accounted. And, this is just what we mean by "variables affecting our thoughts": dissonance theory is most useful in generating predictions about the *conditions* under which you are or are not likely to change your thoughts about the patient for whom you must care. Incidentally, George Bernard Shaw once wrote about living in undesirable circumstances and making the best of the way things are: "If you cannot get rid of the family skeleton, you may as well make it dance."

Self-Perception and Self-Attribution

Our behavior toward others may influence our feelings through self-attribution. Essentially, this is what happens when we convince ourselves that we must like someone because of what we did for him: "If I went to all that trouble for him, then I must like him." Bem's (1965) theory of self-perception makes this very prediction (see Chapter Three). If Bem's theory is correct, then we determine our liking for another person by observing our own behavior in relation to him. After noting our actions as they relate to the other, we make attributions to our own feelings as well as beliefs. This simple notion also appears to have utility in advancing our understanding of the bases for attraction. Its applicability seems to be especially useful in those situations where individuals are uncertain about how they feel toward someone. It could be that they eliminate their uncertainty by acknowledging their own actions and drawing inferences from observations.

According to self-perception theory, we are not as adept at recognizing our feelings as we might think we are. There are even times when we're caught by surprise at our reactions to another person. For example, perhaps you have found yourself responding to romantic persuasions in ways quite different from what you would have expected, and, if not, you have most likely heard this line, which seems to be a standard reaction of characters in novels and movies: 'I didn't realize how much I cared for you until just now when you kissed me." Or, you may have discovered at one time or another how you were denying resentments toward someone, until you finally blew up in anger. Coming to understand how we feel about some persons can be truly challenging and confusing at times. Self-perception theory proposes that insight into our feelings and, hence, a reduction of confusion can be gained when we move from a preoccupation with internal experience to a consideration of our actions. And, it seems that we can learn even more about our attraction to someone when we look at the *context* of our behavior: the relationship itself. Thus, if we look at our *interactions*—the back-and-forth, give-and-take, reciprocal exchange of behaviors in the context of relationships—we may learn more about our feelings toward someone than we would if we limited our exploration only to private reactions.

Interactional Theory

Each of the models discussed to this point represents analyses of the single individual and her behavior. An alternative approach, known as interactional theory, focuses not on the single individual, but on the interaction between *two* individuals. The interactional approach represents less of a theory in the formal sense and more of a descriptive framework for looking at the relationship aspects of attraction and liking. Within this framework, Levinger and his colleagues (Levinger, 1974; Levinger and Snoek, 1972; Huston and Levinger, 1978) have utilized reinforcement and social-exchange concepts to account for the effects of various factors at different points in the relationship. Thus, their approach is one which views attraction developmentally, as something that evolves between two persons over time within the context of their relationship. They have identified different levels of relationships in which factors specific to each level exert primary influences on attraction. Levinger and his colleagues based their analysis on the premise that "real-life" attraction is not a matter of snap judgements and first impressions, but something affected by different variables at different points in time. An example which may clarify this premise is the fact that the simple exchange of greetings and pleasantries may be sufficient to maintain relationships with health care administrators, but totally insufficient to maintain a marital relationship. Each of these relationships involves different degrees of intimacy, for one thing, and one's liking for the administrator is presumably less intense than one's liking for the spouse, because the relationships are on different levels and under the influence of factors more intrinsic to their respective levels. The levels of relationship described by Levinger and Snoek (1972) are depicted in Figure 9.2.

Figure 9.2 shows the levels through which a relationship is seen to pass if two people move toward greater closeness. Attraction between two individuals can range from total unawareness of one another to deep, mutual interaction. At the lowest level of *no contact* (0), two individuals are simply strangers, ignorant of each other's existence. At the level of *unilateral awareness* (1), the two persons become aware of one another and begin to form impressions, even though they have still not interacted. For example, you may see someone at work each day, and that person may see you as well, but you may not move beyond the level of awareness of one another to speak and introduce yourselves. It is assumed that if you receive positive information at this level (e.g., a smile, opinions from a third person), the likelihood of your attempt to move to the next level is increased, and increased further if the other person received positive information about you. *Surface contact* (2) occurs when two people interact in a relatively superficial way. Various factors affect the interaction at this level, including each person's social/professional role and the conditions under

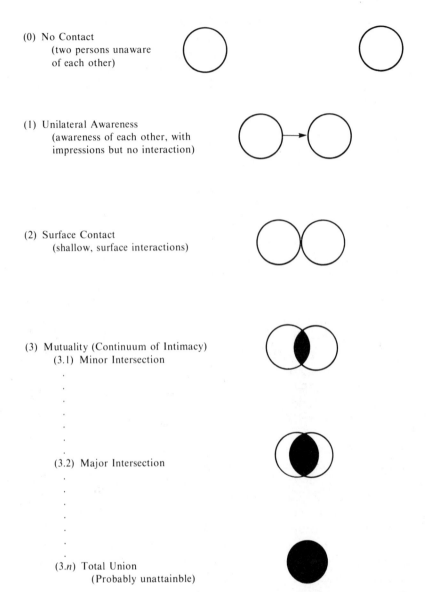

(0) No Contact
     (two persons unaware
     of each other)

(1) Unilateral Awareness
     (awareness of each other, with
     impressions but no interaction)

(2) Surface Contact
     (shallow, surface interactions)

(3) Mutuality (Continuum of Intimacy)
     (3.1) Minor Intersection
     .
     .
     .
     .
     .
     (3.2) Major Intersection
     .
     .
     .
     .
     (3.n) Total Union
     (Probably unattainble)

Figure 9.2   The levels of relationship described by Levinger and Snoek (1972), ranging from zero contact (0) between two persons who are unaware of each other's existence to varying degrees of intimacy and closeness in which there is an overlapping of their lives (3.1–3.2). A total overlapping of two lives is presumed to be unattainable (3.n). (From Levinger and Snoek, 1972.)

which they come into contact. As you might expect, it is at this level that self-presentation and impression management are likely to be important for each person. During surface contacts, each person tries to convey a particular image of herself and, at the same time, elicit as much information about the other person as possible. This is the kind of interaction that characterizes your first encounters with instructors, colleagues, patients, supervisors, and so on. At these times, you acquire some basic knowledge about them, and you use this information to decide about future interactions—whether you want to interact with them again, how you will approach them the next time, or even what other information about yourself to disclose. At the level of *mutuality* (3), there is more intimacy, mutual disclosure, openness, and deeper degrees of overall involvement with the other. This level is seen to exist along a continuum of interdependence between interacting persons. As the lives of the two individuals begin to overlap more and more, each person's thoughts, feelings, and behavior are increasingly influenced by the other's thoughts, feelings, and behavior. For example, increasing mutuality often occurs between nurses and patients who are receiving long-term care. Over time, nurses and patients develop deeper degrees of involvement with one another, to a point where there may be a *minor intersection* (3.1). If the relationship continues to move toward increasingly greater mutuality, a *major intersection* (3.2) is approached, where there is a deep overlapping of attraction. This is a level of intense feelings for one another, from deep respect and compassion to romantic love. From what we know of human relationships, we can say that once people have reached certain levels, they do not necessarily stay there. Just as relationships can move toward greater mutuality, so also can they move *backward* in the direction of surface contact or even no contact, and even back again!

The Utility of Models of Attraction

Most of us usually have little difficulty explaining why we like some people and not others. We seem to feel confident that we know exactly why we like and dislike certain people, and when we're asked about our reasons, we proceed with relative ease to itemize the desirable qualities of those we like and the undesirable qualities of those we dislike. The readiness with which we respond would almost suggest that all we have to do in identifying the determinants of interpersonal attraction is to ask people to list their reasons for liking others. However, as Berscheid and Walster (1978) noted, there is a major flaw in this kind of approach—namely, most people would leave the most important determinant out of their lists: *themselves*.

If we are to understand why a person likes one individual and dislikes the next, we need to know as much about the perceiver as we do about the perceived. The models reviewed here give us some perspectives for understanding the experience of perceivers. Independently, they may be unable to account for the true complexity of one's attraction to another. Collectively, they offer useful insights into factors intrinsic to perceivers which influence their attraction to others. At present, no one theory appears to be without some difficulty in interpreting the data from research on interpersonal attraction. Again, several models appear to be necessary.

The models outlined here rightly stress the role of perceivers in determining attraction. It is safe to assume, however, that specific situational factors not incorporated into the models play important roles. One task for research, then, has been to identify the *conditions* under which liking or disliking occur. Some of the findings in this regard are explored in the next section. Another task for research has been to identify *perceived person characteristics* that weigh heavily in interpersonal attraction. Recognizing that these factors cannot be overlooked, most researchers have concentrated on identifying what it is about an individual that makes others like or dislike him. We will now turn to this problem.

Determinants of Attraction

If you were to pause and think of all the students you know in this course, you could probably cite a variety of reasons for why you like some of them better than others. Included in your list of reasons might be preferences for those who:

Have similar interests and like the things you like
Share your views and see things as you do
Have pleasant personalities and qualities you like
Are neat-appearing and pleasant-looking
Possess some particular talents, skills, or competencies
Like you in return

Some or all of these may be on your list in one form or another; if they are, you have identified what research has found to be important determinants of personal attraction. But, the research is much more informative than the simple list above, for it has revealed numerous qualifications for each of these conditions. Furthermore, there are additional factors not listed above. Perhaps you have some of them on your own list, and, if not, you should find the data to be particularly interesting.

Opportunity to Interact

The most fundamental basis for interpersonal attraction is the *opportunity to interact with another person*. Obviously, if you never see or talk to a person—if you never get to the level of surface contact—it is unlikely that you will be attracted to one another. It would hardly require empirical research to demonstrate such a conspicuous fact. But, it has required research to point up the relationships between interpersonal attraction and factors which increase or decrease the opportunity to interact. One broad category of factors relates to the physical environment, where research has focused on propinquity, or *proximity.*

Physical Proximity and Architecture

Several years ago, I lived in an apartment building shaped just like the one on the left in Figure 9.3. Within a very short time after moving into that apartment, I had come into contact with virtually every other person living in the building. I made a number of friends among my neighbors, and I was sad to

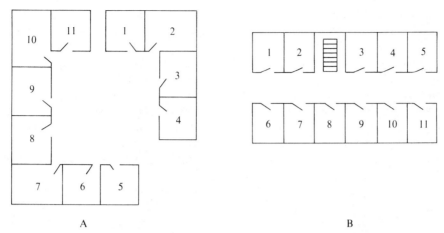

A   B

Figure 9.3   Architectural arrangements affect opportunities to interact and, consequently, interpersonal attraction and relationships. The design of the building on the
left (*A*) facilitates interaction among residents. Even though they are separated by equal
distances, residents of apartments 2 and 7 in building *A* are more likely to interact with
each other than are the residents of apartments 1 and 11 in building *B*. The design of
building *B*, on the right, minimizes opportunities for interaction. Residents of apartments 1 and 11 are less likely to interact, also, because their nearest neighbors provide
alternative opportunities. Given these designs, we would also expect that building *A*
provides less "privacy" than building *B*. When privacy is important, the design on the
right may be much more desirable. Since privacy is more important than interaction (for
patients) in hospital settings, more hospitals are designed with patient units arranged in
the side-by-side pattern similar to building *B*. Imagine a hospital floor plan similar to
that of building *A*. What effects do you think the architectural arrangement would have
on your interactions with colleagues? With patients on the floor? Among patients themselves? Are there certain departments (e.g., medical-surgical, intensive care, administra-
tive services) for which one design may be more appropriate than the other?

leave them when I moved into a different aparment building some time later.
That building was shaped like the one on the right in Figure 9.3. My apartment
was located at the top of a stairway. After living in that building for over a
year, I still had met only a handful of my neighbors. On occasion, I was even
surprised when I met someone by accident in a different location and learned
that the person lived right down the hall from me! On those occasions, we usually exchanged apologies for not being "good neighbors." But, truthfully, I
didn't really feel like such a bad neighbor, nor did I necessarily think that my
new acquaintances were antisocial. Being a psychologist sometimes has its advantages, and one advantage for me was that I knew about the findings of Festinger, Schachter, and Back (1950) and other studies which showed that architecture has a direct influence on human interactions. I realized that the first
apartment building was laid out in such a way as to promote contact between
residents, while my current apartment building was simply not conducive to interaction among tenants. So, none of us were entirely to blame for not getting
to know one another. According to the findings of Festinger, Schachter, and
Back, I had a different advantage over my neighbors: I lived at the top of the
stairs. The advantage, if you want to see it as such, increased the likelihood

that I would run into people more frequently than others down the hall. And, Festinger and his colleagues found that persons living in centralized locations within apartment buildings tend to be more widely known among other tenants and more popular. Since I didn't study the phenomenon in my own apartment building, I have no way of knowing how well-known I really was, nor can I say that my popularity was greater than anyone else's. What I *do* know is that attraction and popularity involve much more than simply getting yourself an apartment in the middle of a building! Most of us are not so eager to make new friends, so desperate to like someone, that we become attracted to others just because we happen to come into frequent contact. Life and living in apartment buildings are not that simple.

Notwithstanding the complexity of interpersonal attraction, research in social and environmental psychology has repeatedly demonstrated that the physical setting can increase or decrease the opportunity to interact with others. People tend to become friends with their closest neighbors (Merton, 1947; Rosow, 1961, Whyte, 1956), college students tend to be more attracted to those who share classes or living quarters than to those who are slightly farther away (Byrne and Beuhler, 1955; Byrne, 1961; Nahemow and Lawton, 1975; Maisonneuve, Palmade, and Fourment, 1952), clerical workers develop closer relationships with those whose desks are nearby (Gullahorn, 1952), and even bomber crews tend to become more attracted to one another as a function of proximity of seats (Kipnis, 1957).

If the physical environment is conceived as a collection of features which can promote or prevent interactions and, hence, interpersonal liking, it would seem that the interior designs of buildings may be basic determinants of attraction. Many office buildings are now being "landscaped" (see Howard, 1972; Sommer, 1974) with strategic placements of barriers and partitions in order to have optimal effects on privacy and interactions. And, even the effects of furniture arrangements have been shown to have direct relationships to social interaction (e.g., Sommer and Ross, 1958; Mehrabian and Diamond, 1971).

Given that physical proximity contributes to one's liking for another, it is equally possible that it can have the reverse effect: physical proximity can lead to interpersonal hostility and conflict. For example, racial desegregation—the process of bringing members of different races into closer contact with one another—has not had entirely positive results. Mere contact is no guarantee that people will come to have favorable interactions, let alone develop attractions for one another. An important variable relates to the *conditions surrounding* interpersonal contact: interpersonal contact can have positive results under favorable conditions and negative results under unfavorable conditions. It would be impossible to identify all of the possible contextual factors which could make situations favorable or unfavorable, but one example may give an idea of how the design of buildings can bring people into close proximity and at the same time decrease opportunities to interact, limit the range of behavioral alternatives available to people, and contribute to interpersonal tension and conflict. In 1955, the Pruitt-Igoe housing project was built in St. Louis, Missouri under an urban renewal program which created 33 high-rise apartment buildings for low income families (Newman, 1973). After three years, the buildings had physically deteriorated from neglect and decay; crime rates increased; vandals, criminals, and juvenile delinquents roamed the grounds; and many families began to vacate their apartments. The city recognized that the project was a miserable failure and had the buildings torn down. Subsequent research indicated that part of the failure was due to the design of the buildings. For example, narrow hallways and few formal gathering places precluded casual interactions, residents couldn't supervise their children playing below because the buildings were so tall (11 stories) and, in general, the architecture prohibited residents from meeting and interacting with one another as they had been used to doing with neighbors in their former housing projects. One effect was a feeling of isolation among the residents (Yancey, 1971). Now, from the research findings cited above, you might expect that residents developed friendships with their closest neighbors. Many of them probably did. Yet, the overall conditions were unfavorable. Thus, the context in which people were brought together may have precluded the development of close relationships. As Berkowitz (1980, p.222) noted, contact will lead to increased attraction to the extent that the encounter is rewarding "and will create greater enmity if the meeting occurs under unpleasant circumstances." While we shall not attempt a sociological analysis of the Pruitt-Igoe failure, it is worthwhile to consider the negative effects which unfavorable physical surroundings exerted on the formation of interpersonal relationships.

In summary, if you are aware of media accounts of crime as well as data pertaining to those crimes, you know that most crimes are committed against people who are in close proximity to the perpetrator. Contrary to popular belief, perpetrators usually strike in the vicinity in which they live, and frequently they know their victims personally. About 40 percent of all murders are committed by persons who are relatives, friends, or close acquaintances of their victims (U.S. Department of Justice, *Uniform Crime Reports*, 1978). Thus, while proximity may be a necessary condition for liking, it also seems to be a necessary condition for hating (Berscheid and Walster, 1978). Proximity by itself is hardly "sufficient" for either liking or disliking. It increases the opportunities for interaction and greater familiarity, which may lead to liking or disliking. Various conditions can determine whether the individual's familiarity with someone leads to increased liking or disliking. For example, Berkowitz (1980) posited that our existing attitudes are important factors. If we come to dislike a certain person, further contact brings us into repeated exposure to an unpleasant experience and this, he believed, strengthens our negative feelings. The same principle is also assumed to hold for individuals we like. Actually, the most conservative statement to be made about the effects of proximity is that the closer our proximity to someone, the more familiar we become with that person, and familiarity may breed liking or contempt, depending on numerous other factors to be considered. In summary, however, the research suggests that proximity is more likely to promote attraction than its opposite (Berscheid and Walster, 1978)—an encouraging outlook.

Similarity

Do "birds of a feather flock together"? Most people seem to take it for granted that this timeworn adage is true. Folk wisdom has it that we like people who are similar to ourselves more than those who are dissimilar. Indeed, this may be one of the reasons for Carol's liking for Christine in the following example:

> Carol had recently enrolled in a social work program and was invited to attend a party sponsored by the Social Work Department. She went to the party, hoping that she would meet other students in the program and perhaps make some new friends. After spending several hours at the party, Carol returned to her apartment, where she was met by her roommate who was eager to learn if Carol met any interesting people. "I did meet some pretty nice people," said Carol, "like Christine. She and I are taking some classes together, and we really seem to have a lot in common. In fact, I couldn't believe how much we're alike. She even comes from a town just outside of Springfield where I lived. She feels the same way as I do about being here in California: she's having a hard time adjusting to the life-style out here, like me, and we both noticed how different a lot of the people are, like this guy, named Burt, whom we met at the party. He's into body-surfing and hang gliding, and he's got this sort of laid-back, mellow, free-spirit style about him. He's an anti-intellectual person who identifies with all of the latest experiential fads in pop-psychology. I suppose his approach to social work is like his approach to everything else, you know, 'just go with the flow and do your thing; whatever it happens to be is all right, as long as you feel good.' Christine and I weren't very impressed with him."

It should be clear in the above example that Carol and Christine were attracted to one another on the basis of their similar interests, attitudes, and values, and that neither of them were attracted to Burt because of the differences they perceived to exist on the same dimensions. Countless studies, especially the dozens conducted by Byrne (e.g., 1969, 1971), have shown repeatedly that we are attracted to and like people whose attitudes, interests, and values appear to agree with ours, and we tend to dislike those who appear to disagree. In fact, many of the same studies indicate that if all you know about a person is that her positions on various issues are similar to yours, you will be attracted to her more than you would to a person whose views are dissimilar. Aronson (1976) cited two possible reasons why similarity is important to us.

One reason, according to Aronson, relates to the validation the other person provides for our views. If the other person's views are similar, she makes us feel that we are right. The reward provided by the other in this way tends to increase our liking for her. Being in new surroundings and having some uncertainty about the validity of one's perceptions of those surroundings could have been conditions which paved the way for Carol's attraction to Christine in the above case. Christine's views about those surroundings may have validated Carol's perceptions and vice versa. By reinforcing each other's views, Carol and Christine could both feel that they were right. Their mutual rewards thus increased their mutual attraction. Aronson also noted that if a person disagrees with us, he is indicating that we may be wrong, and this is punishing. Since we don't like to be punished, we may come to dislike those who disagree with us. However, this requires some qualifications which are discussed below. A second reason why similarity is important may relate to the kinds of inferences we make about those who disagree with us. Specifically, if a person disagrees with us on a substantive issue, we are likely to make some negative inferences about his personality. His contrasting viewpoint may indicate to us that he is just like others whom we have found to be ignorant, obnoxious, or stupid. In the example above, Carol and Christine may have disliked Burt for either one or both of the reasons cited here. On the one hand, he expressed interests, attitudes, and values consistent with the life-style that Carol and Christine found to be objectionable. Thus, Burt may have been suggesting to them that their perceptions were inaccurate and that their own perferred life-styles were questionable. On the other hand, Carol and Christine may have seen Burt as a person who was simply ignorant or obnoxious. From the example, it certainly seems clear that this latter possibility played a role, since Carol made some pretty direct inferences about Burt's overall personality, and those inferences were negative by her evaluative criteria.

Qualifications on the Similarity Variable

At the risk of seeming facetious around the "birds of a feather" notion, we might entertain the question of which comes first—the chicken or the egg." That is, does similarity lead to attraction, or does attraction lead to similarity? It could be that friends have similar attitudes because similarity led them to like one another in the first place, or it could be that attraction leads to agreement (Baron, Byrne, and Griffit, 1974). Berscheid and Walster (1978) reviewed a body of research on this issue and concluded that there is considerable evidence that *similarity generates attraction.* This is not to suggest, however, that individuals who are attracted to one another do not move toward increasing similarity. It seems that people who like one another routinely perceive themselves as being more similar than they actually are. Apparently, there are many times when our mutual attraction leads us to distort the amount of real similarity between us (Stephan, 1973). To maintain cognitive consistency or to satisfy our needs for close relationships, we often make others out to be similar to us. Clearly, there is a difference between *actual* similarity and *perceived* similarity, and, when our strong attraction to someone is based on other factors, there is a likelihood that we will come to assume that we have *more things in common with that person than we really do* (Berscheid and Walster, 1978). However, there is an additional possibility. *Real* attitude similarity may develop between two people as they continue to interact more frequently. The more often they exchange their views, the greater the likelihood that they will reconcile initial differences and develop a common outlook (Berkowitz, 1980).

The question still remains as to whether or not disagreement and dissimilarity are so undesirable. Do we necessarily dislike those who disagree with us? There are various ways of approaching this issue, but the answer is no, we do not necessarily dislike those who disagree with us. For one thing, it depends on the *basis* of our disagreement or dissimilarity. For example, you share many things in common with other health professionals—you are in the same general field, you offer similar services, you wear similar uniforms, you have five toes on each foot, and so on. There are thousands of variables on which people share similarities. The fact is that some similarities are more important than others. You may work on the same floor as 20 other health professionals, but that doesn't mean you'll be attracted to all of them. Conversely, you may like the food in the hospital cafeteria and some of your colleagues may hate that food, and yet you don't yell and scream at one another because of your different tastes. Disagreements and dissimilar tastes are largely irrelevant under those conditions. Thus, for disagreement and dissimilarity to lead to disliking—and for agreement and similarity to lead to attraction—*the issues must be important to you or they won't matter*; they won't "count." Thus, it may be irrelevant that someone likes the color blue, and you don't, but highly significant if that same person says he thinks your best friend is a jerk!

Let's imagine that you have nothing to do one evening, and you decide to attend a meeting dealing with the problem of "burn-out" among health professionals. When you arrive at the meeting, you are informed that participants will first split up into two groups in order to prepare different arguments for debate in the larger assembly one hour later. Let's imagine, further, that the position of one group is that there is really no such thing as "burn-out"; the group's argument is that health professionals break down under prolonged stress only if they are predisposed to it because of already existing emotional problems. The other group contends that "burn-out" is a real phenomenon and a serious problem among health professionals in general, regardless of personality predispositions. On the basis of what we have discussed to this point, you would probably expect that (1) the issue must be important enough to those who came to the meeting, or else they would not have attended and (2) participants would meet with the group whose position on the "burn-out" issue was consistent with their individual views. The stage is now set: the issue is important and you can join either group. You will probably meet with the group consisting of others with similar attitudes and beliefs. Now, what if you are told that one group (the one you are inclined to join because of similar views) consists entirely of health professionals who have already "burned-out" at least once and that each person has had a history of emotional problems? Will you still want to join that group? I don't know. But, the research of Novak and Lerner (1968) showed in a study with this kind of design, investigating a very similar question, that subjects were more willing to interact with attitudinally similar others than with attitudinally dissimilar others, *except when similar others indicated that they had histories of emotional disturbance*. Apparently, there are circumstances where similarity can carry *disagreeable implications* for individuals. There are times when similarity can carry *disagreeable implications* for individuals. There are times when similarity is not rewarding and, hence, does not lead to attraction, but to disliking. In your work with patients, you may run into this phenomenon numerous times. For example, in drug and alcoholism treatment, it is common for patients in a state of denial to become angry and hostile at the mere suggestion that they are dependent on drugs or alcohol. They do not want to be tagged as an "addict" or an "alcoholic"; they do not want to be seen as "one of *them*." They may even express their resentments toward other patients who are being treated for *the same problem*. In no way is similarity desirable for such persons. The same thing may happen in other departments, for example, with paraplegics, quadriplegics, and persons with various physical disabilities who do not want to be seen as "handicapped" or "disabled." As with alcoholic persons, similarity to others with the same kinds of problems is disturbing because of the social stigmas attached to certain disorders, including emotional disorders. So, in the example above, you may not elect to join the group you thought you'd join if you think that others will "by association" assume that you, too, are a "burned-out" health professional who has experienced significant emotional problems. However, it all depends on the implications which you perceive similarity to have for you.

It should be clear by now that the relationship between similarity and attraction is not as simple as the folk wisdom of "birds of a feather" would have us believe. Similarity is *not* always desirable, it does *not* always lead to attraction, it does *not* always lead to affiliation. When two individuals meet, they usually have some things in common from the outset; in fact, their similarities may bring them together in the first place. The fact that they may come to like one another does not automatically suggest that it is due to their similarities. Rather, their developing attraction could evolve out of repeated exposure and increased familiarity, which may, in some cases, lead them to believe that they have more things in common than they really do. Finally, similarity "counts" as a determinant of attraction when individuals agree in important areas (Berscheid and Walster, 1978). With all of these qualifications, one might question the actual role of similarity in interpersonal attraction. However, in spite of these and other exceptions, most researchers agree that when we meet others who hold similar attitudes, we tend to like them more than those who are dissimilar.

Reciprocal Liking

The most important determinant of your liking for another person is whether or not that person likes you. When others communicate their liking for us, they are indicating approval, which is an extremely potent form of reinforcement (as you will recall from Chapter Seven). As a form of reinforcement, it should be especially potent when individuals have been deprived of approval and less potent when they have been saturated with approval. An individual's self-concept and level of self-esteem are usually affected by the provision and withdrawal of social approval. So, the real effect of being liked by someone is contingent upon how we feel about ourselves at any given moment. When our self-esteem is high, we may not be overly responsive to those who indicate their liking for us, but when out self-esteem is low, we are in need of affection and approval, and we tend to be most appreciative of those who communicate their liking for us (Bersheid and Walster, 1978). Under these same conditions, we should be able to tolerate being disliked much more when our self-esteem is high than when it is low. Thus, we also tend to dislike people who reject us when our self-esteem is low. As Aronson (1976, p. 223) put it, "we like to be liked—and the more insecure we feel, the more we appreciate being liked and, consequently, the more we like someone who likes us."

There must be some exceptions to this principle of "liking leads to liking," for there always seem to be conditions under which principles do not hold. The reciprocal liking principle is no exception. From a cognitive consistency viewpoint, Deutsch and Solomon (1959) argued that the crucial variable is not whether people "need" to be liked, but whether they think they "deserve" to be liked. They maintained that people with high self-esteem generally accept the expressed liking from others at face value because they feel that they deserve to be liked anyway. Conversely, people with low self-esteem feel uncomfortable when others express their liking for them; they're suspicious of the other's motives because they don't feel that they deserve to be liked. This hypothesis runs counter to the position above, since it assumes that we like those who like us *only if we like ourselves*, and that we dislike people whose liking for us is inconsistent with our feelings about ourselves. Shrauger (1975) reviewed the research generated by the reinforcement position and the cognitive consistency position. He concluded that we do have a desire to think well of ourselves and we tend to like those who like us more than those who dislike us, because people who like us help us to keep a positive view of ourselves. Shrauger also concluded that we, nevertheless, do have preferences for consistent evaluations of ourselves, and we tend to like those whom we believe are being "up front" with us about their feelings toward us. When other's feelings toward us do not match our own feelings about ourselves, we see them as being inconsistent, inaccurate, or ingratiating. Thus, when we perceive others in any of these ways, our liking for them decreases. As you will recall from Chapter Seven, for example, praise and favors do not always function as rewards. So, if an individual praises a person who does not see the praise as being warranted, that individual may end up being disliked instead of liked. We like to be praised—and praise usually reflects another's liking for us—but we do not like to be manipulated.

Complementarity

If you think about all of the folk "wisdom" in our culture, you probably realize that for every old adage there is at least one which contradicts it. "Patience is virtue" is complemented by "he who hesitates is lost," and, in the area of interpersonal attraction, "birds of a feather flock together" is refuted by "opposites attract." The "opposites attract" notion is no less indiscriminate than its counterpart, so we will have to examine the conditions under which people opposite characteristics are attracted to one another by virtue of *complementarity*.

According to the notion of complementarity, it is not similarity which facilitates one person's liking for another, it is *dissimilarity*. More specifically, if you perceive another person to be different from you—with qualities opposite yours—that person will be more attractive to you. The major qualification of this notion is that the other person will be more attractive to you *if the opposite qualities meet your needs in a complementary way*.

There are contradictory findings among the studies on complementarity effects, and inability clearly to establish this factor as a determinant of attraction has prompted some researchers to conclude that it has *no* effect on interpersonal attraction. However, it seems to me that Aronson's (1976) conclusion is more prudent and less absolute: that whether opposites attract depends on which personality characteristic is under consideration. For example, if you are a supervisor of an emergency department and you place a strong emphasis on neatness, stressing the importance of "a place for everything and everything in its place," then you may not be overjoyed with staff who are careless about where they put surgical instruments, nor would you have a strong attraction to staff who are slovenly and fail to keep the EOR clean and tidy. They probably wouldn't be too happy with you, either. Similarly, when two patients share a room, they may not get along with one another if one of them likes to talk all the time and the other one does not. However, there are certain characteristics which complement each other in such a way as to promote interpersonal liking. For example, a person who is highly dependent should be attracted to others who are nurturant, while being dissatisfied in relationships with other dependent persons who want to be taken care of but can't give. In professional practice, it sometimes happens that persons of equal status—persons with equivalent positions and roles—do not get along as well with one another as they do with their own superiors and subordinates, where professional roles complement one another.

From what we have discussed so far, you might think that if we like those who are *similar* and if we like those who *like us*, then we should be most strongly attracted to people who are both similar and who like us. Jones, Bell, and Aronson (1971) found that the two factors are not additive. That is, while it is rewarding to be liked by persons who share our views, it is even more rewarding to be liked by someone who does not share our views. It seems that if we encounter people who *like us in spite of our differences*, that is especially rewarding to us. The awareness that we can differ in our views about things and still be liked by others is a factor which adds to our liking for those who "like us for ourselves," for who and what we are, independent of our stand on various issues of mutual importance.

Physical Attributes

In an earlier chapter, we noted the value placed on physical appearance in our culture. People seem to go to great extremes to ensure that their physical appearance is acceptable; some even go so far as to have their appearances altered through cosmetic surgery. In virtually all cases, they seek to become more physically attractive. Physical attractiveness has long been recognized as a factor contributing to one's likability, and, in our culture, physically attractive people tend to be liked more than physically unattractive people. Moreover, we attribute numerous good qualities to physically attractive people—qualities which they may not really have. Perhaps this is because we have learned to associate pleasant feelings and experiences with attactive people, and those associations may predispose us to evaluate handsome people positively. Apparently, there is indeed an implicit assumption in our society that "what is beautiful is good" (Dion, Berscheid, and Walster, 1972). In a sense, there is also a converse assumption that "what is good is beautiful." Several studies (e.g., Gross and Crofton, 1977; Owens and Ford, 1978) have shown that when we are given information that certain persons have pleasing personalities, we are more inclined to infer that those persons are also physically attractive (the tendency appears to be much more common for males, however).

It seems that beauty is not only "skin-deep," it is deeper. Because we tend to assume that physically attractive people also have good personalities and various admirable qualities, we tend to be much more lenient in judging them when they do something wrong (e.g., Dion, 1972) and more likely to do favors for them than for unattractive persons (e.g., Benson, Karabenick, and Lerner, 1976).

Competence

We tend to like people who are capable, intelligent, and competent more than we like people who are not. But, there appear to be limits to our liking for competent people (Bramel, 1969), in that extremely competent persons often make us feel uncomfortable and self-conscious if we casually compare ourselves with them. Perhaps you have felt somewhat uncomfortable around a brilliant physician, a psychologist who seemed perfectly adjusted, or even the best dressed, most physically attractive woman in your class. If you felt uncomfortable each time you were with them, chances are you did not develop a strong liking for them. You may have admired them, but you may not have liked them a great deal. For you to like persons who make you feel uncomfortable because of their comptence or perceived "superiority," something else must become involved. One thing that might help is for them to demonstrate some human failings, some evidence of fallibility, some indication that they can make mistakes and blunders like the rest of us. You might feel more comfortable and like them better if the physician would say something absurd or even dumb every once in a while, if the psychologist showed some signs of nervousness now and then, or if the attractive woman came to class in wrinkled clothes and had a few hairs out of place on occasion. There is some evidence that when a person of recognized, consistent competency demonstrates that he or she can fail at something, his or her attractiveness may actually increase (Aronson, Willerman, and Floyd, 1966). Aronson (1976) referred to this phenomenon as the *pratfall effect*, in which evidence of fallibility increases the attractiveness of a person who is already moderately attractive by virtue of his or her competence.

Helmreich, Aronson, and LeFan (1970) found that the observer's level of self-esteem was a factor in determining whether a competent person became more attractive after committing a blunder. Specifically, persons of "average self-esteem" came to like a "superior" person who committed a blunder, whereas persons with "high self-esteem" and persons with "low self-esteem" reacted differently. For them, the blunder served to decrease the attractiveness of the competent "superior." The researchers hypothesized that persons with average self-esteem developed a greater liking for the superior because, for them, the blunder "humanized" the superior and brought him closer to the "average" person. Those with high self-esteem saw themselves as equally competent to the superior and might identify with him as long as he maintained a superior image. Persons with low self-esteem were attracted to the superior at first because they needed someone to look up to, a hero of sorts. Thus, individuals with high self-esteem became less attracted to the superior, presumably because they wished to dissociate their identities from the superior, and persons with low self-esteem became less attracted because they had been let down and disappointed by a person they could no longer perceive as an ideal. In a related study, Deaux (1972, p. 20) identified an additional factor, which was reflected in the title, *"To Err is Humanizing: But Sex Makes a Difference."* Her findings suggested that the pratfall effect applies most directly to *males*. Mettee and Wilkins (1972) found that persons with superior *intellectual ability* were unattracted to another superior person who committed a blunder, while persons with average intellectual ability were neither more nor less attracted to the superior person following a blunder. And, since other researchers have been unable to replicate earlier findings (e.g., Kiesler and Goldberg, 1968), it has yet to be determined unequivocally if the pratfall effect is a more frequent occurrence than its opposite, where blunders *reduce* liking rather than increase it.

Determinants of Attraction: The Rewards Health Professionals Provide

By virtue of their responsibilities, most health professionals have a unique distinction of being able to provide people with medical care *and* emotional comfort. For most recipients, both of these function as rewards—very powerful rewards if you consider the special needs of health care clients. There is a large body of evidence that, in our day-to-day lives, we favor people who help to reduce our feelings of loneliness, sadness, disappointment, fear, anxiety, and even stress. In general, we tend to like persons who help to make our lives more rewarding and satisfying. In light of this fact, it would seem that the tendency may be even more pronounced in health care settings. As indicated earlier in this text, hospitalized patients are persons under stress who may be experiencing a wide range of emotions, including the ones listed above. Under such conditions, health professionals are indeed in a unique position of being able to provide certain psychological rewards to patients. In the routine performance of your duties, your mere presence may help a patient to feel a little less lonely, a kind word may provide some comfort in her sadness, a minute of your time to listen may help her to express her disappointments, a piece of information may relieve some of her fear, a smile may even temporarily reduce some of her anxiety, and casual conversation can sometimes divert her attention from stressful conditions. Your role in the treatment process can have highly rewarding consequences for patients, even without your awareness. Anything you can do to relieve, even temporarily, the physical and emotional discomfort a person is experiencing can make her life a bit more pleasant, if only for a moment. Given these kinds of rewards which health professionals provide, it is hardly surprising that patients typically have positive feelings toward their caretakers.

The Reduction of Loneliness

One of the oldest, most fundamental, and commonly accepted beliefs about human beings relates to the tendency of all individuals to participate in social interaction. It seems to be an almost prehistoric conclusion that human beings are "innately" gregarious. Although contemporary views do not see humanity as "instinctively" motivated to seek the company of others, there can be no question that the tendency to affiliate with others is one of the most basic of all human activities. And, it would be difficult to find a person in wholehearted disagreement with the centuries-old dictum that "It is not good for man to be alone" (Genesis 2:18). There is a wealth of evidence from psychological research that prolonged isolation from other people can have profoundly negative effects on individuals. Even short-term isolation can produce symptoms of emotional distress among many people. If you have ever been exposed to winter snowstorms in the East or Midwest, then you probably know what it's like to develop "cabin fever" when weather conditions confine you to your home. It may be rather enjoyable to stay home for a day, maybe even two days, but sooner or later you get very uncomfortable when you can't go out and be around other people. Similar feelings are experienced by patients confined to hospital beds, their own units, or even the floor they are on. In effect, they are isolated from the larger social context, they have restricted freedom of movement, and they have few behavioral alternatives available for making their hospitalization less constraining. Visitors may alleviate some of the isolation they feel, but the hospital environment itself imposes inescapable restraints. Of course, not all patients are visited by others during their hospitalization, and some people may have few and infrequent visits. Contact with the "outside world" comes mainly through attending health professionals, and it is this form of contact that can be highly rewarding to isolated patients.

One of the general rewards others provide through our affiliation with them is *stimulation*. Research has clearly demonstrated that for normal functioning an adequate amount of stimulation is necessary. When it is not available—when we are isolated from others—we tend to begin *creating our own stimulation*. We may do this by thinking about people, dreaming about them, and, on occasion, even hallucinating about people. The mere presence of others can prevent this, since they provide the stimulation we need.

For most people, isolation at first leads to loneliness, which is quite painful. Over time, however, as the pain becomes greater and greater, there may be a point in many cases where the emotional pain sharply declines (e.g., Schachter, 1959) and apathy sets in. This may sometimes occur among patients who have been isolated for prolonged periods. At some point, it seems as if they have reached a threshold of discomfort and are simply no longer distressed by their isolation. This is not to suggest that they suddenly feel good about their life circumstances. It is to suggest that they may reach a point of *indifference, detachment, withdrawal*—conditions which may impede their recovery or, in some cases, prove to be life threatening.

What all of this suggests for health professionals is that you must be alert to the effects of social isolation on your patients. You are in a position to alleviate, to varying degrees, those effects. Your very presence may have tremendous stimulus value for patients who feel alone and lonely. By being in simple contact with patients, you can, in many cases, provide rewards which increase your overall attractiveness to them. By going a step further to interact with isolated persons on other levels, their liking for you may be increased even more. Why should their *liking* for you matter? To answer a question with another question, what did it matter *to you* when *you* felt very lonely at certain times and someone cared enough to be with you? You may have felt that life is worth living after all.

The Reduction of Fear

Have you ever noticed that on examination days some of your classmates talk to one another more? Although I haven't measured it, I have repeatedly observed more ongoing interactions among my students when I entered the classroom to give an exam (or return corrected exams) than on any other day in any given semester. This has been my observation, and research findings indicate that my observation is accurate. The explanation for this kind of phenomenon is that individuals often try to affiliate with others when they are nervous, afraid, or unsure of themselves, because other people may help them to alter those feelings.

The initial study investigating this hypothesis was conducted by Schachter (1959). His findings confirmed that when people are *fearful*, they are especially inclined to seek the company of others. He also found that the desire to affiliate with others increases as fear increases. However, in subsequent investigations, Schachter (1959) found that individuals are selective about the company with whom they seek to affiliate; just *anybody* will not suffice. It seems that "misery loves *miserable company*"—but not *too* miserable (Rabbie, 1963). When individuals are fearful, they prefer to affiliate with others who are also fearful, but they do not wish to affiliate with people who are extremely afraid because that might cause their own fear to escalate. Various explanations have been offered for the stronger tendency to affiliate with others when one is emotionally upset. Among those explanations are five possible reasons cited by Schachter:

1. *Escape*—when a person is in a stressful situation she may expect that talking with others who are in the same situation will help her figure out a way to get out of the situation.
2. *Cognitive clarity*—if a situation is ambiguous the person may turn to others for information which will help her to gain a perspective on it.
3. *Direct anxiety reduction*—when people are exposed to the same fate—in the "same boat" so to speak—they can provide one another with support and reassurance.
4. *Indirect anxiety reduction*—a person may affiliate with others in order to get her mind off her anxiety and the events to come.
5. *Self-evaluation*—by interacting with others, a person may be able to compare her own feelings against those expressed by others and thereby determine if her feelings are justified and reasonable.

There appears to be considerable evidence lending support to the *self-evaluation* hypothesis (e.g., Firestone, Kaplan, and Russell, 1973; Zimbardo and Formica, 1963). Other people may provide cues about the most appropriate reaction under the circumstances, and those cues are used by individuals to assess their own feelings. Schachter also favored this interpretation as well as the direct anxiety reduction hypothesis. Subsequent research, however, has pointed up that the individual's desire to affiliate with others depends on *why* he is upset and *how upset* he is (Berscheid and Walster, 1978). Apparently, *fear* (as a response to a realistically threatening stimulus) increases one's desire to be together with others who are also fearful, but, the greater the *anxiety* (as a response to objectively innocuous stimuli), the greater is one's desire to be *alone* (Sarnoff and Zimbardo, 1961). It seems that when individuals are upset about a stressful event but embarrassed about their reaction (thinking it to be inappropriate), they do not want to be around others who can see the reaction. The evidence also indicates that when a particularly strong emotion is aroused by a stressful event, individuals may prefer to be alone.

In general, the mere presence of others can help to reduce feelings of fear and anxiety. However, as we have seen, the effect of others' presence is often contingent upon other factors. In some instances, the presence of others may not be rewarding, but punishing, in that it may be embarrassing for individuals to show their feelings publicly. This seems to depend on the particular feelings one has in certain situations and how intense those feelings are. With this in mind, it should become possible for you to be alert to the emotional experience of health care clients and respond by approaching or temporarily withdrawing from contact. In some cases, patients might be terribly afraid of the surgery they must have, and you may be able to provide some information which helps them to cope with the experience. In other cases, patients may be nervous about minor surgery or innocuous forms of treatment and at the same time embarrassed about feeling the way they do: "I know it's just a simple procedure and nothing to be afraid of, but I can't help being apprehensive about it." Your reactions to their fears and anxieties can be rewarding and helpful, or punishing. In any event, your response will have an effect on their reactions to you as a person.

The Reduction of Stress

The evidence seems to be mounting that the presence of other people helps us to cope with various stressful conditions. Epley (1974) noted evidence that individuals who are placed in stressful situations show more severe physiological disturbance when they are alone than when others are present with them. Psychologists and other mental health professionals have long recognized the importance of "support systems" for persons experiencing crises. Support systems consist of people with whom individuals can talk and express their concerns about stressful events in their lives. Persons who make up an individual's support system tend to make it a little easier to cope with the "hard times." Physical illnesses represent some of the "hard times" in our lives— times when we are under significant stress. It is at such times when we can all benefit from the support which others can provide. The support which health professionals can lend to their patients during *their* stressful experiences can go a long way toward enhancing the image of the health professional in the eyes of those they serve. Finally, it should be recognized that "stress" conditions cover a lot of ground. People who are in isolation, people who are lonely or fearful, people who are sad, and even people who are hospitalized for routine tests are all exposed to varying degrees of stress by virtue of their current physical conditions and the novelty of the hospital environment. Anything that can be done to make their lives more pleasant under those conditions will function as rewards. And, the rewards *you provide* "will" come back to you. Often, health professionals fail to see the rewards that have come back to them, even though the rewards are right there in front of them. From what we have covered in this chapter, you should realize by now that one of the most obvious rewards you'll receive is the appreciation of those people you help. They will usually leave the hospital with positive feelings for you—and *you know* that being liked by someone is a powerful reward indeed!

Summary

Interpersonal attraction is an individual's tendency to evaluate another person in a positive or negative way. *Liking* is the term we use most often in everyday language to indicate our preference for and attraction to another person. Six models were presented as different frameworks for conceptualizing interpersonal attraction. The *reinforcement-affect model* is based on the premise that our liking for an individual is determined by the positive feelings we associate with that person, while our disliking for someone is based on negative feelings we associate with that person. *Social-exchange theory* holds that individuals remain attracted to one another in a relationship if the rewards from the relationship are greater for each person than the costs are for each person. *Equity theory* assumes that every person tries to get as much as possible out of life, and he will remain attracted to others in relationships as long as he believes he is receiving as much as he is giving. When inequities develop in relationships, individuals become less attracted to the other. *Cognitive dissonance theory* is a convenient model for interpreting one's attraction to another when rewards provided by the other are not readily apparent. *Self-perception and attribution models* were discussed as approaches which view the causes of attraction to be inferred by individuals upon observing their own behavior. *Interactional theory* represents a framework for viewing interpersonal attraction from the context of a two-person relationship. The basic premise of interactional theory is that different factors affect interpersonal attraction at different levels of relationships. Determinants of attraction were presented, and they include: physical proximity, similarity, reciprocal liking, complementary needs, physical attributes, competence. The final section of the chapter addressed the special rewards health professionals provide health care clients through the reduction of loneliness, fear, and stress. When health professionals are able to make life more comfortable and pleasant for patients, they are providing rewards which increase their attractiveness in the eyes of those they serve. Because "being liked by someone" is a powerful reward in itself, it can be seen as one of the intrinsic rewards for health professionals as they carry out their duties.

References

Adams, J. Inequity in Social Exchange, in *Advances in Experimental Social Psychology*, vol. 2, ed. L. Berkowitz, pp. 267-99. New York, Academic Press, 1965.

Aronson, E., *The Social Animal*, 2d ed. San Francisco, W. H. Freeman, 1976.

Aronson, E., and Mills, J. The effect of severity of initiation on liking for a group. *Journal of Abnormal and Social Psychology* **59**:177–81 (1959).

Aronson, E.; Willerman, B.; and Floyd, J. The Effect of a Pratfall on Increasing Interpersonal Attractiveness, *Psychonomic Science*, **4**:227–28 (1966).

Baron, R. and Byrne, D. *Social Psychology: Understanding Human Interaction*, 2d ed. Boston, Allyn and Bacon, 1976.

Baron, R. A.; Byrne, D.; and Griffitt, W. *Social Psychology: Understanding Human Interaction*. Boston, Allyn and Bacon, 1974.

Bem, D. J. An Experimental Analysis of Self-Persuasion, *Journal of Experimental Social Psychology*, **1**:199–218 (1965).

Benson, P.; Karabenick, S.; and Lerner, R. Pretty Pleases: The Effects of Physical Attractiveness, Race and Sex on Receiving Help, *Journal of Experimental Social Psychology*, **12**:409–15 (1976).

Berkowitz, L. *A Survey of Social Psychology*, 2d ed. New York, Holt, Rinehart, and Winston, 1980.

Berscheid, E., and Walster, E. *Interpersonal Attraction*, 2d ed. Reading, Massachusetts, Addison-Wesley, 1978.

Bramel, D. Interpersonal Attraction, Hostility, and Perception, in *Experimental Social Psychology*, ed. J. Mills, pp. 1–120. New York, Macmillan, 1969.

Byrne, D. Interpersonal Attraction and Attitude Similarity, *Journal of Abnormal and Social Psychology*, **62**:713–15 (1961).

Byrne, D. Attitudes and Attraction, in *Advances in Experimental Social Psychology*, vol. 4, ed. L. Berkowitz, New York, Academic Press, 1969.

Byrne, D. *The Attraction Paradigm*. New York, Academic Press, 1971.

Byrne, D., and Beuhler, J. A. A Note on the Influence of Propinquity Upon Acquaintanceships, *Journal of Abnormal and Social Psychology*, **51**:147–48 (1955).

Byrne, D., and Clore, G. L. A Reinforcement Model of Evaluative Responses, *Personality: An International Journal*, **1**:103–28 (1970).

Deaux, D. To Err is Humanizing: But Sex Makes a Difference, *Representative Research in Social Psychology*, **3**:20–28 (1972).

Deutsch, M., and Solomon, L. Reactions to Evaluations by Others as Influenced by Self-Evaluations, *Sociometry*, **22**:93–112 (1959).

Dion, K. Physical Attractiveness and Evaluation of Children's Transgressions, *Journal of Personality and Social Psychology*, **24**:207–13 (1972).

Dion, K.; Berscheid, E.; and Walster, E. What is Beautiful is Good, *Journal of Personality and Social Psychology*, **24**:285–90 (1972).

Epley, S. W. Reduction of the Behavioral Effects of Aversive Stimulation by the Presence of Companions, *Psychological Bulletin*, **81**:271–83 (1974).

Festinger, L. *A Theory of Cognitive Dissonance*. Stanford, Stanford University Press, 1957.

Festinger, L.; Schachter, S.; and Back, K. *Social Pressures in Informal Groups: A Study of Human Factors in Housing*. New York, Harper and Row, 1950.

Firestone, I. J.; Kaplan, K. J.; and Russell, J. C. Anxiety, Fear, and Affiliation With Similar-State Versus Dissimilar-State Others: Misery Sometimes Loves Nonmiserable Company, *Journal of Personality and Social Psychology*, **26**:409–14 (1973).

Griffitt, W., and Guay, P. "Object" Evaluation and Conditioned Affect, *Journal of Experimental Research in Personality*, **4**:1–8 (1969).

Gross, A. E. and Crofton, C. What is Good is Beautiful, *Sociometry*, **40**:85-90 (1977).

Gullahorn, J. T. Distance and Friendship as Factors in the Gross Interaction Matrix, *Sociometry*, **15**:123-34 (1952).

Helmreich, R.; Aronson, E.; and LeFan, J. To Err is Humanizing—Sometimes: Effects of Self-Esteem, Competence, and a Pratfall on Interpersonal Attraction, *Journal of Personality and Social Psychology*, **16**:259-64 (1970).

Howard, P. Office Landscaping Revisited, *Design and Environment*, Fall:40-47 (1972).

Huston, T. L., and Levinger, G. Interpersonal Attraction and Relationships, *Annual Review of Psychology*, **29**:115-56 (1978).

Jones, E.; Bell, L.; and Aronson, E. The reciprocation of attraction from similar and dissimilar others: A study in person perception and evaluation. In C. G. McClintock (Ed.). *Experimental Social Psychology*, New York: Holt, Rinehart, and Winston, 1971, pp. 142-83.

Kiesler, C. A., and Goldberg, G. N. Multidimensional Approach to the Experimental Study of Interpersonal Attraction: Effect of a Blunder on the Attractiveness of a Competent Other, *Psychological Reports*, **22**:693-705 (1968).

Kipnis, D. M. Interaction Between Members of Bomber Crews as a Determinant of Sociometric Choice, *Human Relations*, **10**:263-70 (1957).

Levinger, G. A. A Three-Level Approach to Attraction: Toward an Understanding of Pair Relatedness, in *Foundations of Interpersonal Attraction*, ed. T. L. Huston, pp. 99-120. New York, Academic Press, 1974.

Levinger, G. A., and Snoek, J. D. *Attraction in Relationship: A New Look at Interpersonal Attraction*. New York, General Learning Press, 1972.

Maissonneuve, J.; Palmade, G.; Fourment, C. Selective Choices and Propinquity, *Sociometry*, **15**:135-40 (1952).

Mehrabian, A., and Diamond, S. Effects of Furniture Arrangement, Props, and Personality on Social Interaction, *Journal of Personality and Social Psychology*, **20**:18-30 (1971).

Merton, R. K. The Social Psychology of Housing, in *Current Trends in Social Psychology*, ed. W. Dennis, pp. 163-217, Pittsburgh, Pittsburgh University Press, 1947.

Mettee, D. R., and Wilkins, P. C. When Similarity "Hurts": Effects of Perceived Ability and a Humorous Blunder on Interpersonal Attractiveness, *Journal of Personality and Social Psychology*, **22**:246-58 (1972).

Nahemow, L., and Lawton, M. P. Similarity and Propinquity in Friendship Formation, *Journal of Personality and Social Psychology*, **32**:204-13 (1975).

Newman, O. *Defensible Space*. New York, Macmillan, 1973.

Novak, D., and Lerner, M. J. Rejection as a Consequence of Perceived Similarity, *Journal of Personality and Social Psychology*, **9**:147-52 (1968).

Owens, G., and Ford, J. G. Further Consideration of the "What Is Good Is Beautiful" Finding, *Social Psychology*, **41**:73-75 (1978).

Rabbie, J. M. Differential Preference for Companionship Under Threat, *Journal of Abnormal and Social Psychology*, **67**:643-48 (1963).

Rosow, I. The Social Effects of the Physical Environment, *Journal of the American Institute of Planners*, **27**:127-33 (1961).

Sarnoff, I. R., and Zimbardo, P. G. Anxiety, Fear, and Social Affiliation, *Journal of Abnormal and Social Psychology*, **62**:356-63 (1961).

Schachter, S. *The Psychology of Affiliation*. Stanford, California, Stanford University Press, 1959.

Shrauger, J. S. Response to Evaluation as a Function of Initial Self-Preception, *Psychological Bulletin*, **82**:581–96 (1975).

Sommer, R. *Tight Spaces*. Englewood Cliffs, New Jersey, Prentice-Hall, 1974.

Sommer, R., and Ross, H. Social Interaction on a Geriatrics Ward, *International Journal of Social Psychiatry*, **4**:128–33 (1958).

Stephan, C. Attributions of Intention and Perception of Attitude as a Function of Liking and Similarity, *Sociometry*, **36**:463–75 (1973).

Thibaut, J. W. and Kelley, H. H. *The Social Psychology of Groups*. New York, Wiley, 1959.

U.S. Department of Justice, Federal Bureau of Investigation. *Uniform Crime Reports*. U.S. Government Printing Office, Washington, D.C., 1978.

Walster, E.; Berscheid, E.; and Walster, G. W. The Exploited: Justice or Justification?, in *Altruism and Helping Behavior: Social Psychological Studies of Some Antecedents and Consequences*, ed. J. Macaulay, and L. Berkowitz, pp. 179–204. New York, Academic Press, 1970.

Walster, E., and Walster, G. W. Interpersonal Attraction, in *Social Psychology: An Introduction*, ed. Seidenbert, B. and Snadowsky, A., pp. 279–308. New York, Free Press, 1976.

Walster, E.; Walster, G. W.; and Berscheid, E. *Equity: Theory and Research*. Boston, Allyn and Bacon, 1978.

Whyte, W. H. Jr. *The Organization Man*. New York, Simon and Schuster, 1956.

Wrightsman, L. S. *Social Psychology* (2nd ed.) Monterey Ca.: Brooks/Cole, 1977.

Yancey, W. L. Architecture and Social Interaction: The Case of a Large-Scale Public Housing Project, *Environment and Behavior*, **3**:3–21 (1971).

Zimbardo, P. G., and Formica, R. Emotional Comparison and Self-Esteem as Determinants of Affiliation, *Journal of Personality*, **31**:141–62 (1963),

---

CHAPTER TEN

Protecting Impressions: The Effects of Accidents, Harmdoing, and Self-Fulfilling Prophecies

With how much ease believe we what we wish!
Whatever, is, is in its causes just.

John Dryden, *Oedipus*

In spite of everything I still believe that
people are really good at heart.

Anne Frank, *Diary of a Young Girl*

When we relate our impressions of others, we usually describe certain characteristics which we believe they possess. We identify salient features of their personalities, appearance, and behavior. Rarely do we cite our own evaluative tendencies as determinants of those impressions. It is just as unlikely that we fail to recognize additional influences on our impressions: our own behavior in relation to others and events affecting the lives of others.

Things that happen to people, even chance occurrences beyond their control, may have a strong effect on our impressions. For example, you may have a friend who seems to get all the breaks; good things always seem to happen for that person. Another friend may seem to be plagued by personal misfortunes; that person never gets a break. In both cases, your impressions of and attraction to these persons are affected by such events. *Accidental consequences* imply chance events which affect the lives of individuals for better or for worse. Chance occurrences affecting people for the worse often include illness and injury. In this chapter, we will examine the effects of accidental consequences, including illness and injury, or perceivers' reactions to "victims." Given the nature of your duties as a health professional, it is highly appropriate that attention be focused on such reactions.

The way we treat people also has a strong effect on what we think of them and how we feel about them. We have already seen how individuals tend to like those who reward them and dislike people who punish them. We have also accounted for our attraction to people *we* have rewarded; i.e., when we benefit others, they tend to become more attractive to us, as we justify our actions by convincing ourselves that they are likable and deserving. But, the opposite may also happen. We often come to *dislike* those people we have harmed. Therefore, the second section of this chapter addresses the effects of harmdoing on our impressions of and liking for persons we have harmed. Whether our actions are intentional or unintentional, whether they cause others bruised lips or bruised egos, harmdoing is usually socially unacceptable, professionally objectionable, and personally disturbing. Of course, no dedicated, self-respecting health professional would intentionally harm health care recipients. Harmdoing is the antithesis of that for which the health professions stand. Yet, it would be naive and irresponsible to suggest that no harm has ever been caused to health care recipients or that you will never have to concern yourself with the possibility of being involved in treatment which does more harm than good. Health professionals must recognize that they have the potential to harm people, just as they have the power to help them. It is imperative that you acknowledge this potential in yourself, becasue the failure to do so may have serious implications for continued medical practice—implications which lead to justified harmdoing and maltreatment of health care recipients. In this chapter, we are therefore concerned with the effects of harmdoing on impressions of others and, ultimately, how interpersonal relations and health care practice are affected.

The final section of the chapter examines the effects of perceiver *expectations* on the behavior of actors. *Self-fulfilling prophecies* occur when individuals force others to behave in ways which confirm those expectations. For example, most of us have the capability of acting foolishly. If others around us treat us as foolish persons, it will bring out more of our foolish behavior than our sensible behavior. We probably don't see ourselves as being foolish in most situations, but others may conclude that we are—and we might then begin to think they are right. As with the other topics of this chapter, there are important implications for health professionals.

Accidental Consequences

Suppose that a patient under your care is being treated for injuries sustained in an automobile accident. The patient is a nice young man, 21 years old, and his injuries are not serious. The automobile accident was the first in which he had ever been involved; it was a single-car accident in which he was the driver and the sole occupant of the vehicle. Your impression of this person will be influenced to some degree by this information. My guess is that your impression will be generally favorable (all other things being equal) and that you will feel some sympathy and compassion for him, given his unfortunate circumstances. After all, accidents can happen to anyone, including yourself. If you have ever been involved in a car accident, you know this from personal experience. Furthermore, anyone can make a mistake while driving and thus cause a mishap, so even if it was the young man's fault, you don't blame him too much because those things can happen. In short, perhaps your view is that "accidents are accidents'': they are misfortunes that happen to people by pure chance or by unintentional mistakes on someone's part. So, you don't hold it against any person involved in an accident, or do you?

If I tell you that this was *not* the first accident in which the young man has been involved, but his *fifth one this year*, your impression of him will be entirely different. You may feel less sympathy and compassion for him, and your overall impression will most likely be more negative. But, how could this be? How could you form a negative impression of an accident victim? Remember, you think that "accidents are accidents," or must you now qualify that view—i.e., "accidents are accidents, *sometimes*"?

When we hear about an accident or any other severe consequences that a person suffers, we usually want to know about the cause. We know there has to be one, and, in fact, we *need to know* that there is a reliable explanation for the events. Without a causal explanation, our world appears much less predictable in the face of pure chance occurrences. It is not very comforting to think that we may be vulnerable to chance consequences, especially when those consequences are severe. So, when we learn of someone's misfortune, we usually feel sorry for them—we even empathize with them—because we realize that misfortune can befall anyone through no fault of his own ("There but for the grace of God go I"). However, as the seriousness of the misfortune increases, it becomes harder and harder to acknowledge that this is something that could happen to anyone (Walster, 1966). To admit that anyone could have five automobile accidents in a single year, for example, is to admit one's own vulnerability to very serious misfortunes. Such an admission is not at all comforting. The odds are entirely against five accidents in a single year; chance occurrences (accidents) just don't happen that frequently. So, where is the cause? Well, under these kinds of circumstances, we seem to conclude that the cause is with the individual—the victim (Berscheid and Walster, 1978; Walster, 1966). We assume that there must be something wrong with this person; he must have done something to bring these things upon himself. If we can convince ourselves that the cause does lie with the victim, we have assured ourselves that we are therefore different, that we would act differently under similar circumstances, and that we are protected from similar misfortunes. Now, when we attribute the cause of misfortunes to dispositional characteristics of the victim, we are, of course, assigning responsibility to the victim and not to chance. Convinced that something is wrong with the victim, our impressions of him become more negative, and our liking for him decreases. In the case of your patient—the young man injured in his fifth automobile accident—you would probably infer that he is reckless and irresponsible. If you think that your impression would *not* be any different than if he had been involved in only one accident—that you would feel just as compassionate, just as sympathetic, and that you wouldn't judge him in either case—then let me ask you a simple question: Knowing that he has had five accidents this year, would you be just as willing to accept a ride from him?

In the course of your career as a health professional, you will come into repeated, daily contact with victims of misfortune. The misfortunes that have befallen your patients are illnesses and injuries. Anyone can become ill, and anyone can be injured. Anyone can be hospitalized through no fault of his own.

You know this very well, so in the vast majority of cases you will probably avoid dispositional attributions for the medical conditions of your patients, but there are some situations where you may find yourself feeling less compassionate, less sympathetic, and less committed to certain patients. If you examine your reactions, you may discover that you have assigned responsibility to the person for his or her own problems. In what instances might this occur? It is impossible to list all of the conceivable circumstances, but consider these:

> A middle-aged man who has been hospitalized several times for emphysema. His physician has insisted for several years that he quit smoking, yet he continues to smoke three packs a day.
> A woman admitted for hypertension and diabetes. She is obese and has made no attempt to lose weight.
> A man in his second admission for treatment of an enlarged liver. With proper nutrition and abstinence from alcohol, the condition was reversed following his first hospitalization nin months ago. Resumption of heavy drinking again caused an accumulation of triglycerides in hepatic cells.

In instances such as these, you would probably recognize the self-defeating patterns which have led to physical illness. You would not attribute their illnesses to chance misfortunes, but to the individuals themselves. One of the dangers is that you might come to believe that they got what they deserved. This is a realistic possibility with a high probability of occurrence.

Several years ago, Lerner (1965) introduced the *just world hypothesis*. Lerner was teaching at a medical school in the South, and he noticed that many of the students who were required to work in a clinic resented that they had to offer treatment to indigent patients. An obvious question that occurred to him was why medical students held such an attitude, given their chosen field. Upon investigating this phenomenon, Lerner (1970) found that many of the medical students believed that the poor people who sought treatment at the clinic were victims of their own negligence and ignorance, that they had somehow brought their illnesses upon themselves. In effect, the medical students *blamed the victims* for their suffering. They decided that the indigent patients deserved their lot in life. Subsequent research by Lerner and his colleagues revealed that this sort of phenomenon occurs in a variety of situations and among a wide range of people. The phenomenon reflects individuals' beliefs that the world is basically a just place and that things happen for a reason that is somehow just. The belief in a just world is an implicit assumption that, for the most part, people get what they deserve.

Imbedded in our culture is the belief that hard work and virtue pay off. Our religious and economic institutions communicate these messages, which are further inculcated within the family context. Most persons come to accept that hard work and virtue do have their rewards. They may even believe that if the rewards are not accrued in this life, then they will be in the next. Yet, when misfortunes happen to someone who is hardworking and virtuous, that person and most observers wonder why such awful things should happen to him or her. The often heard rhetoric ''What did he ever do to deserve that?'' implies the underlying belief that there must be justice somewhere and that things don't happen without some good reason. Therefore, when bad things happen to someone, we assume that there must be some logical explanation, and, often, we then infer that there is some form of justice in injustice. Chance occurrences may then be seen as determined and not accidental, fortuitous, or unexplainable. Usually, this leads us to conclude that the victim deserved what he or she got.

What about when good things happen to people? If we assume that people get what they deserve, then we should attribute their good fortune to their own efforts. This is only partially true. It seems that is something good happens to someone else, we infer either that the person deserved it or that his good fortune isn't all that great (Brickman, Coates, and Janoff-Bulman, 1978). We may also attribute his or her good fortune to chance if we are highly motivated to avoid giving credit to the individual: "He was just lucky, that's all." If good fortune happens to us, however, we are more inclined to make an attribution to ourselves; e.g., our hard work, virtuosity, sacrifice, our special abilities, or our intelligence. Now, when misfortune befalls us, we avoid attributions to ourselves and point to situational forces, including chance. Only persons with the most inadequate self-concepts would favor painful, self-derogating statements, like, "I'm no good, rotten, inept, and deserving of all the bad things that happen to me." Most people don't see themselves as "Calamity Janes or Johns," wringing havoc from every circumstance as they go through life.

Not everyone blames a victim for his misfortunes, nor does everyone assume that fortuitous events are necessarily deserved. Through dissonance-reduction, it is possible to maintain a belief in a just world and still be aware of injustices occurring all around. Indeed, we all know how unjust the tax structure is in this country, and we all know that people can be treated completely unfairly. In the health professions, as well, we know that nurses are overworked, understaffed, underpaid, have high accountability with little authority, and have no parity with physicians. Given these circumstances, even hospital administrators could still maintain an assumption of fairness. For example, they may argue that changes will not be made, because existing conditions are really not incongruous with the expected working conditions of other "second-class" professionals (of course, they would probably avoid the term "second-class," but the message is there). Thus, administrators may take it for granted that physicians have more authority and respect because they deserve it: "Those who have, deserve." Nurses, on the other hand, have less authority and respect: "Those who do not have, do not deserve."

Dehumanization in a Just World

Health care practice can be tedious and stressful to very high degrees. Over time, the tedium can lead to symptoms of emotional and mental exhaustion: *burn-out*. Part of the burn-out syndrome often involves the appearance of negative feelings about others, including patients. Health professionals who are "burning-out" may find themselves being less concerned about patient welfare and less aware that those patients are persons, just like themselves, with the same complement of human attributes. Patients may be converted into disease entities, devoid of humanity, and somehow synonymous with the afflictions of their bodies. When this occurs, patients have been *dehumanized*. One result is that they are then treated as if they didn't matter. This is a singularly dangerous consequence for everyone concerned, as it represents a form of *arbitrary derogation* which makes negligence and maltreatment more likely. Once we have dehumanized people—reduced them to subhuman or nonhuman entities—it becomes much easier to justify actions on our parts that may be harmful to them. It also becomes easier to justify any harm we may already have caused. We may even resort to our just world beliefs and conclude that they actually deserved whatever happened to them.

Millman (1977), for example, suggested that health professionals have developed techniques for justifying treatment errors and minimizing apparent injuries to patients. Often, these techniques are observable in group interactions during case conferences. Unforeseen consequences (discussed in greater detail later) may be cited during mortality conferences where the deaths of certain patients are being discussed. The group's review of circumstances may proceed in such a way as to justify earlier decisions made by physicians. Furthermore, errors may be excused by *blaming the patient: derogating the victim*. Responsibility can be shifted away from the attending physician and staff by establishing the patient as uncooperative, mentally incompetent, or as having somehow done something to undermine treatment or render it less effective. The patient is then seen as deserving of the fate which befell him or her.

This sort of tactic is not restricted to health professionals. Mental health professionals may resort to such justificatory sleights-of-hands on occasions when certain clients terminate therapy prematurely or claim that they have not been helped. All the counselor has to do is reach in his or her bag of therapeutic concepts and pull out the attribution of *resistance*, thereby explaining away the failure by blaming the client. The counselor may attribute to the client a lack of *motivation* for treatment. Motivation is usually interpreted by counselors to mean the individual's willingness to explore himself, to confront unpleasant feelings and negative aspects of his personality, and, in general, to endure the pain of change. Because change is usually a lengthy process, individuals who seek a quick remedy to their difficulties are often seen as being unrealistic and lacking the necessary motivation. But, motivation is also inferred on the basis of the client's willingness to make financial sacrifices. When the client is believed to be unwilling to make the required commitments to therapy and to change, he is assumed to be lacking the motivation to change. If he is seen as lacking motivation, then it becomes much easier to conclude that he therefore *deserves* to live with the problems causing him so much pain. The assumption often appears to be that the client has "made his own bed," so to speak. If he is not willing to change it, then he deserves to "lie in it."

Individuals prefer to make self-attributions for bringing about desirable outcomes in relation to others. Undesirable outcomes are usually attributed to situational factors or to the dispositional characteristics of others. Even in health care settings, individual staff members would be more willing to accept credit for improvements in patients' conditions than they would be to accept blame for their decompensation. The greater tendency is to shift the blame onto the patient for deterioration or lack of improvement. As we have seen, one result is that health professionals (and mental health professionals) may convince themselves that the recipients of ineffective or contraindicated services actually deserved their fate. "Victims" are derogated, and they become less valued in the eyes of their accusers. It therefore becomes much easier to be negligent in the provision of further services. When this occurs, the potential for engaging in actual harmdoing increases. And, it is much easier to harm someone who has been dehumanized into a nameless, faceless, insignificant organism that is nothing but a problem taking up space. It is much easier to cause harm to "what's-his-name," and "who-cares-anyway?"

Causing Harm to Others

A few years ago, one of my students attributed the relationship between cognitive dissonance and the self-concept to a "need to make ourselves right." This was a rather cogent observation concerning the basis for dissonance-reducing behavior. The student clearly recognized our need to see ourselves as decent, responsible persons. He added some personal observations which suggested his further recognition that this need can exert a potent influence on our impressions of and attraction to others:

> I think I'm a pretty decent guy. I try to treat people like I'd want to be treated. Of course, there have been times when I haven't treated people so well. I hurt them by something I said or did to them, and that made me feel pretty bad. Usually, I try to make it up to people if I know I was wrong. But, sometimes it's like there's nothing I can do to patch things up; no matter what I do, it's not good enough for them. It's like they want blood or something—I don't know what they expect. But, I do know that sometimes I end up getting mad at them all over again. I guess I've even told a few people to go to hell, and I wouldn't have anything to do with them anymore. Now that I think about it, it's kind of strange, you know, because I would be mad at them, but I didn't feel bad about myself anymore. I probably made myself right by finally deciding that they got what they deserved.

This person's experiences are not unlike the experiences of most of us who have, at one time or another, caused some sort of harm to others. The awareness of hurting someone is incompatible with our views of ourselves as decent persons. These conflicting cognitions produce a state of dissonance which we may experience as "guilt" or "shame." Like the student above, a typical response for most of us is to try to make amends to our "victims." Making restitution often helps us to reduce our guilt feelings and prove to ourselves and others that we really are decent people after all. However, it sometimes happens that our attempts at restitution are unsuccessful—or it may happen that we bypass restitution altogether—and the dissonance remains. But, usually we don't carry around our guilt feelings for too long in such cases, because we have other strategies we can use. For one thing, we may reduce dissonance as the student did, by *derogating* the victims of our harmdoing.

It is necessary to describe the conditions under which we are most likely to pursue such a course, for there are important implications for interpersonal relations when we decide that our victims "got what they deserved." First, there is abundant evidence that *our attraction to those we have harmed usually decreases, and, in some cases, we actually come to dislike them.* This is especially likely to happen when we convince ourselves that they deserved to suffer. Second, as Berscheid, Boye, and Darley (1968) argued, *when harmdoers justify the harm they have done, they effectively deny responsibility for it, convince themselves that their behavior was acceptable, and become more inclined to engage in harmdoing in the future.* And, it becomes easier to harm someone you have hurt previously and come to dislike than it is to harm someone you have not hurt before and do not dislike. Third, if these are likely consequences of justified harmdoing, then *it should be desirable to make restitution instead.* If harmdoers make amends to their victims, they accept responsibility for the victims' suffering, acknowledge that the behavior was unacceptable, and should then be less willing to do the same thing again. Harmdoers should also maintain more positive evaluations of their victims, and attraction should not decrease.

Derogating Victims of Harmdoing

Davis and Jones (1960) were among the first to demonstrate that individuals often justify harmdoing by *derogating* or "putting down" their victims. These researchers hypothesized that the more responsible an individual feels for *choosing* to harm someone, the more dissonance that person will feel and the more motivated she will be to reduce it by derogating her victim.

This hypothesis was tested in an experiment in which subjects observed an individual being interviewed in an adjoining room and then rated the interviewee in terms of favorableness of first impressions. Subjects were then told that the experimenter wanted to investigate people's reactions to positive and negative feedback about themselves. Some subjects were asked to *volunteer* to give harsh feedback to the person they had observed being interviewed. Other subjects were simply told that they *must* give harsh feedback to the interviewee (who was actually a confederate of the experimenter). In addition, some subjects were told that they would have a chance to meet the interviewee after the experiment (at which time they could retract their criticisms if they wished), while remaining subjects were told that there was no possibility of meeting the interviewee later (thus precluding the chance to retract their criticisms). Each subject met individually with the interviewee and gave him very harsh feedback to the effect that he was shallow, uninteresting, untrustworthy, and generally unlikable. After giving this feedback, each subject was asked to indicate again his impressions of the interviewee. A principal finding was that subjects who volunteered (those who had a choice to insult the interviewee) convinced themselves that they *really didn't like* the victim of their cruelty. These subjects came to believe that the interviewee deserved the insults. Comparisons of their impressions from before and after the feedback indicated that these subjects found the interviewee to be less attractive *after* insulting him. There are numerous other findings from this study which lend support to the derogation tendency, but Davis and Jones offered two main conclusions from their data. First, they concluded that the tendency to derogate victims of cruelty is greatest when we believe that we had some *choice* in the matter (i.e., when we know that we didn't *have to* harm the person). Secondly, the tendency is also great when we realize that we *cannot deny the harmdoing* in the eyes of the person we have hurt (i.e., when we know that we *won't have a chance to retract* what we said or did to hurt the person). Under these conditions, then, our subsequent *liking for our victims is lowest*.

Further research on the derogation process has identified other conditions which appear to set limits on this tendency. According to Glass (1964), one factor is related to *self-esteem*. Glass found that the derogation tendency is strongest among persons with high self-esteem and less strong among persons with low self-esteem. Apparently, persons with low self-esteem do not see their harmdoing as being totally inconsistent with their view of themselves. Because harmdoing is not something in which they are shocked to find themselves involved, they experience less dissonance and feel less of a need to derogate their victims. Conversely, individuals with high self-esteem experience considerable dissonance because harmdoing is so incompatible with the view of themselves as fine, upstanding persons. Glass argued that persons with high self-esteem therefore become highly motivated to justify their actions by "running down" their victims.

The harmdoer's *relationship* with the victim is another factor which limits the derogation tendency. Derogation is more likely to occur when the victim is a *stranger* to the harmdoer and least likely to occur when the victim happens to be an *intimate friend*. As Berscheid and Walster (1978, Chap. 8) noted in their review of exploiters' reactions to their victims, a friend's characteristics are well-known to the harmdoer and, if the harmdoer tries to run down his victim by distorting those characteristics to justify his actions, he will be confronted by *disconfirming facts*. Furthermore, intimates are capable of *challenging* the harmdoer's justifications and distortions and destroying his credibility. Strangers, on the other hand, are persons whom the harmdoer may never have to face again, so he can make all kinds of justifications with minimal threat of being challenged and contradicted. The harmdoer can also distort the stranger's personality characteristics, knowing that he will encounter no information to disprove his projections. Finally, intimate friends or those with whom the harmdoer comes into frequent contact probably have the *capacity to retaliate*. To minimize the threat of retaliation, the harmdoer may avoid derogating the victim altogether. Adding insult to injury can sometimes cause victims to become very intent on revenge.

Berscheid and Walster (1978) viewed the derogation process from an equity theory perspective and suggested that harmdoers who seek to restore equity to relationships with victims will weigh the costs and benefits of restitution against the costs and benefits of justification. The assumption is that the harm one person causes another to suffer produces distress for both persons, who find themselves in an unjust relationship to one another. Whether the harmdoer elects to compensate the victim or justify her actions instead, depends on which alternative she judges to be the *most adequate* and *less costly* way to restore equity. Our main concern here is with justification, but it is worthwhile to note that restitution will be attempted if the harmdoer believes that it is *sufficient* to cover the harm done and if restitution can be made at *lit-*

tle cost to herself. Of course, this does not mean that restitution is necessarily acceptable to the victim. The response that "I said I was sorry! What more do you want?" is often made by the individual who is failing at restitution, like the young man who tries to smooth things over with his date whom he has stood up for three consecutive nights. Under the circumstances, this form of compensation is not sufficient in the eyes of his date, even though he assumes (albeit unwittingly, perhaps) that it is adequate. From your own experience in similar circumstances involving inadequate compensation, you have probably learned that conflicts intensify and broader gaps often develop in the relationships. Upon failing at restitution, harmdoers may resort to self-justification, just as the student did in the earlier example when he eventually told his victims to "go to hell" and avoided further contact with them. In short, if compensation fails—or if it is avoided altogether—impressions of the victim tend to become more negative.

Other Available Justification Tactics

In addition to derogating victims, harmdoers usually have other justificatory options available to them. For example, individuals may try to "play down" or *minimize the harm* they have caused to others. A physician may misdiagnose a patient's illness and prescribe certain medications which have no effect on the symptoms but which cause the patient to experience continual drowsiness and lowered efficiency. If the real problem is finally diagnosed, the physician is minimizing the seriousness of his error if he passes it off as an "honest mistake" and claims that the misprescribed medications were harmless. Individuals can also minimize their harmdoing by contending that the victims are insignificant or unimportant. This is a form of justification similar to that which permitted Nazis to murder millions of Jews during World War II. It is also the kind of justification used by bigots who discriminate against persons from ethnic and racial minorities. And, it is the kind of justification many individuals use to excuse the deplorable living conditions to which human beings are exposed in many of our state hospitals, nursing homes, and correctional institutions. The attitude seems to be that we needn't be concerned about this form of harmdoing because it's really not harmdoing at all: the people in these institutions are "dangerous," "senile," or "insane" anyway. The logic which permits individuals to view others' suffering as justifiable on the grounds that those persons are "insignificant" and don't matter is a form of *irrationality* which encourages further maltreatment. Indeed, one might even wonder who are *really* the "dangerous" and "insane."

Another common form of justification is to claim that "others have done worse" or that "I'm not the only one." This involves a process of social *comparison* in which the individual weighs her own situation against those of others who have done similar things and who were not punished (Schlenker, 1980). The individual tries to convince herself and others that her actions were not so bad and that no one should "point the finger" solely at her. As Schlenker (1980) suggested, the person turns the tables on her accusers and forces them into a position of having to explain why they consider her actions to be any different. The harmdoer, of course, implicitly and automatically hopes that they won't be able to give a decent explanation. If others insist that neither her actions nor the actions of those who have done similar things are acceptable— and, therefore, that her attempted comparison with others is also unacceptable—then the individual may try to justify her actions by insisting that some larger force, like society as a whole, must take the blame for making such behavior a norm.

By emphasizing the *context* in which an individual hurts another, the event can be made to seem less negative than it may actually be (Schlenker, 1980). Health professionals often administer medical treatments which are anything but pleasant experiences for patients. Even when giving a tetanus shot to a child, the circumstance and context provide ample justification for causing some pain in order to help her in the long run. But, even when there is sufficient *external* justification, individuals may still experience some dissonance. Such is the case with psychotherapists who recognize that their jobs sometimes require them to cause people to feel uncomfortable and painful enough to change. It's never easy to hurt others, even in a professional capacity where circumstances justify and perhaps necessitate it. Health professionals and mental health professionals alike must often resort to dissonance-reduction by reminding themselves of the "greater good" and the long-range goals.

As indicated in our discussion of attribution processes, individuals are held most responsible for actions in which they are seen to have engaged *intentionally*. When observers infer intentionality to the actor, they assume that the behavior reveals something about his personality. If the consequences of his behavior are negative, such as physical or emotional injury to another person, negative dispositional characteristics are usually attributed to the perpetrator. Furthermore, the actor may expect negative repercussions above and beyond personality attributions. To avoid such repercussions, the individual may try to justify his actions by using various kinds of *excuses*. Although it can be argued that excuses are indistinguishable from other forms of justifications, Schlenker (1980) treated excuses as attempts by individuals to *minimize their responsibility* for events with which they do not want to be associated.

Unforeseen Consequences

Schlenker (p. 141) maintained that individuals can try to reduce responsibility for negative events by insisting that they "*could not possibly have foreseen* or *merely did not foresee* the consequences." A clear example would be in the health professions where practitioners disclaim responsibility for the deterioration of certain patients because they could not possibly have foreseen the course which the patients' illnesses would take. Therefore, there is nothing which they could have been reasonably expected to do, other than to provide the care they provided. It must be acknowledged that in a small number of unfortunate cases, health professionals may, if fact, cause *iatrogenic* illnesses (disease caused by treatment). In virtually all of those cases, however, health professionals do not foresee the consequences of their actions. If they had foreseen the consequences, they would not have acted as they did. Thus, by arguing this point, the culpable persons may avoid attributions, by self and others, of *full* responsibility. Essentially, this kind of excuse attributes the consequences to *chance*, *accidents*, or *mistakes*. In health care settings, great efforts are taken to reduce the probability of chance occurrences which harm patients. Accidents can happen, but they are not supposed to. And, mistakes are not tolerated very well because they may cost a patient his or her life. So, health professionals who attribute the consequences of their actions to these factors are treading on thin ice. In other contexts, however, accidents and mistakes may be more appropriate explanations. Anyone can spill a glass of red wine on the host's carpet and claim it was an accident. The host may be upset about the stain, but he or she will probably not throw the violator out of the party. *But*, as we will see shortly, when accidents happen to particular individuals with increasing frequency, those consequences are less likely to be seen as true accidents and more likely to be seen as the results of an individual's *faults*. Thus, if the same person spills red wine every time he or she is at the host's house, that person may be excluded from the guest list next time around.

Extenuating Circumstances

Schlenker cited a second category of excuses which involves an individual's explanation that the act was performed under *extenuating circumstances*. The circumstances are identified as factors which either reduced the individual's choices of how to act *or* reduced his or her competence at the time. One of the most popular ploys in this connection is for the individual to claim that he just wasn't himself because he was worried, tired, under a lot of pressure, or even drunk. The exact circumstances cited by an individual vary in their effectiveness as justifications. By claiming extenuating circumstances, the individual makes a *situational attribution* which will rarely help to absolve her completely of responsibility for an event (see Figure 10.1). However, she hopes that at least some of the responsibility can be shared with some other feasible cause.

Extenuating circumstances are common justifications when the consequences of the person's behavior have serious implications for herself as well as for others. In criminal proceedings, for example, persons accused of felonies for which they cannot deny some involvement may plead that the acts were committed under circumstances of duress, impaired functioning, or insanity. Such circumstances are not always judged as acceptable, even if the individual truly believes that they are. In such cases, juries make *dispositional attributions* concerning the locus of responsibility and discount the situational forces pleaded by the defendant.

Individuals may even *create their own extenuating circumstances* and cite them later in situational attributions intended to justify their actions. In his study of domestic violence, for example, Gelles (1972) argued that alcohol allows the aggressor, the victim, and other family members to acknowledge that violence has occurred while, at the same time, enabling them to maintain a view of the family as being normal by putting the blame on the alcohol as the cause of the violence. Drunkenness represents a time-out from socially acceptable behavior, a time when the intoxicated person is not responsible for his actions. Virtually everyone is at least implicitly aware of this. According to Gelles (p. 118), the person who wishes to carry out a violent act may become

Figure 10.1 Individuals may point to extenuating circumstances when making situational attributions for their behavior. Perceivers may nevertheless discount extenuating circumstances, in favor of dispositional attributions.

intoxicated in order to perform the act and then later attribute the violence to the effects of alcohol: "These justifications also may play a causal role in family violence by *providing, in advance, an excuse for behavior. . . .*"

Summary

At various times in our lives, our self-images are threatened when we realize we have harmed someone. This realization produces dissonance, and we try to "make ourselves right" again. In many cases, we try to compensate those we have harmed. At other times, we resort to justifications for our actions. To the extent that our justifications are effective, our liking for the victims of our harmdoing decreases. As indicated, there is abundant evidence that we often come to dislike people we have harmed. When this occurs, the likelihood of future transgressions increases. The likelihood is greatest when we justify our behavior on the grounds that our victims got what they deserved. What, then, can be done to offset this tendency? It is difficult to say what strategies individuals can use "across the board" in all cases where they have harmed someone. It is easier to say that it is very hard to derogate a victim or otherwise justify harmdoing when we have the skill to *see the event as the other person sees it.* That is, it is incompatible with derogation to be *empathic.* The empathic individual cannot derogate someone he has harmed, and he cannot easily justify or excuse his behavior. He can, however, work toward a restoration of a mutually rewarding relationship if he chooses to suspend his own frame of reference for a moment and gain a different perspective on his actions. This may cause the individual to see some things in himself that he does not want to see. But, if the relationship is to continue and if he is to recognize those aspects of himself which may be in need of change, he must *risk a little more dissonance* by looking at the event from the victim's standpoint. It may seem almost unimaginable that a person shift from a highly judgemental attitude after harming another person to a nonjudgemental stance. Indeed, it *is* incomprehensible for the individual who has not enhanced his or her ability to be empathic. When empathy is achieved after harmdoing, it becomes more probable that the harmdoer and the victim can cooperatively identify the conditions of their relationship that move them toward conflict. Once identified, those conditions can be changed. For persons who have developed their empathic skills, this outcome is neither inconceivable nor unattainable.

To try never to be angry at anyone is quite unrealistic and, in fact, impossible. To be mature enough to take a look at what is really going on in the relationship is certainly something we can all do. Perhaps it is the best that any of us can do.

Self-Fulfilling Prophecies

Let's project you five or ten years into the future and imagine that you are the supervisor of an emergency department in a large metropolitan hospital. Over the years, you have provided emergency treatment to persons from every age and almost every racial and ethnic group. Let's also suppose that you have found it difficult to be tolerant and sympathetic with patients from a particular ethnic minority. You see most persons from this group as demanding, obstinate, and uncooperative; they make your job more difficult than it should be. As a result of your impressions, you have come to expect—and, in fact, you can even predict—the same kind of behavior from every person of that group who seeks emergency medical care. Now, do you think it is at all possible that you might respond to those persons in ways that actually *cause* them to confirm your expectations? Is it conceivable that *you* might draw demanding, obstinate, and uncooperative behavior from them? It is not only possible, it is quite likely that that is exactly what you do.

Individuals often fail to recognize the effects of their own behavior on other people and how their behavior ultimately influences their evaluations of and liking for others. There is a concept which describes this type of occurrence, where an actor is "set up" to act in ways which confirm the perceiver's impressions. *Self-fulfilling prophecy* (Merton, 1957) is a term describing the fact that the perceiver's expectations about an interaction produce behavior from the perceiver that ensures the fulfillment of the expectations. According to Merton (1957, p. 423):

> The self-fulfilling prophecy is, in the beginning, a *false* definition of the situation evoking a new behavior which makes the originally false conception come *true*. The specious validity of the self-fulfilling prophecy perpetuates a reign of error. For the prophet will cite the actual course of events as proof that he was right from the very beginning.

The perceiver imposes her expectations on the actor in such a way as to force the actor to confirm those expectations. In expectation of demanding, obstinate, and uncooperative behavior, you may assert yourself from the very beginning of the interaction and communicate in direct or indirect ways that you are not about to tolerate such behavior. By asserting your power and authority, by acting surly and insensitive, by appearing less accessible, or by acting officious and condescending, you may establish yourself in an antagonistic, inimical, and adversary position that effectively draws out the kind of behavior you dislike so much.

Now, if I were to point out your actions to you and tell you that you appear to be rather short and brusque with certain patients, you would probably tell me that you don't treat everyone that way. You'd probably tell me that it's just "these people." By responding to my observation in this way, you have indicated clearly that a *situational* attribution has been made for your own behavior, whereas a *dispositional* attribution has been made for the behavior of "these people": *they* are demanding, obstinate, and uncooperative in general, while *you* are brusque only because of the circumstances. What do you think this scene looks like from the patients' perspectives? Well, as members of an ethnic minority, they have no doubt been subjected to frequent differential treatment. They have probably been treated with disrespect many times and probably have their own expectations of discrimination and oppression in various contexts. Their own experience with health professionals may have caused them to expect unpleasant encounters with uncaring, insolent, irritable, and grouchy emergency personnel. This expectancy may produce highly defensive, insistent behavior toward health professionals. Is it possible, then, that these patients act in ways which cause *you* to confirm *their* expectations? Indeed, it is.

If we were now to look at an encounter between you and a patient from the ethnic group, we might very well see an interaction in which *both of you* act in ways which cause the other to confirm incorrect attributions. You would be brusque (causing the patient to become defensive and insistent), or the patient may be demanding (causing you to become intolerant and somewhat insolent). In a sense, both of you *pull* hostility from one another. Both of you fulfill the other's expectations, but neither of you recognize your own behavior as causal factors in drawing out the expectancy-confirming actions of the other. Incorrect attributions thus become reinforced as each person fulfills the other's prophecy. That is, you attribute the patient's behavior to dispositional factors, and the patient attributes your behavior to dispositional factors. Both of you attribute your own behavior to situational factors because both of you know that you don't act that way with everyone. If both of you could be made to see that your mutual antagonism is *produced by the situation* and *not by personality dispositions*, you could move away from your adversary positions.

The expectancy-confirmation effect has been demonstrated repeatedly in a range of contexts, from classrooms to factories to mental hospitals. In an ingenious study, "On Being Sane In an Insane Place" (Rosenhan, 1973), the expectancies of hospital staff were found to influence impressions of college students admitted to mental hospitals. As part of their clinical training, students were asked to have themselves "voluntarily" committed through the court to mental hospitals for a short time. Hospital staff were not informed that students were undergoing a training experience and, therefore, assumed that admission diagnoses were accurate. Within a short period, "real" patients recognized that the students were not actually disturbed, but staff continued to see them as disturbed. So strong were staff's beliefs that some students even had great difficulty in obtaining their discharge. Imagine yourself as a staff member. How would you react if a person whom you had already established as mentally disturbed confided in you that he or she was really a clinical psychology student involved in a training experience? This is obviously part of the person's delusional system! Such a claim is just what you might expect from persons who are out of touch with reality!

It should be emphasized here that the very context in which an individual is perceived can easily lead to dispositional attributions and expectations. People in our mental institutions are expected to behave in abnormal ways—to act like mental patients. People in our correctional institutions are expected to behave in deviant, antisocial ways—to act like "convicts." People in medical settings are often expected to act "sick." In these environments, once a person has been established as "psychotic," "criminal," or "ill," numerous forms of behavior can be taken as symptoms which confirm prophecies. This can occur in health care settings, for example, when health professionals unknowingly reinforce dependency among patients and do things for them which they are quite able to do for themselves. The message to patients is that they are too sick to help themselves even in small ways. The health professional has the power to define the situation for the patient, who fulfills the prophecy by yielding to professionals who "must know best." This does not always happen, nor is it always damaging, but it can impede and prolong recovery by interfering with the patient's attempts to take care of himself. If he is not allowed to take increasing responsibility for his own health *before* discharge, the immediate posthospitalization period could be quite stressful for him.

Even when people are discharged from institutions and health care settings, expectancies often linger. For example, persons discharged from psychiatric treatment often have a *stigma* attached to their identities, like a scarlet letter. They are treated differently by almost anyone who knows of their past. Other people seem to associate that past with probabilities for future breakdowns, outbursts, or odd behavior. Family, friends, and acquaintances often become vigilant of any sign that the individual's former problems are resurfacing. They may avoid certain topics of discussion, go to great lengths to appease the individual, and generally patronize her. Anything out of the absolute ordinary that she does may be attributed to her "condition." As a result, she is under tremendous pressure to behave in the most conforming fashion imaginable. This pressure applied by others often puts her under sufficient strain eventually to produce behavior which fulfills the prophecy. These situations are usually "no-win" situations for former psychiatric patients, because to be so well-adjusted—much better than before or during hospitalization—is to be "different": their normal behavior is seen as abnormal.

Fulfilling Prophecies Through Social Interaction

In the back-and-forth exchange of behavior between two individuals, each person is actively involved in constructing impressions of the other and in managing her own images. In this process, each person also develops certain expectancies of the other. Figure 10.2 illustrates the social interaction process, which may be seen as a sequence of steps leading to an interaction loop or reentry into an ongoing process. Within this framework, it is possible to identify various expectancy-related events at different steps.

As shown in Figure 10.2, the actor behaves in relation to the perceiver (1); the perceiver interprets the actor's behavior, begins forming expectancies about the actor, and bases her response on those assessments (2); the perceiver then behaves toward the actor (3); the actor perceives and interprets the perceiver's behavior (4); and again acts toward the perceiver (5); the perceiver interprets the actor's response against existing expectancies (6); and behaves toward the actor (7); the actor perceives the other's behavior and reenters the interaction sequence (8). Through this sequence, both persons also perceive their own behavior and are likely to make inferences about themselves from those observations. In relation to self-fulfilling prophecies, each step appears to be important for confirmation of expectancies, but self-observation by the actor may have special significance.

In each encounter between two individuals, both persons are at the same time actors and perceivers. In a general interaction sequence, the designation of one person as the actor and one person as the perceiver is actually quite arbi-

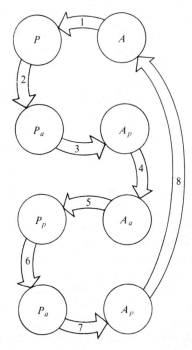

Figure 10.2   The *interaction sequence*, where the actor (*A*) behaves in relation to the perceiver (*P*) at the outset of their encounter (1). *P* interprets *A*'s behavior at stage 2 and bases his response (P_a) on those evaluations. *A* perceives and interprets (A_p) *P*'s behavior and responds to those actions at stage 5. *P* then interprets (P_p) *A*'s response and again acts (P_a) toward *A*, who again has shifted to a perceiver (A_p). Stage 8 represents a reentry into the sequence loop. Both *P* and *A* perceive *their own behavior* during the interaction, and this feedback from self-perception is also used in interpreting each other's behavior. For example, *P* may note that he responded to *A* with anger and thereby infer that he would not have acted that way if *A* were not being obnoxious.

trary. In relation to self-fulfilling prophecies, however, these designations are *not* arbitrary. According to Darley and Fazio (1980), the "perceiver" in the self-fulfilling prophecy sequence is usually the person who has the *power* to define the situation and impose that definition on the other, thereby affecting the life of the other in potentially significant ways. Thus, in an interaction between a supervisor and subordinate, the supervisor has more power to define the nature of their interaction and can exert more power over the subordinate than the subordinate can exert over her. While each person may have his or her own expectancies of the other, it is the supervisor's expectancies of the subordinate that carry more important consequences, since the life and career of the subordinate may be affected. Expectancy-confirmation situations therefore involve interactions between persons who are usually in nonequal roles. The actor is the target of the prophecy, and the perceiver is the prophet.

Perceiver Expectancies

Perceivers can develop expectancies about actors through vicarious, or indirect, experience. A perceiver may have no direct contact with an actor and still develop expectancies based on the actor's reputation or demographic characteristics. For example, if you knew that a nurse from the intensive care unit was being transferred to your department because she had "burned out" and needed a change, you, as a supervisor, may develop some expectations about the nurse's efficiency in your department. Even if you don't know her and have never seen her, your knowledge that she was no longer able to cope with her former situation may predispose you to look for indications of burn-out from her performance in your department. The limited knowledge that an actor is "burned-out," white, middle-aged, male, or similar in any other respect to persons grouped into categories within your implicit personality theory may lead you to draw inferences about the actor which extend beyond the information available. Thus, from your knowledge that a person has experienced burn-out, you may infer that the actor possesses certain personality traits and will exhibit behavior consistent with those traits. If you associate burn-out with disillusionment, cynicism, pessimism, physical and emotional exhaustion, loss of interest, and low morale, you will probably come to expect the actor to put forth minimal effect in her job, neglect some of her duties, and be inconsistent and perhaps unreliable. Of course, it all depends on your implicit personality theory and how far you go in making predictions from inferred traits. And, by no stretch of the imagination do your inferences *necessarily* lead to *accurate* expectancies concerning the behavior of the actor.

Perceivers can also develop expectancies through *direct experience* with an actor. In the interaction process described in Figure 10.2, the perceiver observes a sample of the actor's behavior at step 1. This sample may be sufficient to lead the perceiver to form an expectancy about the actor's future behavior in the interaction and elsewhere. The inferences drawn by the perceiver are not necessarily accurate, nor are they always warranted by the actor's behavior. Nevertheless, the perceiver's expectancy arises, guides his actions toward the actor, and influences the course of the interaction (Darley and Fazio, 1980). The perceiver's actions may thus terminate or facilitate interaction.

The interaction may be *terminated* if the perceiver forms a negative expectancy about the actor's behavior. Imagine being introduced to someone who refuses to shake hands with you. At that point, you would probably expect an unpleasant interaction, were it to continue. But, you may decide at that point to avoid any further interaction with the person. When this happens, your impression of the actor is negative and firm. Without further interaction to disconfirm your impression, you will maintain an expectancy for unrewarding encounters on future occasions. If and when those occasions present themselves, you will most likely turn away from the actor as soon as you can, or you may refuse to enter into any sort of encounter. Negative expectancies formed by perceivers during initial encounters where a job is at stake may have profound consequences for the actor. Perhaps you have had an experience of going through a brief interview with a potential employer who, on the basis of this one interaction, determines that you are not the kind of person for whom he or she is looking. Even if the perceiver does form a negative expectancy, it is possible that he will continue the interaction with the actor. Of course, continued interaction would be more likely when expectancies are positive, but, whatever form the expectancy takes, it will affect the course of the interaction if it continues.

The Actor's Impression of the Perceiver

During the interaction, the actor forms an impression of the perceiver. According to Darley and Fazio (1980), the actor may use one of four possible kinds of attributions in interpreting the perceiver's behavior. *Dispositional attributions* may be made directly to the perceiver. When the actor attributes the perceiver's behavior to dispositional characteristics, she develops an expectation that the perceiver behaves similarly in a wide range of situations. The actor may make a *situational attribution* instead. As Darley and Fazio pointed out, this kind of attribution is more likely to be made when the actor is trying to understand how the situation might have affected the perceiver. When situational attributions are made, the actor develops expectancies about the perceiver's behavior in similar circumstances but not across a range of situations. Thus, a subordinate may attribute his supervisor's reprimands to pressure from her superiors and not to her authoritarian personality. He thereby expects that as pressure decreases or in contexts other than the work environment, the supervisor's behavior will be different. Based on this expectancy, the subordinate can then adjust his own behavior according to the situation. *Self-attributions* can be made by the actor when he believes that the perceiver's behavior toward him is in response to something about himself. For instance, the person who introduces himself to others as a psychologist is usually aware that their reactions may be influenced by his occupation: "I'll bet you've got me all figured out," "What's the difference between a psychologist and a psychiatrist anyway?"; "I'd better be careful of what I say around you"; or "I've got this friend, and he's been having these problems. . . ." *Complex attributions* (multiple attributions; see Chapter Six) are made by the actor who assumes that all of the above factors interactively affect the perceiver's behavior. For example, the psychologist does not expect everyone to respond to him in the same way at a party. Certain individuals will seize the opportunity to ask all sorts of questions, while others are not affected one way or another. Thus, expectancies are based on dispositional and situational attributions as well as the awareness of one's own characteristics.

Darley and Fazio (1980) noted that when the actor assumes that it is something about himself that caused the perceiver to behave as she did, he will try to dispel her impression of him if it appears to be inaccurate and if her impression of him is important. He will try to reinforce her impression of him if it appears that the impression is favorable and accurate. If the actor is uncertain about how closely the perceiver's impression actually describes him, he may, in some cases, accept the perceiver's impression as being accurate, especially if the perceiver is seen as someone who is experienced at making accurate judgements. For example, you may have been told several times by someone whose opinions you respect that you should pursue a career in the health professions. You may have confirmed his or her impressions and expectations by doing so. If attributions are made to situational factors or to the perceiver's disposition—and not to anything about oneself—the actor may act like the perceiver acted. That is, if the perceiver acted friendly, the actor will act friendly; if the perceiver was hostile, the actor will be hostile; if the perceiver was cooperative, the actor will be cooperative, and so on. However, as Darley and Fazio pointed out, the actor will behave in a contrary fashion if he perceives the perceiver's actions to be incompatible with his own goals and motives. Thus, if the perceiver wants to tell ethnic jokes and the actor doesn't want to hear them, the actor may withdraw from the interaction.

Confirmation and Disconfirmation of the Prophecy

To this point, the discussion has considered the perceiver's expectancies, the actor's impressions of the perceiver, and the actor's response to the perceiver. Now, the actor's response may cause the perceiver to develop new expectancies, or the actor's behavior may confirm or refute the perceiver's initial expectancies. The principal concern here is with confirmation and disconfirmation.

As you know from earlier discussions of attribution, individuals are inclined to make dispositional attributions to *other's* behavior. When this is done, perceivers tend to view the actor's behavior as characteristic of a person with particular dispositional traits. The actor's behavior is seen as "typical" and thus expected, given the kind of person he is. Once the perceiver defines the actor as a certain kind of person, she may conclude that his behavior accurately reflects his overall personality. Even if the actor's behavior cannot, in any objective way, be construed as consistent with the perceiver's dispositional attribution, initial impressions and expectancies may persist. Behavior that violates the perceiver's expectancy may be attributed to situational factors: "He was just lucky this time," "Sure, he might seem nice to you, but when you get to know him, you'll see what I mean," "I can't understand it—she's so smart; she must have had something on her mind today that upset her."

In self-fulfilling prophecy situations, it may not matter what the actor does, nor does it necessarily matter that the actor clearly disconfirms the perceiver's expectancy. The perceiver's tendency is to interpret the actor's behavior as confirming the expectancy, regardless of the facts. Once established, the perceiver maintains the expectancy through perceptual selection and resolves inconsistencies through dissonance-reduction. By attributing inconsistent behavior by the actor to situational forces or chance, the perceiver minimizes its relevance. Sooner or later, the predicted behavior is likely to occur, and, when it does, the perceiver takes it as confirmation of the prophecy. Even if the predicted behavior rarely occurs-or if it, in fact, never occurs as predicted—the perceiver may still distort the evidence and interpret it as confirmatory. Therefore, in self-fulfilling prophecy situation, the crucial element seems to be the perceiver's *belief* that the expectancy is confirmed. Confirmation is most likely to occur through perceptual *biasing* by the perceiver.

All of this is not to suggest that actors never objectively fulfill the prophecy. In many instances, the behavior of the perceiver may truly cause the actor to do so (this was pointed up in the earlier example involving the emergency department encounter). Perceivers can and frequently *do* "set up" actors by acting toward them in ways which guarantee fulfillment of the prophecy. The behavioral evidence is then even more convincing in the eyes of the perceiver as confirmation of the prophecy.

Consequences for the Actor

There are potentially significant consequences for actors involved in self-fulfilling prophecies. For example, how do you think children are affected when their teachers hold expectations about their academic performance? Rosenthal and Jacobson (1968) demonstrated in a series of experiments that children taught by teachers who were led to believe these children were more intelligent than other children actually performed better on subsequent intelligence tests. Apparently, the teachers spent more time with children they thought were bright and rewarded their efforts more often than children they saw as less intelligent. Further research suggested that when teachers believe children have strong intellectual potential, they create a warm, stimulating climate for those children, give them more feedback, teach them a wider range of material, and give them more opportunities for learning than are given to children considered less capable (Rosenthal, 1973). Students believed to be average or below average may be ignored, and, should they achieve in spite of their teachers' expectancies, they may be labeled as troublemakers (Rosenthal and Jacobson, 1968).

A group of people can hold unfavorable attitudes toward another group; those attitudes ultimately lead to a fulfillment of a prophecy through the actions of the target group. Confirmation then provides justification for the behavior of the former group toward the target group. For example, let's pretend that males claim women are unqualified to be physicians and therefore will not admit women to medical schools. Lo and behold, women then remain unqualified for such occupations. Women come to believe that they are unqualified because they have been discriminated against, and their attitude is justified. The attitudes of men are also justified because there is no evidence that women can function as physicians. Without evidence to the contrary, the practice of barring women from medical schools is justified. Now, let's extend the fantasy a bit further. Let's envision a time when this practice is loosened somewhat, a time when some women are granted admission to medical school. Males still object to their admission on the grounds that women are not cut out to be physicians, but they decide to admit a few women into school just to appease the protests of discrimination and, at the same time, perhaps to prove, once and for all, that women cannot be physicians. Do you think medical school will be more difficult for the women admitted for study? You can bet your last dollar it will be, but it won't be difficult "because they are unqualified." It will be difficult because males eager to prove their point will make it hard for the women to succeed. Those who fail confirm the prophecy, while those who succeed in the face of special pressure are "exceptions." Traces of this "fantasy" continue to exist from a time when it was hard reality. Indeed, some may even cite the greater ratio of men over women in medical schools today as evidence that women are still not qualified to be physicians. The female-dominated nursing profession may be pointed to as the area wherein women are more qualified. Now, the relationships between nurses, on the one hand, and physicians and hospital administrators, on the other, often include other kinds of self-fulfilling prophecies with important consequences for nurses. For example, if physicians and administrators see nurses as unqualified to challenge or override physicians' decisions, they will impose rules on nurses prohibiting such behavior. The rules will dictate that even the nurse with 30 years of experience cannot override a decision made by a first year intern. In compliance with those rules, nurses then refrain from challenging physicians. By so doing, they reinforce the physicians' beliefs and fulfill the prophecy because they have not demonstrated through their behavior that they can be any more perceptive than physicians. By virtue of their role-conformity, nurses may communicate an acceptance of the expectation concerning their lack of qualifications.

The range of potential consequences befalling actors in self-fulfilling prophecy situations is endless. One important consequence pertains to the effect of self-observation on the self-concepts and future behavior of actors. Although individuals favor situational attributions for their own behavior, self-perception theory (Bem, 1965, 1972) and cognitive dissonance theory (Festinger, 1957) suggest that, under certain conditions, they may also make inferences about themselves. In the self-fulfilling prophecy, actors may make self-attributions after perceiving their own behavior and infer that they are the kind of persons who respond in certain ways in particular situations. For example, when Nancy is the target of frequent teasing by her friends, she may come to believe that being the brunt of their hazing doesn't bother her at all if they have added at various times, "You're such a good sport Nancy—nothing bothers you at all." After hearing these types of comments, Nancy might take note of the way she comes across to her friends when they tease her. Upon realizing that she usually laughs right along with them, even joking about herself at times, she may conclude that they are right. This conclusion could represent an inaccurate self-attribution which causes her to see herself *as others have defined her*, not as she has defined herself. Consequently, in certain situations (i.e., those in which she is the target of jokes), the self-attributions prompt *continuing confirmation of her friends' expectancies*. This kind of behavior could generalize to other situations as she makes new friends who make similar comments which reinforce earlier self-attributions, thus provoking similar expectancy-confirming behavior.

Self-observation may also lead the actor to infer particular feelings toward a perceiver, which influence behavior that confirms the perceiver's expectancy. For instance, if you are a medical patient and your attending nurse acts as if she is unconcerned about your health and comfort, you may interpret her behavior as due to her disposition. You may become all the more convinced of her dispositional qualities when you note your own negative reaction to her ("I don't talk to her and I don't try to be friendly *because* she acts as if she doesn't care anyway"). Your feelings about the nurse are likely to influence subsequent behavior toward her, which may represent continuing confirmation of her expectancies of you (i.e., she expects you to be quiet and nonconversant, and you are). Thus, she continues to go about her business without expressing her concern for your welfare and you remain silent and, hence, give no indication that there is anything about which she should be concerned. The nurse's behavior is probably similar to the "professional manner" of numerous health professionals exposed to continuous human suffering. She may have detached herself from most patients as a way of preventing herself from experiencing emotional pain and stress. By not allowing herself or you to develop any more than the most necessary superficial relationship, she can insulate herself from your suffering and discomfort. Consequently, she acts distant and unaffected as a means of preventing you from expressing feelings which she may be unable or unwilling to handle. Upon seeing her behavior, you close yourself off to her, and her expectations are fulfilled. Again, by inferring a negative feeling toward the perceiver, based on observations of your reactions to the perceiver, your subsequent behavior may very well fulfill the perceiver's prophecy. It must be noted, of course, that this same process applies to positive feelings as well.

A Final Note on the Self-Fulfilling Prophecy

In self-fulfilling prophecy situations, the behavior of actors is modified by the expectations held by perceivers via actions of perceivers toward actors. The actors behave in ways which confirm perceiver expectancies. The behavior of actors may not objectively confirm the expectancies, but the perceivers interpret those actions as confirmatory in any event. A consequence for perceivers is that they can maintain stable impressions of actors, impressions which are highly resistant to change. Their liking for actors can also be maintained and, in fact, justified through expectancy-confirmation processes. A consequence for actors is that they may continue a pattern of behavior whenever certain perceivers or certain situations are encountered—a pattern of behavior which is in the service of expectancy confirmation. Another consequence for actors is that their self-concepts may be altered in various ways when they observe their actions and infer that those actions are particularly self-revealing. As Darley and Fazio (1980) argued, the perceiver's expectancy can exert an influence which extends far beyond the original interaction: it can affect the life of the actor for better or for worse. They fear, as do many others involved in expectancy-confirmation research, that it is often for the worse.

An argument that self-fulfilling prophecies cannot adversely affect the lives of individuals would be hard to devise. In Chapter Two, a version of the self-fulfilling prophecy was described in a case involving a young sailor named Kevin. Kevin assumed that the world was a cruel place and that he was an inherently unlikable person. He had experienced rejection many times in his life—so many times, in fact, that he came to expect it whenever he met someone. So firm were his expectations for rejection that he set out to fulfill his prophecies and reinforce his beliefs about himself and the world around him. His expectancy-confirming behavior became apparent in group therapy sessions, where he manipulated group members' impressions by conveying a negative image. He forced them to become angry at him, and, within a short time, he had successfully caused the entire group to exclude him from daily interactions. Kevin accomplished this by learning about personal issues that were especially problematic for each person in the group and then making fun of their sensitivities. Kevin claimed that he was being treated unfairly, that no matter what he tried to do, people still disliked him. Convinced of the futility of trying to change, Kevin could then justify his drinking problem to his own satisfaction and unwittingly pursue a course leading to chronic alcoholism and perhaps death. In cases like Kevin's, individuals respond to others in ways which force others to display expectancy-confirming actions. Their distorted views of the world, other people, and themselves are reinforced by "setting up" others for confirmation. They can then justify their maladaptive behavior, which, by the way, is intuited to be less painful than change.

Summary

The first section of this chapter examined the effects of accidental consequences on individuals' impressions of victims of misfortune. When the magnitude and/or frequency of misfortunes befalling others increases, so also does the tendency among observers to attribute responsibility to the victims. As a result, victims appear less desirable in the eyes of observers, whose impressions have grown increasingly negative. This tendency appears to stem from a pervasive belief among individuals that the world is a *just* place where people are somehow deserving of the consequences affecting them. Minor misfortunes can happen to anyone, but major misfortunes are not often seen as events that can happen to anyone. Therefore, observers infer that victims must have brought their misfortunes upon themselves. These inferences enable perceivers to feel secure in the belief that they are different, that they would have acted differently, and that, therefore, they are not vulnerable to the same chance events. Health care recipients are victims of one sort or another, and it was noted that, under certain conditions, health professionals may conclude that those persons deserved their fates. The problem of *dehumanization* was discussed as a potential consequence of burn-out, which, in turn, may lead to justifications of negligence and harmdoing.

The second section addressed the problem of *harmdoing*, its effects on perceivers' self-concepts, impressions of those they have harmed, and subsequent behavior toward victims of earlier transgressions. The recognition of having caused harm to another person is inconsistent with one's view of self as a decent person. When harmdoers cannot deny or minimize the harm they have done, they may attempt to make restitution to their victims. When restitution is ineffective in compensating the victim for his or her suffering or when restitution is bypassed altogether, harmdoers may then *derogate* their victims and convince themselves that their victims got what they deserved. Derogation is most likely to occur when harmdoers believe they had some choice between harming and not harming the victims and when they realize that they cannot undo the effects of their actions. Various conditions were identified as limiting the derogation tendency. Among those conditions are the harmdoer's level of self-esteem, the relationship between harmdoers and their victims, the victim's capacity to retaliate, and the availability of adequate compensations. Even if harmdoers do not elect to derogate their victims, other justifications may be used to reduce dissonance. They may attempt to minimize the actual harm done, compare their actions to those who have done similar things, point to the context in which the harmdoing occurred, claim unforeseen consequences or extenuating circumstances. It was emphasized that individuals who have achieved the capacity for *empathy* will find it hard to justify harmdoing because they can see the event from the victim's perspective.

The final section reviewed *self-fulfilling prophecies*, which occur when individuals' expectancies about others produce behavior evoking responses from the others which then confirm the expectancies. Perceiver expectancies may develop through vicarious or direct experience with particular actors. Their expectancies are not necessarily accurate. Perceivers' impressions of actors may be based on distorted and/or limited information. During interactions, actors also form impressions of perceivers. The perceiver's behavior may be attributed by the actor to dispositional, situational, or multiple causes. Actors may also infer that the perceiver's behavior was caused by characteristics of their own (the actors). The behavior of actors may or may not objectively confirm perceiver expectancies, but perceivers usually interpret such behavior as confirmatory. Consequences for perceivers include the reinforcement of their impressions of actors and an increased likelihood of similar responding toward the actors on future occasions. Similar consequences accrue for actors, although they are subject to consequences that are potentially negative. Various undesirable consequences for actors were discussed, including the alteration of their self-concepts. Throughout the chapter, examples were used which pointed to direct implications for health professionals in their interactions with patients, colleagues, and other professionals.

References

Bem, D. J. An Experimental Analysis of Self-Persuasion, *Journal of Experimental Social Psychology*, **1**:199–218 (1965).

Bem, D. J. Self-Perception Theory, in *Advances in Experimental Social Psychology*, vol. 6, ed. L. Berkowitz. New York, Academic Press, 1972.

Berscheid, E.; Boye, D.; and Darley, J. M. Effects of Forced Association Upon Voluntary Choice to Associate, *Journal of Personality and Social Psychology*, **8**:13–19 (1968).

Berscheid, E., and Walster, E. *Interpersonal Attraction*. Reading, Massachusetts, Addison-Wesley, 1978.

Brickman, P., Coates, D., Janoff-Bulman, R. Lottery winners and accident victims: Is happiness relative? *Journal of Personality and Social Psychology,* **36**:917–27 (1978).

Darley, J., and Fazio, R. Expectancy Confirmation Processes Arising in the Social Interaction Sequence, *American Psychologist*, **35**:867–81 (1980).

Davis, K. E., and Jones, E. E. Changes in Interpersonal Perception as a Means of Reducing Cognitive Dissonance, *Journal of Abnormal and Social Psychology*, **61**:402–10 (1960).

Festinger, L. *A Theory of Cognitive Dissonance*. Evanston, Illinois, Row, Peterson, 1957.

Gelles, R. J. *The Violent Home: A Study of Physical Aggression Between Husbands and Wives*. Beverly Hills, California, Sage Publications, 1972.

Glass, D. C. Changes in Liking as a Means of Reducing Cognitive Discrepancies Between Self-Esteem and Aggression, *Journal of Personality*, **32**:520–49 (1964).

Lerner, M.J. Evaluation of performance as a function of performer's reward and attractiveness. *Journal of Personality and Social Psychology,* **1**:355–61 (1965).

Lerner, M.J. The desire for justice and reactions to victims. In J. Macaulay and L. Berkowitz (Eds.), *Altruism and Helping Behavior.* New York, Academic Press, 1970.

Merton, R. K. *Social Theory and Social Structure.* New York, Free Press of Glencoe, 1957.

Millman, M. *The Unkindest Cut: Life in the Backrooms of Medicine.* New York, Morrow, 1977.

Rosenhan, D. On Being Sane in an Insane Place, *Science,* **179**, (4070) (1973).

Rosenthal, R. On the Social Psychology of the Self-Fulfilling Prophecy: Further Evidence for Pygmalion Effects and Their Mediating Mechanisms, in *Reading and School Achievement: Cognitive and Affective Influences,* ed. M. Kling. Eighth Annual Spring Reading Conference, Rutgers, New Jersey, Rutgers University, 1973.

Rosenthal, R., and Jacobson, L. *Pygmalion in the Classroom.* New York, Holt, Rinehart, and Winston, 1968.

Schlenker, B. R. *Impression Management: The Self-Concept, Social Identity, and Interpersonal Relations.* Monterey, California, Brooks/Cole, 1980.

Walster, E. The assignment of responsibility for an accident. *Journal of Personality and Social Psychology,* **3**:73–79 (1966).

CHAPTER ELEVEN

Skills Assessment and Applications for Part Two

More skillful in self-knowledge, even more pure,
As tempted more; more able to endure,
As more exposed to suffering and distress.

William Wordsworth,
Character of the Happy Warrior

In this chapter, you will have the opportunity to further assess your interpersonal skills. The skills which represent the focus of this chapter are not observable skills. They are primarily cognitive and perceptual skills. You are provided with structured inventories and exercises which are designed to assist you in recognizing characteristics of your own cognitive style and perceptual tendencies. In particular, the content of this chapter is intended to help you focus on:

The impressions you form about other people
Your general mode of self-presentation
Your personal values
Attitudes which you hold on certain issues
Beliefs which you hold about people and behavior
Attributions which you may make to others' behavior
The rewards and punishments you may provide others
The rewards and punishments others provide you

Most of the exercises provided here are designed for individual use. However, many are recommended for interpersonal use. Those exercises which you complete on an individual basis may, of course, become the subjects of group or two-person interactions. The exercises themselves are only to stimulate your thinking. You may find it helpful to alter them in various ways.

Your Impressions of Others

To stimulate examination of the general impressions you form of other people, read each of the questions below and take time to consider your responses. You may find it enlightening to do this exercise with at least one other person.

1. When you meet someone for the first time, what do you look for first?
2. Regardless of what you look for, what do you usually notice first? (For example, some people always seem to notice others' hair, clothes, teeth, or posture.)
3. Think about what you usually notice first. What does this suggest about some of your values and sensitivities?
4. What characteristics do you usually associate with the following?

   a. Paramedics (EMTs)
   b. Psychiatrists
   c. Geriatric patients
   d. Orderlies
   e. Female nurses
   f. Surgeons
   g. Chiropractors
   h. Paraplegics
   i. Chaplains
   j. Osteopaths
   k. Alcoholic patients
   l. Candy stripers
   m. Administrators
   n. Male nurses
   o. Interns
   p. Nurse practitioners
   q. Social workers
   r. Terminally ill patients
   s. Auxiliary volunteers
   t. Psychiatric patients

5. What factors are important to you in the impressions you form (i.e., to what do you usually assign significant weight)?
6. For you, are first impressions usually "lasting impressions"?
7. Identify three occasions when your impressions of people were not accurate. Why were your impressions inaccurate? What happened to change your impressions? Were there any similarities in these experiences?
8. From among your classmates, select one who is a real mystery to you, someone you just can't figure out. Why is it difficult for you to form a clear impression of that person? What information would you want, and how can you get it?
9. How are your impressions usually affected when you hear unflattering gossip about others? How much faith do you put in the gossip (assuming that the source is reliable)? Do you ever try to check out the accuracy of that information by going to the subject, the person talked about?
10. Do you think you are a "good judge of character"? How do you know?
11. Can you detect impression management from others' behavior?

12. Describe the public image of the health professional.
13. What person in your life has made the strongest impression on you (apart from your family), whether positive or negative? Why?
14. Think back to your childhood and recall one of your elementary teachers. Whom did you recall? What stands out in your memory about this person? Why do you think you've remembered what you did?
15. Think back to your last psychology course (assuming that you've had one; if not, think back to your last English course). What do you remember about your instructor? Why do you remember that?
14. When you meet others for the first time, what do you want them to notice about you?
15. What do you want others to think of you?
16. How do you want others to feel about you?
17. What do you do to encourage those impressions?
18. Under what kinds of circumstances in the last week have you engaged in purposeful impression management? (Identify three.)
19. What do you want your professional role to say about you as a person?
20. Under what kinds of circumstances are you not your "real self" with others?
21. If you could create an ideal reputation for yourself, what would it be?
22. What do you want others *not* to notice about you most of the time?
23. Of what physical characteristics of yours are you most proud?
24. What kinds of things do you like to hear about yourself?
25. Under what conditions do you enjoy opening up to people?
26. How do you encourage others to open up to you?
27. How do you discourage others from being psychologically intimate with you?
28. How are your impressions of yourself different from the impressions others have of you?
29. What kinds of impressions do you think medical patients "should" have of health professionals?
30. What kind of impression do you think your profession needs to convey to the general public? Is your profession successful? If not, why not?

Impressions You Convey to Health Care Recipients

Many beginning health professionals have a need to be approved of by their clients or patients. To gain that approval, they may engage in excessive sharing of personal information. They may talk about themselves in detail, regardless of how appropriate it is for given clients. Sometimes, this is done in hopes that openness will make them seem more human and promote trust. It is possible that for some of these persons, denying the professional role may make them appear more *inauthentic* than authentic. Consequently, their professional effectiveness is limited. Other beginning health professionals strive to appear professional at all times, perhaps believing that a solid image adds to their effectiveness or perhaps believing that if they don't act consistently with professional objectivity, they will be perceived for what they are: inexperienced. Pause for a moment and reflect on the following items, so that you may begin clarifying your own criteria for impression management.

1. How important is it that persons under your care perceive you as being human?

2. How important is it that persons under your care like you?

3. How much of your personal life are you willing to share with persons under your care? What are the limits?

4. For what reasons would you disclose personal information to health care recipients?

5. What positive effects can you see for patients to whom you disclose personal information?

6. If you were experiencing personal distress around some problem in your life, under what conditions would you *and* would you *not* share that experience with someone under your care?

7. What are your attitudes toward remaining neutral and objective at all times and avoiding expressions of personal feelings toward persons under your care?

8. What kinds of feelings can you *not* see yourself sharing with persons under your care?

Personal Values

The following exercises and questions are intended to stimulate further clarification of some of your values. Some of the exercises to follow are adapted from *Values Clarification* by S. B. Simon, L. W. Howe, and H. Kirschenbaum (New York, Hart, 1978). There are countless ways in which individuals can explore values. This section begins by presenting you with additional questions.

1. Do you have a personal saying or motto by which you live?
2. What do you like most about your training?
3. What do you prize most about life?
4. Do you have a hero or heroine? Who? Why?
5. Identify an important role-model in your life. What is it about her/him that you admire?
6. What is one thing you would like to learn between now and the day you die?
7. If you have any financial savings, for what are you saving your money?
8. Are you more or less religious than you were five years ago?
9. How do you feel about visiting a funeral home?
10. What is the most important thing for you to be able to continue doing throughout your life?
11. How do you spend your free time on weekends?
12. When you have brief periods of free time, how do you usually use it?
13. What are your favorite kinds of novels, magazines, movies, television shows?
14. What do you like least about your current education?
15. If you were a college professor, how would you teach your classes?
16. What is it about you that makes your friends like you?
17. In your lifetime, what person has helped you the most, aside from a family member? How did that person help you?
18. What do you want to be doing five years from now? Ten years? Twenty years?
19. If you could have three wishes come true, what would they be?
20. If you could change one thing about a particular relationship you have, what would it be? why?
21. What is the most pressing decision you must make in your life right now?
22. What is your main ambition in life?
23. What makes you dislike a person just on sight?
24. Are you proud of your sex? Race? Ethnicity? Age? Marital status?

25. What are your most prized possessions?
26. What are your most prized accomplishments?
27. Under what circumstances in your life were you more proud of yourself than you had ever been?
28. Under what circumstances can you see yourself as being more proud of yourself than you have ever been?
29. When are you most embarrassed about yourself?
30. What five things can you do better than other people you know?

Ten Things I Love to Do

A crucial issue in the exploration of personal values is whether or not you are getting what you want out of life. To encourage your thinking on this issue, list 10 things that you love to do, and then do the following:

Place a dollar sign ($) next to those things that cost you five dollars or more each time you do them.

Place the letter A next to those things that you usually prefer doing along.

Place the letter P next to those things that you usually prefer doing with one or more other persons.

Place the letter M next to those things you would like to do more often.

Place the letter B next to those things you would like to do better.

Place a minus five (—5) next to those things that you think you may *not* be able to do five years from now.

For each activity you have listed, identify the approximate number of times you have actually done them in the last month.

After following these instructions, examine your list carefully and then complete these sentences:

I was surprised to discover _____

I learned that _____

Ranking Options

Place the number 1 next to your first choice, 2 (second choice), 3 (least desirable).

1. Which is most important in a friendship?

_____ honesty
_____ loyalty
_____ respect

2. If you were given a $100 bill, what would you do with it?

_____ buy something for myself
_____ share it with someone
_____ give it to someone who needed it more than I

3. What kind of pet would you rather have?

_____ dog
_____ cat
_____ hamster

4. Which would you least like to be?

_____ physically ill
_____ mentally disordered
_____ incarcerated in prison

5. When you worry about failing an exam, about whom do you think?

_____ yourself
_____ your parents
_____ your future

6. Which do you like most about yourself?

_____ my face
_____ my personality
_____ my athletic skill

7. Which learning format do you prefer?

_____ experimentation
_____ lecture
_____ discussion

8. If you had one hour to spend with a dying person, what would you do?

_____ sit in the corner
_____ sit quietly next to the person
_____ sit next to the person and talk, even if he/she couldn't hear me

9. If you learned that a colleague intentionally neglected a patient, would you:

_____ report him/her to the supervisor
_____ confront him/her directly
_____ have nothing else to do with him/her

10. What would be your duty shift preference?

_____ first shift
_____ second shift
_____ third shift

11. Which would you most like people to think of you?

_____ that I am genuine
_____ that I am understanding
_____ that I am sensitive

12. Which would you least like people to think of you?

_____ that I am uncaring
_____ that I am not very smart
_____ that I am physically unattractive

13. Which would you least like to do?

_____ work in intensive coronary care
_____ work in the emergency department
_____ work on a medical/surgical floor

14. Which would you least like to do?

_____ learn how to improve my communication skills
_____ learn how to enhance my social life
_____ learn how to improve my appearance

15. Which would you least like to be?

_____ blind
_____ deaf
_____ paralyzed

16. Which would be the most difficult for you to accept?

_____ the death of a friend
_____ your own death
_____ the death of a parent

17. About which would you be most concerned as you gain professional experience?

_____ getting incremental salary raises
_____ getting promotions
_____ getting professional recognition

18. During a seminar, where would you be seated?

_____ at the front
_____ in the back
_____ in the middle

19. To which person would you be most attracted?

_____ a person my own age
_____ a younger person
_____ an older person

Your Own Social Group

This exercise may be conducted individually, but it is preferable that six or seven persons share their individual responses in a group discussion and decision-making session. There are many variations to the theme of this exercise, but the story line is this:

> You have a small group of friends in your neighborhood. You have all been working on a neighborhood improvement project, and you have discovered that you need at least five more people to help. Since you all happen to be friends anyway, you decided that you don't want "just anybody" from the neighborhood to join your group. You have been approached by 10 people who want to join and participate in the project. Your group has decided that you will vote on who gets in and who does not. Because, you all see this project as a way of bringing you closer together and because you are all more committed to that objective than actually to bringing about the proposed neighborhood improvements, you are not particularly interested in the potential members' organizing or problem-solving abilities.
>
> You are all about to leave the get-together and return to your own homes. You only have 30 minutes to vote on who is to be accepted into the group. You don't have time for much more than superficial descriptions of the "applicants." You must decide before you go home. These are the "applicants," so rank your choices from "most desirable" to "least desirable":
>
> 1. Black male; political activist; first year medical student
> 2. 36-year-old female attorney; single; gay
> 3. 42-year-old retired prostitute; living on her annuities
> 4. 50-year-old male policeman; carries gun; several suspensions for brutality
> 5. 25-year-old female; single parent of one child; frequent male overnight guests
> 6. Male chemist; heavy drinker; known spouse abuser
> 7. Male factory worker; arrested twice for sale of narcotics
> 8. 66-year-old widowed woman; retired professor of English literature
> 9. 30-year-old male; avowed bigot; suspected member of Ku Klux Klan
> 10. 48-year-old mother of nine; recently discharged from mental hospital

Ticket Agent

You are a ticket agent for a flight which has only one remaining seat available. Five people are at the counter, and all are requesting that you give them the last ticket. The flight is to leave in 15 minutes. You have only the following information, and you must use it to decide who gets the ticket.

1. A businesswoman who must make this flight, or she will be unable to keep an appointment. If she misses the appointment, she will be fired from her job—a job which she has worked 10 years to get.
2. A young soldier who has a 48-hour pass to go home. He has not seen his family in one year. In 48 hours, he will be sent overseas for a one-year tour of duty.
3. A middle-aged man whose son was seriously injured in a yachting accident. He does not know if his son will live or die. He is willing to pay you any amount you want for the ticket. Money is no object.
4. A young woman who has been visiting her parents after an argument with her husband. Her husband telephoned and told her that if she was not back home before morning, he would leave her forever.
5. A recent college graduate who has been invited to interview for her first job. She has been unable to find employment commensurate with her education. This is the first opportunity she has had. She has threatened to kill herself if she doesn't land this job.

Raisin River

Read the following story, and then rate each of the characters from the most offensive character to the least objectionable character. The person you consider the most reprehensible should be rated first, then the second most objectionable, and so on.

> Once upon a time, there was a woman named Maudine, who was in love with a man named Tyrone. Maudine and Tyrone lived on opposite sides of the raging Raisin River. The bridge across the river had been washed away during a flood. Maudine was desperate to see Tyrone, since they hadn't been together since the bridge collapsed two weeks earlier. One day, Maudine approached Billy Jim and asked him to transport her across the river in his boat. Billy Jim agreed to do so, but only on the condition that Maudine go to bed with him. Maudine refused and went to a friend, Leland, to explain her plight. Leland said he did not want to get involved in the situation. Maudine felt that her only alternative was to agree to Billy Jim's terms. Billy Jim fulfilled his promise to Maudine and took her across the Raisin River in his boat. Upon reaching the other side and embracing her lover, Maudine told Tyrone what happened. Tyrone immediately pushed Maudine away, and, in his anger, he told her he never wanted to see her again. Heartsick and dejected, Maudine walked down the river bank, where she found her friend Clyde. Maudine related her tale of woe to Clyde, who then sought out Tyrone and beat him mercilessly. Maudine was pleased at the sight of Tyrone getting his due. She and Clyde then walked arm in arm down the bank of the raging Raisin River.

In a group of six to seven people, share your rankings. What do your reactions suggest about your own values and the values of others in the group?

Return to Raisin River

In your group (or individually), consider the following questions concerning the Raisin River story:

1. What additional information would you need in order to feel more confident in the ranking you made?
2. What do your ratings suggest about *inferences* you have made from limited information? How much have you "read into" this story?
3. What do you really know about this case? What do you *not* know?
4. What specific *assumptions* have you made?
5. What does this story suggest to you about making *judgements* of people?

Personal Attitudes

It is important that you become aware of what many of your attitudes are, since they are predispositions to your behavior. In this section, you are provided with various opportunities to examine your attitudes toward various things. First, read each of the following questions and try to identify exactly where you stand on each of the issues. Any of these may be selected for discussion in a group setting. It should be helpful for you to hear some other people's attitudes and even more helpful to learn to understand those attitudes. In group situations, you should not try to "argue" your position, but only present it and then listen to the substance of other's attitudes. Do not judge them right or wrong. Listen!

My attitude Toward . . . Is . . .

1. My attitude toward people who seek abortions is _____

2. My attitude toward active euthanasia is _____

3. My attitude toward passive euthanasia is _____

4. My attitude toward continuing education is _____

5. My attitude toward professional competition is _____

6. My attitude toward personal freedom is _____

7. My attitude toward self-disclosure is _____

8. My attitude toward civil rights is _____

9. My attitude toward exercise is _____

10. My attitude toward dieting is _____

11. My attitude toward divorce is _____

At this point, you may want to identify three of your strongest attitudes relative to some issue or person not cited above. How did you acquire these attitudes? Do you want to change them? Are these attitudes different from what they were five years ago? How did they change? How were they reinforced (if they did not change)?

Ranking Some Attitudes

Rank your attitudes toward the following items. At the top of your list should be your *strongest* attitude, and at the bottom of the list should be your weakest attitude. The issue about which you feel most strongly should be rated number one. Give reasons for why your rankings appear as they do.

Smoking   1. _____

Drug abuse   2. _____

Gossip   3. _____

Cheating   4. _____

Sexism   5. _____

Homosexuality   6. _____

Recreation   7. _____

Marriage   8. _____

Spouse abuse   9. _____

Child abuse   10. _____

Role Reversals

Share your list from the preceding exercise with six or seven people in a group discussion. In your group, have each person spend five minutes role playing an attempt to persuade another person to a particular point of view. The view each person is to defend and argue is the view which is the exact *opposite* of his strongest attitude. Each person should then advocate a position opposite to his weakest attitude. What was the experience like in each counterattitudinal argument? Was it difficult to defend a position to which you are so opposed? Was it easy to defend a position about which you don't care too much? Were your attitudes altered in any way by the counterattitudinal positions you assumed? Which position had the greatest effect on; your existing attitudes?

Attitudes Toward Death and Dying

Your profession deals with issues of life and death. You should therefore clarify some of your attitudes and values relative to these issues. The following questions should help to stimulate that process.

1. Should people take the time to talk about their feelings about death, or should they avoid it because it would be too upsetting for them?
2. To what extent do you believe in a life after death? How does your view in this regard impact on your overall attitude toward dying?
3. Regardless of what you believe about life after death, what is your wish?
4. What does death mean to you?
5. Should people be allowed to choose their own manner of dying?
6. Should life be preserved at all costs?
7. When do people die (i.e., what defines it)?
8. What has exerted the strongest effect on your current attitude toward death?
9. How often do you think about your own death?
10. What aspect of your own death is most unpleasant to think about?
11. Have you ever wanted to die?
12. If you could pick your date of death, when would it be?
13. Would you want to know when you are going to die?
14. What kind of death would you most prefer? Least prefer?
15. How does your least preferred form of death affect your attitude toward those who happen to die that way (i.e., how do you feel when you learn someone has died that way)?
16. If you knew you only had three months to live, what would you do? Why aren't you doing it now?
17. How do you feel about having an autopsy performed on your body?
18. What are your attitudes toward (1) burial, (2) cremation, (3) donation?
19. How important do you believe it is to go through a process of grief and mourning? Should it be encouraged? Discouraged?
20. When you die, how do you want people to react?
21. Should dying persons be encouraged to talk about dying?
22. Is it hard for you to conceive of your own mortality? Is it just everyone else who dies?
23. What is the first experience with death that you can recall?

24. What kind of impression did that first experience leave on you?
25. Have you ever seen a person die? How did it affect you? If you have not seen a person die and expect that in your job you will, how do you think it will affect you at the time? Do you think you will ever get used to it? Should you get used to it?

PART THREE

The Health Professional
and Interpersonal
Communication: Promoting
Satisfactory Relationships

Having now reached Part Three of the text, it should now be reemphasized that the material presented in the three major parts is not mutually exclusive. Direct and indirect references have been made to communication throughout the text. Further, an emphasis across all chapters has been on developing and maintaining satisfactory relationships. So, we have not actually arrived at a portion of the text that is distinct from that which preceded it. Neither have we reached a point where material merely can be repeated.

Part Three includes chapters which deal fairly exclusively with *sending* verbal and nonverbal messages to others. In Chapter Twelve, a basic model of communication is outlined in which the role of the "sender" is stressed. To that end, the chapter discusses processes of *encoding* and *transmitting messages* as well as primary obstacles to effective transmission. In regards to the latter, the chapter pays special attention to the speaker's language, emotions, and intentions, conflicting messages, and other factors effecting poor transmission of messages to another person.

Chapter Thirteen provides some useful guidelines for *attending* and *listening* to others. Physical attending behavior is described as essential for effective communication, as it suggests to the other person that you are involved with her and what she is saying. In reality, this chapter could be placed conveniently in Part One, for the behaviors and skills outlined have as much to do with perception as with overt communication. The chapter concludes with a consideration of *active listening*—what to listen "for," what to listen "to," and how to show you are truly hearing what another person is saying.

Chapter Fourteen describes the necessary conditions which are prerequisite for effective communication and relationships. The communication of *respect* for others is described in terms of actual behaviors which show them that you have positive regard for them as human beings. *Facilitative genuineness* as a core condition for relationships is presented in terms of the observable behaviors that characterize it. The latter portion of Chapter Fourteen represents a necessary return to the communication of *empathy*, a third core condition for facilitative interpersonal relationships. In this section, the emphasis is on common problems in communicating empathic understanding.

Chapter Fifteen outlines some basic conversational skills which tend to have strong positive effects on most relationships. These skills include *concrete* communication, *immediacy*, and several categories of verbal statements, such as recognition responses, restatement, reflection, clarification, interpretation, explanations, and silence. Special sections are reserved for the issue of how to use questions appropriately and how to handle advice and suggestions in a relationship.

Chapter Sixteen is a basic introduction to *assertive* behavior, although a good portion of the material in the text deals with assertion. Basic forms of assertive behavior are described, along with some guidelines for using those responses.

The final chapter of the text provides an opportunity for skills assessment and application of the material in Part Three.

CHAPTER
TWELVE

The Process of Interpersonal Communication

What we've got here is a failure to communicate.

Donn Pearce, *Cool Hand Luke*,
screenplay, 1967

In recent years, there has been a surge of writings on the processes and problems of human communication. On the positive side, this attention has produced a heightened awareness of the centrality of interpersonal communication in human service professions. One effect has been an increased emphasis on the development of effective communication "skills," which are seen as prerequisite to facilitative interactions with service-delivery consumers. On the negative side, a brief survey of proliferating publications suggests that the range of activities subsumed under the heading of communication has been expanding toward a point of encompassing virtually all of human social behavior. The study of human communication often appears to rule out nothing as its proper subject matter. When communication is conceived so broadly as to include human behavior in general, there are no limits to the skills one must learn in order to communicate. Indeed, "communicating" has been the word of the day for so long as to produce an irony bordering on a loss of real meaning. The concept has been defined, dissected, discussed, and displayed in so many ways that when the communication literature is taken as a whole, it would appear that nothing short of complete resocialization suffices for skills development.

Some authors (e.g., Dance, 1970; Mortensen, 1980) have noted the confusion existing in the study of human communication. They have observed that this confusion is due to an exhaustive collection of concepts that have made the boundaries of communication phenomena imperceptible. The view that "all behavior is communication" is one which may even erase those boundaries. It seems to me that all behavior is *not* communication. All behavior may have communication "value," which may or may not be recognized, depending on whether or not it is perceived and assigned meaning. The analogy of the tree falling in the forest when no one is around seems appropriate in this connection: does it make a noise? The answer, of course, is no, because no one picks up the auditory vibrations. In a similar vein, human behavior is not communication if it is not perceived and given meaning. Boundaries must be established for the communication process. To clarify the range of phenomena that can be said to define communication, Mortensen (1980) argued for the specification of conditions necessary for an act of communication to occur. In other words, what are the conditions under which individuals attach meaning and significance to behavior? The first part of this chapter addresses this issue. It is not the aim of the chapter to offer yet another definition of communication, nor to introduce a different model. Rather, it is the intent of the chapter to examine some fundamental characteristics of behavior that appear to belong to the study of interpersonal communication. Some general characteristics of interpersonal communication are outlined, followed by a basic model of the communication process. Obstacles to effective communication are identified and suggestions for enhancing communication skills are provided.

General Characteristics

Analysis of different definitions of communication suggests that it is something which includes three "families": animal communication, human speech communication, and effective communication (Dance, 1970). Given that the concern here is with the second and third of these conceptual families, a broad definition of communication might be that it is the *process of creating meaning between two or more people* (Tubbs and Moss, 1980). As such, this process may be thought of as taking place in any one of three ways.

The simplest view of communication is from a *linear* perspective, which is a unidirectional, or one-way, view. From a linear perspective, communication begins at point A and ends at point B. An individual simply transmits a message to another person. Such a view suggests that the receiver simply accepts the message "as is." But communication goes far beyond linearity to tremendous *interactional* complexity. That is, communication involves reciprocal behavior between individuals within the context of a relationship. This means that there is not only a back-and-forth flow of behavior, there are many things going on simultaneously. For example, both persons are simultaneously acting and perceiving; they transmit messages verbally, vocally, and nonverbally; intentionally and unintentionally; actions and reactions occur in response to private experience, verbal and nonverbal feedback, time and place influences, and the past and current status of the relationship. Furthermore, the very act of creating a message may affect the sender more than the communicated message affects the receiver. This means that senders communicate messages to themselves as well as to the persons with whom they interact. From a *transactional* perspective, then, communication is defined in relation to all existing influences on interacting persons.

The kind of communication we experience most frequently is called *dyadic* communication; two persons face-to-face. It tends to have three general characteristics: (1) both persons are in close proximity to one another, (2) both persons send and receive messages, and (3) the messages have verbal, vocal, and nonverbal components to which meaning can be assigned. As a dyadic process, communication is *effective* only to the extent of close correspondence between a message *as sent* by one person and the message *as received* by the other. Tubbs and Moss (1980) suggested that effective communication is a larger issue which relates to the kinds of *outcomes* we produce from our messages. That is, communication effectiveness is also a function of whether or not we bring about outcomes we intended to produce. They suggested that five communication outcomes are common for most individuals: (1) understanding on the part of the receiver, (2) an impact on the receiver's attitudes, (3) improved relationship between the sender and receiver, (4) influencing action from the receiver, and (5) pleasure or enjoyment.

In general, the closer the correspondence between the message as sent and the message as received, the more effective communication is. However, because of the inherent differences in the frames of reference of interacting persons, perfect correspondence is not achievable. It is only as strong as the weakest link in the communication chain. The hypothetical links in the communication process are depicted in Figure 12.1; the diagram is not intended to convey a linear process, but only to identify some of the important variables or links in the chain. To appreciate the interdependence of these links, it is useful to think of the communication process in terms of *who says what to whom, how, under what circumstances, and with what effects.* This approach suggests at least six elements of the interpersonal communication process: (1) the *source* or sender of the communication (who says it), (2) the *message* (what he says), (3) the *delivery* (how he says it), (4) the *receiver* (to whom he says it), (5) the *context* (physical environment and social circumstances), and (6) the *consequences* of the communication (how changes in any one or more of the elements affect all other elements).

A Basic Model of Communication

The illustration above represents one of the most fundamental ways of conceptualizing communication processes. It is a model, a metaphor of sorts, which is used to symbolize what many believe to be the major elements in the communi-

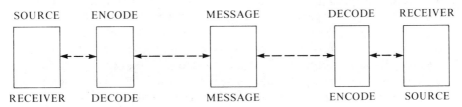

Figure 12.1   An initial model of the communication process.

cation process. The model is offered here only as a guide in examining basic verbal exchanges between two people. Although there are numerous models, most of them include the same basic elements and represent human communication with varying degrees of similarity, depending on their levels of abstraction. The model described here is not an extremely sophisticated model from a conceptual standpoint, and there is good reason for keeping it simple. Specifically, it is intended as a basic framework from which you can develop a perspective on the chief characteristics of dyadic communication. It may be used as a convenient conceptual tool for use in your repertoire of cognitive skills. It can be applied with relative ease in those situations where it is important to you to understand barriers to communication. As something akin to a conceptual template or overlay, the model provides a means of viewing and analyzing an interaction and identifying weak links in the communication chain.

The Source: Encoding and Transmitting

In any model of communication, it is arbitrary to designate one person as a source of a message and another person as the receiver. In earlier chapters, it was noted that actors are perceivers at one and the same time; they are simultaneously acting and perceiving. In communication terms, actors are *sources, senders*, or *speakers*, and perceivers are destinations, or *receivers*. Thus, sources are also receivers in any interaction. They not only send messages, they receive them as well. In the present model, this means that they encode *and* decode messages.

For the sake of organization, the source of a communication can be seen as an individual involved in sending a message to another person. A communication begins when the source converts private experience into a form that can be transmitted. Since private experience consists of information available only to the individual, it cannot be shared until it is transformed into a message suitable for transmission. *Encoding* is the process by which the individual transforms thoughts and feelings into communicable forms. Encoding involves two stages in this model.

The first stage is *identification*, and it requires that the source use appropriate word symbols from his language system to label particular thoughts and feelings. This enables the source to begin formulating the content of the messages he wants to send. As you might expect, communication problems often originate at this point when individuals cannot identify what they want to say; they can't find the right words. Communication problems can also arise at the second stage of encoding, when individuals cannot decide *how* to say what they want to say. *Preparation* is the second stage. It can be conceived as something like a "packaging" operation, analogous to the marketing function once a product has been identified for distribution. Having formulated the message content, the source prepares it for transmission by trying to put it in the most meaningful form, a form which can be understood by the receiver. In most situations, the source has various message options available, and he can choose among the different alternative ways of delivering the message content. The actual transmission process is discussed shortly. However, it is important to recognize that the encoding process precedes delivery, so various decisions are often made at this stage about how to express ideas and feelings. This is not to say that encoding is always a conscious process, for it may be habitual, seemingly automatic, and performed below the threshold of awareness. Furthermore, we often send messages unintentionally. Some of the skills necessary for effective communication are applied at the level of encoding, where individuals exercise greater control over the messages they wish to send. Improved encoding often results in a reduction in the number of unintentional messages sent to others.

At the encoding stage of communication, cognitive skills are quite important. Common sense would point to the need for adequate intellectual skills in order to encode effectively. Social knowledge is equally important. However, the primary tools for accomplishing both phases of the encoding operation—and part of the bases for general and social knowledge—are words. Without the necessary and appropriate word symbols to attach to thoughts and feelings, the process of getting information "up and ready" is greatly hindered. Just as surgical tasks are performed most efficiently when the best instruments are available, so also is the encoding operation performed efficiently when the individual has a good repertoire of language tools. In health care practice, it often happens that patients do not possess sufficient language tools for encoding their experiences effectively. They may have difficulty describing pain or emotions because they can't find the right labels. In many cases, the health professional can be of assistance merely by offering some words for them to use: if they don't have the necessary language tools, you can let them use some of yours.

Proper encoding is important to effective communication in general and may be crucial in some instances of patient care. It is often hard to provide the best possible treatment when patients are unable to articulate complaints in ways which can be understood. Your own language skills can be used to compensate for these deficits. From an opposite perspective, health professionals frequently encode messages in technical terms and then transmit those same terms to patients who simply do not understand what is being said. For example, a physician may know the exact nature of a patient's illness, but she will have to prepare her diagnosis in terms the patient can understand, lest the patient become thoroughly confused or unnecessarily frightened by such sophisticated jargon. Of critical significance here is the individual's capacity for appreciating the experiential field of the person with whom he is communicating. In order for the source's message to have any correspondence to the meaning attached by the receiver, the source must be in tune with the receiver.

One of the most important requirements for effective communication is that the sender and receiver are in tune with each other. The sender must encode in light of the receiver's field of experience. When the source and receiver's fields of past and current experience overlap, there is common ground for meaningful communication to take place (see Figure 12.2). The larger the overlap, the broader the grounds for communication. In order to get her intended message across, the source *must operate within that common area*. For instance, proper encoding has not occurred and, hence, poor communication results when a surgeon uses exclusively technical terms to describe an operation to a patient who has had no medical training. The surgeon might as well be speaking a foreign language, and, indeed, he might be to the person who does not understand the terms. If the surgeon described the same procedure in the same way to a colleague, proper encoding would have taken place. Should he use exclusively nonmedical terms under those circumstances, he would not be operating within the common ground he has with his medical colleague.

In health care practice, you cannot afford complacency in communications. It cannot be taken for granted that, simply because you know what you are saying, someone else also understands. One key is proper encoding. You are responsible for the messages you send, and that responsibility is based partly on the effort you expend in formulating clear and meaningful messages.

The Messages: Decoding and Feedback

Messages are transmitted subsequent to encoding by the source. Messages can be thought of as verbal, vocal, and nonverbal stimuli that have information value; that is, they mean something. The meanings of messages are comprised of signs which hold significance for the sender and/or receiver. Unfortunately, no two persons have exactly the same system of signs, simply because they have not had exactly the same experiences in life. So, the message as encoded by the sender cannot have perfect correspondence to the message as *decoded* by the receiver. But, in most of our interactions, the correspondence is sufficiently close for understanding to be achieved. When I describe my dog to you, for example, you and I will be in sufficient correspondence if you understand that he has four short legs, a beautiful auburn coat with snow-white markings, and long ears that perk up every time he hears the word "treat." Each of these descriptors are signs that have some meaning to you, meaning which probably overlaps to varying degrees with the meaning they have for me. However, your particular responses to these signs are probably different from mine because we have learned through different experiences to respond somewhat differently. It is at this point that we must adjust the model somewhat.

The fact that you respond at all—such as your response to my description of my dog Sam—suggests that you decode or interpret the message and assign meaning to it *and then encode*. As Schramm (1980, p. 21) stated, "the meaning that results from your decoding of a sign will start you *en*coding. Exactly *what* you encode will depend on your choice of the responses available in the situation and connected with the meaning." Natural barriers preclude an overt communication from you subsequent to your encoded response. You simply cannot communicate back to me right now. If we were involved in a dyadic communication, you could respond, if you chose to. Regardless of how you choose to respond, the fact still remains that you are constantly decoding signs from your environment, assigning meaning to these signs, and then encoding something as a result (Schramm, 1980). Your output reflects the input you have received.

In dyadic communication, individuals have the opportunity to respond to the sender's messages. Each person can decode the messages, encode their own messages, and then respond with *feedback*. Many of the verbal responses described in the next several chapters are feedback responses designed to communicate specific messages back to speakers. If speakers are attentive to the feedback responses, then they can use those messages as input for preparing follow-up responses. That is, they can use the input to change their own output in some way. The interesting thing about feedback is that we do not necessarily require others to provide it. We are capable of decoding and responding to our own messages. We can hear ourselves talk, correct misstatements, change words, or alter our conversational approach altogether. Figure 12.2 illustrates the various ways in which we can send and receive information (including feedback from ourselves).

What Figure 12.2 does not show is that we rarely send or receive messages through a single *channel*. A message channel is the medium through which information is transmitted. In interpersonal communication there are three primary channels which have already been examined in different contexts: *verbal statements, vocalization*, and *nonverbal behavior*. All of these channels are used in encoding and decoding messages as well. One of the problems in interpersonal communication is that messages from one channel can contradict messages from another channel. Effective communication occurs when the speaker coordinates signals for transmission in each of the three channels. Receivers then find it easier to decode the messages because they are not incompatible with each other. The meaning attached to one sign from one channel is consistent with the meaning attached to another sign from a different channel. When there is correspondence between the messages sent through each channel, there is a higher probability of correspondence between the meaning as intended by the speaker and the meaning as received by the receiver.

In this model of action and reaction, perhaps the critical variable is that the sender and receiver share a common coding system. Their experiential fields may overlap somewhat, and they may be able to interact and communicate within their common ground, but underlying this must be an encoding and

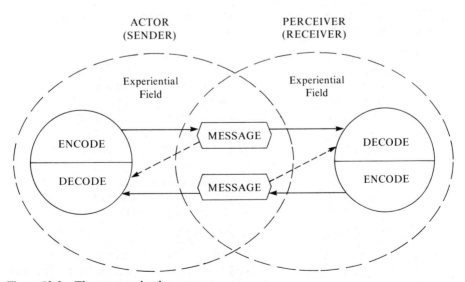

Figure 12.2 The communication process.

decoding system of the speaker which corresponds to the decoding and encoding system of the receiver. When there is minimal correspondence, communication problems result because there is a built-in obstacle for creating meaning between them. There are various obstacles to effective communication. The model presented here is useful in pointing up some of the more common ones.

Obstacles to Effective Communication

There are certain barriers, or obstacles, that are common to all forms of communication between two persons. To understand communication breakdowns, we can examine some of the more common factors leading to such undesirable consequences. Those factors usually can be identified within the process model described in the preceding section.

The Speaker's Language

As indicated, encoding processes require the translation of experience into forms which can be understood by the receiver. This means that the words chosen should capture the essence of what the sender wishes to communicate. If those words mean something different to the receiver, then there is low correspondence between the meaning intended and the meaning received. To prevent miscommunication, the speaker should select words whose meanings are *shared* by the receiver. Chances are that the vast majority of your interactions will take place with people with whom you share the same meanings for most words. However, consider for the moment the possibility that you provide health care services to someone who uses numerous terms from what we call "drug language" or "street language." As an exercise in shared meaning, take a little test. Cover the items on the right below and see if you can identify the proper synonym for the items on the left.

1. Candy	1. Cocaine
2. Dust	2. Cocaine
3. Head	3. Drug user or advocate of drug use
4. Heat	4. Police
5. Key	5. About 2.2 pounds of marijuana (1 kilogram)
6. Roller	6. Vein that won't stay in position for injection
7. Hog	7. Phencyclidine (PCP)
8. Snoopy	8. LSD on a blotter or stamp or seal
9. DOA	9. Phencyclidine (PCP)
10. Window pane	10. LSD on clear plastic

These are street names that are used in various parts of the country. But there is variability around the country as well, since the same referent (what the word represents) may have many different word symbols. For example, soft drinks are identified with different labels, often depending on from what part of the country you are. What do you call them in your part of the country: "pop," "soda," "cola," "tonic"? If you use words without taking into account how the receiver may interpret them, you may be increasing your chances of miscommunication. One means for avoiding this potential problem is to ask yourself: "This is what it means to *me*, but does it or will it mean the same to *her*?" It is also helpful to remember that words per se do not *contain* meaning. If they did, all you would have to do is present the words, and the other person would naturally get the meaning handed to him. Words are vibrations, marks, dots, and so on, *to which people attach meaning*. Meaning comes from human beings, not from the symbols themselves. You may know what you mean, but what do you think your traveling companion hears when you are approaching a roadside diner next to a gas station, and you say: "Let's eat here and get gas."

There are countless problems in the use of words. One which is discussed in detail in Chapter Sixteen concerns the use of ambiguous, nonspecific language that is open to various interpretations (see Figure 12.3). Consider the following:

> Karen, I've been noticing *your work lately*, and you don't seem to be getting *things* done. You seem to be *slacking off*. *Things* get pretty scattered around here when *people* aren't *holding up their own*. So, I'd like you to get *back on track* so we can *get things moving* around here.

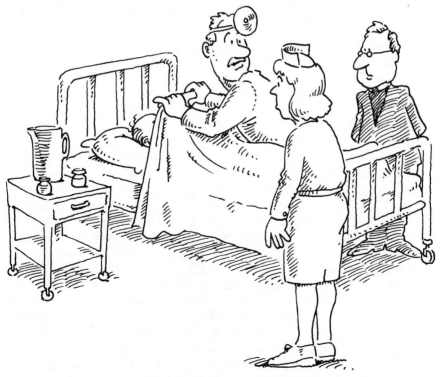

"He said, 'I told you I was sick'."

Figure 12.3 Concrete communications are unambiguous and clear.

If you were Karen, you might have an inkling to what this person was referring, but that's probably all you'd have. It's impossible to tell about what this person was talking. *Concreteness* is specificity of communication, and it avoids this kind of problem:

> Karen, your last two reports were incomplete. In each one, you failed to include cost-benefit analyses. Without that information, the rest of the staff can't consult with clients. We're at a standstill until you provide those figures. I would like your cost-benefit analyses on both projects by Friday.

The Speaker's Emotions and Intentions

If the speaker does not clearly express the emotional context of the message along with the particular verbal content, the receiver is not likely to respond in the manner intended by the speaker. For example, suppose that a series of medical tests revealed that a patient was in serious danger of heart attack unless he radically changed his diet and quit smoking. Suppose, further, that the patient's physician informed him of the need to do both. If the message to the patient communicates the physician's serious concerns about the risk of heart attack, the patient will respond differently from the way he would if he thought the physician was simply trying to get him to take better care of his health.

A similar problem can occur when the speaker does not *admit* to emotions or intentions underlying the message. In some instances, individuals hide their feelings and try not to reveal them in the communication. This is usually dishonest, although not always inappropriate. Whether appropriate or inappropriate, the concealment of feelings detracts from the full significance of a message.

Conflicting Messages

In interpersonal communication, we send messages through three principal channels. When verbal messages are not in sync with nonverbal or vocal cues, receivers may become confused as to the meaning of the verbal statement, or they may discount the verbal statement altogether. For example, during an interview, a client may tell you, "Things are going great. I feel just fine. Lately I've been relaxed, and nothing seems to bother me." Now, suppose that she delivered these verbal messages while sitting on the edge of her chair, wringing her hands, with her head tilted downward, breaking eye contact as she spoke. Postural cues, hand, head, and eye movements would all suggest that she is not as relaxed and trouble-free as she would have us believe by her statements. Suppose, further, that she delivered the verbal messages very slowly, hesitantly, and with difficulty, clearing her throat and swallowing. More conflicting cues! A reliable inference from all of these signals is that she is preoccupied with something. As Ralph Waldo Emerson once said, "What you are speaks so loudly that I cannot hear what you say."

The more channels being used in communication, the more information there is being transmitted to the receiver. Consequently, the possibility becomes greater that the speaker may transmit unintentional messages, which must then be decoded by the receiver. As your communication skills improve, so also does your ability to prevent unintended or conflicting messages from being transmitted.

Ineffective Transmission

Some people have difficulty with verbal communication because they talk too fast or too slowly, or they mispronounce words or misplace them within sentences. We have all probably slurred words at times, failed to emphasize important points, provided too much detail and irrelevancy, and jumped from one thought to another without connecting them properly. In these instances, we introduced *noise* into the communication channels. Noise is channel interference, which is anything that distorts the transmitted message to the receiver. Perhaps you know some persons who consistently introduce noise into their communications. For example:

> NURSE A: How long before we change the site of Mr. Jones's IV?
> NURSE B: As you know, IV sites should be changed after 48 to 72 hours. In some cases, like with Mr. Jones, an IV has to remain in place for more than 72 hours. Since he's had the IV in that site for almost 72 hours now, you should keep checking it just to make sure there are no signs of infection.

For Nurse A, Nurse B's last sentence was the essence of the message. Everything else is noise. To avoid introducing noise into your communication, it is important to remember that excessive detail may detract from the essential information you want to transmit. Truly, when we are asked for the time, we are impeding communication if we proceed to describe how a watch is made!

Receiver's Judgement

Rogers (1961, p. 330) proposed that "the major barrier to mutual interpersonal communication is our very natural tendency to judge, to evaluate, to approve or disapprove, the statement of the other person, or the other group." For example, suppose that after reading this section, you tell a friend about Roger's contention. There is a high probability that your friend's reply will be one of agreement or disagreement. Either she'll respond something like, "Yeah, I can understand that. That makes sense to me," or else she'll say something like, "Oh, I don't believe that. I can think of lots of other reasons why people fail to communicate." Or, take a different example. Suppose that you express a personal opinion about nurses having parity with physicians. It is quite predictable that your opinion will be evaluated by the person to whom you express it. It is equally predictable that he will then communicate approval or disapproval of your position. Rogers suggested that this tendency to judge another's statements becomes even stronger when feelings and emotions are involved. When our feelings influence us to evaluate another person's statements, we shift from listening to the person to a preoccupation with our own judgements. We retreat into our own frames of reference, which precludes understanding from the other's point of view. The logical means for correcting this tendency, or at least keeping it in check, is to work on achieving empathy. This is accomplished through *active listening*, which is described fully in the next chapter.

Summary

Communication is a phenomenon which has been conceptualized in so many ways as to cloud the meaning of the concept. In this chapter, some generally accepted characteristics of interpersonal communication were described. As a *process of creating meaning between two or more people*, communication may be seen as a *linear, interactional, or transactional* process. The kind of communication explored in this text is called *dyadic* communication—face-to-face communication between two persons. Dyadic communication is effective only to the extent of close correspondence between a message *as sent* by one person and the message *as received* by the other. Effective communication is also contingent upon specific outcomes or consequences pertaining to *understanding*, *attitude influence*, the *relationship* between interacting persons, *behavioral influence*, and *pleasure* or enjoyment. The correspondence between the message as sent and the message as received is only as strong as the weakest link in the communication process. This process is defined in terms of who says what to whom, how, under what circumstances, and with what effects. The process therefore involves at least six elements: the *source*, speaker, or sender of the message, the *message content, message delivery,* the *receiver,* the *context* of communication, and the *consequences* of the communication.

A model of the communication process was outlined in order to provide a general framework for examining specific factors which contribute to effective or ineffective communication. *Encoding* is the process by which the sender transforms thoughts and feelings into communicable forms. It consists of two stages: identification and preparation. One of the most important aspects of encoding and transmitting messages is that the speaker operate within an area of overlap between his own field of experience and that of the receiver. *Decoding* is a process of translating signals into messages. The receiver decodes signals sent by the speaker through any one or more of three channels: verbal, nonverbal, and vocal. When signals are decoded into messages, the individual then encodes a message for response. Response to the speaker's message is called feedback. Both speaker and receiver are at the same time encoders and decoders of information. The designation of one person as speaker and the other as receiver is arbitrary and only offered for purposes of discussion. Both perform the same communication activities in actual interactions.

Some obstacles to communication include improper or vague language used by the speaker, the failure or unwillingness to express emotions or intentions with verbal statements, conflicting messages, the introduction of noise into the communication channel, and the tendency to evaluate the statements of the other person during an interaction. Many other obstacles to communication are discussed in the contexts of the remaining chapters of the text, and so also are suggestions for improved communication. The last five chapters of the text are concerned exclusively with enhancing communication effectiveness.

References

Dance, F. E. X. The Concept of Communication, *Journal of Communication*, **20**:201–10 (1970).

Mortensen, C. D. Communication Postulates, in *Messages: A Reader in Human Communication*, 3d ed., S. B. Weinberg. New York, Random House, 1980.

Rogers, C. R. *On Becoming a Person*. Boston, Houghton Mifflin, 1961.

Schramm, W. How Communication Works, in *Messages: A Reader in Human Communication*, 3d ed., S. B. Weinberg, New York, Random House, 1980.

Tubbs, S. L., and Moss, S. *Human Communication*, 3d ed., New York, Random House, 1980.

CHAPTER THIRTEEN

Attending and Listening
in Health Care Services

*No one cares to speak to an unwilling listener. An arrow
never lodges in a stone: often it recoils upon the sender
of it.*

St. Jerome, *Letter 52*

Bore, n. a person who talks when you wish him to listen.

Ambrose Bierce, *The Devil's Dictionary*

During our interactions with others, we want and expect them to pay attention
th what we have to say. While we express ourselves, we usually remain alert to
cues as to whether or not they are tuned-in and listening. We look for signs that
our messages are being received and understood. How exasperating, sometimes painful, and always frustrating it is when feedback is clear that we're not
being heard (see Figure 13.1). Despite the rejection we sense from being ignored, sometimes it is equally disturbing to end up as sounding boards for
someone's patronizing platitudes or critical judgements. Feedback of this sort
can make us feel impotent and insignificant because it systematically discounts
or discredits the experiences we are trying to relate. As a result, we may try
harder to get our points across, or we may even give up and withdraw from
those who are communicating that our thoughts and feelings are unimportant
or unwelcome. In any case, our initial reaction is to be distracted by cues suggesting that those with whom we are interacting are not really with us or fully
involved in the interaction. Our train of thought is interrupted, and the intended message often becomes lost amidst ensuing accusations ("You're not
even listening to me!") and rebuttals ("I am too! I can repeat everything you
just said!").

What does it mean to say that we want others to give us their undivided
attention when we communicate our thoughts or feelings? Generally speaking,
it means that we want the *respect* to which we are entitled as human beings
with legitimate thoughts and feelings. More specifically, it means that we want
others to suppress their own concerns for the moment, participate in the here
and now of the interaction, concentrate and understand our concerns as we re-

Figure 13.1

late them, and *prove it* by displaying a physical posture of involvement and by responding intelligently and sensitively to what we have to say. This doesn't seem like much to expect. Yet, casual observation of most interactions would suggest that we may be expecting quite a lot, because most people are simply not skilled at or used to paying close attention and listening. In conversations, it is common for listeners to shift their focus to their own thoughts and what they plan to say when the speaker stops talking. It is just as common for listeners to deal with only a single issue raised by the speaker—to seize upon one bit of information to the exclusion of a full range of communications. And, listeners often become preoccupied with searching for an opening in the conversation—just the right moment to cut in, cut off the speaker, and relieve themselves of their own views. If you take a look at people in conversation, you will probably also see them in postures suggesting only partial involvement in the interaction.

It is always easier to appreciate the above points by looking at what other people do. It is more challenging and sometimes threatening to think about similarities between their interpersonal behavior and your own. The reality is that you and I are victims of the same communication habits and tendencies as those "other people" alluded to above. One difference may be that you and I have opportunities to use this chapter as a means for correcting some of our habits, avoiding many future communication pitfalls, and improving our skills of attending and listening. We have a challenge to look at our own skills and make those changes that are necessary for enhanced interpersonal effectiveness.

This chapter is concerned exclusively with the basic skills of attending and listening. *Attending* is an inclusive concept which incorporates various perceptual and communication activities. As used here, it refers to specific skills of focusing on and responding to the range of messages sent by a speaker. Some of these skills involve *physical attending*, which is examined in the following section in terms of the ways in which you use your body to enhance your receptivity to communications and to show others that you are with them and centered on what they have to say. *Psychological attending* is what you do while you attend physically. It involves a full psychological participation in the thoughts and feelings communicated by the speaker. Psychological attending is an active mode of involvement with another person in an interaction, and, as such, it is contingent upon *active listening*. Whether or not you respond appropriately during an interaction often depends on the extent to which you are participating psychologically through active listening. The listening skills which facilitate this kind of involvement in an interaction are discussed in the second section of the chapter.

There are no more basic nor essential communication skills to master than those of attending and listening. These are the skills upon which all others rest. They must precede whatever else is done in human interactions. Within your profession, these are skills which you must have available at all times.

Health professionals devote a great portion of their work days making observations. Observation is a process which includes listening. In a very real sense, a significant percentage of the salaries paid to health professionals is for skilled observations involving intelligent, critical, and empathic listening. Unfortunately, it would appear that compensation for these kinds of skills is not always justified by actual performance. In terms of listening efficiency, there is an absence of data showing that health professionals are significantly better skilled than other professional or white-collar workers. In most cases, their listening efficiency is no greater than 50%. This means that health professionals may be listening *only half as well as they could.* By direct implication, this also suggests that observations, in general, may not be as accurate as we would expect. For example, a brief article by Patton (1976) described her futile efforts to inform the entire health care team that she was not feeling well four days postoperatively. She told all members of that team how she was feeling, yet no one listened. Finally, one staff member did listen and discovered the cause of her problem to be an infection! In all probability, this is far from an isolated case of listening inefficiency. It should not be hard to conceive of similar circumstances where the consequences for health care recipients were much more serious. If nothing else, the potential effects *for patients* of failures by health professionals to attend and listen to their expressed concerns constitutes a firm and incontrovertible rationale for learning and practicing the skills presented here.

Most health professionals would no doubt recognize the potentially adverse effects of poor listening efficiency. Those effects could ripple or even billow through the entire health care organization. But what about the "positive effects" of *effective* listening? The most readily apparent consequence for listeners is a better understanding of what speakers are saying. Another way of stating this is that effective listeners obtain more accurate and valid information about the situations or experiences speakers are trying to relate. Their observations are more reliable than those of poor listeners. Consequently, they have a more legitimate and serviceable knowledge base for making decisions about how to respond. Effective listeners are effective responders.

Paying attention and listening closely to other people—whether they be patients, colleagues, or administrators—improves not only your understanding of what they are saying, it improves your understanding of those people as human beings. With deeper interpersonal understanding comes an increasingly positive attitude or attraction to others. Your behavior in relation to those persons thus tends to become more facililtative, in that it promotes, enhances, and feeds into the growth and quality of the relationships. For those to whom you show your care and respect by listening, your attentiveness itself functions as a powerful reinforcer. It is gratifying to be listened to and enlivening to be listened to with sensitivity. When you demonstrate to others that you are attending and listening out of respect for their thoughts and feelings, they will tend to feel renewed in their desire to talk about those things that are on their minds. They will sense from your behavior that it is permissible to be more open with you because you appear to be truly interested. People who have been listened to without being interrupted often become less defensive because the experience helps to reduce their fears of having their ideas and feelings criticized, discounted, or rejected. The effective listener is one who can foster such feelings in others because she refrains from judging their statements and contaminating the authenticity of their experiences through the imposition of her own values. The effective listener is a person who listens intently for the full meaning of the facts and feelings communicated by others. She seeks a special kind of understanding. She seeks not merely an intellectual grasp of the words in a message. She wants to see things from the speaker's point of view. She seeks empathic understanding.

From an organizational standpoint, whatever helps individuals helps the entire organization. When individuals listen to one another—when they take the time to respond to each other's communication needs—they come to feel less isolated and often less compelled to keep their thoughts and feelings buried under a mound of existing pressures. The health care team tends to become a more cohesive unit, with improved morale and greater cooperation within a healthier, interpersonal climate. With a reduction in unnecessary pressures, there is often a positive impact on performance efficiency and the quality of health care services. A carry-over effect should occur in patient care when members of the health care team learn to attend to one another. The obverse could also be expected when health professionals improve their ability to attend and listen to patients' communications. Paying attention and listening to others require specific skills. Although these skills are vital to competent health care practice, the decision to spend the time and energy developing them is a decision you must ultimately make for yourself.

Attending to Others

Susan is a psychiatric nurse who had been working overtime daily in an understaffed mental health unit. She had become disillusioned, discontented, emotionally drained, and felt trapped in a highly stressful position. During one of her infrequent breaks, she decided to talk about her feelings with another staff member, Teresa.

Teresa was in the supply room, preparing medications for patients on the unit, when Susan walked up behind her. Teresa looked over her shoulder at Susan and then turned her eyes back to the medications in front of her.

"As usual," said Teresa, "I'm late in getting these out. Why can't the pharmacy prepare the cart like they're supposed to? Why do we have to do their work for them? It's as if we didn't have enough to do. Seems like they could at least get us a medical tech to do this. When are they going to get us some help up here anyway?"

"Well," Susan replied, "that's sort of what I wanted to talk to you about." Susan leaned against the supply cabinet and faced Teresa, who was busy filling the medication cups.

"Lately, I've been feeling so tired and frustrated, and I don't know how long I can keep up this pace. It's effecting my home life, Tony is upset because I never get out of work on time, I'm never in the mood to go out, and he's so angry that he insists I should quit. I just don't know what to do, Teresa!"

Teresa, still looking down at her work, shook her head, "Well, *I'm* going to quit if they don't get someone else to do this! My God, look at all these orders I have to fill!"

Later that afternoon, Susan was standing at the nursing station when Marilyn, another staff member, walked up. "Susan, I'll bet I've made five trips down to

Mr. Smith's room in the last hour. He keeps turning on the call light and, when I get down there, he complains about a different pain every time. I need a break. So, how's everything going with you? I haven't seen Tony in a long time; how is he?''

"Marilyn, do you have a minute?" Susan asked, "I've got something on my mind that's really been bothering me lately."

"Sure, if I'm not interrupted with another call. What's the matter?"

Susan proceeded to relate her feelings as she did to Teresa. All the while she talked, Marilyn kept shifting her eyes toward the corridor and nervously tapping her fingers against her folded arms. Finally, Marilyn stopped Susan.

"Look, Susan, you've been here long enough. You ought to know that you can't let things get to you around here. You just have to take things as they are. They're never going to change, so forget about it and just do what you have to do and don't go out of your way looking for problems. Listen, I'll talk to you later. I can't believe Mr. Smith hasn't turned his light on again. I've got to see what's going on down there now."

After talking things over with Tony that evening, Susan decided to go to the Director of Nursing, Ms. Jones, and let her know about the conditions in the unit; maybe she could do something that Susan's supervisor hadn't been able to do. Susan knew that her supervisor had complained to the administration before, and with no luck. When Susan told her supervisor that she needed to see the Director, Ms. Brown said she thought it may be a good idea if staff provided some direct input to Ms. Jones.

When Susan entered the Director's office, Ms. Jones was working at her desk. She greeted Susan and informed her that she would be with her in a moment. After Ms. Jones finished writing, she kept her pen in her hand and simply looked across her desk at Susan.

"Now, what can I do for you?" she asked.

As Susan began talking, Ms. Jones rested her elbow on the desk and raised her forearm to place her hand under her chin, as if she were tired and in need of supporting her head. With her right hand still on the desk and holding her pen, Ms. Jones appeared to scribble lines on a pad of paper. Susan continued speaking while Ms. Jones shifted her eyes from her desk to Susan and back again. Ms. Jones suddenly changed her posture and leaned far back into her chair and folded her arms, occasionally uncrossing them to slide a hand onto the desk to shuffle some papers around.

"My God, she's not even listening to me!" Susan thought to herself. "What is it with everyone around here? No one pays attention, no one listens, no one seems to care what I say!" In futility, Susan stopped talking. When Ms. Jones took her eyes off her desk and looked at Susan, Susan despondently concluded her conversation.

"I don't want to take up any more of your time, Ms. Jones. I just thought that maybe it would help to talk to you about my job, but I guess there isn't much to say anymore."

"Susan," replied Ms. Jones, "I know that your department is understaffed and that you're all under a lot of pressure up there. We're trying to work out some transfers from other departments to yours, but it takes time. So, I ask that you be patient and do the best you can."

Ms. Jones rose from her chair and walked around the desk to the office door. Opening the door, she turned to Susan. "I'm glad you came in to see me, Susan. I care about my nurses, and I want to stay on top of things and know what's happening with all of you. My door is open when any of you wants to see me. I'm always willing to listen and do what I can."

Susan's experience is not at all unlike the experiences of many health professionals working in demanding jobs which *seem* to preclude taking time to attend and listen to one another. With most of their time devoted to caring for patients, it often seems to health professionals that there is just no time to care for one another, no time to stop and pay attention to what may be bothering a colleague. If health professionals recognize the extent of their commitment to the welfare of human beings, then they must realize that such a commitment does not end with patient care. If they are able and willing to take the time to care for patients, then they must be willing to find the time to care for one another. *The health and well-being of health care providers are no less important than the health and well-being of those they serve.*

Effective health care services means that patients are receiving close and careful attention. In a similar way, effective communication means that interacting persons are closely and carefully attending to one another. Just as there is no health service provided when there is no attention, neither is there communication without attention. Effective communication is grounded in understanding, and understanding is contingent upon attention. In the above case, there are numerous examples to be discussed where verbal and nonverbal cues suggested an absence of attention on the parts of Susan's colleagues. Because Susan was unsuccessful in securing their attention, she finally yielded to her frustration and, during her encounter with Ms. Jones, began to withdraw from further disclosure. Given her conclusion that no one really cared what she had to say, the option to quit her job probably received more serious consideration. Such a possibility could have been avoided if any one of her colleagues had responded by adopting a posture of involvement with her. In the following section, the nonverbal behavior of Susan's colleagues is discussed, common problems in physical attending are examined, and suggestions are offered as means for preventing similar communication pitfalls in your own relationships.

Physical Attending

Physical attending involves the use of your body to convey the message that you are involved in an interaction. It also entails the use of your body to enhance your receptivity, to listen, and to make appropriate verbal responses. As you know, what you do with your body can sometimes say more than any words coming from your mouth. Most importantly, you communicate whether or not you are *oriented* to the other person—i.e., whether your attention is directed toward that person or somewhere else. If you are to communicate understanding, you must first demonstrate that you are oriented to the experience of the speaker, and one of the first things you do is take control of those features of the immediate environment that constitute distractions.

Controlling Distractions

Environmental distractions can make it difficult, if not impossible, to pay attention and listen to another person. Many distractions are beyond our control, but those which can be eliminated or reduced must be, if satisfactory interactions are to take place.

Anything which causes a shift of your attention away from the speaker is a distraction. Needless to say, the number of potential distractors is limitless. Nevertheless, we can take a look at the contexts in which Susan approached her colleagues and note some commonly overlooked factors. Teresa, for example, was distracted by the duties she was performing when Susan entered the supply room. She was pressed for time, but her behavior was similar to the actions of most of us when we fail to put aside some activity in order to attend to someone speaking to us. It often seems as if we think we can concentrate on two or more things at the same time: whatever it is we're doing and whatever it is the other person is saying. Even if we had such a capability—which we don't—the message would still go out to the other person that we have divided our attention. The reality is that our attention can focus only on one thing at a time. In Teresa's case, her task received attention, while Susan's words were largely ignored. She could not process Susan's messages efficiently while focusing on her job. A message to Susan was probably that Teresa's task was more important than anything Susan had to offer. By not *stopping what we are doing*— thereby controlling a distraction—attending does not occur, active listening is not possible, information is poorly processed, and understanding is neither achieved nor communicated.

Marilyn was also distracted. She was hyperalert and vigilant over the corridor, where she expected to see Mr. Smith's light go on at any moment. Under these circumstances, it is little wonder that she was unable to attend to Susan. Marilyn failed to control potential distractions, and she could have gained control in at least two simple ways. First, she could have suggested to Susan that they move to a place where the chance of being interrupted was minimized. A suggestion like this would have communicated to Susan that Marilyn recognized her general concern about some issue and that she was willing to give Susan her undivided attention. Second, Marilyn could have turned her body away from the corridor, thus ignoring the distractor and not Susan. In doing so, Marilyn could have freed herself to become more involved with Susan. By turning her back to the corridor and facing Susan squarely, she could have increased her chances of listening and hearing. Eye contact with Susan would have been facilitated, and the temptation to shift her gaze in response to expected distractions would have been controlled. The mere repositioning of her body could have also helped to reduce her level of nervous anticipation about being suddenly interrupted. In a very real sense, Marilyn expected to be distracted and disengaged from the interaction at any moment, and this expectancy represented a significant distraction in and of itself.

Ms. Jones remained seated behind a desk which was a physical barrier between herself and Susan. Genuine person-to-person interactions rarely take place when people are separated by physical barriers such as desks. A desk symbolizes professional role relationships, where the person behind the desk is usually in a position of greater power. Persons who consistently protect their power positions from behind their desks tend to communicate that they are not fully available to those with whom they are conversing. The message often is that they prefer role-defined interactions where open expression of feelings is typically absent. By staying behind desks when circumstances call for closer personal involvement with others, we may be saying, ''I am available to you, *but I do not choose to get too involved with you.''* Ms. Jones also had papers strewn across her desk, as one might expect an administrator to have. It is neither realistic nor necessary to clear one's desk each time a person enters the office, but it is clearly reasonable to assume that the papers on one's desk represent potential distractions. For Ms. Jones, they were indeed distractions, and they were not only visible, they were within reach and manipulable. By sitting at her desk, Ms. Jones permitted those distractions to exist in the visual field between herself and Susan. Then, she gave into the ever-present cues tempting her to shift her attention away from Susan. From a communication standpoint, it may be irrelevant if she actually read those papers during the interaction, because the acts of touching them and lowering her eyes to look at them would suggest a predominant interest in that business and not in Susan's communications. It's hard enough to show real involvement with another person and virtually impossible when the individual remains seated behind a status-enforcing desk while playing ''paper chase'' as the other is speaking. If interactions are to be personalized, barriers which impose unnecessary structure on the interchange should be avoided and so also should potentially distracting stimuli in the perceptual field.

Finally, Ms. Jones held a distractor in the palm of her hand: a pen. You will recall from Chapter Two that artifacts belonging to individuals often have sign value for observers. Although Ms. Jones's pen obviously served a useful function for her, it had no useful function during her interaction with Susan. Consequently, by holding it in her hand throughout the encounter, Ms. Jones may have unknowingly communicated to Susan that she had not fully shifted her attention from her work. Of course, artifacts such as pens, pipes, toothpicks, paper clips, or cigarettes do not necessarily distract others during an interaction, but the probability of distracting the speaker and oneself is certainly much greater than if one's hands are free of objects. I believe there is a very good reason for giving up such props during our interactions with others: we communicate respect for them. By putting artifacts away, we may be able to show that we are literally dropping what we are doing in order to give our full presence to what they have to say. In a small way, we may be able to demonstrate that we appreciate the importance of their thoughts and feelings. Imagine being in Susan's place. You enter Ms. Jones's office and begin speaking. She still has her pen in her and and is sitting behind the desk, moving papers, and changing her posture frequently. I venture to say that you may begin to feel as if you're imposing on her time, that she is awaiting your departure so she can get back to work, and that what you have to say is not really welcome. Clearly, Ms. Jones's nonverbal behavior appears to be saying to you, ''I'm busy and what you have to say is not important to me. I am not interested in listening, and I am not committed to helping you.'' With nonverbal messages like these, verbal statements to the contrary may be meaningless.

Bodily Orientation and Posture

Physical attending means that interacting persons adopt a posture of involvement with one another (Egan, 1975). We communicate a posture of involvement with others when we *face them squarely and orient our bodies directly toward them*. If you think of your body being on an axis, you are physically oriented to another person when the axis of that individual is parallel to yours. If someone is facing you while your shoulder is at a 90° angle to hers, then you are oriented in a different direction. You are "giving the shoulder." When you are positioned at a 90° angle, the interaction will tend to be less personal and less intimate than it might be if you were standing face-to-face. Usually, people turn their bodies on an axis and increase the angle of orientation when they are feeling less intimate. At 180° they have turned their backs, usually indicating withdrawal from the interaction. Therefore, to communicate attention and involvement, it is necessary to maintain a parallel positioning of your body with the axis of the other person. In addition to demonstrating our involvement in the interaction, the face-to-face orientation increases the likelihood that we will perceive and process the speaker's communications accurately.

Most of our interactions take place within what Edward Hall (1964, 1966) called the *casual-personal zone*. This is an area of space extending outward from 1½ feet to 4 feet from each individual. Most people in our culture seem to consider the area within 1½ feet of their bodies to be an intimate zone, and the majority of people with whom they interact are not allowed into that zone. With casual acquaintances and strangers, individuals tend to feel increasingly uncomfortable as the intimate zone is penetrated and physical contact appears imminent. The area beyond 4 feet and up to 12 feet is called the "social-consultative" zone (Hall, 1966). Interactions within the social-consultative zone tend to be relatively impersonal. They also preclude the optimal use of our perceptual apparatus to pick up cues from one another that may be important to the interaction. So, it seems that the casual-personal zone permits some degree of intimacy while, at the same time, preventing personal discomfort. Physical and psychological attending may be best achieved and communicated when you position your body at a distance enabling you to see and hear clearly, without engaging other senses (i.e., smell, touch, and taste) to the point of becoming overloaded with sensory information and increased anxiety.

The way you stand or sit during an interaction may tell others a lot about you and how you feel about the situation. Your *posture* will give cues to your level of involvement. For example, folded arms and rigid stance may be taken as an indication of defensiveness; leaning backward, reclining, or slouching in a chair could be read as disinterest; or resting your feet on a desk or your head in your hands could be interpreted as apathy, boredom, or indifference. Conversely, an "open" posture is a nondefensive position which is usually taken as a sign that you are receptive to the other person and what she has to say. It is a posture defined primarily by open arms—arms that are not crossed in front of you, hands that are exposed and not in your pockets or behind your back. It is a posture which is also characterized by a *forward lean* of the upper body. When two people are truly involved with one another their upper bodies tend to lean forward. You can witness this for yourself in almost any social setting. Go to the school or hospital cafeteria and observe people who are engaged in conversation at their tables. You will probably notice that they're leaning forward as a nonverbal sign of the attention they're giving to one another. You may also see people sitting at tables, leaning back, and looking around the room, attending to everything else but each other.

In our case example, Teresa gave Susan "the shoulder." She stood at a 90° angle to Susan while Susan faced her directly. This orientation away from Susan represented a nonverbal cue that she was involved in her work and not in what Susan was communicating. Although Marilyn faced Susan, she folded her arms and nervously tapped her fingers. Susan may have perceived this as one sign that Marilyn was not really open to the interaction and Susan's plight. She managed to prove it by preaching and chastising Susan for the feelings Susan expressed. At a social-consultative distance from Susan, Ms. Jones revealed a preference to deal with Susan on an impersonal, professional level, despite Susan's expressions of deeply personal concerns. Her frequent postural shifts and bodily movements suggested impatience and a preoccupation with other matters as well as a general reluctance to participate in extensive interpersonal exchange. As she walked to the door, Ms. Jones oriented her body away from Susan. She turned her back and increased the distance between them, thus indicating to Susan that, as far as she was concerned, there was little more to discuss. Verbally, Ms. Jones's attempt to placate Susan, infer conciliatory promises, and sidestep the personal issues Susan presented by citing her concern for "my nurses" and "all of you" were oral reinforcements of her nonverbal expressions of detachment and disinterest in Susan's unique circumstances.

Eye Contact

Our eyes are principle sensory organs which permit the focusing of visual attention of objects and events in our environment. Often, the extent to which we are actually attending can be easily inferred by others when they observe the direction of our gaze. Our eye behavior can reveal a great deal about that in which we are interested and that in which we are not. In most interpersonal situations, good eye contact is essential in order to perceive, process, and respond to important cues from others. It is also essential as an expression of our attention and involvement.

During most interactions, individuals look at each other between 25 and 75% of the time (Harrison, 1974). Eye contact tends to increase when interacting persons like each other, when they are interested in what is being said, and when they are paying close attention to one another. It tends to decrease when individuals dislike each other, when something is being rejected, when sensitive subjects are brought up, when individuals are physically very close to each other, (Harrison, 1974), or when individuals purposely avoid acknowledging something said or done during the interaction—when an implicit norm of "civil inattention" (Goffman, 1963) induces them to break eye contact, as if to suggest a failure to recognize what occurred. Eye contact is a much more intricate and complex phenomenon than most people seem to realize. It is influenced by numerous cultural, individual, and interpersonal factors. In fact, Harrison (1974, p. 126) described eye contact as "a choreographed exchange that depends on the mutual activity of both partners."

Eye contact is one of the most important expressions of feelings and willingness to participate fully in an interaction. Unfortunately, many individuals find it difficult to maintain eye contact with others. A result is that they are often perceived as nervous, embarrassed, uncomfortable, disinterested, or preoccupied. In many cases, these perceptions are probably accurate (at least in our culture, where we expect people to "look us in the eye"). Therefore, to prevent others from making similar inferences about us and, more importantly, to show that we are paying close attention, it is necessary to limit the frequency of averted gazes during our interactions. This does not mean that we should fixate on them, for this would most likely suggest that we are staring. Rather, it means that we maintain *appropriate eye contact through direct eye-to-eye correspondence interspersed with occasional averted gazes*. Numerous exercises are provided in Chapter Eighteen, and they are aimed at helping to enhance your visual attention skills by learning to regulate eye contact in social interactions.

In the case example, Teresa made eye contact with Susan only briefly when Susan entered the supply room. Upon turning and focusing on the medications in front of her, Teresa clearly demonstrated where her visual attention was directed. Susan, quite literally, was not even "in the picture." Marilyn, on the other hand, did achieve some eye contact with Susan, although she repeatedly and consistently shifted her eyes toward the corridor. If you have observed similar eye behavior during some of your interactions, you can probably recall being distracted eventually by roving eyes. Perhaps you, too, began looking in the same direction, searching for whatever lured their attention away from you. Ms. Jones's eye behavior probably gave Susan the impression that she was thinking about something else, as she frequently broke her gaze to look down at the papers on her desk. In touching and moving the papers about, her hand movements tended to complement and reinforce eye behavior suggesting divided attention. It was noted earlier that stimuli in the visual field between Ms. Jones and Susan (i.e., papers on the desk) were lingering distractions which had not been controlled by Ms. Jones.

Relaxation

A posture of involvement should be *in*tense, but not tense. Our bodies should communicate that we are relatively at ease and relaxed with the persons with whom we interact. This means that we should avoid rigid stances and postures, tapping fingers, gripping the arms of chairs, and tightly gripping ourselves—as some people do when they fold their arms, clasp their hands together, or interlock their fingers and hold their folded hands across or against one leg that has been crossed over the other. These are "tight" postures which suggest some degree of discomfort in the interaction. The longer these postures are sustained, the more likely it is that other persons begin feeling vaguely uncomfortable themselves. Being outwardly tense and rigid signals nervousness and discomfort, which are infectious and almost inevitably lead to strained interactions. Being relaxed and letting your body show it tends to put others at ease, and it makes them feel a bit more comfortable with us. A relaxed posture often tells other people that we feel safe with them, that we are not being defensive, and that we feel no threat in being open with them. Relaxation also enhances your ability to pay attention and process information. Anxiety and tension may interfere with the reception of sensory information and cause you to be less efficient than you might be if you were more relaxed.

Under different circumstances, perhaps Teresa and Marilyn could be more relaxed with Susan. Given the existing circumstances, however, neither could relax enough to pay full attention to Susan. Teresa felt pressured to fill the prescriptions, while Marilyn was apprehensive about being interrupted. Neither Teresa nor Marilyn seemed able to disengage themselves from their preoccupations, and it is a safe bet that their tension was at least to some degree contagious for Susan. It is difficult to imagine how Susan could have felt comfortable with either person under those circumstances. Had Teresa and Marilyn been able to shift their attention, even momentarily, they probably would have experienced a reduction in their levels of tension, and this would have been apparent to Susan. As for Ms. Jones, her bodily shifts and eye and hand movements suggested impatience and restlessness—the opposite of relaxation. Her fidgeting was incompatible with any attempt she could have made to appear at ease with Susan. It would be no stretch of the imagination to assume that Susan felt constrained by these nonverbal messages.

CLOSER

The skills of physical attending are essential for efficient reception and processing of information. Moreover, the skills of physical attending help to create a *climate of support and trust* between people (Egan, 1977). The development of mutual trust in a relationship implies increasing intimacy or closeness, which evolves as individuals move toward greater understanding of the thoughts and feelings each person expresses. Individuals grow closer because they come to understand and appreciate the meanings and significance of each other's experience of living. To stress the importance of these outcomes, and to integrate the major elements of physical attending, it should be useful for you to remember a simple acronym: CLOSER. This acronym represents the principal elements of the skills discussed here. It also represents one of the ultimate goals of physical attending. It can serve as a helpful reminder of the six basic things you can do with your body to let others know you are attending and fully involved with them.

C: CONTROL distractions that threaten to shift your attention.
L: LEAN slightly toward the person with whom you are interacting.
O: Maintain an OPEN, nondefensive posture.
S: Position yourself so that you are facing the person SQUARELY.
E: Maintain appropriate EYE contact.
R: Try to be comfortable and RELAXED.

In summary, a good communicator is a person who is flexible in adjusting to undesirable environmental conditions. She fights and resists distractions, and if they cannot be controlled easily, she strives harder to concentrate. She orients herself to speakers by facing them squarely, leaning slightly forward, and assuming an open posture of involvement. She looks directly at others as they speak, neither staring nor avoiding mutual gaze. Her eye contact is appropriate and facilitates further disclosure from others. She is physically relaxed and psychologically comfortable in communication interactions, while at the same time exerting concentrative effort to stay on top of what is being expressed. Underlying her attending behavior is a genuine interest in achieving deeper understanding of others and a true respect for them as human beings. Furthermore, she recognizes that understanding cannot be reached without attention and that attention is enhanced by exercising control over her body. She knows that her body is always communicating and that her nonverbal behavior is a system of communication that sends messages which are open to numerous interpretations. With this in mind, she is sensitive to what her body may be saying at any given moment, but she is neither hyperalert to her own actions nor hyperreflective about their possible effects on others. She is not a spectator of her own performances, but a manager of her behavior. Finally, she is keenly aware of a broad range of verbal, vocal, and nonverbal messages being communicated by persons with whom she interacts: she pays attention and proves it to those with whom she wishes to become CLOSER.

Psychological Attending and Active Listening

We can think of physical attending in at least two ways—first, as a core of nonverbal behaviors necessary for communicating involvement with others and, second, as a means for actually becoming involved psychologically. True involvement is shown and genuine understanding is achieved only to the extent that physical attending is accompanied by psychological attending. The key process on which all of this depends is *listening*.

Real listening is far different from "hearing," which is a relatively passive and automatic physiological process of recieving auditory stimuli. Hearing is obviously a component of listening, but the two are not synonymous. Hearing does not require much conscious effort for most of us, while listening demands considerable concentrated effort. There are various ways of listening to others. Tubbs and Moss (1980), for example, described "pleasurable listening" as that which takes place when your aim is to enjoy a communication. Although still not comparable to passive hearing, pleasurable listening requires less effort than "discriminative listening," which is attempted when you want to comprehend and remember something. Even more effort is required for "critical listening"—the effort to determine if a message is being communicated accurately and honestly, with undistorted information. Discriminative listening is the kind you use when you are taking notes during a lecture, when you are given orders for patient care, and when a supervisor is explaining a new technique for neurological assessment. Critical listening is often used to discern whether a patient is distorting information about how he feels, to discover the exact combination of substances taken by a person suffering an adverse drug reaction, or to resolve incongruencies between the reports of a mother and the reports of a father in suspected cases of child abuse. Different modes of listening may be necessary in different situations. In circumstances where a patient may be afraid to describe the full range of her physical symptoms—which may occur when she is terrified of learning that she has cancer—discriminative listening would not suffice. Critical listening is needed in those situations where a person's feelings or interests make it hard for her to be objective about her medical condition. Nonetheless, the ability to listen in both discriminative and critical ways are essential for competent health care practice.

There is another kind of listening that represents the topic of this section. It is a form of listening which may facilitate one's ability to listen critically and discriminatively. Moreover, it is a mode of listening which improves the quality and validity of information received from a speaker, promotes deeper levels of understanding, and facilitates the development of open, fulfilling relationships. This kind of listening is called *active listening*, and it is the means through which we can participate psychologically in our interactions with others.

Active listening is a *total effort to grasp the meaning and significance of the facts and feelings communicated by others*. The "active" listener is fully alert, oriented to the here and now of the interaction, interested in the speaker and what he has to say, and tuned-in to the full range of channels through which messages are sent. She "listens" to nonverbal messages which confirm, refute, reinforce, or qualify vocal cues and verbal statements. She works at processing information from each of these sources, because she is striving to understand not just the facts being stated, but the speaker's feelings about those facts. In other words, she listens to the *content* of the message and the *feelings* expressed because she is committed to understanding the *essence* of the speaker's experience.

How to Listen "Actively"

Active listening is a difficult skill to learn and to practice consistently. Most of us are simply not used to putting so much effort into listening. Like any other skill, though, active listening can become part of your interpersonal behavior with a little hard work at first. All skills are hard to learn at first. With practice and self-discipline, they can usually become almost second nature.

What to Listen "For"

Most messages sent by an individual have two components: content and feelings. Active listening requires that you recognize each component and communicate your understanding of both. The content of a message can be thought of as information about experiences in a person's life that give rise to his or her feelings. As such, content may represent statements about situations, events, ideas, facts, people, or behavior. Very often, content is comprised of *cognitive* message units pertaining to the speaker's thoughts or knowledge about the subject of his communication. For example, suppose a colleague related the following to you:

> I find a consistent challenge in my work. The range of medical problems I encounter forces me to be alert and on top of things. The patients themselves are so differ-

ent from one person to the next. I never seem to have a dull moment, and I never seem to get tired of it. In a way, it's like I thrive on the challenge. It's really stimulating to me—it keeps me going!

The content of this message is reflected in the factual information he offered. That is, he "finds" (*sees, discovers, thinks,* or *believes* there is) challenge in his work; medical problems are diverse (*statement of fact*); those problems necessitate competent performance (*fact*); patients are different (*fact*); he does not "seem" (*does not notice or think*) to tire of his work. This is all information describing his work experience.

The above communication also contains information about the health professional's feelings. He appears to be *excited, interested,* fulfilled, and *attracted* to his work. These feelings are revealed in the latter part of the communication, which contains *affective* message units. The full meaning of his communication cannot be understood without recognizing both cognitive and affective elements. The full meaning, or the *essence,* of his communication is that he is highly stimulated by the diversity and variety in his work. This is precisely for what active listening requires you to listen: the full meaning or essence of a person's communication. Both content and feelings give meaning to a message. To understand that meaning, you must listen for both. When you do, you can understand the speaker's feelings and what he thinks gives rise to those feelings.

The primary goal of active listening is to understand the situation as the other person sees it. In other words, the task is to achieve empathic understanding. *Therefore, to grasp the essence of the speaker's communications, you must attend to and use the raw data from his messages to re-create his experience within your own frame of reference.* It is often useful to ask yourself during the interaction, "What is this person feeling, and why is he feeling that way?" This simple question can serve as a useful guide in identifying the *what* and *why* of the speaker's experience. Your answer can be inserted into a simple format, such as, "This person feels . . . *because.* . . ."

In active listening, you are indeed trying to see things from the speaker's point of view, but you are not seeking to understand the full meaning of his communications because you want to "figure him out" in a diagnostic sense. The purpose is not to play psychologist and uncover deeply buried reasons for his feelings. The purpose is to achieve a level of understanding that can be *demonstrated to the other person.* You must *communicate* your understanding and respond in a way that tells the other person you understand how he sees the situation. Even if you think he is not seeing the whole picture clearly, you must, nevertheless, suspend your judgment and communicate that you are seeing things through his eyes.

Although both feelings and content give meaning to messages, either one may be more important at any given time. Some messages may be predominantly cognitive, and feelings may be extremely weak and barely evident. Still, it is important to listen for feelings in any message, because it is only when you discriminate both that you are able to recognize what is uppermost in the person's consciousness at any given moment. You must attend to both and rely on moment-to-moment communications from the speaker as signs of what is foremost in his awareness. Even if the essence of a message is defined primarily by its content, it is still necessary to perceive feelings accurately. As Ivey (1980) suggested, emotions are central to intellectual life, so a clear understanding of an individual's feelings provides an important basis for understanding his thoughts, attitudes, and decisions.

What to Listen "To"

In listening for the full meaning of a communication, you must tune in to all channels through which messages come. Verbal statements consist of spoken words that are vital sources of information revealing the speaker's feelings as well as the causes and consequences of those feelings. Psychologists have found, however, that the meanings of words can be modified substantially by the speaker's vocalizations (paralinguistic behavior) and nonverbal behavior. Therefore, to grasp the essence of the speaker's communications, it is necessary that we listen for cues to meaning from all of these sources. Active listening requires that we also attend to the context of the interaction—physical, social, and emotional. That is, we must be alert to the "background" of verbal, vocal, and nonverbal messages so that we can interpret them in the context of the situation facing the speaker.

Engage your empathic skills, and suppose, just for the moment, that you are in the hospital as a patient undergoing tests to determine the reasons for your gradual weight gain despite loss of appetite, your feelings of general malaise and weakness, a distended abdomen, and gastrointestinal hemorrhaging. You have other visitors in your room when I stop by to see how you're doing. While I'm visiting with you and your friends, I notice that you seem somehow detached from the group interaction. You say that you're feeling just fine, but you haven't convinced me that all is well with you. Your head turns away from the group, and your eyes seem fixated on some distant object outside your window. When you do make contact with your visitors, it appears halfhearted and obligatory, because your smiles disappear quickly from your face, your statements are short and concise, and the tone of your voice decreases noticeably at the end of each sentence. As I talk with your friends, it occurs to me that they don't seem to notice your behavior, because they keep talking to you as if you were fully involved in the interaction. Perhaps they're not listening to you and reading your behavior in the same way I am. Perhaps they have not recognized the emotional context of the interaction. Perhaps they don't realize, as I do, that you are faced with fear and uncertainty about your life, your survival. I can understand your behavior in this interaction, because I can read all of the messages you're sending. And, I can put those messages in a meaningful perspective by putting them *in the context* of your current medical situation. The effective listener knows *for* what to listen and *to* what to listen. She listens *for* the full meaning of a communication, and, to apprehend that meaning, she listens *to* verbal statements, vocalizations, nonverbal behavior, and the physical, social, and emotional context of the communication.

Verbal Messages. Verbal messages come in the form of words stated and put together by the speaker. These words help to define the content of the communication and the feelings associated with it. Words are probably used more by speakers to relate content than they are to express feelings. This is not to say that verbalized feelings are rare. Rather, many people find it much easier to discuss their thoughts than their feelings. Often, people don't come right out and state how they feel. Their feelings are woven beyond words into vocalizations and nonverbal expressions. Nevertheless, valuable information is obtained about the meaning of the speaker's messages when we pay careful attention to verbal ingredients of communications.

Verbal communication can be approached in various ways (see Chapters Two and Twelve, for example). In relation to active listening, our concern here is with three aspects of verbal communication: verbal *referents*, *meaning*, and *focus*.

Words are symbols that refer to objects, events, ideas, people, relationships, and so on. *Referents* are those things to which words refer. For example, the word "surgery" represents the medical treatment of disease, injury, or deformity by manual or operative methods. The medical treatment itself is a referent, the process for which the word stands. The word surgery has meaning when it is attached to a referent that we recognize. In our interactions with others, the speaker may use the plural pronoun "they" to indicate a focus on others, or he may use names to identify specific people. "We" or "us" may indicate a focus on the experience of a group to which the speaker may belong or identify. It may also suggest a focus on the immediate relationship with the receiver. Finally, the speaker can use specific nouns to focus on a topic, such as hematology, stress, professional development, and so on.

The speaker's preferred temporal focus is important to identify through active listening. She can speak in the past, present, or future tense: "It *was* just marvelous," "I *am* nervous," "They *will never* meet our demands." The temporal, or time, focus taken by the speaker may suggest to you whether the past, present, or future is uppermost in her mind. It frequently happens that an overemphasis by the speaker on the past or future indicates an avoidance of present thoughts and feelings. Discussions of past and future events are normal and necessary in human interactions. Yet, in many of our interactions, we neglect the here and now. From the listener's standpoint, it is important to be in touch with what the speaker is feeling at the moment, even though she may be talking about past or future events. In the next chapter, we will examine the ways in which a focus of immediate experience can facilitate more satisfactory interactions. Here it is sufficient to note that, in active listening, attention must be paid to the experience of the speaker in the present physical, social, and emotional context. It is her behavior in the here and now of the interaction that may add more meaning to her communications than any information about the past or the future.

Vocalizations. Words represent the verbal messages sent by individuals, but the *ways* in which they are delivered can modify their meanings altogether. The *vocalizations*, or *paralinguistic cues*, which accompany words are the behavioral counterparts of exclamation points, question marks, periods, and punctuations in written communications. As Egan (1977) suggested, the speaker's vocalizations can confirm, deny, emphasize, and add emotional color to what is being said. For example, if you tell me in a halting, cracking, strained voice that you are terribly afraid of failing this course, I'll probably believe you (all other things being equal, of course), because the way in which you are delivering the message tends to *confirm* the validity of your words. If I invited you to attend a lecture with me next week and you replied by dragging your words out slowly, hesitantly, as if wavering and faltering with your answer— "Oh!—that—sounds interesting—uh—yeah, okay—uh—I don't think I have any commitments that night, but—uh . . ."—then I would probably not press the issue and either leave it up to you to let me know of your interest later or I would merely suggest that we make it some other time, perhaps. This is because your manner of responding tended to *deny* what you were stating. Let's suppose that you are ill and you decide to call your supervisor to tell her you will not be in for work toady. When you talk to her over the telephone, chances are that you'll want to leave no doubt as to just how sick you really are. So, as you deliver your message in something of a whining, moaning, sorrowful way, you are *emphasizing* the gravity of your illness. After all, you're sick; so, you don't want to sound as healthy as you do every other day! *Emotional color* is added to the speaker's verbal statements when she stresses certain words, for example, "I *r-e-a-l-l-y* feel *s-o-o-o* happy for you!"

Active listening means that you attend to the ways in which paralanguage qualifies verbal statements. It means that you are listening closely for vocal cues which add to the full meaning of the communication. You are not merely listening to words, you are listening to the *ways* in which they are delivered. Listen to the "language of language," and attend to cues such as the individual's range of voice, resonance, speech tempo and control, voice qualifiers (see Chapter Two). Chapter Two also identifies other paralinguistic cues to which you should listen (e.g., vocal emblems, illustrators, regulators, adaptors, and verbal affect displays). A review of that chapter should be helpful in orienting you to the kinds of vocal cues that add to the meaning of the speaker's communications. It should help you to recognize the range of vocal cues to which you should listen.

Another common problem encountered by many ineffective listeners is that they assume prematurely that they understand the precise referents of words used by speakers. They take it for granted that they know exactly about what the speaker is talking. Conversely, the effective listener is alert to possible multiple meanings of words. In those circumstances where words may have various connotations, other cues often help to clarify the intended meaning. If not, it becomes necessary to ask for clarification by stating your uncertainty about what the speaker means. Again, however, you need not be preoccupied with the words per se, but with their referents. The referents are what you are seeking to understand. Chapters Fourteen and Fifteen offer some suggestions for responding to speaker messages in ways which ensure the accuracy of what you hear the speaker saying.

The words used by a speaker also reveal the particular *focus* he wishes to take during an interaction. If he talks primarily about factual information, then he probably prefers a content focus for the moment. If he talks mainly about feelings, then he may prefer an affective focus. The words representing the subjects of sentences can tell you where the speaker wants to focus his messages. For example, if the speaker constantly uses the pronouns "I," "me," or "myself," the focus of his communication is on the self. The pronoun "you" can indicate a focus on the receiver, or it may refer to people in general. Rather than bringing a direct focus to themselves, speakers may rely on this pronoun as a means of detaching themselves from their own experience during the conversation and putting it at a safer distance:

> Well, when this kind of thing happens to *you*, *you* get pretty upset. *You* don't want to talk to anyone because *you're* do damned mad, and, besides, there's nothing anyone can say that makes *you* feel better. *You* just keep it to *yourself* and deal with it the best *you* can.

When pronouns are used in this way, it implies that the speaker does not wish to take sole ownership of his own concerns. He talks about them as if they also belonged to someone else. This is a very common way of neutralizing the impact of our feelings and avoiding revelations of just how we're being affected. The words speakers use are for the purpose of giving *meaning* to specific referents. The words are *not* the things about which they speak. We are concerned with comprehending words only as means for understanding those things to which they refer. When there is correspondence between the referent you have for a word and the referent the speaker has for the same word, then you have shared meaning, and you can both understand the same referent. Communication can take place. Sometimes, however, there is not exact correspondence between the meaning intended by the speaker and the meaning attached by the receiver because their referents are slightly different. This is very common when words are used as symbols for feelings. This emotional experience to which the speaker refers when she uses the word "repulsed" may not have the same meaning to you when you hear her tell about her reaction to the unkempt appearance of a mutual friend. This is because the word is used as a referent to *her* particular experience of repulsion: the way her body reacts, what happens inside of her, what she feels like doing. Given this fact, perhaps you can appreciate how important empathy is in active listening. To increase the level of shared meaning in a feeling word—to bring your respective referents into closer correspondence—you must be able to see what that word means to the speaker. You must use your own referent as an anchor, a basis for elaborating the meaning of the referent to the speaker.

You cannot understand feeling referents—and you cannot, therefore, grasp the full meaning of the speaker's words—if you do not understand what your own feelings are like (a review of Chapter Four should be helpful for you in this connection). When you cannot recognize your own feelings and thus label them accurately, interpersonal communication comes close to being an exchange of private meanings. Consider the following passage from Lewis Carroll's *Through the Looking Glass*:

> "But 'glory' doesn't mean 'a nice knock-down argument,' " Alice objected.
>
> "When *I* use a word," Humpty Dumpty said, in a rather scornful tone, "it means just what I choose it to mean—neither more nor less."
>
> "The question is," said Alice, "whether you *can* make words mean so many different things."
>
> "The question is," said Humpty Dumpty, "which is to be master—that's all."

Alice could not understand the referents to Humpty Dumpty's words, not that she was obliged to, because he had created a private language which he could use in any way he liked. Still, they could not communicate effectively until they shared the same meanings for specific referents. Just as we cannot communicate with anyone until we have let them know what the referents are, neither can we understand others' communications when we cling rigidly to the singular meanings we have assigned to words. Again, active listening demands that we try to understand the meanings words have for the speaker and, in particular, those words representing feelings.

One of the problems faced by ineffective listeners is that they have not learned to label feelings accurately. They are not skilled in attaching words to feelings and, therefore, have difficulty recognizing affective message components. A good listener is one who has an extensive *feeling vocabulary*. She has a full range of feeling words that enable her to understand the experiences of persons using those same words in their verbal messages. She can identify and relate to others' emotional states because she has learned, labeled, and categorized her own. Table 13.1 provides a list of commonly used feeling words. These are words that are frequently found in the affective parts of verbal messages. You can use this table to begin expanding your own feeling vocabulary. You should have no difficulty recognizing the words themselves, but you may find it a bit harder to articulate the emotional experiences to which they refer: their experiential referents. Therefore, take a moment to look at each word and think about what it is like for you to feel each of these ways. Recall situations in which you have actually experienced each one of these feelings, and then try to describe to yourself exactly what those feelings were like for you at the time.

Table 13.1   Commonly Used Feeling Words: Describe the Experiential Referents for These Words by Asking Yourself, *"What is it like for me when I feel. . . ."*

Accepted	Daring	Glad	Pessimistic
Affectionate	Defensive	Good	Pleased
Afraid	Delighted	Guilty	Puzzled
Ambitious	Dependent	Happy	Rejected
Angry	Depressed	Hopeful	Relaxed
Annoyed	Despondent	Hostile	Resentful
Anxious	Determined	Hurt	Responsible
Awkward	Disappointed	Impatient	Sad
Bewildered	Discouraged	Impulsive	Satisfied
Bitter	Disillusioned	Inferior	Shy
Bored	Dismayed	Insecure	Suspicious
Bothered	Disoriented	Intimate	Sympathetic
Capable	Elated	Jealous	Tense
Carefree	Enthusiastic	Joyful	Threatened
Cheerful	Excited	Kind	Thrilled
Confident	Foolish	Lonely	Trusting
Confused	Friendly	Loving	Uneasy
Contented	Frustrated	Miserable	Unhappy
Courageous	Furious	Mistrustful	Uptight
Cynical	Fussy	Nervous	Worried

Nonverbal Behavior.   Considerable attention was devoted to nonverbal behavior in earlier chapters. It is sufficient to note here that nonverbal behavior constitutes an extremely valuable source of information in the communication process, and the perception of that information is part of the task of active listening. Active listening involves a total focus on all sources of messages, not the least of which is the nonverbal modality. Facial expressions, hand and body movements, gestures, postures, and use of space, and even physical appearance provide cues which can underscore or override verbal and vocal messages. Typically, nonverbal responses of the speaker *add* meaning to verbal statements and vocalizations in the same ways that vocal cues confirm, deny, emphasize, or emotionally color the words spoken. A minute facial gesture, moistened eyes, tensing posture, quick and shallow breathing, and fidgeting hands may even hold more communicative value than anything the speaker is saying at the moment.

The basic purpose of attending to nonverbal behavior in the process of active listening is to see how it supports or contradicts other messages. You "listen" to nonverbal behavior, not as a detective of silent clues, but as an involved participant in a *whole* human interaction.

Summary: Pulling It Together

Paying attention and listening to another person communicate her thoughts and feelings require skill. They demand an ability to use social intelligence effectively and readily in performing specific behaviors and avoiding others. First, as a receiver of a communication, you must *attend physically.* This means that you must use your body to enhance your receptivity to messages and, at the same time, demonstrate a posture of involvement with the speaker. To do this, it is necessary to *control distractions* that threaten to disrupt your attention to the speaker. Physical attending also means that you *orient your body toward the speaker and face him squarely, lean slightly forward* with your upper body, maintain *appropriate eye contact*, and *relax*. These nonverbal behaviors are among the outward signs of your perceptual focus on the speaker. *Psychological attending* is what you do while you are attending physically. It is more than a perceptual activity, for it requires the full psychological participation in your interaction with the speaker. Psychological attending is achieved through *active listening*, which is a *total effort to grasp the meaning and significance of the facts and feelings communicated by the speaker.* In active listening, you listen for the *full meaning*, or *essence*, of the speaker's messages, which is revealed through the cognitive and affective components of his communications: the *content* and *feelings* revealed in his communications. When listening for the content and feelings of messages, you are attempting to understand the speaker's emotional experience and the antecedents (causes) and consequences (effects) of that experience. In other words, you are listening for the factors underlying the speaker's feelings. To grasp the full meaning of communications in this way, you must listen to *verbal statements, vocalizations,* and *nonverbal cues.* Active listening requires that you listen to all of these sources of information, so that you may *re-create the experience of the speaker within your own frame of reference.* The primary task of active listening, then, is to achieve and communicate *empathic understanding.*

The fact remains that you may practice all of the above and still not be a good listener. *Listening is ineffective if it is only a receptive act.* It is nothing more than a sterile process of hollow listening. As Egan (1977) argued, the ultimate proof of good listening is *good responding.* In the next chapter, we examine the kinds of responses that suggest good listening. In particular, we will examine these responses against the framework of interpersonal relationships in general, since their performance also stands as vital to the quality of our relationships at work and in our personal life.

References

Egan, G. *The Skilled Helper: A Model for Systematic Helping and Interpersonal Relating.* Monterey, California, Brooks/Cole, 1975.

Egan, G. *You and Me: The Skills of Communicating and Relating to Others.* Monterey, California, Brooks/Cole, 1977.

Hall, E. T. Silent Assumptions in Social Communication, *Disorders of Communication*, **42**:41–55 (1964).

Hall, E. T. *The Hidden Dimension.* New York, Doubleday, 1966.

Harrison, R. P. *Beyond Words: An Introduction to Nonverbal Communication.* Englewood Cliffs, New Jersey, Prentice-Hall, 1974.

Goffman, E. *Behavior in Public Places.* New York, Free Press, 1963.

Ivey, A. E. *Counseling and Psychotherapy: Skills, Theories, and Practice.* Englewood Cliffs, New Jersey, Prentice-Hall, 1980.

Patton, M. A. I Told Them All, *American Journal of Nursing*, **76**:113 (1976).

Tubbs, S. L., and Moss, S. *Human Communication*, 3d ed. New York, Random House, 1980.

CHAPTER FOURTEEN

Facilitative Conditions
for Effective Communication
and Relationships

*The meeting of two personalities is like the contact of
two chemical substances: if there is any reaction, both
are transformed.*

Carl Gustav Jung,
Modern Man in Search of a Soul

The nature of interpersonal communication assures that "when two personalities meet," there is indeed a "reaction." From the convergence of two individuals during an encounter, there emerges a third entity—an alliance formed for the purpose of communication. This alliance is known as the interpersonal relationship, and it is within the context of their relationship that each person may be "transformed" intellectually, emotionally, and even physically. The extent to which individuals experience a transformation of any kind, for better or for worse, often depends on a core of conditions which set the climate of the relationship and constitute a major force in influencing the behavior of each person. In other words, there appear to be certain basic dimensions of relationships which collectively influence the climate and flow of communication between interacting persons and, consequently, the nature and degree of change experienced by each individual.

We have found that in counseling relationships where helpers provide high levels of *empathy, respect,* and *genuineness,* the helpee's inherent capacity for open and clear communication usually manifests itself (e.g., Carkhuff, 1969, 1972; Carkhuff and Berenson, 1967, 1977; Rogers, 1962; Truax and Carkhuff, 1967). While being genuinely herself, the counselor demonstrates a deep respect for and empathic understanding of the client. Virtually all approaches to counseling reflect the same recognition of the necessity to promote communication by providing these or similar conditions within the context of the counseling relationship. The conditions supersede any theory or any techniques the counselor may use (Hansen, Stevic, and Warner, 1977). Training in the skills of providing these conditions has been offered primarily within the counseling professions, although there is no acceptable justification for continuing such a practice. The skills of promoting satisfactory relationships are the exclusive domain of *no* single discipline and are needed wherever human beings seek to improve the quality of their interactions. Such skills are indispensable to all human service professions where interpersonal relationships represent the mediums for effecting desired changes. Across the health care professions, in particular, there is a growing awareness that relationship-building and helping skills have special applicability to a whole range of service delivery areas (O'Brien and Johnson, 1977). Health professionals can profit greatly from learning the same kind of fundamental skills that are integral to counseling (Bartnick and O'Brien, 1980; Rosen and Wiens, 1979). The broadening scopes of both counseling and health care professions now mandate the sharing of particular areas of expertise. The time has come for counselors to impart their knowledge of human relationships, because health professionals are being asked to be more than technical experts. They are being asked to be experts in interpersonal relations as well. Learning how to develop and maintain relationships would be immediately helpful to health professionals individually, subsequently helpful to their colleagues, and ultimately to those they serve.

You should keep in mind that your understanding of the skills presented here as well as your ability to implement them can facilitate other people's entrance into alliances with you. In health care practice, the quality of those alliances may very well account for a notable share of the outcomes of medical treatment, for it is through them that you apply your technical knowledge and skill. In most cases, the better your relationships with patients, the better your mutual communication is and the better the quality of care you provide. It can be argued, I believe, that, as a health professional, you must be, first and foremost, an expert in interpersonal relationships—a person who has the know-how to create the best possible alliances for accomplishing health care objectives.

The Attitude and Communication of Respect

Most people would probably agree that mutual *respect* is necessary for satisfactory relationships. Beyond this point of initial agreement, they may be at odds as to what the condition really means. Like all fundamental concepts, respect seems to elude precise definition. It often means different things to different people and different things to the same persons under different circumstances. Here the concept is put into a perspective which hopefully limits the range of possible connotations it has for you. Respect is defined in two ways—first, as an orientation or attitude toward others and, second, as a way of acting toward them.

The Orientation of Respect

We can "respect" other people in various ways. We can admire their intelligence, defer to their judgement, avoid interfering with something they are doing, pay close attention when they speak, or fawn obsequiously at their status. Whenever we respect others, we usually feel approving about some set of characteristics. We note something about them, evaluate it positively, and label our judgement "respect." Most of the time, our respect is "conditional" and reserved only for those qualities we judge to be worthy of our admiration, reverence, or deference.

There is another way of looking at respect, however. It is used here in a broader sense, as *a pervasive, nonconditional attitude of acceptance of persons in their totalities. It is an orientation toward people, defined by unqualified acceptance of and positive regard for the humanness and uniqueness of others.* It is a prizing of the essence of humanness in people, a prizing of individuals *because* they are individuals. Such an orientation, of course, implies that there is something about being human that is worthy of respect, something about humanity that is to be cherished for its own sake. As such, this form of respect for humanness is grounded in our systems of value priorities. For example, you may hold unconditional positive regard (Rogers, 1957) for a person, partly to the extent that you hold "individuality" as a primary value—that is, your acceptance that individuals are to be prized for their differentness and separateness and not for their conformity to stereotyped standards of social desirability. Conceptualized in this way, respect means that individuals are valued as persons with negative as well as positive characteristics. There is no demand that individuals become different in order to gain your acceptance. There is simply no attachment of conditions of worth to their characteristics (see Chapter Three). As Jourard (1974) said, respect means that you see others' unique qualities as "priceless and irreplaceable."

True respect for the humanness of another person does not mean that you are obliged to approve of everything she does. It means that you may indeed disapprove of certain of her actions, while, at the same time, recognizing her as a person worthy of respect for her humanness, regardless of the unacceptability of her behavior. You may not like what she does, and you may even dislike what she *is*, but you nevertheless accept that she is *who* she is—a distinctly different human being with those specific qualities. An attitude such as this is one which preserves the integrity and autonomy of the other, even if it means a dissolution of the relationship.

The notion of respect as unconditional positive regard for the other's humanness does not, then, mean that you completely relinquish your own set of values and accept everything as appropriate. This approach would be inconsistent with the sincere concern and honesty that characterize deep respect. An attitude of respect includes a willingness to share personal reactions concerning the other's behavior, not the denial of genuine and perhaps negative feelings. A willingness to share genuine feelings when they arise is often a measure of respect for others (as we shall see in the next section). It is unrealistic to assume that we always have positive feelings about those with whom we interact. We simply feel differently about different people, and our feelings toward the same persons often change as circumstances change. Respect does not imply that you ignore those feelings, nor does it mean that you must like everyone. To the contrary, respect involves the effort to identify and be aware of the feelings that do exist. It is important that we recognize how we feel about different people when we are interacting with them and to think about the meaning of those feelings for us and for those persons. Carkhuff and Berenson (1977) maintained that respect has its origin in the respect we have for ourselves. The significance and meaning of the feelings we have for others may, then, relate directly to the feelings we have about our own selves. Where negative feelings are concerned, Rogers (1967) indicated that, most of the time, those reactions somehow relate to our own concerns and our own values. Consequently, we may in fact learn a great deal about the respect we have for ourselves by noting the respect we have for others. In general, if you accept your own person as defined by faults as much as strengths, you should find it much easier to accept the same in others.

Unconditionality of positive regard is an ideal proposed by Rogers (1957) to suggest a nonevaluative attitude toward others as human beings. It is a positive attitude which is maintained in spite of their behavior. The behaviors of individuals represent important "parts" of their whole selves, but they are more than a sum of their respective actions. Respect does *not* necessarily require a suspension of judgement concerning those "parts"—those *behaviors*. It is entirely possible to disapprove of an individual's behavior and still maintain a positive acceptance of the *person*. Indeed, the quality of human relationships often rides on people's ability to make this critical distinction, for, all too often, we seem ready to judge the whole person, when it is his or her behavior that we so strongly reject. In relationships, if there ever are situations comparable to "throwing out the baby with the bath water," these are lamentably close.

The Communication of Respect

An attitude of respect is nonobservable and must therefore be inferred from outward behavior. In the final analysis, it is how you translate respect into action and communicate it to the other person that counts. Moreover, your behavioral indications of respect must be accurately perceived by others. To communicate respect for another individual, it is your responsibility to demonstrate it in the presence of that person by doing certain things and avoiding others. Some suggestions are provided here, but they are by no means inclusive of all the ways to communicate respect. You may want to include some of your own.

Physical Attending

The same physical attending skills used to communicate involvement with a speaker also reveal positive regard for that person. You demonstrate nonverbally that you are interested in and committed to understanding her communications because *she is worth the effort*. Egan (1975, p. 95) commented that, "In the case of respect, actions literally speak louder than words." One of the least ambiguous ways in which you can loudly proclaim your respect for the other is by using your body to tell her you are involved in the interaction. By itself, physical attending is an excellent cue to the positive regard you hold for that person, for it indicates that nothing else is more important to you at the moment than actively participating with her in the interaction. Resisting distractions, facing her squarely with an open posture, leaning slightly forward, maintaining appropriate eye contact, and being relaxed are all signals that you consider her worth listening to.

Active Listening

If you are listening actively, your responses are keener, more insightful, and more appropriate than if you are passively hearing verbal statements. Those responses tend to indicate your concerned focus and your full psychological participation with the other. Normally, the other person will sense that you really care about what she has to say. She may begin to realize that, if you respect her feelings and experiences, they must be worth something. When you continue to show your respect for her as a person, her own sense of self becomes reinforced and she tends to find it easier to accept those feelings as rightfully hers. Ultimately, she finds it easier to accept similar feelings in others, and her increasing self-regard generalizes to a more accepting attitude toward those with whom she interacts. The respect which you communicated tends to be reciprocated by her in your subsequent interactions, and your relationship tends to become more rewarding for both of you.

Waiting Patiently

Good listeners know how to wait and keep their mouths shut when the situation calls for it. In fact, Plato seemed to recognize the social intelligence required of good communicators when he commented, "Wise men talk, because they have something to say; fools talk, because they have to say something." Perhaps he also meant that it takes a measure of social know-how to recognize when to keep quiet. During our interactions, there are times when speakers need to pause and stop talking. This does not necessarily signal that we should rush to fill the void of silence. The speaker may need time and room to sort out his thoughts and feelings, he may need a moment to rest and recover from a painful experience he has related, or he may be confused as to where to go with his message. There are many reasons for pauses in communications, and it is important to be able to understand the reasons for those interludes. If you are listening actively, it is not difficult to recognize when the speaker simply needs silence. Preserving that silence for the speaker is a way of communicating respect. It shows that you care about what he is experiencing at the moment and that you are not preoccupied with your own discomfort. Waiting patiently for the speaker to resume his communication is often hard for people to do. In some cases, silence is more discomfortable than the verbal message itself. Sometimes, it seems as if people considered silence as a breach of etiquette. However, waiting patiently may be more beneficial than anything you would interject. To communicate respect, then, it is necessary, first, to recognize when silence is appropriate, second, to preserve it as needed, and, third, to interrupt it sensitively if the speaker is unable to resume the communication. In the next chapter, silence is discussed as a conversational skill. Here, it is sufficient to note that it may well be a critical means for demonstrating your respect for the speaker.

Nonjudgemental Responding

It has been emphasized elsewhere in this text that the tendency to evaluate the statements of another person represents one of the major obstacles to the achievement of empathy and to communication in general. The act of expressing those judgements is also an obstacle to the communication of respect when the judgements are made about the speaker's feelings and experiences. Although we are not used to thinking in such terms, it seems to me that the standards by which we judge feelings—right and wrong, good and bad—are rarely applicable to those human experiences. These are moral standards of judgement which do not apply to human feelings. In and of themselves, there simply are no "right" or "wrong" feelings. It is when we recognize that human feelings cannot be evaluated in such terms—and it is when we suspend the tendency to attach our own values to other people's feelings and experiences—that we communicate respect. Nonevaluative responding is a message to the other person that we have not attached conditions of worth to his experience of living. It is a way of showing that we acknowledge his perfect right to his own feelings and that we are choosing not to shape him into our image of the acceptable person. Consider the differences between the following responses:

TIM: I feel so incompetent! After all my training, I feel like I still don't know enough—like I don't know as much as I should. I haven't seen anyone else having problems with their jobs—at least, they don't say anything about it. God, am I the only one who feels this way? Am I really as inept as I feel?

JAN: No, you're not. Don't get down on yourself. You shouldn't feel incompetent just because you don't know everything. Other people just out of training probably feel the same way. If they don't, then there's something wrong. It's only normal to feel insecure at first. You'll get over it—it's just a phase you're going through now.

BETH: You're feeling really discouraged and unsure of yourself because you're not an "expert" like you think you should be. Everyone else seems so confident in knowing exactly what to do, and that makes you feel even more inadequate.

Jan responded in an evaluative way by speaking to Tim's competency and to the appropriateness of his feelings. She chastised him for having legitimate feelings and then minimized their significance by judging them "normal" and attributing them to a "phase." The message probably came across to Tim that it was silly to acknowledge a genuine experience. Jan was essentially telling Tim, "Forget it!" She was obviously unmindful of him and had never gained sight of his feelings because she didn't think them *worth* either her or his attention. Beth responded in a nonjudgemental fashion to both the feelings and content of Tim's message. The immediate issue was not his competence, it was his experience of inadequacy, uncertainty, and discouragement. Beth managed to communicate an appreciation for the issue of competency which *underlay* Tim's feelings. She did not ignore that issue, but gave it secondary importance by attending first to his feelings of the moment. Most importantly, she neither criticized nor condoned Tim's feelings. By simply reflecting the essence of his communication, she demonstrated respect and, at the same time, empathy.

Communicating Empathy

One of the best ways of showing respect is by communicating empathic understanding of the speaker's feelings, thoughts, and behavior. All communications of empathy are simultaneous communications of respect for the other person. Those behaviors associated with empathic listening and communications reveal a willingness to take the time and effort required to understand a person. And, as understanding increases, so also does respect tend to increase. This is because an appreciation of the other's uniqueness is enhanced to the extent that empathic understanding is achieved. The more you understand the differentness and separateness of an individual human being, the more accepting you tend to become of his or her distinctiveness from others.

In health care practice, communicating empathic understanding may be one of the best ways of helping some patients regain a measure of self-respect which has dwindled because of illnesses shattering their sense of dignity. Giving your full attention, your time, and your energy is a compliment to most patients and helps them to recover a sense of worth. By demonstrating your respect for them, you may promote a level of self-respect that not only subsidizes treatment efforts, but contributes to their total well-being.

Disagreement and Confrontation

Respect does not mean that you always agree with the other person and lapse into a detached frame of mind where you communicate that anything he does or says is all right. It does not mean backing down from disagreements and necessary confrontations. Sometimes, it is necessary to communicate respect by challenging the other person, confronting an issue, or bringing something out in the open. Failure to do these things when necessary often reveals an attitude of indifference, an absence of real caring or concern, because the other person is just not worth the "hassle." Perhaps you can recall from your own experience, as I can from mine, instances when you thought it wasn't worth the bother to disagree or confront someone. Speaking for myself, I realize that those have been instances where I did not hold sufficient regard for those persons or where the issues were not central to our relationships. Confrontation is discussed in detail in the next chapter, but here it should be understood that it is not conceived as an "aggressive" response of attacking others' communications. There are many ways to confront and challenge others in adaptive ways. The task is responsibly and sensitively to point up to another person various discrepancies you perceive between the person's statements and her actions, between your thoughts or feelings and hers, or between past and present experiences. Perceptive and sensitive disagreements and confrontations suggest an openness and honesty associated with true respect and empathy. Knowing when and how to challenge others supplements your ability to demonstrate both.

Genuineness

Genuineness is discussed in the next section as a quality of congruence and authenticity of behavior. The genuine person puts on no "front" for others.

By interacting as one's real self, and not as some role-defined entity, respect is communicated. The individual says, in effect, "I have no need to hide behind a social facade when I am with you. I am not pretending to be something or someone else, because I respect you and do not wish to manipulate our interactions or exploit our relationship."

Implementing the Condition of Respect

Carkhuff (1969) revised an earlier scale (Truax, 1962b) for measuring the "communication of respect in interpersonal processes." It is a five-point scale similar to the kind described in Chapter Four for the measurement of empathic understanding. There are five levels at which the communication of respect may be identified, ranging from minimally facilitative levels at points 1 and 2 to communications of deep respect for the other's worth as a person (at level 5).

Level One

At this level, the verbal and behavioral expressions of the first person show a clear lack of respect for the second person. The first person communicates to the second person that her feelings and experiences are not worthy of consideration. At this level, the first person may even try to become the focus of attention or actively offer judgements and advice:

PATIENT: Can't I just go into the bathroom and give myself a bath? I don't know why I couldn't do that—and besides, I just don't like being treated like a child who can't take care of himself!

NURSE: Well, Mr. Smith, the reality is that we can't take a chance on you hurting yourself. Right now you shouldn't be walking around, because you're just too weak. Now, you just relax and let us do our job until you're stronger. You're not being treated like a child, anyway. We do this for other people who are too weak to take care of themselves, and they don't complain—they like being pampered.

At this level, an individual may communicate repeatedly that the experiences of the other are of little or no consequence to him:

STUDENT: Next month, my practicum begins and—I—uh, don't really know if I can—if I will, uh—

ADVISOR: Be able to take it?

STUDENT: Yeah, I mean I've never really had to be so involved in services—I mean seeing people suffer every day and—

ADVISOR: Isn't it kind of late to be thinking about whether or not you can cut it?

STUDENT: Well, it's not like I never thought about it before.

ADVISOR: So, why is it such a big thing now? You can't let everything drop at this point. You've just got to put it in the back of your mind and do what you have to do—that is, if you really want to complete your training.

STUDENT: Oh, I want to complete my training. It's just that—

ADVISOR: [Interrupting] It's just that you don't know if you can stomach the practicum experience, I know.

STUDENT: It's just that I don't want to be so upset by what I see that I won't be able to do my job. I don't think there's anything wrong with feeling this way right now—I mean, didn't you feel like this when you were in training?

ADVISOR: If I did, I don't remember it because I probably got over it very quickly, just like you will if you want to graduate.

Level Two

At level two, the first person responds to the second person in such a way as to demonstrate little respect for his feelings and experiences. She may respond passively or mechanically, or she may even ignore many of his feelings. When communications of respect would be expected, the first person shows a lack of positive regard for the second person.

PATIENT: He doesn't have to come in here several times a day, but at least one visit doesn't seem like much to ask for. I thought—I think maybe he doesn't care what happens to me. My God, I expected him to come up here and see me!

PHYSICIAN: Um, hm.

PATIENT: It's only 10 minutes from the hospital. It wouldn't take him more then 10 minutes to get here. And, he wouldn't have to stay long. I don't want him to stay that long, anyway.

PHYSICIAN: Um, hm.

PATIENT: It's been 6 days; I thought he'd be here 6 days ago.

PHYSICIAN: That's a long time.

PATIENT: It seems like an eternity to me. When you love someone as much as I love him, 6 days apart is a long separation—even longer when he stays away and only calls on the phone.

PHYSICIAN: Hm, well, maybe when he calls, you can work it out. In the meantime, I want you to get some rest. Being upset isn't helping your blood pressure any. We may have to do something about that. We'll see in the morning.

Level Three

At level three, the first person communicates a positive respect and concern for the second person. She communicates in various ways that who the second person is and what he has to say do matter to her. Carkhuff identified this level as the *minimal level of facilitative interpersonal functioning*. Ideally, the communication of respect should not fall below this level. Individuals should attempt to be even more effective in demonstrating positive regard (at levels four and five), but they should prevent their communications of respect from being at less than minimally acceptable levels.

PATIENT: For a long time there, I didn't know if I was ever going to make it. Every improvement I made was followed by a setback—like one step forward and two steps backward, you know?

NURSE: Um, hm, I remember.

PATIENT: And, I felt like I'd been condemned or doomed or something. Like I'd be in and out of here for the rest of my life, never really getting any better. I'd see other patients and compare my problems with theirs, and it seemed like I was always the one coming up on the short end of the stick. Then, I'd see some people I knew were dying. I'd see them laying in their beds, and I just knew it. And when I looked at them, I'd see myself somewhere down the road—and not too far off. That's all I could really see in my future—death—and probably soon.

NURSE: You didn't see any hope for yourself at all, did you?

PATIENT: Not a bit of hope! None at all! In fact, there were times when I—when I—I thought about ending it all—I mean times when I even thought of suicide. It was that bad. I just didn't want to live if it meant going on like I had been. For such a long time—so long—I had no reason to live.

NURSE: No purpose—nothing to keep you going.

PATIENT: Nothing—[sigh]—Well, I guess I just had to keep on somehow—guess there must've been a reason. Maybe now I'm starting to know what it was—what it is.

NURSE: Looking back on everything and knowing where you are now—well, I guess there's a lot for you to think about.

Level Four

Persons communicating respect at level four are demonstrating a deeply positive regard for others. The first person shows a nonevaluative and unconditional warmth toward the second person. There may be some traces of conditionality in the first person's responses to very personal and private experiences of the second person, but the second person is given ample freedom to express himself and experience acceptance.

ELAINE: I don't know. I guess I've always thought I should keep my work relationships separate from my social relationships. It just seems to make it easier for me to work with other staff if I don't have outside relationships with them.

KAREN: You really wouldn't be comfortable with us going out together after work or getting together for dinner.

ELAINE: It's not that I wouldn't be open to that, Karen. You and I get along fabulously here at work, and I'm sure we'd get along just as well socially. I feel so awful to say all this, I don't want you to get the wrong idea—I mean your friendship means a lot to me. But, I—well, I've been burned a few times by people I got too close to away from work.

KAREN: It's really hard for you to imagine that not happening again. After a few bad experiences, I guess we do get leery.

ELAINE: Yeah, that's right. See, Karen, relationships are special things to me. Maybe I take them too seriously, and maybe I'm too sensitive and afraid of being hurt. I think that's it. I think I'm still afraid to take a risk and develop new relationships, because I expect to be hurt sometime.

KAREN: Taking a risk means making yourself vulnerable, and right now, you're afraid of relationships. You sound like you want them, but, at the same time, they scare you. It must be pretty hard for you to have to be on guard and so careful all the time—never letting anyone get close enough to hurt you—or care for you.

Level Five

At level five, the first person communicates the very deepest respect for the second person's worth as a person. The second person is permitted to be freely and openly himself. The first person is willing to enter into the other's experiential world and share his joys as well as his depressions, his achievements as well as his failures, his strengths, and his limitations. At this level, the first person may even influence the second person to communicate highly personal information.

PATIENT: Nothing—nothing's the matter.

PHYSICIAN: I sort of sensed that something was bothering you today. You know, when you feel like it—if you feel like it—I'd be glad if you

PATIENT: [Abrupt interruption] *What?*

PHYSICIAN: I said, when and if you want to, I'd be glad if you shared some of your feelings.

PATIENT: [Abrupt interruption] Hey whoa, whoa, wait a minute—hey, let's just stop the music for a minute! What's this "sharing your feelings" stuff, huh? Since when did you become a shrink? I'm not bending your ear when you're charging me more money all the while I do it. All I ask from you is that you treat my medical needs.

PHYSICIAN: Well, I'd say that's a fair request. I have no interest in playing "shrink," as you say. And, I can see that you're really against sharing your feelings with me.

PATIENT: Right you are! Nothing against you personally, Doc. But I just don't like people trying to pry into my affairs. If I've got things on my mind, I can get them off my mind by myself. I can work out my own problems without any kind of professional help.

PHYSICIAN: I guess I sometimes feel that way myself. But I really didn't have "professional" help in mind when I said I'd be glad if you shared your feelings. I'm not a "shrink," so I'm not offering "professional" help. I just meant to offer my ear.

PATIENT: Okay, I appreciate that. Thanks anyway, Doc, but I still prefer to handle my own problems.

PHYSICIAN: And that's fine with me. I just wanted you to know that you seemed troubled by something and that I'm interested in listening if you wanted it.

Facilitative Genuineness

In our culture, it is sometimes difficult to determine whether it is a value to be unpretentious, real, and genuine or whether the value is a manufactured image of social acceptability. It may also be difficult to define exactly what we mean by "genuine," since even the manufactured models of social desirability are designed to appear authentic and "natural."

Rogers (1957, 1962) postulated *congruence* as a core condition for interpersonal relationships. According to Rogers, the term describes human behavior which is without facade or front and reflective of what and who the individual really *is*. By congruence, Rogers meant to denote that the feelings and thoughts being experienced by an individual are available to his awareness, that he is able to live these thoughts and feelings in the relationship, and that he is able to communicate them where appropriate. Furthermore, congruence was used to suggest that the individual *is himself in a person-to-person encounter* with another. He is role-free and "able to *be* the complexity of his feelings without fear'' (Rogers, 1962, p. 417). This condition has since become known as *genuineness.*

The "genuine" person is *for real.* She is open, sincere, honest, and truly involved in the relationship. She is freely and deeply and *responsibly* herself. Most people have a notion of what it means to be genuine or "real," but usually the connotation is somewhat different from that implied by the way the term is used by psychologists. To many people, being real means "doing your own thing" and not worrying about what others may think, regardless of how you may affect them. To others, it simply means the absence of pretense, the opposite of phoniness. However, to most psychologists, the meaning of the term runs deeper. First, the concept of genuineness is typically used in the vein suggested by Rogers. It does not encompass the "mellow," "let it all hang out," "if it feels good do it," "I gotta be me," "free-spirit" clichés inflicted on us by those who seek to use a guise of genuineness to cloak self-enhancing interests. Genuineness means exactly the opposite, in the sense that *responsibility* is integral to its achievement. The real, congruent person recognizes and responds to her sense of interpersonal responsibility and is sensitive to how her behavior may affect others. She is appropriately open in her interactions, and she "matches" her behavior with her true thoughts and feelings. She is aware of her feelings and communicates messages that are consistent and compatible with each other.

The condition of genuineness has special applicability to relationships in health care practice. The health professional is genuine to the extent that she can step out of her "professional manner" or role and into an honest person-to-person interaction when appropriate. A value assumption I am making here is that most human interactions in health care settings would be more effective and more productive for all parties concerned *if they were role-free and not role-defined.* I do not mean to suggest that there is no room for role-defined interactions where treatment objectives must be accomplished, nor do I mean to negate the value of communicating some degree of "expert" status to patients, for this may often have positive therapeutic effect. What I do mean to say is that one can be "professional" without falling back on her credentials. As Carkhuff (1971) argued, there is a difference between *credentialed professionals* and *functional professionals.* Credentialed professionals are those persons who have degrees and certificates indicating that they have completed formal training programs and to whom a stamp of approval (e.g., a license to practice) has been granted. Functional professionals are those persons who possess the skills of interpersonal communicating and relating. They may or may not be credentialed. Conversely, credentialed professionals may or may not be functional. One can be professional and genuine at the same time, provided that part of the professionalism is of a functional nature. To be a genuine person *and* a competent professional, one must avoid taking refuge in credentials and roles. Health care recipients want to be treated as people *by* people, not by technical experts.

There is a qualification to all of this, however, for even genuineness may not *always* be desirable. For example, it is highly unlikely that the health professional who is genuinely listless, dogmatic, resentful, skeptical, or pessimistic is very therapeutic for patients. Carkhuff and Berenson (1977) commented on this kind of problem among psychotherapists. They differentiated the construct of genuineness from the notion of *facilitative genuineness*. Genuineness, per se, may in some cases be destructive when the individual's only genuine way of responding is negative and harmful to the other. In other words, some people are simply destructive when they are genuine. If the individual is truly aware of his own experience (i.e., if he is aware of his potential destructiveness), then he must alter his responses to the other in order to communicate constructively. He alters his communications so as to not make the other's experience more unpleasant than it may be. He is sensitive to the condition of the other person and actively communicates *facilitative genuineness*—genuineness that has constructive effects, not destructive effects, on the relationship.

The Communication of Genuineness

It is necessary to comprehend the meaning of genuineness if you are to *be* genuine. And, it is assumed here that genuineness is a value which is worth pursuing—that to be genuine is a valued way of *being*. However, this way of "being" means very little until it is translated and reinforced through *behavior*. The principal concern here is with the communication of genuineness. Egan (1975) identified *spontaneous, nondefensive, consistent,* and *self-disclosing* behaviors as those which communicate genuineness. These behaviors are described below, with the addition of two other behavioral indications of genuineness: *flexibility* and *immediacy*.

It is important to note at the outset that it is often difficult to practice these behaviors consciously and appear genuine at the same time. For example, how does one "practice" spontaneity? Does not the attempt to be "spontaneous" interfere with its achievement? The reality seems to be that the great effort people often put into being genuine leads to a phony genuineness (Patterson, 1974). Usually, the more people deliberately try to be genuine, the less genuine they become. In some instances, their "genuineness" is little more than a facade of disinhibition—a spectacle of controlled exhibitions. In other instances, what comes under the mask of genuineness is irresponsible assertiveness—"shooting from the hip" with careless and thoughtless communications. In my opinion, the more a person strives to be genuine, the more likely he is to miss it. I do not see how genuineness can be attained or communicated when it is made an end in itself. Rather, the communication of genuineness must occur as a by-product of something else. It must be an effect, not of revealing ourselves to others, but of *revealing ourselves to ourselves*. Indeed, that is the true meaning of genuineness.

Spontaneity

The genuine person is not always focused on himself, and he is not always weighing what he is going to say. He is appropriately "spontaneous" in the sense that he does not censor and filter his communications for social acceptability. Being responsibly assertive, the genuine person is free but not impulsive and thoughtless with his communications. Egan (1975) compared the genuinely spontaneous individual to a skilled basketball player who has acquired an entire repertoire of moves for any given game situation. Almost instinctively, he uses those moves as needed. Virtually no time is taken to weigh the options, because he is so skilled as to be able to select instantly the best response under the circumstances. His spontaneity is almost second nature. To carry the analogy further, the grace and agility of the basketball player is comparable to that of the truly genuine person, who is agile and graceful interpersonally. Those who take refuge behind roles or cling to rigid ways of interacting lack the necessary spontaneity of expression which gives meaning to genuineness. Like the unskilled basketball player, they are limited in the repertoires of response options available to them. And, the responses that are available to them are often unresourceful and sometimes ungracious.

Spontaneity does not mean that you blurt out every thought and feeling that comes to awareness. It does not mean that you react off the top of your head or totally from the pit of your stomach. Unfortunately, this is a specious notion, largely perpetuated by some quasi— and psuedopsychological sources. The very notion of *facilitative genuineness* is incompatible with unrestrained expression. Skilled spontaneity is grounded in perceptiveness and social intelligence—the ability to tell when responses will have constructive or destructive effects on the relationship. Rogers (1957) advised that when negative feelings arise, for example, they should not necessarily be expressed. It is Rogers's contention that negative feelings should be given expression *if they persist or if they restrict your capacity to communicate empathy and positive regard.*

Nondefensiveness

According to Egan, the genuine person is nondefensive in her relationships with others. She recognizes her strengths as well as her limitations and feels no compulsion to guard or hide those deficits. She is not threatened by appearing fallible, nor is she threatened by expressions of hostility from others. For example, if a medical patient told a physician that she didn't think she was being helped at all by his treatment strategy, he could respond in several ways.

SAMPLE A: I think I know what's best for you, so why don't you let me be the judge of what's effective and what's not?

SAMPLE B: Well, it's up to you. But you'd better be prepared to go through the same thing with another physician if you decide to change. He'll see right away how you don't follow instructions.

SAMPLE C: You haven't felt any better since we began. I know it must seem like all of this is worthless. No change, no improvement—I guess I'd begin wondering myself, if I were you.

Samples A and B reflect defensive postures taken by the physician. Sample C is a nondefensive response. He does not appear to be threatened by her challenge, because he is probably at ease with himself and his treatment strategies—their advantages and limitations. A response such as this may indicate that this physician is in the best position to help his patient because his "ego" is not wrapped up in his role. He does not feel a need to defend either himself or his treatment decisions, and he is probably open to suggestions. Furthermore, he is sensitive to the patient's frustration and discouragement, and his communication suggested empathic understanding and respect.

Consistency

The characteristic of consistency probably comes closest to what Rogers had in mind with the original concept of congruence. Egan describes consistency as the manifestation of few discrepancies—between one set of "notional" values (good ideas) and another set of "real" values (suggested by the person's actions), between thinking or feeling one way and saying another, or between acting with discretion one time and indiscretion on another occasion. For instance, if a colleague asked you what you really thought of him, how would you respond? Consider some possibilities:

SAMPLE A: Well, to tell you the truth, I think you're a total bore. You're always talking about your wife and your "darling" little children, as if everyone around here came to work just to find out how they're doing. You never want to hear about anything we do, and I'm sick and tired of it—and that includes you and your cute little family.

SAMPLE B: Oh, well—I think you're—uh—really a—great—guy. Why are you asking me this, anyway? I mean, what do you want me to say?

SAMPLE C: To be honest with you, I don't see a lot of value in that sort of thing, but I'm glad that you asked me because your uncertainty about my feelings tells me that maybe we ought to take a look at what's going on between us—both ways.

The response from Sample A is painfully blunt and probably destructive. A response like this is like an accident waiting to happen—except it's no accident, it's deliberate. Responses like these suggest that the person welcomes the opportunity to unload his thoughts and feelings without regard for their consequences. Sample B is so halting and hesitating as to communicate that the speaker is not really honest about his true feelings. The second sentence is defensive, in that the speaker is trying to find an "out" by answering the question with another question. He's "begging" the question, as they say. Sample C suggests that the speaker recognizes the person's desire for feedback, but the response tactfully shifts from an evaluative, judgemental mode to a proposal that they work together in taking a look at what's going on between them. The speaker seems to know that evaluations of this kind are potentially destructive to the relationship and that it is probably not in the other person's best interest to reveal everything as requested. As Egan (1975, p. 94) stated: "The phony is filled with discrepancies: he feels things but does not express his feelings, he thinks things but does not say them, he says one thing and does another. The phony is inconsistent."

Self-Sharing

Genuineness implies the capability for deep but appropriate self-disclosure. As a genuine interpersonal response, self-disclosure is offered for the benefit of the relationship and not as a self-satisfying end in itself. Since self-disclosure as the sharing of private information about oneself involves some degree of personal risk and assertiveness, it will be examined in greater detail in the context of responsibly assertive behavior in Chapter Sixteen.

Flexibility

In some ways, the notion of spontaneity suggests an ability to be flexible, to adapt your behavior to meet the demands of different situations. In a narrower sense, however, flexibility of thought and feelings often characterizes the genuine person. That is, the genuine person is not only able to adapt his behavior outwardly, he is capable of shifting his way of thinking and "going with" feelings as they arise. He does not rigidly adhere to a single way of looking at things, approaching things, or thinking about things. His empathic skills enable him to look at, approach, and think about things as the other person might. Where feelings are concerned, he is able to get in touch with them as they emerge, and, as they change, he is in tune with his transforming personal experience. Just as he does not cling to a single way of thinking, neither does he fail to follow the course of changing feelings within him.

Flexibility also involves the ability to shift attention on demand. The genuine person is capable of shifting focus from herself to others and back, as needed. She listens neither solely to the other nor solely to herself during an interaction, for she can attend to the other's communications as well as her own reactions to those messages. In brief, she adapts cognitively and affectively to the total flow of communication.

Immediacy

Immediacy, the focus on the here and now of the interaction, is a condition to be discussed separately later. Here, it is useful to note that immediacy involves the individual's reflection upon a *current* aspect of (1) some thought or feeling within herself, (2) some thought or feeling about the other, or (3) some aspect of the relationship. The outward expression of immediacy may take various forms—all of which appear to be elements of genuineness. The individual's constructive expression of experiences in the here and now of an interaction represents an effort to bring out in the open something that has not been readily apparent or brought up by the other. This kind of genuine expression of covert experiences tends to facilitate communication and promote the further development of the relationship. In many instances, unexpressed feelings about the other or about the relationship may inhibit open and effective communication. For example, consider the obstacles to communication between two people in the exchange below. Aaron and Nick have been working together in the same department for several years, and they know each other fairly well. After being on duty for two hours one evening, Aaron approaches Nick:

> AARON: Nick, we've been here for 2 hours and you haven't said a single word to me. You haven't even looked me in the eye tonight. Whenever I come near you, I get the feeling, like I feel right now, that you're mad at me. I feel really uncomfortable even mentioning it, because I don't know what's going on with you tonight.

NICK: What's *"going on"* with me? Nothing's *"going on"* with me! If I don't speak for a while, does there have to be something "going on" with me? Maybe there's something "going on" with you! [Turns and walks away]

From the dialogue itself, we could safely assume that Nick was inhibiting the expression of whatever thoughts and feelings he was experiencing. His communication posed an obstacle to open and genuine interaction because he was not being congruent in what he was experiencing and what he was saying. His nonverbal behavior also suggested a lack of congruence. Aaron, on the other hand, expressed his feelings of the moment in an attempt to bring out in the open whatever it was that Nick was not expressing directly. Aaron was also trying to generate discussion about their relationship in the here and now. In doing this, Aaron communicated genuineness, since he was not hiding or covering up his current experience of Nick.

Implementing the Condition of Genuineness

Carkhuff (1969) revised a tentative scale for measuring genuineness, originally developed by Truax (1962a). Both Truax and Carkhuff (1967) indicated that the measurement of genuineness is perhaps the most difficult of all the core conditions of relationships. The format of the scale for measuring "facilitative genuineness in interpersonal processes" (Carkhuff, 1969) is the same as that used to measure respect and empathy. It is a scale which defines five levels of genuineness, beginning at a very low level where the individual presents a facade or defends and denies private experience and continuing to a high level of congruence where the individual is freely and deeply herself.

Level One

At level one, there is evidence of a considerable discrepancy between the individual's private experience and his verbal communications. Where there is no discrepancy, the individual's responses are used in a destructive fashion.

At level one, the individual is clearly defensive and his verbalizations are unrelated to what he is feeling at the moment, or his only genuine responses to the other person are negative. There may also be notable contradictions between the individual's verbal statements and vocal or nonverbal cues (e.g., an individual who says he is not angry while his jaw clenches, his lips purse, his body tenses, and the knuckles on his clenched fists are white).

PATIENT: Can I ask you a question?

NURSE: Sure, fire away.

PATIENT: Well, it's about the way I acted when I was withdrawing—when I—you know, when I was going through the "DTs." I guess I made it pretty hard on all of you—I mean, having to be strapped down and all

NURSE: [Interrupts] No, it wasn't any big thing.

PATIENT: Well, I'm just so embarrassed—humiliated is more like it. I guess I just wanted to know some things about what I did. No one told me why I had to be restrained. I mean, what was I doing? I know I was out of it for a while, but it's all confusing to me. Did I act really crazy?

NURSE: No, you were just a little disorganized and confused about things.

PATIENT: People don't get strapped to their beds just because they're "a little confused." You were here, what did I do?

NURSE: Look, I don't think you'd really want to know. It would probably upset you. Just forget about it. It's all in the past. No one around here probably remembers, anyway, so let it go. I'll be in to check on you later; now get some rest.

NURSE: [At the nursing station] Hey, Helen, you know that patient in 502? You know, the one who had the DTs the other night?

HELEN: Of course I know him. We were all talking about him at lunch today. It'll be a long time before any of us forget that guy.

NURSE: Well, I was just in his room. He wanted me to tell him all about what he did the other night. Can you imagine that?

HELEN: So what did you tell him?

NURSE: I didn't tell him anything, are you kidding? I'm not going to fill in his memory for him. After all the trouble he caused, he deserves to set with his amnesia.

Level Two

At level two, the individual's responses are slightly unrelated to what she is feeling at the moment, or, when her responses are genuine, they are negative in regard to the other person. The individual may respond in a "professional" manner that has a canned, rehearsed quality to it. Responses are usually based on the individual's prescribed role and not on what she really thinks or feels.

DR. H.: Mrs. J., how do you do. I'm Dr. H. I'm pleased to make your acquaintance. Would you be so kind as to follow me, and we'll go back to my office where we can discuss your referral to this clinic.

[Later]

MRS. J.: . . . So that's basically why I asked to be referred somewhere else. I just couldn't accept what Dr. R. told me. I've been a nervous wreck all week—I'm even nervous now, sitting here with you.

DR. H.: Well, Mrs. J., your anxiety is quite understandable.

MRS. J.: Not to me, it isn't! I'm even taking a tranquilizer three times a day, and I'm still so nervous all the time.

DR. H.: Hm—I see.

MRS. J.: I'm just scared to death that you're going to tell me that I'm psychotic or something—that that's why my medications aren't helping me.

DR. H.: Psychosis is a general term which may refer to any one of a number of gross disorganizations of personality functioning, Mrs. J. From this interview, I have been unable to observe any symptoms suggesting that a diagnosis reflecting gross impairment is warranted.

MRS. J.: Well, at least I'm not psychotic. That's some relief.

DR. H.: Yes, I suppose it would be.

MRS. J.: So what's the verdict? What's my problem? I mean, you said I wasn't crazy, but you can't leave me hanging like this—I mean—I don't feel any different, and I don't think things are going to be any better for me just knowing what my problem *isn't*!

DR. H.: A formal diagnosis seems quite important to you. But, I'm not sure that a diagnosis is really going to tell you what your problem *is*. You see, a diagnosis is a label we attach to a cluster of symptoms that fit together in some consistent way. It is only a name for your problems. Naming those problems won't change them.

Level Three

Level three is the minimally facilitative level of genuineness. The individual may be implicity either defensive or professional, but no "explicit" cues are given to indicate incongruence. She provides no negative cues between what she says and what she feels, but neither does she provide positive cues to communicate a truly genuine response. The individual may listen and follow the second person but really commits nothing of herself to the interaction. Responses appear to be appropriate and sincere, but they do not reflect a deep involvement with the second person.

ADMINISTRATOR: Harold, do you share Lorraine's concerns?

HAROLD: Yes, I'm pretty much in agreement with Lorraine on this. I think we have to give parity to the nursing staff. It's long overdue. I know we're going to have problems if we implement this policy, but I'm optimistic enough—and realistic enough—to believe that we can get it running smoothly.

ADMINISTRATOR: I appreciate your optimism, Harold.

LORRAINE: I think we have to have that kind of attitude. I know I feel very optimistic, and I've felt even more optimistic since last week when you agreed to meet with us. I want you to know that I take it as a positive sign from you. I feel some support from you already, and it's something that, in all honesty, I haven't felt from you before.

ADMINISTRATOR: Historically, the administration's position on this issue has had to remain firm. I can see where our differences would lead you to feel unsupported.

HAROLD: Well, the administration's stance has naturally seemed unreasonable to us because of our conviction that parity is called for by virtue of the nature of the nursing function itself. I, for one, have felt isolated and alienated from the administration, partly because of what I have seen as your rejection of that function. Unlike Lorraine, I can't say as I now feel real support from you. Not yet, anyway. I guess I still feel somewhat alienated, and I feel like it's all up to you to "walk like you're talking."

ADMINISTRATOR: Seems like "trust" is an issue for you.

The administrator was listening and following Harold and Lorraine, and he gave no evidence of incongruence between his words and his thoughts or feelings. Yet, he never gave of himself during the interaction. Both Harold and Lorraine shared some of their personal feelings. While the administrator's responses seemed appropriate, those responses failed to suggest a deep involvement with each person's experiences.

Level Four

At level four, the individual provides neither implicit nor explicit evidence of incongruence. She gives no indication of defensiveness or the presence of a facade. There are positive cues suggesting a genuine response in a nondestructive manner. The individual responds with many of her own feelings, and there is little doubt as to whether she really means what she says.

ALICE: You know, for the last couple of years, I've been thinking about how nice it would be it I could find a job somewhere away from this part of the country. I'd love to move to a city where no one knew me—where I'd have to make new friends and sort of start out all over again.

ALEX: Sounds kind of exciting, and scary, too.

ALICE: Yeah, it is pretty scary. I guess that's what holds me back. The unknown aspect is hard to get around. I'm pretty comfortable here, and everything seems so safe and secure. It'd be hard to give that up—you know, leave everything that's familiar and safe, and then go someplace where everything is strange and different. But, I could always move back here if things got too rough for me. It wouldn't be like I was making a move that was one-way and final.

ALEX: Right. I guess I'd want to know for myself—if I was moving away—that I could move back if I wanted to.

ALICE: Then again, I'd really have to resist that temptation, probably. It's just too easy to turn around and retreat from things when the going gets rough.

ALEX: You'd have to stick with it as long as you could, I guess.

ALICE: Alex, you're from the West coast. Wasn't it hard for you when you moved here? I mean, you ought to know just what it's like.

ALEX: Well, I know what it was like for *me*. I was scared, and I didn't know anyone. I felt all alone. Just now as you were talking about it, it was like those feelings came back to me. It's been a long time, and I don't feel at all like I did when I came here. But, it's not hard for me to remember what it was like—it's not hard to get in touch with feeling lonely and scared.

Level Five

Level five responses suggest that the individual is freely and deeply herself, without pretense or facade. She is open to her own as well as the other's experiences and feelings, whether pleasant or emotionally painful. There are no traces of defensiveness or a retreat to a professional role. At this level, it is not essential that the individual express personal feelings, since her responses to the other's communications make it clear that she is being very much herself.

PATIENT: I'm sure you know all about it, don't you?

NURSE: Well, I guess after working here for so long, I sometimes secretly wish that someone would take care of me and tend to my needs. So, yeah, I know it can be really nice in some ways—that is, to have so many people paying close attention to you. But the other side of the coin for me is that, when someone has to take care of me, I have to do what *they* say—not what I want to do.

PATIENT: It's like you always have to give up something—like you can't have both—you can't do what you want to do and what they tell you to do.

NURSE: Yeah, if you're independent, no one takes care of you, and if you're dependent on somebody—like when you're in the hospital—you're not you're own boss in some ways. It's like, one way or another, you're giving up something.

Empathy

In this text, a strong emphasis has been placed on the centrality of empathy in interpersonal relations—first, as a perceptual skill involving the ability to look at the experiences of another person *as he sees them* and, second, in terms of communicating one's *understanding* of the essence of the other's experiences. Many of the perceptual and communication skills characterizing empathic understanding in interpersonal processes have already been reviewed (see Chapters Four and Thirteen). At this point, you should have a firm grasp of the meaning of those skills and their significance to interpersonal relationships. The perceptual and communication skills basic to empathy are the same skills used to build and maintain facilitative relationships. In this section, empathy is examined from a different perspective. Various potential obstacles to providing the core condition of empathy are outlined for the purpose of orienting you more keenly toward some of the common problems experienced by individuals as they try to communicate empathic understanding.

It is worthwhile to examine potential obstacles to empathy, because when empathy is not achieved or when it is not communicated, other core conditions are adversely affected and the relationship may suffer. What this suggests is that anything affecting empathy also affects the other conditions. The converse also holds, since the core conditions are *interdependent*. For instance, the communication of empathy can be hollow or threatening if the individual is not genuine. In turn, empathy must be based on respect (Patterson, 1974). Increased or decreased understanding may lead to increased or decreased respect and genuineness. The deeper the understanding an individual has of another, the more respect he tends to have for that person and the less need there is to put up a facade. The more genuine and nondefensive the individual is, the easier it is for him to listen actively and achieve and communicate understanding and respect. These conditions, then, are clearly interrelated. As Patterson (1974) suggested, the core conditions appear to interact in such a way as to increase each other. Regardless of the initial level at which each condition is provided, they all grow together—each contributing to the increased levels of the others. Thus, while the following discussion examines obstacles to empathy, it should be noted that these obstacles ultimately impact upon all of the core conditions.

Common Problems in Communicating Empathy

As indicated in the preceding chapter, a common obstacle to the achievement and communication of empathy is the *failure to attend and listen* to the other. One can hardly hope to communicate empathy if he is not paying attention and trying to understand the other person. An individual would also find it almost impossible to be empathic *when he holds little respect* for the other as an individual. Without a measure of respect, the individual may simply not care enough to listen for understanding. And, if a person is *not genuine*, he cannot accurately re-create the experience of the other within his own frame of reference, because that frame of reference is distorted in the first place; second, he cannot get out of his facade or role long enough to put himself in the other's shoes—he's too preoccupied with his own shoes! These are basic and easily recognizable obstacles to empathy. There are others, however, which may be less apparent at first.

Failure to Attain the Minimally Facilitative Level of Empathy

An individual may fail to communicate empathy at the minimally facilitative level (Level Three; see Chapter Four). It is at this level that the expressions of the individual in response to the communicated feelings of the other are essentially "interchangeable" with those of the other, in that they express essentially the same affect and meaning. Below this level, responses may detract noticeably from the expressed feelings and thoughts of the other person. To point up some of the common kinds of responses reflecting the failure to achieve level three empathy, consider the responses (below) to the following communication:

PATIENT: What's really bothering me is how people are going to react to me when they see me. You know—with my face this way—the burns, the—scars. God, I know I look awful! I mean, who can stand to look at this? [Begins sobbing]

HP₁ *Oh, come on, now. Don't cry. It won't be as bad as you think. You're just a little self-conscious right now. It'll be just fine, you'll see.*

HP₂ *That's all right—lot's of people feel just as you do after being burned so badly. But they all get over it sooner or later.*

HP₃ *You don't look so awful to me. What makes you think that other people are going to be turned off?*

HP₄ *Hmm—wish I could do something to make it easier for you.*

In the first example, the health professional (HP₁) was actually responding more to his own discomfort than to the patient's feelings. He attempted to *minimize* the severity and significance of the patient's feelings after first trying to shift her away from what was so urgent to her. Then he *detracted* noticeably from the patient's experience by offering a euphemistic *rationalization* for the radical transformation of her self-image ("You're *just a little self-conscious* . . ."). Finally, he implied *promises* that everything would be fine—almost as a last-ditch effort to cover all the bases to try to get her to inhibit her feelings. For this health professional, it was minimization, detraction, rationalization, and false assurances. HP₁ gave the impression of patronizing the patient, trying to placate her with condescension and expert explanations of the "real" facts—facts which he tried to convince the patient he could see clearly. This health professional may have been better off not responding at all, for at least in that way, he may have left a measure of doubt in the mind of the patient as to whether or not he truly understood.

HP₂ communicated only a vague understanding of the patient's experience. He put the patient's experience in the context of all other burn victims and related to her as one among many and little different from the rest. In essence, he *stereotyped* her experience and failed to respond to her individuality. His response appeared to be inauthentic, for it smacked of cliches.

HP₃ ignored the patient's feelings entirely and responded solely to the message *content*. Then he focused on "other people" and probably forced the patient into a defensive posture by challenging her. But he challenged her with an inane question, for it suggested that he had not understood her communication. had he attended to the feelings and content of the message, he would have known what made her think that other people are going to be turned off.

HP₄ probably had a fleeting sense that the patient was troubled, but he gave no indication of appreciating the real depth of her emotional pain. His statement is reminiscent of the passerby who looks upon someone in need for help and reacts by thinking that someone ought to do something. He was perfectly capable of listening, at the very least. That is a beginning, and that would communicate much more empathy than he suceeded in doing. As it happened, he simply failed to hear beyond the words spoken.

Each of the above sample responses reflects common problems in achieving empathy. Frequently, obstacles take the forms of:

Minimizing the experience of the other by imposing one's own frame of reference to make improper judgements.

Explaining away the other's experience through unjustified rationalizations.

Stereotyping the other's experience by placing it in a broad category of uniformly similar experiences.

Responding solely to message content while ignoring concomitant feelings.

General failure to engage in active listening.

Had these obstacles been avoided in relation to the patient's communications, each of the health professionals could have understood the person's profound sense of helplessness concerning what she perceived as her unsightly and perhaps even hideous disfigurement. They may have also recognized the overwhelming fear, dread, and even terror she felt in anticipation of being some sort of monstrous freak in eyes of others—that her facial deformity would repulse others and cause them to avoid and reject her. Perhaps they would have understood her fear of the unknown and her feelings of hopelessness and despair at being unable to project herself into a future which held anything promising. And, maybe they would have recognized that this tragic mutilation of her face had shaken her entire body-image and overall self-concept—that a radical upheaval of her experience of herself had disorganized her view of herself as a human being. In short, perhaps they would have understood the meaning and significance of her experience.

Faking Empathy

It is not at all uncommon to have difficulty following what someone is saying, even if you're paying close attention. Sometimes a speaker is emotionally excited, distracted, confused, or unable to find and use the right words to express his thoughts. These and other kinds of speaker conditions can adversely affect the effectiveness of his communications. At other times, the listener may not be attending, as was noted earlier. Regardless of the reasons for misapprehensions, it is inadvisable to pretend to understand when you really don't. Faking understanding or empathy tends to lead to greater misunderstanding. The speaker assumes from your pretense that he may proceed with additional information, and you, in turn, become even more lost because you are unable to see the connections between what he is adding and what he has already said. Misunderstanding begets further misunderstanding *unless you admit to it and try to get back on track.* By admitting that you are lost—instead of just going along, shaking your head and saying, "hmm" and "uh-huh"— you communicate to the speaker that you are genuinely interested in getting at the essence of his messages. You also communicate a real interest and involvement with the other person when you reveal your confusion: "I guess I'm lost here. Can you go over that again?"; "I'm sorry. I must have missed something. Can you help me out?"

In their training, counselors are often reminded that they should not take their understanding for granted. They should not automatically assume that they understand everything the person is saying. In everyday interactions, we would be well-advised to keep this in mind, since there are numerous occasions when we think we *probably* understand, but we still have some trace of confusion. In those situations, there are various ways in which we can clarify our understanding and remove our doubts: "Let me see if I've got this straight," "I think what I hear you saying is that . . . ," "I don't know, I may need some help here, but you seem to be saying that. . . ." In each of these examples you demonstrate a tentative understanding which is contingent upon clarification or reinforcement from the speaker. You don't communicate *mis*understanding, but, at the same time, you don't affirm your own understanding—you leave it up to the speaker to affirm it. You try to match your understanding with that of the speaker, who lets you know how close you really are. If you're not very close, then the speaker will let you know one way or another. He may state that what you heard is not what he meant, he may shift his focus and try to understand what is going on with you and why you are having difficulty with his communication, he may cease his communications, or he may even change the subject:

NURSE: You'd think I wasn't able to do anything on my own. She's always checking up on me, following me around, seeing if I did this right and making sure I didn't forget that. It's like she has no faith in me—no trust in my ability to do the job!

TECHNICIAN: That's pretty frustrating for you. I can imagine how irritated you must feel. It's like in training, where you're always being watched. Like everyone knows you're inexperienced, and they all want to make sure you don't screw up. It's like "Big Brother" always has his eye on you wherever you go in the hospital.

NURSE: Well, it's not that bad. I don't feel like *everyone* is watching over me all the time, just her. Even in training, it wasn't like this. My supervisor then was really nice. She gave me room to make mistakes and learn from them. Like the time when. . . .

The technician in this example didn't misunderstand completely; it's just that he was inaccurate and assumed that he understood better than he did. His response influenced the nurse's eventual shift away from her immediate experi-ence and onto a recollection of her training experience.

Technical and Colloquial Language

Empathy is communicated most effectively when your language is in sync with the language of the speaker. That is, your choice of words should reflect that you have assumed the other person's frame of reference.

> PATIENT: I don't know what my doctor thinks of me. Sometimes I get the impres-sion that he thinks I'm crazy—that my problems are all in my head. He treats me like that, sometimes, and I end up wondering if he's right. At other times, he makes it seem as if I'm really on top of my physical condi-tion. He tells me that other people should be as conscious of their health as I am. It's like I get lots of mixed messages from him, and I never know what to expect.
>
> NURSE: Your *perplexity* becomes rather intense when his behavior *obfuscates* the issue of his attitudes toward you.

This kind of response is overly formal and stilted. The average patient may be-come just as confused about the nurse as he might be about his physician. The reality is that sophisticated terms and concepts are not the norm for most peo-ple in our society. They are not used frequently in ordinary conversation, and they are rarely used when relating feelings. There is really no place for these "$10" words in interactions in which feelings are at issue. Words like "obfus-cate" are simply not the kind of terms that communicate empathic understand-ing. Formal, stilted language also suggests detachment from the raw experience of the speaker, and so also does the overreliance on technical terms:

> PATIENT: I don't know why I couldn't have done all this at home. She told me what I needed to do, and I was going to be checking in with her regularly, any-way. Now, here I am laying in a hospital bed—for what?
>
> NURSE: I know it must seem pointless for you to have to follow a *therapeutic re-gime* like that in this *milieu*.

Egan (1975) cautioned counselors against relying on overused formulas for communicating empathy, for this may also constitute an obstacle to what is seeking expression. The same caveat is applicable for health professionals. As an example, consider the following:

> MARY: I can't believe it! I never thought I'd do so well on that exam! Oh, my goodness, it's such a relief to know I passed!
>
> NANCY: You feel elated because you did better than expected.
>
> MARY: You know it! I was so afraid of that exam, I thought I would fail it for sure. I was really uptight all the while I took it.
>
> NANCY: You were afraid because you thought you'd fail it.

Nancy's response has a canned, rigid quality to it. It also borders on "parrot-ing" Mary's exact words. It is as if she was mechanical in inserting Mary's words into the formula described in Chapter Thirteen: "You feel . . . because. . . ." This formula has considerable value when used as an aid in understand-ing the feelings and content of others' communications. It helps you to get fo-cused on the essence of a speaker's messages; but to use the formula as a sole framework for responding is inappropriate and ineffective because it soon appears to others as mechanical, forced, artificial, and just *not you*. It makes you respond "out of character," in an unnatural way. Egan suggested that this formula be used to get at the core of the other's communications, but that it be altered to fit your style of expression. That is, use your own terms—terms that are part of your conversational style. Match those terms with the language used by others, and you'll be more effective in communicating empathy.

There are qualifications to this, however. You should not adopt a conversational style that is characteristic of the other person and not you. This would mean that you avoid using language with which you're not at all comfortable. Communicating empathy does not mean that you sound like the other person, as Rick does in the following example:

> JOHN: Oh, wow, man! Like this place has really got me bummed out, ya' know? Like I'm not into being laid up in the hospital. How about you, man?
>
> RICK: Hey, man, I'm hip to that. You're really freaked, because it's a drag being down, man. I know where you're coming from.

Rick probably could have avoided sounding ludicrous if he had not adopted the same vague jargon John used. It is indeed surprising to me that either one of them could have communicated any meaningful messages by using such a nebulous system of symbols. One can only guess where the experiential referents are for these two people. In this example, we have a clear demonstration of the use of nonspecific language which has minimal communicative value. Problems of language nonspecificity are considered in more detail in the next chapter. Here, it should be clear how empathy is difficult to achieve and communicate when the common symbols are so ambiguous and nondescriptive.

Rambling

Rambling is another obstacle to avoid. Rambling responses are long and involved communications that are much more elaborate than they need to be. They run on and on and gradually shift the focus away from the other person onto oneself. As the individual rambles with what she believes to be an empathic response, the other person becomes inundated with feedback which must be sorted out and reintegrated back into her original train of thought. Being smothered with feedback, the person often feels confused and doesn't know to what to react. The end result often is a curtailment of further self-disclosure. For example, the colleague's response below is long-winded and takes the focus of the interaction from the nurse's experience to his own thoughts. Perhaps while intending to communicate empathy, the colleague became lost in his own ramblings.

> NURSE: I just don't think I'll make a very good supervisor. There are a lot of other people around here who would do so much better than I could in that position. Knowing my limitations as I do, I can't help thinking that I don't have what it takes to fill the position.
>
> COLLEAGUE: What I hear you say is that you're feeling pretty inadequate because of things you know you can't do very well. I've sensed that from you before, like in the staff meetings when you try not to disagree with the

others. It's like, if you do disagree and you're wrong, then everyone will think you're incompetent. But if you just don't say anything, then no one will ever know if you are or aren't. It's really painful for you to be wrong. In some ways, I guess I share those feelings about myself. I know how I've felt a few times when I suggested something at a meeting and everyone shot down the idea. I felt pretty low, and I felt like I didn't want to say another thing.

The colleague started off with a fairly good empathic response, but she spoiled it by carrying it beyond a point of communicating concise understanding. She could have stopped at the end of the first sentence; the rest of her communication was unnecessary and distracting to the nurse. To be effective, empathic responses should be brief, accurate, and specific.

Long-winded, rambling responses should be avoided. At the same time, it is useful to prevent the other person from doing the same, or else the entire interaction takes on the appearance of two monologues being delivered one right after the other. You can prevent the other person's rambling messages by cutting down on the frequency of reactions which reinforce and encourage rambling: "uh-huh"; "really?"; "hmm"; "yeah"; "I see"; and nonverbal reinforcers, such as head nods and smiles. Then you should interject relatively frequent empathic responses. At times, of course, it is necessary to permit the other person to relate his experiences at great length. Under those circumstances, it is best to remain attentive while listening for the central *themes* in what the person is saying. By listening to the pervading themes in her communications, the listener may be able to pull together the salient issues revealed by the speaker. In this way, the listener would not have to respond to each substantive comment made by the speaker. Rather, he could respond to the few significant and overriding affective and cognitive themes communicated by the speaker.

Summary

The obstacles discussed above represent but a select few of the many potential problems in the communication of empathy. To be sure, there are many other common barriers to demonstrating deep understanding: e.g., asking too many questions; cutting off the speaker and jumping in too soon in an effort to prove your understanding; getting too far ahead of the speaker and communicating deep understanding when that level of empathy is not yet appropriate; not getting your vocalizations and nonverbal behavior in tune with your verbal statements; offering interpretive insights based on misapplied psychological theories. Many of these obstacles to empathy are common communication errors in general. They are discussed in relation to conversational skills in the next chapter.

References

Bartnick, R. W. and O'Brien, C. R. Health Care and Counseling Skills, *The Personnel and Guidance Journal*, **58** (10):666–67 (1980).

Carkhuff, R. *Helping and Human Relations. Selection and Training*, vol. 1. New York, Holt, Rinehart, and Winston, 1969.

Carkhuff, R. R. *The Development of Human Resources*. New York, Holt, Rinehart, and Winston, 1971.

Carkhuff, R. R. *The Art of Helping*. Amherst, Massachusetts, Human Resources Development Press, 1972.

Carkhuff, R. R., and Berenson, B. G. *Beyond Counseling and Therapy*. New York, Holt, Rinehart, and Winston, 1967.

Carkhuff, R. R., and Berenson, B. G. *Beyond Counseling and Therapy*, 2nd ed. New York, Holt, Rinehart, and Winston, 1977.

Egan, G. *The Skilled Helper: A Model for Systematic Helping and Interpersonal Relating*. Monterey, California, Brooks/Cole, 1975.

Hansen, J. C.; Stevic, R. R.; and Warner, R. W. Jr. *Counseling: Theory and Process*, 2nd ed. Boston, Allyn and Bacon, 1977.

Jourard, S. M. *Healthy Personality: An Approach from the Viewpoint of Humanistic Psychology.* New York, Macmillan, 1974.

O'Brien, C. R., and Johnson, J. L. Paraprofessional Support for the Hospitalized Patient, *Dimensions in Health Service*, **54**:37–39 (1977).

Patterson, C. H. *Relationship Counseling and Psychotherapy*. New York, Harper and Row, 1974.

Rogers, C. R. The Necessary and Sufficient Conditions of Therapeutic Personality Change, *Journal of Consulting Psychology*, **21**:95–103 (1957).

Rogers, C. R. The Interpersonal Relationship: The Core of Guidance, *Harvard Educational Review*, **32** (4):416–28 (1962).

Rogers, C. R., ed. *The Therapeutic Relationship and Its Impact*. Madison, The University of Wisconsin Press, 1967.

Rosen, J. C., and Wiens, A. N. Changes in Medical Problems and the Use of Medical Services Following Psychological Intervention, *American Psychologist*, **34**:420–31 (1979).

Truax, C. B. A Tentative Scale for the Measurement of Therapist Genuineness or Self-Congruence, *Discussion Papers, Wisconsin Psychiatric Institute, University of Wisconsin*, **35** (1962a).

Truax, C. B. A Tentative Scale for the Measurement of Unconditional Positive Regard, *Psychiatric Institute Bulletin. Wisconsin Psychiatric Institute, University of Wisconsin* **2**:1 (1962b).

Truax, C. B., and Carkhuff, R. R. *Toward Effective Counseling and Psychotherapy*. Chicago, Aldine, 1967.

CHAPTER
FIFTEEN

Conversation and Other Relationship Skills

*"Then you should say what you mean," the March
Hare went on.*
*"I do," Alice hastily replied; "at least—at least I
mean what I say—that's the same thing, you know."*
*"Not the same thing a bit!" said the Hatter. "Why,
you might just as well say that 'I see what I eat' is the
same thing as 'I eat what I see'!"*

Lewis Carroll,
Alice's Adventures in Wonderland

A great portion of our lives is spent conversing with other people. We talk with family, friends, colleagues, patients, casual acquaintances, and strangers. In all of those interactions, we spend time and energy trying to express ourselves in the best ways we can. We want to be understood. Most of us communicate our thoughts and feelings by using expressive styles acquired through casual social experience and some formal language training. From casual experience, we have learned some of the informalities of communication, and from formal education, we have learned how to conform to established practices of speaking. Inasmuch as either one or both forms of communication bring about intended results, they are effective. That is, so far as a person's language furthers his intentions, it is effective. The problem is that we often experience considerable difficulty communicating with people in conversations: we often have a hard time or fail in producing the intended effects of our messages. One of the reasons is that our learned ways of conversing are often ineffective. We have learned how to talk, but we have not necessarily learned how to talk and listen to one another effectively. The plain fact is that, while we may be good at casual chitchat or conventional discourse, many of us are at a loss to know what to say once we have covered the weather, sporting events, literary critiques, or double-digit inflation. Since we spend so much time interacting with people, it is peculiar that we have spent so little time learning how to converse and build solid relationships.

It is just as necessary to have a repertoire of conversation skills as it is to have a wardrobe of clothes. In dress, to follow this parallel, we all develop tastes and preferences for work, sport, and formal clothing. We wear what is attractive to us, what is comfortable, and what is appropriate for different occasions. We need to have and be able to wear various kinds of clothes, and we need to recognize when they are and when they are not appropriate. In a similar way, if we are going to interact with other people, we need to have a repertoire of various communication skills, and we need to know when they are most appropriate. Furthermore, we need to be comfortable in using those skills; they have to "fit" our personalities. An underlying assumption of this chapter is that the kinds of conversational and relationship skills presented here can fit comfortably with most people. They are appropriate whenever people meet people. Like all-purpose clothing, they have a wide range of applicability. If some of these skills are not in your repertoire of communication skills now, they can become readily available to you with a little "tailoring": *practice.* No doubt, some tailoring will be necessary in order to have these skills fit your interpersonal style. Chapter Eighteen provides some useful exercises designed to enhance your chances for improving and/or integrating the specific verbal skills described here.

The first part of this chapter describes the skills of *concreteness* and *immediacy*, two classes of responses which can have strong positive effects on the quality of your relationships. The second part of the chapter reviews a number of specific *verbal* responses which aid in communicating and establishing the core relationship conditions described in the last chapter. Special attention is given to the use of *questions, advice-giving,* and *suggestions.* There are so many components to conversational behavior that it is impossible to consider them all. This chapter outlines many of the more basic skills that contribute to the enhancement of communication and relationships in a variety of settings, not the least of which includes the health care organization.

Concreteness

Have you ever kind of wondered about things? Have you ever felt a little funny about yourself? Have you ever read vague questions that leave you confused about what the writer is getting at? If you're really concentrating on what you're reading here, the first two questions should leave sufficient doubt as to what is meant. The questions are broad, general, ambiguous, indirect, incomplete, and similar to many communications you've probably received and even sent in some of your interactions with others. When the terms comprising the verbal content of messages are vague, they strip the communication of clear meaning. Vague, nonspecific communications lead to vague understanding. Whether the speaker intentionally or unintentionally speaks in broad generalities, the outcomes are the same: listeners are without precise understanding of the messages. Listening to people speak in vague generalities can be frustrating and confusing, not to mention boring. The psychological distance between people becomes greater when ambiguous language precludes understanding and promotes frustration. Though it is not always possible to prevent this from happening by trying to say exactly what you mean, it is possible to improve your overall communication effectiveness by learning how to be clear and specific.

The skill of being clear and specific in communication is called *concreteness*. Carkhuff and Berenson (1977, p. 13) defined concreteness as specificity of expression involving the "fluent, direct, and complete expression of specific feelings and experiences, regardless of their emotional content." It entails the use of specific terminology, rather than general or abstract terminology, in the communication of thoughts and feelings. Truax and Carkhuff (1964) proposed concreteness as a fourth condition for facilitative interpersonal relationships. It is a facilitative relationship condition in that it serves three important functions: (1) it keeps the listener's responses close to the speaker's feelings and experiences; (2) it fosters accurate understanding of the speaker, permitting early corrections or clarifications of misunderstandings; and (3) it encourages the speaker to attend to specific issues (Carkhuff and Berenson, 1977).

When an individual communicates in nonspecific ways that leave you uncertain as to at what she is trying to get, you may help her to get at personally relevant material by responding concretely. This does not mean that you should launch into an interrogation aimed at "just the facts." Concreteness is not synonymous with objective, impartial probing and questioning—i.e., asking the person to be specific about the particulars of who, what, where, when, and how. Information of this sort is available from the individual, and it may be communicated without extensive probing from you. Simple and concrete reflective statements and clarifications from you are often sufficient to influence concreteness from the other person. When they are not effective in pulling out specific terms from the other, questions may then be necessary. But, asking for specifics should be kept at a minimum because of the tendency for the interaction to turn into a question-and-answer session where you are guiding and taking responsibility for the flow of communication. As we will see later, excessive questioning—even in the service of specificity—tends to establish a pattern where the other person accepts a role of answering and you take the role of asking, and when you don't ask anything, the other person may do nothing.

Implementing the Condition of Concreteness

What are the verbal responses which suggest concreteness and which encourage concrete communications from others? Carkhuff (1969) presented a scale for measuring "concreteness or specificity of expression in interpersonal processes." By proceeding through the five levels of this scale, you should be able to get some "concrete" ideas about what constitutes a concrete message, and you should be able to see how specificity tends to beget specificity from others.

Level One

At level one, the first person leads or allows discussions involving only vague and indefinite generalities. The interacting parties may discuss everything strictly on an abstract or highly intellectual level. The listener makes no attempt to move the discussion toward specific thoughts or feelings that are personally relevant to the speaker or to himself. In the following dialogue, Jim is a medical technician who reinforces an orderly's superficial and ambiguous messages. Ben, the orderly, intimates that something is troubling him at a much deeper level than he is able or willing to get at. Neither of them gets at the personally relevant thoughts and feelings that underlie each other's metaphorical communications.

> BEN: Sometimes it seems like you can never be sure about people. You know, like one time you think they're going to do one thing and they do the other, and the next time you think they're going to do something and they don't. No matter what you think they're going to do, it always seems to come out differently than you expected.
>
> JIM: Yeah, I know. They're so unpredictable at times. It really makes you wonder.
>
> BEN: No kidding! I mean, you need to be able to predict *some* things, right? But, man, when you're striking out all the time, you begin wondering about how well you can play the game, you know?
>
> JIM: I know! It's like you're expecting a fast ball and you get a curve. You can't ever be sure when they're going to throw you a curve. But if you wait for it all the time, they'll keep blowing fast balls by you.

Both of these individuals seem to be skirting some personally significant issues about their relationships with specific people in their lives. They are implying that things have happened to them in other relationships, but it is not at all clear what those things are or how they really feel about them. Ben kept his own experiences at a distance and played it safe by not "owning" them. He continuously referred to "you," which is a popular method for denying ownership to one's thoughts and feelings. He used "people" instead of naming the individuals who violated his expectancies; he avoided labeling the specific feelings he was experiencing, as if the events to which he alluded had no emotional impact on him; he spoke about his thoughts and feelings in global terms. Jim, like Ben, relied on abstract metaphors, even when giving feedback. It seemed as if he was talking more about a baseball game than about human experiences. He helped Ben to remain at a safe distance from his feelings by referring to "they" and to "you" as *indefinite references*. If Jim understood Ben at all, it was only in the most fleeting sense.

Level Two

At level two, the first person may lead or allow discussions of material that is personally relevant to the speaker, but the discussions are carried out on an abstract or intellectual level. The interacting persons may identify significant feelings, but they discuss them "intellectually," almost as if the feelings were objects or even subjects for impartial analysis. In the example below, the first nurse encourages a discussion of personally relevant material concerning death, but specific thoughts and feelings are kept at an abstract level.

> NURSE ONE: I really believe that you have to come to terms with your own mortality if you're going to work in this field.
>
> NURSE TWO: I agree completely. I think we all have to take some time every once in a while and think about how we're being affected by the death and dying we're exposed to around here.
>
> NURSE ONE: I think I know how *I'm* being affected—at least I'm pretty sure I do. For one thing, it seems like seeing someone die makes you appreciate health all the more. It's interesting that I sort of take things for

granted and go along without giving much thought to how important life is to me, and then all of the sudden one of my patients dies, and it changes things—I mean it makes you take a different look at things.

NURSE TWO: How true! That's happened to me lots of times. You go along doing your job without giving it much thought, and then something sort of jolts you, and you begin thinking "What's this all about, anyway?"

NURSE ONE: And you can't come up with a good answer, either! Sometimes you even wonder what good it does to be trying to help people when, for who knows what reason, they die. So what have you done for them? Anything? That's another thing you start wondering about.

The first nurse initiated the interaction, and she helped to keep it at a safe level, where neither of them really had to disclose their personal problems around the experience of death and dying. No other issue is more difficult for people to talk about than that of death, particularly their own. No doubt, the nurses' frequent exposure to death brought them close to their own private thoughts and feelings about their own deaths. Perhaps to insulate themselves from the frightening and disturbing realities of their own mortality, the nurses avoided concrete expressions of their personal and deep thoughts and feelings. They talked "about" general effects and reactions to death, without getting down to the essence of their experiences with it.

Level Three

Level three is the minimally facilitative level of concreteness. At this level, the listener will occasionally make it possible for the discussion to center around things that are personally relevant to the speaker. However, there continue to be areas that are not dealt with concretely and areas which the speaker does not develop fully by being specific. Consider the following:

SHARON: I don't know. It's been a lousy day. Things just haven't gone right since I got up this morning. You know, one of those days when nothing goes right.

CLAIRE: Sounds like you're pretty discouraged because everything that could go wrong has gone wrong.

Claire's response is fairly good. It's empathic, and it concretely identifies Sharon's feelings. At this point in their interaction, Claire still doesn't know exactly what has happened to Sharon; she doesn't know the experiences underlying her discouragement. But her response is an invitation for Sharon to elaborate and move to specifics.

SHARON: Well, not *everything*, but a lot of things have gone wrong. A couple of run-ins with my family before coming to work, and then some hassles with a few patients. And, just a few minutes ago, I had a big argument with the payroll office.

CLAIRE: Gee, Sharon, you seem like you have the bases covered with your hassles today!

Claire's response here is lacking specificity. Sharon started to become more concrete in discussing the bases for her discouragement, but Claire took the message back to a vague level. Had Claire reflected a clear recognition of

Sharon's conflicts at home, with patients, and with the payroll office, Sharon may have been encouraged to develop her thoughts and feelings more concretely. As it happened, Claire probably dissuaded Sharon somewhat.

Level Four

At level four, the listener is frequently helpful in enabling the speaker to develop fully in concrete and specific terms almost all instances of concern. The listener is frequently able to guide the discussion to specific feelings and experiences. At this level, the listener provides concrete feedback, which enables the speaker to focus on specific instances of important and personally relevant feelings and experiences.

STUDENT A: I think I really blew it with the instructor.
STUDENT B: You feel like you made a bad impression because of something you did?
STUDENT A: I know I made a bad impression, and I just know it's going to cost me.
STUDENT B: You think he's going to lower your grade because of what you did.
STUDENT A: Right! I mean, I can't say as I blame him. I acted pretty disrespectful to him.
STUDENT B: Sounds like you think you offended him and he'll punish you for it.
STUDENT A: I must have offended him. I was talking with him about my grade on the last exam, and he said something that made me mad—so, I told him off. I just couldn't control myself, I was so mad at him for what he said.
STUDENT B: He must have said something that really hit a sore spot, if you got that mad.
STUDENT A: Yeah, he sure did. He told me that he didn't think I would pass the course. But, it was the *way* he said it! He acted so smug and arrogant! Who does he think he is, treating me like I'm some insignificant dolt who doesn't even belong here!

Level Five

Level five is very difficult to maintain because it is the level at which the individual is *always* helpful in guiding the discussion. He is always concrete in his communications and enables the other person to discuss fluently, directly, and completely specific feelings and experiences. Regardless of their emotional content, the individual involves the other person in discussion of specific feelings, situations, and events.

Achieving Concreteness

As the preceding discussion would suggest, you can help other people communicate more concretely if you are as concrete as possible in your responses. Since it is unlikely that most of us function at level five, where we are consistently concrete across situations, level four seems to be a realistic goal to achieve. But there are other ways in which we can facilitate concreteness from others.

One way is by not allowing the other person to ramble (Egan, 1975). If the other person engages in long, drawn out storytelling, she will necessarily include a good deal of vague and irrelevant material. Sometimes people may need to talk on, for various reasons. But, most of the time, it is not necessary and not conducive to deep understanding to reinforce long-windedness. Ideally, interactions should include a significant amount of dialogue. You can come closer to this ideal if you respond frequently, concisely, and concretely. This usually enables the other individual to gain some sense of direction in his communications.

Another way to achieve concreteness is to come right out and ask the person for specifics. This approach may indeed be indicated when you are not getting direct clarification of vague information. There are many ways to elicit specific information without resorting to a barrage of questions. For example, "I was wondering what he did that annoyed you so much," "Please tell me about those habits you have a hard time breaking," "I'm not really sure what you mean by 'far out.' " And, even when questions are used, they can be asked in ways which require the other person to speak clearly and in detail, so that further questioning becomes unnecessary.

Immediacy: "Processing" the Interaction

If you speak to me and then I speak to you, we've made a communication "loop." We have interacted verbally. Let's imagine that this loop begins with your intention to let me know that you like me. You feel comfortable enough with me to show your liking by kidding around and joking. But let's say that I see your kidding around as inappropriate, and I become annoyed with your behavior. Now, even though I'm annoyed and want you to know it, I may not want to hurt your feelings. So, I try to let you know as delicately as I can that I don't appreciate your humor at the moment. You, in turn, think that I didn't understand your intentions, and you feel embarrassed and hurt. As the communication loop draws to an end, you begin feeling more distant from me, and you apologize and become silent. If we were to let things settle in this way, we might have a hard time with each other in subsequent encounters. However, we may be able to improve our relationship by "processing" our current interaction.

Immediacy refers to the ability to discuss the current interaction between yourself and another person. It involves direct and mutual processing of how you are feeling and behaving in relation to one another. The processing may focus on where you stand in relation to the other person and where she stands in relation to you. Or, it may involve a discussion of what is happening "right here and right now" in *this* interaction context. The latter emphasis is not on where you stand with one another generally, but on what is taking place in the immediate present of the conversation.

Carkhuff (1969) viewed immediacy as one of the most critical factors in terms of communicating an understanding of the complexity of events between two persons. It is a complex response, in that it appears to be contingent upon the proper integration of certain other skills. Immediacy seems to be related to *empathy* in the sense that one must understand oneself and the other in order to recognize and call attention to the current interaction. The open expression of one's experience of the other and of the interaction itself appears to be an aspect of *genuineness*. That same expression is an aspect of *self-disclosure*. And, pointing up the effects of the other's behavior in relation to oneself may often require skills of *confrontation*. Finally, the communication of all of these in the here and now of an interaction takes "guts"—it requires a measure of responsible *assertiveness* to come forth with one's thoughts and feelings as they pertain to the other person.

Pulling together the above skills to communicate immediacy is a very difficult task. Immediacy is perhaps one of the most difficult communication skills to master. Most people are not used to focusing on the immediate present of their interactions, let alone calling attention to the interpersonal process. When relevant thoughts and feelings arise during our interactions, it is much more common for us to block their expression. Sometimes, of course, this is the most appropriate thing to do; it is neither practical nor necessary always to focus on the here and now. But there are many occasions when we could benefit greatly from using immediacy responses in our interactions with others. As to exactly when immediacy should be used is rather hard to say, for it depends on your perception of the current situation, your social intelligence in judging what is and what is not appropriate, and your interest or willingness to facilitate more satisfactory relationships with particular people. Some occasions when immediacy is usually helpful are described later. In general, however, immediacy is typically used as a form of *invitation* to another person to deal openly with some issue that would allow both of you to become more satisfactorily involved with each other. The invitation comes in the form of a *disclosure of your thoughts or feelings about the issue, your perceptions of how the relationship stands right now*, and a *direct or indirect challenge to the other to deal with the issue now so that the relationship will not be adversely affected*. This kind of invitation frequently promotes a dialogue enabling individuals to take a look at what is going on between them for better or for worse. By calling attention to the immediate interaction, they can come to recognize what they are doing in relation to each other and thereby free themselves to move forward in and with that relationship.

Implementing the Skill of Immediacy

Early scales for measuring immediacy in interpersonal relationships (Mitchell and Mitchell, 1966; Leitner and Berenson, 1967) were revised by Carkhuff (1969). Like the other scales developed by Carkhuff, the scale for measuring "immediacy of relationship in interpersonal processes" is a five-point scale ranging from low to high or facilitative levels of immediacy.

Level One

At level one, the verbal and behavioral expressions of the first person disregard the content and effect of the second person's expressions that have the potential for relating to the first person. The first person may ignore any communication that deals with her relationship to the other person. In brief, the individual simply passes over all messages that are related to her. The patient representative (PR) in the dialogue below ignores a patient's messages that are quite direct and deal with their relationship.

> PATIENT: I'm not sure if I want to continue with all of this. I don't think we're getting anywhere because I don't feel that you're interested in helping me that much. You seem to have such a blasé attitude about all of this, and I haven't seen anything being done since you first came to see me. I just don't think you're helping me.
>
> PR: I know you're probably wanting to see some results, and I can understand how it can all seem so futile. We've had some personnel changes recently, and that has slowed things down on our end. Just try to be a little patient. Things will work out.

Level Two

The verbal and behavioral expressions of the first person disregard "most" of the second person's expressions that have potential for relating to the first. Even if the second person, for example, a patient, is talking about health professionals in general, the health professional to whom she is talking may remain silent or just not relate the message content to herself. At this level, the first person may consciously choose to ignore most of the communications that are related to her, as seems to be the case with the nurse in the following interchange:

> PATIENT: I've spent a few times in hospitals in my day, and one thing that just irks me to no end is to have someone come in like you just did and wake me up to give me a damned pill!
>
> NURSE: Here, Mr. Black, you need to take this.
>
> PATIENT: I have to take it, I have to take it! You are always coming in here and telling me what I "have" to do! You're like some kind of robot when you come in here—no "hello, how are you today"—nothing but orders! Do you ever talk to people?
>
> NURSE: Well, if you don't take this pill now, I'll just have to come back again in a few minutes.
>
> PATIENT: Back again with more orders—no thanks! I'll take it! Hey, why don't you have that other nurse do this stuff for you? She's nice and friendly. I get along pretty well with her.
>
> NURSE: Hmm, maybe I will.

Level Three

At level three, the verbal and behavioral expressions of the first person may *appear* to resemble immediacy, but they do not relate to what the second person is saying about the *immediate moment*. The first person may make literal responses to the other person's expressions—responses which suggest that she has missed the other person's reference to her, specifically. In the example below, Randy is not closed to expressions of immediacy, but he does not go beyond a minimally facilitative level of communicating immediacy:

> PAUL: Randy, I feel really good about what you said in there just now. I feel like you're supporting me, and I really need it. I didn't get the support I expected from the others, but you weren't afraid to say what you thought.

RANDY: That's all right, Paul. You've got some legitimate points, and I just think they're too strong to ignore.

PAUL: Well, I think so, too. But I don't think the others want to admit it. I didn't think I had a friend in the world in there, until you defended my position. I guess I just feel like I can really trust you.

RANDY: I'm glad you feel that way, Paul. Thanks for your confidence. But, again, you deserved to be supported. I agree with every point you brought up in there.

Level Four

At level four, the verbal and behavioral expressions of the first person appear cautiously and tentatively to relate the other person's expressions directly to their relationship. She tries to relate the other person's responses to herself but does so in a rather guarded and provisional manner. Level four immediacy is reflected in the responses of a newly appointed supervisor in the dialogue below:

SUPERVISOR: Mary, I get the impression that you're trying to tell me something.

MARY: Okay, I'll come right out with it. I don't see how you qualify for this job. You've been here only three years, and I've been here for ten. We've worked together on the floor, and now I'm supposed to take orders from you. I can't accept that.

SUPERVISOR: You can't accept me in a position of authority.

MARY: I can't accept the fact that you give me orders. It's like, all of the sudden, we're different—we're not equal anymore.

SUPERVISOR: All of the sudden I'm "more equal" than you?

MARY: Put it any way you like. The fact is that I have a hard time relating to you as my supervisor. Even standing here right now, it really bothers me.

SUPERVISOR: Maybe it's the position. I mean, you and I got along before. I get the feeling that you might be jealous of my position, and maybe I'm not coming across to you as I used to. Maybe I'm acting differently, and I don't know it.

The supervisor appeared to be willing to deal with Mary's immediate concerns, but she was rather cautious about it. Her final responses included an accusation of jealousy, and such accusations often have the effect of bringing more negative feelings to surface in the other. She could have admitted her own confusion about how she was coming across without blaming or suggesting that Mary was jealous.

Level Five

At level five, the verbal and behavioral expressions of the first person relate the second person's expressions directly to their relationship. The first person may also directly and explicitly relate the other's expressions to himself. He is not hesitant in making explicit interpretations of his behavior, the other's behavior, and/or their relationship as it stands at the moment. In the dialogue below, Steve communicates immediacy at level five.

RICHARD: I'm never sure where I stand with anyone around here.

STEVE: That also means right here, doesn't it, Richard?

RICHARD: Yeah, I suppose so. I've thought about mentioning it before, but I—well, I didn't think it'd do any good, I guess.

STEVE: You're saying that you didn't know if I'd be up front with you. Like right now, you don't seem to be all that sure of me—you don't know if I'll be honest with you.

RICHARD: I want to trust you, and I want to be able to hear what you have to say—but—I—

STEVE: You don't feel all that comfortable with me yet. There's still some doubts about me and where you stand with me. Coming right out and asking about it doesn't guarantee that I'm going to be honest with you.

RICHARD: Yeah, it's like, if I came right out and asked you what you thought of me, well, I figured you'd be on the spot and you'd just say what you thought I wanted to hear. But if I didn't ask, I felt like I'd never know one way or the other.

STEVE: Well, Richard, right now I feel good that you let me know what you were thinking. I don't feel like I have to hide anything from you, because I really don't feel like you've put me on the spot. I guess I've wondered at times about where I stand with *you*. So, I'm actually glad you took the initiative. Because you did, I feel pretty comfortable with talking about our relationship. It's funny—I guess I feel a little closer to you already.

The issue of trust is one which often calls for the use of immediacy responses. Dealing with the here and now of the interaction is a useful way of entering into a dialogue which enhances interpersonal trust. There are other occasions, however, where immediacy is equally helpful.

Special Occasions for Immediacy

Immediacy is appropriate when you see that either you or the other person are not giving voice to thoughts and feelings having relevance to the current interaction. The following are some sample immediacy responses in different situations where they might be useful. These occasions for the use of immediacy are by no means all-inclusive. Furthermore, they are *general* occasions when certain issues seem to be involved in the relationship. The sample responses themselves are taken out of context, and, as you know, the context of the interaction may determine their appropriateness as communications.

Dependency

In relationships where you perceive others to be overly dependent on you for taking responsibility which is rightly theirs or which should be shared, immediacy may be a useful means for bringing the issue out in the open. In some cases it may be useful in relationships with patients, but you will need to exercise careful judgement and recognize the potential negative effects of calling attention to a condition (dependency) which is common to some degree among most patients. That is, some patients may need to be dependent on you psychologically.

SAMPLE COMMUNICATION: You know, these staff meetings are for us to deal with whatever you people want to deal with. But as I sit here today, thinking back on the meetings we've had this month, it occurs to me that *I* have been the one to choose all of the topics. I'm thinking that you're waiting for me to bring up *another* topic today—and I guess I just have! What's happening in here?

Personality "Clashes"

Sometimes, when we don't know why two people aren't getting along with one another, we attribute their interpersonal conflicts to "personality clashes" (as if that explained it!). No doubt, you have been involved in some of these "clashes," and you'll probably find yourself in conflict with someone again. Unable to find the reasons for your difficulties, you may have resigned to irreconcilable differences and continued to interact with those persons in cold or even antagonistic ways. One way with which similar problems can be dealt in the future is by using immediacy carefully to get at the unverbalized issues that underlie the so-called personality clashes. (Here we are only concerned with immediacy as *one* approach to conflict resolution.)

> SAMPLE COMMUNICATION: It's obvious that you and I have some different approaches to things around here. We seem to go in different directions, and, at times, we even seem to work against one another. Your approach seems to be orderly and "by the book," and my approach is pretty flexible. I prefer doing things in my own flexible style, and when you're so controlled and orderly, I get frustrated, because I don't feel like we're making as much progress.

Resistance or Reluctance

Certain patients are resistant to various facets of medical treatment. They may be angry about having to be hospitalized, and they may be resentful of being ill. Certain other patients may not be resistant, but they may be reluctant to assume the role of patient in the first place. Indeed, if given the choice, most patients would avoid such a role. When in that role, however, resistance or reluctance may take many shapes. Obvious examples include open hostility, uncooperativeness, noncooperative silence, defensiveness, strained civility, and even sarcasm. Less obvious forms of resistance or reluctance include overcompliance, attempts at distraction, denial of experiences or physical symptoms that are apparent to others, and even ingratiation. In using immediacy to work through resistance or reluctance, you must first realize that *you are not the cause*. You just happen to be the most convenient target for its expression. The patient's resistance is *not* your responsibility; it is his. But you may begin to lower that resistance by relating to the person in the here and now of your experience of him.

> SAMPLE COMMUNICATION: I sense from the way you've acted since I've been in here that you're pretty angry. At least, that's how you come across to me. I feel kind of uncomfortable about it, because I was hoping that we could get along with each other.

A Final Word on Immediacy

The decision to use immediacy responses should be based on various considerations. For one thing, you should ask yourself during the interaction, "What is she (he) trying to tell me that she (he) is not putting into words?" If you suspect that the answer has relevance to the interaction and to the relationship in general, immediacy may be quite useful in digging it out. Second, overuse of immediacy is just as inadvisable as not using it at all. Relationships hardly go anywhere when individuals are "stuck" in the here and now—they can see neither where they have come from nor where they may be headed. In fact, in the early phases of relationships, immediacy may be contraindicated because of the danger of "coming on too strong" to the other person. As relationships are just beginning to develop, individuals may find such directness rather threatening. Effective use of immediacy rests upon other skills, such as observation, listening, social intelligence, communication know-how, as well as the ability to integrate empathic understanding with genuineness, self-disclosure, confrontation, and assertiveness—no easy task, indeed!

Basic Verbal Responses

There are specific classes of verbal responses that are frequently used to implement the core conditions of relationships. This section describes those responses primarily in terms of their verbal *content*, on the assumption that "what" is said to another person is of paramount significance to the relationship, in general, and to the immediate interaction, in particular. The content of a person's speech transmits important information about what she thinks, how she feels, and how well she understands and respects her own as well as another's experience. Inasmuch as there are limitless possible responses which facilitate communication, no attempt is made here to be comprehensive. Rather, seven classes of verbal responses are presented: *recognition responses, restatement and paraphrasing, reflection, clarification, interpretation, explanations,* and *silence.*

Recognition Responses

Recognition responses are simple indications of basic understanding. They tell the other person that you are listening and that you are following and involved in what she is saying. Brief statements, such as "Yes," "I see," "I understand," or "I hear you" are examples of recognition responses. More common, however, are vocal utterances, such as "uh-huh" and "mm-hm." Although not words, these sounds are commonly taken as expressions of understanding. They may also indicate encouragement from the listener to continue with a verbal communication:

> SPEAKER: I talked with her husband, thinking that he may be able to get through to her—

LISTENER: Mm-hm.
SPEAKER: And he said he'd do whatever he could to help us out.

Recognition responses, particularly vocal utterances, are used so frequently and automatically that they may at times have uncalculated effects. For example, "mm-hm" may be taken by the speaker as an indication that the listener approves of what he is saying, that he agrees with his views, or that he is being urged to continue taking the discussion in an irrelevant direction. Recognition responses like these function as reinforcers for the speaker. Therefore, it is important to avoid overusing these kinds of responses because of the potential for inadvertently communicating something you do not intend. Moreover, it is necessary to be aware of your *stimulus value* in general: your potential for influencing the communications of others through all of the messages you may send—verbally, vocally, and nonverbally. It may be hard to believe, but a simple "mm-hm" can indicate that you have made a judgement, even if you really haven't. If you want to communicate respect for the other person, if you want to demonstrate a nonjudgement attitude, then you should be alert to the possibility that such a minor utterance can at times suggest the exact opposite of what you intend. Simply consider the possible effects of this health professional's communication:

PATIENT: I've been living with this pain for so long, I can't remember when I didn't have it. I guess, after a while, you just learn to live with it.
HP: Mm-hm.
PATIENT: But that doesn't make living any easier. I mean, it'd be so much better if I didn't ache all the time.
HP: Mm-hm.
PATIENT: The microsurgery I had last year helped for a little while, but now it's worse than ever. I don't want to stay on pain killers, and I don't want anything my doctors have recommended. A friend of mine said he could get some DMSO for me, so I'm just going to start using that and forget all this other nonsense.
HP: Mm-hm.

While this health professional may have communicated a basic understanding of the patient's plight, he may also have unwittingly reinforced her decision to substitute self-administered DMSO for medical treatment.

Restatement and Paraphrasing

Simply put, *restatement* involves using the other person's words to echo exactly what she said to you. This type of response is effective when it is used *infrequently*. Otherwise, you will sound like a parrot, unable to respond in any way but the most mundane and mechanical fashion. When used infrequently and at carefully selected places during an interaction, restatement responses have the potential for serving a "mirroring" function. They may allow the other person to hear what she has said and perhaps reflect on her own words to determine if they actually communicate what she means to communicate. Restatement responses may also say to the person that her words are appropriate and expressive, that there is nothing wrong with the way she is verbally communicating.

To communicate empathic understanding, however, restatement should be used sparingly because it does not always indicate that *you* understand the essence of the message. Continuous use of restatement may be a corruption of empathy and a genuine annoyance to the speaker, who begins thinking that you're playing games with him: "I know, I just said that!"

Paraphrasing is one step removed from direct restatement. It is a form of translation in which you pull together the chief points expressed by the speaker and then reword the verbal content. As you might expect, this, too, can have adverse effects on an interaction when used excessively:

> MIKE: If I have to cover for him one more time—He's always expecting me to cover for him—and I always do. I never say no. Doesn't do him any good, and it makes me furious!
>
> BILL: He always wants you to cover for him, and you do. You never say no, and that makes you really mad and doesn't do him any good, either.
>
> MIKE: Doesn't do either of us any good. I mean, I'm just prolonging it by protecting him. He's got to face up to his responsibilities sooner or later. I'm not going to take him by the hand all the time!
>
> BILL: It doesn't help either of you when you protect him all the time, and he doesn't accept his responsibilities. He's got to learn to stand on his own two feet.
>
> MIKE: That's right. That's what I said. Something wrong with my words or something?

Reflection

Reflection goes beyond recognition and paraphrasing. It is a form of responding which lets the other person know that you hear and understand the content of the message *and what is behind it*. It is a form of responding which implies recognition and which may include elements of paraphrasing. Reflection involves a grasp of the full meaning of a message and a verbal statement which reflects the essence of that message. The essence of the speaker's message is found in both the cognitive and affective components. It is easy to reflect the message content back to the speaker by stating the basic thoughts or facts he expressed, and it is easy to fake understanding by doing so. But the key to the kind of response described here is *empathic* understanding, which is hard to fake. It is hard to fake an understanding of another person's deep feelings and the meaning of those feelings to that person. One cannot use reflection effectively if the significance of the other's feelings is not understood.

The technique of reflecting feelings was first clarified by Rogers (1942) in his book *Counseling and Psychotherapy*. It entails uncovering and summarizing the feelings that lie beneath the other person's comments. It is a technique that has been alluded to in previous chapters in terms of using the formula *"You feel . . . because. . . ."* This kind of response is a reflection response. As indicated earlier, however, this format for responding reflectively should not be overworked. The above phrase can wear thin during interactions. It is probably best to use this phrase *covertly* as a guide and then *overtly* in combination with other verbal openers and introductory phrases, for example:

Seems like you . . .
I hear you saying that . . .
Sounds like you . . .
You sure are . . .
It's like you feel . . .
As I get it, you . . .
So, you're saying that . . .

As Schulman (1978) suggested, when an individual regularly reflects feelings with any one phrase, the result is either the other person's deaf ear or communications of annoyance. Reflection is more effective if the verbal openers are varied and not rote or mechanical. In addition to using verbal openers like the ones above, reflection may take the form of direct labeling of the feelings communicated, as in the following example:

LESLIE: Doctor, I am so tired of having to do *everything* around the house. If I don't see that things get done, they just don't get done—period! Sometimes, I just feel like screaming! My blood pressure soars, I know! I'm just fed up with it all!

DOCTOR: You've had it. You're frustrated, tired, you feel used, and you're really uptight about all of it. It can be very depressing for you when it seems that no one cares about the price you have to pay for them.

Another alternative is to speak as if you were the other person:

HARRIET: Maybe I'm self-conscious—too self-conscious. I don't know. I just don't feel like I can relax around them, you know. I just never know what they're thinking.

LAURA: I feel like I have to be "on" when I'm with the other nurses. There's something about them that makes me uptight. I never know where I stand with them. Maybe they don't like me.

When restating and paraphrasing the speaker's communications, you focus more on content, and when reflecting, you focus on feelings as well. You attempt to put into words what the other person has stated intellectually or descriptively. You do not interpret her communications in the analytic sense, for you add nothing of your own to those communications *except your empathic understanding and sensitivity*. Nor do you guess or assume that the person means something or is feeling something that she may not mean or feel. You simply voice the emotions that are there. How can you be sure what emotions *are* there? If you are truly attending and listening, and if you are able to re-create the other's experience in your own frame of reference, *you will know* what the person is experiencing. If you're not attending, you can't be sure what she is feeling. As you can see, all of these responses—including reflection—are dependent on basic attending and listening effectiveness.

Clarification

Clarification involves untangling, unraveling, clearing out, and illuminating what the other person has said or tried to say. It is a response which is used when the speaker's messages are confusing or generally unclear. Clarification responses may take the form of a question beginning with "do you mean that . . ." or "are you saying that . . ." along with a rephrasing of all or part of the other person's message (Cormier and Cormier, 1979). For example:

> GARY: I tell you, things have gotten a lot more stressful for me since I took this position. I feel so unsure of myself. I keep wondering if I'm doing all right—if I'm making it, you know? I've never had to made so many decision; someone else always made them for me. I'm having a hard time sleeping at night, I'm drinking more than I used to—everything just gets all jumbled up. And, I've lost 20 pounds. I look like hell, I know. Do I look like a person who's really together and on top of things?
>
> JOEL: Are you saying that things are really stressful because you don't feel confident enough to make decisions without worrying about whether you've done the right thing?

Joel used this clarification response to make Gary's message explicit and to check out the accuracy of his own perceptions of the message. Making the speaker's message explicit is one of the purposes of clarification. But the second purpose is to check out what you heard. Therefore, clarification responses should be tentative and not final or absolute. You simply can't be sure if your perception of the speaker's message is accurate. You need the speaker to confirm for accuracy. When using clarification, then, avoid jumping to quick conclusions about the speaker's message. Present your clarification response in a way which gives the speaker room to verify what is and what is not accurate. You may do this in various ways, without using the above verbal interrogatives as openers. The following are some examples of other clarification responses to Gary's communication:

> You mean, since you took this job, you feel like you have all the responsibilities and decisions on your shoulders?

> One thing for sure is that you're really worried about how well you're doing. I think I hear you saying that the hardest thing about it is having confidence in your decisions. Right?

With either of these responses, you could check out the accuracy of what you heard Gary say. These responses could also encourage Gary to elaborate his thoughts and feelings and move you both toward a clearer understanding of his current experience.

Interpretation

There is a fine line between clarification and interpretation (Patterson, 1974). Clarification is used to sort through implicit or explicit message elements in order to eliminate ambiguity or confusion. Interpretations go beyond this in dealing with the *implicit* parts of messages only. Moreover, interpretations of the speaker's implicit messages are *hypotheses* about the meanings of the facts or experiences which the speaker does not talk about directly. An interpretation, then, is a statement about the possible relationships among various explicit and implicit messages. As such, interpretation requires that you put something of yourself into the response. It means that you impose meaning as you see it. The responses described to this point do not require that you do this—they do not require you to speak from your own frame of reference to provide the other person with different insights and perspectives.

Actually, not all interpretations are based in your own frame of reference. When you interpret the meaning of the speaker's communication in terms of the possible meaning it has *for him*, you are responding partly from his frame of reference. Conversely, when you interpret his communication in terms of what it means *to you*, you are responding mainly from your own frame of reference. When the latter form of interpretation is used, you expect the other person to respond *to you*. By interpreting in terms of how things seem to you, you shift the focus from the speaker to yourself. It makes a difference whether you interpret meaning for yourself or for the other person. If it is his experience that is the focus of the interaction and you then interpret that experience for what it means to you, that person must then turn his attention to *your understanding of his experience*. It may be important that you understand that experience, but it is probably more important that he understand his own experience, so that he can become clearer in subsequent messages. Another purpose of interpretation is to help the speaker to entertain different ways of looking at his own experience, so that self-understanding may improve and facilitate more effective communication of experience.

There appear to be some dangers in using interpretations. They can be threatening to the other person, suggesting that you are analyzing her and making her the curious object of speculation. The other person may even get the impression that you know more about her than she does, and that can be disturbing because it can make her feel transparent and vulnerable. It could influence her to let you do all the talking because you seem to have all the answers. The effects of interpretations vary, depending on the quality of the relationship, the speaker's willingness to deal with other points of view, and the accuracy of the interpretation itself. For your purposes as a health professional, it is probably more appropriate to use interpretation responses with colleagues than with patients whom you may not know as well. To people who are not familiar with you, interpretations can be quite threatening. Even with colleagues, interpretation may be inadvisable if your relationships are not strong enough to support them.

Cormier and Cormier (1979) suggested some "ground rules" for using interpretation responses. The first ground rule is to be careful about *timing*. Interpretation should be used after you and the other person have become comfortable with each other. Also, if the other person appears to be ill at ease with what is being discussed, she may not be ready for or receptive to interpretations. Therefore, if you suspect that your interpretation may cause the other to feel anxious, then you should probably avoid it. You simply do not want to offer an interpretation for something that is too painful for the other person to deal with. Finally, you may find it more helpful to use interpretations when you know there is ample time remaining for both of you to process and follow up on the other person's reaction to your hypothesis. It is usually not advisable to offer an interpretation just before you end the interaction, for you may leave the other person "hanging" with a statement that is perplexing and bothersome. You need time to check for accuracy.

A second ground rule is to make sure that your interpretation is *supported by the speaker's actual message* instead of your own biases and projections. As Cormier and Cormier (1979, p. 89) put it, you must "be aware of your own blind spots." As an example, if you have had an unfortunate experience with a certain physician and are biased against that physician, be alert to the possibility that this bias could affect the way you interpret other people's statements about the physician. If you aren't careful, you could easily suggest to a patient, for example, that she would do well to find another physician. This may be in the best interest of no one.

Third, don't use interpretations to "show off" your perceptiveness or psychological expertise. It is not helpful. Interpretations are used to present helpful information; they are not vehicles for mental exhibitionism or, as Ivey and Gluckstern (1976, p. 135) call it, "psychological imperialism."

Finally, interpretations should be offered in much the same way as clarification responses. They should be stated as *tentatively as possible*. For example, you might start the interpretation with "Could it be that . . .," "Do you think that . . .," "I'm wondering if . . .," "Maybe you . . .," or "Something that occurs to me is . . . ." Once your interpretation has been delivered, check for accuracy, just as you do upon offering clarification responses.

Explanations

The fine line between clarification and interpretation continues through explanation responses. Explanations are not statements about how things *might be* (i.e., interpretations); rather, they are statements about how things *are*. As such, explanations are generally impersonal, logical, and matter-of-fact (Benjamin, 1969). Statements about the way things are are often helpful in encouraging the other person and yourself to take a look at reality and stay there. Explanations can take various forms: statements about causes; statements about behavior; statements about your thoughts, feelings, or position on an issue; or statements about situations or relationships. They are useful when it is apparent that you and the person with whom you are interacting would benefit by recognizing some specific facts. As you might expect, they are more effective when provided in concrete terms.

Silence

In their authoritative text, *Pragmatics of Human Communication*, Watzlawick, Beavin, and Jackson (1967) pointed out that one cannot *not* communicate. Even when you are silent, you are responding to the here and now of an interaction. "Silence is never silent" (Yalom, 1975; p. 386). It is a response which has meaning in the context of the interaction and may therefore communicate as much, if not more, than verbal statements. What silence actually communicates depends on how it is perceived by the other person. To someone who is quite vocal, silence on the part of the other person may be welcome. To someone who requires frequent feedback, silence may be ambiguous and confusing. Indeed, for the latter individual, silence may suggest that the listener is not really listening, that she is not interested, or that she does not understand what is being expressed. Uncertainty about the meaning of the listener's silence may lead the speaker to terminate the conversation. Or, if the speaker concludes that the listener's silence indicates that she is not open to or disapproving of what is being revealed, he may close himself off to subsequent interactions with that person. It is hard to say how silence will be perceived by a speaker. It is not hard to predict, however, that if silences are not punctuated by verbal or vocal indications of understanding and acceptance, the effects will be largely negative.

Unless you are very certain of how your silence is being perceived, you should not remain quiet for long periods. Even one minute of silence while the speaker is talking can be very lengthy, depending on the circumstances and the needs of the speaker (see Figure 15.1). This is not to suggest that you should always avoid long silences. Rather, you should be alert to the possible interpretations given to your silence and adjust your behavior accordingly. This requires that you pay close attention to the speaker and learn to be sensitive to how she is reacting to you as you say nothing. Keep in mind, however, that, as a properly used and timed response, silence may leave the speaker with the thought that "someone actually took the time to listen to me."

Using Questions Appropriately and Effectively

It is commonly accepted that the logical bridge between confusion and understanding is a question. "If you don't understand something, *ask*" is the maxim we have internalized. Surely, you'll get the answers you need, if only you ask; if not, ask more questions! After all, if one question is good, more are better! "You'll never know unless you ask" is what we have learned. While the intent of these directives seems clear enough, observation of people in conversation would often suggest that something has been lost from translation to practice. Simply consider what we do with our questions to others: we ask questions where we already *know* the answers, we ask questions where we *want no* answers, we ask questions where there *are no* answers, we ask questions which *confuse* people, we ask questions that are *irrelevant*, we ask questions that put others on the *defensive*, we ask questions which beget only *more questions*. Moreover, the ease and frequency with which we ask questions often makes our interactions look like cross-examinations—question and answer sessions where our interest in digging out the facts overrides our concern for promoting real understanding.

The issue is not whether we should eliminate questions from our interactions. Obviously, questions serve a purpose, and they are necessary at times. The issue can be stated, as a matter of fact, in the form of a question: "Will the question I am about to ask this person be *helpful* in increasing *his* understanding *and mine*?" The plain fact is that sometimes questions are just not helpful in this regard. Therefore, some ground rules for using questions appropriately and effectively might include:

> Challenging the value of the question you are about to ask.
> Determining if other responses can elicit the same information.
> Recognizing the potential effects of your question on the other person and on the flow of communication.
> Deciding on the type of question to use.

This section provides some suggestions on the use of questions. Something to keep in mind is that questions are usually more effective in facilitating communication from others when they are used as *supplements* to responses, like reflection, clarification, and interpretation. In any event, they should be used sparingly and only as part of your verbal responsiveness.

Open and Closed Questions

The *open* question is broad and allows the other person sufficient latitude in interpreting and responding to the request for information. It is a question which places no restrictions on what views or feelings he may express. The open question is useful in getting the other person to discuss a broad range of personal information. Some examples of open questions would be: "What are your thoughts about the surgery you're scheduled for?"; "The new schedule is something we'll have to adjust to. What do you think about it?"; "Would you tell me about what happened last night?"

The *closed* question is narrow and usually limits the other person to a direct and specific answer. Often, closed questions require simple yes or no answers. Contrast the above open questions with the following closed questions: "Are you concerned about your surgery?"; "Do you think you'll have any problems adjusting to the new schedule?"; "Do you want to tell me about what happened last night?" Clearly, the closed question is less effective in encouraging the other person to talk openly about an issue of concern to either of you.

Direct and Indirect Questions

Open questions are also *direct* questions. They are to the point, and there is little doubt as to the information requested. Closed questions may also be direct and to the point. Direct questions are outright requests for information, and they may be open or closed.

> *Open-Direct:* Would you tell me about your previous experience?
> *Closed-Direct:* Do you have any previous experience?

Indirect questions do not appear to be questions at all. They don't sound like questions, but they are nevertheless implicit and perhaps disguised requests for information. Indirect questions give the other person full reign to take the responses into any and all personally relevant dimensions of his answer. Now, contrast the following indirect questions with the open and closed questions from above:

> You're scheduled for surgery in the morning. You must have a lot of things running through your mind.
>
> With your surgery coming up, I suppose it's a pretty stressful time for you right now.
>
> I'm wondering what you think about the new schedule.
>
> This new schedule is a big change for all of us. You must have some thoughts about it.
>
> I'm really curious about what happened last night.
>
> You were here last night. I'd sure like to know what happened.

Again, although indirect questions may not seem like questions at all, they show an interest in learning available information. They leave the door wide open for the other person to respond.

Loaded Questions

Loaded questions are forms of closed questions that are sometimes used to back another person into a corner. The person asking the question already knows the answer, so she has stacked the deck against the respondent by implying the desired answer (Tubbs and Moss, 1980). Most of the time, loaded questions are emotion-laden and force the other person into a defensive posture. They also tend to annoy the other person. An example of a loaded question is: a psychology graduate student to a professor in class, "Isn't it true that personality tests are not always reliable?" In situations like these, by the way, I have found it useful to respond to the implicit message and not to the question itself. It is sometimes helpful to respond to that message by asking your own *indirect* question: "I'm actually hearing a statement from you and not a question. I'm also wondering about the point you're trying to make." Responses such as these tend to bring the issues out in the open for further discussion. Besides, when you're the target of a loaded question, it may be necessary to turn the tables.

If you're concerned about building or preserving quality relationships, then it is advisable to not ask loaded questions like the ones above.

Restrictive Questions

I have chosen the word "restrictive" to describe the question which puts absolute restrictions on how the other person may answer. Restrictive questions may sometimes be rhetorical and at other times steer the respondent toward agreement just to avoid the questioner's disapproval. In the former case, such questions are actually more than rhetorical, because the questioner presumes that his answer is the one which the respondent would give had she really been asked a legitimate question (e.g., "No one would deliberately mix up those medications, would they?"; "We all know what the administration is up to, don't we?"). In the latter instance, restrictive questions may force the respondent to agree with the questioner if she knows what's good for her (e.g., "It's either a layoff or you go on second shift. You don't mind second shift do you?"; "You don't want to go against your doctor's orders, do you? You're upset right now, but you don't want to go and do something that's going to make your condition worse, do you?").

Double Questions

Double questions present the respondent with two inquiries at the same time. They force the individual to choose between the inquiries and respond to one and then the other, if he can remember what the other one was by the time he finishes responding to the first: "What was the other part of that question?" Under these circumstances, double questions can be quite confusing for the respondent and, subsequently, for the questioner:

> NURSE: Are you feeling better now? Do you want some water?
> PATIENT: No.
> NURSE: You don't want any water?
> PATIENT: No, I do want some water. I mean, yes, I want some water. I'm not feeling well.

When questions need to be asked, they should be asked one at a time, not together.

Multiple Questions

Multiple questions, whether "fired" one right after another or successively after each answer, trap the respondent in a bombardment of inquiries that leave her confused and perhaps even irritated. Here is an extreme example of rapid-fire questions that hardly promote rapport between the questioner and the respondent: "Why don't you tell me? Don't you trust me? Are you mad at me or something? Is it something I said? Is there something you want me to do differently? Can't you say something? Are you just going to close yourself off to me?" With all of these questions, the respondent may indeed close himself off. If he responds to any of these questions, it would depend on which of them happened to "stick' in his short-term memory.

When each answer is followed by another question, the questioner is still bombarding the respondent. What tends to happen is that a pattern of question and answer is established, where the respondent learns to wait for a question before responding. He may adjust to the pattern in such a way that, when no questions are posed, he remains silent. Think for a moment about what might happen when a person presents a problem to you, and you fall into a pattern of asking one question after another. After asking all of your questions, that person might then expect you to come up with a solution, or at least offer a brilliant insight—and why not? You've gotten all the information you need. If you have no solution, if you can't offer something to enhance the person's understanding of his problem, what you have accomplished by asking so many questions? The other person may wonder about this, but even if he doesn't, *you probably will.* After asking all those questions and eliciting so much information, you may feel obliged to say something insightful, even though you do not know where to go with that information. More often than not, we feel compelled to give some expert advice, regardless of how well we really understand the situation. We will turn to an examination of advice-giving shortly. First, it is important to give special attention to a question that is used more frequently than any other: "why."

"Why" Questions

"Why" is an interrogative that is used in the search for causes and reasons. It is a word which serves a useful purpose in our search for information. But, it also is a word which frequently connotes blame, condemnation, disapproval, or displeasure (Benjamin, 1969). Because of these implications, the word often forces individuals into defensive postures in which they feel as if they are being challenged to explain themselves. The word "why" tends to put people on the spot: "Why did you let him talk to you like that?"; "Why didn't you set that IV?"; "Why did you do that?" Questions like these are probes that ask for information the person may not have or which he may be unwilling to share. Consider the effects of this question, for example: "Why do you feel that way?" This is a judgemental response presented in the form of a question. By implication, the person should not feel as she does. The individual therefore may become defensive, hostile, close herself off, feel ashamed or embarrassed, try to muster up all the explanations and rationalizations of which she can think. Regardless of other reactions, one effect is to take her *away* from the experience of those feelings (when feelings are at issue) and force her to *think* about them. In other words, she is diverted from an affective experience to an intellectual exercise where she must present causal explanations. She may be robbed of an opportunity to understand those feelings by "staying with" them.

The word "why" may have a place in interpersonal communication, however. It can probably be used effectively when the respondent perceives no threat from the questioner—when the question is seen as a genuine and simple attempt to get information. This may require that the relationship is characterized by high levels of the core conditions. Nevertheless, the same information you seek with the word "why" can be obtained with other questions using the words *what* or *how*. For example, instead of asking, "Why are you so upset about that?", "Why do you bother with him?", or "Why didn't you follow instructions?", you can get the same information in these ways:

> What is it that is upsetting you so much?
> How is it that this has upset you like it has?
>
> How is it that you tolerate so much from him?
> What do you think makes you put up with him?

What do you suppose influenced you to disregard the instructions?
How did you happen to bypass the instructions?

Of course, you needn't start your questions with either "what" or "how." Indirect questions may work even better.

A Final Note on the Use of Questions

Some summary statements can be offered on the use of questions. First, it is important to formulate meaningful questions and to use them for a specific purpose. Therefore, it is helpful to question your questions. Determine if they are necessary, be aware of their possible side effects, and choose the most appropriate form for stating your questions. Second, remember that open questions and indirect questions tend to elicit more information than closed or direct questions. Third, avoid loaded questions, double and multiple questions, and restrictive questions. Fourth, the fewer questions you ask the better; you will avoid setting a pattern where your role is seen as inquisitor and the other person as respondent. Fifth, avoid "why" questions where possible.

Questions should be stated as clearly, concretely, and succinctly as possible. Once you have used them, *listen* to the response. After all, you have asked for information, so you will need to pay attention to the answer. If you find that you're not listening closely to the answers provided by the other person, then maybe you should give some thought to the real purpose of your questions.

Advice and Suggestions

In your position as a health professional, some of your responsibilities necessarily involve giving advice. Directly or indirectly, threateningly or non-threateningly, you will need to tell someone what to do and what not to do from time to time. In the vast majority of your relationships—whether those relationships are professional or personal—you will neither need nor be expected to render advice. People may need advice when they are incapable of making decisions on their own. But most people are capable of making their own decisions. Whether advice should be offered under those circumstances is a matter of debate. In my opinion, advice-giving should be kept out of most of our relationships most of the time, even when it is requested. Listening and showing involvement may be more important to people than any advice you may offer (Figure 15.1). The reasons for my position are many, but I would like to stimulate your thinking on this issue by inviting you to take some time to consider each of the following questions. After thinking about each question, you should be able to appreciate the bases for my position on this issue.

1. What are the *grounds* that give you the right to offer advice?
2. Are people capable of surviving *without* your advice?
3. Can people benefit from advice they cannot understand from *their own* frames of reference?

Figure 15.1

4. Are you *really helping* someone by giving advice?
5. Does this person have the *resources* to follow through on your advice?
6. Do you *know enough* about the person's situation to give meaningful advice?
7. Do you have enough factual *information* and sufficient *knowledge* to give sound advice?
8. Is it important to you to give advice? If so, what is the basis for the *value* you place on advice-giving? From where does your need to give advice come?

9. How do you feel when your advice is *rejected*?
10. How do you feel when your advice is *accepted*—and *doesn't work*?
11. What if your advice does work and the individual keeps *returning* to you for more advice?
12. What effect does *bad advice* have on your relationship?
13. If you like to give advice, is it because you regard your way of doing things as the *best way*? Do you want others to be like you?

No one can benefit from advice unless it is meaningful to her and unless she can understand it from her own frame of reference, not in terms of how *you* see the situation. Even if a person asks for advice, she is not receptive to it until and unless she has had the opportunity to express her concerns to the point of then being able truly to *listen* to the advice she claims she wants. Many times, people will seek advice, and, when they get it, *they run with it*. They try it out, and if it fails, then they may never seek you out again. Other people ask for advice and then systematically reject each piece of advice offered: "I've tried that"; "No, that won't work"; "I've tried everything." If they had actually tried everything, then they wouldn't be asking for advice; they would have found the answer for which they were looking. Still others do not want to take responsibility for their own behavior, so if they fail at one of their own solutions, they have only themselves to blame. It is much more convenient to put the responsibility on someone else, because if they fail, then they can blame the advice-giver. By falling into the trap of giving advice, you may be communicating to the other person that you have no faith in his ability to work things out for himself: "Yes, I will tell you what to do, because you are not competent enough to discover your own solution." There are most assuredly numerous dimensions to advice-giving, most of which contribute nothing of positive value to interpersonal relationships.

Suggestion is related to advice-giving, but it is toned down, tentative, and sometimes vague (Benjamin, 1969). Suggestion is a means by which an individual offers a *possible* course of action for another, but it is left up to the other person to accept, reject, or entertain his own ideas. Moreover, the purpose of suggestion is not really to give solutions, but to stimulate the other person's thinking, so that he may decide for himself:

> I have a suggestion to make, if you'd like to hear it. It's just an idea, for what it's worth. If you put together the rough draft of the proposal by next week, you could show it to the staff during the staff meeting. They could give you some feedback, and then you could make any changes that were necessary. With their input, you'd have a better chance of addressing the major issues as thoroughly as possible. I don't know what you think of the idea; I'm sort of thinking out loud. Think it'd do you any good?

Contrast this with direct advice-giving:

> What you need to do is to get the draft prepared by the next staff meeting. Then bring it in and get some input from the others. Take their ideas and use them in beefing up the proposal, so you've got all the bases covered. Really, that's what I think you should do.

Granted, there may be a fine line between advice-giving and suggestion; but you should be able to see that suggestion is a process which involves the other person in decision-making. It is a way of throwing out possible courses of action for the other individual to weigh and do with whatever he chooses. It neither demands agreement and compliance nor does it present the other person with a threat of criticism should he choose to reject the suggestion. You simply state your opinion and then process it with the other person.

Summary

The skill of being clear and specific in communication is called *concreteness*. Concreteness is also a facilitative relationship condition that fosters accurate understanding of the speaker, keeps the listener's responses close to the speaker's feelings and experiences, and encourages the speaker to attend to specific issues. A five-point scale was outlined as a guide for assessing the level of concreteness in interpersonal communication, and *level three* was identified as the minimally facilitative level. Concreteness is achieved by being specific in one's own statements to oneself, by preventing the speaker from rambling and discussing irrelevancies, and by directly asking for specific information.

Immediacy is a response involving a process commentary of the here and now of an interaction. It is a mutual processing of participants' behaviors in relation to one another in the immediate present of an interaction. Immediacy is a complex response contingent upon skills of empathy, genuineness, self-disclosure, confrontation, and assertiveness. On a five-point scale of immediacy in interpersonal processes, level three is the minimally facilitative level. Occasions for the use of immediacy include, but are not limited to, dependency relationships, personality clashes, and resistance or reluctance.

Seven classes of verbal responses were discussed in the chapter. *Recognition* responses were described as basic indications of understanding. *Restatement* and *paraphrasing* were defined in terms of echoing or translating the speaker's words. *Reflection* goes beyond recognition and paraphrasing to let the other person know that you hear and understand the message and what is behind it. *Clarification* responses involve illuminations of what the other person has said or has tried to say. *Interpretation* goes beyond clarification to deal with the implicit portion of messages. Interpretations are essentially hypotheses about the way things might be. *Explanations* are statements about the way things are. *Silence* was described as a nonverbal communication with important implications for both participants in an interaction.

A separate section was devoted to the use of questions in interpersonal interactions. Different kinds of questions were discussed: *open* and *closed* questions, *direct* and *indirect* questions, *loaded* questions, *restrictive* questions, *double* questions, *multiple* questions, *"why"* questions. Some suggestions for the use of questions were offered.

The final section addressed the issues of *advice* and *suggestions*. It was argued that advice-giving is usually invaluable and even potentially damaging to interpersonal relationships, whereas suggestions may be justified when presented in ways which allow the other person sufficient leeway to choose whether or not to follow them.

References

Benjamin, A. *The Helping Interview.* Boston, Houghton Mifflin, 1969.

Carkhuff, R. R. *Helping and Human Relations. Selection and Training*; vol. 1. New York, Holt, Rinehart, and Winston, 1969.

Carkhuff, R. R., and Berenson, B. G. *Beyond Counseling and Therapy*; 2nd ed. New York, Holt, Rinehart, and Winston, 1977.

Cormier, W. H., and Cormier, L. S. *Interviewing Strategies for Helpers: A Guide to Assessment, Treatment, and Evaluation.* Monterey, California, Brooks/Cole, 1979.

Egan, G. *The Skilled Helper: A Model for Systematic Helping and Interpersonal Relating.* Monterey, California, Brooks/Cole, 1975.

Ivey, A., and Gluckstern, N. *Basic Influencing Skills: Participant's Manual.* Amherst, Massachusetts, Microtraining Associates, 1976.

Leitner, L., and Berenson, B. G. *Immediate Relationship Scale: A Revision.* Unpublished research scale, State University of New York at Buffalo, 1967.

Mitchell, R., and Mitchell, K. M. *The Therapist Immediate Relationship Scale.* Unpublished research scale, Michigan State University, 1966.

Patterson, C. H. *Relationship Counseling and Psychotherapy.* New York, Harper and Row, 1974.

Rogers, C. R. *Counseling and Psychotherapy.* Boston, Houghton Mifflin, 1942.

Schulman, E. D. *Intervention in Human Services*, 2nd ed. St. Louis, C. V. Mosby, 1978.

Truax, C. B., and Carkhuff, R. R. Concreteness: A Neglected Variable in the Psychotherapeutic Process, *Journal of Clinical Psychology*, **20**:264–67 (1964).

Tubbs, S. L., and Moss, S. *Human Communication*, 3rd ed. New York, Random House, 1980.

Watzlawick, P.; Beavin, J. H.; and Jackson, D. D. *Pragmatics of Human Communication.* New York, Norton, 1967.

Yalom, I. *The Theory and Practice of Group Psychotherapy*, 2nd ed. New York, Basic Books, 1975.

CHAPTER
SIXTEEN

Toward Responsible Assertive Behavior

Ofttimes nothing profits more
Than self-esteem, grounded on just and right
Well managed.

John Milton, *Paradise Lost*

In what ways are socially skilled persons different from unskilled persons? Psychologists have studied this question for several years, and research findings have pointed up various behavioral differences. Identifying precise behavioral differences depends on one's definition of social skill, characteristics of persons being studied, interpersonal situations studied, and the measures being used to assess those differences. With all of these variables and no fine and clear distinction, the research has suggested that skilled and unskilled individuals are probably best differentiated on global impressionistic ratings by trained observers. And, when trained observers give their impressions of skilled versus unskilled persons, a frequent common denominator is *assertiveness*. Observation suggests that socially skilled people tend to be more assertive than unskilled people. What this means is that skilled people usually evidence more pronounced emotional expression and more forceful speech, communicate their thoughts more clearly, initiate and maintain conversations more frequently, listen more carefully to others, demonstrate respect for others and for themselves, disclose personal information more freely, strive to meet their own needs without violating the rights of others, and demonstrate willingness to help others meet their needs without violating their own rights. Socially skilled people are neither passive nor aggressive; they are assertive.

The socially skilled health professional is a *responsibly* assertive person. She acts in her own best interests and in the best interests of health care recipients and staff by communicating openly, honestly, appropriately, and without being overly self-conscious and anxious. Some unskilled health professionals are nonassertive, and their relative passivity reinforces their sense of frustration and powerlessness in a health care system where they feel like an insignificant cog in a gigantic wheel. They often tend to feel sorry for themselves because of their perceived victimization and inability to exercise any control over events. With increased resignation and nonassertion, many of these individuals finally explode into angry outbursts, burn out, or break down. Others simply continue to plod along, never quite meeting their own needs as they want, and never quite wanting to meet others' needs. Some health professionals are not at all passive; they are generally aggressive. They interact in domineering, controlling, and authoritative ways which leave others feeling that their dignity has been violated in some way. They find it difficult to establish and maintain relationships wherein there is mutual understanding, respect, and trust. Their interpersonal contacts may be just as unrewarding as those of the nonassertive person.

Being a responsibly assertive person is not a matter of "can or can't." It is a matter of *choice*. As Douglas and Bevis (1979, p. 258) suggested, the health professional who chooses assertion as a plan of action "will increase self-confidence, maintain individuality, be accountable for quality care to clients, and not hesitate to negotiate with those in control of organizations." Assertion makes it possible to enhance other interpersonal skills in ways which facilitate the processes of meeting one's own needs and the needs of others.

In this chapter, assertion is discussed in terms of a limited range of skills. It is beyond the scope of the chapter to provide a comprehensive examination of the numerous components of assertion and assertion training. For example, a basic skill underlying assertive behaviors is the ability to reduce one's own level of anxiety. This skill is not examined here, but a means for learning to control anxiety in situations where assertion is appropriate is described in Chapter Seventeen, and so also are exercises for *rehearsing* assertive responses. A cognitive understanding of the skills presented here will not suffice: practice is necessary.

What Is Assertion?

In one of the foremost texts on assertive training, Lange and Jakubowski (1976, p. 38) defined *assertion* as follows: "Assertion involves standing up for personal rights and expressing thoughts, feelings, and beliefs in direct, honest, and appropriate ways which respect the rights of other people." Assertive messages about what one thinks, how one feels, and how one sees a situation are expressed *responsibly*, in that no attempt is made to overpower or degrade another person. At the same time, assertion involves respect for one's needs and rights as well as those of others. A goal of responsible assertive behavior is to get and give respect in ways which preserve the integrity of oneself and others and which leave room for satisfying each other's needs. This view of assertion contrasts somewhat with the popularized notion that it is a way of getting what you want without consideration for the rights and feelings of others. Such behavior is not only irresponsible, it is not assertive.

A central issue in the definition of assertion has been the distinctions between "assertive," "nonassertive" (passive), and "aggressive" behavior. *Nonassertion* is the failure to express honest thoughts, feelings, and beliefs when such expression would be appropriate. It involves passivity and a subordination of one's own rights to expression. Nonassertion may involve the assumption of a subservient role in an interaction, where the individual expresses herself in a manner which can be easily disregarded by others. She may be diffident, apologetic, and communicate, in effect: "My thoughts and feelings don't matter. Yours do. I don't count. You do. I am inferior; you are superior." Another term for acting in a subservient manner is deference. Deferent behavior is often seen in those situations where the individual acts as if the other person is right or better by virtue of age, experience, sex, race, or any number of other characteristics, including professional "status." For example, deference is often observable in the ways in which some nurses permit certain physicians to dominate them or unjustly assert their authority. Nonassertion shows a lack of respect for one's own needs and rights, or it may reveal a lack of respect for another person's ability to deal with disappointments, handle her own problems, take responsibility, and so on (Lange and Jakubowski, 1976). The usual purpose of nonassertion is to avoid conflict by appeasing or placating the other person.

Aggression is often mistaken for assertion. However, aggression is typically distinguished from assertion in terms of its disregard for the rights of others. Although an individual may stand up for personal thoughts or beliefs, he is doing so in an aggressive way if he humiliates, belittles, or degrades the other person in the process. This mode of expression is inappropriate and dishonest. The goal is to win out over the other person, to dominate or control, to establish oneself as superior in some way, and to weaken the other person's ability to express herself. Aggressive communications say to the other person, "This is what I think, and that is all that matters. If you think differently, then you are a fool. What I am is important; what I want counts. You do not matter because you are nothing." The following statement is an aggressive communication reflecting the speaker's attempt to overpower and embarrass the listener:

> What do you mean, "We've done it that way for years?" So what? Are you so stuck in tradition that you can't see any other ways of doing things? It's time for a change. We have to find new ways of doing things. Your attitude burns me up! It's people like you that perpetuate the problem!

Other distinctions have also been suggested. For example, Rich and Schroeder (1976) argued that assertion is the skill to seek, enhance, or maintain *reinforcements* in interpersonal situations through expressions made in the face of risks of losing those reinforcements or perhaps even incurring punishment for open expression. Bandura (1977) considered *expectation* to be an important aspect of assertion—that is, what the individual expects the other person to do as a result of his personal assertion. Some writers (e.g., Cheek, 1976) have stressed that assertion in one *context* may have a different meaning in other contexts. Assertive messages of a black ghetto person may have a different effect when delivered to a middle-class white than they would to a black peer. In health care settings, assertive expressions of nurses that go beyond traditional role behavior would probably be defined differently by people having different expectations of what is and is not appropriate nursing behavior for that context. And, as McFall and Twentyman (1973) suggested, the *appropri-*

ateness of assertive behavior can be assessed only according to its *effects on others*.

Reasons for Nonassertion and Aggression

Lange and Jakubowski (1976) pointed up five major reasons for nonassertive behavior. One reason stems from the *inability to distinguish assertion from aggression*. Assertiveness is often equated with aggressiveness, which, in turn, is viewed as socially dangerous. Consequently, many individuals suppress their assertive needs, because open expression is considered socially unacceptable. A second reason is an *inability to distinguish nonassertion from politeness*. According to Lange and Jakubowski, many people act nonassertively under the mistaken notion that such behavior defines politeness and consideration for others. They have learned, for example, that it is impolite to end a telephone conversation with someone who has called them, to enter ongoing conversations between two other people, to ask dinner guests to leave when the evening has grown late, to agree with compliments, or to praise themselves. These sorts of behaviors are neither impolite nor aggressive; they are assertive. Third, people often act nonassertively because they *believe they have no right to act otherwise*. They may feel that they are not entitled to express certain thoughts or feelings. For example, nurses often see themselves as second-class professionals without the right to act on *their own* convictions in strategic circumstances (Douglas and Bevis, 1979). Fourth, individuals may *fear negative consequences* of assertion. In health care settings, this may involve a fear of criticism, reprimand, or undue conflict and stress. Fifth is the mistaken belief that one is being *helpful to another person by acting nonassertively*. This frequently occurs in families of alcoholics where no one confronts the alcoholic about his drinking. It is assumed that it is better to be quiet and not address the problem. In point of fact, this kind of nonassertion is "enabling," in that it tends to reinforce the alcoholic's drinking. He assumes that, since no one has confronted him, his drinking is not problematic. To these bases for nonassertive behavior we might add that some people may simply *know of no other way to act*. They have learned an interpersonal style of passivity, and they are devoid of the skills to act differently.

Aggression is a multidimensional phenomenon with no single set of antecedents or consequences. It is not possible to identify all of the possible reasons why someone would communicate in an aggressive manner. Some conditions do appear to be more common than others, however. For example, some individuals may communicate aggressively as a means for overcoming and *compensating* for actual feelings of powerlessness and inferiority. Responding aggressively to others is a way of trying to gain control and achieve a sense of competency and superiority. Second, some people may act aggressively during an interaction because they are ashamed of acting *nonassertively on previous occasions*. They may feel as if they have allowed people to dominate them in the past, and, weary of this, they overcompensate by going to the other extreme. They may also act aggressively as a check against passivity. If they don't come across strongly and forcefully, they assume, others will naturally take control of the interaction. Third, we have all noticed people acting aggressively when such behavior was "out of character" for them. Because they usually don't respond in such a way, current aggressiveness is probably due to *emotional difficulties* or, as many of us like to say, "stress": "It's just not like her to act that way. She must be under a lot of stress." Fourth, some people believe that aggression is the best *means to an end*. It is taken for granted that if you want to get ahead, you have to be aggressive and "step on a few toes." They may believe that it is the only way to get through to people. Just as nonassertion can represent an ingrained pattern of relating to the world, so also can aggressiveness. Finally, there are those persons whose interpretations of assertion have been distorted by "pop psychology" versions of the concept. Many popular "self-improvement" books seem to convey a vision of reality which informs people of their perfect right to act in any way they choose in furthering their own interests. Manipulation, intimidation, and seduction are seen as strategies for exploiting relationships under the guise of assertiveness. Such behavior is not assertive; it is irresponsible aggression.

Reasons for Assertion

A major rationale for assertive behavior is that it tends to increase one's *self-respect*. Responsible assertive behavior supports the individual's perception of herself as a valuable human being who is entitled to her own experience of self, an experience which need not be subordinated at the expense of a loss of self-respect or dignity. All too often, individuals are preoccupied with securing the respect or, more specifically, the approval of others. To secure others' approval, it is often considered necessary to be nonassertive, to deny and suppress honest thoughts and feelings which, if openly expressed, would result in disapproval. However, not only does nonassertiveness fail to guarantee approval, it may even produce disapproval. The nonassertive person may be pitied rather than approved, with pity eventually turning into irritation and even disgust (Jakubowski-Spector, 1973). With increased assertiveness comes increased self-respect and increased self-confidence. The person who respects herself is not dependent on the approval of others. Being freer to respect her own self, she becomes freer to respect others, their needs, wants, expectations, beliefs, feelings, and values. Because she does not force her own experience into subservience, neither does she disregard the experience of others.

A second major reason for assertion is that it enables the individual to *meet his own needs and wants*. Many nonassertive people are so concerned with meeting the needs of others, protecting others feelings, and fulfilling other's expectations, they eventually become bitter and resentful because they have not attended to their own needs. There is most assuredly nothing wrong with meeting other people's needs—as long as individuals do not continuously devalue their own.

A third reason for assertion is that it tends to promote open, honest relationships characterized by *mutuality*, or give-and-take. The assertive person realizes that to have her own needs met in a relationship, she must be ready to meet the needs of the other. To the extent that she is able to satisfy some of her needs, she finds it easier to satisfy the other person's needs. Taking care of oneself and nourishing the other tend to have a reciprocal effect, and each person increasingly moves out toward the other with caring, respect, and understanding. For persons who are basically assertive, taking care of themselves tends to occur simultaneously with nourishing others (Cotler and Guerra, 1976). Of course, assertion does not automatically mean that individuals will always have their needs met, but it does increase the likelihood that both parties in a relationship can at least partially achieve their goals and have their needs satisfied (Lange and Jakubowski, 1976).

Fourth, assertion has a much higher probability of effecting better relationships than either aggression or nonassertion. Aggression and nonassertion contribute to imbalanced relationships. Successful aggression puts the aggressor in a dominant position, while nonassertion keeps the individual in a submissive role. Assertion promotes balance and equality because no one is forced into a defensive or offensive posture through force or manipulation.

Basic Forms of Assertive Behavior

The fact that assertive behavior can take so many forms necessarily limits the range of behaviors considered here. Two major forms of assertion are examined—*confrontation* and *self-disclosure*—followed by a discussion of other useful assertive responses: *urging, refusal, commanding, giving and receiving compliments, self-praise, sorting issues, apologizing,* and *nonverbal assertion.*

Confrontation

Confrontation is something which most people seem to equate with opposition, antagonism, defiance, or attack. It is frequently associated directly or indirectly with aggression. As an assertive behavior, however, confrontation has a different meaning. It is a *statement about some discrepancy or distortion apparent in a person's messages or behavior or both*. Assertive confrontation involves pointing up these discrepancies, bringing them to the other person's attention, and, sometimes, even challenging the person. Egan (1977) viewed confrontation as an invitation for the other person to look at her behavior in relation to others.

Confrontation is an expressive skill that is *situationally* appropriate, in that it may fit one interpersonal situation and not another. No definitive statement can be made on what and when to confront, but some general guidelines are offered here so that you may have some bases for deciding on the place of confrontation in your relationships. Some guidelines on the process of confrontation are also provided.

General Goals of Confrontation

Pete worked in the personnel department of a large health care organization that offered a human relations training program for employees. During the initial session, participants were shown a film of several people interacting in a group en-counter. After viewing the film, the participants were asked for comments about what they observed. Responding first, Pete declared, "There was a lot of bull go-ing on in that group, especially from that one guy in the blue sweater! He was play-ing games with everybody! I'd have confronted the hell out of him! I wouldn't let him get away with that nonsense! *I'd have gone right for the jugular!*"

This might seem like an interesting caricature, were it not for the fact those same words were actually spoken by an individual in a slightly different context (names and contexts are changed for "Pete's" sake!). This kind of frontal approach to other people is hostile, punishing, and ultimately has nega-tive consequences for all parties concerned. The real purpose for the con-fronter is to relieve himself of anger, not to promote constructive change in the way another person is communicating or acting.

A primary goal of confrontation is to call attention to obstacles that are threatening to disrupt your interaction and, thereby, prevent you from satisfy-ing your communication needs. It is also a goal of confrontation to effect an increase in the other person's understanding of his own behavior and how it is affecting you and your relationship with him. By *describing*—not interpret-ing—discrepancies or distortions apparent in an individual's messages or be-havior or both, you offer information which can be used by the other person to enhance his self-awareness. Self-awareness should become a forerunner of changes in the way he relates to you. Ultimately, it is a constructive change in the patterns of interactions between you that constitutes an overriding goal of confrontation. Your effectiveness in realizing this goal depends on what and how you confront.

Guidelines on "What" to Confront

Confrontation involves pointing up discrepancies and distortions. These are the general subjects of confrontation. *Discrepancies* often come in the form of mixed messages. Cormier and Cormier (1979) outlined four major types of mixed messages that may be confronted.

Verbal and Nonverbal Behavior.   Discrepancies may exist between what a person verbally states and what her body communicates. We have dealt with this phenomenon in other contexts, so you should appreciate how these kinds of mixed messages are often in need of confrontation. For example, a person may tell you that she feels very comfortable with you, but she assumes a rigid posture and discloses nothing personal about herself. A simple confrontation might be: "I hear you say that you feel comfortable with me, yet your body looks tense, and you haven't told me anything about yourself."

Verbal Messages and Subsequent Action.   Confrontations may be war-ranted when an individual states an intention to do something and then fails to carry it out or else does so in a manner different from what he described. For example, a person may tell you that he is going to meet you at five o'clock, but he doesn't arrive until seven o'clock and offers no explanation for his lateness. "You said you'd meet me here at five, so I've been waiting for you for two hours."

Incongruent Verbal Messages.   Individuals occasionally contradict themselves by stating two opposing messages. When stated inconsistencies are apparent, it is useful to bring them to the person's attention—for example, "It doesn't make any difference to me if they *force* me onto second shift (first message), but it seems like they could find someone else besides me (second message)." These messages contradict one another and may call for a confrontation: "First you say that you don't mind being put on second shift, and then you say that they ought to find someone else." This message may also reflect incongruence between the verbal message and vocal cues, such as that suggested by the emphasis the speaker placed on the word "force." In other circumstances, individuals may make a single verbal statement that contradicts itself by virtue of the words chosen: "I don't mind if you treat me like a *child*," "I'll find plenty of things to do, *sitting here all alone by myself all night*," "Just as long as you're happy, it doesn't matter how much I *suffer*." These kinds of messages are actually games which may need to be confronted, as discussed later.

Incongruent Nonverbal Messages.   When nonverbal messages contradict one another, they may need to be brought to the person's attention—for example, a patient may be wiping tears from her eyes and smiling at the same time: "You're smiling and yet drying your tears at the same time." Or, a person may keep nodding his head as you talk, and at the same time focus in a different direction: "You keep nodding your head, but you're looking over there while I talk."

It was noted in earlier chapters that people may distort reality when they cannot face it comfortably. They may alter their experience of the world in order to fit their needs or to maintain a stable self-concept. For example, a person may explain her verbal assault on another as mere confrontation done for the other person's own good. In an instance like this, a real confrontation to her attempts to describe her distorted perception and suggests an alternative way of looking at her own behavior: "You see what you did as being helpful, yet I'm wondering if you really wanted to let loose with your anger." This kind of confrontation points to the individual's view of her own behavior and also offers a different way of seeing it. Alternative frames of reference can be helpful if they are accurate.

Egan (1975) suggested that confrontation is useful in situations where individuals are playing *games*. An individual is playing games with people if he manipulates them to meet his own needs. There are countless games that people can play. I have known people, for example, who were "dumb as foxes." They pretended to be uniformed, slow, incompetent, and generally not too sharp. These people conveyed images with those characteristics just so they could escape responsibility or keep others from expecting too much from them. They threw up smoke screens to cover themselves. Confrontations may help to clear away the smoke and expose the game:

NURSE A: You've spent a lot of energy around here letting us know how helpless you are. Yet, you only have to be shown how to do things once. And, if no one shows you, you manage to do them anyway.

NURSE B: I guess I know how to do more things than I thought.

NURSE A: Maybe you do. But I've seen you work, and I've gotten the impression that you're really a very good nurse. There really doesn't seem to be much that you truly don't know how to do.

NURSE B: I suppose my biggest problem is not that I don't know how to do things, but that a lot of times I'd rather someone else did them. I guess I haven't been very fair to the others.

Confronting game behavior is not an easy thing to do. Sometimes the confrontation can backfire and reinforce the game playing. For example, a health professional may claim that he can't work because he's tired, upset, or ill, even though he isn't. He claims symptoms in order to disguise his real reasons for not wanting to work. Challenging him could influence him to emphasize his symptoms even more. In this connection, I am reminded of a mother who once told me that her daughter refused to eat the beets on her plate at dinner. The child claimed they would make her sick. Not believing this, the mother forced the child to eat the beets. As the mother turned her back to the child and walked toward the kitchen, the child stuck her finger in her throat and induced vomiting. Counterconfrontations can take many forms, too.

Guidelines on "How" to Confront

If you determine that confrontation is warranted, the issue becomes one of *how* to confront. Because confrontation is a potentially powerful assertive response, some guidelines on its use should be helpful. Some cautions should also be noted.

Describe the Message and/or Behavior. As Egan (1975) noted, confrontation should be used in the spirit of empathy. It should be based on an empathic understanding of the other person. This suggests that confrontation should not involve judgements or evaluations of the other person. Rather, confrontational statements should be *descriptive*: they should be neutral statements of the discrepancy or distortion. Were the confrontation to have a judgemental quality, the other person would be much more likely to become defensive. She would probably view the confrontation as an attack on her person. The intention of confrontation is to note something about messages and/or behavior, not about the personality of the individual. In confrontation, statements about the other's personality should be avoided in most cases (e.g., "You just said that to make me feel better, but you don't mean it. You're *insensitive*, and you don't care about anyone but yourself").

Give Concrete Evidence. Confrontations should be as concrete as possible. A vague and poorly expressed confrontation would be something like this: "You say you want to move up in the organization, but you're really slacking off lately," or even worse, "You've been slacking off lately; let's get with it, Bill." Everything that applies to concreteness in general applies to confrontation as well. For it to be effective, confrontation should include specific examples of the messages or behavior in question: "Bill, I hear you say that you'd like a promotion, but for the last month you've been coming late to work, taking long lunches, and four of your reports are still overdue," or "Bill, I understand that you want to be promoted, and I'm wondering if one of the obstacles has to do with your hanging back in meetings, not speaking your views and not showing people what you can do."

Be Tentative.   Leave room in your confrontation for response from the other. Just as clarifications and interpretations are tentative, so also should confrontations be stated tentatively. The idea is to provide a statement about which the other person can think and with which he can work. He will be unable to do so if confrontations are absolute and come on like "gangbusters." Overpowering the person with a confrontative statement usually throws him off stride, disorients him somewhat, and forces him to try to recover from the blow, rather than process the message. The failure to be tentative often comes from the confronter's interest in proving herself right: "You don't really want to hear what I have to say because your mind is already made up." Of course, this sort of confrontation could also be a manipulation used to make the other person even more open to a following message to which he was not closed in the first place. He may feel as if he has to defend himself and prove that his mind is *not* already made up by accepting what the confronter subsequently suggests.

Assess the Relationship.   The relationship should be able to hold up under the strain of the confrontation. If the relationship is not a close or solid one—that is, characterized by at least moderate levels of the core conditions—the other person may not be as receptive to your words as she might be if the relationship were otherwise. If there is little rapport between you and the other person, you may want to give serious thought to the advisability and necessity of confrontation. This is not to suggest that good rapport must exist even where confrontation takes place around an issue of importance to two relative strangers. It is only to suggest that you should assess the state of your relationship—whatever it may be—before you confront the other person.

Be Aware of the Other Person.   If the other person is in a state of confusion, emotional distress, or if he is otherwise preoccupied, confrontation may not be effective. To be effective, the other person must be psychologically capable of receiving and processing your message. If he is currently disorganized for some reason, the confrontation may have either no effect at all or it may further disorganize him.

Beware of the "Mum" Effect.   An ancient Persian story has it that a messenger ran for miles to his king's encampment with news of the army's defeat in battle. As payment for delivering this message, the king had the messenger executed. The messenger was the bearer of bad tidings, and he paid the price. Today, we don't execute people who bring us bad news, but we don't like the news any better. It seems that many of us are very reluctant to bring bad news to others. We know we're not going to be killed, but we usually feel quite uncomfortable, nonetheless. The bad news we bear usually makes the receiver feel bad, and we, in turn, feel bad because we were the "messengers." Consequently, we often realize that it may be to our advantage not to relay unpleasant messages. The costs are seen as being too great, especially when the bad news is about the other person in some way. Tesser and Rosen (1975) demonstrated that people often prefer to keep mum rather than tell someone about *her* misfortune. Aptly, they labeled this phenomenon the *mum effect.*

Tesser and Rosen found that people are less inhibited in talking about bad news in general and more inhibited when the message pertains directly to the receiver. The mum effect seems to characterize many individuals' reactions to confrontation. They don't want to upset another person, so they often fail to respond in an assertive way. As Egan (1977) suggested, if you find yourself giving in to the mum effect, you may need to ask yourself how committed you really are to the person you refuse to confront. Are you avoiding confrontation because of your own discomfort? Is this not nonassertion? Sometimes people are afraid to confront others simply because they fear their responses or because they are uncertain about how to handle others' reactions to the confrontation. Let's examine some of the usual responses to confrontation.

The Reactions of the Person Who Is Confronted

Confrontation usually causes the person confronted to feel somewhat disorganized (Carkhuff, 1969). Another way of describing the person's experience is in terms of *cognitive dissonance*. From earlier discussions, you will recall that a state of dissonance exists when an individual receives information that is not compatible with her existing beliefs or knowledge. Confrontation leads to this experience when the individual is presented with contradictory information. When dissonance is experienced, the individual seeks to reduce it, and she can do so in numerous ways. She can convince herself that the contradictions do not really exist (i.e., she can *deny* the subject of the confrontation); she can attempt to discredit the confronter (i.e., by *projecting* illicit motives to the confronter or by challenging his credibility); she can try to persuade the confronter to see things differently (i.e., by *rationalizing*); she can turn from the confronter and seek affirmation from others (i.e., by *displacing* her response and eliciting support). She may also listen to what the confronter has to say and then examine the facts with the confronter. As a result, she may change. Regardless of how the individual responds, confrontation requires *follow-up*. Once discrepancies or distortions are pointed up, they should be discussed openly. This reduces the person's tendency to take a defensive posture. Of course, the key variable here is the quality of the relationship i.e., if the core conditions exist at levels which facilitate such discussion. When the core conditions do exist, the substance of the confrontation can usually be dealt with mutually and constructively. In the context of counseling, for example, we have found that counselors functioning at high levels on the core conditions tend to use confrontation more frequently and more effectively than low-level functioning counselors (Carkhuff and Berenson, 1967). Furthermore, high-level functioning counselors confront their clients more often with their *assets* and *resources* than with their limitations (Carkhuff and Berenson, 1967).

A Final Note on Confrontation

Carkhuff and Berenson (1977) suggested that confrontation is not a technique to be used by those persons who cannot master basic relationship skills and who cannot manage their own lives with honesty, skill, and responsibility. They insisted that facilitative confrontation is a set of skills emerging from a broad base of relationship and communication skills. Confrontation without empathic understanding is likely to be inaccurate at best and destructive at worst (Berenson and Mitchell, 1974). Empathic understanding is a prerequisite condition for facilitative confrontation in interpersonal relationships. It promotes interpersonal trust, which provides a foundation for effective confrontation. Respect is also a prerequisite condition, for, without it, confrontation may easily resemble aggression or nonassertion. That is, when an individual holds little respect for another, he is more likely to be antagonistic, as opposed to responsibly confrontive, or he may have a pact of "mutual nonexposure" (Carkhuff and Berenson, 1977) with the other person. Neither person confronts the other because they have made an implicit agreement to be less than what they can be. They do not want to be challenged for being that way. Over time, this pact leads to contempt for the other and contempt for oneself (Carkhuff and Berenson, 1977). Genuineness is also necessary for confrontation. The confronter must be willing to risk full exposure of himself during an experiential confrontation with another person. Confrontation may sometimes result in counterconfrontations, and this possibility demands that the individual is willing to examine the observations of the other about him. The inauthentic person closes himself off to reciprocity.

Self-Disclosure

Self-disclosure has been examined in relation to self-perception (Chapter Three) and self-presentation (Chapter Seven). It is discussed here because it also represents a form of expression that is often synonymous with assertion. Disclosing oneself to another human being requires assertiveness as much as anything. It usually takes guts. As an offering of free personal information, self-disclosure often involves the expression of thoughts, feelings, attitudes, beliefs, or experiences having direct relevance to one's own needs within a relationship. At times, self-disclosure can also be solely for the benefit of another person.

While self-disclosure usually involves some element of risk, this is not always the case. Perhaps you have sat next to a stranger on an airplane and listened to that person tell about problems she was having at work, which were related to medical problems brought on by marital and family difficulties. Maybe the circumstances were different for you, but the fact remains that individuals have much less to lose by revealing personal information to strangers than if they were to disclose the same things to co-workers, neighbors, relatives, or other acquaintances. In a real sense, they can disclose themselves and remain anonymous. There are no repercussions to fear from self-disclosures to strangers. Most self-disclosures are not made to strangers, however. In this section, we are concerned with self-disclosure within the contexts of existing relationships—contexts wherein individuals may indeed perceive risks to self-revelation. Because of such risks, self-disclosure in existing relationships is an aspect of assertion.

Actually, we reveal a good deal of information about ourselves even if we don't intend to. We may send nonverbal cues of which we are not aware until someone brings them to our attention. We may send numerous messages that tell others what we are feeling. As discussed here, self-disclosure is a *purposeful* act. It serves various purposes for individuals. It may be used to let another person know how she is affecting you; it may be used to reduce the distance between you and another person; it may be used to encourage similar disclosures from someone; it may be used to communicate empathy, genuineness, respect, and trust; it may be used to let the other person know that she is not alone in what she is experiencing. Self-disclosure may be gradual or sudden. In most relationships, it tends to increase gradually as two people begin developing more trust in one another (Wheeless and Grotz, 1976). Early in relationships, self-disclosures are more impersonal, but sometimes an individual will suddenly reveal something extremely personal, perhaps more than the receiver really wants to know at that stage of the relationship. When this happens, it is common to wonder about the person's reasons for being so free with intimate information. The self-disclosures may seem so inappropriate and poorly timed that negative evaluations of the person are made, and what he may have intended as a means for promoting closeness actually puts greater distance between himself and the receiver. Self-disclosure is not simply a matter of exposing oneself indiscriminately to anyone under any circumstance. Most people are aware of this, but most people are not necessarily skilled in self-disclosure, either. They may be skilled at "underdisclosure," and "overdisclosure" is not a realistic concern for them. But *appropriate* self-disclosure—that which fits the relationship and the situation—may be a bit more difficult. Luft (1969) suggested that self-disclosure is appropriate when it meets five conditions:

1. When it is a function of an ongoing relationship
2. When it occurs reciprocally
3. When it is timed to fit what is happening
4. When it concerns what is happening within and between interacting persons
5. When it moves by gradual increments

Guidelines for Self-Disclosure

Self-disclosure rests on acceptance of, trust in, and respect for another person. It also tends to enhance each of these conditions. Consequently, self-disclosure is often a good index of the depth and quality of a relationship. People who trust, accept, and respect each other tend to reveal more personal information about themselves. Those disclosures, in turn, tend to increase trust, acceptance, and respect. Each person becomes freer to be genuine in relation to the other. In this connection, Carkhuff (1969, p. 209) commented that self-disclosure is one facet of genuineness and that "spontaneous sharing on the part of both parties is the essence of a genuine relationship." As a facet of assertiveness, self-disclosure can be used primarily for one's own benefit or for the benefit of another person. In either case, when used appropriately, self-disclosure promotes increased openness and honesty in communication.

One guideline for appropriate self-disclosure pertains to the *amount* of information disclosed. Too little disclosure may maintain the distance that exists between two people, while too much disclosure may have the same effect for different reasons. When individuals reveal very little about themselves, they are offering very little upon which to build a relationship. The message may be that they want to secure their privacy and prevent the relationship from moving toward increased involvement. On the other hand, when individuals indiscriminately dump their experiences on others, they are often seen as lacking discretion, tact, judgement, or common sense. Equally possible is that they may be perceived as preoccupied and in need of help. It appears, therefore, that a *moderate* amount of material has more positive effects on relationships than too much or too little self-disclosure. In judging what is "moderate," it is usually helpful to gauge self-disclosures against the free information offered by the other person during an encounter. Cues can be perceived and used as signals for what is and what is not an appropriate amount of information to reveal.

Another guideline concerns the *duration* of self-disclosure: the amount of time spent in giving free information about oneself. Usually, duration correlates with amount, in that the longer you speak, the more you usually say. From a different perspective, the longer you speak, the less time there is for the other person to reciprocate with self-disclosure. If the situation calls for mutual sharing of personal information, then it would seem that conciseness is important.

A third guideline pertains to the *intimacy* of the disclosure. It is usually most appropriate to keep your disclosures at about the same level of intimacy or depth as those of the other person and gradually increase the level of intimacy. Your disclosures should be similar in terms of *content* and *affect* when mutual sharing is taking place. The experiences you relate should roughly parallel those of the other person, and the mood conveyed should parallel the feelings expressed by the other.

Fourth, it is important to prevent mutual sharing from turning into *story swapping* and "one-upsmanship": "Oh, you think that's bad, you should've been with me the other day when. . . ." This can occur, even in initially intimate encounters, when individuals escalate reciprocal self-disclosures so rapidly that they can't see where it is taking them. Before they know it, they've reached a point where they are recounting stories or private reminiscences. Neither is really attending to the other, because both are caught in the web of their own memories.

"I" Messages in Self-Disclosure and Confrontation

Using the personal pronoun "I" is a useful guide for disclosing personal thoughts and feelings. This pronoun communicates ownership to the substance of disclosures. In his book *Parent Effectiveness Training*, Thomas Gordon (1970) described "I" language as a four-part statement for revealing feelings about another person's behavior. The individual first describes the other person's behavior, then he describes how her behavior specifically affects his feelings or his life, he then describes the specific feelings, and he completes the disclosure with a description of what he wants:

1. *Behavior* . . . ("When you are absent from our staff meetings, . . . ")
2. *Effects* . . . (" . . . we miss valuable input about patients, . . . ")
3. *Feelings* . . . (" . . . and I feel frustrated and concerned, . . . ")

4. *Change* . . . (" . . . so you could help us all by attending the meetings.")

Notice that this disclosure addresses the ways in which the receiver's behavior affects the speaker. The speaker takes ownership of the feelings revealed and does not engage in blaming and accusations which usually result from "you" messages:

> You make me so frustrated when you're absent from the staff meetings. Don't you know we need your input about patients?

Unlike "I" messages, "you" messages refer to the other person, who is held responsible for the feelings which the speaker rightly owns. Gordon (1977) argued that most "you" messages are potentially damaging to relationships because they put blame on the other person and may make her feel guilty. Or, they may make the other person defensive and motivated to retaliate. At the very least, they may fail to influence that person to change what is so offensive to the speaker. Again, this is because the speaker puts sole responsibility for *his* feelings onto the receiver.

More recently, in *Leader Effectiveness Training*, Gordon (1977) suggested that people can learn to send "I" messages when they practice a three-part message formula: *Behavior + Feelings + Effects*. Gordon believed that leaving off the statement about what the speaker wants the receiver to do may have the advantage of giving the receiver more room to offer her own ideas for dealing with the situation. However the individual prefers to use the formula—three-part or four-part—it is only a framework for learning how to take ownership to feelings and to disclose them. Just as the format for reflection and active listening ("You feel . . . because . . . ") is a guide for initial practice, so also is the "I" language format intended for modification by each individual so that it matches his own interpersonal style.

It should be noted that the example above is not only a self-disclosure, it is a form of confrontation. Although a useful mode of confrontation, it does not guarantee that the person confronted will be open to the message. However, contrast the two statements below, and decide for yourself to which one the receiver would be more open.

> #1: You really irritate me when you butt in while I'm talking with a patient. Can't you see I'm busy? What's wrong with you?
>
> #2: When I'm interrupted while I'm talking with a patient, I get irritated and upset, and I lose my train of thought.

I think there is a high probability that you would judge the second statement as being less offensive and less accusatory. Still, it does not insure that the receiver will be open to the message that her behavior is inappropriate. No matter how it is worded, she may still become defensive. As Gordon (1977) recommended, a defensive response calls for a shift by the speaker to active listening in order to work through the communication barrier.

When you use "I" messages, you declare ownership to feelings, and you are more assertive. You are also being more concrete, more genuine, and you communicate more respect for the other person. You also demonstrate more self-respect because you are taking the steps to meet your needs in a relationship.

Levels of Self-Disclosure

Self-disclosures vary from the absence of personal information to deep and detailed revelations. At the least facilitative level, the individual tries to *remain unkown* to another person. He avoids self-disclosure altogether. This avoidance can take the form of nonassertion (total passivity due to fear of consequences), or it may be a passive-aggressive response (intentional stubbornness, obstructionism, or undermining the interaction). If the individual gives self-disclosure at all, it is likely to be in a way that is incompatible with the other person's disclosures; it is safe and unrelated to the communications of the other person. Another tactic at this level is the individual's attempt to divert the other's attention away from requests for personal information.

At a slightly higher level of self-disclosure, the individual may not actively avoid revealing personal information, but, at the same time, he does not go out of his way to volunteer it. When another person asks for personal information, the individual may respond hesitantly and provide no more than that for which the other person asked. Disclosures are short, superficial, without detail, and often vague.

At a moderate level of disclosure, the individual may volunteer free personal information. However, it may be rather vague and lacking concrete information which describes the individual's uniqueness. Self-disclosures are not resisted, yet the content of revelations may not go beyond his reactions to the other person in the immediate context. That is, little information may be provided which tells about other dimensions of the individual's experience of living.

At a high level of self-disclosure, the individual *freely volunteers personal information in depth and in detail.* When conditions determine that such disclosures are appropriate, they tend to have strong positive effects on the relationship. There is depth and detail when the information describes the individual's differentness, separateness, and uniqueness as a human being. It may even be that, under different circumstances or if the receiver were to relay the disclosures to an outsider, the information would be very embarrassing to the individual. He trusts in the other person, however. The self-disclosures usually imply that trust. Since he therefore holds nothing back in talking about himself, he is opening himself up and exposing his personality in a responsibly assertive way.

Intentional self-disclosure is something that is not necessary in all of our relationships. High levels of self-disclosure are probably inappropriate for most of them. As indicated in Chapter Seven, it may be sufficient to be able to disclose oneself to at least one other person. First, it is helpful to be able to disclose oneself *to oneself*. Self-disclosure to the self and to one other person is the least we can expect from ourselves. When both are achieved satisfactorily, it becomes easier to move out toward others. When they are not achieved, it is not possible to be self-disclosing in other relationships. That is, when we have not disclosed ourselves to ourselves, we have very little, if anything, to share about ourselves in any meaningful way. The assertive person implicity or explicitly understands this. She also understands that to communicate high levels of self-disclosure, whatever the circumstances, certain other conditions must also be met.

It is necessary to know *why* you are disclosing personal information.

It is necessary to know *what* you want to achieve through self-disclosure.

It is necessary to keep the *depth* and *detail* of disclosures related to your goals.

It is necessary to assess the *appropriateness* of self-disclosure in each interaction.

It is necessary to exercise some *control* over disclosures in order to avoid irrelevancies and overloading the listener.

If appropriate, it is most beneficial to relationships to disclose *feelings toward other people as they arise* and not keep them buried and out of sight.

Assertive Skills for Conversations

The conversational skills described in the previous chapter obviously require a measure of assertiveness. It is probably arbitrary to separate those verbal responses from the ones outlined here. However, this section describes additional conversational skills which are often practiced in assertion-training workshops and seminars—ostensibly because they are among the verbal responses with which people often have the most trouble. Whether they are or not is another issue. Nevertheless, the verbal responses dicussed here are ones which we have all used, but not necessarily effectively. Frequently, we use these responses in either nonassertive or aggressive ways. This discussion may suggest to you some ways of using these verbal skills more assertively.

General Persuasion

Persuasion is an intentional process of attempting to influence individuals toward particular attitudinal positions or courses of actions. It is a process which has been extensively researched, theorized, and even popularized in the literature. As an assertive process, persuasion is something that people often have trouble accomplishing. Frequently, people either do not know how to influence others without being aggressive. Lange and Jakubowski (1976) introduced two principles designed to help people maximize their impact on others when giving opinions, particularly in group settings: *timing* and *tact*.

According to Lange and Jakubowski, before deciding on the best time to assert one's opinions, the individual needs to determine the particular issues which have top priority and warrant an assertive stance. When issues are not ranked, individuals may end up talking at length and rambling about every related matter. You may have witnessed this in staff or other group meetings where an individual forcefully expresses her positions on all of the issues. She talks far too long, and eventually the rest of the group begins to tune out and grow frustrated with her. It typically happens that she is tagged with a label of some sort and in subsequent meetings her opinions are not taken seriously.

Lange and Jakubowski suggested that once the individual identifies the precise issues she wants to influence, her opinions should be stated after one-third to one-half of the group members have expressed theirs. The reasoning is that it is at that point in the interaction that individuals have a clearer sense of the group's position. Furthermore, group members can more easily consider the points which have already been raised. When the individual expresses her opinions, they should be stated concretely, convincingly, and without reducing credibility by making self-effacing comments. It seems to me that the same approach would also be appropriate in two-person enounters.

Tact is considered by Lange and Jakubowski to be essential in assertive persuasion. They describe tact in terms of prefacing one's opinion with a statement about some merit in the other person's point of view. An example of this kind of tact is illustrated in the following example.

> Your suggestion that we rotate the schedule so that everyone does cardiac monitoring is well-taken. That would probably work out well for all of us, if only we all understood the cardiac monitoring system. Some of us haven't had that training.

This approach communicates to the other person that the individual understands his point and considers some aspect of it to be valuable. Then the individual expresses her viewpoint.

Urging

Urging is a form of persuasion that is often compared to coaxing and cajoling. In a more general sense, urging is an attempt to influence another person toward some course of action that the person has already implicitly or explicitly indicated as appropriate. An urging response represents an effort to prevent the person from evading what you believe he should not evade. It also involves supporting the person in going through with whatever course of action has been discussed. For example, in one of your interactions, you and a friend may agree that she would benefit by taking an assertion-training workshop. If she does nothing about it, the whole issue remains academic. To move her toward action, an urging response may be helpful—but, not necessarily.

Even though you think assertion training would be helpful for her and even though she may have verbalized her agreement with you, her refusal to budge may mean that she's not really convinced. Maybe she is letting you know that the idea itself is sound, but *for her* it's not practical. If you continue to urge her to participate in assertion training, you may be influencing more resistance from her. The point to all of this is that effective urging rests upon accurate perception. You must be alert to the possible effects which urging may have. Are you asserting your beliefs because you have an investment in proving their value? Are you urging your own case and thereby imposing your own frame of reference on the other person? As a responsibly assertive communication, urging must be based on respect for the other person. Therefore, when urging is not having the intended impact on the other, it is probably best to back off—to back up and discuss with the individual her concerns about the proposed course of action.

VIRGINIA: Gloria, I really think you'd get a lot our of that workshop. I know you won't find it as bad as you think.

GLORIA: You're probably right. I know I could learn a lot that would help me. But, I don't know—I just—there's just something about it that holds me back.

Here, Virginia would be helpful is she responded to Gloria's vagueness and to the mixed messages she's sending.

VIRGINIA: I hear you saying that, on the one hand, you want to go, and, on the other hand, you don't. I know why you would like to go, but I don't know what it is that's holding you back.

GLORIA: I'm not sure, either. Maybe it's the thought of being in a group of people—being in front of people who are going to tear you down and tell you what you're not doing right.

VIRGINIA: Sounds like you see assertion training as a pretty frightening experience—people tearing you down and all.

GLORIA: Well, yes and no. I mean, that's what I'm afraid of—that's what I'm afraid will happen. But, I know it's not really like that at all.

VIRGINIA: You're right. It's really *not* like that at all. I thought the same thing before I attended a workshop. I was nervous and afraid of what might happen—maybe just because of the kind of workshop it was—you know—*"assertiveness."* I thought I'd get pushed around and humiliated, but it was great—people were so sensitive and understanding. I think that's exactly what you'd find if you went through it.

Refusal

Assertion sometimes requires us to support our personal rights by refusing requests that infringe upon us, although we also have the right sometimes to choose not to assert those rights in particular situations (Lange and Jakubowski, 1976). In some situations, we may judge it more appropriate to comply with requests than to refuse them. When requests appear to be unreasonable and when it seems appropriate to refuse them, assertive refusal is necessary.

Saying no is difficult for many people and saying no to a persistent person is even harder. The persistent person comes on stronger with each refusal, thus making the target person either more irritated or less resistant. What often happens to the person who initially refuses a request is that, when the other person comes back with a stronger, more forceful request, she assumes that the initial explanation was not good enough. She then tries to come up with a better explanation in hopes that the requester will accept it. Unfortunately, this scrambling for better reasons often leads to flimsy excuses which are then disputed by the requester, leaving the "refuser" in a one-down position (Lange and Jakubowski, 1976). Some refusers, of course, might fear that continued refusals will make the requester angry and decrease his liking for the refuser.

There are various ways of responding to presistent requests. One which I tend to favor is using *immediacy to confront what the person is doing*. That is, rather than focusing on the request itself, the refuser shifts to what the requester is doing in the *process*. For example:

> As you continue to persist, I'm getting irritated that you have chosen to ignore my decision.
>
> You do not seem to be respecting my decision, and I am getting angrier as you become more persistent.
>
> I am getting more annoyed, because your persistence tells me that I am not being heard.

Another approach is to move from a communication of understanding to a basic assertion and then to a confrontation response, if necessary. For example, assume that the spouse of a patient came to the central nursing station and requested that the patient be allowed to have four visitors at a time (two more than the limit). An empathic assertion might be something like this:

> I know you would like your wife to be able to visit with more than two people at a time, but I have a responsibility to the other patient, as well. I cannot allow four people in the room.

If the person ignored this refusal, a basic assertion could follow:

> I cannot allow four people to visit your wife at one time.

The person could then be confronted if he persisted with the unreasonable request:

> I think I have made myself clear on this matter, Mr. J. If there is any confusion, perhaps you can let me know what it is.

If all else fails, you might make a request that the person change his behavior:

> I would appreciate it if you'd accept what I said, Mr. J., and I'd like you to please stop persisting, will you?

Commanding

Commanding is a response in which the individual orders another person to follow her instructions. Obviously, health professionals are required to do considerable commanding in their practices. That being the case, it should be done tactfully and assertively, not aggressively. First, the individual needs to be clear on the orders she needs to give. Do they need to be given? Exactly what are they? Can the objectives be accomplished without a command?

When giving a command, the health professional usually responds out of her professional role and position of authority. Sometimes, a command is more effective when it comes unambiguously from a position of authority. At other times, it is equally or more effective if it is not delivered from a strong power position. Because nonverbal and vocal cues are important elements in giving orders, it is difficult to present an example. When other communication and relationship skills are within the "commander's" repertoire, however, giving orders can be done assertively, without undue pressure, authority, and even agressiveness.

Giving and Receiving Compliments

Some people feel uneasy when they give compliments to others. Many people seem to feel uneasy when compliments are given *to them*. How often have you heard (or given) these kinds of responses to compliments: "Oh, this old thing?"; "It was really nothing"; "You've got to be kidding." Have you ever stopped to think that these kinds of responses are *rejections*? They negate the compliments. They also call into question the complimenter's judgement.

Being able to give genuine compliments to another person requires assertiveness. Giving those compliments tends to bring you a bit closer to that person. Conversely, receiving compliments can have the same effect. Unfortunately, we all seem to have learned from the time we were children that it is important to be humble and modest and, for many people, this has translated into an inability to accept compliments. Indeed, in some cases it generalizes into an inability to see anything worthwhile in oneself. From this learned norm of humility and modesty, most of us have acquired a habit of refuting compliments. One effect for us is that we deprive ourselves of a chance to feel good about ourselves and about those who compliment us. When we continuously reject compliments, people tend to quit giving them, and all we may be left with is our humility, which somehow doesn't make us feel satisfied.

Assertion in relation to giving and receiving compliments does not mean that you should become an ingratiating backslapper or a boastful egotist. It means that you are capable of offering honest praise to others and of accepting the same without embarrassment or self-depreciation.

Self-Praise

In my experience as a therapist and as a professor, I have found that one of the hardest things for people to do is to list without embarrassment 10 things they really like about themselves. It seems much easier to list faults. Indeed, people often find it much easier to recognize and share their faults and weaknesses with others than to disclose their strengths and good qualities. Assertion-training programs try to reverse this tendency. After all, who wants to hear only negative information from someone? Who wants constantly to listen to someone disclose his shortcomings? Negative personal information to the exclusion of positive personal information may influence others to form slanted impressions biased by supposed imperfections. If a person cannot see herself in a positive light, how can she expect that others would perceive her any differently?

Learning to recognize personal strengths and assets and resources is an important step toward increasing one's liking for oneself. It is also a vital step toward having something positive to share with others. It seems that one of the chief obstacles to expressing one's positive qualities relates to a fear of violating the implicit norm of humility. Again, however, assertive self-praise is not a transition into a swaggering braggart. Rather, it is a step toward increased *self-respect*. If you haven't already, you might take a moment to list 10 things that *you really like about yourself*.

Sorting Issues

Sometimes, during our interactions, messages get crossed and issues run together. Consider the following dialogue:

ALBERT: Hey, Joan, I'd like to leave work a little early tomorrow. Would you mind if I made up the time on Thursday?

JOAN: Normally, I wouldn't mind at all, but I'll be in a conference all afternoon tomorrow, so I'm going to need you to stick around and watch over things in my absence.

ALBERT: Oohh—come on, Joan! Someone else can cover for you, can't they? I don't ask for favors very often.

JOAN: I know you don't, Albert, but I really need *you* to fill in for me tomorrow afternoon. How about taking the next afternoon off?

ALBERT: No, it's got to be tomorrow. Come on, Joan, I thought you were a friend I could count on.

JOAN: Albert, I am a friend, and I hope you can count on me at times. But, tomorrow I need to have you here all day.

ALBERT: Sure—if you were really my friend and if I could really count on you, then you'd let me leave early tomorrow.

JOAN: Albert, I am your friend. But our friendship is not the issue here. The issue is that I can't be here tomorrow, and I need you to fill in.

In this dialogue, Joan sorted the issue of friendship from the issue of Albert's filling her position in her absence. You have probably encountered a similar experience where two or more issues ran together and were not properly separated. You may have left the interaction feeling frustrated and confused. If you were nondiscriminating and nonassertive, you may have gone for the "hook" (e.g., "If you were really my friend, you would . . . "; "If you really loved me, then you would . . . "; "Don't you care about the patients? Why do you . . . "). You may have given in to the manipulation because you felt guilty or ashamed.

An assertive response under these kinds of circumstances is to separate the different issues before you. You are then in a better position to ascertain what is being communicated by the other person. Upon discriminating what his request is from what he is implying, you may be in a much better position to decide on the most appropriate response—one that will clear the air and leave nothing unsettled.

Apologizing

In some situations, guilt feelings serve adaptive purposes. For example, when a person feels guilty or ashamed for hurting someone's feelings unnecessarily, those feelings may induce the individual to offer an apology to the injured party. This seems to be an appropriate action which can help the person to prevent similar harmdoing in the future. The experience of guilt can sometimes lead to behavior which has positive effects on relationships.

Some people either don't feel guilt or (probably in the majority of these cases) they simply do not show it by offering apologies. Some people simply make very few apologies for their actions, even when they know their actions have been harmful. Conversely, there are people who make excessive apologies, even when they're not warranted or appropriate. They either experience too much pervasive guilt or they are so desperate for approval that they apologize for everything in order to avoid expressions of disapproval. No apologies may reflect passive-aggressive behavior, while excessive apologies may indicate non-assertion. For apologies to be effective, they should be communicated assertively. But, if assertion is a means for maintaining self-respect, how can a person maintain or enhance self-respect by apologizing?

Essentially, this can be accomplished by apologizing for the *behavior* that was abusive to the other person, without communicating that the *person* making the apology is generally harmful or undignified (Cotler and Guerra, 1976). Before offering an apology, then, individuals should identify what it was that they *did*—exactly in what actions did they engage—that produced the undesirable effect for another person. The effect on the other should also be accounted for in the apology statement: "I apologize for making you cry by telling you that you were stupid." Specifying the behavior and its effects along with your expression of guilt can indicate to the other person that you are sincere in what you are saying—*as long as vocal and nonverbal cues reinforce that message.* They will, if you're truly sincere.

Nonverbal Assertion

All of the nonverbal attending skills discussed in Chapter Thirteen are also assertive skills. They do not need to be reviewed here. But, if you return to Chapter Thirteen and reexamine each of the physical attending skills, you should be able to see how these responses can be used to enhance verbal assertiveness. In assertion, it is necessary to have all message channels in tune with each other. Verbal statements alone do not demonstrate assertiveness.

Summary

The health professional who chooses assertion as a mode of interaction can profit in terms of increased self-confidence, personal autonomy, interpersonal sensitivity, and self-respect. *Assertion* is a process of standing up for personal rights and expressing thoughts, feelings, and beliefs in direct, honest, and appropriate ways which respect the rights of other people (Lange and Jakubowski, 1976). A central issue in the definition of assertion is the distinction among assertive, nonassertive, and aggressive behavior. *Nonassertion* is the failure to express thoughts and feelings when expressions would be appropriate. *Aggression* is typically differentiated from assertion in terms of its disregard for the rights of others.

Reasons for nonassertion include the inability to distinguish assertion from aggression, the inability to distinguish nonassertion from politeness, the belief that one is not entitled to act assertively, a fear of negative consequences, the belief than one is being helpful to others by acting nonassertively, and the limited range of social skills available to some persons. Some reasons for acting aggressively include overcompensation, emotional concerns, learned aggression, and misunderstood assertion. The major reasons for acting assertively include increased self-respect, the meeting of one's own needs and wants, mutuality of give-and-take, and the probability of enhancing the quality of relationships.

Confrontation is an assertive response which is a statement about some discrepancy or distortion apparent in a person's message or behavior or both. A primary goal of confrontation is to call attention to obstacles that are threatening to disrupt interactions and relationships. Guidelines for "what" and "how" to confront were presented. *Self-disclosure* is another assertive behavior that invovles the revelation of personal information about oneself. Guidelines for self-disclosure was outlined, along with an emphasis on the use of *"I" language*. Different levels of self-disclosure were then described. Additional assertive skills for use in conversation were outlined: *general persuasion, urging, refusal, commanding, giving and receiving compliments, self-praise, sorting issues, apologizing,* and *nonverbal assertion.*

References

Bandura, A. Self-Efficacy: Toward a Unifying Theory of Behavioral Change, *Psychological Review*, **84**:191–215 (1977).

Berenson, B. G., and Mitchell, K. M. *Confrontation for Better or Worse!* Amherst, Massachusetts, Human Resources Development Press, 1974.

Carkhuff, R. R. *Helping and Human Relations. Practice and Research*, vol. 2. New York, Holt, Rinehart, and Winston, 1969.

Carkhuff, R. R., and Berenson, B. G. *Beyond Counseling and Therapy*. New York, Holt, Rinehart, and Winston, 1967.

Carkhuff, R. R., and Berenson, B. G. *Beyond Couseling and Therapy*, 2nd ed. New York, Holt, Rinehart, and Winston, 1977.

Cheek, D. K. *Assertive Black . . . Puzzled White.* San Luis Obispo, California, Impact, 1976.

Cotler, S. B., and Guerra, J. J. *Assertion Training: A Humanistic-Behavioral Guide to Self-Dignity.* Champaign, Illinois, Research press, 1976.

Cormier, W. H., and Cormier, L. S. *Interviewing Strategies for Helpers: A Guide to Assessment, Treatment, and Evaluation.* Monterey, California, Brooks/Cole, 1979.

Douglas, L. M., and Bevis, E. O. *Nursing Management and Leadership in Action*, 3rd ed. St. Louis, C. V. Mosby, 1979.

Egan, G. *The Skilled Helper: A Model for Systematic Helping and Interpersonal Relating.* Monterey, California, Brooks/Cole, 1975.

Egan, G. *You and Me: The Skills of Communicating and Relating to Others.* Monterey, California, Brooks/Cole, 1977.

Gordon, T. *Parent Effectiveness Training.* New York, Peter H. Wyden, 1970.

Gordon, T. *Leader Effectiveness Training.* New York, Bantam Books. 1977.

Jakubowski-Spector, P. Facilitating the Growth of Women Through Assertive Training, *The Counseling Psychologist*, **4**:75–86 (1973).

Lange, A. J., and Jakubowski, P. *Responsible Assertive Behavior: Cognitive Behavioral Procedures for Trainers.* Champaign, Illinois, Research Press, 1976.

Luft, J. *Of Human Interaction.* Palo Alto, California, National Press, 1969.

McFall, R. M., and Twentyman, C. T. Four Experiments on the Relative Contributions of Rehearsal, Modeling, and Coaching to Assertion Training, *Journal of Abnormal Psychology*, **81**:199–218. (1973).

Rich, A. R., and Schroeder, H. E. Research Issues in Assertiveness Training. *Psychological Bulletin, (Nov.),* **83**(6):1084–96 (1976).

Tesser, A., and Rosen, S. The Reluctance to Transmit Bad News, in *Advances in Experimental Social Psychology*, vol. 8, ed. L. Berkowitz. New York, Academic Press, 1975.

Wheeless, L. R., and Grotz, J. The Measurement of Trust and Its Relationship to Self-Disclosure, *Human Communication Research,* **2**:338–46 (1976).

CHAPTER
SEVENTEEN

Skills Assessment and Applications for Part Three

One must learn by doing the thing; for though you think
you know it, you have no certainty, until you try.

Sophocles

The final chapter of this text is intended for those persons who wish to continue testing the personal relevance and conceptual bases of text material. Like Chapters Five and Eleven, the present chapter is designed to focus on skills assessment and practice in order to bring interpersonal relation concepts to life. You are not deluged with exercises and interpersonal experiences here, since it is assumed that there are sufficient experiential applications to move you toward bridging the gap between academic learning and actual practice in social/professional contexts. That is the ultimate test of relevance: the extent to which you are successful in bridging the gap.

A common complaint of both textbook material and structured exercises is that neither is "real." "Things don't work that way in 'real' life," some would contend. If you have any degree of skepticism, you can conduct your own tests of relevance as you sample these exercises. That is what the exercises are for: to bring textbook learning to interpersonal living. You can be your own witness to applicability, but as you know from earlier chapters, you may need to check your perceptions for accuracy. That is one reason why many of the exercises involve participation in dyads or groups of four people. Interpersonal exercises offer valuable opportunities for learning from one another.

In a very real sense, you have a responsibility to take control of your own learning. Texts and exercises can only suggest and stimulate. The meaningfulness of concepts and skills is demonstrated in your response to those suggestions. *You* are the one to demonstrate applicability and meaningfulness in relation to your own life. The material in this text only points you in a certain direction. You have to find your own way through the woods, as it were. You can take the first step by gaining *firsthand* experience of the major concepts presented here. The exercises are designed around those concepts, and they should help you to generate some of your own data about the significance of the concepts. The exercises should also stimulate further questions to be explored, issues to be resolved, and skills to be developed.

The exercises in this chapter place a heavy emphasis on relationship skills. The rationale for developing such skills has already been discussed at several points in the text. Some may still argue, however, that we have a behavioral technology for changing specific responses, so why waste time with all this stuff about relationships. One reason rests upon a value assumption—an assumption that there is something worthwhile in learning how to establish and maintain satisfactory relationships. There is something to be said for taking the time to enter another person's world in order to better understand what living is like for that person. There is something of great value in people themselves, which can never be appreciated without moving out to them with understanding and true commitment. There is something of great value in ourselves, which can never be recognized without holding our relationships in the highest regard. Interpersonal relationships are the substance of social and professional living. The conditions upon which they are built and maintained are not expendable pleasantries or academic minutiae. They are conditions which may seem ideal and artificial only because they are conditions which do not characterize the majority of relationships between human beings. To promote and advocate the skills underlying these conditions, then, is to promote the means for developing relationships which are more "real" than those to which we are accustomed.

Communicating Understanding of Feelings

Assume that you are interacting with each of the persons whose statements are given below. Your objective is to communicate an understanding of each person's feelings. In the space provided, you can insert exactly what you would say to each person. You are not to indicate what you would *do*, or what you would advise the other to do. *Write down the exact words you would say to each of these persons.* You will note that not much space is provided for your answers. That is because empathic responses should be "neat and trim," as you will recall from preceding discussions.

1. FEMALE PATIENT: I don't know if I can talk about it. Right now my world is just upside-down. I never expected the doctor to give me a report like the one he just gave me.

   You feel _____.

2. STUDENT NURSE: I just know she's going to ask me to stand up there in

front of everyone and demonstrate how to insert an IV. I'll die if she calls on me. I can't get up in front of the class like that.

You feel _____.

3. MALE PATIENT: No one ever told me anything about what these tests were supposed to be like. I've had all these enemas, and now I've got to have one of those barium enemas. I don't know what else they can do to me.

You feel _____.

4. LAB TECHNICIAN: I've been up here to this floor seven times today taking blood samples. It seems like someone could get things coordinated around here, for gosh sakes!

You feel _____.

5. STAFF NURSE: When I got word that she wanted to see me, I got so nervous. I was sure someone had told her about me doing something I wasn't supposed to do. She never wants to see me unless I do something wrong. But when I got to her office, she said she just wanted me to give some input on the new rotation!

You feel _____.

6. EMERGENCY PATIENT: You people are all alike! You don't care about us! All you care about is having your damned forms filled out. I could die waiting around for someone to take care of me!

You feel _____.

7. STAFF NURSE: We're always told about how "understanding" we have to be. But nobody seems to care if anyone understands our problems!

You feel _____.

8. ADMINISTRATOR: I can't figure it out. I just don't know where to go with this matter you've brought up. I've never encountered anything like it in all of my years in hospital work.

You feel _____.

9. FEMALE PATIENT: Two years ago, my son was killed in a car accident. My husband never seemed to get over it. Then, last year—he died of a heart attack. It was strange. He died almost exactly one year after our son.

You feel _____.

10. STAFF NURSE: I've been working overtime and Saturdays for three months. I haven't had any time off. I've managed to handle all of my work at home, and I don't know *how* I've done it.

You feel _____.

For a twist in this exercise, you might make up some of your own statements and have others in the class make up some of their own statements. Each person should write her preferred responses on a separate sheet of paper. Exchange statements and write your responses. Check your responses with those recommended by the persons making up the statements. Discuss differences of opinion.

Communicating Understanding of Content

Follow the same instructions as those given in the preceding exercise, with the exception that this time you are to respond to *content* only.

1. STUDENT NURSE: I guess I'm a little self-conscious, being the only minority student in the class. Usually, it doesn't bother me at all. But for some reason, I feel so conscious of myself in here.

You feel _____.

2. MINISTER: The poor lady has been so strong through her terrible ordeal. I look at her and feel so inadequate in my own weaknesses.

You feel _____.

3. ALCOHOLIC: I appreciate all you've tried to do, but I keep telling you that I don't need it. There's nothing wrong with me. Like I said, I don't have any drinking problem.

You feel _____.

4. RECEPTIONIST: Some of these people are so demanding. They call up here and want this and want that—and they want it *right now*! I get so tired of it!

You feel _____.

5. ORDERLY: I've always wanted to be a nurse, but I guess I'm just not cut out to be one. I can't get accepted into any programs, and it really hurts!

You feel _____.

Communicating Understanding of Feelings and Content

Read the following statements and give your responses in the same manner as above, with the change being that you should now reflect both feelings and content. The format "You feel . . . because . . . " is inserted into the first three response spaces as a guide. You may want to alter your response style to fit your own approach.

1. STUDENT NURSE: I can't go on duty today. Please understand. I just can't handle it today—so many things have happened today—I'm just a nervous wreck. Everything's gone wrong!

   You feel _____ because _____ .

2. PATIENT: This is the absolute worst food I've ever eaten. They must have marinaded this salad in a leech bed! They must want to keep everyone sick!

   You feel _____ because _____ .

3. STAFF NURSE: I should have known better than to request a transfer to this department. No matter where you go in this hospital, everything is the same.

   You feel _____ because _____ .

4. COLLEAGUE: You know, the one point that really sticks with me is the one about "genuineness." I know that some of the best relationships I've ever had were ones where nobody was putting on any false fronts. That really means a lot to me.

   You feel _____ because _____ .

5. COLLEAGUE: It was wonderful, just wonderful! I watched that little boy get out of that bed and walk across the room. I never thought he'd ever be able to do that. Oh, you should have been there! It was so heartwarming!

   You feel _____ because _____ .

6. MALE PATIENT: I haven't talked about personal stuff like that in years. And now you're asking me to tell you about my sexual behavior!

   You feel _____ because _____ .

7. MALE PATIENT: I don't know about others, but I guess that being Jewish has made me think more about Tay-Sachs. Sometimes I get frightened. Sometimes I get mad when I think about it.

   You feel _____ because _____.

8. FEMALE PATIENT: I was really nervous before I came in here, but this interview isn't anything like I thought it was going to be. I don't mind it at all. It's kind of interesting.

   You feel _____ because _____.

9. FEMALE PATIENT: It feels good to talk to someone. You know, I don't get many visitors, so I enjoy it when you take the time to talk with me.

   You feel _____ because _____.

10. MALE PATIENT: So, I don't get any visitors. Who cares? I don't need their damned sympathy! To hell with them all, anyway!

    You feel _____ because _____.

Clarification

Assume that the statements below are directed to you. Each of the statements contains either ambiguous messages or several messages. Clarification responses would probably be appropriate in each case. In the spaces provided, write your clarification responses exactly as you would say them to the persons making the statements.

1. PATIENT: I wish I didn't have to do all of these physical therapy exercises. They seem so pointless to me.

   _____.

2. STUDENT NURSE: I haven't heard from my family in two weeks, and my grades are slipping. I don't know what to do about it.

   _____.

3. FEMALE PATIENT: This mastectomy has ravaged me. I hardly feel like a woman anymore. I feel like I won't be able to look at people, and I'm afraid of being alone with my husband. I feel like my whole life has been turned inside out and my body along with it. I don't see what can be lying ahead for me.

   _____.

4. NURSE: My health is such that I'm going to have to quit my job. I don't want to, because I've loved my job for so many years. I don't know what I'm going to do with my time now. Maybe I can do some volunteer work. I don't know, I just keep thinking about the past. I can't really get oriented to the future and not working here anymore.

_____.

5. CHILD PATIENT: I don't want the operation. It'll hurt me. I don't care if I get sick, I don't want an operation. I want to get better some other way. How come I have to have an operation and nobody else does. Jimmy didn't have one when he was here.

_____.

Questions

Read the following "why" questions and change them into different types of questions. You may want to use indirect questions, or you may elect to substitute "what" or "how" at the beginnings of each question. This exercise should influence you to begin thinking of other ways of getting information without resorting to the starter "why."

1. Why do you think the doctor is not going to be in to see you today?

_____

2. Why do you keep looking at the floor while I'm talking to you?

_____

3. Why can't you get things organized around here?

_____

4. Why are you looking at me like that?

_____

5. Why don't you ever stop and think before you do these things?

_____

6. Why haven't you taken the medications I left for you?

_____

7. Why is it so important that we document everything that happens?

_____

8. Why do you feel that way?

_____

9. Why do you think no one has come to visit you?

_____

10. Why should you avoid asking "why" questions?

_____

Concreteness

Below are several vague statements dealing with behaviors, experiences, or feelings. They are probably not unlike statements you could very well have made on various occasions. Draw from your own experience, put yourself in the place of the speaker, and turn these vague statements into concrete ones. For example, you could use your own experience to make this statement concrete: "Things are going pretty well between us these days." You could make it concrete by being specific: "We have spent at least an hour each night talking to one another about our relationship and what we want from it. We've had no arguments for over one month because we're identifying conflicts when they arise." Of course, you could fill in your own examples.

1. I've been messing up at work lately.

_____

_____

2. I'm really not comfortable with that suggestion.

_____

_____

3. Sometimes I wonder about you.

_____

_____

4. Things are really in an uproar at work.

_____

_____

5. Sometimes things just get all turned around.

_____

_____

6. Sometimes school really gets me down.

_____

_____

Immediacy

Read each of the statements below and imagine yourself in an interaction with the speaker. Use immediacy responses as invitations to the speaker to deal with some aspect of your relationship. Your immediacy responses should "process" the interaction by calling attention to your own feelings, your perceptions of the other person and the relationship, and some ways in which the issues may be worked through between you.

1. PATIENT: It's really hard for me to talk to you about this. I trust you—I mean I know you can't go blabbing everything around to everyone. But, I've been burned before, and I just don't open up very easily. I don't know you that well, and I don't know if I want to talk about what's bothering me.

_____

_____

_____

2. COLLEAGUE: You and I work well together, but sometimes I wish you'd be a bit more responsible and not leave me hanging. I don't mean to criticize you, but I would appreciate a little more help now and then. Don't get me wrong, I do like working with you, I just get a little upset at times. I'm not upset now. It doesn't bother me at all right now, but sometimes you really irk me.

_____

_____

_____

3. FRIEND: Yeah, that's right, Andy, he's a real "great guy." Aren't you, Greg? Just tell us how great you are! Come on "great" one [sarcastically]—tell us!

_____

_____

_____

4. COLLEAGUE: Nothing's wrong. I just don't have anything to say to you. So, if you'll excuse me, I have a lot of things to do—that is, if it's all right with you.

_____

_____

_____

Communication Exercises

The exercises described in this section provide you with structured formats for practicing and assessing skills related to the following: physical attending, active listening, communicating core conditions, concreteness, immediacy, specific verbal responses, and assertion.

Exercise 1: Sender-Receiver

On a sheet of paper, draw a picture of a jack-o-lantern, but do not show the figure to anyone. Ask one person to stand facing the chalkboard and a second person to sit with her back to the first (approximately 10 feet away). If a chalkboard is not available, arrange the two persons back to back in chairs at least 2–3 feet apart. Designate the person facing the chalkboard as the "receiver." Give the jack-o-lantern figure to the second person and designate her the "sender." Give the following instructions to both persons:

Your task as the sender is to describe to the receiver the figure at which you are now looking. You are to describe the figure without stating what it is and without defining its parts. Your objective is to have the receiver reproduce that figure on the chalkboard. [Turn to the receiver] Your task as the receiver is to reproduce the figure as described to you by the sender. You may ask no questions. You may request no clarification.

When the sender and receiver agree that the task is completed, compare the stimulus figure with the reproduction. Open discussion by asking sender, receiver, and participant observers to identify implications for interpersonal communication. For example, was the message as sent in correspondence to the message as received? Were there apparent problems in encoding, decoding, transmission? Did the receiver impose his own frame of reference and complete details not communicated by the sender? Did the sender introduce noise into the communication channel? How could the results be different if the receiver were allowed clarification and feedback? How would the sender benefit from feedback?

Draw another simple geometric figure and have two other persons participate as sender and receiver. This time allow them to talk back and forth during the task.

Exercise 2: Nonverbal Communication at Different Distances

To point up the effects of distance on nonverbal attending behavior, have two people sit facing each other at a distance of 15–20 feet. Instruct them to carry on a discussion of something of common interest. After three minutes, move the interactants to within three feet of one another, and instruct them to continue their discussion. After three minutes of conversation, terminate the interaction and discuss your observations of each person's physical attending behavior. As they moved physically closer, did they assume a CLOSER (see Chapter 13) attending posture?

Exercise 3: Horizontal and Vertical Orientations

Instruct one person to lie down on the floor and carry on a conversation with a second person who is seated in a chair at his side. The first person should lie on his back. After three minutes, instruct the interactants to change positions. After three more minutes, terminate the interaction, and ask each participant for his/her reactions to his/her vertical and horizontal orientations. What was it like to lie in a supine position and talk "up" to another person? What was it like to talk "down" to the other person?

Exercise 4: Attending to Physical Attending

Carry on a conversation with someone for five minutes, and then discuss each other's perceptions of the other's physical attending behavior. Did each person believe the other was attending physically? Give feedback in terms of CLOSER.

Other variations of this exercise may require observers to record nonverbal behaviors of the interacting persons. Observers can then provide additional feedback on possible nonverbal messages being sent by each person.

Exercise 5: Listening to Another Person

For five minutes, listen to another person (whom you do not know very well) tell about his life. You are to ask no questions nor make any statements. After five minutes, feed back what you heard, as precisely as you can. Two other observers should use pencil and paper to take notes during the five minute talk. They should be able to verify your feedback for accuracy, as should the original speaker.

During this exercise, you can make nonverbal replies as the speaker talks. The observers and the speaker should give you feedback on your nonverbal communication and your attending behavior. During 15 minutes of processing the experience, also discuss your reactions to remaining silent for five minutes. How well did you use silence as a response? Switch roles and repeat the exercise.

Exercise 6: Reactions to Nonattending

During this exercise, you and a partner are to carry on a conversation for five minutes. You are to assume various positions that clearly communicate nonattending. After five minutes, elicit the other person's reactions to your physical nonattending. Reverse roles and repeat the exercise. How does it feel to be ignored?

Exercise 7: Listening and Paraphrasing

Select an issue for debate with another person. Each of you is to express your own views in a conversation about an issue of mutual significance. The one rule is that before you state your own views, you must paraphrase the views of the other person. Before each of your statements, you must paraphrase the statements just made by the other person. This is an excellent exercise which may help you to improve your active listening skills because it forces you to pay close attention. Oh, there *is* one other rule: after paraphrasing your partner's statement, you still cannot express your own views until your partner is satisfied that you have paraphrased her correctly.

Exercise 8: Listening and Reflection

During five minutes of discussion, your only verbal responses are to be reflection responses in which you capture the feelings and content of the other's message and then feed it back to the person in your own words. You may want to practice the format "You feel . . . because . . . " for a while, but you will also want to alter the format to fit your own style. Elicit feedback from your partner on how accurately you reflected thoughts and feelings and how you came across in using the reflection response.

Exercise 9: Communicating the Core Conditions

In a group of three of four persons, two people are to function as observers, while one person role-plays a health care client with a specific problem. Assume the role of the fourth person, a health professional interacting with the client. The role-play should proceed for at least 20 minutes. After ending the role-play, elicit feedback from the "client" as to your communication of empathy, respect, and genuineness. The observers should then share their observations, using the kind of recording sheet illustrated in Figure 17.1. Note: It is essential that you all understand the scales for assessing levels of empathy, respect, and facilitative genuineness (see Chapter Fourteen for the criteria).

Exercise 10: Verbal Responses

In a format similar to the one above, practice the verbal responses of reflection, clarification, and silence. Observers should record specific responses and then provide their feedback after the 20-minute interaction.

Exercise 11: Concreteness and Immediacy

Again, in the same interaction format, have observers give feedback on your use of concreteness and immediacy. They may use recording sheets similar to the one in Figure 17.2.

Condition	Level				
	1	2	3	4	5
Empathy					
Respect					
Genuineness					

Figure 17.1   Recording sheet for observation of core conditions.

Condition	Level				
	1	2	3	4	5
Concreteness					
Immediacy					

Figure 17.2   Recording sheet for observation of concreteness and immediacy.

Exercise 12: Using Questions

Pair off with another person; one of you begin with a succession of open-ended questions to which the other is to respond genuinely. Reverse roles and repeat. During each 5-minute interaction, try to integrate open-ended questions with indirect questions. Eliciting information from the other will require you to respond to that information, so you should be prepared to practice other verbal responses as well, including your own self-disclosures.

Exercise 13: Transfer of Training

Transfer of training refers to the generalization of learning to real life situations. Each day for one week, practice three of the core conditions. That is, select situations in which you can practice communicating empathy, respect, and facilitative genuineness. It should be noted that it is not possible to practice either respect or genuineness by itself. To integrate these skills, it is usually advisable to practice empathic listening. With practice, the other two skills should begin to manifest themselves. Practicing empathy in real life, or *in vivo*, is something which can be assisted by some of the other exercises in this chapter and by practice in small groups.

Exercise 14: "I Am . . ."

Take the words "I am . . . " and complete the sentence in 10 different ways. Do this with one other person. Then look at the criteria for appropriate self-disclosure in Chapter Sixteen to see which of the items are appropriate to share with your partner. Elicit feedback from your partner and urge specificity.

Exercise 15: "UP"

Sometimes in situations calling for assertion, individuals feel powerless or powerful, depending on their perceptions and beliefs about the situations.

Think of a situation in which you must assert yourself—a situation in which you frequently find yourself. How powerful or powerless do you feel in that situation? Try to put a value on your experience by using the UP (units of power) scale, which is nothing more than a scale from 1 to 10, with 1 representing total powerlessness and 10 representing complete powerfulness. Five represents a balance between the two experiences. Identify situations in which you feel powerless and assign your feelings in those situations a number from the scale. Identify situations in which you feel powerful; assign those experiences a numerical value. Practice using this scale in assertion-related situations in order to monitor your feelings at the time. Feelings of powerlessness (low values) may indicate a need to respond assertively. Feelings of powerfulness, however, may not necessarily mean that you are powerful or have behaved responsibly. Aggression may make people feel powerful if the consequences place others in subordinate positions. Assess the situation to determine if your feelings of powerfulness have come from assertion or aggression.

Exercise 16: "SUDS"

An assessment device which has been found to be useful in assertion training is the SUDS scale.* SUDS stands for subjective units of discomfort scale. The scale is totally subjective, with 0 representing the most comfortable a person can remember ever having been and 100 being the most uncomfortable. "Discomfort" in this scale is actually a term for anxiety. Most lay persons call anxiety "nervousness," although the synonym is not completely accurate. At any rate, anxiety, nervousness, or discomfort is seen as a subjective experience which often occurs in situations individuals perceive as somehow threatening. The experience is variable from person to person and from one situation to the next, but some common characteristics can be noted:

Physiologic and Motor Signs

Muscular tension	Dizziness or faintness
Facial flushing	Intestinal distress
Dry mouth	Felt need to urinate
Pounding heart	Palmar sweat
Perspiration	Reduced hand temperature
Shallow breathing	Mild to moderate tremors
Heart palpitations	Incoordination
Feelings of weakness	Freezing or "drawing a blank"

Cognitive and Affective Signs

Feelings of panic	Self-consciousness
Agitation	Impaired concentration
Distractibility	Forgetfulness
Inattention	Feelings of dread
Worrying	Irritability

*Wolpe, J., and Lazarus, A. A. *Behavior Therapy Techniques*. New York, Pergamon, 1966.

At point zero on the SUDS scale, the individual is not aware of any of these signs. At 50, there is perceived to be a moderate level of discomfort, but a good balance between too much and too little. Coincidentally, this tends to be the level at which task performance is facilitated: too little anxiety leaves the person "unmotivated," while too much anxiety interferes with smooth and efficient functioning. At any given point in time, your SUDS level can range from 0 to 100. To experiment with the scale, find your zero point by recalling a situation where you felt totally at ease and comfortable (e.g., sitting at home reading a novel, walking along the beach, meditating, lying in bed in the morning). Now, find a situation at the other end of the scale that would lead to a state of extreme discomfort or panic. Use this experience as your anchoring point at the discomfort end of the scale. Now, take a moment to figure out where your SUDS level is right now in the immediate present. Assign a number to your experience. Do not say "somewhere around 30 or 40." Give it a precise number: 32, 55, 70, for example. See if you can identify signs of discomfort from your body; *listen to what your body is telling you.* Practice using the scale at different times during the day. Tune in to your body's messages and assign point values to your different feeling states at different times. Use the SUDS recording form illustrated in Figure 17.3 as a means for increasing your awareness of comfort/discomfort (relaxation/anxiety). This recording sheet may help you

1. Describe the situation in which you feel "discomfort."	
2. Describe the behavior of others in that situation (i.e., how he/she or they typically act).	
3. Describe your behavior in that situation (i.e., how you usually act).	
4. What is your usual SUDS level in that situation? (Be specific.)	
5. At what level would you like your SUDS to be?	
6. What is your usual UP level and where would you like it to be?	
7. Identify at least one assertive response that may help you change your SUDS and UP levels.	
8. What is your usual SUDS level when you use that response?	

Figure 17.3 Recording sheet for describing SUDS and UP levels in specific situations where a more assertive response is appropriate.

to identify characteristics of situations that lead to your feelings of anxiety. It should also help you to begin thinking about some ways in which you might reduce your SUDS levels in those situations.

Exercise 17: Teaching Yourself to Relax

There are countless techniques for inducing relaxation. You probably have some of your own already. If not, discuss relaxation techniques with others, and listen to their suggestions. They may have some useful ideas. Without describing specific procedures for relaxation, I will refer you to references under the headings of: *relaxation training, self-hypnosis, yoga, meditation, autogenic training, biofeedback, rational restructuring, desensitization,* and *assertion training*. If you are truly committed to learning how to relax, these are options for you. It requires that you first *take control of your own learning*.

Exercise 18: Practicing Assertive Responses

Review the assertive responses described in Chapter Sixteen. With one other person, practice each of those responses. Spend five minutes on each trial. After each response is practiced, provide feedback to one another on your performances. Before you practice a response, note your SUDS level, note it as you are demonstrating the response, and note it after giving the response. Record your SUDS levels and compare them for each response. Do some responses make you more uncomfortable than others? Did you become more relaxed with practice? Were your SUDS levels higher before, during, or after performing the responses?

Identify the assertive responses which seem to be most difficult for you. Practice those with your partner. Continue recording SUDS levels until you note a significant decrease in your levels of discomfort.

Exercise 19: Assertive Role-Plays

In a dyad, each person should have an opportunity to practice the following kinds of responses. One person should "set up" the situation so that the other may practice the assertive response. Reverse roles, note your SUDS levels, process the experience, and move on to the next structured role-play.

1. Refuse to lend a dollar to an acquaintance when you don't have it.
2. Refuse to lend a dollar to an acquaintance when you do have it.
3. Terminate a conversation with an acquaintance without an excuse.
4. Introduce yourself to a fellow student you have never met.
5. Offer free information about yourself to a person you have just met.
6. Compliment an acquaintance for having the highest exam score.
7. Compliment a friend for being there when you need her.
8. Spend two minutes praising yourself for realistic strengths and assets.

9. Spend two minutes in self-disclosures using only "I" statements.
10. Give an order to a subordinate.
11. Confront a colleague who has been late for work.
12. Confront a friend for failing to keep an appointment with you.
13. Make a concise apology to a patient for responding late to her call light.

Exercise 20: Real-Life Assertion

When you are comfortable with certain assertive responses, practice them in "real life" situations. Some suggestions are indicated below. Remember to monitor your SUDS levels.

1. Initiating a conversation with a cashier at a check out
2. Complimenting a waiter or waitress for good service (if it is)
3. Asking open-ended questions of a clerk in a store
4. Saying something good about yourself to a gas station attendant
5. Going into a market, buying a single item, and then asking the person with a full basket in front of you if you can go ahead in the checkout line
6. Going into a restaurant and sending food back that is not the way you ordered it

Note: when practicing these or other assertive responses in life situations, avoid situations that are real problems for you at this time. Also, select situations that hold a high probability of success. Finally, remember that assertion is responsible if it does not infringe upon the rights of others; do not exploit others or violate their personal rights.

Exercise 21: Practice Your Deficits

In a group of four persons, discuss specific skills deficits that you have. Each person should discuss at least one skill deficit: a skill that he or she currently is not able to perform efficiently and effectively. This skill should also be one which is associated with a relatively high SUDS level (e.g., stating your opinions before a group). Each person should describe the skill deficit as concretely as possible: what makes it a deficit? what does he usually do? what is his SUDS level when performing the response? For example, you might say, "I get so nervous in front of a group. I just clam up. When I do try to express myself, I hesitate, I stammer and stutter, and I'm always fidgeting with my hands. I just know everyone can tell I'm nervous, because I'm so clumsy and uncoordinated in those situations."

After you have identified a specific skill deficit, *practice it*. Practice doing exactly what you don't want to do. Show the others how well you can stammer and stutter, for example, and how hesitant, fidgety, and clumsy you are. Did you find this hard to do? Was it amusing to you? Did you think it was silly?

Did you find yourself more relaxed under these circumstances] The fact is that sometimes we try so hard to do something that the act of trying interferes with actually doing it! Conversely, sometimes we try so hard *not* to do something that we end up doing exactly what we're trying to avoid. This exercise may be hard for you to do. There is a high probability, however, that as you try to do what you don't want to do, you will become more relaxed. There is humor in this, and humor goes a long way toward relaxing people.

INDEX